ASP.NET Core 6 and

Fifth Edition

Full-stack web development with ASP.NET 6 and Angular 13

Valerio De Sanctis

BIRMINGHAM—MUMBAI

ASP.NET Core 6 and Angular
Fifth Edition

Copyright © 2022 Packt Publishing

Senior Publishing Product Manager: Suman Sen

Acquisition Editor – Peer Reviews: Saby Dsilva

Project Editor: Parvathy Nair

Content Development Editors: Georgia Daisy van der Post and Alex Patterson

Copy Editor: Safis Editing

Technical Editor: Aniket Shetty

Proofreader: Safis Editing

Indexer: Sejal Dsilva

Presentation Designer: Ganesh Bhadwalkar

First published: October 2016

Second edition: November 2017

Third edition: February 2020

Fourth edition: January 2021

Fifth edition: April 2022

Production reference: 1290322

Published by Packt Publishing Ltd.

Livery Place

35 Livery Street

Birmingham

B3 2PB, UK.

ISBN 978-1-80323-970-5

www.packt.com

Contributors

About the author

Valerio De Sanctis is a skilled IT professional with more than 20 years of experience in lead programming, web-based development, and project management using ASP.NET, PHP, and Java. He has held senior positions at a range of financial and insurance companies, most recently serving as Chief Technology Officer, Chief Security Officer, and Chief Operating Officer at a leading after-sales and IT service provider for multiple top-tier life and non-life insurance groups. He's also a Microsoft Most Valuable Professional (MVP) for Developer Technologies & Cloud and Datacenter Management.

He has written various books on web development, many of which have become best-sellers on Amazon, with tens of thousands of copies sold worldwide

I would like to thank those who supported me in writing this book: my beloved and beautiful wife, Carla, for her awesome encouragement and invaluable support; my children, Viola and Daniele; as well as my parents and my sister. Last but not least, I would like to thank you, the reader, for picking up this book. I really hope you will enjoy it!

About the reviewer

Wouter Huysentruit is a seasoned software developer and architect with more than 20 years of experience in many different fields. He strives for solutions that are easy to understand and maintain. His current interest is in developing user-friendly web applications based on Microsoft technologies and Angular in addition to working on many open-source projects for which he also received the Microsoft MVP award.

A big thanks goes out to my wife and kids for supporting me during the review of this book.

Table of Contents

Chapter 14: Real-Time Updates with SignalR 625

Chapter 15: Windows, Linux, and Azure Deployment 643

Preface

ASP.NET Core is a free and open-source modular web framework developed by Microsoft that runs on top of the full .NET Framework (Windows) or .NET Core (cross-platform). It has been made specifically for building efficient HTTP services that can be reached and consumed by a massive range of clients, including web browsers, mobile devices, smart TVs, web-based home automation tools, and more.

Angular is the successor of AngularJS, a world-renowned development framework born with the aim of providing the coder with the toolbox that is needed to build reactive and cross-platform web-based apps that are optimized for desktop and mobile. It features a structure-rich template approach based upon a natural, easy-to-write, and readable syntax.

Technically, these two frameworks have little or nothing in common: ASP.NET Core is mostly focused on the server-side part of the web development stack, while Angular is dedicated to covering all the client-side aspects of web applications, such as the **User Interface (UI)** and **User Experience (UX)**. However, both of them came into being because of a common vision shared by their respective creators: the HTTP protocol is not limited to serving web pages; it can also be used as a viable platform upon which to build web-based APIs to effectively send and receive data. This is the notion that slowly made its way through the first 20 years of the World Wide Web's life and is now an undeniable, widely acknowledged statement and also a fundamental pillar of almost every modern web development approach.

As for the reasons behind this perspective switch, there are plenty of good ones, the most important of them being related to the intrinsic characteristics of the HTTP protocol: it's rather simple to use, and flexible enough to match most of the development needs of the ever-changing environment that the World Wide Web happens to be in. This is not to mention how universal it has become nowadays: almost any platform that we can think of has an HTTP library, so HTTP services can reach a broad range of clients, including desktop and mobile browsers, IoT devices, desktop applications, video games, and so on.

The main purpose of this book is to bring together the latest versions of ASP.NET Core and Angular within a single development stack to demonstrate how they can be used to create high-performance web applications and services that can be used seamlessly by any clients.

Who this book is for

This book is for intermediate and experienced developers who already know about ASP.NET Core and Angular and are looking to learn more about them and understand how to use them together to create a production-ready **Single-Page Application** (SPA) or **Progressive Web Application** (PWA) using SQL Server and Entity Framework Core.

However, the fully documented code samples (also available on GitHub) and the step-by-step implementation tutorials make this book easy to understand even for beginners and developers who are just getting started.

What this book covers

Chapter 1, *Introducing ASP.NET and Angular*, introduces some of the basic concepts of the frameworks that we are going to use throughout the book, as well as the various kinds of web applications that can be created (SPAs, PWAs, native web apps, and more).

Chapter 2, *Getting Ready*, explains how to create the ASP.NET Core projects that will be used for the rest of the book using the templates provided by Visual Studio for both the back-end (ASP.NET Core Web API) and the front-end (Standalone Angular App).

Chapter 3, *Looking Around*, is a detailed overview of the various back-end and front-end elements provided by the .NET Core and Angular template shipped with Visual Studio, backed up with some high-level explanations of how they can work together in a typical HTTP request-response cycle.

Chapter 4, *Front-End and Back-End Interactions*, provides a comprehensive tutorial for building a sample ASP.NET Core and Angular app that provides diagnostic info to the end user by querying health check middleware using a Bootstrap-based Angular client.

Chapter 5, *Data Model with Entity Framework Core*, constitutes a journey through Entity Framework Core and its capabilities as an **Object-Relational Mapping** (ORM) framework, from SQL database deployment (cloud-based and/or local instance) to data model design, including various techniques to read and write data from back-end controllers.

Chapter 6, *Fetching and Displaying Data*, covers how to expose Entity Framework Core data using the ASP.NET Core back-end web API, consume that data with Angular, and then show it to end users using the front-end UI.

Chapter 7, *Forms and Data Validation*, details how to implement the HTTP PUT and POST methods in back-end web APIs in order to perform insert and update operations with Angular, along with server-side and client-side data validation.

Chapter 8, *Code Tweaks and Data Services*, explores some useful refactoring and improvements to strengthen your app's source code and includes an in-depth analysis of Angular's data services to understand why and how to use them.

Chapter 9, *Back-End and Front-End Debugging*, looks at how to properly debug the back-end and front-end stacks of a typical web application using the various debugging tools provided by Visual Studio to their full extent.

Chapter 10, ASP.NET Core and Angular Unit Testing, comprises a detailed review of the **Test-Driven Development (TDD)** and **Behavior-Driven Development (BDD)** development practices and goes into how to define, implement, and perform back-end and front-end unit tests using xUnit, Jasmine, and Karma.

Chapter 11, Authentication and Authorization, gives you a high-level introduction to the concepts of authentication and authorization and presents a narrow lineup of some of the various techniques, methodologies, and approaches to properly implementing proprietary or third-party user identity systems. A practical example of a working ASP.NET Core and Angular authentication mechanism based upon ASP.NET Identity and IdentityServer4 is included.

Chapter 12, Progressive Web Apps, delves into how to convert an existing SPA into a PWA using service workers, manifest files, and offline caching features.

Chapter 13, Beyond REST – Web API with GraphQL, introduces the concept of the GraphQL query language, explains its pros and cons, and shows how to implement a GraphQL-based API using HotChocolate (for the back-end) and Apollo Angular (for the front-end).

Chapter 14, Real-Time Updates with SignalR, is dedicated to SignalR, a free and open-source library that can be used to send asynchronous notifications to client-side web applications, and explains how to implement it in ASP.NET Core and Angular.

Chapter 15, Windows, Linux, and Azure Deployment, teaches you how to deploy the ASP.NET and Angular apps created in the previous chapters and publish them in a cloud-based environment using a Windows Server 2019 or a Linux CentOS virtual machine, as well as covering Azure App Service deployment.

To get the most out of this book

These are the software packages (and relevant version numbers) used to write this book and test the source code:

- Visual Studio 2022 Community Edition 17.0.4 with the optional ASP.NET and web development workload (it can be selected from the Workloads section within the Visual Studio installer app)
- Microsoft .NET 6 SDK 6.0.101
- TypeScript 4.3
- NuGet package manager 6.0
- Node.js 14.15.0 (we strongly suggest installing it using **Node Version Manager**, also known as **nvm**)
- Angular 13.0.1

For deployment on **Windows:**

- **Internet Information Services (IIS)** (Windows Server)
- **ASP.NET Core Runtime 5 and Windows Hosting Bundle Installer for Win64** (ASP.NET official website)

For deployment on **Linux**:

- **ASP.NET Core Runtime 5 for Linux** (YUM package manager)
- **.NET 5 CLR for Linux** (YUM package manager)
- **Nginx HTTP Server** (YUM package manager)

Download the example code files

The code bundle for the book is hosted on GitHub at `https://github.com/PacktPublishing/ASP.NET-Core-6-and-Angular`. We also have other code bundles from our rich catalog of books and videos available at `https://github.com/PacktPublishing/`. Check them out!

Download the color images

We also provide a PDF file that has color images of the screenshots/diagrams used in this book. You can download it here: `https://static.packt-cdn.com/downloads/9781803239705_ColorImages.pdf`.

Conventions used

There are a number of text conventions used throughout this book:

`CodeInText`: Indicates code words in text, database table names, folder names, filenames, file extensions, pathnames, dummy URLs, user input, and Twitter handles. For example: "Navigate to the `/ClientApp/src/app/cities` folder."

A block of code is set as follows:

```
<mat-form-field [hidden]="!cities">
<input matInput (keyup)="loadData($event.target.value)"
placeholder="Filter by name (or part of it)...">
</mat-form-field>
```

When we wish to draw your attention to a particular part of a code block, the relevant lines or items are highlighted:

```
import { FormGroup, FormControl } from '@angular/forms';

class ModelFormComponent implements OnInit {
    form: FormGroup;

    ngOnInit() {
        this.form = new FormGroup({
            title: new FormControl()
        });
    }
}
```

Any command-line input or output is written as follows:

```
> dotnet new angular -o HealthCheck
```

Bold: Indicates a new term, an important word, or words that you see on screen. For example, words in menus or dialog boxes appear in the text like this. Here is an example: "A simple **Add a new City** button will fix both these issues at once."

Warnings or important notes appear like this.

Tips and tricks appear like this.

Get in touch

Feedback from our readers is always welcome.

General feedback: Email feedback@packtpub.com, and mention the book's title in the subject of your message. If you have questions about any aspect of this book, please email us at questions@packtpub.com.

Errata: Although we have taken every care to ensure the accuracy of our content, mistakes do happen. If you have found a mistake in this book we would be grateful if you would report this to us. Please visit, http://www.packtpub.com/submit-errata, selecting your book, clicking on the Errata Submission Form link, and entering the details.

Piracy: If you come across any illegal copies of our works in any form on the Internet, we would be grateful if you would provide us with the location address or website name. Please contact us at copyright@packtpub.com with a link to the material.

If you are interested in becoming an author: If there is a topic that you have expertise in and you are interested in either writing or contributing to a book, please visit http://authors.packtpub.com.

Share your thoughts

Once you've read *ASP.NET Core 6 and Angular, Fifth Edition*, we'd love to hear your thoughts! Scan the QR code below to go straight to the Amazon review page for this book and share your feedback.

https://packt.link/r/1803239700

Your review is important to us and the tech community and will help us make sure we're delivering excellent quality content.

1

Introducing ASP.NET and Angular

Over the first two chapters of this book, we'll build the basics of our ASP.NET and Angular journey by mixing theoretical coverage of their most relevant features with a practical approach. More specifically, in the first chapter, we'll briefly review the recent history of ASP.NET/.NET Core and Angular frameworks, while in the second chapter, we'll learn how to configure our local development environment so we can assemble, build, and test a sample web application boilerplate.

By the end of these chapters, you'll have gained knowledge of the path taken by ASP.NET and Angular to improve web development in the last few years and learned how to properly set up an ASP.NET and Angular web application.

Here are the main topics that we are going to cover in this chapter:

- **Two players, one goal**. How ASP.NET and Angular can be used together to build a modern, feature-rich, and highly versatile web application
- **The ASP.NET Core revolution**. A brief history of ASP.NET's most recent achievements
- **What's new in Angular**. A recap of the Angular development journey, from its origins to the most recent days

Technical requirements

These are the software packages (and relevant version numbers) used to write this book and test the source code:

- Visual Studio 2022 Community edition 17.0.0 with the optional *ASP.NET and web development* workload (it can be selected from the **Workloads** section within the Visual Studio installer app)
- Microsoft .NET 6 SDK 6.0.100
- TypeScript 4.3
- NuGet package manager 6.0
- Node.js 14.15.0 (we strongly suggest installing it using **Node Version Manager**, also known as **nvm**)
- Angular 13.0.1

We strongly suggest using the same version used within this book – or newer, but at your own risk! Jokes aside, if you prefer to use a different version, that's perfectly fine, as long as you are aware that, in that case, *you may need to make some manual changes and adjustments to the source code*.

The code files for this book can be found here: `https://github.com/PacktPublishing/ASP.NET-Core-6-and-Angular`.

Two players, one goal

From the perspective of a fully functional web-based application, we can say that the Web API interface provided with the ASP.NET framework is a programmatic set of server-side handlers used by the server to expose a number of hooks and/or endpoints to a defined request-response message system. This is typically expressed in structured markup languages (XML), language-independent data formats (JSON), or query languages for APIs (GraphQL). As we've already said, this is achieved by exposing **application programming interfaces** (APIs) through HTTP and/or HTTPS protocols via a publicly available web server such as IIS, Node.js, Apache, or NGINX.

Similarly, Angular can be described as a modern, feature-rich, client-side framework that pushes the HTML and ECMAScript's most advanced features, along with the modern browser's capabilities, to their full extent by binding the input and/or output parts of an HTML web page into a flexible, reusable, and easily testable model.

Can we combine the *back-end* strengths of ASP.NET and the *front-end* capabilities of Angular in order to build a modern, feature-rich, and highly versatile web application?

The answer, in short, is yes. In the following chapters, we'll see how we can do that by analyzing all the fundamental aspects of a well-written, properly designed, web-based product, and how the latest versions of ASP.NET and/or Angular can be used to handle each one of them. However, before doing all that, it might be very useful to backtrack a bit and spend some valuable time recollecting what's happened in the last 8 years in the development history of the two frameworks we're going to use. It will be very useful to understand the main reasons why we're still giving them full credit, despite the valuable efforts of their ever-growing competitors.

The ASP.NET Core revolution

To summarize what has happened in the ASP.NET world within the last decade is not an easy task; in short, we can say that we've undoubtedly witnessed the most important series of changes in .NET Framework since the year it came to life. This was a revolution that changed the whole Microsoft approach to software development in almost every way. To properly understand what happened in those years, it would be useful to identify some distinctive key frames within a slow, yet constant, journey that allowed a company known (and somewhat loathed) for its proprietary software, licenses, and patents to become a driving force for open source development worldwide.

The first relevant step, at least in my humble opinion, was taken on April 3, 2014, at the annual Microsoft Build conference, which took place at the Moscone Center (West) in San Francisco. It was there, during a memorable keynote speech, that Anders Hejlsberg – father of Delphi and lead architect of C# – publicly released the first version of the .NET Compiler Platform, known as Roslyn, as an open source project.

It was also there that Scott Guthrie, executive vice president of the Microsoft Cloud and AI group, announced the official launch of the .NET Foundation, a non-profit organization aimed at improving open source software development and collaborative work within the .NET ecosystem.

From that pivotal day, the .NET development team published a constant flow of Microsoft open source projects on the GitHub platform, including Entity Framework Core (May 2014), TypeScript (October 2014), .NET Core (October 2014), CoreFX (November 2014), CoreCLR and RyuJIT (January 2015), MSBuild (March 2015), the .NET Core CLI (October 2015), Visual Studio Code (November 2015), .NET Standard (September 2016), and so on.

ASP.NET Core 1.x

The most important achievement brought by these efforts toward open source development was the public release of ASP.NET Core 1.0, which came out in Q3 2016. It was a complete reimplementation of the ASP.NET framework that we had known since January 2002 and that had evolved, without significant changes in its core architecture, up to version 4.6.2 (August 2016). The brand-new framework united all the previous web application technologies, such as MVC, Web API, and web pages, into a single programming module, formerly known as MVC6. The new framework introduced a fully featured, cross-platform component, also known as .NET Core, shipped with the whole set of open source tools mentioned previously, namely, a compiler platform (Roslyn), a cross-platform runtime (CoreCLR), and an improved x64 Just-In-Time compiler (RyuJIT).

Some of you might remember that ASP.NET Core was originally called ASP.NET 5. As a matter of fact, ASP.NET 5 was no less than the original name of ASP.NET Core until mid-2016, when the Microsoft developer team chose to rename it to emphasize the fact that it was a complete rewrite. The reasons for that, along with the Microsoft vision about the new product, are further explained in the following Scott Hanselman blog post that anticipated the changes on January 16, 2016: `http://www.hanselman.com/blog/ASPNE T5IsDeadIntroducingASPNETCore10AndNETCore10.aspx`.

For those who don't know, Scott Hanselman has been the outreach and community manager for .NET/ASP.NET/IIS/Azure and Visual Studio since 2007. Additional information regarding the perspective switch is also available in the following article by Jeffrey T. Fritz, program manager for Microsoft and a NuGet team leader: `https://blogs.msdn. microsoft.com/webdev/2016/02/01/an-update-on-asp-net-core-and-net-core/`.

As for Web API 2, it was a dedicated framework for building HTTP services that returned pure JSON or XML data instead of web pages. Initially born as an alternative to the MVC platform, it has been merged with the latter into the new, general-purpose web application framework known as MVC6, which is now shipped as a separate module of ASP.NET Core.

The 1.0 final release was shortly followed by ASP.NET Core 1.1 (Q4 2016), which brought some new features and performance enhancements, and also addressed many bugs and compatibility issues affecting the earlier release.

These new features include the ability to configure middleware as filters (by adding them to the MVC pipeline rather than the HTTP request pipeline); a built-in, host-independent URL rewrite module, made available through the dedicated `Microsoft.AspNetCore.Rewrite` NuGet package; view components as tag helpers; view compilation at runtime instead of on-demand; .NET native compression and caching middleware modules; and so on.

For a detailed list of all the new features, improvements, and bug fixes in ASP.NET Core 1.1, check out the following links:

- **Release notes:** `https://github.com/aspnet/AspNetCore/releases/1.1.0`
- **Commits list:** `https://github.com/dotnet/core/blob/master/release-notes/1.1/1.1-commits.md`

ASP.NET Core 2.x

Another major step was taken with ASP.NET Core 2.0, which came out in Q2 2017 as a preview and then in Q3 2017 for the final release. The new version featured a wide number of significant interface improvements, mostly aimed at standardizing the shared APIs among .NET Framework, .NET Core, and .NET Standard to make them backward-compatible with .NET Framework. Thanks to these efforts, moving existing .NET Framework projects to .NET Core and/or .NET Standard became a lot easier than before, giving many traditional developers a chance to try and adapt to the new paradigm without losing their existing know-how.

Again, the major version was shortly followed by an improved and refined one: ASP.NET Core 2.1. This was officially released on May 30, 2018, and introduced a series of additional security and performance improvements, as well as a bunch of new features, including SignalR, an open source library that simplifies adding real-time web functionality to .NET Core apps; Razor class libraries; a significant improvement in the Razor SDK that allows developers to build views and pages into reusable class libraries, and/or library projects that could be shipped as NuGet packages; the Identity UI library and scaffolding, to add identity to any app and customize it to meet your needs; HTTPS support enabled by default; built-in **General Data Protection Regulation (GDPR)** support using privacy-oriented APIs and templates that give users control over their personal data and cookie consent; updated SPA templates for Angular and ReactJS client-side frameworks; and much more.

For a detailed list of all the new features, improvements, and bug fixes in ASP.NET Core 2.1, check out the following links:

- **Release notes:** `https://docs.microsoft.com/en-US/aspnet/core/release-notes/aspnetcore-2.1`
- **Commits list:** `https://github.com/dotnet/core/blob/master/release-notes/2.1/2.1.0-commit.md`

Wait a minute: did we just say Angular? Yeah, that's right. As a matter of fact, since its initial release, ASP.NET Core has been specifically designed to seamlessly integrate with popular client-side frameworks such as ReactJS and Angular. It is precisely for this reason that books such as this exist. The major difference introduced in ASP.NET Core 2.1 is that the default Angular and ReactJS templates have been updated to use the standard project structures and build systems for each framework (the Angular CLI and NPX's `create-react-app` command) instead of relying on task runners such as Grunt or Gulp, module builders such as webpack, or toolchains such as Babel, which were widely used in the past, although they were quite difficult to install and configure.

Being able to eliminate the need for these tools was a major achievement, which has played a decisive role in revamping the .NET Core usage and growth rate among the developer communities since 2017. If you take a look at the two previous installments of this book – *ASP.NET Core and Angular 2*, published in mid-2016, and *ASP.NET Core 2 and Angular 5*, out in late 2017 – and compare their first chapter with this one, you will see the huge difference between having to manually use Gulp, Grunt, or webpack, and relying on the integrated framework-native tools. This is a substantial reduction in complexity that would greatly benefit any developer, especially those less accustomed to working with those tools.

Six months after the release of the 2.1 version, the .NET Foundation came out with a further improvement: ASP.NET Core 2.2 was released on December 4, 2018, with several fixes and new features, including an improved endpoint routing system for better dispatching of requests, updated templates featuring Bootstrap 4 and Angular 6 support, and a new health checks service to monitor the status of deployment environments and their underlying infrastructures, including container orchestration systems such as Kubernetes, built-in HTTP/2 support in Kestrel, and a new SignalR Java client to ease the usage of SignalR within Android apps.

For a detailed list of all the new features, improvements, and bug fixes in ASP.NET Core 2.2, check out the following links:

- **Release notes:** `https://docs.microsoft.com/en-US/aspnet/core/release-notes/aspnetcore-2.2`
- **Commits list:** `https://github.com/dotnet/core/blob/master/release-notes/2.2/2.2.0/2.2.0-commits.md`

ASP.NET Core 3.x

ASP.NET Core 3 was released in September 2019 and came with another bunch of performance and security improvements and new features, such as Windows desktop application support (Windows only) with advanced importing capabilities for Windows Forms and **Windows Presentation Foundation (WPF)** applications; C# 8 support; .NET Platform-dependent intrinsic access through a new set of built-in APIs that could bring significant performance improvements in certain scenarios; single-file executable support via the `dotnet publish` command using the `<PublishSingleFile>` XML element in project configuration or through the `/p:PublishSingleFile` command-line parameter; new built-in JSON support featuring high performance and low allocation that's arguably two to three times faster than the JSON.NET third-party library (which became a de facto standard in most ASP.NET web projects); TLS 1.3 and OpenSSL 1.1.1 support in Linux; some important security improvements in the `System.Security.Cryptography` namespace, including AES-GCM and AES-CCM cipher support; and so on.

A lot of work has also been done to improve the performance and reliability of the framework when used in a containerized environment. The ASP.NET Core development team put a lot of effort into improving the .NET Core Docker experience on .NET Core 3.0. More specifically, this is the first release featuring substantive runtime changes to make CoreCLR more efficient, honor Docker resource limits better (such as memory and CPU) by default, and offer more configuration tweaks. Among the various improvements, we could mention improved memory and GC heap usage by default, and PowerShell Core, a cross-platform version of the famous automation and configuration tool, which is now shipped with the .NET Core SDK Docker container images.

.NET Core 3 also introduced Blazor, a free and open source web framework that enables developers to create web apps using C# and HTML.

Last but not least, it's worth noting that the new .NET Core SDK is much smaller than the previous installments, mostly thanks to the fact that the development team removed a huge set of unnecessary artifacts included in the various NuGet packages that were used to assemble the previous SDKs (including ASP.NET Core 2.2) from the final build. The size improvements are huge for Linux and macOS versions, while less noticeable on Windows because that SDK also contains the new WPF and Windows Forms set of platform-specific libraries.

For a detailed list of all the new features, improvements, and bug fixes in ASP.NET Core 3.0, check out the following links:

- **Release notes:** `https://docs.microsoft.com/en-us/dotnet/core/whats-new/dotnet-core-3-0`
- **ASP.NET Core 3.0 releases page:** `https://github.com/dotnet/core/tree/master/release-notes/3.0`

ASP.NET Core 3.1, which is the most recent stable version at the time of writing, was released on December 3, 2019.

The changes in the latest version are mostly focused on Windows desktop development, with the definitive removal of a number of legacy Windows Forms controls (*DataGrid*, *ToolBar*, *ContextMenu*, *Menu*, *MainMenu*, and *MenuItem*) and added support for creating C++/CLI components (on Windows only).

Most of the ASP.NET Core updates were fixes related to Blazor, such as preventing default actions for events and stopping event propagation in Blazor apps, partial class support for Razor components, and additional *Tag Helper Component* features; however, much like the other *.1* releases, the primary goal of .NET Core 3.1 was to refine and improve the features already delivered in the previous version, with more than 150 performance and stability issues fixed.

A detailed list of the new features, improvements, and bug fixes introduced with ASP.NET Core 3.1 is available at the following URL:

- **Release notes:** `https://docs.microsoft.com/en-us/dotnet/core/whats-new/dotnet-core-3-1`

.NET 5

Just when everyone thought that Microsoft had finally taken a clear path with the naming convention of its upcoming frameworks, the Microsoft developer community was shaken again on May 6, 2019, by the following post by Richard Lander, Program Manager of the .NET team, which appeared on the Microsoft Developer Blog: `https://devblogs.microsoft.com/dotnet/introducing-net-5/`.

The post got an immediate backup from another article that came out the same day written by Scott Hunter, Program Management Director of the .NET ecosystem: `https://devblogs.microsoft.com/dotnet/net-core-is-the-future-of-net/`.

The two posts were meant to share the same big news to the readers: .NET Framework 4.x and .NET Core 3.x would converge in the next major installment of .NET Core, which would skip a major version number to properly encapsulate both installments.

The new unified platform would be called .NET 5 and would include everything that had been released so far with uniform capabilities and behaviors: .NET Runtime, JIT, AOT, GC, BCL (Base Class Library), C#, VB.NET, F#, ASP.NET, Entity Framework, ML.NET, WinForms, WPF, and Xamarin.

Microsoft said they wanted to eventually drop the term "Core" from the framework name because .NET 5 would be the main implementation of .NET going forward, thus replacing .NET Framework and .NET Core; however, for the time being, the ASP.NET Core ecosystem is still retaining the name "Core" to avoid confusing it with ASP.NET MVC 5; Entity Framework Core will also keep the name "Core" to avoid confusing it with Entity Framework 5 and 6. For all of these reasons, in this book, we'll keep using "ASP.NET Core" (or .NET Core) and "Entity Framework Core" (or "EF Core") as well.

From Microsoft's point of view, the reasons behind this bold choice were rather obvious:

- Produce a single .NET runtime and framework that can be used everywhere and that has uniform runtime behaviors and developer experiences
- Expand the capabilities of .NET by taking the best of .NET Core, .NET Framework, Xamarin, and Mono
- Build that product out of a single code base that internal (Microsoft) and external (community) developers can work on and expand together and that improves all scenarios

 The new name could reasonably generate some confusion among those developers who still remember the short timeframe (early to mid-2016) in which ASP. NET Core v1 was still called ASP.NET 5 before its final release. Luckily enough, that "working title" was ditched by the Microsoft developer team and the .NET community before it could leave noticeable traces on the web.

.NET 5 was released on General Availability in November 2020, a couple of months after its first Release Candidate, thus respecting the updated .NET schedule that aims to ship a new major version of .NET once a year, every November:

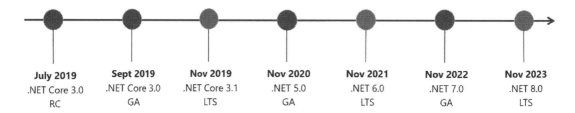

.NET Schedule

July 2019	Sept 2019	Nov 2019	Nov 2020	Nov 2021	Nov 2022	Nov 2023
.NET Core 3.0	.NET Core 3.0	.NET Core 3.1	.NET 5.0	.NET 6.0	.NET 7.0	.NET 8.0
RC	GA	LTS	GA	LTS	GA	LTS

- .NET Core 3.0 release in September
- .NET Core 3.1 = Long Term Support (LTS)
- .NET 5.0 release in November 2020
- Major releases every year, LTS for even numbered releases
- Predictable schedule, minor releases if needed

Figure 1.1: .NET schedule

In addition to the new name, the .NET 5 framework brought a lot of interesting changes, such as:

- *Performance improvements and measurement tools*, summarized in this great analysis performed by Stephen Toub (.NET Partner Software Engineer) using the new Benchmark.NET tools: https://devblogs.microsoft.com/dotnet/performance-improvements-in-net-5/.

- *Half Type*, a binary floating point that occupies only 16 bits and that can help to save a good amount of storage space where the computed result does not need to be stored with full precision. For additional info, take a look at this post by Prashanth Govindarajan (Senior Engineering Manager at LinkedIn): `https://devblogs.microsoft.com/dotnet/introducing-the-half-type/`.

- *Assembly trimming*, a compiler-level option to trim unused assemblies as part of publishing self-contained applications when using the self-contained deployment option, as explained by Sam Spencer (.NET Core team Program Manager) in this post: `https://devblogs.microsoft.com/dotnet/app-trimming-in-net-5/`.

- *Various improvements in the new System.Text.Json API*, including the ability to ignore default values for value-type properties when serializing (for better serialization performance) and to better deal with circular references.

- *C# 9 and F# 5 language support*, with a bunch of new features such as *Init Only Setters* (that allows the creation of *immutable* objects), *function pointers*, *static anonymous functions*, *target-typed conditional expressions*, *covariant return types*, and *module initializers*.

And a lot of other new features and improvements besides.

> A detailed list of the new features and improvements and a comprehensive explanation of the reasons behind the release of ASP.NET 5 are available at the following URL:
>
> - **Release notes:** `https://docs.microsoft.com/en-us/dotnet/core/dotnet-five`
> - For additional info about the C# 9.0 new features, take a look at the following URL: `https://docs.microsoft.com/en-us/dotnet/csharp/whats-new/csharp-9`.

.NET 6

.NET 6 came out on November 8, 2021, a year after .NET 5, as expected by the .NET schedule. The most notable improvement in this version is the introduction of the *Multi-platform Application UI*, also known as *MAUI*: a modern UI toolkit built on top of Xamarin, specifically created to eventually replace Xamarin and become the .NET standard for creating multi-platform applications that can run on Android, iOS, macOS, and Windows from a single code base.

The main difference between *MAUI* and *Xamarin* is that the new approach now ships as a core workload, shares the same base class library as other workloads (such as *Blazor*), and adopts the most recent *SDK Style project system* introduced with .NET 5, thus allowing a consistent tooling and coding experience for all .NET developers.

In addition to *MAUI*, .NET 6 brings a lot of new features and improvements, such as:

- *C# 10 language support*, with some new features such as *null parameter checking*, *required properties*, *field keyword*, *file-scoped namespaces*, *top-level statements*, *async main*, *target-typed new expressions*, and more.

- *Implicit using directives*, a feature that instructs the compiler to automatically import a set of using statements based on the project type, without the need to explicitly include them in each file.

- *New project templates*, which are much cleaner and simpler since they do implement (and demonstrate) most of the language improvements brought by C# version 9 and 10 (including those we've just mentioned).

- *Package Validation tooling*, an option that allows developers to validate that their packages are consistent and well-formed during package development.

- *SDK workloads*, a feature that leverages the concepts of "workloads" introduced with .NET Core to allow developers to install only necessary SDK components, skipping the parts they don't need: in other words, it's basically a "package manager" for the SDKs.

- *Inner-loop performance improvements*, a family of tweaks dedicated to the performance optimization of the various tools and workflows used by developers (such as CLI, runtime, and MSBuild), thereby aiming to improve their coding and building experience. The most important of them is the *Hot Reload*, a feature that allows the project's source code to be modified while the application is running, without the need to manually pause or hit a breakpoint.

For a comprehensive list of the new C# 10 features, check out the following URL: `https://docs.microsoft.com/en-us/dotnet/csharp/whats-new/csharp-10`.

This concludes our journey through the recent history of ASP.NET. In the next section, we'll move our focus to the Angular ecosystem, which experienced a rather similar turn of events.

What's new in Angular?

If following in the footsteps of Microsoft and the .NET Foundation in recent years has not been an easy task, things were not going to get any better when we turned our eyes to the client-side web framework known as Angular. To understand what happened there, we have to go back 10 years, to when JavaScript libraries such as jQuery and MooTools were dominating the client-side scene; the first client-side frameworks, such as Dojo, Backbone.js, and Knockout.js, were struggling to gain popularity and reach wide adoption; and stuff such as React and Vue.js didn't even exist.

Truth be told, jQuery is still dominating the scene to a huge extent, at least according to BuiltWith (`https://trends.builtwith.com/javascript/javascript-library`) and w3Techs (`https://w3techs.com/technologies/overview/javascript_library/all`). However, despite being used by 74.1% of all websites, it's definitely an option chosen less often by web developers than it was 10 years ago.

GetAngular

The story of AngularJS started in 2009 when Miško Hevery (now senior computer scientist and Agile coach at Google) and Adam Abrons (now director of engineering at Grand Rounds) were working on their side project, an **end-to-end** (E2E) web development tool that would have offered an online JSON storage service and also a client-side library to build web applications depending on it. To publish their project, they took the GetAngular.com hostname.

During that time, Hevery, who was already working at Google, was assigned to the Google Feedback project with two other developers. Together, they wrote more than 17,000 lines of code in 6 months, slowly sinking into a frustrating scenario of code bloat and testing issues. Given the situation, Hevery asked his manager to rewrite the application using GetAngular (the side project mentioned previously), betting that he could do that alone within 2 weeks. His manager accepted and Hevery lost the bet shortly thereafter, as the whole thing took him 3 weeks instead of 2; however, the new application had only 1,500 lines of code instead of 17,000. This was more than enough to get Google's interest in the new framework, which was given the name AngularJS shortly thereafter.

 To listen to the full story, take a look at the following Miško Hevery keynote speech at ng-conf 2014: https://www.youtube.com/watch?v=r1A1VR0ibIQ.

AngularJS

The first stable release of AngularJS (version 0.9.0, also known as dragon-breath) was released on GitHub in October 2010 under an MIT license; when AngularJS 1.0.0 (also known as temporal domination) came out in June 2012, the framework had already achieved huge popularity within the web development communities worldwide.

The reasons for such extraordinary success can hardly be summarized in a few words, but I'll try to do that nonetheless by emphasizing some key selling points:

- **Dependency injection:** AngularJS was the first client-side framework to implement it. This was undeniably a huge advantage over the competitors, including DOM-manipulating libraries such as jQuery. With AngularJS, developers could write loosely coupled and easily testable components, leaving the framework with the task of creating them, resolving their dependencies, and passing them to other components when requested.
- **Directives:** These can be described as markers on specific DOM items such as elements, attributes, and styles: a powerful feature that could be used to specify custom and reusable HTML-like elements and attributes that define data bindings and/or other specific behaviors of presentation components.
- **Two-way data binding:** The automatic synchronization of data between model and view components. When data in a model changes, the view reflects the change; when data in the view changes, the model is updated as well. This happens immediately and automatically, which makes sure that the model and the view are updated at all times.

- **Single-page approach:** AngularJS was the first framework to completely remove the need for page reloads. This provided great benefits at both the server-side (fewer and smaller network requests) and client-side level (smoother transitions, a more responsive experience), and paved the way for the single-page application pattern that would also be adopted by React, Vue.js, and the other runner-up frameworks later on.

- **Cache-friendly:** All the AngularJS magic was meant to happen on the client side, without any server-side effort to generate the UI/UX parts. For this very reason, all AngularJS websites could be cached anywhere and/or made available through a CDN.

 For a detailed list of AngularJS features, improvements, and bug fixes from 0.9.0 through 1.7.8, check out the following link:

- **AngularJS 1.x Changelog:** `https://github.com/angular/angular.js/blob/master/CHANGELOG.md`

Angular 2

The new release of AngularJS, released on September 14, 2016, and known as Angular 2, was a complete rewrite of the previous one, entirely based upon the new ECMAScript version 6 (officially ECMAScript 2015) specifications. Just like the ASP.NET Core rewrite, the revolution brought such a number of breaking changes at the architectural level and for HTTP pipeline handling, the app life cycle, and state management that porting the old code to the new one was nearly impossible. Despite keeping its former name, the new Angular version was a brand-new framework with little or nothing in common with the previous one.

The choice to not make Angular 2 backward-compatible with AngularJS clearly demonstrated the intention of the author's team to adopt a completely new approach, not only in the code syntax but also in their way of thinking and designing the client app. The new Angular was highly modular, component-based, and came with a new and improved dependency injection model and a whole lot of programming patterns its older cousin had never heard of.

Here's a brief list of the most important improvements introduced with Angular 2:

- **Semantic versioning:** Angular 2 is the first release to use semantic versioning, also known as SemVer: a universal way of versioning the various software releases to help developers track down what's going on without having to dig into the changelog details. SemVer is based on three numbers – $X.Y.Z$, where X stands for a *major* version, Y stands for a *minor* version, and Z stands for a *patch* release. More specifically, the X number, representing the *major* version, gets incremented when incompatible API changes are made to stable APIs; the Y number, representing the *minor* version, gets incremented when backward-compatible functionality is added; and the Z number, representing a *patch* release, gets incremented when a backward-compatible bug is fixed. Such improvements can be easily underestimated, yet it's a must-have for most modern software development scenarios where **Continuous Delivery (CD)** is paramount and new versions are released with great frequency.

- **TypeScript:** Seasoned developers will probably already know what TypeScript is. Those who don't won't need to worry since we're going to use it a lot during the Angular-related chapters of this book. For now, let's just say that TypeScript is a Microsoft-made superset of JavaScript that allows the use of all ES2015 features (such as Default, Rest, and Spread parameters; template literals; arrow functions; Promises; and more) and adds powerful type-checking and object-oriented features during development (such as class and type declarations). The TypeScript source code can be transpiled into standard JavaScript code that all browsers can understand.

- **Server-side rendering (SSR):** Angular 2 comes with Angular Universal, an open source technology that allows a *back-end* server to run Angular applications and serve only the resulting static HTML files to the client. In a nutshell, the server will render a first pass of the page for faster delivery to the client, and then immediately refresh it with client code. SSR has its caveats, such as requiring Node.js to be installed on the host machine to execute the necessary pre-rendering steps, as well as having the whole `node_modules` folder there, but can greatly increase the app's response time for a typical internet browser, thus mitigating a known AngularJS performance issue.

- **Angular Mobile Toolkit (AMT):** A set of tools specifically designed for building high-performance mobile apps.

- **Command-line interface (CLI):** The new CLI introduced with Angular 2 can be used by developers to generate components, routes, services, and pipes via console/terminal commands, together with simple test shells.

- **Components:** These are the main building blocks of Angular 2, entirely replacing the controllers and scopes of AngularJS, and also taking on most of the tasks previously covered by the former directives. Application data, business logic, templating, and the styling of an Angular 2 app can all be done using components.

 I did my best to explore most of these features in my first book, *ASP.NET Core and Angular 2*, which was published in October 2016, right after the final release of the two frameworks: `https://www.packtpub.com/product/asp-net-core-and-angular-2/9781786465689`.

Angular 4

On March 23, 2017, Google released Angular 4: the number 3 version was skipped entirely in order to unify all the major versions of the many Angular components that had been developed separately before that date, such as Angular Router, which already was at version 3.x at the time. Starting with Angular 4, the entire Angular framework was then unified into the same MAJOR.MINOR.PATCH SemVer pattern.

The new major version brought a limited number of breaking changes, such as a new and improved routing system, TypeScript 2.1+ support (and a requirement), and some deprecated interfaces and tags. There were also a good number of improvements, including:

- **Ahead-of-time (AOT) compilation:** Angular 4 compiles the templates during the build phase and generates JavaScript code accordingly. That's a huge architectural improvement over the JIT mode used by AngularJS and Angular 2, where the app was compiled at runtime.

For example, when the application starts, not only is the app faster since the client doesn't have to compile anything, but it throws/breaks at build time instead of during runtime for most component errors, thus leading to more secure and stable deployments.

- **Animations npm package:** All the existing UI animations and effects – as well as new ones – were moved to the @angular/animations dedicated package instead of being part of @angular/core. This was a smart move to give non-animated apps the chance to drop that part of code, thereby being much smaller and arguably faster.

Other notable improvements included a new form validator to check for valid email addresses, a new paramMap interface for URL parameters in the HTTP routing module, and better internalization support.

Angular 5

Released on November 1, 2017, Angular 5 featured TypeScript 2.3 support, another small set of breaking changes, many performance and stability improvements, and a few new features, such as the following:

- **New HTTP Client API:** Starting from Angular 4.3, the @angular/http module was put aside in favor of a new @angular/common/http package with better JSON support, interceptors, immutable request/response objects, and other stuff. The switch was completed in Angular 5 with the previous module being deprecated and the new one recommended for use in all apps.

- **State Transfer API:** A new feature that gives the developer the ability to transfer the state of the application between the server and the client.

- **A new set of router events for more granular control over the HTTP life cycle:** ActivationStart, ActivationEnd, ChildActivationStart, ChildActivationEnd, GuardsCheckStart, GuardsCheckEnd, ResolveStart, and ResolveEnd.

November 2017 was also the release month of my *ASP.NET Core 2 and Angular 5* book, which covers most of the aforementioned improvements: https://www.packtpub.com/product/asp-net-core-2-and-angular-5/9781788293600.

In June 2018, that book was made available as a video course: https://www.packtpub.com/product/asp-net-core-2-and-angular-5-video/9781789531442.

Angular 6

Released in April 2018, Angular 6 was mostly a maintenance release, more focused on improving the overall consistency of the framework and its toolchain than adding new features. Therefore, there were no major breaking changes. RxJS 6 supports a new way to register providers, the new providedIn injectable decorator, improved Angular Material support (a component specifically made to implement material design in the Angular client-side UI), more CLI commands/updates, and so on.

Another improvement worth mentioning was the new CLI ng add command, which uses the package manager to download new dependencies and invoke an installation script to update our project with configuration changes, add additional dependencies, and/or scaffold package-specific initialization code.

Last, but not least, the Angular team introduced Ivy, a next-generation Angular rendering engine that aims to increase the speed and decrease the size of the application.

Angular 7

Angular 7 came out in October 2018 and was certainly a major update, as we can easily guess by reading the words written by Stephen Fluin, developer relations lead at Google and prominent Angular spokesman, on the official Angular development blog upon the official release:

"This is a major release spanning the entire platform, including the core framework, Angular Material, and the CLI with synchronized major versions. This release contains new features for our toolchain and has enabled several major partner launches."

Here's a list of the new features:

- **Easy upgrade:** Thanks to the groundwork laid by version 6, the Angular team was able to reduce the steps that need to be done to upgrade an existing Angular app from an older version to the most recent one. The detailed procedure can be viewed by visiting `https://update.angular. io`, an incredibly useful Angular upgrade interactive guide that can be used to quickly recover the required steps, such as CLI commands and package updates.

- **CLI update:** A new command that attempts to automatically upgrade the Angular application and its dependencies by following the procedure mentioned previously.

- **CLI prompts:** The Angular CLI has been modified to prompt users when running common commands such as `ng new` or `ng add @angular/material` to help developers discover built-in features such as routing and SCSS support.

- **Angular Material and CDK:** Additional UI elements such as virtual scrolling; a component that loads and unloads elements from the DOM based on the visible parts of a list, making it possible to build very fast experiences for users with very large scrollable lists; CDK-native drag-and-drop support; improved drop-down list elements; and more.

- **Partner launches:** Improved compatibility with a number of third-party community projects such as Angular Console, a downloadable console for starting and running Angular projects on your local machine; AngularFire, the official Angular package for Firebase integration; Angular for NativeScript, integration between Angular and NativeScript – a framework for building native iOS and Android apps using JavaScript and/or JS-based client frameworks; some interesting new Angular-specific features for StackBlitz, an online IDE that can be used to create Angular and React projects, such as a tabbed editor and integration with the Angular Language Service; and so on.

- **Updated dependencies:** Added support for TypeScript 3.1, RxJS 6.3, and Node 10, although the previous versions can still be used for backward compatibility.

The Angular Language Service is a way to get completions, errors, hints, and navigation inside Angular templates: think about it as a virtuous mix between a syntax highlighter, IntelliSense, and a real-time syntax error checker. Before Angular 7, which added the support for StackBlitz, such a feature was only available for Visual Studio Code and WebStorm.

For additional information about the Angular Language Service, take a look at the following URL: `https://angular.io/guide/language-service`.

Angular 8

Angular 7 was quickly followed by Angular 8, which was released on May 29, 2019. The new release is mostly about Ivy, the long-awaited new compiler/runtime of Angular: despite being an ongoing project since Angular 5, version 8 was the first one to officially offer a runtime switch to actually opt into using Ivy, which would become the default runtime starting from Angular 9.

To enable Ivy on Angular 8, the developers had to add an `"enableIvy"`: `true` property to the `angularCompilerOptions` section within the app's `tsconfig.json` file.

Those who want to know more about Ivy are encouraged to have an extensive look at the following post by Cédric Exbrayat, cofounder and trainer of the Ninja Squad website and now part of the Angular developer team: `https://blog.ninja-squad.com/2019/05/07/what-is-angular-ivy/`.

Other notable improvements and new features included:

- **Bazel support:** Angular 8 was the first version to support Bazel, a free software tool developed and used by Google for the automation of building and testing software. It can be very useful for developers aiming to automate their delivery pipeline as it allows incremental builds and tests, and even the possibility to configure remote builds (and caches) on a build farm.
- **Routing:** A new syntax was introduced to declare the lazy-loading routes using the `import()` syntax from TypeScript 2.4+ instead of relying on a string literal. The old syntax was kept for backward compatibility but may be dropped soon.
- **Service workers:** A new registration strategy was introduced to allow developers to choose when to register their workers instead of doing it automatically at the end of the app's start up life cycle. It's also possible to bypass a service worker for a specific HTTP request using the new `ngsw-bypass` header.
- **Workspace API:** A new and more convenient way to read and modify the Angular workspace configuration instead of manually modifying the `angular.json` file.

In client-side development, a service worker is a script that the browser runs in the background to do any kind of stuff that doesn't require either a user interface or any user interaction. If you're new to the concept, don't worry – we'll extensively talk about them in *Chapter 12*, *Progressive Web Apps*, where we'll build our very own service worker.

The new version also introduced some notable breaking changes – mostly due to Ivy – and removed some long-time deprecated packages such as @angular/http, which was replaced by @angular/common/http in Angular 4.3 and then officially deprecated in 5.0.

A comprehensive list of all the deprecated APIs can be found in the official Angular deprecations guide at the following URL: https://angular.io/guide/deprecations.

Angular 9

Angular 9 was released in February 2020 after a long streak of release candidates through 2019 Q4 and was the most recent version for only 4 months before being replaced by its successor (Angular 10).

The new release brought the following new features:

- **JavaScript bundles and performance**: An attempt to fix the very large bundle files, one of the most cumbersome issues of the previous versions of Angular, which drastically increased the download time and brought down the overall performance.
- **Ivy compiler**: The new Angular build and render pipeline, shipped with Angular 8 as an opt-in preview, is now the default rendering engine.
- **Selector-less bindings**: A useful feature that was available to the previous rendering engine, but missing from the Angular 8 Ivy preview, is now available to Ivy as well.
- **Internationalization**: Another Ivy enhancement that makes use of the Angular CLI to generate most of the standard code necessary to create files for translators and to publish an Angular app in multiple languages, thanks to the new i18n attribute.

The new i18n attribute is a numeronym, which is often used as an alias for internationalization. The number 18 stands for the number of letters between the first *i* and the last *n* in the word *internationalization*. The term seems to have been coined by the **Digital Equipment Corporation** (**DEC**) around the 1970s or 1980s, together with l10n for localization, due to the excessive length of the two words.

The long-awaited Ivy compiler deserves a couple more words, being a very important feature for the future of Angular.

As the average Angular developer already knows, the rendering engine plays a major role in the overall performance of any *front-end* framework since it's the tool that translates the actions and intents laid out by the presentation logic (in Angular components and templates) into the instructions that will update the DOM. If the renderer is more efficient, it will arguably require fewer instructions, thus increasing the overall performance while decreasing the amount of required JavaScript code at the same time. Since the JavaScript bundles produced by Ivy are much smaller than the previous rendering engine, Angular 9's overall improvement is relevant in terms of both performance and size.

February 2020 was also the release month of my *ASP.NET Core 3 and Angular 9* book, featuring a whole new set of source code snippets and project samples that can also be found in this book: `https://www.packtpub.com/product/asp-net-core-3-and-angular-9-third-edition/9781789612165`.

Angular 10

Angular 10 was released on June 24, 2020, just a few months after Angular 9. The short timeframe between Angular 9 and 10 was explained by the Angular development team as an attempt to get the framework back on its regular schedule since Angular 9 got delayed by a few weeks.

The new release was mostly focused on fixing issues: more than 700 issues were fixed and over 2,000 were touched on in the process. However, there were still quite a few important updates to be aware of:

- *Upgrade to TypeScript 3.9*, as well as TSLib 2.0, and TS Lint v6. It's worth noting that earlier versions of TypeScript are no longer supported because they are not compatible with some potentially breaking changes in the `tsconfig.json` file structure (see below).
- *Angular Material improvements*, including a new date range picker.
- *Additional warnings when using CommonJS imports*, as they can result in both larger and slower applications.
- *Optional stricter settings*: Developers are now able to create new projects with a *strict* flag that enables stricter listing rules and bundle sizes, thereby resulting in more efficient tree-shaking (a term commonly used in JavaScript contexts for dead-code elimination using the `import` and `export` module syntax).

For additional info about the improved `tsconfig.json` file structure (namely, *"Solution Style" tsconfig.json files*), take a look at the following paragraph from the TypeScript 3.9 release notes: `https://www.typescriptlang.org/docs/handbook/release-notes/typescript-3-9.html#support-for-solution-style-tsconfigjson-files`.

To know more about the meaning of the term "tree-shaking," check out the following guide: `https://developer.mozilla.org/en-US/docs/Glossary/Tree_shaking`.

Angular 11

Angular 11 was released on November 11, 2020, the same release day of .NET 5. The new release added the following features:

- *Component Test Harnesses*, a set of classes that lets a test interact with a component via a supported API. By using the Harness API, a test insulates itself against updates to the internals of a component, such as changing its DOM structure: such an idea comes from the `PageObject` pattern, which is commonly used for integration testing.
- *Updated Hot Module Replacement Support*: HMR is a mechanism that allows modules to be replaced without a full browser refresh; configuring HMR in Angular 11 is a lot easier, and they also introduced a new `--hmr` CLI command to enable it.
- *TypeScript 4.0 Support*: While TypeScript 3.9 (and lower) support has been dropped, this important upgrade allows Angular 11 apps to build much faster than previous versions.
- *Webpack 5 support*, although it is still experimental since the new version has only been released recently and might still not be entirely stable.
- *TSLint to ESLint migration*: This is one of the most important changes to this version since TSLint and Codelyzer have been officially deprecated, and they will definitely be removed in the next release. To help developers to deal with such an update, the Angular team has introduced a three-step method that can be used to seamlessly migrate from TSLint to ESLint using the CLI.
- *Dropped support for Internet Explorer 9 and 10*, as well as IE mobile.

Other new features included updated Language Service Preview, new automated migrations and schematics, some service worker improvements, lazy-loading support for named outlets, resolve guard generation via the Angular CLI, stricter types for built-in pipes, and ISO 8601 week-numbering year format support in the `formatDate` function.

Angular 12

Angular 12 came out on May 12, 2021, after numerous beta releases and release candidates. The major update to this version is the long-announced deprecation of the legacy View Engine compilation and rendering pipeline in favor of the now stable and objectively superior Ivy technology, thus granting faster Ahead-Of-Time compilation.

Other notable improvements include:

- *Nullish Coalescing operator* (??) in Angular templates.
- *Style improvements*, thanks to inline Sass support in Components (within the `styles` field of the `@Component` decorator).
- *Deprecating support for IE11*, which will be removed in Angular 13.
- *HTTP improvements*, such as human-readable `HttpStatusCode` names and some new methods for dealing with HTTP parameters and metadata more efficiently.

- *Strict mode by default*. The Angular strict mode is now enabled by default in the CLI: this flag will enable several source code consistency checks in the TypeScript compiler as well as in Angular. Writing code with strict mode enabled helps developers to catch bugs early, reduce bundle size, avoid allocating unnecessary memory, follow best practices and get better IDE support, thus improving the maintainability of the app.

Angular 13

Last, but not least, we come to Angular 13, which was released on November 3, 2021, and is currently the most recent version.

The new features list includes:

- *FormControlStatus*, a new type that will seamlessly include all possible status strings for form controls.
- *View Engine*, which was already deprecated in Angular 12, has been removed, thus leaving the new *Ivy* rendering engine as the only choice. View Engine removal also means that *IE11* support has been dropped as well.
- *Angular Package Format (APF)* has been redesigned, removing *View Engine*-specific metadata, matching the format of ES2020, and adding support for *Node Package Exports*.
- *New Component API*, which allows developers to create components with less boilerplate code.
- *Persistent Build Cache* support has been enabled by default.
- *RxJS dependency version* has been updated from 6.x to 7.4.
- *TestBed performance improvements* that lead to faster, less memory-intensive, less interdependent, and more optimized tests.

This concludes our brief review of the recent history of the ASP.NET Core and Angular ecosystems. In the next sections, we'll summarize the most important reasons that led us to choose them in 2021-2022.

Reasons for choosing .NET and Angular

As we have seen, both frameworks have gone through many intense years of changes. This led to a whole refoundation of their core and, right after that, a constant strain to get back on top – or at least not lose ground against most modern frameworks that came out after their now-departed golden age. These frameworks are eager to dominate the development scene: Python, Go, and Rust for the server-side part, and React, Vue.js, and Ember.js for the client-side part, not to mention the Node.js and Express ecosystem, and most of the old competitors from the 1990s and 2000s, such as Java, Ruby, and PHP, which are still alive and kicking.

That said, here's a list of good reasons for picking ASP.NET Core in 2022:

- **Performance:** The new .NET web stack is considerably fast, especially since .NET Core 3.1, with further improvements in .NET 5 and .NET 6.
- **Integration:** It supports most, if not all, modern client-side frameworks, including Angular, React, and Vue.js.

- **Cross-platform approach**: .NET web applications can run on Windows, macOS, and Linux in an almost seamless way.

- **Hosting**: .NET web applications can be hosted almost anywhere: from a Windows machine with IIS to a Linux appliance with Apache or NGINX, from Docker containers to edge-case, self-hosting scenarios using the Kestrel and WebListener HTTP servers.

- **Dependency injection:** The framework supports a built-in dependency injection design pattern that provides a huge number of advantages during development, such as reduced dependencies, code reusability, readability, and testing.

- **Modular HTTP pipeline**: ASP.NET middleware grants developers granular control over the HTTP pipeline, which can be reduced to its core (for ultra-lightweight tasks) or enriched with powerful, highly configurable features such as internationalization, third-party authentication/ authorization, caching, routing, seamless integration with industry-standard APIs, interfaces, and tools such as *SignalR*, *GraphQL*, *Swagger*, *Webhooks*, and *JWT*.

- **Open source:** The whole .NET stack has been released as open source and is entirely focused on strong community support, thus being reviewed and improved by thousands of developers every day.

- **Side-by-side execution:** It supports the simultaneous running of multiple versions of an application or component on the same machine. This basically means that it's possible to have multiple versions of the common language runtime, and multiple versions of applications and components that use a version of the runtime, on the same computer at the same time. This is great for most real-life development scenarios as it gives the development team more control over which versions of a component an application binds to, and more control over which version of the runtime an application uses.

As for the Angular framework, the most important reason we're picking it over other excellent JavaScript libraries such as React, Vue.js, and Ember.js is the fact that it already comes with a huge pack of features out of the box, making it the most suitable choice, although maybe not as simple to use as other frameworks/libraries. If we combine that with the consistency benefits brought by the TypeScript language, we can say that Angular, from its 2016 rebirth up to the present day, has embraced the framework approach more convincingly than the others. This has been consistently confirmed in the last few years, with the project undergoing six major versions and gaining a lot in terms of stability, performance, and features, without losing much in terms of backward compatibility, best practices, and overall approach. All these reasons are solid enough to invest in it, hoping it will continue to keep up with these compelling premises.

Now that we have acknowledged the reasons to use these frameworks, let's ask ourselves the best way to find out more about them: the next chapter should give us the answers we need.

Summary

Before moving on, let's do a quick recap of what we just talked about in this chapter.

We briefly described our platforms of choice – ASP.NET and Angular – and acknowledged their combined potential in the process of building a modern web application.

We spent some valuable time recalling what's happened in these last few years and summarizing the efforts of both development teams to reboot and improve their respective frameworks. These recaps were very useful to enumerate and understand the main reasons why we're still using them over their ever-growing competitors.

In the next chapter, we will deal with the typical challenges of a full stack developer: define our goals, acquire the proper mindset, set up the environment, and create our first ASP.NET and Angular projects.

Suggested topics

For further information, we recommend the following topics: ASP.NET Core, .NET Core, .NET 6, Angular, Angular 13, Tree-shaking, Angular Ivy, tsconfig.json, Roslyn, CoreCLR, RyuJIT, NuGet, npm, ECMAScript 6, JavaScript, TypeScript, webpack, SystemJS, RxJS, Cache-Control, HTTP Headers, .NET middleware, Angular Universal, server-side rendering (SSR), ahead-of-time (AOT) compiler, service workers, web manifest files, and tsconfig.json.

References

- *ASP.NET 5 is dead – Introducing ASP.NET Core 1.0 and .NET Core 1.0*: `http://www.hanselman.com/blog/ASPNET5IsDeadIntroducingASPNETCore10AndNETCore10.aspx`

- *An Update on ASP.NET Core and .NET Core*: `https://blogs.msdn.microsoft.com/webdev/2016/02/01/an-update-on-asp-net-core-and-net-core/`

- *ASP.NET Core 1.1.0 release notes*: `https://github.com/aspnet/AspNetCore/releases/1.1.0`

- *ASP.NET Core 1.1.0 Commits list*: `https://github.com/dotnet/core/blob/master/release-notes/1.1/1.1-commits.md`

- *ASP.NET Core 2.1.0 release notes*: `https://docs.microsoft.com/en-US/aspnet/core/release-notes/aspnetcore-2.1`

- *ASP.NET Core 2.1.0 Commits list*: `https://github.com/dotnet/core/blob/master/release-notes/2.1/2.1.0-commit.md`

- *ASP.NET Core 2.2.0 release notes*: `https://docs.microsoft.com/en-US/aspnet/core/release-notes/aspnetcore-2.2`

- *ASP.NET Core 2.2.0 Commits list*: `https://github.com/dotnet/core/blob/master/release-notes/2.2/2.2.0/2.2.0-commits.md`

- *ASP.NET Core 3.0.0 release notes*: `https://docs.microsoft.com/en-us/dotnet/core/whats-new/dotnet-core-3-0`

- *ASP.NET Core 3.0 releases page*: `https://github.com/dotnet/core/tree/master/release-notes/3.0`

- *ASP.NET Core 3.1.0 release notes*: `https://docs.microsoft.com/en-us/dotnet/core/whats-new/dotnet-core-3-1`

- *.NET Core is the future of .NET*: `https://devblogs.microsoft.com/dotnet/net-core-is-the-future-of-net/`

- *The Evolution from .NET Core to .NET 5*: `https://docs.microsoft.com/en-us/dotnet/core/dotnet-five`

- *Introducing .NET 5*: https://devblogs.microsoft.com/dotnet/introducing-net-5/
- *Performance improvements in .NET 5*: https://devblogs.microsoft.com/dotnet/performance-improvements-in-net-5/
- *Introducing the Half Type*: https://devblogs.microsoft.com/dotnet/introducing-the-half-type/
- *App Trimming in .NET 5*: https://devblogs.microsoft.com/dotnet/app-trimming-in-net-5/
- *What's new in C# 9.0*: https://docs.microsoft.com/en-us/dotnet/csharp/whats-new/csharp-9
- *BuiltWith: JavaScript Library Usage Distribution*: https://trends.builtwith.com/javascript/javascript-library
- *Usage of JavaScript libraries for websites*: https://w3techs.com/technologies/overview/javascript_library/all
- *Miško Hevery and Brad Green – Keynote – NG-Conf 2014*: https://www.youtube.com/watch?v=r1A1VR0ibIQ
- *AngularJS 1.7.9 Changelog*: https://github.com/angular/angular.js/blob/master/CHANGELOG.md
- *ASP.NET Core and Angular 2*: https://www.packtpub.com/application-development/aspnet-core-and-angular-2
- *ASP.NET Core 2 and Angular 5*: https://www.packtpub.com/application-development/aspnet-core-2-and-angular-5
- *ASP.NET Core 2 and Angular 5 – Video Course*: https://www.packtpub.com/web-development/asp-net-core-2-and-angular-5-video
- *Angular Update Guide*: https://update.angular.io
- *Angular Language Service*: https://angular.io/guide/language-service
- *Angular Deprecated APIs and Features*: https://angular.io/guide/deprecations
- *What is Angular Ivy?*: https://blog.ninja-squad.com/2019/05/07/what-is-angular-ivy/
- *Solution Style tsconfig.json files*: https://www.typescriptlang.org/docs/handbook/release-notes/typescript-3-9.html#support-for-solution-style-tsconfigjson-files
- *Tree Shaking*: https://developer.mozilla.org/en-US/docs/Glossary/Tree_shaking

2

Getting Ready

In this second chapter, we'll switch from theory to practice: more specifically, we will choose the kind of web application that we want to build and how we can do it in accordance with the expectations of a typical product owner.

In the second part of this chapter, we'll start our development journey by setting up our local development environment and create our first Angular and ASP.NET Core projects.

Here's a full breakdown of the topics we're going to cover:

- **A full-stack approach**: The importance of being able to learn how to design, assemble, and deliver a complete product
- **Multi-page applications (MPAs), single-page applications (SPAs), native web applications (NWAs), and progressive web applications (PWAs)**: Key features of and the most important differences between the various types of web applications, as well as how well ASP.NET and Angular could relate to each one of them
- **A sample SPA project**: What we're going to do throughout this book
- **Preparing the workspace**: How to set up our workstation to achieve our first goal – implementing a simple Hello World boilerplate that will be further extended in the following chapters

By the end of the chapter, we'll have everything we need to start our full-stack development journey.

Technical requirements

In this chapter, we're going to need all the technical requirements listed in the previous chapters, with no additional resources, libraries, or packages.

The code files for this chapter can be found here: `https://github.com/PacktPublishing/ASP.NET-Core-6-and-Angular/tree/main/Chapter_02`.

A full-stack approach

Learning to use ASP.NET Core and Angular together means being able to work with both the *front-end* (client side) and *back-end* (server side) of a web application; to put it in other words, it means being able to design, assemble, and deliver a complete product.

Eventually, in order to do that, we'll need to dig through the following:

- *Back-end* programming
- *Front-end* programming
- UI styling and UX design
- Database design, modeling, configuration, and administration
- Web server configuration and administration
- Web application deployment

At first glance, it can seem that this kind of approach goes against common sense; a single developer should not be allowed to do everything by themselves. Every developer knows that the *back-end* and the *front-end* require entirely different skills and experience, so why in the world should we do that?

Before answering this question, we should understand what we really mean when we say *being able to*. We don't have to become experts on every single layer of the stack; no one expects us to. When we choose to embrace the full-stack approach, what we really need to do is raise our awareness level throughout the whole stack we're working on; this means that we need to know how the *back-end* works, and how it can and will be connected to the *front-end*. We need to know how the data will be stored, retrieved, and then served through the client. We need to acknowledge the interactions we will need to layer out between the various components that our web application is made from, and we need to be aware of security concerns, authentication mechanisms, optimization strategies, load balancing techniques, and so on.

This doesn't necessarily mean that we have to have strong skills in all these areas; as a matter of fact, we hardly ever will. Nonetheless, if we want to pursue a full-stack approach, we need to understand the meaning, role, and scope of all of them. Furthermore, we should be able to work our way through any of these fields whenever we need to.

MPAs, SPAs, PWAs, and NWAs

In order to demonstrate how ASP.NET and Angular can work together to their full extent, we couldn't think of anything better than building some small SPA projects with most, if not all, PWA features. The reason for this choice is quite obvious: there is no better approach to demonstrate some of the best features they have to offer nowadays. We'll have the chance to work with modern interfaces and patterns such as the HTML5 pushState API, webhooks, data transport-based requests, dynamic web components, UI data bindings, and a stateless, AJAX-driven architecture capable of flawlessly encompassing all of these features. We'll also make good use of some distinctive PWA features such as service workers and web manifest files.

If you don't know the meaning of these definitions and acronyms, don't worry, we are going to explore these concepts in the next couple of sections, which are dedicated to enumerating the most relevant features of the following types of web applications: MPAs, SPAs, PWAs, and NWAs. While we're there, we'll also try to figure out the most common product owner's expectations for a typical web-based project.

Multi-page applications

Multi-page applications, also known as **MPAs**, are those web applications that work in a traditional way: each time the user asks for (or submits) data to the server, they render a new page that is sent back to the browser.

This is how all websites used to work during the first 20 years of the World Wide Web, and is still the most widely used approach nowadays due to a number of advantages that MPAs can still provide: excellent SEO performance, a fast and steady learning curve, the ability to manage and customize static and dynamic content, and a lot of great **content management systems** (**CMSes**), frameworks, and UI themes – such as WordPress, Joomla, and the like – that can be used to build them from the ground up in a few minutes.

However, MPAs also come with some significant cons: the required server-side roundtrips tend to make them quite expensive in terms of bandwidth; moreover, front-end and back-end development are often tightly coupled, thus making them harder to maintain and update. Luckily enough, most of these issues have been mitigated throughout the years, thanks to various browser features and technology improvements such as CDN, server-side caching, AJAX requests, and so on. At the same time, such techniques add more complexity to the development and deployment phases; that is, unless we choose to rely upon one of the CMS platforms that we talked about early on, thus giving up on most of the coding aspects – with all that that implies.

Single-page applications

To put it briefly, an SPA is a web-based application that tries to provide the same user experience as a desktop application. If we consider the fact that all SPAs are still served through a web server and thus accessed by web browsers, just like any other standard website, we can easily understand how that desired outcome can only be achieved by changing some of the default patterns commonly used in web development, such as resource loading, DOM management, and UI navigation. In a good SPA, both content and resources – HTML, JavaScript, CSS, and so on – are either retrieved within a single page load or are dynamically fetched when needed. This also means that the page doesn't reload or refresh; it just changes and adapts in response to user actions, performing the required server-side calls behind the scenes.

These are some of the key features provided by a competitive SPA nowadays:

- **No server-side round trips**: A competitive SPA can redraw any part of the client UI without requiring a full server-side round trip to retrieve a full HTML page. This is mostly achieved by implementing the **separation of concerns** (**SOC**) design principle, which means that the data source, the business logic, and the presentation layer will be separated.

- **Efficient routing**: A competitive SPA is able to keep track of the user's current state and location during its whole navigation experience using organized, JavaScript-based routers. We'll talk more about that in the upcoming chapters when we introduce the concepts of server-side and client-side routing.

- **Performance and flexibility**: A competitive SPA usually transfers all of its UI to the client, thanks to its JavaScript SDK of choice (Angular, jQuery, Bootstrap, and so on). This is often good for network performance as increasing client-side rendering and offline processing reduces the UI impact over the network. However, the real deal brought by this approach is the flexibility granted to the UI as the developer will be able to completely rewrite the application's *front-end* with little or no impact on the server, aside from a few of the static resource files.

This list can easily grow, as these are only some of the major advantages of a properly designed, competitive SPA. These aspects play a major role nowadays, as many business websites and services are switching from their traditional MPA mindset to fully committed or hybrid SPA-based approaches.

Progressive web applications

In 2015, another web development pattern pushed its way into the light when Frances Berriman (a British freelance designer) and Alex Russel (a Google Chrome engineer) used the term PWAs for the first time to refer to those web applications that could take advantage of a couple of new important features supported by modern browsers: service workers and web manifest files. These two important improvements could be successfully used to deliver some functionalities usually only available on mobile apps – push notifications, offline mode, permission-based hardware access, and so on – using standard web-based development tools such as HTML, CSS, and JavaScript.

The rise of PWAs began in March 19, 2018, when Apple implemented support for service workers in Safari 11.1. Since that date, PWAs have been widely adopted throughout the industry thanks to their undeniable advantages over their "non-progressive" counterparts: faster load times, smaller application sizes, higher audience engagement, and so on.

Here are the main technical features of a PWA (according to Google):

- **Progressive**: Works for every user, regardless of browser choice, using progressive enhancement principles
- **Responsive**: Fits any form factor: desktop, mobile, tablet, or forms yet to emerge
- **Connectivity independent**: Service workers allow offline use, or use on low-quality networks
- **App-like**: Feels like an app to the user with app-style interactions and navigation
- **Fresh**: Always up to date due to the service worker update process
- **Safe**: Served via HTTPS to prevent snooping and ensure content hasn't been tampered with
- **Discoverable**: Identifiable as an application by a web manifest (`manifest.json`) file, and a registered service worker, and discoverable by search engines
- **Re-engageable**: The ability to use push notifications to maintain engagement with the user
- **Installable**: Provides home screen icons without the use of an app store
- **Linkable**: Can easily be shared via a URL and does not require complex installation

However, their technical baseline criteria can be restricted to the following subset:

- **HTTPS:** They must be served from a secure origin, which means over TLS with green padlock displays (no active mixed content)
- **Minimal offline mode:** They must be able to start even if the device is not connected to the web, with limited functions or at least displaying a custom offline page
- **Service workers:** They have to register a service worker with a fetch event handler (which is required for minimal offline support, as explained previously)
- **Web manifest file:** They need to reference a valid `manifest.json` file with at least four key properties (`name`, `short_name`, `start_url` and `display`) and a minimum set of required icons

> For those interested in reading about this directly from the source, here's the original link from the Google Developers website:
>
> `https://developers.google.com/web/progressive-web-apps/`
>
> In addition, here are two follow-up posts from Alex Russell's Infrequently Noted blog:
>
> `https://infrequently.org/2015/06/progressive-apps-escaping-tabs-without-losing-our-soul/`
>
> `https://infrequently.org/2016/09/what-exactly-makes-something-a-progressive-web-app/`
>
> For those who don't know, Alex Russell has worked as a senior staff software engineer at Google since December 2008.

Although they have some similarities, PWAs and SPAs are two different concepts, have different requirements, and differ in many important aspects. As we can see, none of the PWA requirements mentioned previously refer to SPAs or server-side round trips. A PWA *can* work within a single HTML page and AJAX-based requests (thus also being an SPA), but it *could* also request other server-rendered (or static) pages and/or perform standard HTTP GET or POST requests, much like an MPA. It's also the opposite: any SPA can implement any single PWA technical criteria, depending on the product owner's requirements (more on that later), the server-side and client-side frameworks adopted, and the developer's ultimate goal.

Native web applications

The first good definition of **native web applications** (also known as **NWAs**) available on the web can arguably be found in Sam Johnston's blog post written on January 16, 2009, which went like this:

> *A Native Web Application (NWA) is a web application which is 100% supported out of the box by recent standards-compliant web browsers.*

A similar approach was used 6 years later (January 22, 2015) by Henrik Joreteg to describe the defining feature of NWAs:

> *The thing these apps all have in common is that they all depend on the native web technologies: HTML, CSS, and JavaScript (arguably, you could add WebGL to that list).*

These definitions help us to understand that we're dealing with a rather generic term that encompasses SPAs, MPAs, and even PWAs – since they all depend on native web technologies that are supported out of the box by all recent browsers; however, due to the emphasis given to the *recent* keyword and the existence of the more specific web application types, the term NWA is mostly used to identify those web applications that, although being built using modern web-based technologies, cannot be classified as MPAs, SPAs, or PWAs because they tend to adopt a *hybrid* approach.

Since we're going to use Angular, which is all about developing SPAs and has also shipped with a strong and steady service worker implementation since version 5, we are fully entitled to take advantage of the best of both worlds. For this very reason, we're going to use service workers – along with the benefits of increased reliability and performance they provide – whenever we need to, all while keeping a solid SPA approach. Furthermore, we're definitely going to implement some strategic HTTP round trips (and/or other redirect-based techniques) whenever we can profitably use a microservice to lift off some workload from our app, just like any good NWA is meant to do.

Are all these features able to respond to modern market needs? Let's try to find it out.

Product owner expectations

One of the most interesting, yet underrated, concepts brought out by many modern Agile software development frameworks, such as Scrum, is the importance given to the meanings and definitions of roles. Among these roles, there's nothing as important as the product owner, also known as the customer in the Extreme Programming methodology, or customer representative elsewhere. They're the ones who bring to the development table the expectations we'll struggle to satisfy. They will tell us what's most important to deliver and when they will prioritize our work based on its manifest business value rather than its underlying architectural value. They'll be empowered by management to make decisions and make tough calls, which is sometimes great, sometimes not; this will often have a big impact on our development schedule. To cut it short, they're the ones in charge of the project; that's why, in order to deliver a web application matching their expectations, we'll need to understand their vision and feel it as if it were our own.

This is always true, even if the project's product owner is our dad, wife, or best friend: that's how it works.

Now that we have made that clear, let's take a look at some of the most common product owner expectations for a typical web-based SPA project. We ought to see whether the choice of using ASP.NET and Angular will be good enough to fulfill each one of them, as follows:

- **Early release(s)**: No matter what we're selling, the customer will always want to see what they're buying. For example, if we plan to use an Agile development framework such as Scrum, we'll have to release a potentially shippable product at the end of each sprint, or if we are looking to adopt a Waterfall-based approach, we're going to have milestones. One thing is for sure, the best thing we can do in order to efficiently organize our development efforts will be to adopt an iterative and/or modular-oriented approach.

ASP.NET and Angular, along with the strong separation of concerns granted by their underlying MVC- or MVVM-based patterns, will gracefully push us into the mindset needed to do just that.

- **GUI over back-end**: We'll often be asked to work on the GUI and *front-end* functionalities because they will be the only things that are viewable and measurable for the customer. This basically means that we'll have to mock the data model and start working on the *front-end* as soon as possible, delaying the back-end implementation as much (and as long) as we can. Note that this kind of approach is not necessarily bad; we just won't do that just to satisfy the product owner's expectations.

On the contrary, the choice of using ASP.NET along with Angular will grant us the chance to easily decouple the presentation layer and the data layer, implementing the first and mocking the latter, which is a great thing to do. We'll be able to see where we're going before wasting valuable time or being forced to make potentially wrong decisions. ASP.NET's Web API interface will provide the proper tools to do that by allowing us to create a sample web application skeleton in a matter of seconds using the controller templates available within Visual Studio and in-memory data contexts powered by Entity Framework Core, which we'll be able to access using Entity models and code first. As soon as we do that, we'll be able to switch to GUI design using the Angular presentation layer toolbox as much as we want until we reach the desired results. Once we're satisfied, we'll just need to properly implement the Web API controller interfaces and hook up the actual data.

- **Fast completion**: None of the preceding things will work unless we also manage to get everything done in a reasonable time span. This is one of the key reasons to choose to adopt a server-side framework and a client-side framework that work together with ease. ASP.NET and Angular are the tools of choice, not only because they're both built on solid, consistent ground, but also because they're meant to do precisely that – get the job done on their respective sides and provide a usable interface to the other partner.
- **Adaptability**: As stated by the Agile Manifesto, being able to respond to change requests is more important than following a plan. This is especially true in software development where we can even claim that anything that cannot handle change is a failed project. That's another great reason to embrace the separation of concerns enforced by our two frameworks of choice, as this grants the developer the ability to manage—and even welcome, to some extent—most of the layout or structural changes that will be expected during the development phase.

A few lines ago, we mentioned Scrum, which is one of the most popular Agile software development frameworks out there. Those who don't know it yet should definitely take a look at what it can offer to any results-driven team leader and/or project manager. Here's a good place to start:

`https://en.wikipedia.org/wiki/Scrum_(software_development)`

For those who are curious about the Waterfall model, here's a good place to learn more about it:

`https://en.wikipedia.org/wiki/Waterfall_model`

That's about it. Note that we didn't cover everything here as it would be impossible without the context of an actual assignment. We just tried to give an extensive answer to the following general question: if we were to build an SPA and/or a PWA, would ASP.NET and Angular be an appropriate choice? The answer is undoubtedly yes, especially when used together.

Does this mean that we're done already? Not a chance, as we have no intention of taking this assumption for granted. Conversely, it's time for us to demonstrate this by ceasing to speak in general terms and starting to put things in motion. That's precisely what we're going to do in the next section: prepare, build, and test an example SPA project.

An example SPA project

What we need now is to conceive a suitable test case scenario similar to the ones we will eventually have to deal with – an example SPA project with all the core aspects we would expect from a potentially shippable product.

In order to do this, the first thing we need to do is to become our own customer for a minute and come up with an idea, a vision to share with our other self. We'll then be able to put our developer shoes back on and split our abstract plan into a list of items we'll need to implement; these items will be the core requirements of our project. Finally, we'll set up our workstation by getting the required packages, adding the resource files, and configuring both the ASP.NET and Angular frameworks in the Visual Studio IDE.

Not your usual Hello World!

The code we're going to write within this book won't be just a shallow demonstration of full-stack development concepts; we won't throw some working code here and there and expect you to connect the dots. Our objective is to create solid, realistic web applications – with server-side web APIs and client-side UIs – using the frameworks we've chosen, and we're also going to do that following the current development best practices.

Each chapter will be dedicated to a single core aspect. If you feel like you already know your way there, feel free to skip to the next one. Conversely, if you're willing to follow us through the whole loop, you'll have a great journey through the most useful aspects of ASP.NET and Angular, as well as how they can work together to deliver the most common and useful web development tasks, from the most trivial ones to the more complex beasts. It's an investment that will pay dividends as it will leave you with a maintainable, extensible, and well-structured project, plus the knowledge needed to build your own. The following chapters will guide us through this journey. During the trip, we'll also learn how to take care of some important high-level aspects, such as SEO, security, performance issues, best coding practices, and deployment, as they will become very important if/when our applications are eventually published in a production environment.

To avoid making things too boring, we'll try to pick enjoyable themes and scenarios that will also have some usefulness in the real world: to better understand what we mean – no spoilers here – you'll just have to keep reading.

Preparing the workspace

The first thing we have to do is set up our workstation; it won't be difficult because we only need a small set of essential tools. These include Visual Studio 2022, an updated Node.js runtime, a development web server (such as the built-in IIS Express), and a decent source code control system, such as Git. We will take the latter for granted as we most likely already have it up and running.

 In the unlikely case you don't, you should really make amends before moving on! Stop reading, go to www.github.com, www.bitbucket.com, or whichever online **Source Code Management (SCM)** service you like the most, create a free account, and spend some time learning how to effectively use these tools; you won't regret it, that's for sure.

In the next sections, we'll set up the web application project, install or upgrade the packages and libraries, and build and eventually test the result of our work. However, before doing that, we're going to spend a couple of minutes understanding a very important concept that is required to properly use this book without getting (emotionally) hurt – at least in my opinion.

Disclaimer – do (not) try this at home

There's something very important that we need to understand before proceeding. If you're a seasoned web developer, you will most likely know about it already; however, since this book is for (almost) everyone, I feel like it's very important to deal with this matter as soon as possible.

This book will make extensive use of a number of different programming tools, external components, third-party libraries, and so on. Most of them (such as TypeScript, npm, NuGet, most .NET frameworks/packages/runtimes, and so on) are shipped together with Visual Studio 2022, while others (such as Angular, its required JavaScript dependencies, and other third-party server-side and client-side packages) will be fetched from their official repositories. These things are meant to work together in a 100% compatible fashion; however, they are all subject to changes and updates during the inevitable course of time. As time passes by, the chance that these updates might affect the way they interact with each other, and the project's health, will increase.

The broken code myth

In an attempt to minimize the chances of broken code occurring, this book will always work with fixed versions/builds of any third-party component that can be handled using the configuration files. However, some of them, such as Visual Studio and/or .NET SDK updates, might be out of that scope and might wreak havoc in the project. The source code might cease to work, or Visual Studio could suddenly be unable to properly compile it.

When something like that happens, a less experienced person will always be tempted to put the blame on the book itself. Some of them may even start thinking something like this: *There are a lot of compile errors, hence the source code must be broken!*

Alternatively, they may think like this: *The code sample doesn't work: the author must have rushed things here and there and forgot to test what he was writing.*

It goes without saying that such hypotheses are rarely true, especially considering the amount of time that the authors, editors, and technical reviewers of these books spend in writing, testing, and refining the source code before building it up, making it available on GitHub, and often even publishing working instances of the resulting applications to worldwide public websites.

The GitHub repository for this book can be found here:

`https://github.com/PacktPublishing/ASP.NET-Core-6-and-Angular`

It contains a Visual Studio solution file for each chapter containing source code (`Chapter_02.sln`, `Chapter_03.sln` and so on), as well as an additional solution file (`All_Chapters.sln`) containing the source code for all the chapters.

Any experienced developer will easily understand that most of these things couldn't even be done if there was some broken code somewhere; there's no way this book could even attempt to hit the shelves without coming with a 100% working source code, except for a few possible minor typos that will quickly be reported to the publisher and thus fixed within the GitHub repository in a short while. In the unlikely case that it looks like it doesn't, such as raising unexpected compile errors, the novice developer should spend a reasonable amount of time trying to understand the root cause.

Here's a list of questions they should try to answer before anything else:

- Am I using the same development framework, third-party libraries, versions, and builds adopted by the book?
- If I updated something because I felt like I needed to, am I aware of the changes that might affect the source code? Did I read the relevant changelogs? Have I spent a reasonable amount of time looking around for breaking changes and/or known issues that could have had an impact on the source code?
- Is the book's GitHub repository also affected by this issue? Did I try to compare it with my own code, possibly replacing mine?

If the answer to any of these questions is *No*, then there's a good chance that the problem is not ascribable to this book.

Stay hungry, stay foolish, yet be responsible as well

Don't get me wrong: if you want to use a newer version of Visual Studio, update your TypeScript compiler, or upgrade any third-party library, you are definitely encouraged to do that. This is nothing less than the main scope of this book – making you fully aware of what you're doing and capable of, way beyond the given code samples.

However, if you feel you're ready to do that, you will also have to adapt the code accordingly; most of the time, we're talking about trivial stuff, especially these days when you can Google the issue and/or get the solution on Stack Overflow.

Have they changed the name of a property or method? Then you need to load the new spelling. Have they moved the class somewhere else? Then you need to find the new namespace and change it accordingly, and so on.

That's about it – nothing more, nothing less. The code reflects the passage of time; the developer just needs to keep up with the flow, performing minimum changes to it when required. You can't possibly get lost and blame someone other than yourself if you update your environment and fail to acknowledge that you have to change a bunch of code lines to make it work again.

Am I implying that the author is not responsible for the source code of this book? It's the exact opposite; the author is always responsible. They're supposed to do their best to fix all the reported compatibility issues while keeping the GitHub repository updated. However, you should also have your own level of responsibility; more specifically, you should understand how things work for *any* development book and the inevitable impact of the passage of time on any given source code. No matter how hard the author works to maintain it, the patches will never be fast or comprehensive enough to make these lines of code always work in any given scenario. That's why the most important thing you need to understand – even before the book's topics – is the most valuable concept in modern software development: being able to efficiently deal with the inevitable changes that *will* always occur. Whoever refuses to understand that is doomed; there's no way around it.

Now that we've clarified these aspects, let's get back to work.

Setting up the project(s)

Assuming we have already installed Visual Studio 2022 and Node.js, here's what we need to do:

1. Download and install the .NET 6 SDK
2. Check that the .NET CLI will use that SDK version
3. Install the Angular CLI
4. Create a new .NET and Angular project
5. Check out the newly created project within Visual Studio
6. Update all the packages and libraries to our chosen versions

Let's get to work.

Installing the .NET 6 SDK

The .NET 6 SDK can be downloaded from either the official Microsoft URL (`https://dotnet.microsoft.com/download/dotnet/6.0`) or from the GitHub official release page (`https://github.com/dotnet/core/tree/master/release-notes/6.0`).

The installation is very straightforward – just follow the wizard until the end to get the job done, as follows:

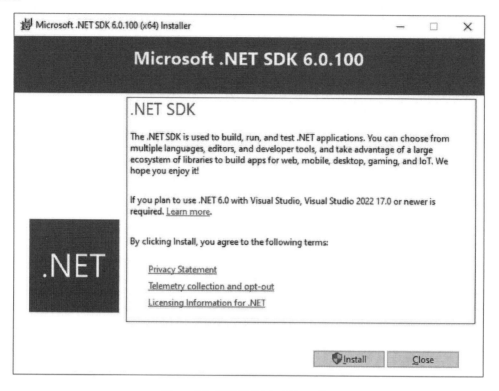

Figure 2.1: .NET SDK 6.0.100 installer

The whole installation process shouldn't take more than a couple of minutes.

Checking the SDK version

Once the .NET SDK has been installed, we need to confirm that the new SDK PATH has been properly set and/or that the .NET CLI will actually use it. The fastest way to check that is by opening Command Prompt and typing the following:

```
> dotnet --help
```

Be sure that the .NET CLI executes without issue and that the version number is the same as we installed a moment ago.

 If the prompt is unable to execute the command, go to **Control Panel | System | Advanced System Settings | Environment Variables** and check that the C:\Program Files\dotnet\ folder is present within the PATH environment variable; manually add it if needed.

Installing Node.js and Angular CLI

The next thing we must do is to install the *Angular Command-Line Interface* – better known as the **Angular CLI**. In order to do that we have to install **Node.js**, so that we can access npm and use it to get the official Angular packages.

If you're on Windows, we strongly suggest installing Node.js using **nvm for Windows** – a neat Node.js version manager for the Windows system. The tool can be downloaded from the following URL: `https://github.com/coreybutler/nvm-windows/releases`.

Once Node.js has been installed, the Angular CLI can be installed using the following command:

```
npm install -g @angular/cli@13.0.1
```

After doing that, you should be able to type `ng --version` and get the Angular CLI ASCII logo containing the installed packages version. If that's not the case, you might have to add the Node.js and/or npm `/bin/` folder to your `PATH` environment variable.

Creating the .NET and Angular project

Now that our frameworks have been installed, we can create our first .NET and Angular project – in other words, our first app. Visual Studio 2022 gives us multiple options for doing this:

- Use the **ASP.NET Core with Angular template**, which was the default (and only) option up to Visual Studio 2019: a single project hosting both the front-end Angular app and the back-end ASP.NET Core API.
- Use the new **Standalone TypeScript Angular Template** together with the **ASP.NET Core Web API template**, a new approach introduced with Visual Studio 2022 that allows to keep the front-end Angular app and the back-end ASP.NET Core API in two separate projects, although fully able to interoperate with each other.

Both approaches have their pros and cons. The single-project approach might probably seem simpler to maintain at first; however, it has two relevant flaws:

- It doesn't help new developers to fully understand the importance of decoupling the front-end and the back-end architecture (as well as codebases), which is a pivotal concept when dealing with SPAs.
- It doesn't allow us to create the front-end app using the Angular CLI version installed on the computer.

For these two reasons, we're going to choose the multi-project approach throughout the whole book: this option will help the reader to better understand the distinct underlying logic of both frameworks, not only during development but also when we'll have to eventually publish and deploy our app(s).

Creating the Angular project

Let's start with the front-end Angular project, which will also provide the name for our Visual Studio 2022 solution.

For those who don't know the Visual Studio naming conventions, a *solution* is basically a collection of multiple projects: in our multi-project approach we'll end up having two projects (the front-end Angular App and the back-end ASP.NET Core Web API) within a single solution.

Launch Visual Studio, then click on the **Create a new project** button: use the search textbox near the top of the window to look for the **Standalone TypeScript Angular Template**, just like shown in the following screenshot:

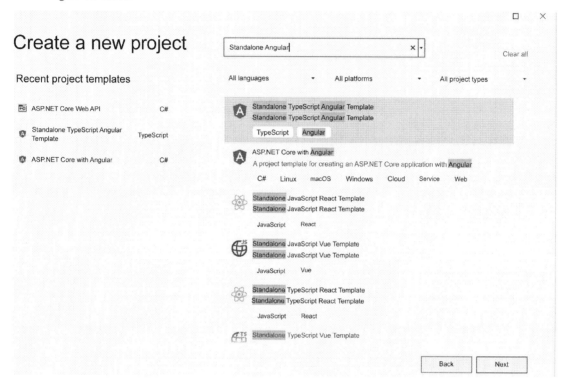

Figure 2.2: Creating a new Standalone TypeScript Angular template

Select that template and click **Next** to access the **Configure your new project** screen. In the following screenshot, fill the form with the following values:

- **Project name:** HealthCheck
- **Location:** C:\Projects\
- **Solution name:** HealthCheck
- **Place solution and project in the same directory:** No (uncheck this flag)

There's a good reason for calling our project *HealthCheck*, as we're going to see in a short while (no spoilers, remember?).

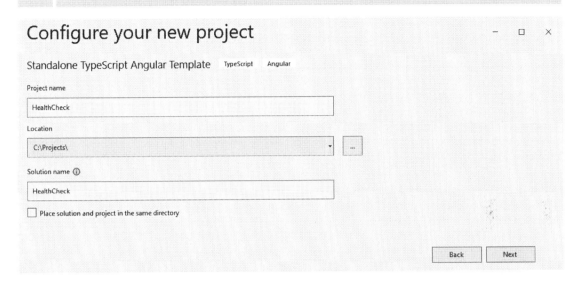

Figure 2.3: Standalone TypeScript Angular template configuration wizard

It goes without saying that these are only suggested choices: however, in this book we're going to use these names – which *will* impact our source code in terms of class names, namespaces, and so on – and \Projects\ as our root folder: non-experienced developers are strongly advised to use the same names and folder.

 Choosing a root-level folder with a short name is also advisable to avoid possible errors and/or issues related to path names being too long: Windows 10 has a 260-character limit that can create some issues with some deeply nested npm packages.

When done, click the **Next** button again to access the third and last section of the wizard: **Additional information.**

Here, we need to be sure to check the **Add integration for Empty ASP.NET Web API Project** option. This option will add some important files to our Angular template so that it can be hooked up with the ASP.NET Core project, which is what we'll create in a short while.

As soon as we'll hit the **Create** button to complete the wizard, Visual Studio will start to create and pre-pare our new project: when everything is set and done, the development GUI will appear with the new project's files clearly visible in the **Solution Explorer** window, as shown in the following screenshot:

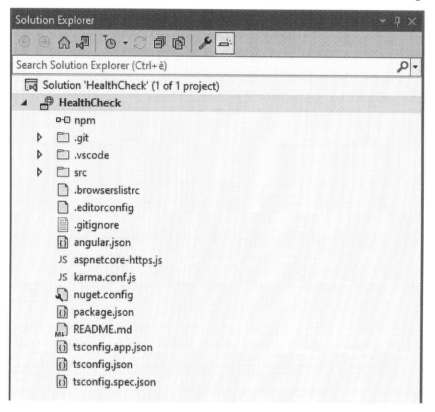

Figure 2.4: Solution Explorer window

Now we can proceed with the next step, which is creating our *ASP.NET Core Web API* project.

Creating the ASP.NET Core Web API project

The process of adding our second (and last) project is quite similar to what we just did, therefore we'll just briefly mention the relevant steps:

1. In the **Solution Explorer**, right-click on the solution node (**Solution 'HealthCheck'**), then select **Add > New Project**.

2. When the wizard appears, use the search textbox to find the **ASP.NET Core Web API** project, select it, and click **Next**.

3. Give the new project the following name: HealthCheckAPI. Also, be sure to create it in the solution folder we've created with the Angular project (it should be C:\Projects\HealthCheck\, unless we've used a different path). Once this is done, click **Next** to go to the next section of the wizard.

4. Choose the **.NET 6** Framework, then leave the default options as they already are: **Authentication type: None, Configure for HTTPS**: checked; **Enable Docker**: unchecked, **Use controllers**: checked, **Enable OpenAPI support**: checked, as shown in the following screenshot.

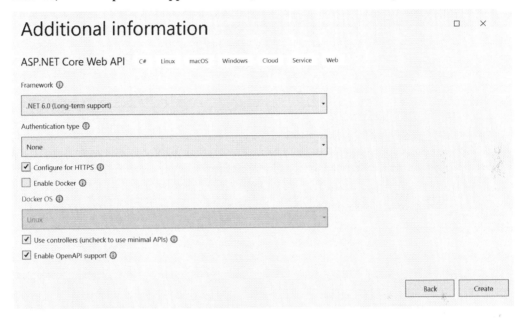

Figure 2.5: ASP.NET Core Web API template configuration wizard

Once this is done, hit **Create** to complete the wizard. The **HealthCheckAPI** project will be added to the existing solution, right below the **HealthCheck** project.

Now we have the front-end project and the back-end project ready within the same solution: we just need a few tweaks to their configuration settings so that we can get them to work together.

Connecting the two projects

Let's start with the Angular project.

From **Solution Explorer**, right-click on the **HealthCheck** project (the Angular one), then select **Properties**.

In the modal window that opens, go to **Configuration Properties** > **Debugging**, then select the **launch. json** debugger, as shown in the following screenshot:

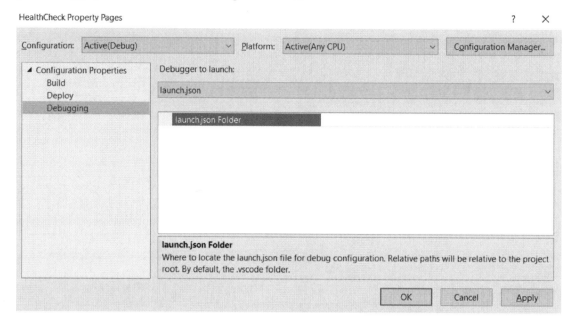

Figure 2.6: Angular project's configuration properties window

Now it's time to deal with the ASP.NET Core Web API project. This time, instead of using the GUI, we'll just modify the underlying settings file.

From **Solution Explorer**, open the *HealthCheckAPI* project node (the ASP.NET one), then open the / Properties/ folder and double-click the launchSettings.json file to open it in the text editor.

Once you're there, perform the following changes:

- Set all the "launchBrowser" settings to false.
- Replace the random-generated HTTP and HTTPS ports with fixed values: we're going to use 40080 for HTTP and 40443 for HTTPS.

>
>
> The reason to use fixed ports is that we'll have to deal with some framework features (such as internal proxies) that require fixed endpoints. In the unlikely event that these ports end up being busy and/or cannot be used, feel free to change them: just be sure to apply the same changes throughout the whole book to avoid getting HTTP 404 errors.

Here's what our launchSettings.json file should look like after these changes (updated lines are highlighted):

```
{
    "$schema": "https://json.schemastore.org/launchsettings.json",
```

```
  "iisSettings": {
    "windowsAuthentication": false,
    "anonymousAuthentication": true,
    "iisExpress": {
      "applicationUrl": "http://localhost:40080",
      "sslPort": 40443
    }
  },
  "profiles": {
    "HealthCheckAPI": {
      "commandName": "Project",
      "dotnetRunMessages": true,
      "launchBrowser": false,
      "launchUrl": "swagger",
      "applicationUrl": "https://localhost:40443;http://localhost:40080",
      "environmentVariables": {
        "ASPNETCORE_ENVIRONMENT": "Development"
      }
    },
    "IIS Express": {
      "commandName": "IISExpress",
      "launchBrowser": false,
      "launchUrl": "swagger",
      "environmentVariables": {
        "ASPNETCORE_ENVIRONMENT": "Development"
      }
    }
  }
}
```

Now we just need to tell Visual Studio how to properly run our projects.

Setting the startup project(s)

Last but not least, we need to make good use of one of the most important, yet less-known features introduced with the latest versions of Visual Studio, at least for SPAs: the ability to set up multiple startup projects:

1. From **Solution Explorer**, right-click on the *HealthCheck* solution (the top-level node) and select **Set Startup Projects**.
2. In the modal window that opens, change the startup project radio button from **Single startup project** to **Multiple startup projects**, then select **Start** for each project's action.

3. Finally, operate with the two arrows to the right to move the **HealthCheckAPI** (ASP.NET) project above the **HealthCheck** (Angular) project, so that it will be launched first.

4. Here's what the *Multiple startup project* settings should look like after these changes:

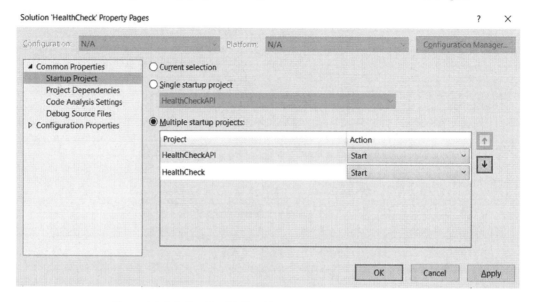

Figure 2.7: Solution 'HealthCheck' startup project settings window

Once this is done, we can move to the next (and last) step. Remember when we said that we would be dealing with fixed endpoints? Here's the first one we need to take care of.

From the **HealthCheck** project, open the `/src/proxy.conf.js` file, which is the configuration file for the proxy that will be used by the Angular Development Server to reach our ASP.NET API project URLs when running our projects in *debug* mode. Don't worry about these concepts for now; we'll explain them in a short while. For the time being, we just need to ensure that the proxy will route the API requests to the correct URL, including the HTTPS port.

For that reason, change the `target` URL to match the fixed HTTPS port that we've configured in the ASP.NET Core API project, which should be `50433` (unless we changed it):

```
const PROXY_CONFIG = [
  {
    context: [
      "/weatherforecast",
    ],
    target: "https://localhost:40443",
    secure: false
  }
]

module.exports = PROXY_CONFIG;
```

Let's take the chance to choose a fixed HTTPS port for the Angular Development Server as well.

Open the `/.vscode/launch.json` file and change the default HTTPS port to 4200, as shown in the following highlighted code:

```json
{
  "version": "0.2.0",
  "configurations": [
    {
      "type": "chrome",
      "request": "launch",
      "name": "localhost (Chrome)",
      "url": "https://localhost:4200",
      "webRoot": "${workspaceFolder}"
    },
    {
      "type": "edge",
      "request": "launch",
      "name": "localhost (Edge)",
      "url": "https://localhost:4200",
      "webRoot": "${workspaceFolder}"
    }
  ]
}
```

> **IMPORTANT:** Your `launch.json` file might be different if you have Chrome and/or MS Edge installed. Just keep the configuration blocks for the browser you have on your system and plan to use to debug your app and remove (or avoid adding) the others, otherwise your project will crash on startup. In this book, we're going to use Chrome and MS Edge, hence we'll keep the file as it is.

Now we're finally ready to launch our project(s) and see how well they work together... unless we want to spend a couple of minutes investigating the alternative "single-project" approach.

Single-project approach

If you're happy with the new "multiple-project" approach, you might as well skip this section and move to the next one. However, those who prefer to go with the "classic" **ASP.NET Core with Angular template** alternative are free to do that and won't suffer from that choice, since all the code samples contained in this book are fully compatible with both approaches.

Despite the flaws we talked about a short while ago, our template still provides a convenient starting point for creating an ASP.NET Core and Angular app, adding all the required files and a general-purpose configuration that we'll be able to customize to better suit our needs.

The most efficient way to create a solution using the **ASP.NET Core with Angular template** is to use the dotnet CLI.

Open a command-line terminal, create a root folder that will contain our project(s) – such as \Projects\ – and get inside it.

Once you're there, type the following command to create the Angular app:

```
> dotnet new angular -o HealthCheck
```

This command will create a fully-fledged ASP.NET Core and Angular app in the C:\Projects\ HealthCheck\ folder.

With this template, all the Angular-related files (including the settings files) are contained within the /ClientApp/ folder instead of being hosted in a separate project: some rather compact boilerplate that contains all the required .NET and Angular configuration files, resources, and dependencies.

As we can see by looking at the various folders, the working environment contains the following:

- The default ASP.NET MVC /Controllers/ and /Pages/ folders, both containing some working samples.
- The /ClientApp/src/ folder with some TypeScript files containing the source code of an example Angular app.
- The /ClientApp/e2e/ folder, containing some example E2E tests built with the Protractor testing framework.
- The /wwwroot/ folder, which will be used by Visual Studio to build an optimized version of the client-side code whenever we need to execute it locally or have it published elsewhere. That folder is initially empty, but it will be populated upon the project's first run.

If we spend some time browsing through these folders and taking a look at their content, we will see how the .NET developers did a tremendous job of easing the .NET experience with the Angular project setup process. If we compare this boilerplate with the built-in Angular 2.x/5.x templates shipped with Visual Studio 2015/2017, we will see a huge improvement in terms of readability and code cleanliness, as well as a better file and folder structure.

Also, those who fought with task runners such as Grunt or Gulp and/or client-side building tools such as webpack in the recent past will most likely appreciate the fact that this template is nothing like that: all the packaging, building, and compiling tasks are entirely handled by Visual Studio via the underlying .NET and Angular CLIs, with specific loading strategies for development and production.

All in all, those who are used to working with the back-end and the front-end within the same project might still prefer using this template. However, getting used to the multi-project approach – and splitting the server-side and the client-side parts into two separate projects – will greatly help us to understand the overall logic that drives the modern microservice-based architectures and thus is a chance that we shouldn't miss if we want to become better developers.

Before moving on, we should perform a quick test run to ensure that our project is working properly. This is what the next section is all about.

Performing a test run

The best way to see if our multiple-project approach is working as expected is to perform a quick test run by launching our projects in *Debug* mode. To do that, hit the Visual Studio **Start** button or the *F5* key to start compiling and running our app.

After a few seconds, we'll be asked to trust a self-signed certificate that ASP.NET Core will generate to allow our app to be served through HTTPS (as shown in the following screenshot): let's just click **Yes** to continue.

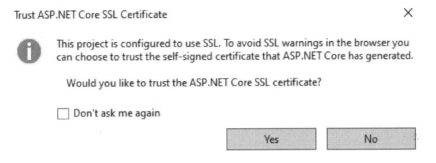

Figure 2.8: Trust ASP.NET Core SSL Certificate popup

 If we don't want to have to authorize the ASP.NET Core self-signed SSL certificates, we can flag the **Don't ask me again** checkbox right before hitting **Yes**.

Right after that, Visual Studio will launch three separate processes:

- The **ASP.NET Core Server**, a web server that will serve the server-side APIs. This web server will be *Kestrel* (the default) or *IIS Express*, depending on the project configuration. Either of them will work for our purposes, since we've wisely configured both to use the same fixed endpoints and HTTP/HTTPS ports.

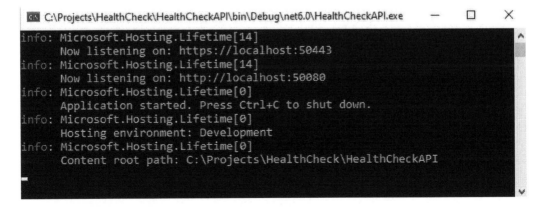

Figure 2.9: Kestrel web server for the ASP.NET Core Web API project

- The **Angular Live Development Server**, a console application acting as a web server that will host our Angular application's files using the ng serve command from the Angular CLI.

Figure 2.10: Angular Live Development Server for the Standalone TypeScript Angular project

- Our favorite **web browser**, such as *MS Edge*, *Mozilla Firefox*, or *Google Chrome* (we're going to use *MS Edge* from now on), which will interact with the **Angular Live Development Server** through the fixed HTTPS endpoint we configured a while ago.

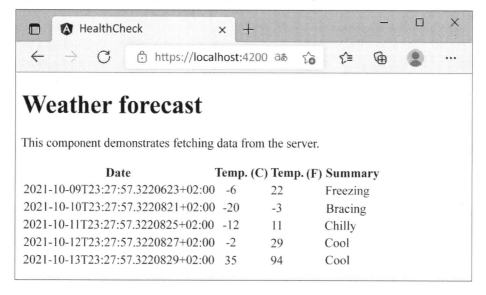

Figure 2.11: MS Edge web browser for the Standalone TypeScript Angular project

The page we're going to see in the web browser shows a basic Angular component performing a simple data fetching retrieval task from the ASP.NET Core Web API project: a tiny, yet good (and fully working) example of what we'll be doing from now on.

What we just did was an excellent consistency check to ensure that our development system is properly configured. If we see the page shown in the preceding screenshot, it means that we're ready to move on.

Troubleshooting

In the unlikely case we don't, it probably means that we're either missing something or that we've got some conflicting software preventing Visual Studio and/or the underlying .NET and Angular CLIs from properly compiling the project. To fix that, we can try to do the following:

- Uninstall/reinstall Node.js, as we possibly have an outdated version installed.
- Uninstall/reinstall Visual Studio, as our current installation might be broken or corrupted. The .NET SDK should come shipped with it already; however, we can try reinstalling it as well.

If everything still fails, we can try to install Visual Studio and the previously mentioned packages in a clean environment (either a physical system or a VM) to overcome any possible issues related to our current operating system configuration.

 If none of these attempts work, the best thing we can do is to ask for specific support on the .NET community forums at:

`https://forums.asp.net/default.aspx/7?General+ASP+NET`

Architecture overview

Before moving on to the next chapter, let's spend a couple more minutes to fully understand the underlying logic behind the *development* environment that we've just built.

We've already seen that when Visual Studio starts our projects in the *development* environment, three processes are launched: the standalone Angular project (*HealthCheck*), the ASP.NET Core Web API (*HealthCheckAPI*), and the web browser that will interact with them.

Here's a simple diagram that summarizes how these three processes work together and interact with each other:

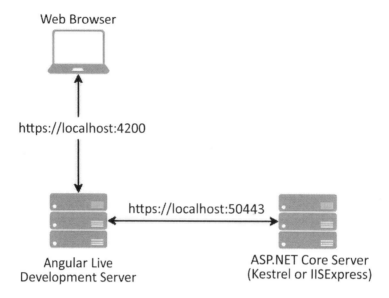

Figure 2.12: HealthCheck (front-end) and HealthCheckAPI (back-end) projects interaction in the development setup

As we can see from the previous diagram, the web browser will call the **Angular Live Development Server** (which listens to HTTPS port 4200), which will deal with them in the following way:

- Directly serve all the requests for the Angular pages and static resources.
- Proxy all the API requests to the Kestrel web server hosting the ASP.NET Core Web API (which listens to the HTTPS port 40443).
- It's important to understand that the **Angular Live Development Server** is only meant for local development, where it will allow the use of most *debug* tools and greatly speed up the coding experience with features such as *hot reload*. Whenever we want to deploy our app(s) in production, or in any environment other than local development, we're going to build our app into *production bundles* and deploy them to a front-end web server (or a CDN) that will basically take its place in the preceding diagram. We'll talk about all this extensively in *Chapter 15, Windows, Linux, and Azure Deployment*, when we'll learn how to publish our apps.

Summary

So far, so good; we've just set up a working skeleton of what's about to come. Before moving on, let's do a quick recap of what we just did (and learned) in this chapter.

First of all, we learned the differences between the various approaches that can be adopted to create web apps nowadays: SPAs, MPAs, and PWAs. We also explained that since we'll be using .NET and Angular, we'll stick to the SPA approach, but we'll also implement most PWA features, such as service workers and web manifest files. In an attempt to reproduce a realistic production-case scenario, we also went through the most common SPA features, first from a technical point of view, and then putting ourselves in the shoes of a typical product owner while trying to enumerate their expectations.

Last, but not least, we learned how to properly set up our development environment; we chose to do that using the latest Angular SPA template shipped with the .NET SDK, thus adopting the standard ASP. NET Core/.NET 6 approach. Then, we created our Standalone Angular project and the ASP.NET Core back-end API project using Visual Studio, configured them to be able to work together, and tested the overall result to ensure that everything was working properly. Finally, we spent some valuable time to fully understand how the *development* architecture that we've just built works.

In the next chapter, *Chapter 3*, *Looking Around*, we'll take an extensive look at the app we just created to properly understand how the .NET *back-end* and the Angular *front-end* perform their respective tasks and what they can do together.

Suggested topics

For further information, we recommend the following topics: Single-Page Application (SPA), Progressive Web Application (PWA), Native Web Application (NWA), Multi-Page Application (MPA), Scrum, Agile Manifesto, ASP.NET Web API, Angular CLI, Node.js, npm, nvm for Windows, Visual Studio 2022, and Visual Studio Project Templates.

References

- *Native Web Apps, Henrik Joreteg, 2015*: `https://blog.andyet.com/2015/01/22/native-web-apps/`

- *Manifesto for Agile Software Development, Kent Beck, Mike Beedle, and many others, 2001*: `https://agilemanifesto.org/`

- *Progressive Web Apps*: `https://developers.google.com/web/progressive-web-apps/`

- *Progressive Web Apps: Escaping Tabs Without Losing Our Soul*: `https://infrequently.org/2015/06/progressive-apps-escaping-tabs-without-losing-our-soul/`

- *What, Exactly, Makes Something A Progressive Web App?*: `https://infrequently.org/2016/09/what-exactly-makes-something-a-progressive-web-app/`

- *Scrum (software development)*: `https://en.wikipedia.org/wiki/Scrum_(software_development)`

- *Waterfall model*: `https://en.wikipedia.org/wiki/Waterfall_model`

- *CLI-Based Front-End Project Templates*: `https://devblogs.microsoft.com/visualstudio/the-new-javascript-typescript-experience-in-vs-2022-preview-3/#cli-based-front-end-project-templates`

- *NVM for Windows*: `https://github.com/coreybutler/nvm-windows/releases`

3
Looking Around

Now that our project has been created, it's time to take a quick look around and try to understand some of the hard work that the .NET and Angular SPA template has done to make it work.

Hey, wait a minute! Shouldn't we skip all these setup technicalities and just jump into coding?

As a matter of fact, yes, we'll definitely be jumping into the coding in a little while. However, before doing so, it's wise to highlight a couple of aspects of the code that have been put in place already so that we'll know how to move effectively within our project in advance: where to find the *server-side* and *client-side* code, where to put new content, how to change our initialization parameters, and so on. It will also be a good chance to review our basic knowledge of the Visual Studio environment and the packages we will need.

That's precisely what we're going to do in this chapter. More specifically, the following are the main topics we're going to cover:

- **Solution overview**: A high-level summary of what we'll be dealing with
- **The ASP.NET back-end**: An overview of the ASP.NET Core Web API project (*HealthCheckAPI*): controllers, configuration files, and so on
- **The Angular front-end**: An overview of the Angular project (*HealthCheck*): the workspace, the /src/ folder, the Angular initialization cycle, and so on
- **Creating a new front-end app with the Angular CLI**: Installation, creation, and testing
- **Getting to work**: Changing the Web API endpoints, adding new Angular components, implementing a basic navigation and routing system, and so on

IMPORTANT! The sample code we're reviewing here is the code that comes with the default Visual Studio templates shipped by .NET 6 SDK at the time of writing: in the (likely) event that this sample code is updated in future releases, ensure you get the former source code from the web using this book's official GitHub repository and use it to replace the contents of your project folder.

Caution: failing to do this could result in you working with different sample code from the code featured in this book.

Technical requirements

In this chapter, all of the previous technical requirements listed in *Chapter 2*, *Getting Ready*, will apply, with no additional resources, libraries, or packages.

The code files for this chapter can be found here: https://github.com/PacktPublishing/ASP.NET-Core-6-and-Angular/tree/master/Chapter_03/.

Solution overview

The first thing that catches the eye is that, as we've already mentioned, the layout of a standard ASP. NET Core solution is quite different from what it used to be in ASP.NET 5 and earlier versions. The most notable thing is that we have two different projects – one for Angular (*HealthCheck*) and one for the ASP.NET Core Web API (*HealthCheckAPI*) – that start together and need to interact with each other. If we have previous "classic" ASP.NET single-project experience, we could find such an approach quite different from what we were used to working with.

The best thing about the new approach is that we're instantly able to distinguish the ASP.NET *back-end* part from the Angular *front-end* part, which could be troublesome with the previous, single-project experience, when the two stacks were often intertwined.

Let's quickly review their overall structure to better understand how each one of them works.

The ASP.NET back-end

The ASP.NET *back-end* stack is contained in the following folders:

- The Dependencies virtual folder, which basically replaces the old References folder and contains all the internal, external, and third-party references required to build and run our project. All the references to the NuGet packages that we'll add to our project will also be put there.
- The /Controllers/ folder, which has been shipped with any MVC-based ASP.NET application since the preceding release of the MVC framework: such a folder contains a single controller – WeatherForecastController.cs – which is responsible for serving the sample weather forecast data that we briefly saw in *Chapter 2*, *Getting Ready*, during our final test run.
- The root-level files–Program.cs and appsettings.json–that will determine our web application's configuration, including the modules and middlewares, compilation settings, and publishing rules; we'll address them all in a while.

If you hail from the ASP.NET MVC framework(s), you might want to know why this template doesn't contain a /Pages/ or /Views/ folder: where did our Razor Pages and views go?

As a matter of fact, this template doesn't make use of pages or views. If we think about it, the reason is quite obvious: a Web API project doesn't need any of them, since its main purpose is to return JSON data.

Configuration files

Let's start by taking a look at the root-level configuration files and their purpose: Program.cs and appsettings.json. These files contain our web application's configuration, including the modules and middlewares, as well as environment-specific settings and rules.

Those who are already familiar with ASP.NET Core will notice that we're not mentioning the `Startup.cs` file, which was a pivotal configuration element along with the `Program.cs` file. The reason for that is fairly simple: it's not required anymore. The new .NET 6 framework introduces a new hosting model for ASP.NET Core applications that unifies `Startup.cs` and `Program.cs` in a single file experience that takes advantage of the new C# *top-level statements* feature (which we briefly mentioned in *Chapter 1, Introducing ASP. NET and Angular*) to reduce the amount of boilerplate code required to get the app up and running.

For additional info regarding this change, check out the **Migration to ASP.NET Core in .NET 6** development notes by David Fowler (ASP.NET Team Software Architect) at the following URL:

https://gist.github.com/davidfowl/0e0372c3c1d895c3ce195ba983b1e03d

The `WeatherForecast.cs` file contains a strongly typed class designed to be returned from the `Get` method of `WeatherForecastController`: this model can be seen as a View Model, as it will be serialized into JSON by the ASP.NET Core Framework. In our humble opinion, the template authors should have put it within the `/ViewModel/` folder (or something like that) instead of leaving it at the root level. Anyway, let's just ignore it for now, since it's not a configuration file, and focus on the rest.

Program.cs

The `Program.cs` file will most likely intrigue most seasoned ASP.NET programmers, as it's not something we usually see in a web application project. First introduced in ASP.NET Core 1.0, the `Program.cs` file's main purpose is to create a *builder*: a factory object used by the .NET Core runtime to set up and build the interface that will host our web application.

In the first ASP.NET Core versions (up to 2.2), the builder was called `WebHostBuilder` and the hosting interface was known as `IWebHost`; in .NET 3.0, they became `HostBuilder` and `IHost`, respectively, due to the introduction of the *generic host*, a more versatile host that can support other workloads like worker services, gRPC services, and Windows services.

That's great to know, but what is a host? In just a few words, it is the execution context of any ASP.NET Core app. In a web-based application, the host must implement the `IHost` interface, which exposes a collection of web-related features and services that will be used to handle the HTTP requests.

The preceding statement can lead to the assumption that the web host and the web server are the same thing. However, it's very important to understand that they're not, as they serve very different purposes. Simply put, the host is responsible for application startup and lifetime management, while the server is responsible for accepting HTTP requests. Part of the host's responsibility includes ensuring that the application's services and the server are available and properly configured.

We can think of the host as being a wrapper around the server: the host is configured to use a particular server, while the server is unaware of its host.

For further info regarding the `IHost` interface, as well as the whole ASP.NET Core initialization stack, check out the following guide: `https://docs.microsoft.com/en-us/aspnet/core/fundamentals/`.

In .NET 6, the *generic host* approach can still be used, but the recommended way to set up a web application is the new hosting model introduced with this version that we briefly mentioned a moment ago. The new approach relies upon a new `WebApplicationBuilder` class with a built-in implementation of `IHostBuilder` and `IHost`: this small, yet effective, improvement makes the `Program.cs` overall logic much simpler for new developers to understand without changing the underlying host-based approach.

If we open the `Program.cs` file and take a look at the code, we can see what the new minimal template looks like:

```
var builder = WebApplication.CreateBuilder(args);

// Add services to the container.

builder.Services.AddControllers();
// Learn more about configuring Swagger/OpenAPI at https://aka.ms/aspnetcore/
swashbuckle
builder.Services.AddEndpointsApiExplorer();
builder.Services.AddSwaggerGen();


var app = builder.Build();

// Configure the HTTP request pipeline.
if (app.Environment.IsDevelopment())
{
    app.UseSwagger();
    app.UseSwaggerUI();
}


app.UseHttpsRedirection();


app.UseAuthorization();


app.MapControllers();


app.Run();
```

As we can easily see, the new code is mostly about executing the following tasks:

- Instantiate a `WebApplicationBuilder` (line 1)
- Add some services (lines 5-8)
- Use the builder to create a `WebApplication` object (line 10)
- Configure the app with the required middleware (lines 13-23)
- Run the app (line 25)

The `IHost` interface that we've just talked about is implemented by the `WebApplication` object and can be accessed by the `Host` public property (`app.Host`).

If we compare the new `Program.cs` code with the old `Program.cs` plus `Startup.cs` approach, which was the default until .NET 5, we can immediately see a huge difference in terms of overall complexity.

Here's what a typical ASP.NET 5 `Program.cs` file looked like:

```
public class Program
{
    public static void Main(string[] args)
    {
        CreateHostBuilder(args).Build().Run();
    }

    public static IHostBuilder CreateHostBuilder(string[] args) =>
        Host.CreateDefaultBuilder(args)
            .ConfigureWebHostDefaults(webBuilder =>
            {
                webBuilder.UseStartup<Startup>();
            });
}
```

And here's the source code of the corresponding `Startup.cs` file:

```
public class Startup
{
    public Startup(IConfiguration configuration)
    {
        Configuration = configuration;
    }

    public IConfiguration Configuration { get; }

    // This method gets called by the runtime. Use this method to add services
to the container.
    public void ConfigureServices(IServiceCollection services)
```

```
    {
        services.AddControllersWithViews();
        // In production, the Angular files will be served from this directory
        services.AddSpaStaticFiles(configuration =>
        {
            configuration.RootPath = "ClientApp/dist";
        });
    }


    // This method gets called by the runtime. Use this method to configure the
HTTP request pipeline.
    public void Configure(IApplicationBuilder app, IWebHostEnvironment env)
    {
        if (env.IsDevelopment())
        {
            app.UseDeveloperExceptionPage();
        }
        else
        {
            app.UseExceptionHandler("/Error");
            // The default HSTS value is 30 days. You may want to change this
for production scenarios, see https://aka.ms/aspnetcore-hsts.
            app.UseHsts();
        }

        app.UseHttpsRedirection();
        app.UseStaticFiles();
        if (!env.IsDevelopment())
        {
            app.UseSpaStaticFiles();
        }

        app.UseRouting();

        app.UseEndpoints(endpoints =>
        {
            endpoints.MapControllerRoute(
                name: "default",
                pattern: "{controller}/{action=Index}/{id?}");
        });
```

```
            app.UseSpa(spa =>
            {
                // To learn more about options for serving an Angular SPA from ASP.
    NET Core,

                // see https://go.microsoft.com/fwlink/?linkid=864501

                spa.Options.SourcePath = "ClientApp";

                if (env.IsDevelopment())
                {
                    spa.UseAngularCliServer(npmScript: "start");
                }
            });
        }
    }
```

As we can see, the old approach looks a lot more complicated than the new version: we had to deal with a whole bunch of nested lambdas, pay attention to many configuration-aware overloads, and, most importantly, there was a huge amount of source code; maybe too much for a bootstrapping class, especially for a newcomer. No wonder the ASP.NET Core team did its best to try and simplify the whole thing.

Let's get back to that new approach and take a closer look at what the improved Program.cs file does after instantiating WebApplication in the app local variable:

```
// Configure the HTTP request pipeline.
if (app.Environment.IsDevelopment())
{
    app.UseSwagger();
    app.UseSwaggerUI();
}

app.UseHttpsRedirection();

app.UseAuthorization();

app.MapControllers();

app.Run();
```

The code is very readable, so we can easily understand what happens here: the first comment line clearly explains it: we're configuring the HTTP request pipeline by loading the required middlewares and services that will be used by our web application.

In detail, here's what we have:

- An `if` statement that registers a couple of middlewares only if the app is being run in a *development* environment: these "development" middlewares are both related to **Swagger**, which is something that we'll talk about in a short while.

- Another block of middlewares that will be used with any environment: `HttpsRedirection`, which will handle HTTP-to-HTTPS redirects; `Authorization`, which allows access to some API requests to be restricted to authorized users only. Note how these methods are called with no parameters: this just means that their default settings are more than enough for us, so there's nothing to configure or override here.

- After the environment-specific and always-on middlewares, there's a call to the `MapControllers` method, which adds the endpoints required by the controller's action methods to handle the incoming HTTP requests. We'll extensively talk about that in upcoming chapters, when we deal with *server-side* routing aspects. For now, let's just note that the method is called without any parameters, meaning that we're not specifying any custom route here: this means that we're just using the default routing rules enforced by the framework's naming conventions, at least for now.

- Last but not least comes the call to the `Run` method, which executes the application and blocks the calling thread until the `IHost` shutdown.

 It's worth noting that middlewares and services added to the HTTP pipeline will process incoming requests in registration order, from top to bottom. This means that `HttpsRedirection` will take priority over `Authorization`, which will take place before the `MapControllers` method, and so on. Such behavior is very important and could cause unexpected results if taken lightly, as shown in the following Stack Overflow thread: `https://stackoverflow.com/questions/52768852/`.

It's worth noting that the `Program.cs` file doesn't contain any reference to the `StaticFiles` middleware, meaning that our Web API won't be able to serve any static files such as TXT, CSS, JS, images, and videos. This is no surprise since we plan to serve all these files from the Angular app (or through a third party, such as a *Content Delivery Network*). This is another big difference with the single-project approach, where we would have been forced to add static files support to serve all the Angular files, bundles, and resources – at least during the *development* phase.

appsettings.json

The `appsettings.json` file is just a replacement for the good old `Web.config` file; the XML syntax has been replaced by the more readable and considerably less verbose JSON format. Moreover, the new configuration model is based upon key/value settings that can be retrieved from a wide variety of sources, including, but not limited to, JSON files, using a centralized interface.

Once retrieved, they can be easily accessed within our code using **dependency injection** via literal strings (using the `IConfiguration` interface).

This can be demonstrated by opening the `WeatherForecastController.cs` file and modifying the constructor in the following way (new/updated lines are highlighted):

```
public WeatherForecastController(
    ILogger<WeatherForecastController> logger,
    IConfiguration configuration
    )
{
    _logger = logger;
    var defaultLogLevel = configuration["Logging:LogLevel:Default"];
}
```

If we place a breakpoint by the end of the constructor and run our project in *Debug* mode, we can check that the `defaultLogLevel` variable will contain the `"Information"` string, which is precisely the value specified in the `appsettings.json` file.

> Those who don't like to deal with string literals to access configuration files could take the chance to define a custom `POCO` class that will internally read the `IConfiguration` values and return them as named properties: however, since we won't need to access those values frequently, for the sake of simplicity, we're going to avoid implementing such *strongly typed* logic and just use the literal approach shown above.

appsettings.Development.json

It's worth noting that there's also an `appsettings.Development.json` file nested below the main one. Such a file serves the same purpose as the old `Web.Debug.config` file, which was widely used during the ASP.NET 4.x period. In a nutshell, these additional files can be used to specify additional configuration key/value pairs (and/or override existing ones) for specific environments.

To better understand the concept, let's take the chance to slightly modify the default logging behavior of the *Development* environment.

Open the `appsettings.Development.json` file and update the following lines:

```
{
  "Logging": {
    "LogLevel": {
      "Default": "Debug",
      "Microsoft.AspNetCore": "Warning"
    }
  }
}
```

After performing this change, every time our Web API project is launched in a *Development* environment the default log level will be set to **Debug** instead of **Information**, which will still be the default log level for the other environments – until we create other appsettings.<EnvironmentName>.json files to override it.

Assuming we understood everything here, let's move on to the main players of any ASP.NET Core project: the *Controllers*.

Controllers

Controllers are the backbone of most ASP.NET Core applications since they are entitled to handle the incoming HTTP requests. More specifically, a controller is used to define a set of actions (or action methods), which are basically the methods that get called by the routing middleware to handle the requests mapped to them through routing rules.

Controllers logically group similar actions together: such aggregation mechanisms allow developers to conveniently define common sets of rules, not only for routing, but also for caching, authorization, and other settings that can benefit from being applied collectively.

 As per ASP.NET Core convention, each controller class resides in the project's root-level /Controllers/ folder and is suffixed with the Controller keyword.

In a typical ASP.NET MVC project, *controllers* are mostly used to serve the *views* to the client, which contains static or dynamic HTML content. That's not the case in Web API projects, where their main purpose is to serve JSON output (REST APIs), XML-based responses (SOAP web services), a static or dynamically created resource (JPG, JS, and CSS files), or even a simple HTTP response (such as an HTTP 301 redirect) without the content body.

In a typical ASP.NET MVC project, all the controllers derive from the Controller class, which adds support from views; in Web API projects, since they don't need to serve views, it's better to have them extend the ControllerBase class instead, which is more lightweight.

 This approach is also followed by the ASP.NET Core Web API project template we're using: if we look at the WeatherForecastController source code, we can see that it derives from the ControllerBase class.

The only exception to this good practice comes if we plan to use the same controller to serve both views and Web APIs: when that's the case, deriving it from Controller is the most logical and convenient choice.

WeatherForecastController

By acknowledging all this, we can already infer that the single sample WeatherForecastController contained in the /Controllers/ folder is there to expose a set of Web APIs that will be used by the Angular *front-end*. To quickly check it out, hit *F5* to launch our project(s) in *Debug* mode and execute the default route by typing the following URL: https://localhost:40443/weatherforecast.

If we remember what we did in the previous chapters, we already know that this is the URL endpoint for the local *Kestrel* (or *IISExpress*) web server hosting the Web API projects.

 The actual port number may vary, depending on the SPA Proxy Server URL assigned by Visual Studio and stored within the project configuration files. If you want to use different HTTP and/or HTTPS ports, follow the instructions that we supplied in *Chapter 2, Getting Ready*.

This will execute the Get() method defined in the WeatherForecastController.cs file. As we can see by looking at the source code, such a method has an IEnumerable<WeatherForecast> return value, meaning that it will return multiple objects of the WeatherForecast type.

If we copy the preceding URL into the browser and execute it, we should see a JSON array of randomly generated data, as shown in the following screenshot:

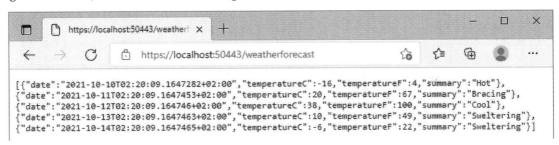

Figure 3.1: JSON array of weather data

It's easy to imagine who'll be asking for these values: the answer is... our Angular app.

Introducing OpenAPI (Swagger)

Before moving on to the Angular *front-end* project, there's another *back-end* feature we should familiarize ourselves with: **OpenAPI**, formerly known as **Swagger**.

Those who have some experience with web services should have already heard such a name: in very short terms, the OpenAPI Specification (OAS) is a language-agnostic specification to document and describe REST APIs. Its main role is to allow computers, as well as humans, to univocally understand the capabilities of a REST API without having direct access to the source code.

The OpenAPI Specification was initially known as *Swagger* since its development (2010): the name was officially changed on January 1, 2016, when the Swagger specification was renamed the OpenAPI Specification (OAS) and was moved to a new GitHub repository, which is still there today.

The OpenAPI Specification GitHub repository is available at the following URL:

`https://github.com/OAI/OpenAPI-Specification`

Adding OpenAPI support to a RESTful Web Service project will grant some relevant benefits, such as:

*   Minimizing the amount of work needed to connect decoupled services
*   Reducing the amount of time needed to accurately document the service

If we consider how important these aspects have become in the last few years, we can easily understand why OpenAPI can be included by default in most Visual Studio API templates: the one we've used to create our **HealthCheckAPI** project makes no exception, as we've seen in *Chapter 2, Getting Ready*, and early on in this chapter, when we were looking at the middlewares included in the `Program.cs` file.

More precisely, the default OpenAPI implementation added by our template is called **Swashbuckle** and is made available with the **Swashbuckle.AspNetCore** NuGet package. However, since we checked **Enable OpenAPI Support** when we created our project back in *Chapter 2, Getting Ready*, we don't need to explicitly add it: it's already included in our project.

To check whether the **Swashbuckle.AspNetCore** NuGet package is already installed, right-click on the *HealthCheckAPI* project node from **Solution Explorer** and select **Manage NuGet Packages**. The package should be clearly visible in the **Installed** tab, as shown in the following screenshot:

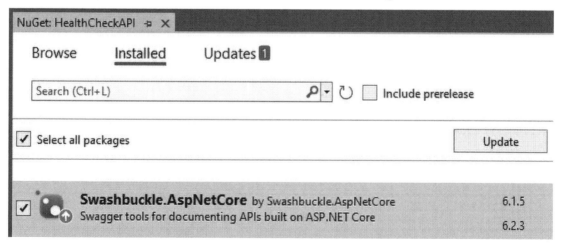

Figure 3.2: Swashbuckle.AspNetCore NuGet package

However, we could take the chance to upgrade the package to the most recent version.

In this book, we'll use version **6.2.3**, which is currently the most recent release: as always, we strongly suggest that you use it as well.

Adding Swashbuckle to our project allows us to use three different components:

- **Swashbuckle.AspNetCore.Swagger**: a middleware that can be used to expose SwaggerDocument objects as JSON endpoints
- **Swashbuckle.AspNetCore.SwaggerGen**: a generator that builds SwaggerDocument objects directly from the app's routes, controllers, and models
- **Swashbuckle.AspNetCore.SwaggerUI**: a user interface that uses the Swagger JSON to create a rich and customizable user experience to visually document the Web API

If we look again at our existing `Program.cs` source code, we can see that these components are already present in our app's initialization pipeline: however, the `SwaggerUI` is currently only available in our *Development* environment – which kind of makes sense, since we don't know if we want to publish it (yet). Publicly documenting a Web API service might be a good thing if we want third-party services to consume it, but can be a major security, privacy, and/or performance flaw if we want to keep our endpoints (and data) for our eyes only.

As a matter of fact, keeping the `SwaggerUI` only available during development seems a good idea, at least for now: let's use this opportunity to take a good look at it.

To do that, hit *F5* to launch our project(s) in *Debug* mode and execute the Swagger UI default endpoint:

```
https://localhost:40443/swagger
```

As soon as we hit *Enter*, the default Swashbuckler Swagger UI should appear in all its glory, as shown in the following screenshot:

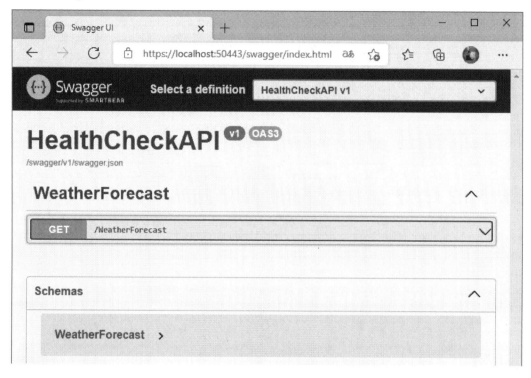

Figure 3.3: Swagger UI for HealthCheckAPI

As we can see, the SwaggerEndpoint that we configured in the Program.cs file is mentioned within a hyperlink right below the main title. If we click on that hyperlink, we'll be able to see the auto-generated swagger.json file, which contains a comprehensive description of our single (for now) /WeatherForecast action method: accepted HTTP methods, input parameters, return types of the various JSON values, and so on.

We can easily understand how such an auto-documentation feature can be an invaluable resource for other back-end developers that don't have much experience with the project's code base – not to mention any third party who wants (or needs) to integrate with our Web API without having access to the source code.

That's enough for now: we'll come back to Swagger/OpenAPI in the upcoming chapters when we add more controllers and action methods to our Web API project.

Now that we're done inspecting the ASP.NET Core *back-end* part, we can finally move on to the Angular *front-end* project.

The Angular front-end

The Angular *front-end* project comprises the following stuff:

- The /src/ folder, which contains the Angular app source code files, as well as some static assets (HTML, CSS, and the like). If we look at the source code files, we can see that they have a .ts extension, which means we'll be using the **TypeScript** programming language (we'll say more about this in a bit)
- A bunch of root files, which contain the Angular configuration settings, the required npm packages to run the app, and the scripts to build the development and production bundles to host it

The *front-end* part of the template will probably be seen as more complex to understand, because Angular—just like most *client-side* frameworks—has evolved at a dramatic pace, thus experiencing many breaking changes in its core architecture, toolchain management, coding syntax, template, and setup.

For this very reason, it's very important to take our time understanding the role of the various files shipped with the template. This brief overview will start with root-level configuration files, which will also be updated with the latest versions of the Angular packages (and their dependencies) that we'll need to use.

The root files

The Angular workspace is the file system place containing the Angular files: a collection of application files, libraries, assets, and so on. In most ASP.NET Core and Angular project templates this type of workspace is located within the /ClientApp/ folder: however, since we opted for a Standalone Angular template, our workspace is located within the project's root folder.

 The workspace is created and initialized by the Angular CLI command used to create the app. Since we've used the Visual Studio GUI, we didn't see that part with our own eyes because it was executed in the background. However, we're going to fully experience it later on, when we manually create a new app with the Angular CLI.

Any CLI commands operating on the app and/or their libraries (such as adding or updating new packages) will be executed from within the workspace.

angular.json

The most important role within the workspace is played by the angular.json file, created by the CLI in the workspace root. This is the workspace configuration file and contains workspace-wide and project-specific configuration defaults for all build and development tools provided by the Angular CLI.

The first few properties at the top of the file define the workspace and project configuration options:

- version: The configuration file version
- newProjectRoot: The path where new projects are created, relative to the workspace root folder. We can see that this value is set to the projects folder, which doesn't even exist (no need to worry about that: we won't create any new Angular projects anyway)

- `projects`: A container item that hosts a sub-section for each project in the workspace, containing project-specific configuration options
- `defaultProject`: The default project name—any CLI command that doesn't specify a project name will be executed on this project

> It's worth noting that the `angular.json` file follows a standard generic-to-specific cascading rule. All configuration values set at the workspace level will be the default values for any project and can be overridden by those set at the project level. These, in turn, can be overridden by command-line values available when using the CLI.
>
> It's also worth mentioning that, before **Angular 8**, manually modifying the `angular.json` file was the only way to make changes to the workspace config.

That's all we need to know, at least for the time being. All the configuration values are already good enough for our scenario, hence, we'll just leave them as they are for now.

> Up to **Angular 7**, manually modifying the `angular.json` file was the only way to make changes to the workspace config. This changed with **Angular 8** with the introduction of the **workspace API**, which now allows us to read and modify these configurations much more conveniently. For additional info regarding this new feature, we suggest taking a look at the following page: `https://github.com/angular/angular-cli/blob/master/packages/angular_devkit/core/README.md#workspaces`.

package.json

The `package.json` file is the **Node Package Manager** (**npm**) **configuration file**. It basically contains a list of **npm packages** that the developer wants to be restored before the project starts. Those who already know what npm is and how it works can skip to the next section, while those who don't should definitely keep reading.

npm started its life as the default package manager for the JavaScript runtime environment known as **Node.js**. During recent years, though, it has also been used to host a number of independent JavaScript projects, libraries, and frameworks of any kind, including *Angular*. Eventually, it became the *de facto* package manager for JavaScript frameworks and tooling. Those who have never used it can think of it as the *NuGet* for the JavaScript world.

Although npm is mostly a *command-line* tool, the easiest way to use it from Visual Studio is to properly configure a `package.json` file containing all the npm packages we want to get, restore, and keep up to date later on. These packages get downloaded in the `/node_modules/` folder within our project directory, which is hidden by default within Visual Studio; however, all retrieved packages can be seen from the npm virtual folder. As soon as we add, delete, or update the `package.json` file, Visual Studio will automatically update that folder accordingly.

In the Angular SPA template we've been using, the shipped `package.json` file contains a huge number of packages—all **Angular** packages—plus a good bunch of dependencies, tools, and third-party utilities such as **Karma** (a great test runner for JavaScript/TypeScript).

Before moving ahead, let's take a further look at our `package.json` file and try to get the most out of it. We can see how all packages are listed within a standard JSON object entirely made up of *key-value* pairs. The package name is the *key*, while the *value* is used to specify the version number. We can either input precise build numbers or use the standard **npmJS** syntax to specify *auto-update rules* bound to custom version ranges using supported prefixes, such as the following:

- **The Tilde** (~): A value of "~1.1.4" will match all 1.1.x versions, excluding 1.2.0, 1.0.x, and so on
- **The Caret** (^): A value of "^1.1.4" will match everything above 1.1.4, excluding 2.0.0 and above

This is another scenario where *IntelliSense* comes in handy, as it will also visually explain the actual meaning of these prefixes.

 For an extensive list of available npmJS commands and prefixes, it's advisable to check out the official npmJS documentation at `https://docs.npmjs.com/files/package.json`.

Upgrading (or downgrading) Angular

As we can see, the Angular SPA template uses fixed version numbers for all Angular-related packages; this is definitely a wise choice since we have no guarantees that newer versions will seamlessly integrate with our existing code without raising some potentially breaking changes and/or compiler errors. Needless to say, the version number will naturally increase over time because template developers will definitely try to keep their good work up to date.

That said, here are the most important Angular packages and releases that will be used throughout this book (not including a small bunch of additional packages that will be added later on):

```
"@angular/animations": "13.0.1",
"@angular/common": "13.0.1",
"@angular/compiler": "13.0.1",
"@angular/core": "13.0.1",
"@angular/forms": "13.0.1",
"@angular/platform-browser": "13.0.1",
"@angular/platform-browser-dynamic": "13.0.1",
"@angular/router": "13.0.1",

"@angular-devkit/build-angular": "13.0.1",
"@angular/cli": "13.0.1",
"@angular/compiler-cli": "13.0.1"
```

The former group can be found in the `dependencies` section, while the latter is part of the `devDependencies` section. As we can see, the version number is mostly the same for all packages and corresponds to the latest Angular final release available at the time of writing.

The version of Angular that we use in this book was released a few weeks before this book hit the shelves. We did our best to use the latest available (non-beta, non-rc) version to give the reader the best possible experience with the most recent technology available. That said, that freshness will eventually decrease over time and this book's code will start to become obsolete. When this happens, try not to blame us for that!

If we want to ensure the highest possible level of compatibility between our project and this book's source code, we should definitely adopt that same release, which, at the time of writing, also corresponds to the latest stable one. We can easily perform the upgrade—or downgrade—by changing the version numbers; as soon as we save the file, Visual Studio *should* automatically fetch new versions through **npm**. In the unlikely scenario that it doesn't, manually deleting the old packages and issuing a full rebuild should be enough to fix the issue.

As always, we're free to overwrite such behavior and get newer (or older) versions of these packages, assuming that we properly understand the consequences according to the **Disclaimer** in *Chapter 2, Getting Ready*.

If you encounter problems while updating your `package.json` file, such as conflicting packages or broken code, ensure that you download the full source code from the official GitHub repository of this book, which includes the same `package.json` file that has been used to write, review, and test this book. It will definitely ensure a great level of compatibility with the source code you'll find here.

Upgrading (or downgrading) the other packages

As we might expect, if we upgrade (or downgrade) Angular to the latest available version (at the time of writing), we also need to take care of a series of other npm packages that might need to be updated (or downgraded).

Here's the full package list (including the Angular packages) we'll be using in our `package.json` file throughout the book, split into `dependencies` and `devDependencies` sections. The relevant packages are summarized in the following snippet—be sure to triple-check them!

```
"dependencies": {
  "@angular/animations": "13.0.1",
  "@angular/common": "13.0.1",
  "@angular/compiler": "13.0.1",
  "@angular/core": "13.0.1",
  "@angular/forms": "13.0.1",
  "@angular/platform-browser": "13.0.1",
  "@angular/platform-browser-dynamic": "13.0.1",
```

```
    "@angular/router": "13.0.1",
    "rxjs": "7.4.0",
    "tslib": "2.3.1",
    "zone.js": "0.11.4",
    "jest-editor-support": "*"
  },
  "devDependencies": {
    "@angular-devkit/build-angular": "13.0.1",
    "@angular/cli": "13.0.1",
    "@angular/compiler-cli": "13.0.1",
    "@types/jasmine": "3.8.0",
    "@types/node": "^12.11.1",
    "jasmine-core": "3.8.0",
    "karma": "6.3.0",
    "karma-chrome-launcher": "3.1.0",
    "karma-coverage": "2.0.3",
    "karma-jasmine": "4.0.0",
    "karma-jasmine-html-reporter": "1.7.0",
    "typescript": "4.4.4"
  }
}
```

It's advisable to perform a manual command-line npm install followed by an npm update from the project's root folder right after applying these changes to the package.json file in order to trigger a batch update of all the project's npm packages. Sometimes, Visual Studio doesn't update the packages automatically, and doing that using the GUI can be tricky.

Those who run into **npm** and/or **ngcc** compilation issues after the npm update command can also try to delete the /node_modules/ folder and then perform an npm install from scratch.

Upgrading the Angular code

It's worth noting that our updated package.json file might not include some of the packages that were present in the Visual Studio default ASP.NET and Angular SPA project template. The reason for that is quite simple: those packages are either deprecated, obsolete, or not required by the code samples we'll be working with from now on.

tsconfig.json

The tsconfig.json file is the TypeScript configuration file. Again, those who already know what TypeScript is won't need to read all this, although those who don't should.

In fewer than 100 words, TypeScript is a free, open source programming language developed and maintained by Microsoft that acts as a JavaScript superset; this means that any JavaScript program is also a valid TypeScript program. TypeScript also compiles to JavaScript, meaning it can seamlessly work on any JavaScript-compatible browser without external components.

The main reason for using it is to overcome JavaScript's syntax limitations and overall shortcomings when developing large-scale applications or complex projects. Simply put, it makes the developer's life easier when they are forced to deal with non-trivial code.

In this project, we will definitely use TypeScript for a number of good reasons. The most important ones are as follows:

- TypeScript has several advantageous features compared with JavaScript, such as static typing, classes, and interfaces. Using it in Visual Studio also gives us the chance to benefit from the *built-in* IntelliSense, which is a great benefit and often leads to a remarkable productivity boost.

- For a large *client-side* project, TypeScript will allow us to produce more robust code, which will also be fully deployable anywhere a plain JavaScript file would run.

Not to mention the fact that the Angular SPA template we chose already uses TypeScript. Hence, we can say that we already have one foot in the water!

Jokes aside, we're not the only ones praising TypeScript; this has been acknowledged by the Angular team itself, considering the fact that *the Angular source code has been written using TypeScript since Angular 2*, as was proudly announced by Microsoft in the following MDSN blog post in March 2015: `https://devblogs.microsoft.com/typescript/angular-2-built-on-typescript/`.

This was further emphasized in this great post by *Victor Savkin* (cofounder of Narwhal Technologies and acknowledged Angular consultant) on his personal blog in October 2016: `https://vsavkin.com/writing-angular-2-in-typescript-1fa77c78d8e8`.

Getting back to the `tsconfig.json` file, there's not much to say; the option values used by the Angular template are just what we need to configure both Visual Studio and the **TypeScript compiler (TSC)** to properly transpile the TypeScript code files included in the `/src/` folder, hence there's no need to change it.

 For additional info about the `tsconfig.json` file and all the available options, visit the following URL: `https://angular.io/config/tsconfig`.

Other workspace-level files

There are also other notable files created by the CLI in the workspace root. Since we'll not be changing them, we'll just briefly mention them in the following list:

- `.browserlistrc`: a file used by the build system to adjust CSS and JS output to support various browsers.

- `.editorconfig`: a workspace-specific configuration for code editors.

- `.gitignore`: a text file that tells Git—a version-control system you most likely know quite well—which files or folders to ignore in the workspace. These are intentionally untracked files that shouldn't be added to the version control repository.

- `/node_modules/`: a (hidden) folder containing all the **npm** packages for the entire workspace. This folder will be populated with packages defined in the `package.json` file located on the workspace root; since it's excluded from the project by default, we can only see it if we click on the **Show All Files** button at the top of **Solution Explorer**.

- `aspnetcore-https.js`: a script that sets up HTTPS for the application using the ASP.NET Core HTTPS certificate. Remember the HTTPS authorization popup that appeared in *Chapter 2, Getting Ready*, during our first test run? We've just found what triggered it.

- `karma.conf.js`: an application-specific *Karma* configuration. Karma is a tool used to run *Jasmine*-based tests. We can safely ignore the whole topic for now, as we'll get to it later on.

- `nuget.config`: a NuGet configuration file: we can safely ignore it.

- `package-lock.json`: provides version information for all packages installed in the `/node_modules/` folder by the **npm** client. If you plan to replace **npm** with **Yarn**, you can safely delete this file (the `yarn.lock` file will be created instead).

> **Yarn** is a package manager for the JavaScript programming language developed and released by Facebook in October 2016 to address some of the limitations that **npm** had at the time, and is meant to be a drop-in replacement for **npm**. For further info, read here: `https://yarnpkg.com/`.

- `README.md`: introductory documentation for the workspace. The `.md` extension stands for **Markdown**, a lightweight markup language created by *John Gruber* and *Aaron Swartz* in 2004.

- `tsconfig.*.json`: project-specific configuration options for various aspects of our app: `.app.json` for *application-level*, `.server.json` for *server-level*, and `.spec.json` for *tests*. These options will override those set in the generic `tsconfig.json` file in the workspace root.

Now that we know the basics of various workspace-level files, we can move on to examining Angular's source code files.

The /src/ folder

It's time to pay a visit to the Angular app and see how it works by looking at its source code files. Rest assured, we won't stay for long; we just want to get a glimpse of what's under the hood.

By expanding the `/src/` directory, we can see that there are the following sub-folders:

- The `/src/app/` folder, along with all its sub-folders, contains all the TypeScript files related to our Angular app; in other words, the whole *client-side* application source code is meant to be put here.

- The `/src/assets/` folder is meant to store all the application's images and other asset files. These files will be copied and/or updated *as-is* in the deployment folder whenever the application is built.

- The `/src/environments/` folder contains build configuration options that target specific environments; this template, just like any Angular new project default, includes an `environment.ts` file (for development) and an `environment.prod.ts` file (for production).

There is also a bunch of root-level files:

- `favicon.ico`: a file containing one or more small icons that will be shown in the web browser's address bar when we visit the Angular app, as well as near the page's title in various browser components (tabs, bookmarks, history, and so on).
- `index.html`: the main HTML page that is served when we access the Angular app. The CLI automatically adds all JavaScript and CSS files when building our app, so we typically don't need to add any `<script>` or `<link>` tags here manually.
- `karma.conf.js`: application-specific Karma configuration. Karma is a tool used to run Jasmine-based tests. We can safely ignore the whole topic for now, as we'll get to it later on.
- `main.ts`: the main entry point for our application. Compiles the application with the JIT compiler and bootstraps the application's root module (`AppModule`) to run in the browser. We can also use the AOT compiler without changing any code by appending the `--aot` flag to CLI build and serve commands.
- `polyfills.ts`: provides polyfill scripts for improving browser support.
- `proxy.conf.ts`: the Angular Live Development Server's proxy configuration settings. We've already seen it in *Chapter 2, Getting Ready*, when we've changed the HTTPS port to the single rule currently present: the one that redirects all the HTTP requests to `/weatherforecast` to the API web server. In short, we're going to update that rule to make it more generic so that it will redirect all the API HTTP requests to the Web API server.
- `styles.css`: a list of CSS files that supply styles for a project.
- `test.ts`: the main entry point for the project's unit tests.

Let's start our coding review with the `/src/app/` folder's content.

The /src/app/ folder

Our template's `/src/app/` folder follows Angular folder structure best practices and contains our project's logic and data, thereby including all Angular *modules*, *services*, and *components*, as well as *templates* and *styles*. It's also the only sub-folder worth investigating, at least for the time being.

AppModule

As we briefly anticipated in *Chapter 1, Introducing ASP.NET and Angular*, the basic building blocks of an Angular application are **NgModules**, which provide a compilation context for components. The role of NgModules is to collect related code into functional sets: therefore, the whole Angular app is defined by a set of one or more NgModules.

NgModules were introduced in Angular 2 RC5 and are a great, powerful way to organize and bootstrap any Angular application; they help developers consolidate their own set of **components, directives**, and **pipes** into *reusable* blocks. As we said previously, every Angular application since v2 RC5 must have at least one module, which is conventionally called a **root module** and is thus given the `AppModule` class name.

Any Angular app requires a *root module*—conventionally called AppModule—that tells Angular how to assemble the application, thus enabling bootstrapping and starting the initialization life cycle (see the diagram that follows). The remaining modules are known as **feature modules** and serve a different purpose. The *root module* also contains a reference list of all available components.

The following is a schema of the standard **Angular Initialization Cycle**, which will help us better visualize how it works:

Angular Initialization Cycle

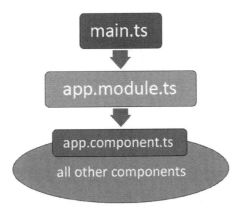

Figure 3.4: The Angular initialization cycle

As we can see, the main.ts file bootstraps app.module.ts (AppModule), which then loads the app. component.ts file (AppComponent); the latter, as we'll see in a short while, will then load all the other components whenever the application needs them.

The *root module* of the sample Angular app created by our template can be found in the /src/app/ folder and is defined within the app.module.ts file. If we look at the source code, we can see that our AppModule is split into two main code blocks:

- A list of **import** statements, pointing to all the references (in the form of TypeScript files) required by the application
- The root NgModule block, which is basically a collection of named arrays, each one containing a set of Angular objects that serve a common purpose: **directives, components, pipes, modules, providers,** and so on. The last one contains the component we want to bootstrap, which, in most scenarios—including ours—is the main application component, AppComponent

AppComponent

If NgModules are Angular building blocks, **components** can be defined as the bricks used to put the app together, to the extent that we can say that an Angular app is basically a tree of components working together.

Components define **views**, which are sets of screen elements that Angular can choose between and modify according to your program logic and data, and use **services**, which provide specific functionality not directly related to views. **Service providers** can also be injected into components as *dependencies*, thus making the app code modular, reusable, and efficient.

The cornerstone of these components is conventionally called AppComponent, which is also the only component that—according to Angular folder structure conventions—should be placed in the /app/ root folder. All other components should be put in a sub-folder, which will act as a dedicated *namespace*.

> As we can easily notice, AppComponent is also the only component present in our Stand-alone Angular template: this means that the app currently offers a single view only. On top of that, it also lacks a proper menu and navigation system. In other words, it's *literally* a single-page application! Don't worry, though: we'll soon add other components, as well as perform some UI and UX tweaks to improve its look and feel.

As we can see, our AppComponent consists of four files:

- app.component.ts: defines the component logic, that is, the component class source code.
- app.component.html: defines the HTML template associated with the AppComponent. Any Angular component can have an optional HTML file containing its UI layout structure instead of defining it within the component file itself. This is almost always a good practice unless the component comes with a very minimal UI.
- app.component.css: defines the base CSS StyleSheet for the component. Just like the .html file, this file is optional, yet it should always be used unless the component doesn't require UI styling.
- app.component.spec.ts: contains the unit tests for the app.component.ts source file and can be run using the Jasmine JavaScript test framework through the Karma test runner.

Let's take a brief look at each one of them.

The TypeScript class file

Let's start with the app.component.ts file, which will help us to start familiarizing ourselves with the source code of a typical Angular component class:

```
import { HttpClient } from '@angular/common/http';
import { Component } from '@angular/core';

@Component({
  selector: 'app-root',
  templateUrl: './app.component.html',
  styleUrls: ['./app.component.css']
})
export class AppComponent {
  public forecasts?: WeatherForecast[];
```

```
  constructor(http: HttpClient) {
    http.get<WeatherForecast[]>('/weatherforecast').subscribe(result => {
      this.forecasts = result;
    }, error => console.error(error));
  }

  title = 'HealthCheck';
}

interface WeatherForecast {
  date: string;
  temperatureC: number;
  temperatureF: number;
  summary: string;
}
```

As we can see, the class contains the following coding blocks:

- A list of import statements, much like we've seen in the `AppModule` class.
- The `@Component` decorator, which defines `selector`, as well as the `templateUrl` and `styleUrls` of the component. `selector` is the most important thing defined there as it tells Angular to instantiate this component wherever it finds the corresponding tag in template HTML. In this case, `AppComponent` will be instantiated wherever Angular finds the `<app-root>` tag.
- The TypeScript class for the component, which includes the constructor, local properties, methods, and so on.
- An interface to store the weather forecast JSON data coming from the ASP.NET Core Web API in a typed fashion: ideally, these interfaces should require their own dedicated and separate file – however, for the sake of simplicity, the template we're using puts it here.

Let's now switch to the HTML template file.

The HTML template file

The `/src/app/app.component.html` file contains the HTML required to render the component on the browser's screen. Within these templates, we can use HTML, CSS, and JS code, as well as some special Angular syntax that can be used to add powerful features, such as *interpolation*, *template statements*, *binding syntax*, *property binding*, *directives*, and *reference variables*.

We'll talk more about these features in *Chapter 4, Front-End and Back-End Interactions*, when we create a custom component with a table-based template much similar to this one.

The StyleSheet file

As we can see, the `/src/app/app.component.css` style is currently empty: it just means that the component has no styles applied (yet). For now, we can just leave it as it is: we'll come back to this file later on, when we start styling our Angular app.

The spec.ts file

Before going further ahead, let's spend some time taking a better look at the `app.component.spec.ts` file. Those files, as per the Angular naming convention, are meant to contain **unit tests** for their corresponding source files and are run using the *Jasmine* JavaScript test framework through the *Karma* test runner.

For additional info regarding Jasmine and Karma, check out the following guides:

Jasmine: `https://jasmine.github.io/`

Karma: `https://karma-runner.github.io/`

Angular Unit Testing: `https://angular.io/guide/testing`

While we're there, it could be useful to give them a run to see whether the *Jasmine + Karma* testing framework that has been set up by our template actually works.

Our first test run

Before running the test, it may be useful to understand a little bit more about *Jasmine* and *Karma*. If you don't know anything about them, don't worry—you will soon. For now, just know that **Jasmine** is an open source testing framework for JavaScript that can be used to define *tests*, while **Karma** is a test runner tool that automatically spawns a web server that will execute JavaScript source code against Jasmine-made *tests* and output their respective (and combined) results on a command line.

In this quick test, we'll basically launch **Karma** to execute the source code of our sample Angular app against the **Jasmine** *tests* defined by the template in the `app.component.spec.ts` file; this is actually a much easier task than it might seem.

Open Command Prompt, navigate to the Angular project root folder, and then execute the following command:

```
> npm run ng test
```

This will call the Angular CLI using **npm**.

IMPORTANT: Chrome needs to be installed, otherwise the test won't work.

In the unlikely event that the `npm` command returns a `program not found` error, check that the `Node.js/npm` binary folder is properly set within the `PATH` variable. If it's not there, be sure to add it, and then close and re-open the command-line window and try again.

First testing attempt

Right after we hit *Enter*, a new browser window should open with the Karma console and a list of results for the Jasmine tests, as shown in the following figure:

Figure 3.5: First run of the Jasmine test: epic fail

As we can see, we have three failed tests out of three: that's quite unexpected, since we're using template-generated code that should work right off the bat!

As a matter of fact, the `app.component.spec.ts` file shipped with the Standalone TypeScript Angular template has not been updated properly to reflect the component's HTML template, at least at the time of writing: in other words, it's broken.

To fix it, we need to perform the following changes to the source code (new and updated lines are highlighted):

```
import { TestBed } from '@angular/core/testing';
import { HttpClientTestingModule } from '@angular/common/http/testing';
import { AppComponent } from './app.component';

describe('AppComponent', () => {
  beforeEach(async () => {
    await TestBed.configureTestingModule({
```

```
    imports: [
      HttpClientTestingModule
    ],
    declarations: [
      AppComponent
    ],
  }).compileComponents();
});

it('should create the app', () => {
  const fixture = TestBed.createComponent(AppComponent);
  const app = fixture.componentInstance;
  expect(app).toBeTruthy();
});

it('should have as title 'HealthCheck'', () => {
  const fixture = TestBed.createComponent(AppComponent);
  const app = fixture.componentInstance;
  expect(app.title).toEqual('HealthCheck');
});

it('should render title', () => {
  const fixture = TestBed.createComponent(AppComponent);
  fixture.detectChanges();
  const compiled = fixture.nativeElement as HTMLElement;
  expect(compiled.querySelector('h1')?.textContent).toContain('Weather
forecast');
  });
});
```

In a nutshell, here's what we did:

- Added the `HttpClientTestingModule` to the testing module's import list, as the app requires it to run (and pass the three tests)
- Changed the `'should render title'` test (the last one) so that it will properly match the app title

Once done, we can try to launch the test again and see if we've managed to fix these errors.

Second testing attempt

Again, navigate to the Angular project root folder and execute the `npm run ng test` command. If we did everything properly, we should see something like the following screenshot:

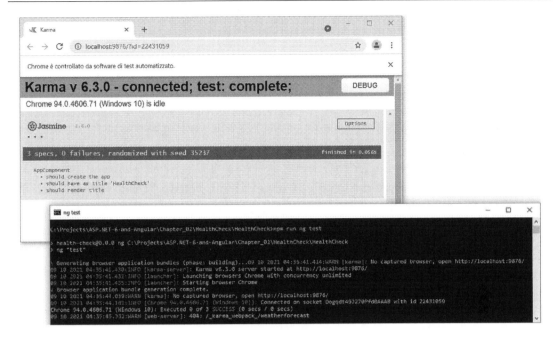

Figure 3.6: Second run of the Jasmine test: success!

All three tests have been completed successfully: well done!

 For the sake of simplicity, we're going to stop here with Angular app tests for the time being; we'll discuss them in far greater depth in *Chapter 9, Back-End and Front-End Debugging*.

Getting to work

Now that we've got a general picture of our projects, it's time to do something. Let's start with two simple exercises that will also come in handy in the future. The first of these will involve the *server-side* endpoints of our Web API project, while the second will affect the *client-side* user experience of our Angular app. Both will help us to ensure we have really understood everything there is to know before proceeding to subsequent chapters.

Changing the API endpoints

If we take another look at Angular's `proxy.conf.js` file, we can easily see that the only existing rule is explicitly mapping the single Web API's action method of our Web API:

```
const PROXY_CONFIG = [
  {
    context: [
      "/weatherforecast",
    ],
    target: "https://localhost:40443",
```

```
      secure: false
   }
]


module.exports = PROXY_CONFIG;
```

This might be OK for our initial testing purposes, but it can become a very unpractical approach as soon as we start to add controllers and action methods: we surely don't want to manually update these rules every time.

The best thing we can do to fix that is to define a single rule that will work for all our API endpoints: this can be done by defining a prefix (such as /api/) that will be used by all of our action methods' endpoints. Such a change needs to be performed in three files:

- The Angular app.component.ts file (*HealthCheck* project), where the HTTP request is issued
- The Angular proxy configuration file (*HealthCheck* project), where the HTTP request is diverted to the Web API web server
- The WeatherForecastController.cs file (*HealthCheckAPI* project), which will respond to the HTTP request with the weather forecast JSON data

Let's start with the Angular project.

Open the /src/app/app.component.ts file and update the existing '/weatherforecast' value in the following way:

```
constructor(http: HttpClient) {
  http.get<WeatherForecast[]>('/api/weatherforecast').subscribe(result => {
    this.forecasts = result;
  }, error => console.error(error));
}
```

Now we need to change the proxy, so the new URL will be properly addressed to the Web API application. Open the /src/proxy.conf.json file and update the existing endpoint in the following way:

```
const PROXY_CONFIG = [
  {
    context: [
      "/api",
    ],
    target: "https://localhost:40443",
    secure: false
  }
]
```

The Angular aspects of our job are done: now every HTTP request starting with /api – including the updated /api/weatherforecast – will be diverted to our *back-end* Web API application.

However, our Web API application doesn't know it yet: if we now try to run our Angular app by hitting *F5*, we'd get no more weather forecast data, since the old /weatherforecast endpoint will return an HTTP 404 (Not Found) error. To fix the issue, we simply need to change it to /api/weatherforecast so that the updated rule will affect it.

Switch to the *HealthCheckAPI* project, open the /Controllers/WeatherForecastController.cs file, and add the api/ prefix to the existing [Route] attribute value (line 6 or so) in the following way:

```
[Route("api/[controller]")]
```

Now we can launch our project(s) in *Debug* mode and see if the Angular app is able to fetch the weather forecast data again.

The good thing about this change is that our Angular proxy now features a *generic* rule that will be valid for any API endpoint – as long as we include the api/ prefix in the controller's route – without having to add a new rule every time.

 For additional info about the *Angular Live Development Server* proxy settings, check out the following URL:

https://angular.io/guide/build#proxying-to-a-backend-server

The changes we've just applied to our endpoint URLs are good enough when running our app(s) in *Development* mode since we can rely upon the Angular proxy and they will work great even when publishing our app(s) in a *Production* environment as long as we can serve the Web API through a proxy using similar techniques.

However, what if our hosting service (or strategy) doesn't allow that? What if we want to publish our *HealthCheck* Angular app and the *HealthCheckAPI* back-end on two completely different domains without being able to proxy the latter through the /api/ folder of the former one? This is a typical scenario of most modern deployment techniques: for example, if we wanted to host our Angular app on a **Content Delivery Network (CDN)** instead of using an actual HTTP server.

If we want our app(s) to support such behaviors, the best thing we can do is to implement an additional baseUrl property and use it as a "prefix" for all our API calls: let's take the chance to do that.

Implementing the baseUrl property

The best place to implement a baseUrl property would be the /src/environments/ folder, which we briefly mentioned earlier. This folder contains two files – environment.ts and environment.prod.ts – that can be used to define environment-specific settings, which is precisely what we need.

 The environment.*.ts files are the Angular counterpart of the ASP.NET Core appsettings.*.json files, and they can be used to fulfill the same requirements: set up configuration values that will be automatically overridden depending on the app's execution environment.

Open the `/src/environments/environment.ts` file and add the `baseUrl` property in the following way:

```
export const environment = {
  production: false,
  baseUrl: "/"
};
```

This is the value that we're going to use in the *Development* environment since we can rely upon the Angular proxy.

Let's now open the `/src/environments/environment.prod.ts` file and set up the `baseUrl` property with a slightly different value:

```
export const environment = {
  production: false,
  baseUrl: "https://localhost:40443/"
};
```

As we can see, this time we've set up a whole URL with a protocol and port. We've used `localhost` for the time being since we don't have any clue about our Web API's *Production* endpoint (yet); however, now that we have the `baseUrl` variable ready, we'll easily be able to replace this value with an FQDN as soon as we have it available. As a matter of fact, we're going to do that in *Chapter 15, Windows, Linux, and Azure Deployment*, when we'll learn how to publish our apps in production.

Refactoring the Angular app

The next thing we're going to do is to refactor our current Angular app to make it a bit more versatile and user-friendly. More specifically, here's what we're going to do:

- **Add two new components**, one for the app's "welcome screen" and another for the existing data fetching example (where we'll move the existing weather forecast implementation)
- **Add a top-level navigation menu**, so that the user will be able to navigate between the new components from the UI
- **Implement a client-side routing system**, so that each choice selected by the user through the navigation menu will be handled by showing the correct components

Let's get to work.

Adding HomeComponent

Let's start by adding `HomeComponent`, which will host our app's home page contents. Given our development workspace, there are two main approaches for doing that:

- Use the Angular CLI
- Use the Visual Studio **Add New Item** feature

The Angular CLI method is considered the most convenient choice since it automatically generates all the required files and references: that's the reason why we're going to use it.

Open Command Prompt and navigate to the Angular project's root folder. It should be /Projects/ HealthCheck/HealthCheck/ if you followed our path naming conventions, and type the following command:

```
> ng generate component Home
```

The preceding command will perform the following tasks, as shown in the following screenshot:

- Create a new /src/app/home/ folder to host the new component files
- Generate the component's ts, css, html, and spec.ts files and fill them with sample data
- Update the app.module.ts file to add a reference to the new component

```
CREATE src/app/home/home.component.html (19 bytes)
CREATE src/app/home/home.component.spec.ts (612 bytes)
CREATE src/app/home/home.component.ts (267 bytes)
CREATE src/app/home/home.component.css (0 bytes)
UPDATE src/app/app.module.ts (575 bytes)
```

Figure 3.7: Output of the ng generate component's Home command

Once done, we can move on to the next steps.

> From now on, we'll always create component files using the Angular CLI throughout the rest of the book. However, those who prefer to use the manual approach are free to do that: just be sure to add the required references to Angular's AppModule, which will be shown in a short while.

The dry run switch

In case we want to see what the preceding ng command does without making any change, we can use the --dry-run switch in the following way:

```
> ng generate component Home --dry-run
```

That switch will prevent the CLI from making any changes to the file system, meaning that we will see what the ng command does without creating or modifying any file. This can be useful whenever we are unsure about what the command might do, since we'll be able to see what it does without the risk of breaking something in our app.

> It's also worth noting that the --dry-run switch is not limited to the ng generate component: it can be used with any Angular CLI command.

Skipping the spec.ts file

In case we want to prevent the creation of the file for the unit tests, we can add the `--skip-tests` switch to the CLI command in the following way:

```
> ng generate component Home --skip-tests
```

This switch will prevent the Angular CLI from creating the `spec.ts` file for the component: we've briefly seen `spec.ts` files in *Chapter 2, Getting Ready*, when we performed our first unit test. Since we're not going to use these files until *Chapter 10, ASP.NET Core and Angular Unit Testing*, when we talk about client-side and server-side testing, for the sake of simplicity, we'll just skip them using the `--skip-tests` switch from now on. For that very reason, in case we have already generated the `home.component.spec.ts` file, we can delete it before going on.

Adding FetchDataComponent

The next thing we're going to do is to create the `FetchDataComponent`, where we'll put the autogenerated data fetch example that currently resides in `AppComponent`.

Again, use Command Prompt from within the *HealthCheck* project root path to issue the following console command:

```
ng generate component FetchData --skip-tests
```

Again, the command will add the required files and update `AppModule` accordingly.

Now we have two (mostly empty) components to play with: however, there's currently no way for the user to reach them since our Angular app lacks a proper navigation menu, as well as a routing mechanism that allows such navigation to work.

Let's solve this problem for good.

Adding the navigation menu

In a typical HTML-based user interface, a navigation menu is an element containing several hyperlinks (or buttons, or tabs) that allows the user to navigate between the various website sections, pages, or views.

If we think of it from an Angular perspective, we can easily see how it's no different than a component, just like `Home` and `FetchData`. For that very reason, we're going to create it with the same technique that we've used until now:

```
ng generate component NavMenu --skip-tests
```

With this, we can finally start to code!

First of all, open the `/src/app/app.module.ts` file to acknowledge the (highlighted) changes automatically performed by the Angular CLI:

```
import { HttpClientModule } from '@angular/common/http';
import { NgModule } from '@angular/core';
```

```
import { BrowserModule } from '@angular/platform-browser';

import { AppComponent } from './app.component';
import { HomeComponent } from './home/home.component';
import { FetchDataComponent } from './fetch-data/fetch-data.component';
import { NavMenuComponent } from './nav-menu/nav-menu.component';

@NgModule({
  declarations: [
    AppComponent,
    HomeComponent,
    FetchDataComponent,
    NavMenuComponent
  ],
  imports: [
    BrowserModule, HttpClientModule
  ],
  providers: [],
  bootstrap: [AppComponent]
})
export class AppModule { }
```

We don't need to do anything here, but it can be useful to understand *what we should have done* if we didn't use the Angular CLI and chose to create these components manually instead.

Let's now create our navigation menu. From Visual Studio **Solution Explorer**, open the *HealthCheck* project, navigate to the /src/app/nav-menu/ folder, select the nav-menu.component.html file, and fill it with the following HTML code, overwriting the existing sample content:

```
<header>
  <nav>
    <a [routerLink]="['/']">Home</a>
    |
    <a [routerLink]="['/fetch-data']">Fetch Data</a>
  </nav>
</header>
```

As we can see, we didn't do much: just the minimal amount of HTML code to implement a hyper-link-based navigation mechanism within a standard <header> element.

The only thing worth noting here is that each hyperlink element contains a reference to a RouterLink – an Angular *directive* that makes that element a link that initiates the navigation to a route. The navigation system that we're going to build will open the routed components in a dedicated <router-outlet> container present on the page.

Updating the AppComponent

The best place to put that <router-outlet> location is AppComponent, which should also contain the NavMenuComponent: that way, AppComponent will truly become the backbone of our Angular app, containing both the navigation component and the container where the routed components will be opened.

However, before doing that, we need to "move" the current AppComponent behavior – showing the weather forecast data – to the dedicated FetchDataComponent that we added a moment ago: since the component's behavior is handled by the source code contained in its TypeScript and HTML files, it means that we need to move the content of those files as well.

 For the sake of simplicity, we can ignore the StyleSheet file for now since it's currently empty.

Open the /src/app/fetch-data.component.ts file and update it in the following way (added/updated code is highlighted):

```typescript
import { HttpClient } from '@angular/common/http';
import { Component, OnInit } from '@angular/core';

import { environment } from '../../environments/environment';

@Component({
  selector: 'app-fetch-data',
  templateUrl: './fetch-data.component.html',
  styleUrls: ['./fetch-data.component.css']
})
export class FetchDataComponent implements OnInit {
  public forecasts?: WeatherForecast[];

  constructor(http: HttpClient) {
    http.get<WeatherForecast[]>(environment.baseUrl + 'api/weatherforecast').
subscribe(result => {
      this.forecasts = result;
    }, error => console.error(error));
  }

  ngOnInit(): void {
  }
}

interface WeatherForecast {
```

```
  date: string;
  temperatureC: number;
  temperatureF: number;
  summary: string;
}
```

As we can see, all the updated code lines are taken from the app.component.ts file: that was expected since we're actually transferring the original behavior of AppComponent to this component.

 We also took the chance to use the baseUrl property we added earlier on as a prefix for the 'api/weatherforecast' endpoint to make it ready for both *Development* and *Production* environments.

The same thing must be done with the /src/app/fetch-data.component.html file, which contains the HTML template for the component. This time, we can just perform a copy and paste from the app.component.html file since we do have no class names to preserve. Here's the updated code:

```html
<h1 id="tableLabel">Weather forecast</h1>

<p>This component demonstrates fetching data from the server.</p>

<p *ngIf="!forecasts"><em>Loading... Please refresh once the ASP.NET backend
has started.</em></p>

<table *ngIf="forecasts">
  <thead>
    <tr>
      <th>Date</th>
      <th>Temp. (C)</th>
      <th>Temp. (F)</th>
      <th>Summary</th>
    </tr>
  </thead>
  <tbody>
    <tr *ngFor="let forecast of forecasts">
      <td>{{ forecast.date }}</td>
      <td>{{ forecast.temperatureC }}</td>
      <td>{{ forecast.temperatureF }}</td>
      <td>{{ forecast.summary }}</td>
    </tr>
  </tbody>
</table>
```

Now that we've "moved" the data-fetching behavior to FetchDataComponent, we can finally update the
AppComponent source code so that it can perform its new "backbone" job.

Here's the updated /src/app/app.component.ts file:

```
import { Component } from '@angular/core';

@Component({
  selector: 'app-root',
  templateUrl: './app.component.html',
  styleUrls: ['./app.component.css']
})
export class AppComponent {
  title = 'HealthCheck';
}
```

And here's the corresponding /src/app/app.component.html modified file:

```
<app-nav-menu></app-nav-menu>
<div class="container">
  <router-outlet></router-outlet>
</div>
```

As expected, the updated AppComponent is just a container for NavMenuComponent and the <router-
outlet> Angular elements.

 It's worth noting that, in order to add a reference to NavMenuComponent, we had to use
the <app-nav-menu> tag, which matches the value of the selector property specified in
the nav-menu.component.ts file.

Updating the test files

Now that we've moved the behavior of AppComponent (and the source code) to FetchDataComponent,
the test defined in the app.component.spec.ts file that looks for the app's title will fail; this can be
easily tested by running Karma with the ng test command and viewing the outcome.

To fix that, we have two options:

- Remove the /src/app.component.spec.ts file
- Comment out the code for that test since we no longer need it

For the sake of simplicity, we'll go with the latter option. Here's how we can do that:

```
// Test removed in Chapter 3,
// since the AppComponent doesn't contain the app's title anymore.
//  it('should render title', () => {
//    const fixture = TestBed.createComponent(AppComponent);
```

```
//    fixture.detectChanges();
//    const compiled = fixture.nativeElement as HTMLElement;
//    expect(compiled.querySelector('h1')?.textContent).toContain('Weather
forecast');
// });
```

With this, all our components are ready: we just need to add the **RouterModule** to our Angular app to make everything work.

Adding the AppRoutingModule

The Angular RouterModule is an optional service that can be used to show a different component when the client URL changes: the component to display will be instantiated and shown within <router-outlet>, the tag we've just added to our HTML template file of AppComponent.

RouterModule can be implemented within the AppModule or in a separate module: however, since using a dedicated module is considered a best practice (more on that later), we'll follow that approach.

From **Solution Explorer**, navigate to the /src/app/ folder and create a new TypeScript file, calling it app-routing.module.ts. Once done, fill it with the following content:

```
import { NgModule } from '@angular/core';
import { Routes, RouterModule } from '@angular/router';
import { HomeComponent } from './home/home.component';
import { FetchDataComponent } from './fetch-data/fetch-data.component';

const routes: Routes = [
  { path: '', component: HomeComponent, pathMatch: 'full' },
  { path: 'fetch-data', component: FetchDataComponent }
];

@NgModule({
  imports: [RouterModule.forRoot(routes)],
  exports: [RouterModule]
})
export class AppRoutingModule { }
```

Once done, open the app.module.ts file and update it in the following way (new/updated lines are highlighted):

```
import { HttpClientModule } from '@angular/common/http';
import { NgModule } from '@angular/core';
import { BrowserModule } from '@angular/platform-browser';

import { AppRoutingModule } from './app-routing.module';
```

```
import { AppComponent } from './app.component';
import { HomeComponent } from './home/home.component';
import { FetchDataComponent } from './fetch-data/fetch-data.component';
import { NavMenuComponent } from './nav-menu/nav-menu.component';

@NgModule({
  declarations: [
    AppComponent,
    HomeComponent,
    FetchDataComponent,
    NavMenuComponent
  ],
  imports: [
    BrowserModule,
    HttpClientModule,
    AppRoutingModule
  ],
  providers: [],
  bootstrap: [AppComponent]
})
export class AppModule { }
```

What we did should be quite straightforward: we've added a new import reference pointing to our new AppRoutingModule file path and added it to the imported modules (the imports array).

Reasons for using a dedicated routing module

We've just said that using a separate, dedicated routing module is considered an Angular best practice, but we still don't know the reasons for this. What are the benefits that will compensate the additional work required to maintain its source code?

As a matter of fact, there are no real benefits for small and/or sample apps. When that's the case, most developers will probably choose to skip the routing module and merge the routing configuration directly in AppModule itself, just like the sample VS app did in the first place.

However, such an approach is only convenient when the app's configuration is minimal. When the app starts to grow, its routing logic will eventually become much more complex, thanks to some advanced features (such as *specialized guard* and *resolver* services) that, sooner or later, we'll want (or have) to implement. When something like this happens, a dedicated routing module will help us to keep the source code clean, simplify and streamline the testing activities, and increase the overall consistency of our app.

The only downside that comes with using multiple modules is that the Angular CLI's ng generate command won't be able to determine which module we want to add the component's references to. For example, if we now try to generate a new component using the following command:

```
ng generate component Test --skip-tests
```

The command will return the following error:

```
Error: More than one module matches.
Use skip-import option to skip importing the component into the closest module.
```

To avoid the above error, we have two choices:

- Use the `--skip-import` switch and add the references manually
- Use the `--module=app` switch to target a specific module

In the upcoming chapters, we'll often use the latter option whenever we need to add further components.

Finishing touches

We're finally ready to test our new components, as well as our minimal navigation and routing system. However, before doing that, let's spend a couple more minutes changing the ultra-minimalistic default HTML template of HomeComponent with a more satisfying welcome message.

Open the `/src/app/home/home.component.html` file and replace its entire contents with the following:

```
<h1>Greetings, stranger!</h1>
<p>This is what you get for messing up with ASP.NET and Angular.</p>
```

Save all the files, run the project in *Debug* mode, and get ready to see the following:

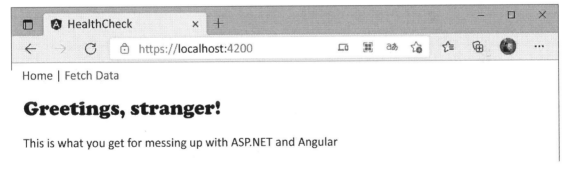

Figure 3.8: Looking at our new home view

It still looks pretty plain and uninspired, but hey... it's just the start of the journey, right?

Test run

Now we can perform our final test run to see if our new components – as well as the routing and navigation system – actually work. If we got something similar to what we can see in the previous screenshot, we can already see that the new AppComponent works since it shows NavComponent and HomeComponent.

We just have to click on the **Fetch Data** link at the top to check whether the navigation and routing system is working as well: if everything has been done properly, we should be able to see our new DataFetchComponent together with the retrieved API data, just like in the following screenshot:

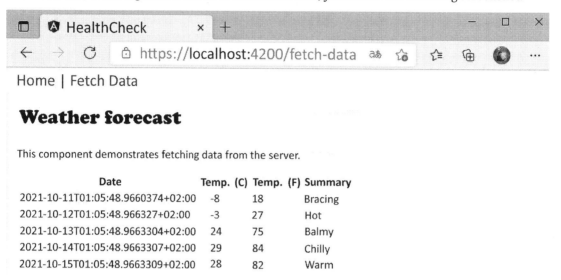

Figure 3.9: Our new FetchDataComponent

That's about it for now. Rest assured, we can easily do better than that in terms of UI, UX, and overall features: we'll greatly improve the look and feel of our sample apps in the following chapters, where we'll start to use StyleSheets (which we didn't even touch yet!), add new components, and so on. However, at least for the time being, we can be happy with what we did: understanding how easy it is to add components and update their content—and also how rapidly Visual Studio, ASP.NET, and Angular will react to our modifications—is good enough.

Summary

In this chapter, we spent some valuable time exploring and understanding our sample project's core components, how they work together, and their distinctive roles. For the sake of simplicity, we split the analysis into two parts: the .NET *back-end* ecosystem, where we've inspected the ASP.NET Core Web API project (*HealthCheckAPI*), and the Angular *front-end* architecture, which was dedicated to the Standalone Angular project (*HealthCheck*). We've seen how each project comes with its own configuration files, folder structure, naming conventions, and overall scope.

At the end of the day, we've met the end goal of this chapter and learned a fair number of useful things: we know the location and purpose of both *server-side* and *client-side* source code files; we are aware of most ASP.NET Core and Angular configuration settings and parameters; we also learned how to change these settings to meet our needs, such as the Web API routing endpoints, and insert new stuff, as we did with the Angular components and routing module.

Part of the chapter was dedicated to the Angular CLI: we've spent a good amount of time learning how to create new components following the Angular best practices. Such time was very well spent since now we know how to set up a new ASP.NET Core and Angular project without having to rely on the Visual Studio default templates or use a manual approach.

Last but not least, we also took the time to perform a quick test run to see whether we're ready to hold our ground against what's coming in upcoming chapters: setting up an improved request-response cycle, building our own controllers, defining additional routing strategies, and more.

Suggested topics

For further information, we recommend the following topics: Razor Pages, the separation of concerns, the single responsibility principle, JSON, web hosts, Kestrel, ASP.NET middlewares, dependency injection, the Angular workspace, Jasmine, Karma, unit tests, server-side rendering (SSR), TypeScript, Angular architecture, the Angular initialization cycle, and the Angular Router Module.

References

- *Introduction to ASP.NET Core*: `https://docs.microsoft.com/en-us/aspnet/core/`
- *Migration to ASP.NET Core in .NET 6*: `https://gist.github.com/davidfowl/0e0372c3c1d89 5c3ce195ba983b1e03d`
- *Angular: Setting Up the Local Environment and Workspace*: `https://angular.io/guide/setup-local`
- *Angular Architecture Overview*: `https://angular.io/guide/architecture`
- *Angular Upgrade Guide*: `https://update.angular.io/`
- *npmJS*: `https://docs.npmjs.com/files/package.json`
- *Yarn Package Manager*: `https://yarnpkg.com/`
- *TypeScript – Modules*: `https://www.typescriptlang.org/docs/handbook/modules.html`
- *TypeScript – Module Resolution*: `https://www.typescriptlang.org/docs/handbook/module-resolution.html`
- *TypeScript Configuration*: `https://angular.io/config/tsconfig`
- *TSLint*: `https://palantir.github.io/tslint/`
- *Angular AoT Compiler*: `https://angular.io/guide/aot-compiler`
- *Karma*: `https://karma-runner.github.io/`
- *Jasmine*: `https://jasmine.github.io/`
- *Angular – Testing*: `https://angular.io/guide/testing`
- *Strongly Typed Configuration Settings in ASP.NET Core*: `https://weblog.west-wind.com/posts/2016/may/23/strongly-typed-configuration-settings-in-aspnet-core`
- *Strongly Typed Configuration Settings in ASP.NET Core without IOptions<T>*: `https://www.strathweb.com/2016/09/strongly-typed-configuration-in-asp-net-core-without-ioptionst/`

- *Strongly Typed Configuration Settings in ASP.NET Core Part II*: https://rimdev.io/strongly-typed-configuration-settings-in-asp-net-core-part-ii/

- *Angular Development Server proxy settings*: https://angular.io/guide/build#proxying-to-a-backend-server

- *Strongly Typed Configuration Settings in ASP.NET Core Part II*: https://rimdev.io/strongly-typed-configuration-settings-in-asp-net-core-part-ii/

4

Front-End and Back-End Interactions

Now that we have a minimalistic—yet fully working—Angular web app up, running, and connected with our ASP.NET Core API, we can start to build some stuff. In this chapter, we're going to learn the basics of client-side and server-side interactions: in other words, how the *front-end* (Angular) can fetch some relevant data from the *back-end* (ASP.NET Core) and display it on screen, in a readable fashion.

As a matter of fact, we should've already got the gist of how it works in *Chapter 3*, *Looking Around*, when we worked with Angular's `FetchDataComponent` and ASP.NET Core's `WeatherForecastController.cs` classes and files. The Angular component (*front-end*) pulls data from the ASP.NET controller (*back-end*) and then puts it on the browser screen (UI) for display.

However, controllers aren't the only way for our ASP.NET Core *back-end* to serve data to the *front-end*: we can also serve static files, or use any other middleware designed to handle requests and output a response stream or content of some sort, as long as we add it into our application pipeline. Such a highly modular approach is one of the most relevant concepts of ASP.NET Core. In this chapter, we'll make use of that by introducing (and playing with) a built-in middleware that has little or nothing to do with .NET controllers, although it is able to deal with requests and responses just like they do: `HealthChecksMiddleware`.

Here's a quick breakdown of what we're going to cover:

- **Introducing ASP.NET Core health checks:** What they are and how we can use them to learn some useful concepts about ASP.NET Core and Angular interactions
- **HealthCheckMiddleware:** How to properly implement it within our ASP.NET Core *back-end*, configure it within our web application's pipeline, and output a JSON-structured message that can be used by our Angular app
- **HealthCheckComponent:** How to build an Angular component to fetch the `HealthCheck` structured data from the ASP.NET Core *back-end* and bring it all to the *front-end* in a human-readable fashion

- **Restyling the UI**: How to improve the look and feel of our Angular app using *Angular Material*, a user interface component library containing a lot of reusable and beautiful UI components

Are you ready? Let's do this!

Technical requirements

In this chapter, we're going to need all the technical requirements listed in the previous chapters, with no additional resources, libraries, or packages.

The code files for this chapter can be found here: `https://github.com/PacktPublishing/ASP.NET-Core-6-and-Angular/tree/master/Chapter_04/`.

Introducing ASP.NET Core health checks

We called our first project `HealthCheck` for a reason: the web app we're about to build will act as a monitoring and reporting service that will check the *health* status of a target server—and/or its infrastructure—and show it on screen in real time.

In order to do that, we're going to make good use of the `Microsoft.AspNetCore.Diagnostics.HealthChecks` package, a built-in feature of the ASP.NET Core framework first introduced in 2.2, refined and improved for the ASP.NET Core 3 release and still available up to the current .NET version. This package is meant to be used to allow a monitoring service to check the status of another running service—for example, another web server—which is precisely what we're about to do.

 For additional information about ASP.NET Core health checks, we strongly suggest reading the official MS documentation at the following URL: `https://docs.microsoft.com/en-us/aspnet/core/host-and-deploy/health-checks?view=aspnetcore-6.0`.

Adding the HealthChecks middleware

The first thing we need to do is to add the `HealthChecks` middleware to our web app. This can be done by opening the `Program.cs` file and adding the following lines:

```
var builder = WebApplication.CreateBuilder(args);


// Add services to the container.

builder.Services.AddHealthChecks();
builder.Services.AddControllers();
// Learn more about configuring Swagger/OpenAPI at https://aka.ms/aspnetcore/
swashbuckle
builder.Services.AddSwaggerGen();


var app = builder.Build();
```

```
// Configure the HTTP request pipeline.
if (app.Environment.IsDevelopment())
{
    app.UseSwagger();
    app.UseSwaggerUI();
}

app.UseHttpsRedirection();

app.UseAuthorization();

app.UseHealthChecks(new PathString("/api/health"));

app.MapControllers();

app.Run();
```

The /api/health parameters we passed to the UseHealthChecks middleware will create a server-side route for the health checks. It's also worth noting that we added that middleware right before MapControllers, so that our new route won't be overridden by any controller that could share that same name in the future.

We can immediately check out the new route by doing the following:

1.   Press *F5* so that our web application will run in *debug* mode
2.   Navigate to the https://localhost:40443/api/health URL and hit *Enter*

As soon as we do that, we should be able to see something like this:

Figure 4.1: Checking our health check

As we can see, our system is Healthy: that's rather obvious since we have no checks defined yet.

How about adding one? That's what we're going to do in the next section.

Adding an Internet Control Message Protocol (ICMP) check

The first check we're going to implement is one of the most popular ones: an **Internet Control Message Protocol (ICMP)** request check to an external host, also known as **PING**.

As you most likely already know, a PING request is a rather basic way to check the presence—and therefore the availability—of a server that we know we should be able to reach within a **local area network (LAN)** or **wide area network (WAN)** connection. In a nutshell, it works in the following way: the machine that performs the PING sends one or more ICMP echo request packets to the target host and waits for a reply. If it receives one, it reports the round-trip time of the whole task; otherwise, it times out and reports a `host not reachable` error.

The `host not reachable` error can be due to a number of possible scenarios, as listed here:

*   The target host is **not available**
*   The target host is **available, but actively refuses TCP/IP communications** of any kind
*   The target host is **available and accepts incoming connections, but it has been configured to explicitly refuse ICMP requests** and/or not send ICMP echo replies back
*   The target host is **available and properly configured to accept ICMP requests and send echo replies back, but the connection is very slow or hindered** by unknown reasons (performance, heavy load, and so on), so the round-trip time takes too long—or even times out

As we can see, this is an ideal scenario for a health check: if we properly configure the target host to accept the PING and always answer it, we can definitely use it to determine whether the host is in a healthy status or not.

Possible outcomes

Now that we know the common scenarios behind a PING test request, we can put down a list of possible outcomes, as follows:

*   `Healthy`: We can consider the host `Healthy` whenever the PING succeeds with no errors or timeouts
*   `Degraded`: We can consider the host `Degraded` whenever the PING succeeds, but the round-trip takes too long
*   `Unhealthy`: We can consider the host `Unhealthy` whenever the PING fails—that is, the check times out before any reply

Now that we've identified these three *statuses*, we just need to properly implement them within our health check.

Creating an ICMPHealthCheck class

The first thing we have to do is create a new `ICMPHealthCheck.cs` class in our project's root folder.

Once done, fill it with the following content:

```
using Microsoft.Extensions.Diagnostics.HealthChecks;
using System.Net.NetworkInformation;
```

```csharp
namespace HealthCheckAPI
{
    public class ICMPHealthCheck : IHealthCheck
    {
        private readonly string Host = $"10.0.0.0";
        private readonly int HealthyRoundtripTime = 300;

        public async Task<HealthCheckResult> CheckHealthAsync(
            HealthCheckContext context,
            CancellationToken cancellationToken = default)
        {
            try
            {
                using var ping = new Ping();
                var reply = await ping.SendPingAsync(Host);

                switch (reply.Status)
                {
                    case IPStatus.Success:
                        return (reply.RoundtripTime > HealthyRoundtripTime)
                            ? HealthCheckResult.Degraded()
                            : HealthCheckResult.Healthy();

                    default:
                        return HealthCheckResult.Unhealthy();
                }
            }
            catch (Exception e)
            {
                return HealthCheckResult.Unhealthy();
            }
        }
    }
}
```

As we can see, we implemented the IHealthCheck interface since it's the official .NET way to deal with health checks: such an interface requires a single async method—CheckHealthAsync—which we used to determine if the ICMP request was successful or not.

In the preceding code, the `ping` variable has been declared with the `using` keyword: this technique is called a *using declaration* and was introduced in C# version 8 as a convenient replacement for the `using` statements/blocks to reduce nesting and produce more readable code.

For further info regarding the *using declaration* feature, take a look at the following URL:

`https://docs.microsoft.com/en-us/dotnet/csharp/language-reference/proposals/csharp-8.0/using`

Those who want to use it are strongly advised to also read this great post by Steve Gordon (Microsoft MVP) to better understand how `using` declarations work under the hood:

`https://www.stevejgordon.co.uk/csharp-8-understanding-using-declarations`

The code is very easy to understand and handles the three possible scenarios we defined in the previous section. Let's go over what the host can be considered to be:

- `Healthy`, if the PING request gets a successful reply with a round-trip time of 300 ms or less
- `Degraded`, if the PING request gets a successful reply with a round-trip time greater than 300 ms
- `Unhealthy`, if the PING request fails or an `Exception` is thrown

One final notice regarding the single line of code that we used to set the `Host` value:

```
Private readonly string Host = $"10.0.0.0";
```

As we can see, we've set `Host` to a non-routable IP address—which might seem rather awkward. We did that for demonstration purposes, so that we'll be able to simulate an "unhealthy" scenario: we're definitely going to change it later on.

That's pretty much it. Our health check is ready to be tested—we just need to find a way to *load* it into our web application's pipeline.

Adding the ICMPHealthCheck

In order to load our ICMP health check into the web application pipeline, we need to add it to the `HealthChecks` middleware. To do that, open the `Program.cs` class again and change the first line we previously added in the following way:

```
// ...existing code...

builder.Services.AddHealthChecks()
    .AddCheck<ICMPHealthCheck>("ICMP");

// ...existing code...
```

That's it.

The `// ...existing code...` comment is just a way to tell us to leave the already-existing code as it is, without altering it. We're going to use that keyword whenever we need to add a few lines of code to an existing block instead of rewriting the unmodified lines.

It's worth noting that, since we added a reference to the `ICMPHealthCheck` class, which we've just created within the `HealthCheckAPI` namespace, we must add a reference to that namespace as well. Here we'll take the chance to use another handy C# 10 feature called *Global Using*: as the name suggests, this feature allows us to define some common `using` statements that will automatically be available for use within the entire project.

To do that, we just need to add the `global` keyword before the `using` statement that we want to make global. Since the `HealthCheckAPI` happens to be our API project's namespace, it seems the perfect candidate for that.

Here's the single line we need to add at the top of the `Program.cs` file:

```
global using HealthCheckAPI;
```

Now, we can hit *F5* and try it out. Here's what we should be able to see:

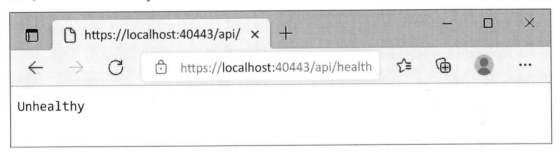

Figure 4.2: Checking our health check

As expected, the hardcoded ICMP request to `10.0.0.0` has failed, hence we get the **Unhealthy** status. That's great, right?

Well, actually, it's not that great. Our health check does indeed work, but comes with the following three major flaws:

- **Hardcoded values:** The `Host` and `HealthyRoundtripTime` variables should be passed as parameters so that we can set them programmatically
- **Uninformative response:** `Healthy` and `Unhealthy` are not that great—we should find a way to have a custom (and better) output message instead
- **Untyped output:** The current response is being sent in plain text—if we want to fetch it with Angular, a JSON content type would definitely be better (and way more usable, as we'll see in the *Health checks in Angular* section later on)

Let's fix these issues, one at a time.

Improving the ICMPHealthCheck class

In this section, we'll improve our ICMPHealthCheck class by adding the host and healthyRoundtripTime parameters, a custom outcome message for each possible status, and a JSON-structured output.

Adding parameters and response messages

Open the ICMPHealthCheck.cs class file and perform the following changes (added/modified lines are highlighted):

```
using Microsoft.Extensions.Diagnostics.HealthChecks;
using System.Net.NetworkInformation;


namespace HealthCheckAPI
{
    public class ICMPHealthCheck : IHealthCheck
    {
        private readonly string Host;
        private readonly int HealthyRoundtripTime;

        public ICMPHealthCheck(string host, int healthyRoundtripTime)
        {
            Host = host;
            HealthyRoundtripTime = healthyRoundtripTime;
        }


        public async Task<HealthCheckResult> CheckHealthAsync(
            HealthCheckContext context,
            CancellationToken cancellationToken = default)
        {
            try
            {
                using var ping = new Ping();
                var reply = await ping.SendPingAsync(Host);

                switch (reply.Status)
                {
                    case IPStatus.Success:
                        var msg =
                            $"ICMP to {Host} took {reply.RoundtripTime} ms.";
```

```
                    return (reply.RoundtripTime > HealthyRoundtripTime)
                    ? HealthCheckResult.Degraded(msg)
                    : HealthCheckResult.Healthy(msg);


            default:
                var err =
                    $"ICMP to {Host} failed: {reply.Status}";
                return HealthCheckResult.Unhealthy(err);
        }
    }
    catch (Exception e)
    {
        var err =
            $"ICMP to {Host} failed: {e.Message}";
        return HealthCheckResult.Unhealthy(err);
    }
}
}
}
```

As we can see, we changed a couple of things, as follows:

- We added a constructor accepting the two parameters we'd like to set programmatically: `host` and `healthyRoundtripTime`. The old *hardcoded* variables are now set by the constructor upon initialization and then used within the class afterward (such as within the main method).

- We created various different *outcome messages* containing the target host, the PING outcome, and the round-trip duration (or the runtime error), and added them as parameters to the `HealthCheckResult` return objects.

> In the preceding code, we've used *string interpolation*, a powerful text formatting feature released in C# version 6 to replace the previous `string.Format` approach. For further info regarding this feature, go to the following URL:
>
> `https://docs.microsoft.com/en-us/dotnet/csharp/tutorials/string-interpolation`

That's pretty much it. Now, we just need to set the `host` name and `healthyRoundtripTime` programmatically since the old *hardcoded defaults* are now gone. In order to do that, we have to update our middleware setup in the `Program.cs` file.

Updating the middleware setup

Open the `Program.cs` file again and change the existing `HealthChecksMiddleware` implementation in the following way:

```
// ...existing code...

builder.Services.AddHealthChecks()
    .AddCheck("ICMP_01",
        new ICMPHealthCheck("www.ryadel.com", 100))
    .AddCheck("ICMP_02",
        new ICMPHealthCheck("www.google.com", 100))
    .AddCheck("ICMP_03",
        new ICMPHealthCheck($"www.{Guid.NewGuid():N}.com", 100));

// ...existing code...
```

Here we go: as we can see, another advantage of being able to programmatically configure the host is that we can add the ICMP health check multiple times—once for each host we'd like to actually check. In the preceding example, we're taking the chance to test three different hosts: `www.ryadel.com`, `www.google.com`, and the same non-existing host we used before, which allows us to emulate an Unhealthy status as well as the Healthy ones.

Now, we could be tempted to hit *F5* and try it out... However, if we were to do that, we would face a rather disappointing outcome, as shown in the following screenshot:

Figure 4.3: Checking our health check

The reason for this is quite obvious: even if we're running multiple checks, we're still relying on the default outcome message, which is nothing more than a Boolean sum of the statuses returned by all the checked hosts. For that very reason, if at least one of them is Unhealthy, the whole check will be flagged as Unhealthy as well.

Luckily enough, we can avoid that sum—and get a much more granular output—by dealing with the third flaw of our `ICMPHealthCheck`: implementing a custom, JSON-structured output message.

Implementing a custom output message

To implement a custom output message, we need to override the `HealthCheckOptions` class. To do that, add a new `CustomHealthCheckOptions.cs` file to the project's root folder and fill it with the following content:

```
using Microsoft.AspNetCore.Diagnostics.HealthChecks;
using System.Net.Mime;
using System.Text.Json;

namespace HealthCheckAPI
{
    public class CustomHealthCheckOptions : HealthCheckOptions
    {
        public CustomHealthCheckOptions() : base()
        {
            var jsonSerializerOptions = new JsonSerializerOptions()
            {
                WriteIndented = true
            };

            ResponseWriter = async (c, r) =>
            {
                c.Response.ContentType =
                 MediaTypeNames.Application.Json;
                c.Response.StatusCode = StatusCodes.Status200OK;

                var result = JsonSerializer.Serialize(new
                {
                    checks = r.Entries.Select(e => new
                    {
                        name = e.Key,

                        responseTime =
                            e.Value.Duration.TotalMilliseconds,
                        status = e.Value.Status.ToString(),
                        description = e.Value.Description
                    }),
                    totalStatus = r.Status,
                    totalResponseTime =
```

```
                                r.TotalDuration.TotalMilliseconds,
                    }, jsonSerializerOptions);
                    await c.Response.WriteAsync(result);
                };
            }
        }
    }
```

The code is quite self-explanatory: we override the standard class—which outputs the one-word output we want to change—with our own custom class so that we can change its ResponseWriter property, in order to make it output whatever we want.

More specifically, we want to output a custom JSON-structured message containing a lot of useful stuff from each of our checks, listed here:

- name: The identifying string we provided while adding the check to the HealthChecks middleware within the Program.cs file: "ICMP_01", "ICMP_02", and so on
- responseTime: The whole duration of that single check
- status: The individual status of a check, not to be confused with the status of the whole HealthCheck—that is, the Boolean sum of all the inner checks' statuses
- description: The custom informative message we configured earlier on when we refined the ICMPHealthCheck class

All these values will be properties of the array items contained in the JSON output: one for each check. It's worth noting that the JSON file, in addition to that array, will also contain the following two additional properties:

- totalStatus: The Boolean sum of all the inner checks' statuses—Unhealthy if there's at least an Unhealthy host, Degraded if there's at least a Degraded host, and Healthy otherwise
- totalResponseTime: The whole duration of all the checks

That's a lot of useful information, right? We just have to configure our middleware to output them, instead of those one-word responses we've seen before.

About health check responses and HTTP status codes

Before going further, it's worth noting that—in the preceding CustomHealthCheckOptions class—we set *ResponseWriter*'s HTTP status code to a fixed StatusCodes.Status200OK. Is there a reason behind that?

As a matter of fact, there is, and it's also quite an important one. The HealthChecks middleware's default behavior returns either HTTP status code 200, if all the checks are OK (Healthy), or HTTP status code 503, if one or more checks are KO (Unhealthy). Since we've switched to a JSON-structured output, we don't need the 503 code anymore, as it would most likely break our *front-end* client UI logic—unless properly handled. Therefore, for the sake of simplicity, we just forced an HTTP 200 response, regardless of the end result. We'll find a way to properly emphasize the errors within the upcoming Angular UI.

Configuring the output message

Open the Program.cs file and change the following lines accordingly (the updated code is highlighted):

```
// ... existing code


app.UseHealthChecks(new PathString("/api/health"),
    new CustomHealthCheckOptions());


// ... existing code
```

Once done, we can finally hit *F5* and properly test it out. This time, we won't be disappointed by the outcome, as shown in the following screenshot:

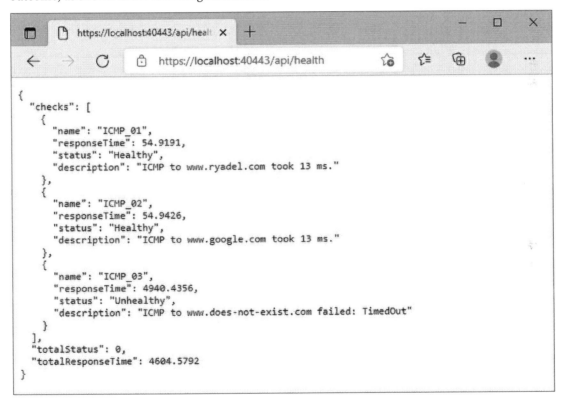

Figure 4.4: A more detailed health check output message

That's a pretty nice response, isn't it?

Now, each and every check is properly documented, as well as the *total* outcome data, in a structured JSON object. This is just what we need to feed some Angular components that we can show on screen in a human-readable (and fashionable) way, which we're just about to do, starting with the next section.

Health checks in Angular

It's now time to build an **Angular component** that is capable of fetching and displaying the structured JSON data we managed to pull off in the previous sections.

As we know from *Chapter 3, Looking Around*, an Angular component is commonly made of four separate files, as follows:

- The **component** (`.ts`) file, written in TypeScript and containing the `component` class, together with all the module references, functions, variables, and so on
- The **template** (`.html`) file, written in HTML and extended with the *Angular template syntax*, which defines the UI layout architecture
- The **style** (`.css`) file, written in CSS and containing the Cascading Style Sheets rules and definitions for drawing the UI
- The **test** (`.spec.ts`) file, written in TypeScript and containing the tests that will be run by **Karma**

Although the aforementioned four-files approach is arguably the most practical one, the only required file is the component one, as both the template and the style files could also be embedded as inline elements within the component file. The choice between using separate files or going inline is a matter of taste; however, since the Angular CLI adopts the four-files approach, we strongly suggest following this good practice. Such an approach will also enforce the separation of concerns embodied within the component/template duality featured by Angular.

Let's now use the Angular CLI to generate the first three files for a new `HealthCheck` component (skipping the test file), just like we did in *Chapter 3, Looking Around*.

Creating the Angular component

Open a Command Prompt, navigate through the `/src/app` folder of our Angular project, and type the following command:

```
> ng generate component HealthCheck --module=app --skip-tests
```

As always, the CLI will create the component files and add the required references to the `AppModule` for us.

It's worth noting that, since our app has multiple modules (`AppModule` and `AppRoutingModule`), every time we create a new module, we need to specify which module to add the component's references to using the `--module` switch (as explained in *Chapter 3, Looking Around*).

As soon as the CLI generates the new component files, we can fill them with the following content.

Health-check.component.ts

Here's the `/src/app/health-check/health-check.component.ts` source code:

```typescript
import { Component, OnInit } from '@angular/core';
import { HttpClient } from '@angular/common/http';

import { environment } from ' ./../../environments/environment';

@Component({
    selector: 'app-health-check',
    templateUrl: './health-check.component.html',
    styleUrls: ['./health-check.component.css']
})
export class HealthCheckComponent implements OnInit {
  public result?: Result;

  constructor(private http: HttpClient) {
  }

  ngOnInit() {
    this.http.get<Result>(environment.baseUrl + 'api/health').subscribe(result
=> {
      this.result = result;
    }, error => console.error(error));
  }
}

interface Result {
    checks: Check[];
    totalStatus: string;
    totalResponseTime: number;
}

interface Check {
    name: string;
    responseTime: number;
    status: string;
    description: string;
}
```

If you're curious about what we did there, here's a breakdown of the most relevant stuff:

- At the start of the file, we made sure to import all the Angular *directives, pipes, services,* and *components*—in one word, *modules*—that we need throughout the whole class.
- In the class declaration, we've explicitly implemented the OnInit interface by adding the implements OnInit instruction to add type-safety: this way, we won't risk typing or spelling mistakes within the ngOnInit lifecycle hook.
- In the component's constructor, we instantiated the HttpClient service using **dependency injection (DI)**.
- Last but not least, we defined two interfaces to deal with the JSON request we're expecting to receive from the HealthChecksMiddleware: Result and Check, which we designed to host the whole JSON resulting object and each element of the internal array, respectively.

Before going further, it could be useful to spend some valuable time expanding on some very important topics we've just met by implementing the preceding code, as follows:

- **Imports and modules**
- **Dependency injection**
- **ngOnInit** (and other lifecycle hooks)
- **Constructor**
- **HttpClient**
- **Observables**
- **Interfaces**

Since we're going to see them all throughout this book, it's definitely advisable to review them now.

Imports and modules

The static import statement that we used multiple times in the preceding HealthCheckComponent is used to import bindings that are exported by other JavaScript modules.

The concept of working with *modules* started with ECMAScript 2015 and has been thoroughly adopted by TypeScript and, therefore, Angular. A *module* is basically a collection of variables, functions, classes, and so on, grouped within a class: each *module* is executed within its own scope, not in the global scope, meaning that all the elements declared within it are not visible from the outside unless they are explicitly *exported* using the export statement.

Conversely, to consume a variable, function, class, interface, and so on contained (and *exported*) within a *module*, that *module* has to be imported using the `import` statement. This is quite similar to what we do with *namespaces* in most programming languages (C# has `using` statements, for example).

As a matter of fact, all the Angular *directives*, *pipes*, *services*, and *components* are also packed into collections of *JavaScript modules*, which we have to *import* into any TypeScript class whenever we want to use them. These collections are basically libraries of modules: we can easily recognize them since their name begins with the `@angular` prefix. Our `packages.json` file (the NPM package file), which we've seen in previous chapters, contains most of them.

> To know more about ECMAScript modules and better understand the module resolution strategy in TypeScript, check out the following URLs:
>
> **TypeScript modules:** `https://www.typescriptlang.org/docs/handbook/modules.html`
>
> **Module resolution:** `https://www.typescriptlang.org/docs/handbook/module-resolution.html`

JavaScript modules should not be confused with Angular's own modularity system, which is based upon the `@NgModule` decorator. As we already know from previous chapters, Angular's *NgModules* are *building blocks*—that is, containers for a cohesive block of code dedicated to an application domain, a workflow, or a common feature set. We know from the aforementioned chapters that each Angular app has at least one `NgModule` class, called the root module, which is conventionally named `AppModule` and resides in the `app.module.ts` file in the application root; additional NgModules will be added in the upcoming chapters.

Unfortunately, the *JavaScript module system* and the *Angular NgModule system* use a rather similar vocabulary (*import* versus *imports*, *export* versus *exports*), which might lead to confusion—especially considering that Angular apps require the developer to use both of them at the same time (and often in the same class file). Luckily enough, although being forced to intertwine these two systems might be a bit tricky at first, eventually, we'll become familiar with the different contexts in which they are used.

Here's a sample screenshot, taken from our `HealthCheck` app's `AppModule` class file, which should help you distinguish between the two different systems:

```
1   import { BrowserModule } from '@angular/platform-browser';
2   import { NgModule } from '@angular/core';
3   import { FormsModule } from '@angular/forms';
4   import { HttpClientModule, HTTP_INTERCEPTORS } from '@angular/common/http';
5   import { RouterModule } from '@angular/router';
6
7   import { AppComponent } from './app.component';
8   import { NavMenuComponent } from './nav-menu/nav-menu.component';
9   import { HomeComponent } from './home/home.component';
10  import { HealthCheckComponent } from './health-check/health-check.component';
11
12  @NgModule({
13      declarations: [
14          AppComponent,
15          NavMenuComponent,
16          HomeComponent,
17          HealthCheckComponent
18      ],
19      imports: [
20          BrowserModule.withServerTransition({ appId: 'ng-cli-universal' }),
21          HttpClientModule,
22          FormsModule,
23          RouterModule.forRoot([
24              { path: '', component: HomeComponent, pathMatch: 'full' },
25              { path: 'health-check', component: HealthCheckComponent }
26          ])
27      ],
28      providers: [],
29      bootstrap: [AppComponent]
30  })
31  export class AppModule { }
```

JAVASCRIPT
MODULE SYSTEM

import {...}

ANGULAR
MODULE SYSTEM

@NgModule({...});

Figure 4.5: Inspecting the AppModule class file

For additional information regarding the Angular module system and the `NgModule` decorator, check out the following URLs:

NgModule: https://angular.io/guide/ngmodules

Angular architecture: NgModules and JavaScript modules: https://angular.io/guide/architecture-modules#ngmodules-and-javascript-modules

Dependency injection (DI)

We've talked about DI a number of times already, and with good reason, because it's an important application design pattern for both ASP.NET Core and Angular, with both frameworks making extensive use of it to increase their efficiency and modularity.

To explain what DI actually is, we must first talk about what *dependencies* are in a class: these can be defined as *services* or *objects* that a class needs to *instantiate* into *variables* or *properties*, in order to perform one or more tasks.

In a *classic* coding pattern, those dependencies are instantiated on the fly within the class itself—for example, during its initialization phase, such as within the constructor method. Here's a typical example of that:

```
public MyClass() {
    var myElement = new Element();
    myElement.doStuff();
}
```

In the preceding example, the myElement variable is an object instance of the Element type, and also a (local) *dependency* of MyClass: as we can see, it gets instantiated in the constructor because we most likely need to use it there. From there, we can either use it as a local variable (and let it die at the end of the constructor's scope) or assign it to a class property to further extend its life span and scope.

DI is an alternative software design pattern in which a class asks for dependencies from external sources rather than creating them itself. To better understand this concept, let's try to rewrite the same code as before with a DI approach, like this:

```
public MyClass(Element myElement) {
    myElement.doStuff();
}
```

As we can see, there's no need to instantiate the myElement variable because this task is already handled by the **dependency injector**—external code that is responsible for creating the *injectable* objects and injecting them into the classes.

The whole DI coding pattern is based upon the concept of **Inversion of Control** (**IoC**), to resolve dependencies. Such a concept revolves around the basic idea that, formally, if ObjectA depends on ObjectB, then ObjectA must not create or import ObjectB directly, but provide a way to *inject* ObjectB instead. In the preceding code block example, ObjectA is obviously MyClass, while ObjectB is the myElement instance.

For additional information about the DI software design pattern, check out the following links:

DI in ASP.NET Core: `https://docs.microsoft.com/en-us/aspnet/core/fundamentals/dependency-injection`

DI in Angular: `https://angular.io/guide/dependency-injection`

In Angular, the DI framework provides declared dependencies to a class when that class is instantiated.

In the preceding HealthCheckComponent class, we used DI in the component's constructor method to inject an HttpClient service instance; as we can see, we also took the chance to assign the private *access modifier* to both of them. Thanks to that modifier, those variables will be accessible through the whole component class.

As per Angular conventions, a parameter injected without an access modifier can only be accessed within the constructor; conversely, if it gets an access modifier such as `private` or `public`, it will be defined as a class member, hence changing its scope to the class. Such a technique is called **variable scoping**, and we're going to use it a lot in our Angular components from now on.

ngOnInit (and other lifecycle hooks)

The `ngOnInit` method that we used in the `HealthCheckComponent` class is one of the component's *lifecycle hook methods*: in this section, we'll try to shed some light on them, since we're going to use them a lot throughout this book.

Each Angular component has a lifecycle, which is managed by Angular. Each time a user visits a view within our app, the Angular framework creates and renders the required *components* (and *directives*) along with their children, reacts to their changes whenever the user interacts with them, and eventually destroys and removes them from the **Document Object Model** (**DOM**) when the user navigates elsewhere. All these "key moments" trigger some lifecycle hook methods that Angular exposes to the developers so that they can perform something when each one of them actually occurs.

Here's a list of the available hooks, in order of execution (when possible, since some of them are called multiple times during the component's lifecycle):

- `ngOnChanges()`: Responds when Angular (re)sets data-bound input properties. The method receives a `SimpleChanges` object of current and previous property values. Called before `ngOnInit()`, and whenever one or more data-bound input properties changes.
- `ngOnInit()`: Initializes the directive/component after Angular first displays the data-bound properties and sets the directive/component's input properties. Called once, after the first `ngOnChanges()` method.
- `ngDoCheck()`: Detects and acts upon changes that Angular can't, or won't, detect on its own. Called during every change detection run, immediately after `ngOnChanges()` and `ngOnInit()`.
- `ngAfterContentInit()`: Responds after Angular projects external content into the component's view/the view that a directive is in. Called once after the first `ngDoCheck()` method.
- `ngAfterContentChecked()`: Responds after Angular checks the content projected into the directive/component. Called after the `ngAfterContentInit()` method and every subsequent `ngDoCheck()` method.
- `ngAfterViewInit()`: Responds after Angular initializes the component's views and child views/ the view that a directive is in. Called once after the first `ngAfterContentChecked()` method.
- `ngAfterViewChecked()`: Responds after Angular checks the component's views and child views/ the view that a directive is in. Called after the `ngAfterViewInit()` method and every subsequent `ngAfterContentChecked()` method.
- `ngOnDestroy()`: Cleans up just before Angular destroys the directive/component. Unsubscribes `Observables` and detaches the event handlers to avoid memory leaks. Called just before Angular destroys the directive/component.

The preceding **lifecycle hook methods** are available for all Angular *components* and *directives*. To make use of them, we can just add them to our component class—which is precisely what we did in the preceding `HealthCheckComponent`.

Now that we have understood the role of `ngOnInit()`, we should take a moment to explain why we put the `HttpClient` source code in the `ngOnInit()` lifecycle hook method instead of using the component's `constructor()` method: shouldn't we have used that instead?

The next section should greatly help us to understand the reason for such a choice.

Constructor

As we most likely already know, all TypeScript classes have a `constructor()` method that will be called whenever we create an instance of that class: since TypeScript is, by all means, a superset of JavaScript, any TypeScript `constructor()` method will be transpiled into a JavaScript `constructor()` function.

The following code block shows an example of a TypeScript class:

```
class MyClass() {
  constructor() {
    console.log("MyClass has been instantiated");
  }
}
```

This will be transpiled into the following JavaScript function:

```
function MyClass() {
  console.log("MyClass has been instantiated");
}
```

If we omit the constructor in TypeScript, the JavaScript transpiled function will be empty; however, whenever the framework needs to instantiate it, it will still call it in the following way, regardless of whether it has the constructor or not:

```
var myClassInstance = new MyClass();
```

Understanding this is very important because it greatly helps us to understand the difference between the component's `constructor()` method and its `ngOnInit()` lifecycle hook, and it's a huge difference, at least from the perspective of the component initialization phase.

The whole Angular Bootstrap process can be split into two major (and subsequent) stages:

- **Instantiating the components**
- **Performing change detection**

As we can easily guess, the `constructor()` method is called during the former phase, while all the lifecycle hooks—including the `ngOnInit()` method—are called throughout the latter.

If we look at these methods from this perspective, it's pretty easy to understand the following key concepts:

- If we need to create or *inject* some *dependencies* into an Angular component, we should use the `constructor()` method; as a matter of fact, this is also the only way we can do that since the constructor is the only method that gets called in the context of the Angular injector.
- Conversely, whenever we need to perform any component *initialization* and/or *update* task— such as performing an HTTP request or updating the DOM—we should definitely do that by using one of the lifecycle hooks.

The `ngOnInit()` method, as its name implies, is often a great choice for the component's initialization tasks, since it happens right after the directive's and/or component's input properties are set. That's why we have used this to implement our HTTP request, using the Angular built-in `HttpClient` service.

HttpClient

Being able to efficiently send and receive JSON data from our ASP.NET Core controllers is probably the most important requirement for our **single-page application (SPA)**. We chose to do that using the Angular `HttpClient` service, first introduced in Angular 4.3.0-RC.0, which is among one of the best answers the framework can give to get the job done. For this very reason, we will use it a lot throughout this book; however, before doing that, it might be advisable to properly understand what it is, why it is better than the former implementation, and how to properly implement it.

The new `HttpClient` service was introduced in July 2017 as an improved version of the former Angular HTTP client API, also known as `@angular/http`, or, simply, HTTP. Instead of replacing the old version in the `@angular/http` package, the Angular development team has put the new classes in a separate package—`@angular/common/http`. They chose to do that to preserve the *backward compatibility* with the existing code bases, and also to ensure a slow, yet steady, migration to the new API.

Those who used the old Angular HTTP service class at least once will most likely remember its main limitations, listed here:

- **JSON was not enabled by default**, forcing the developers to explicitly set it within the request *headers*—and `JSON.parse`/`JSON.stringify` the data—when working with RESTful APIs.
- **There was no easy way to access the HTTP request/response pipeline**, thus preventing the developer from intercepting or altering the *request* and/or *response* calls after they were issued or received by using some ugly and pattern-breaking hacks. As a matter of fact, extensions and wrapper classes were basically the only way to customize the service, at least on a global scope.
- **There was no native strong-typing for request and response objects**, although that could be addressed by casting JSON as interfaces as a workaround.

The great news is that the new `HttpClient` does all of this and much more; other features include testability support and better error handling via APIs entirely based on `Observables`.

It's worth noting that putting the `HttpClient` service within the component itself is not good practice because it will often lead to unnecessary code repetition among the various components that need to perform HTTP calls and handle their results. This is a known issue that greatly affects production-level apps, which will likely require post-processing of the received data, handling errors, adding retry logic to deal with intermittent connectivity, and so on.

To better deal with those scenarios, it's strongly advisable to separate the data access logic and the data presentation role by encapsulating the former in a separate service, which can then be injected into all the components that require it, in a standardized and centralized way. We'll talk more about that in *Chapter 8*, *Code Tweaks and Data Services*, where we'll eventually replace multiple `HttpClient` implementations and centralize their source code within a couple of data services.

Observables

Observables are a powerful feature for managing async data; they are the backbone of the **ReactiveX JavaScript** (**RxJS**) library, which is one of the Angular required dependencies. Those who are familiar with ES6 *Promises* can think of them as an improved version of that approach.

An *observable* can be configured to send literal values, structured values, messages, and events, either *synchronously* or *asynchronously*: the values can be received by subscribing to the *observable* itself using the `subscribe` method hook, meaning that the whole data flow is handled within it—until we programmatically choose to *unsubscribe*. The great thing about this approach is that, regardless of the chosen approach (*sync* or *async*), streaming *frequency*, and *data type*, the programming interface for listening to values and stopping listening is the same.

The great advantages of *observables* are the reason why Angular makes extensive use of them when dealing with data. If we take a good look at our `HealthCheckComponent` source code, we can see how we use them as well when our `HttpClient` service fetches the data from the server and stores the result in the `this.result` local variable. Such a task is performed by calling two consecutive methods: `get<Result>()` and `subscribe()`.

Let's try to summarize what they do, as follows:

- `get<Result>()`: As the name suggests, this method issues a standard HTTP request to our ASP. NET Core `HealthChecks` middleware to fetch the resulting JSON response object. This method needs a URL parameter, which we create on the fly by adding the `hc` literal string (the same string that we set early on within the `Program.cs` file) to the base Web API URL.

- `subscribe()`: This method invokes the *observable* returned by the get call, which will execute two very different actions right after a result and/or in case of an error. Needless to say, all this will be done *asynchronously*, meaning that the app won't wait for the result and keep executing the rest of the code.

Those who want to get additional information can take a look at the following URLs, taken from the RxJS official documentation:

ReactiveX Library—Observables guide: `http://reactivex.io/rxjs/class/es6/Observable.js~Observable.html`

Angular.io—Observables guide: `https://angular.io/guide/observables`

It's very important to understand that we're only scratching the surface of what an *observable* can do. However, this is all we need for now: we'll have the chance to talk more about them later on.

Interfaces

Now that we know how the Angular `HttpClient` service works, we have every right to ask ourselves a couple of questions: why are we even using these interfaces? Can't we just use the raw JSON data sent by the ASP.NET Core `HealthChecks` middleware that we defined early on, consuming them as anonymous JavaScript objects?

Theoretically speaking, we can, just as we can output raw JSON from the controllers, instead of creating all the ViewModel classes like we did instead. In a well-written app, though, we should always resist the temptation to handle raw JSON data and/or to use anonymous objects for a number of good reasons:

- **We have chosen TypeScript over JavaScript because we want to work with type definitions:** Anonymous objects and properties are the exact opposite; they lead to the JavaScript way of doing things, which is something we wanted to avoid in the first place.

- **Anonymous objects (and their properties) are not easy to validate:** We don't want our data items to be error-prone or forced to deal with missing properties.

- **Anonymous objects are hardly reusable:** In other words, they won't benefit from many handy Angular features—such as *object mapping*—that require our objects to be actual instances of an interface and/or a type.

The first two arguments are very important, especially if we're aiming for a production-ready application; no matter how easy our development task might seem at first, we should never think that we can afford to lose that level of control over our application's source code.

The third reason is also crucial, as long as we want to use Angular to its full extent. If that's the case, using an undefined array of properties—such as raw JSON data—is basically out of the question; conversely, using a structured TypeScript interface is arguably the most lightweight way to work with structured JSON data in a *strongly typed* fashion.

It's worth noting that we've not added the `export` statement to our interface: we did that on purpose since we're only going to use this within the `HealthCheckComponent` class. Should we need to change this behavior in the future—for example, to create an external data service—we'll have to add this statement (and, arguably, move each one of them into a separate file) to enable us to `import` them into other classes.

health-check.component.html

Here's the /src/app/health-check/health-check.component.html source code:

```html
<h1>Health Check</h1>

<p>Here are the results of our health check:</p>

<p *ngIf="!result"><em>Loading...</em></p>

<table class='table table-striped' aria-labelledby="tableLabel" *ngIf="result">
  <thead>
    <tr>
      <th>Name</th>
      <th>Response Time</th>
      <th>Status</th>
      <th>Description</th>
    </tr>
  </thead>
  <tbody>
    <tr *ngFor="let check of result.checks">
      <td>{{ check.name }}</td>
      <td>{{ check.responseTime }}</td>
      <td class="status {{ check.status }}">{{ check.status }}</td>
      <td>{{ check.description }}</td>
    </tr>
  </tbody>
</table>
```

As we already know from *Chapter 3, Looking Around,* the *template* part of our Angular component is basically an HTML page, containing a table with some Angular directive. Before moving on, let's have a closer look, as follows:

- ngIf: This is a *structural directive* that conditionally includes the container HTML element, based on the Boolean expression value specified after the equals (=) sign: when such an expression evaluates to *true*, Angular renders the element; otherwise, it doesn't. It can be chained with an else block that—if present—will be shown when the expression evaluates to *false* or *null*. In the preceding code block, we use it within the <table> element so that it only appears when the result internal variable (which we defined in the **component** class earlier on) stops being *undefined*, which will happen after the data has been fetched from the server.

- ngFor: Another *structural directive* that renders a template for each item contained in a given collection. The directive is placed on an element, which becomes the parent of the cloned templates. In the preceding code block, we use it inside the main <table> element to create and show a <tr> element (a row) for each check item within the result.checks array.

- `{{ check.name }}`, `{{ check.responseTime }}`, and so on: These are called *interpolations* and can be used to incorporate calculated strings into the text between HTML element tags and/or within attribute assignments. In other words, we can use them as placeholders for our class variables' property values. As we can see, the *interpolation* default delimiters are the double curly braces, `{{` and `}}`.

To understand more about `ngIf`, `ngFor`, interpolations, and other Angular UI fundamentals, we strongly suggest taking a look at the official documentation:

Displaying data: `https://angular.io/guide/displaying-data`

Template syntax: `https://angular.io/guide/template-syntax`

Structural directives: `https://angular.io/guide/structural-directives`

health-check.component.css

Here's the `/src/app/health-check/health-check.component.css` source code:

```
.status {
  font-weight: bold;
}


.Healthy {
  color: green;
}


.Degraded {
  color: orange;
}


.Unhealthy {
  color: red;
}
```

There's not much to note here; just some vanilla CSS to style out the component template. Notice how we played a bit with the styling of the table cell, which will contain the *status* of the various checks. It's strongly advisable to highlight them as much as we can, so we made them bold and with a color matching the status type: green for Healthy, orange for Degraded, and red for Unhealthy.

Due to space limitations, we won't be able to talk much about CSS styling in this book: we will just take it for granted that the average web programmer knows how to handle the simple definitions, selectors, and styling rules we will use in our examples.

Those who want (or need) to understand more about CSS and CSS3 are encouraged to take a look at this great online tutorial: `https://developer.mozilla.org/en-US/docs/Web/CSS`.

A word on Angular component styling

As a matter of fact, Angular gives us at least two ways to define custom CSS rules for our components:

- Setting them within a `styles` property in the component metadata
- Loading styles from external CSS files by adding a `styleUrls` property in the component metadata

Both of the preceding approaches rely upon properties that need to be added to the component's @ `Component` decorator; the latter is the one used by the default template we reviewed back in *Chapter 3, Looking Around*, and is preferable in most cases, since it allows us to separate the HTML structure from the CSS styling.

If we wanted to migrate to the former, here's how we should set the `styles` property instead:

```
@Component({
  selector: 'app-health-check',
  templateUrl: './health-check.component.html',
  styles: ['
    .status { font-weight:bold; }
    .Healthy { color: green; }
    .Degraded { color: orange; }
    .Unhealthy { color: red; }
  ']
})
```

The only real advantage of such an approach is that it doesn't need the addition of a separate CSS file, which could make it viable enough for small and lightweight components that require little styling: that said, in the vast majority of cases, the `styleUrls` property is definitely the way to go.

It goes without saying that we've only scratched the surface of a huge and complex topic; however, for obvious reasons of space, we won't go much further than this for the rest of the book.

Those who want to know more about *component styling* are strongly encouraged to take a look at the Angular official guide: `https://angular.io/guide/component-styles`.

Now that our component is ready, we need to properly add it to our Angular app.

Adding the component to the Angular app

Since we've generated the component using the Angular CLI, we don't need to update the `app.module.ts` file: all the required changes have been automatically performed by the CLI.

However, if we want our new component to be reachable to our users within our Angular app, we need to make some minimal changes to the following files:

- `app-routing.module.ts`
- `nav-menu.component.ts`
- `nav-menu.component.html`

Let's get this done.

AppRoutingModule

Since we've created a dedicated `AppRoutingModule` to handle routing, we also need to update it by adding the new routing entry, so that our users will be able to navigate to that page.

Open the `/src/app/app-routing.module.ts` file and add the following highlighted lines:

```typescript
import { NgModule } from '@angular/core';
import { Routes, RouterModule } from '@angular/router';
import { HomeComponent } from './home/home.component';
import { FetchDataComponent } from './fetch-data/fetch-data.component';
import { HealthCheckComponent } from './health-check/health-check.component';

const routes: Routes = [
  { path: '', component: HomeComponent, pathMatch: 'full' },
  { path: 'fetch-data', component: FetchDataComponent },
  { path: 'health-check', component: HealthCheckComponent }
];

@NgModule({
  imports: [RouterModule.forRoot(routes)],
  exports: [RouterModule]
})
export class AppRoutingModule { }
```

What we did here is not hard to understand: we've added a dedicated `health-check` route that will handle the navigation to our new component. Once done, we just need to add it to our `NavMenuComponent` so that our users will be able to see and use it within the app's UI, which is what we'll do now.

NavMenuComponent

Adding our new *component* navigation path to RoutingModule was a required step to make sure our users are able to reach it; however, we also need to add a link for our users to click on. Since NavMenuComponent is the component that handles the navigation user interface, we need to perform some stuff there as well.

Open the /src/app/nav-menu/nav-menu.component.html file and add the following highlighted lines:

```html
<header>
  <nav>
    <a [routerLink]="['/']">Home</a>
    |
    <a [routerLink]="['/fetch-data']">Fetch Data</a>
    |
    <a [routerLink]="['/health-check']">Health Check</a>
  </nav>
</header>
```

Now that our new component has been added to our Angular app, we just need to test it out.

Testing it out

To see our new HealthCheckComponent in all of its glory, we just need to do the following:

- Hit *F5* to launch the project in *debug* mode
- When the home view is done loading, click on the new **Health Check** link in the top-left navigation menu

If we did everything correctly, the browser should load the new **Health Check** view, which should look just like the following screenshot:

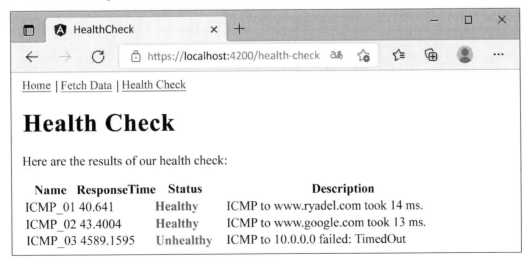

Figure 4.6: Our new HealthCheckComponent

It definitely seems like we did it!

Our health check is up and running, proudly showing us the results of the three ICMP requests we set up within our ASP.NET Core's HealthChecksMiddleware.

That said, we must admit that the look and feel of such a table are not that great. And the rest of the app doesn't look any better. The fact that we're barely using any styling is starting to take its toll in terms of visual experience.

For this reason, before moving forward, it might be useful to spend some valuable time addressing such issues for good. Let's be clear, we're not going to turn our "minimalist" HTML templates into a jaw-dropping layout: we'll just add some minor UI tweaks with the help of a free, open source, and well-known front-end framework.

Restyling the UI

You might think that the framework we're referring to is *Bootstrap*, since it's one of the most used choices when building responsive, mobile-first front-end applications. However, we're not going to use it: we'll opt for **Angular Material** instead, since it natively integrates with most Angular apps, provides a wide set of UI components, and gives a great look and feel, possibly even better than *Bootstrap*.

Introducing Angular Material

Angular Material is a UI component library that implements Material Design in Angular. As you most likely already know, Material Design is a UI design language that Google developed in 2014 that focuses on using grid-based layouts, responsive animations, transitions, padding, and depth effects such as lighting and shadows.

Material Design was introduced by the Google designer Matías Duarte on June 25, 2014, at the 2014 Google I/O conference. To make UI designers familiarize themselves with its core concepts, he explained that "unlike real paper, our digital material can expand and reform intelligently. Material has physical surfaces and edges. Seams and shadows provide meaning about what you can touch."

The main purpose of Material Design is to create a new UI language combining principles of good design with technical and scientific innovation in order to provide a consistent user experience across not only all Google platforms and applications but also any other web applications seeking to adopt such concepts. The language was revamped in 2018, providing more flexibility and advanced customization features based on themes.

As of 2020, Material Design is used on almost all Google web applications and tools—including Gmail, YouTube, Google Drive, Google Docs, Sheets, Slides, Google Maps, and all of the Google Play-branded applications, as well as most Android and Google OS UI elements. Such wide adoption also includes Angular, which has been provided with a dedicated NPM package that can be added to any Angular-based project to implement Material Design into any Angular app; this package is called @angular/material and includes the native UI elements, the **Component Dev Kit** (**CDK**), a set of animations, and other useful stuff.

Installing Angular Material

Installing Angular Material is a rather easy process: the best thing is to follow the official instructions from the following URL:

```
https://material.angular.io/guide/getting-started
```

Which is what we'll do right now.

Let's start with opening a Command Prompt window: once done, navigate to the Angular project's root folder—just like we do when we add a new component—and type the following command:

```
ng add @angular/material@13.0.1
```

The Angular Material installation wizard will start, as shown in the following screenshot:

```
√ Found compatible package version: @angular/material@13.0.1.
√ Package information loaded.

The package @angular/material@13.0.1 will be installed and executed.
Would you like to proceed? Yes
√ Package successfully installed.
? Choose a prebuilt theme name, or "custom" for a custom theme: Indigo/Pink
? Set up global Angular Material typography styles? Yes
? Set up browser animations for Angular Material? Yes
UPDATE package.json (1319 bytes)
√ Packages installed successfully.
UPDATE src/app/app.module.ts (944 bytes)
UPDATE angular.json (3423 bytes)
UPDATE src/index.html (579 bytes)
UPDATE src/styles.css (181 bytes)
```

Figure 4.7: Installing Angular Material using the CLI

The Angular CLI will automatically find the most suitable/compatible version, depending on the version of the CLI itself. That said, it's strongly advisable to use the version used within this book (see above).

The wizard will ask the following questions:

- Choose a prebuilt theme name: **Indigo/Pink**
- Set up global Angular Material typography styles? **Yes**
- Set up browser animations for Angular Material? **Yes**

 As a matter of fact, we're free to choose any default theme and opt-out of the browser animations if we don't want them: however, adding the global typography styles is highly recommended, since we don't have any additional CSS frameworks—and the default browser typography is not great.

Here's what the wizard will do to our Angular app:

- Add the required NPM packages and dependencies to the `package.json` file: `@angular/material` and `@angular/cdk`
- Add the `BrowserAnimationModule` to the `/src/app/app.module.ts` file (if we've answered YES to the "add browser animations" question)
- Add the Roboto font and the Material Design icon found to the `/src/index.html` file
- Add the `mat-typography` CSS class to the `<body>` element of the `/src/index.html` file
- Add some basic styling to the `/src/style.css` files

Once *Angular Material* has been installed, we can start restyling our components.

 For additional info about Angular Material, its setup process, and a list of supported features, check out the following links:

`https://material.angular.io/`

`https://material.angular.io/guide/getting-started`

Adding a MatToolbar

The first component we'll revamp is the `NavMenuComponent`, which doesn't look that great. More precisely, we'll replace its basic HTML template with an Angular Material native component specifically designed to host navigation menus: the **MatToolbar**.

1. To install it, we need to perform the following tasks:
2. Add the required references to the `AppModule` class

Update the `NavMenuComponent`'s HTML template accordingly

Let's do this.

Updating the AppModule

Open the `/src/app/app.module.ts` file and add the following highlighted lines just below the already existing `AppRoutingModule` import statement:

```
import { AppRoutingModule } from './app-routing.module';
import { MatButtonModule } from '@angular/material/button';
import { MatIconModule } from '@angular/material/icon';
import { MatToolbarModule } from '@angular/material/toolbar';
```

Then add the following highlighted lines at the end of the `@NgModule`'s `imports` array:

```
imports: [
  BrowserModule,
  HttpClientModule,
  AppRoutingModule,
```

```
      BrowserAnimationsModule,
    MatButtonModule,
    MatIconModule,
    MatToolbarModule
  ]
```

As we can see, we've added three Angular Material modules:

- MatButtonModule, which adds supports for button components
- MatIconModule, which allows the use of material icons
- MatToolbarModule, the main component we want to add

We're going to use all three of them to revamp our NavMenuComponent template file.

Updating the NavMenuComponent HTML template

Open the /src/app/nav-menu/nav-menu.component.html file and replace all the existing content with the following code:

```html
<header>
  <mat-toolbar color="primary">
    <button mat-icon-button [routerLink]="['/']">
      <mat-icon>
        home
      </mat-icon>
    </button>
    <a mat-flat-button color="primary" [routerLink]="['/fetch-data']">
      Fetch Data
    </a>
    <a mat-flat-button color="primary" [routerLink]="['/health-check']">
      Health Check
    </a>
  </mat-toolbar>
</header>
```

As we can see, we've replaced our previous hand-made implementation—which was based on a plain <nav> HTML element—with a new one relying upon the three modules we've just added:

- The Angular Material module syntax is quite simple to understand: each component has its own tag; for example, the whole toolbar is defined by the <mat-toolbar> tag.
- These components can be styled using standard CSS classes or custom *Attribute Directives*, a specific kind of directive specifically designed to change the appearance or behavior of DOM elements and Angular components: for example, the menu links are styled with the mat-flat-button directive, which applies some CSS classes to the <a> element itself to make it look like a button.

The official documentation of the Angular Material modules that we've used here are available at the following URLs:

`https://material.angular.io/components/button/overview`

`https://material.angular.io/components/icon/overview`

`https://material.angular.io/components/toolbar/overview`

To read more about Angular's *Attribute Directives*, check out the following URL: `https://angular.io/guide/attribute-directives`.

First test run

Let's take a small break from coding and styling to see what we just did. Press *F5* to launch our project(s) in *debug* mode and see if our new top-level navigation menu looks better than before.

If you can't see the updated Angular app after hitting *F5*, you can try to manually close all the console windows (including the one where `ngcc` is running) and then launch the projects again.

If we did everything correctly, we should see something like in the following screenshot:

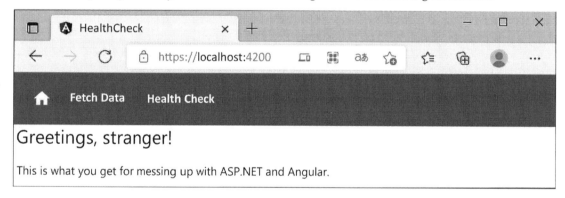

Figure 4.8: Our new top-level navigation menu using Angular Material's MatToolbar component

Not bad at all! Maybe a bit of padding applied to the content below the menu would make it look even better: let's quickly add it before moving on.

Open the `/src/app/app.component.css` file and add the following CSS rule:

```
.container {
  padding: 5px 10px;
}
```

This will create a small spacing between the content and the menu, as well as between the content and the external borders of the page.

Now we can continue styling our other components.

Playing with (S)CSS

The next thing we are about to do is to improve the look and feel of our HTML tables: we currently have two of them, one in the `DataFetchComponent`—which we've moved there from `AppComponent` a while ago—and another one in the `HealthCheckComponent`.

However, before doing that, we're going to take the chance to replace our existing CSS files with SCSS files, so that we can use the extended CSS syntax provided by the powerful **Sass** preprocessor.

Wait a minute? What is **Sass**?

If you feel the urge to ask this question, read the following section: if you already know what we're talking about, you might as well skip it, since you probably already know that story.

Introducing Sass

If you've worked with style sheets within the last few years, there's no chance you haven't heard of Sass; however, for the sake of those who haven't, let's take a few words to talk about it.

Before getting to that though, we must briefly introduce the concept of style sheets.

This section is mostly aimed at those who have never used Sass before. If you have some experience with Sass already or feel like you don't need to know anything else about why we'll use it, you might as well skip it entirely and jump to the next section: **Replacing CSS with Sass.**

A brief history of CSS

Style sheet language, also known as *style language*, is a programming language used to define the presentation layer's UI design rules of a structured document. We can think of it as a skin or a theme that we can apply to a logical item (the structured document) to change its appearance. For example, we can make it look blue, red, or yellow; we can make the characters bigger or smaller and thinner or wider; we can change the text spacing, alignment, and flow; and so on.

Using dedicated style sheet languages gives developers the chance to separate the presentation layer's code and structure (respectively, JavaScript and HTML) from the UI design rules, thus enforcing the **Separation of Concerns (SoC)** principle within the presentation layer itself.

When it comes to web pages, web applications, and anything else that mostly uses HTML, XHTML, XML, and other markup language-based documents, the most important style sheet language undoubtedly is CSS.

It was December 17, 1996, when the **World Wide Web Consortium (W3C)** released the official W3C CSS recommendation for the style sheet language that would be known as CSS1. CSS2 came less than two years later (May 1998), while its revised version, CSS2.1, took considerably more time (June 2011).

Starting from CSS3, things started to become more complex, since the W3C ditched the single, monolithic specification approach by splitting it into separate documents called modules, each one of them following its very own publishing, acceptance, and recommendation history. Starting in 2012, with four of these (Media Queries, Namespaces, Selectors, and Color) being published as formal recommendations and full CSS2.1 backward compatibility, CSS3 quickly became the most adopted style sheet language standard for the development of new websites.

CSS code sample

Regardless of their version, each adding new features while maintaining backward compatibility with the previous one(s), CSS sticks to the following syntax:

```
<selector> [sub-selector] [sub-sub-selector] {
    <property>: <value>;
    <another-property>: <value>;
    <yet-another-property>: <value>;
    /* ... and so on... */
}
This translates as follows:
.container {
  padding: 5px 10px;
}
```

We saw this code a short while ago; it's the `container` class we've just added in the `/src/app/app.component.css` file to add some padding to our app's content.

That class basically says that any HTML element with the `container` class assigned will have a padding of 5 px (top and bottom) and 10 px (left and right).

To assign a CSS class to an HTML element, we can use the `class` attribute in the following way:

```
<div class="container">
    [...some content...]
</div>
```

If the `class` attribute is already present, additional CSS classes can be assigned by separating them with a single space:

```
<div class="container otherClass someOtherClass">
    [...some content...]
</div>
```

Simple enough, isn't it?

What is Sass and why use it?

Sass is a cascading style sheets preprocessor; we can think of it as a "syntax enhancer" for CSS files, enabling us to do a number of things that CSS doesn't support (yet), just like PHP and/or ASP can do for an HTML page.

The following diagram should help us better understand the concept:

- Static content
- Verbose
- Enforces code repetitions
- No Variables
- No Loops / Cycles

- Dynamic content
- Concise
- Enforces code reusage
- Can define Variables
- Allows Loops / Cycles

Figure 4.9: PHP advantages over static HTML pages

These are the main advantages of using a hypertext preprocessor instead of writing raw HTML pages; we're talking about PHP, but the same goes for ASP.NET Web Forms, Razor, and basically everything else.

The following are the advantages of using Sass instead of writing raw CSS files:

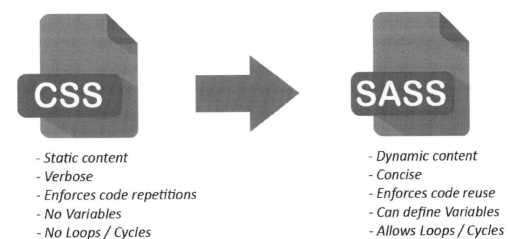

- Static content
- Verbose
- Enforces code repetitions
- No Variables
- No Loops / Cycles

- Dynamic content
- Concise
- Enforces code reuse
- Can define Variables
- Allows Loops / Cycles

Figure 4.10: Sass advantages over standard CSS syntax

As we can see, they serve the exact same purpose in terms of assisting, improving, and enhancing the development effort.

Making the switch from static style sheets to dynamic style sheets is just as easy as switching from static HTML pages to PHP or ASP dynamic pages; they both feature a nested metalanguage that can extend the base static language in a pure backward-compatible fashion. This means that a valid CSS file is also a valid Sass file, just as a valid HTML file is also a valid PHP or ASP file.

There are also some key differences between hypertext preprocessors and style sheet preprocessors, the most important being how web servers deal with them.

Hypertext preprocessors such as PHP and ASP are compiled by the web server upon each request; the web server compiles them on the fly and then serves the resulting HTML for each request/response flow. Conversely, style sheet preprocessor files are usually compiled into standard CSS files before being published; in other words, the web service doesn't know about the existence of these files, as it just serves the resulting CSS-compiled result.

This also means that using a style sheet preprocessor will have no performance impact on the server, unless we choose to install some experimental and still highly inefficient handlers, extensions, modules, or client-side scripts that will compile the source files on the fly.

IMPORTANT NOTE: From now on, we'll take for granted that the reader has a decent knowledge of CSS files, syntax, selectors, and their common use within HTML pages. If this is not the case, we strongly suggest that you learn the core CSS and Sass concepts before going further. The following URLs can greatly help newcomers understand the distinctive features of both languages:

CSS: `https://www.w3.org/Style/CSS/learning`

Sass: `https://sass-lang.com/guide`

Replacing CSS with Sass

As we know from *Chapter 3*, *Looking Around*, the Angular CLI's default behavior is to generate standard CSS files: to perform the switch from CSS to SCSS, the first thing we need to do is to change such behavior.

To do that, open the `angular.json` file and add the following highlighted lines within the existing `"schematics"` section:

```
"schematics": {
  "@schematics/angular:application": {
    "strict": true
  },
  "@schematics/angular:component": {
    "style": "scss"
  }
}
```

That's pretty much it: from now on, whenever we use the Angular CLI to generate our components, Sass files (SCSS) will be created instead of the standard CSS files.

The only thing we need to do now is to rename all the extensions of the style sheet files of our existing components, as well as updating the `styleUrls` references in the component's TypeScript files: in both cases, we need to switch from `.css` to `.scss`.

> Performing the renaming of our components' style sheet files is a rather easy task that can be easily done within the Visual Studio GUI via the **Solution Explorer:** we just need to prepend an `"s"` letter to all the files with the `.css` extensions present within the `/src/app` folder (and subfolders), and then update that file's reference in the corresponding `.ts` file.
>
> Those who need further guidance can check out the GitHub project for this chapter, where all the files have been updated with the proper extension.

After we do that, the only file with the `.css` extension left in the whole project should be the `/src/styles.css` file—the one containing the CSS rules valid for the whole application. We can rename it to `.scss` as well; however—since it's not a component style sheet file—we also need to update its corresponding references within the `angular.json` file in the following way:

```
"styles": [
    "./node_modules/@angular/material/prebuilt-themes/indigo-pink.css",
    "src/styles.scss"
]
```

> **IMPORTANT:** Be sure to update all the references (there are two of them). Also, be sure to manually close all the console windows and relaunch the projects again after updating the `angular.json` file.

Once done, we can finally use Sass syntax (together with CSS syntax) anywhere in our Angular project.

Restyling the tables

Let's immediately take advantage of the Sass syntax by restyling our existing HTML tables. Since we have two of them, we can define a global class within our new (renamed) `/src/styles.scss` files, which hosts our application-wide style sheet rules:

Open that file and append the following highlighted lines to the existing code:

```
html, body { height: 100%; }
body { margin: 0; font-family: Roboto, "Helvetica Neue", sans-serif; }

table {
```

```
  border: 0px;
  border-spacing: 0px;
  border-collapse: collapse;

  tr {
    border-bottom: 1px solid #dddddd;

    &:nth-child(even) {
      background-color: #f4f4f4;
    }

    th, td {
      text-align: left;
      padding: 5px 10px;
    }
  }
}
```

Once done, save the file and hit *F5* to test the new table styling. To see that, we need to navigate to our FetchDataComponent and to our HealthCheckComponent, which can be done using our new Angular Material menu.

If we did everything correctly, we should be able to see the new CSS rules affecting the tables of both components, just like in the following screenshots:

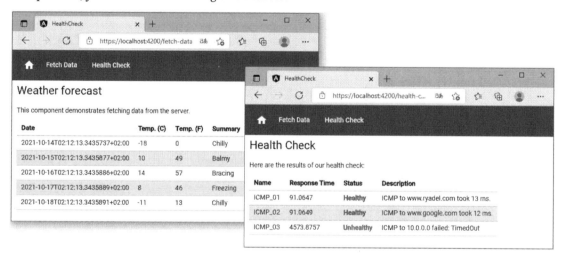

Figure 4.11: HTML tables styled with Sass

That's it: our UI is still not perfect, but we can be satisfied with these improvements, at least for now.

> It's worth noting that, instead of restyling our existing HTML tables, we could have used the Angular Material's **MatTable** component to entirely replace them: by doing that, we would have gained a lot of powerful features, such as filtering, sorting, paging, and so on.
>
> However, for the sake of simplicity, we have opted for a "faster" approach, which also allowed us to integrate Sass in our Angular project. We will make extensive use of the **MatTable** component in the next chapters, when we'll have to deal with more complex (and overly populated) tables.

Now that we've learned the basics, we'll move on to a completely different topic. However, the reader should already be able (and is strongly encouraged) to further expand this sample project with more sophisticated use case scenarios, such as:

- Create additional checks using the same approach that we've adopted for the `ICMPHealthCheck` class: a DBMS connection check, read/write permissions on a UNC folder or resources, the presence/absence of watchdog files, internet connectivity, CPU/memory/bandwidth usage, and so on.

- Proactively handle the different states in our application depending on the various health check results: show a message to our users if the application is not working properly, disable the components of the application that are not working, switch to a fallback alternative, send alert email notifications to the administrators, and so on.

- Extend the `HealthChecksMiddleware` capabilities with **LiteXHealthChecks**, a lightweight, yet powerful, NuGet package with a number of modular add-ons that allow us to check the status of a component in the application, such as a back-end service, database, or some internal state.

Further improve the look and feel of our Angular app by applying additional styling rules using the CSS and/or Sass syntax.

That said, we've just gained some important knowledge regarding *Angular Material* and *Sass*, two very useful tools that we'll definitely use in the upcoming chapters.

Summary

Let's spend a minute briefly recapping what we learned in this chapter. First of all, we acknowledged that *.NET controllers* are not the only tool in the shed: as a matter of fact, any middleware is virtually able to deal with the HTTP *request* and *response* cycle—as long as it is in our application's pipeline.

To demonstrate such a concept, we introduced `HealthChecksMiddleware`, a neat ASP.NET Core built-in feature that can be used to implement status monitoring services, and then we implemented it. We started with the ASP.NET Core *back-end*, refining our work until we were able to create a JSON-structured output; then, we switched to Angular, where we learned how to properly fetch it with a *component* and show it on screen through the browser's HTML-based UI.

Last but not least, we've spent some valuable time improving the UI and UX of our Angular app by adding a couple of powerful layout-based features: *Angular Material* and *Sass*. Eventually, the final outcome was good enough to reward us for our hard work.

That's enough for the *HealthCheck* app, at least for the time being. Starting from the next chapter, we'll bring back the standard .NET *controllers* pattern and see how we can leverage it to learn something new.

Suggested topics

For further information, we recommend the following topics: Health Monitoring, Health Checks, HealthChecksMiddleware, HealthCheckOptions, HTTP Requests, HTTP Responses, ICMP, PING, ResponseWriter, JSON, JsonSerializerOptions, Components, Routing, Modules, AppModule, HttpClient, ngIf, ngFor, Directives, Structural Directives, Interpolations, NgModule, Angular module system, JavaScript module system (import/export), Angular Material, Cascading Style Sheets (CSS), Sass.

References

- *Health checks in ASP.NET Core*: `https://docs.microsoft.com/en-US/aspnet/core/host-and-deploy/health-checks`

- *Request and response operations in ASP.NET Core*: `https://docs.microsoft.com/en-us/aspnet/core/fundamentals/middleware/request-response`

- *ASP.NET Core health monitoring*: `https://docs.microsoft.com/en-us/dotnet/architecture/microservices/implement-resilient-applications/monitor-app-health`

- *"pattern-based using" and "using declarations"*: `https://docs.microsoft.com/en-us/dotnet/csharp/language-reference/proposals/csharp-8.0/using`

- *C# 8.0: Understanding Using Declarations*: `https://www.stevejgordon.co.uk/csharp-8-understanding-using-declarations`

- *String Interpolation in C#*: `https://docs.microsoft.com/en-us/dotnet/csharp/tutorials/string-interpolation`

- *TypeScript modules*: `https://www.typescriptlang.org/docs/handbook/modules.html`

- *Module Resolution*: `https://www.typescriptlang.org/docs/handbook/module-resolution.html`

- *Dependency Injection in ASP.NET Core*: `https://docs.microsoft.com/en-us/aspnet/core/fundamentals/dependency-injection`

- *Angular.io—Dependency Injection*: `https://angular.io/guide/dependency-injection`

- *Angular—Lifecycle Hooks*: `https://angular.io/guide/lifecycle-hooks`

- *ReactiveX Library—Observables*: `http://reactivex.io/rxjs/class/es6/Observable.js~Observable.html`

- *Angular.io—Observables guide*: `https://angular.io/guide/observables`

- *JavaScript—Import statement*: `https://developer.mozilla.org/en-US/docs/Web/JavaScript/Reference/Statements/import`

- *JavaScript—Export statement*: `https://developer.mozilla.org/en-US/docs/Web/JavaScript/Reference/Statements/export`
- *Angular—HttpClient*: `https://angular.io/guide/http#httpclient`
- *Angular—NgModules*: `https://angular.io/guide/ngmodules`
- *Angular—NgModules and JavaScript modules*: `https://angular.io/guide/architecture-modules#ngmodules-and-javascript-modules`
- *Angular—Displaying Data*: `https://angular.io/guide/displaying-data`
- *Angular—Template Syntax*: `https://angular.io/guide/template-syntax`
- *Angular—Structural Directives*: `https://angular.io/guide/structural-directives`
- *Angular Material*: `https://material.angular.io/`
- *CSS—Cascading Style Sheets*: `https://developer.mozilla.org/en-US/docs/Web/CSS`
- *Sass basics*: `https://sass-lang.com/guide`

5

Data Model with Entity Framework Core

The HealthCheck sample app that we've been playing with since *Chapter 2*, *Getting Ready*, is working fine, yet it lacks some important features we would likely make use of in a typical web application; among the most important of them is the ability to read and write data from a **Database Management System (DBMS)** since this is an essential requirement for almost any web-related task: content management, knowledge sharing, instant communication, data storage and/or mining, tracking and statistics, user authentication, system logging, and so on.

Truth be told, even our HealthCheck app could definitely use some of these tasks: tracking the host statuses over time could be a nice feature; user authentication should be a must-have, especially if we plan to publicly release it to the web; system logging is always great to have; and so on. However, since we prefer to keep our projects as simple as possible, we're going to create a new one and grant some DBMS capabilities to it.

Here's what we're going to do in this chapter:

- **Create a brand-new .NET and Angular web application project** called *WorldCities*: a database of cities from all over the world
- **Choose a suitable data source** to fetch a reasonable amount of *real* data to play with
- **Define and implement a data model** using Entity Framework Core
- **Configure and deploy a DBMS engine** that will be used by our project
- **Create the database** using Entity Framework Core's Data Migrations feature
- **Implement a data seeding strategy** to load the data source to the database
- **Read and write data with .NET** using the **Object-Relational Mapping (ORM)** techniques provided by Entity Framework Core

Are you ready to get started?

Technical requirements

In this chapter, we're going to need all of the technical requirements that were listed in the previous chapters, plus the following external libraries:

- `Microsoft.EntityFrameworkCore` NuGet package
- `Microsoft.EntityFrameworkCore.Tools` NuGet package
- `Microsoft.EntityFrameworkCore.SqlServer` NuGet package
- **SQL Server 2019** (if we opt for the local SQL instance route)
- **MS Azure subscription** (if we opt for the cloud database hosting route)

As always, it's advisable to avoid installing these straight away. We're going to bring them in during this chapter so that we can contextualize their purpose within our project.

The code files for this chapter can be found at `https://github.com/PacktPublishing/ASP.NET-Core-6-and-Angular/tree/master/Chapter_05/`.

The WorldCities web app

The first thing we're going to do is create two new projects using the two Visual Studio templates that we used in *Chapter 2, Getting Ready*:

- The *Standalone TypeScript Angular template*, for a new Angular project
- The *ASP.NET Core Web API template*, for a new Web API

In a nutshell, we just need to repeat what we did during the second part of *Chapter 2, Getting Ready*, where we created the **HealthCheck** and **HealthCheckAPI** projects: the only difference is that this time we're going to give them a different name: **WorldCities** for the standalone TypeScript Angular project, and **WorldCitiesAPI** for the ASP.NET Core Web API.

Creating these two projects from scratch will be a great exercise, and a good chance to put into practice what you've learned until now. Let's see if you're able to do that without help!

 If you have issues, you can check out the book's GitHub repository for this chapter and compare its content with what you did.

Once we've created the two projects, the first thing we need to do is to ensure that Visual Studio will start them both by using the *Multiple startup projects* feature – just like we did in *Chapter 2, Getting Ready*. To do that, right-click to the solution node, select the **Set Startup Projects** option from the contextual menu, and act accordingly.

Right after that, we'll need to apply the same upgrades and improvements to our new projects that we did on the **HealthCheck** and **HealthCheckAPI** projects in *Chapter 2, Getting Ready*.

Updating the ASP.NET Core app

Let's start with the ASP.NET Core app, which only requires some minor changes. Here's what we need to do:

- In the launchSettings.json file, change HTTP and HTTPS ports to 40080 and 40443

That's about it.

Updating the Angular app

Let's move on to the Angular app. Here's what we need to do:

- Upgrade (or downgrade) the Angular version in the package.json file
- Edit the /src/proxy.conf.json file to update the Angular proxy context from /weatherforecast to /api, as well as changing the HTTPS port to 40443 to match the ASP.NET Core app
- Add the HomeComponent and the NavMenuComponent using the ng generate Angular CLI command
- Remove the weather forecast data-fetching features from the AppComponent, so that it will only contain the app-nav-menu and router-outlet elements
- Add the AppRoutingModule to separate the routing strategies from the AppModule
- Add the baseUrl property to the /src/environments/environment.ts and environment.prod.ts files, using the "/" and "https://localhost:40443/" values respectively

 As we can see, we didn't mention the FetchDataComponent: we will not use it in our new **WorldCities** Angular app, therefore we can avoid creating it—as well as referencing it in the NavMenuComponent and AppRoutingModule.

While we're there, we can keep the exercise going by applying the UI improvements that we implemented in the *Restyling the UI* section of *Chapter 4, Front-End and Back-End Interactions*:

- Install *Angular Material*
- Add the *MatToolbar* to the NavMenuComponent
- Replace *CSS* with *Sass*

 Again, we can skip the HealthCheckComponent and all its references since we don't need it.

Having to repeat all these steps might seem unpleasant at first, but it's a good way to confirm that we've understood each relevant step. However, if you don't want to practice you can also copy and paste the updated code from the **HealthCheck** Angular app... or directly pull the updated source code from this chapter's GitHub repository.

After making all these changes, we can check that everything is working by pressing *F5* and inspecting the outcome. If everything has been done properly, we should be able to see the following screen:

Figure 5.1: Inspecting our new WorldCities ASP.NET and Angular app

 If you get a different outcome (or run into UI or compilation errors), you might want to compare your new `WorldCities` project against the one present in the GitHub repository for this chapter to ensure that all the updates and refactoring steps have been applied.

Since we don't want to read that "Greeting, stranger!" phrase for the rest of this book, let's take 2 minutes of our time to briefly revamp our new app's home page.

Minimal UI restyling

Open the web browser and go to `www.pexels.com`, a neat website that offers free stock photos and videos shared by talented creators from all over the world. Type `world map` in the search bar and pick a suitable cover image, possibly with landscape proportions.

Here's a good one, taken from `https://www.pexels.com/photo/close-up-of-globe-335393/`:

Figure 5.2: World map for our cover image

Many thanks to **NastyaSensei** for making the preceding image available under Pexel's *free-to-use* license: `https://www.pexels.com/license/`.

You can check out more of her photos here: `https://www.pexels.com/@ nastyasensei-66707.`

Download the photo using the lowest possible resolution available (640x426) and save it in our **World-Cities** app using the following path and name:

```
/src/assets/img/home.jpg
```

In order to do this, we'll have to create the `/img/` folder, because it isn't there yet.

Now that we have our own home cover image, let's update the home view to show it in a proper way; open the `/src/app/home/home.component.html` file and change its contents in the following way:

```
<h1>WorldCities</h1>
<p>
  A sample web application to demonstrate
  how to interact with ASP.NET, Angular,
  Entity Framework Core and a SQL Database.
</p>

<img src="/assets/img/home.jpg" alt="WorldCities"
     class="home-cover" />
```

As we can see from the preceding code, we plan to show our new image using an `<img>` element that also features a `class` attribute: this means that now we need to implement that `home-cover` CSS class using one of the styling component approaches supported by Angular.

As we know from what we've experienced in the previous chapters, we could do that by either adding a `styles` property to the component's metadata by updating the `/src/app/home/home.component.ts` TypeScript file...

```
@Component({
  selector: 'app-home',
  templateUrl: './home.component.html',
  styles: ['.home-cover { display:block; margin:auto; max-width:100%; }']
})
```

... or we could use the separate SCSS file and implement the class there. We also know that this latter approach is almost always preferable, as it will allow us to separate the HTML structure from the CSS styling without messing up the component code, hence we'll do it that way.

From **Solution Explorer**, open the `/src/app/home/home.component.scss` file—which should be empty by now—and fill its contents with the following code:

```scss
.home-cover {
  display:block;
  margin: auto;
  max-width:100%;
}
```

Be sure to check that the `home.component.scss` file is properly referenced in the `styleUrls` property within the component's `/src/app/home/home.component.ts` file in the following way:

```typescript
@Component({
  selector: 'app-home',
  templateUrl: './home.component.html',
  styleUrls: ['./home.component.scss']
})
```

Now that we've updated the SCSS file, let's look at the style sheet rules that we've put in the `home-cover` class: as we can see, we've applied some minimal CSS styling to center the image and make it automatically resize so that its base width (640 px) won't be a hindrance for mobile phones.

Let's now press *F5* and see what our new home view looks like:

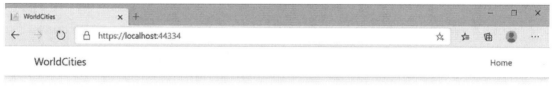

Figure 5.3: Inspecting our cover image

We will never win an award for this layout, but that's OK for our purposes.

If we reduce our browser width to the minimum amount (or use MS Edge's *Mobile Emulation* feature by opening the *Developer Tools* and then pressing *Ctrl + Shift + M*), we can also see how it would look on mobile devices:

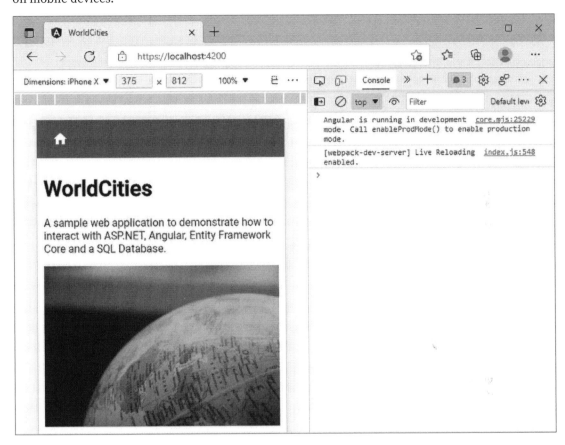

Figure 5.4: Mobile devices view of our cover page

Not that bad, is it?

That's about it: now we have a brand-new .NET and Angular web application to play with. We just need a data source and a data model that can be accessed through a *back-end Web API* to retrieve some data from: in other words, a data server.

Reasons to use a data server

Before we move on, it would be wise to spend a couple of minutes answering the following question: *do we really need a real data server?* Can't we just emulate one somehow? We're only running code samples, after all.

As a matter of fact, we could definitely avoid doing that and skip this entire chapter: Angular provides a neat **in-memory Web API** package that replaces the `HttpClient` module's `HttpBackend` and emulates **CRUD** operations over a RESTful API; the emulation is performed by intercepting the Angular HTTP requests and redirecting them to an in-memory data store under our control.

This package is great and works really well for most test case scenarios, such as the following:

- To simulate operations against data collections that haven't been implemented on our dev/ test server

- To write unit test apps that read and write data without having to intercept multiple HTTP calls and manufacture sequences of responses

- To perform end-to-end tests without messing with the real database, which is great for **Continuous Integration** (**CI**) builds

The *in-memory* Web API service works so well that the entire Angular documentation at `https://angular.io/` relies upon it. However, we're not going to use it for now, for a simple (and rather obvious) reason: this book's focus is not on Angular, but the **client/server interoperability between Angular and .NET**; for that very reason, developing a *real* Web API and connecting it to a real data source through a real data model is part of the game.

We don't want to simulate the behavior of a RESTful *back-end* because we need to understand what's going on there and how to implement it properly: we want to implement it, along with the DBMS that will host and provide the data.

This is the reason why we created the **WorldCitiesAPI** project in the first place, and we definitely plan to use it: that's precisely what we're going to do, starting from the next section.

 Those who want to get additional information about the Angular in-memory Web API service can visit the `in-memory-web-api` GitHub project page at `https://github.com/angular/in-memory-web-api/`.

The data source

What kind of data will our *WorldCities* web application need? We already know the answer: a database of cities from all over the world. Does such a repository even exist yet?

As a matter of fact, there are several alternatives we can use to populate our database and then make it available to our end users.

The following is the free world cities database by DSpace-CRIS:

- **URL:** `https://dspace-cris.4science.it/handle/123456789/31`
- **Format:** CSV
- **License:** Free to use

The following is GeoDataSource's world cities database (free edition):

- **URL:** `http://www.geodatasource.com/world-cities-database/free`

- **Format:** CSV
- **License:** Free to use (registration required)

The following is the world cities database by simplemaps:

- **URL:** `https://simplemaps.com/data/world-cities`
- **Format:** CSV, XLSX
- **License:** Free to use (CC BY 4.0, `https://creativecommons.org/licenses/by/4.0/`)

All of these alternatives are good enough to suit our needs: we'll go with `simplemaps.com` since it requires no registration and provides a human-readable spreadsheet format.

Open your favorite browser, type in or copy the above URL, and look for the **Basic** column of the **World Cities Database** section:

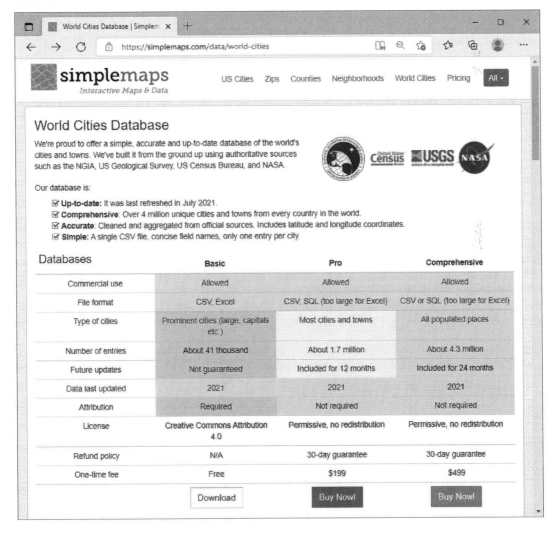

Figure 5.5: Downloading a world cities database from simplemaps.com

Click the **Download** button to retrieve the (huge) ZIP file containing both the .csv and .xlsx files and save it somewhere. That's it for now; we'll deal with these files later on.

Starting with the next section, we'll start the building process of our data model: it's going to be a long, but also very rewarding, journey.

The data model

Now that we have our raw data source, we need to find a way to make it available to our web application so that our users will be able to retrieve (and maybe alter) the actual data.

For the sake of simplicity, we won't waste our precious time by introducing the whole data model concept, as well as the various meanings of these two words. Those of you who are experienced, as well as seasoned developers, will probably be aware of all of the relevant stuff. We'll just say that when we are talking about a data model, we don't mean anything more or anything less than a lightweight, definitely typed set of entity classes representing persistent, code-driven data structures that we can use as resources within our Web API code.

The word persistent has been used for a reason; we want our data structure to be stored in a database. That's rather obvious for any application based on data. The brand-new web application we're about to create won't be an exception since we want it to act as a collection—or a repository—of records so that we can read, create, delete, and/or modify according to our needs.

As we can easily guess, all of these tasks will be performed by some *back-end* business logic (.NET controllers) that's triggered by a *front-end* UI (Angular components).

Introducing Entity Framework Core

We will create our database with the help of **Entity Framework Core** (also known as **EF Core**), the well-known, open-source **Object Relational Mapper (ORM)** for **ADO.NET** that's developed by Microsoft. The reasons for this choice are as follows:

- Seamless integration with the Visual Studio IDE
- A conceptual model based upon entity classes (**Entity Data Model (EDM)**), which will allow us to work with data using domain-specific objects without the need to write data-access code, which is precisely what we're looking for
- Easy to deploy, use, and maintain in development and production phases
- Compatible with all of the major open-source and commercial SQL engines, including **MSSQL**, **SQLite**, **Azure Cosmos DB**, **PostgreSQL**, **MySQL/MariaDB**, **MyCAT**, **Firebird**, **Db2/Informix**, **Oracle DB**, and more, thanks to the official and/or third-party providers and/or connectors available via NuGet

It's worth mentioning that **Entity Framework Core** was previously known as **Entity Framework 7** until its latest RC release. The name change follows the ASP.NET 5/ASP.NET Core perspective switch we already talked about as it also emphasizes the Entity Framework Core major rewrite/redesign if we compare it to the previous installments.

You might be wondering why we're choosing to adopt a SQL-based approach instead of going for a NoSQL alternative; there are many good NoSQL products, such as *MongoDB*, *RavenDB*, and *CouchDB*, that happen to have a C# connector library. What about using one of them instead?

The answer is rather simple: despite being available as third-party providers, they haven't been included in the official **Entity Framework Core Database Providers list** (see the link in the following information box). For that very reason, we're going to stick to the relational database, which may also be a more convenient approach for the simple database schemas we're going to design within this book.

For those who want to know more about the upcoming release and/or feel bold enough to use it anyway—maybe with a NoSQL DB as well—we strongly suggest that you take a look at the following links and docs:

- **Project roadmap:** `https://github.com/aspnet/EntityFramework/wiki/Roadmap`
- **Source code on GitHub:** `https://github.com/aspnet/EntityFramework`
- **Official documentation:** `https://docs.efproject.net/en/latest/`
- **Official Entity Framework Core Database Providers list:** `https://docs.microsoft.com/en-us/ef/core/providers/?tabs=dotnet-core-cli`

Installing Entity Framework Core

To install Entity Framework Core, we need to add the relevant packages to the dependencies section of our project file. We can easily do this using the visual GUI in the following way:

- Right-click on the `WorldCitiesAPI` project
- Select **Manage NuGet Packages**
- Ensure that the **Package source** drop-down list is set to **All**
- Go to the **Browse** tab and search for the packages containing the `Microsoft.EntityFrameworkCore` keyword:

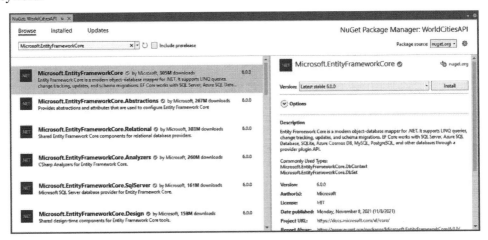

Figure 5.6: Installing Entity Framework Core

Once there, select and install the following packages (the latest at the time of writing):

- `Microsoft.EntityFrameworkCore` version 6.0.0
- `Microsoft.EntityFrameworkCore.Tools` version 6.0.0
- `Microsoft.EntityFrameworkCore.SqlServer` version 6.0.0

These packages will also bring some required dependencies, which we'll need to install as well, and require the acceptance of their license terms:

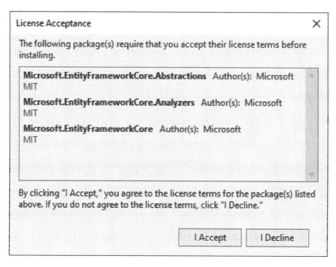

Figure 5.7: Accepting the license

If we prefer to do this using the NuGet Package Manager command line, we can input the following:

```
PM> Install-Package Microsoft.EntityFrameworkCore -Version 6.0.0
PM> Install-Package Microsoft.EntityFrameworkCore.Tools -Version 6.0.0
PM> Install-Package Microsoft.EntityFrameworkCore.SqlServer -Version 6.0.0
```

It's worth noting that the version number, which is the one that's the most recent at the time of writing, might be subject to change: be sure to triple-check it in this book's GitHub repository as well!

The SQL Server Data Provider

Among the installed namespaces, it's worth noting the presence of `Microsoft.EntityFrameworkCore.SqlServer`, which is the **Microsoft SQL Database Provider** for Entity Framework Core. This highly versatile connector provides an interface for the whole Microsoft SQL Server database family, including the latest SQL Server 2019.

DBMS licensing models

Despite having a rather expensive (to say the least) licensing model, there are at least three Microsoft SQL editions that can be used for free, as long as certain requirements are met:

- **Evaluation edition** is free, but comes with no production use rights, meaning that we can only use it on development servers. Additionally, it can only be used for 180 days. After that, we'll have to either buy a license or uninstall it (and migrate to a different edition).

- **Developer edition** is also free and comes with no production use rights. However, it can be used without limitations, providing that we only use it for development and/or testing scenarios.

- **Express edition** is free and can be used in any environment, meaning that we can use it on development and production servers. However, it has some major performance and size limitations that could hinder the performance of a complex and/or high-traffic web application.

> For additional information regarding the various SQL Server editions, including the commercial ones that do require a paid licensing model, check out the following links:
>
> - https://www.microsoft.com/en-us/sql-server/sql-server-2019
> - https://www.microsoft.com/en-us/sql-server/sql-server-2019-comparison

As we can easily see, both the **Developer** and **Express** editions can be a great deal for small web applications like those we're playing with in this book.

What about Linux?

SQL Server 2019 is also available for Linux and officially supported for the following distributions:

- **Red Hat Enterprise Linux (RHEL)**
- **SUSE Enterprise Server**
- **Ubuntu**

Other than that, it can also be set to run on Docker and even provisioned as a virtual machine on Azure, which can often be a great alternative if we don't want to install a local DMBS instance and save our precious hardware resources.

As for the licensing model, all SQL Server products are licensed the same way for all of these environments: this basically means that we can use our license (including the free ones) on the platform of our choice.

SQL Server alternatives

If you don't feel like using Microsoft SQL Server, you're 100% free to pick another DBMS engine, such as MySQL, PostgreSQL, or any other product, as long as it has some kind of Entity Framework Core official (or third-party) support.

Should we make this decision now? This entirely depends on the data modeling approach we want to adopt; for the time being, and for the sake of simplicity, we're going to stick to the Microsoft SQL Server family, which allows us to install a decent DBMS for free on either our local machine (development and/or production) or Azure (thanks to its €200 cost and 12-month free trial): don't worry about this for now—we'll get there later on.

Data modeling approaches

Now that we have Entity Framework Core installed and we know—more or less—which DBMS we are going to use, we have to choose between one of the two available approaches to model the data structure: **Code-First** or **Database-First**. Each one comes with a fair number of advantages and disadvantages, as those of you with experience and those of you who are seasoned .NET developers will almost certainly know. Although we won't dig too much into these, it would be useful to briefly summarize each before making a choice.

Code-First

This is Entity Framework's flagship approach since version 4 and also the recommended one: an elegant, highly efficient data model development workflow. The appeal of this approach can be easily found in its premise; the Code-First approach allows developers to define model objects using only standard classes, without the need for any design tool, XML mapping files, or cumbersome piles of autogenerated code.

To summarize, we can say that going Code-First means *writing the data model entity classes we'll be using within our project and letting Entity Framework generate the database accordingly*:

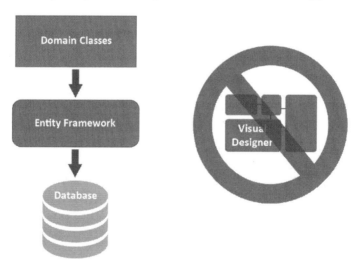

Figure 5.8: The Code-First approach

The pros and cons are explained in the following sections.

Pros

- There is no need for diagrams and visual tools whatsoever, which can be great for small-to-medium-sized projects as it will save a lot of time
- It has a fluent code API that allows the developer to follow a convention-over-configuration approach so that it can handle the most common scenarios, while also giving them the chance to switch to a custom, attribute-based implementation that overrides the need to customize the database mapping

Cons

- Good knowledge of C# and updated EF conventions is required.
- Maintaining the database can often be tricky, as well as handling updates without suffering data loss. Migration support, which was added in 4.3 to overcome this issue and has been continuously updated since then, greatly mitigates the problem, although it also affects the learning curve in a negative way.

Database-First

If we either have an existing database already or don't mind building it beforehand, we could consider an alternative approach that goes the other way around: instead of letting EF Core automatically build the database using the SQL commands generated from the model objects, we generate these objects from an existing database using the dotnet ef command-line tool. This code-generation technique is known as *model scaffolding* and relies upon the following command:

```
> dotnet ef dbcontext scaffold
```

> For additional info about EF model scaffolding and Database-First, visit the following URL:
>
> https://docs.microsoft.com/en-us/ef/core/miscellaneous/cli/dotnet#dotnet-ef-dbcontext-scaffold

We can summarize this by saying that going Database-First will mean *building the database and letting Entity Framework create/update the rest accordingly*:

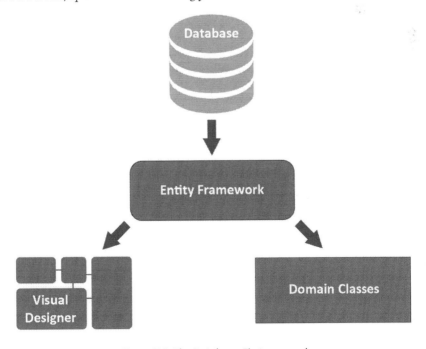

Figure 5.9: The Database-First approach

The pros and cons are explained in the following sections.

Pros

- If we have an already-existing database in place, this will probably be the way to go as it will spare us the need to recreate it
- The risk of data loss will be kept to a minimum because any structural change or database model update will always be performed on the database itself

Cons

- Manually updating the database can be tricky if we're dealing with clusters, multiple instances, or several development/testing/production environments as we will have to manually keep them in sync instead of relying on code-driven updates/migrations or autogenerated SQL scripts
- We will have less control over the autogenerated model classes, therefore managing associations, foreign keys, and constraints will be more difficult

Making a choice

By taking the advantages and disadvantages of these two options into account, there is no such thing as an overall *better* or *best* approach; conversely, we can say that each project scenario will likely have a best-suited approach. That said, considering that Code-First is the recommended approach for Entity Framework Core, especially for new applications and/or whenever the database doesn't exist yet, we have little to no doubt that adopting it will be our best choice.

 Truth be told, the Database-First approach has become less and less popular in recent years, and the framework support for this technique dropped as well: as a matter of fact, such an approach is rarely used nowadays, unless there's an already-existing database structure that can't be easily updated or needs to be preserved the way it already is because other apps and/or services are already accessing it.

Now that we've made our choice, we'll need to create some entities and find a suitable DBMS to store our data: this is precisely what we're going to do in the following sections.

Creating the entities

Now that we have a data source, we can leverage one of the major advantages of the *Code-First* approach we talked about earlier and start writing our **entity** classes early on, without worrying too much about what database engine we'll eventually use.

Truth be told, we already know something about what we'll eventually use. We won't be adopting a NoSQL solution as they aren't officially supported by Entity Framework Core yet; we also don't want to commit ourselves to purchasing expensive license plans, so the commercial editions of Oracle and SQL Server are probably out of the picture as well.

This leaves us with relatively few choices: SQL Server Developer (or Express) edition, MySQL/MariaDB, the community edition of Oracle (known as Oracle XE), or other less well-known solutions such as PostgreSQL. Furthermore, we are still not 100% sure about installing a local DBMS instance on our development machine (and/or on our production server) or relying on a cloud-hosted solution such as Azure.

That being said, adopting Code-First will give us the chance to postpone the call until our data model is ready.

However, to create the entity classes, we need to know what kind of data they are going to contain and how to structure it: that strongly depends on the data source and the database tables that we eventually want to create using Code-First.

In the following sections, we're going to learn how we can deal with these tasks.

Defining the entities

In Entity Framework Core, as well as in most ORM frameworks, an **entity** is a class that maps to a given database table. The main purpose of entities is to make us able to work with data in an object-oriented fashion while using strongly typed properties to access table columns (and data relations) for each row. We're going to use entities to fetch data from the database and serialize them to JSON for the *front-end*. We will also do the opposite, that is, deserializing them back whenever the *front-end* issues POST or PUT requests that will require the back-end to perform some permanent changes to the database, such as adding new rows or updating existing ones.

If we try to enlarge our focus and look at the general picture, we will be able to see how the entities play a central role among the whole bi-directional data flow between the DBMS, the *back-end*, and the *front-end* parts of our web application.

To understand such a concept, let's take a look at the following diagram:

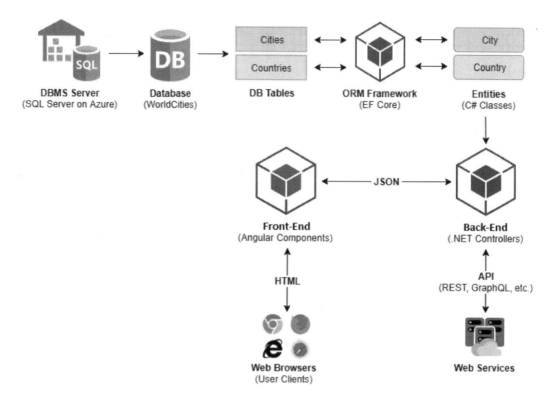

Figure 5.10: The DBMS data lifecycle

As we can clearly see, the main purpose of **Entity Framework Core** is to map the database tables to entity classes: that's precisely what we need to do now.

Unzip the world cities compressed file we downloaded a while ago and open the `worldcities.xlsx` file: if you don't have MS Excel, you can import it on Google Drive using Google Sheets, as shown at the following URL: `http://bit.ly/worldcities-xlsx`.

 Right after importing it, I also took the chance to make some small readability improvements to that file: bolding column names, resizing the columns, changing the background color and freezing on the first row, and so on.

If we open the preceding URL, we will see what the imported spreadsheet looks like:

	A	B	C	D	E	F	G	H	I	J	K
1	city	city_ascii	lat	lng	country	iso2	iso3	admin_name	capital	population	id
2	Malishevë	Malisheve	42.4822	20.7458	Kosovo	XK	XKS	Malishevë	admin		1901597212
3	Prizren	Prizren	42.2139	20.7397	Kosovo	XK	XKS	Prizren	admin		1901360309
4	Zubin Potok	Zubin Potok	42.9144	20.6897	Kosovo	XK	XKS	Zubin Potok	admin		1901608808
5	Kamenicë	Kamenice	42.5781	21.5803	Kosovo	XK	XKS	Kamenicë	admin		1901851592
6	Viti	Viti	42.3214	21.3583	Kosovo	XK	XKS	Viti	admin		1901328795
7	Shtërpcë	Shterpce	42.2394	21.0272	Kosovo	XK	XKS	Shtërpcë	admin		1901828239
8	Shtime	Shtime	42.4331	21.0397	Kosovo	XK	XKS	Shtime	admin		1901598505
9	Vushtrri	Vushtrri	42.8231	20.9675	Kosovo	XK	XKS	Vushtrri	admin		1901107642
10	Dragash	Dragash	42.0265	20.6533	Kosovo	XK	XKS	Dragash	admin		1901112530
11	Podujevë	Podujeve	42.9111	21.1899	Kosovo	XK	XKS	Podujevë	admin		1901550082
12	Fushë Kosovë	Fushe Kosove	42.6639	21.0961	Kosovo	XK	XKS	Fushë Kosovë	admin		1901134407
13	Kaçanik	Kacanik	42.2319	21.2594	Kosovo	XK	XKS	Kaçanik	admin		1901200321
14	Klinë	Kline	42.6217	20.5778	Kosovo	XK	XKS	Klinë	admin		1901230162
15	Leposaviq	Leposaviq	43.1039	20.8028	Kosovo	XK	XKS	Leposaviq	admin		1901974597
16	Pejë	Peje	42.66	20.2922	Kosovo	XK	XKS	Pejë	admin		1901339694
17	Rahovec	Rahovec	42.3994	20.6547	Kosovo	XK	XKS	Rahovec	admin		1901336358
18	Gjilan	Gjilan	42.4689	21.4633	Kosovo	XK	XKS	Gjilan	admin		1901235642
19	Lipjan	Lipjan	42.5217	21.1258	Kosovo	XK	XKS	Lipjan	admin		1901682048
20	Obiliq	Obiliq	42.6869	21.0703	Kosovo	XK	XKS	Obiliq	admin		1901102771
21	Gjakovë	Gjakove	42.3803	20.4308	Kosovo	XK	XKS	Gjakovë	admin		1901089874
22	Pristina	Pristina	42.6666	21.1724	Kosovo	XK	XKS	Prishtinë	primary		1901760068

Figure 5.11: Inspecting the worldcities.xlsx file

By looking at the spreadsheet headers, we can infer at least two database tables we're going to need:

- **Cities**: For columns *A*, *B*, *C*, and *D* (and arguably *K*, if we want to keep those unique IDs)
- **Countries**: For columns *E*, *F*, and *G*

This seems to be the most convenient choice in terms of common sense. Alternatively, we could put everything into a single `Cities` table, but we're going to have a lot of redundant content, which is something we would arguably want to avoid.

If we're going to deal with two database tables, this means that we need two entities to map them on and to create them in the first place, since we plan to adopt the Code-First approach.

The City entity

Let's start with the `City` entity.

From the project's **Solution Explorer**, do the following:

1. Create a new `/Data/` folder at the root level of the `WorldCitiesAPI` project; this will be where all of our Entity Framework-related classes will reside.

2. Create a `/Data/Models/` folder.

3. Add a new **ASP.NET | Code | Class** file, name it `City.cs`, and replace the sample code with the following:

```
using System.ComponentModel.DataAnnotations;
using System.ComponentModel.DataAnnotations.Schema;


namespace WorldCitiesAPI.Data.Models
{
```

```
public class City
{
    #region Properties
    /// <summary>
    /// The unique id and primary key for this City
    /// </summary>
    [Key]
    [Required]
    public int Id { get; set; }

    /// <summary>
    /// City name (in UTF8 format)
    /// </summary>
    public string Name { get; set; } = null!;

    /// <summary>
    /// City Latitude
    /// </summary>
    [Column(TypeName = "decimal(7,4)")]
    public decimal Lat { get; set; }

    /// <summary>
    /// City Longitude
    /// </summary>
    [Column(TypeName = "decimal(7,4)")]
    public decimal Lon { get; set; }

    /// <summary>
    /// Country Id (foreign key)
    /// </summary>
    public int CountryId { get; set; }
    #endregion
}
```

As we can see, we added a dedicated property for each of the spreadsheet columns we identified early on; we also included a CountryId property, which we're going to use to map the *foreign key* for the Country related to the city (more on that later on). We also tried to improve the overall readability of the entity class source code by providing each property with some useful comments that will definitely help us to remember what they are meant for.

Last but not least, it's worth noting that we took the chance to decorate our entity class using some **Data Annotations** attributes as they are the most convenient way to override the default Code-First conventions. More specifically, we used the following annotations:

- [Required]: This defines the property as a *required* (non-nullable) field.
- [Key]: This means that the property hosts the *primary key* of the database table.
- [Column(TypeName="decimal(7,4)"]: This means that the property will require a DB column of the specified type and precision. If we don't provide this information, Entity Framework won't know which precision to set for the database table columns it will create for those properties and will fall back to its default values. This fallback could result in a loss of precision if our actual data has a greater number of decimals.

Additional Data Annotations attributes will be added later on.

Those of you who have some experience with Entity Framework (and relational databases) will most likely understand what those Data Annotations are there for: they are a convenient way to instruct Entity Framework on how to properly build our database when using the Code-First approach. There's nothing complex here; we're just telling Entity Framework that the database columns that were created to host these properties should be set as required and that the primary key should be bound in a one-to-many relationship to other *foreign* columns in different tables.

In order to use the Data Annotations, we have to add a reference to one or both of the following namespaces, depending on the attributes we're going to use:

```
System.ComponentModel.DataAnnotations
System.ComponentModel.DataAnnotations.Schema
```

If we take a look at the preceding code, we will see that both of these namespaces have been referenced with a using statement for convenience, even if the attributes we've used so far ([Key] and [Required]) only require the first one.

> We'll definitely talk more about Data Annotations in this chapter later on. If you want to find out more about Data Annotations in Entity Framework Core, we strongly suggest reading the official documentation, which can be found at the following URL: https://docs.microsoft.com/en-us/ef/core/modeling/.

The Country entity

The next entity will be the one for identifying the countries, which will have a one-to-many relationship with Cities.

> This is hardly a surprise: we're definitely going to expect a single Country for each City and multiple Cities for each given Country: this is what one-to-many relationships are for.

Right-click on the /Data/Models/ folder, add a Country.cs class file, and fill it with the following code:

```csharp
using System.ComponentModel.DataAnnotations;
using System.ComponentModel.DataAnnotations.Schema;

namespace WorldCitiesAPI.Data.Models
{
    public class Country
    {
        #region Properties
        /// <summary>
        /// The unique id and primary key for this Country
        /// </summary>
        [Key]
        [Required]
        public int Id { get; set; }

        /// <summary>
        /// Country name (in UTF8 format)
        /// </summary>
        public string Name { get; set; } = null!;

        /// <summary>
        /// Country code (in ISO 3166-1 ALPHA-2 format)
        /// </summary>
        public string ISO2 { get; set; } = null!;

        /// <summary>
        /// Country code (in ISO 3166-1 ALPHA-3 format)
        /// </summary>
        public string ISO3 { get; set; } = null!;
        #endregion
    }
}
```

Again, there's a property for each spreadsheet column with the relevant Data Annotations and comments.

ISO 3166 is a standard that was published by the **International Organization for Standardization (ISO)** that's used to define unique codes for the names of countries, dependent territories, provinces, and states. For additional information, check out the following URLs:

- `https://en.wikipedia.org/wiki/ISO_3166`
- `https://www.iso.org/iso-3166-country-codes.html`

The part that describes the country codes is the first one (ISO 3166-1), which defines three possible formats: **ISO 3166-1 alpha-2** (two-letter country codes), **ISO 3166-1 alpha-3** (three-letter country codes), and **ISO 3166-1 numeric** (three-digit country codes). For additional information about the ISO 3166-1 ALPHA-2 and ISO 3166-1 ALPHA-3 formats, which are the ones that are used in our data source and therefore in this book, check out the following URLs:

- `https://en.wikipedia.org/wiki/ISO_3166-1_alpha-2`
- `https://en.wikipedia.org/wiki/ISO_3166-1_alpha-3`

Should we (still) use #region blocks?

If we look at the code samples of the two entity classes we've just added, we can see that we've used some #region directives: let's spend a minute talking about them.

As most C# developers already know, regions are preprocessor directives that let the developer specify a block of code that can be expanded or collapsed when using the outlining feature of the code editor.

For additional info about C# regions and common usage samples, read this guide:

`https://docs.microsoft.com/en-us/dotnet/csharp/language-reference/preprocessor-directives/preprocessor-region`

Regions were introduced with the first versions of C# and were praised during the language's early years because they were seen as a viable technique to improve code readability, especially in long and complex classes. However, they can also lure the developer into adopting a number of bad practices, such as shoving "unoptimized" or repeating code to hide it from view instead of refactoring it; dividing a complex method (or class) into multiple "tasks" instead of splitting it into multiple methods (or classes); embedding redundant code instead of making it less redundant; and so on.

Since the potential disadvantages of regions vastly exceed their supposed advantages, regions are now considered a bad practice by most C# developers and their usage has declined.

This opinion has been enforced by **StyleCop**, a great open-source static code analysis tool from Microsoft that checks C# code for conformance to the recommended coding styles and design guidelines, which summarizes its judgment regarding regions in its SA1124 rule:

> *TYPE: SA1124DoNotUseRegions*
>
> *CAUSE: The C# code contains a region.*
>
> *DESCRIPTION: A violation of this rule occurs whenever a region is placed anywhere within the code. In many editors, including Visual Studio, the region will appear collapsed by default, hiding the code within the region. It is generally a bad practice to hide code, as this can lead to bad decisions as the code is maintained over time.*
>
> *HOW TO FIX: To fix a violation of this rule, remove the region from the code.*

This kind of settles it: we should never use regions, period.

Those who want to know more about the `#regions` debate within the C# developer community and the reasons why they are discouraged nowadays might enjoy reading this Stack Overflow thread, which pretty much summarizes it:

`https://softwareengineering.stackexchange.com/questions/53086/are-regions-an-antipattern-or-code-smell`

Again, the verdict was (almost) unanimous: region blocks = code smell, and the best thing you can do to avoid such smell is open a window—and throw regions away.

Although I generally agree with such an "anti-region" approach, I still think that using #regions to group together fields, properties, and so on can be useful in some edge-case scenarios, such as code samples and tutorials (like the classes we're creating and reviewing in this book), because it allows us to distinguish between different parts of code: for example, we're going to use them to help the reader tell apart *standard properties* versus *navigation properties* within an entity type.

This is why in this book we're still using them here and there, even if we're fully aware that good, StyleCop-compliant code won't need them—not even to group together fields, properties, private methods, constructors, and so on: at the same time, I also recommend not using them (or limiting their usage to a minimum amount) in your actual code.

Defining relationships

Now that we have built our main `City` and `Country` entity skeleton, we need to enforce the relationship we know exists between them. We want to be able to do stuff such as retrieving a `Country` and then browsing all of its related `Cities`, possibly in a strongly typed fashion.

To do this, we have to add a couple of new entity-related properties, one for each entity class. More specifically, we will be adding the following:

- A Country property in our City entity class, which will contain a single country related to that city (the *parent*)
- A Cities property in our Country entity class, which will contain a collection of the cities related to that country (the *children*)

If we take a deeper look and try to visualize the relationship between those entities, we will be able to see how the former property identifies the *parent* (from each child's perspective), while the latter will contain the *children* (from the parent's perspective): such a pattern is precisely what we can expect for a *one-to-many relationship* like the one we're dealing with.

In the following sections, we'll learn how we can implement these two *navigation* properties.

Adding the Country property to the City entity class

Add the following code lines near the end of the file, near the end of the *Properties* region (new lines are highlighted):

```
using System.ComponentModel.DataAnnotations.Schema;

// ...existing code...

/// <summary>
/// Country Id (foreign key)
/// </summary>
[ForeignKey(nameof(Country))]
public int CountryId { get; set; }
#endregion

#region Navigation Properties
/// <summary>
/// The country related to this city.
/// </summary>
public Country? Country { get; set; } = null!;
#endregion

// ...existing code...
```

As we can see, other than adding the new Country property, we also decorated the already-existing CountryId property with a new [ForeignKey(nameof(Country))] data annotation. Thanks to that annotation, Entity Framework will know that such a property will host a primary key of a foreign table and that the Country navigation property will be used to host the *parent* entity.

 It's worth noting that the binding that's declared using that [ForeignKey] data annotation will also be formally enforced by creating a constraint, as long as the database engine supports such a feature.

It's also worth noting that we used `nameof(Country)` instead of a mere `"Country"` literal string: we did that to increase the type safety of our code, thus making it less prone to typing errors.

As we can see by looking at the first line of the preceding source code, in order to use the `[ForeignKey]` data annotation we have to add a reference to the `System.ComponentModel.DataAnnotations.Schema` namespace at the beginning of the class in case we didn't already.

Adding the Cities property to the Country entity class

Let's now switch to the `Country.cs` class: once there, add the following right after the end of the `Properties` region:

```
// ...existing code...
#region Navigation Properties
/// <summary>
/// A collection of all the cities related to this country.
/// </summary>
public ICollection<City>? Cities { get; set; } = null!;
#endregion

// ...existing code...
```

That's it. As we can see, no *foreign key properties* have been defined for this entity since *one-to-many* relationships don't need them from the *parent* side: therefore, there's no need to add a `[ForeignKey]` data annotation and/or its required namespace.

Entity Framework Core loading pattern

Now that we have a `Cities` property in the `Country` entity and a corresponding `[ForeignKey]` data annotation in the `City` entity, you may be wondering how we can use these navigation properties to load the related entities. To put this another way: **how are we going to populate the Cities property within the Country entity whenever we need to?**

Such a question gives us the chance to spend a couple of minutes enumerating the three ORM patterns supported by Entity Framework Core to load these kinds of related data:

- **Eager loading:** The related data is loaded from the database as part of the initial query.
- **Explicit loading:** The related data is explicitly loaded from the database at a later time.
- **Lazy loading:** The related data is transparently loaded from the database when the entity navigation property is accessed for the first time. This is the most complex pattern among the three and might suffer some serious performance impacts when not implemented properly.

It's important to understand that, whenever we want to load an entity's *related data*, we need to activate (or implement) one of these patterns. This means that, in our specific scenario, our `Country` entity's `Cities` property will be set to NULL whenever we fetch one or more countries from the database, **unless we explicitly tell Entity Framework Core to load the cities as well.**

This is a very important aspect to consider when dealing with Web APIs because it will definitely impact how our .NET *back-end* will serve their JSON structured data responses to our *front-end* Angular client.

To understand what we mean, let's take a look at a couple of examples.

The following is a standard Entity Framework Core query that's used to retrieve Country from a given Id with the EF Core default behavior (no loading pattern defined or implemented):

```
var country = await _context.Countries
    .FindAsync(id);


return country; // country.Cities is still set to NULL
```

As we can see, the country variable is returned to the caller with the Cities property set to NULL, simply because we didn't ask for it: for that very reason, if we convert that variable into a JSON object and return it to the client, the JSON object would contain no cities either.

The following is an Entity Framework Core query that retrieves country from a given id using **eager loading**:

```
var country = await _context.Countries
    .Include(c => c.Cities)
    .FindAsync(id);


return country; // country.Cities is (eagerly) loaded
```

Let's try to understand what is happening here:

- The Include() method that was specified at the start of the query tells Entity Framework Core to activate the eager loading data retrieval pattern
- As for the new pattern, the EF query will fetch the country as well as all of the corresponding cities in a single query
- For all of these reasons, the returned country variable will have the Cities property filled with all the cities related to country (that is, the CountryId value will be equal to that *country's* id value)

For the sake of simplicity, we're only going to use *eager loading* through this book, using the Include() method whenever we need it; for additional information regarding *lazy loading* and *explicit loading*, we strongly suggest that you take a look at the following URL: https://docs.microsoft.com/en-US/ef/core/querying/related-data.

Defining the database table names

The SQL script generated by EF Core using the Code-First approach, as per its default settings, will create a database table for each entity using the entity's class name: this basically means that we're going to have a City table containing all the cities and a Country table for the countries. Although there's nothing wrong with these names, we might as well change this default setting to create the tables in plural form for consistency reasons: Cities for the cities, Countries for the countries.

To "force" a database table name of our choice for each individual entity, we can add the [Table] data annotation attribute to the entity class in the following way.

For the City entity (the /Data/Models/City.cs file):

```
[Table("Cities")]
public class City
```

For the Country entity (the /Data/Models/Country.cs file):

```
[Table("Countries")]
public class Country
```

Before going further, let's perform this simple update to our classes in order to demonstrate how easy it is to achieve additional control over the autogenerated database.

With this, we're done with the entities, at least for the time being. Now, we just need to get ourselves a DBMS so that we can actually create our database.

Defining indexes

Since we're going to deal with a dataset featuring tens of thousands of records, it could also be wise to add some indexes to our entities. Such a task can be easily done using the [Index] data annotation attribute in the following way.

For the City entity (the /Data/Models/City.cs file):

```
[Table("Cities")]
[Index(nameof(Name))]
[Index(nameof(Lat))]
[Index(nameof(Lon))]
public class City
```

For the Country entity (the /Data/Models/Country.cs file):

```
[Table("Countries")]
[Index(nameof(Name))]
[Index(nameof(ISO2))]
[Index(nameof(ISO3))]
public class Country
```

To use the [Index] attribute, we'll also need to add the following reference in both files:

```
using Microsoft.EntityFrameworkCore;
```

When we generate the database using EF Core's *Code-First* approach, these property attributes will be used to create SQL indexes for the corresponding table columns—which will greatly improve the performance of any lookup query.

Getting a SQL Server instance

Let's close this gap once and for all and provide ourselves with a SQL Server instance. As we already mentioned, there are two major routes we can take:

- **Install a local SQL Server instance** (Express or Developer edition) on our development machine
- **Set up a SQL database (and/or server) on Azure** using one of the several options available on that platform

The former option embodies the classic, cloudless approach that software and web developers have been using since the dawn of time: a local instance is easy to pull off and will provide everything we're going to need in development and production environments... as long as we don't care about data redundancy, heavy infrastructure load and possible performance impacts (in the case of high-traffic websites), scaling, and other bottlenecks due to the fact that our server is a single physical entity.

In Azure, things work in a different way: putting our DBMS there gives us the chance to have our SQL Server workloads running as either a hosted infrastructure (**Infrastructure as a Service**, also known as **IaaS**) or a hosted service (**Platform as a Service**, also known as **PaaS**): the first option is great if we want to handle the database maintenance tasks by ourselves, such as applying patches and taking backups; the second option is preferable if we want to delegate these operations to Azure. However, regardless of the path we choose, we're going to have a scalable database service with full redundancy and *no single-point-of-failure* guarantees, plus a lot of other performance and data security benefits. The downsides, as we can easily guess, are as follows: the additional cost and the fact that we're going to have our data located elsewhere, which can be a major issue in terms of privacy and data protection in certain scenarios.

In the following section, we'll quickly summarize how to pull off both of these approaches so that we can make the most convenient choice.

Installing SQL Server 2019

If we want to avoid the cloud and stick to an "old-school" approach, we can choose to install a **SQL Server Express** (or Developer) on-premises instance on our development (and later, on our production) machine.

To do that, perform the following steps:

1. **Download the SQL Server 2019 on-premises installation package** (we're going to use the Windows build here, but the Linux installer is also available) from the following URL: `https://www.microsoft.com/en-us/sql-server/sql-server-downloads`.

2. **Double-click on the executable file** to start the installation process. When prompted for the installation type, select the **BASIC** option (unless we need to configure some advanced options to accommodate specific needs, provided that we know what we're doing).

The installation package will then start downloading the required files. When it's done, we'll just have to click **New SQL Server stand-alone installation** (the first available option starting from the top, as shown in the following screenshot) to start the actual installation process:

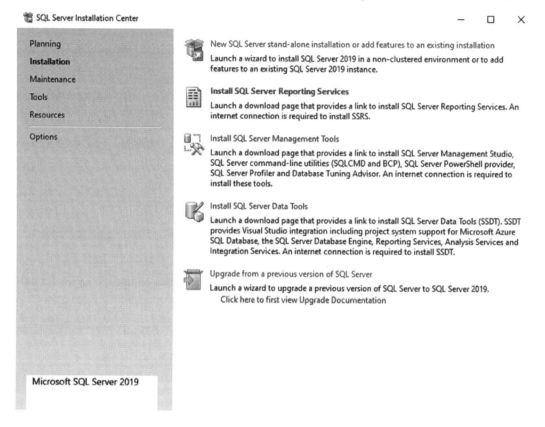

Figure 5.12: Installing SQL Server 2019

Accept the license terms and go ahead, keeping all of the default options and performing the required operations (such as opening the **Windows Firewall**) when asked to.

> If we want to keep our disk space consumption to a minimum amount, we can safely remove the SQL Replication and Machine Learning services from the **Feature Selection** section and save roughly 500 MB.

Set the **Instance Name** to SQLExpress and the **Instance ID** to SQLEXPRESS. Remember that choice: we're going to need it when we have to write down our connection string.

When we're asked to choose an **Authentication Mode** (as we can see in the following screenshot), choose one of the following options:

- **Windows authentication mode**, if we want to be able to have unrestricted access to the database engine only from the local machine (using our Windows credentials)

- **Mixed Mode,** to enable the SQL Server system administrator (the sa user) and set a password for it

These two options can be seen in the following screenshot:

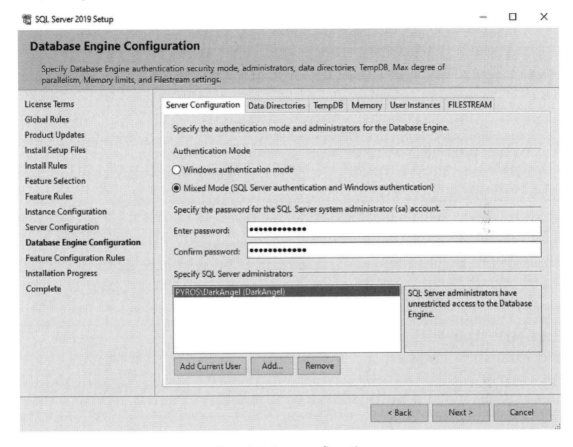

Figure 5.13: Server configuration

The former option is great for security, while the latter is much more versatile—especially if we're going to administer the SQL server remotely using the SQL Server built-in administrative interface, which is the tool we're going to use to create our database.

Those who need a more comprehensive guide to perform the SQL Server local instance installation can take a look at the following tutorials:

- **Installing SQL Server on Windows:** https://docs.microsoft.com/en-US/sql/database-engine/install-windows/installation-for-sql-server
- **Installing SQL Server on Linux:** https://docs.microsoft.com/en-US/sql/linux/sql-server-linux-setup

After the SQL Server installation is complete, we can immediately connect to the newly installed instance using one of the following free-to-use management tools:

- **SQL Server Management Studio**, also known as *SSMS*
- **Azure Data Studio**, also known as *ADS*

Both are software applications that allow connecting to a SQL Server database and managing its contents (tables, users, agents, and so on), as well as performing queries and scripts. SSMS is only available for Windows and has a lot of features that can be performed using the GUI, while ADS embraces a portable, multiplatform, and lightweight design and provides a rather minimal interface that just allows performing SQL queries (at least for now).

For the purpose of this book we're going to use *SQL Server Management Studio*, since it allows a more graceful learning curve for SQL novices; however, *Azure Data Studio* might be a great alternative for seasoned SQL developers who prefer to avoid the GUI-based approach and perform everything through SQL queries and scripts.

Installing the DB Management tool(s)

SQL Server Management Studio can be installed through the SQL Server installation wizard's additional components (the *SQL Server Management tools* section) or downloaded as a standalone package from the following URL:

```
https://docs.microsoft.com/en-us/sql/ssms/download-sql-server-management-studio-ssms
```

Azure Data Studio can be downloaded from the following URL:

```
https://docs.microsoft.com/en-us/sql/azure-data-studio/download-azure-data-studio
```

Before using these tools to connect to our database, we're going to spend some valuable time talking about the Azure path.

Creating a SQL Database on Azure

If you want to get over the DBMS local instances and embrace the *cloudful* **Azure** route, our to-do list entirely depends on which of the main approaches provided by the Azure platform we're going to choose from. The three main options available to end users are, from the least to most expensive, a SQL database, a SQL Managed Instance, and a SQL virtual machine. We'll go through each in turn.

SQL Database

This is a fully managed SQL Database engine based on SQL Server Enterprise edition. This option allows us to set up and manage one or more single relational databases hosted in the Azure cloud with a PaaS usage and billing model: more specifically, we can define it as a **Database-as-a-Service (DBaaS)** approach. This option provides built-in high availability, intelligence, and management, which means it's great for those who want a versatile solution without the hassle of having to configure, manage, and pay for a whole server host.

SQL Managed Instance

This is a dedicated SQL Managed Instance on Azure. It is a scalable database service that provides near 100% compatibility with a standard SQL Server instance and features an IaaS usage and billing model. This option provides all of the same PaaS benefits as the previous one (SQL Database) but adds some additional features and capabilities, such as linked servers, service brokers, database mail, full Azure Virtual Network support, multiple databases with shared resources, and so on.

SQL virtual machine

This is a fully managed SQL Server consisting of a Windows or Linux virtual machine with a SQL Server instance installed on top of it. This approach, which also adopts an IaaS usage and billing model, offers full administrative control over the whole SQL Server instance and the underlying OS, hence being the most complex and customizable one. The most significant difference from the other two options (SQL Database and SQL Managed Instance) is that SQL Server virtual machines also allow full control over the database engine: we can choose when to start maintenance/patching, change the recovery model, pause/start the service, and so on.

Making a choice

All of these options are good and, although very different in terms of overall costs, can be activated free of charge: **SQL Database** is arguably the cheapest one because it's free for 12 months, thanks to the trial subscription plan offered by Azure, as long as we keep its size under 250 GB; both **SQL Managed Instance** and **SQL Virtual Machine** are rather expensive, since they both provide a virtualized IaaS, but they can be activated for free (at least for a few weeks) with the €200 provided by that same Azure trial subscription plan.

> For more information regarding the pros and cons of the Azure options described in the previous sections, we strongly suggest that you read the following guide: https://docs.microsoft.com/en-US/azure/sql-database/sql-database-paas-vs-sql-server-iaas.

In the following sections, we're going to learn how to set up a SQL database since it is the less expensive approach in the long term: the only downside is that we'll have to keep its size under 250 GB... which is definitely not an issue, considering that our world cities data source file is less than 1 GB in size.

If you want to opt for an Azure SQL Managed Instance (option #2), here's a great guide explaining how to do that: https://docs.microsoft.com/en-us/azure/sql-database/sql-database-managed-instance-get-started.

If you wish to set up SQL Server installed on a virtual machine (option #3), here's a tutorial covering that topic: https://docs.microsoft.com/en-US/azure/virtual-machines/windows/sql/quickstart-sql-vm-create-portal.

Setting up a SQL Database

Let's start by visiting the following URL: https://azure.microsoft.com/en-us/free/services/sql-database/.

This will bring us to the following web page, which allows us to create an Azure SQL database instance:

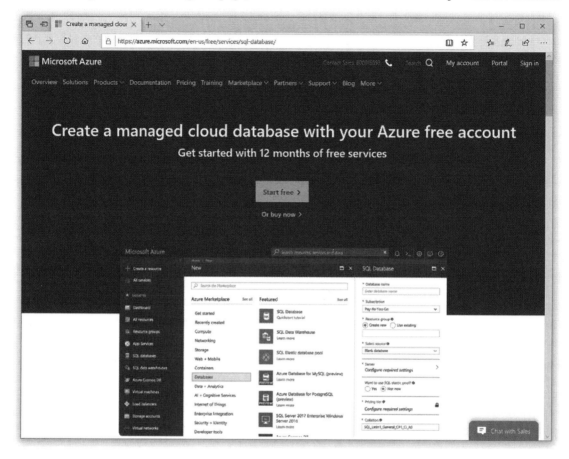

Figure 5.14: Creating a new Azure free account

Click the **Start free** button and create a new account.

 If you already have a valid MS account, you can definitely use it; however, you should only do that if you're sure that you want to use the free Azure trial on it: if that's not the case, consider creating a new one.

After a brief registration form (and/or login phase), we'll be redirected to the Azure portal.

It goes without saying that if the account we've logged in with has already used up its free period or has an active paid subscription plan, we'll be gracefully bounced back:

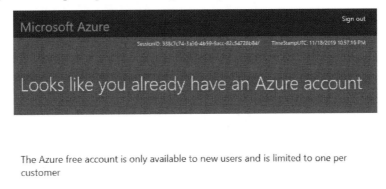

Figure 5.15: View for users who aren't new

Eventually, after we've sorted everything out, we should be able to access the Azure portal (`https://portal.azure.com`) in all of its glory:

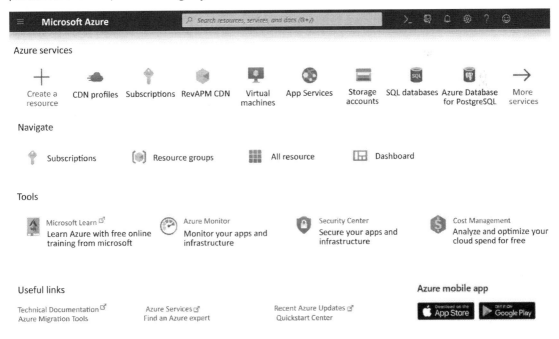

Figure 5.16: The Azure portal

Once there, do the following:

1. Click the **Create a resource** button to access the **Azure Marketplace**.
2. Search for an entry called **Azure SQL**.
3. Click **Create** to access the selection page shown in the following screenshot:

 IMPORTANT: Be careful that you don't pick the **SQL Managed Instances** entry instead, which is the one for creating the SQL Server virtual machine—this is option #2 that we talked about earlier.

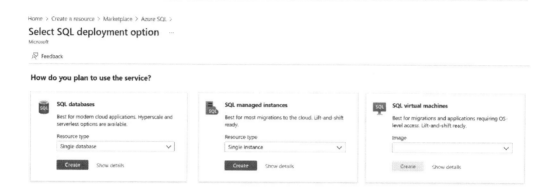

Figure 5.17: Selecting an SQL deployment option

From the preceding selection screen, do the following:

1. Select the first option (**SQL databases**)
2. Set the **Resource type** drop-down list to **Single database**
3. Click the **Create** button to start the **main setup** wizard

During this process, we'll also be asked to create our very first **Azure tenant** (unless we already have one). This is a virtual organization that owns and manages a specific set of Microsoft cloud services. Tenants are identified by unique URLs in the following format: `<TenantName>.onmicrosoft.com`. Just give it a suitable name and go ahead.

Configuring the instance

As soon as we click the **Create** button, we'll be asked to configure our SQL Database with a wizard-like interface split into the following tabs:

*   **Basics:** Subscription type, instance name, admin username and password, and so on
*   **Networking:** Network connectivity method and firewall rules
*   **Security:** Security settings
*   **Additional settings:** Collation and time zone
*   **Tags:** A set of name/value pairs that can be applied to logically organize Azure resources into functional categories or groups sharing a common scope (such as Production and Test)
*   **Review + create:** Review and confirm all of the preceding settings

In the **Basics** tab, we have to insert the database details, such as the database name—which will also be the prefix of the database URL, in the `<NAME>.database.windows.net` format—and the server we would like to use. If this is our first time coming here, we're not going to have any available servers. Due to this, we'll have to create our first one by clicking on the **Create new** link and filling in the pop-over form that will slide to the rightmost side of the screen. Be sure to set a non-trivial **Server admin login** (we will use `WorldCitiesAdmin` in our screenshots) and a complex **Password**.

> It's important to understand that the *Server admin login* is not the account that will be used by our web application to access the *WorldCities* database: we'll create a dedicated user (with fewer rights) for that. The *Server admin login* is the global administrator account of the whole Azure SQL Database service instance: we will mostly use it to perform high-level administrative tasks, such as creating the *WorldCities* database, adding the web application's dedicated user, and so on.

The following screenshot shows an example of how to configure this part of the wizard:

Home > Select SQL deployment option >

Create SQL Database   ···
Microsoft

Basics   Networking   Security   Additional settings   Tags   Review + create

Create a SQL database with your preferred configurations. Complete the Basics tab then go to Review + Create to provision with smart defaults, or visit each tab to customize. Learn more ☐

Project details

Select the subscription to manage deployed resources and costs. Use resource groups like folders to organize and manage all your resources.

Subscription * ⓘ	Microsoft MVP ⌄
Resource group * ⓘ	PacktPub ⌄
	Create new

Database details

Enter required settings for this database, including picking a logical server and configuring the compute and storage resources

Database name *	WorldCities ✓
Server * ⓘ	(new) worldcities-2021 (West Europe) ⌄
	Create new
Want to use SQL elastic pool? * ⓘ	◯ Yes ⦿ No

Figure 5.18: Configuring our SQL database

The last two options in the **Basics** tab will ask us for the **Compute + storage** type and **Backup storage redundancy**: for this specific project, we can definitely choose the minimum possible tier—a locally redundant **Basic** storage type with 2 GB maximum space (see the following screenshot):

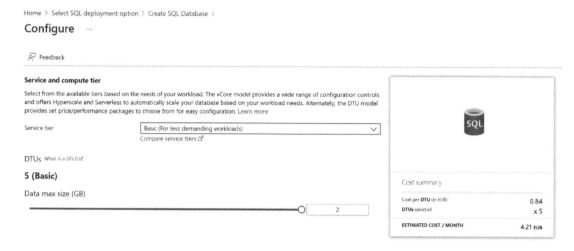

Figure 5.19: Choosing the compute and storage type

However, if we're feeling bold, we can go for a **Standard** type with 250 GB storage instead since it would still be free for 12 months.

In the **Networking** tab, be sure to choose a **Public endpoint** to enable external access from the internet so that we'll be able to connect to our database from all of our environments. We should also set both the firewall rules to **Yes** to *allow Azure services and resources to access the server* and *add our current IP address* to the allowed IPs whitelist.

> Wait a minute: isn't that a major security issue? What if our databases contain personal or sensitive data?
>
> As a matter of fact, it is: allowing public access from the internet is something we should always avoid unless we're playing with open data for testing, demonstrative, or tutorial purposes... which is precisely what we're doing right now.

The **Additional settings** and **Tags** tabs are OK with their default settings: we should only change them if we need to alter some options (such as the collation and the time zone that is most suitable for our language and country) or to activate specific stuff such as the *advanced data security*—which is completely unnecessary for our current needs.

In the **Review + create** tab, we'll have our last chance to review and change our settings (as shown in the following screenshot):

Basics

Subscription	Microsoft MVP
Resource group	PacktPub
Region	West Europe
Database name	WorldCities
Server	(new) worldcities-2021
Authentication method	SQL authentication
Server admin login	WorldCitiesAdmin
Compute + storage	Basic: 2 GB storage
Backup storage redundancy	Locally-redundant backup storage

Networking

Allow Azure services and resources to access this server	Yes
Private endpoint	None
Minimum TLS version	1.2
Connection Policy	Default

Security

Identity (preview)	Not enabled
Transparent data encryption	Service-managed key selected
Advanced data security	Not now
Sql Ledger(Database)	Disabled
Digest Storage	Disabled

Figure 5.20: Reviewing our chosen settings

If we're not sure about them, we have the chance to go back and change them. When we're 100% sure, we can hit the **Create** button and have our SQL database deployed in a few seconds.

 It's worth noting that we can also download a template for automation in case we want to save these settings to create additional SQL databases in the future.

That's it: now, we can focus on configuring our database.

Configuring the database

Regardless of the path we take—a local instance or Azure—we should be ready to manage our newly created Azure SQL database.

The most practical way to do that is to connect to it using one of the two free SQL Server Management GUIs provided by Microsoft that we talked about early on: **SQL Server Management Studio** and **Azure Data Studio**. If you haven't installed it yet, now is the time to do that.

> We're going to use **SQL Server Management Studio** in the following examples and screenshots, as well as through the rest of the book.

Once the tool is installed, launch it: from the main dashboard, click on the **New Connection** link, then fill out the form with your SQL Database data as shown in the following screenshot:

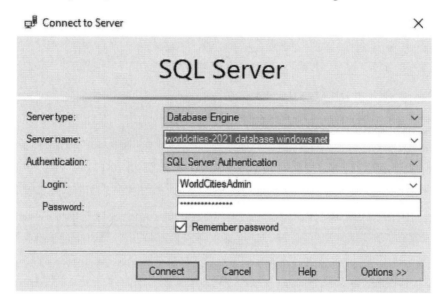

Figure 5.21: Connecting to the SQL Server

More specifically, we need to use the **Server name**, **Login**, and **Password** chosen when we installed our local SQL Server instance or created the SQL database on Azure.

> As we can see by looking at the URL that we wrote in the **Server** field, in the preceding screenshot we're connecting to a typical Azure SQL Database instance: in order to connect to a locally installed SQL Server, we would use `localhost\SQLEXPRESS`, `127.0.0.1\SQLEXPRESS`, or something like that, depending on the instance name that we've chosen during the installation process.

By clicking the **Connect** button, we should be able to log in to our database server. As soon as SSMS connects to the SQL Database server, an **Object Explorer** window will appear, containing a tree view representing the structure of our SQL Server instance. This is the interface we'll use to create our database, as well as the user/password that our application will use to access it.

Creating the WorldCities database

If we took the Azure SQL Database route, we should already be able to see the WorldCities database in the Databases folder of the **Object Explorer** tree to the left:

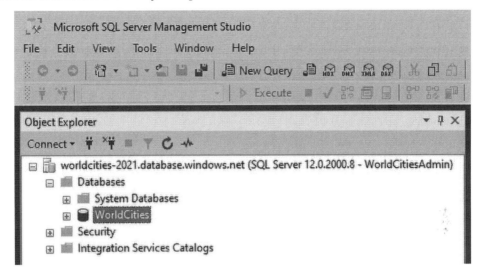

Figure 5.22: Inspecting the WorldCities folder in the Object Explorer

Alternatively, if we installed our local *SQL Server Express* or *Developer* instance, we'll have to manually create it by doing the following:

1. Right-click on the **Databases** folder
2. Choose **Add Database** from the **contextual** menu
3. Type in the **WorldCities** name, then click on **OK** to create it

Once the database has been created, we'll get the chance to expand its tree node by clicking on the plus (+) sign to the left and visually interacting with all its child objects—*tables*, *stored procedures*, *users*, and so on—through the SSMS GUI. It goes without saying that if we do that now, we would find no tables because we haven't created them yet: that's something that Entity Framework Core will do for us later on. However, before doing that, we're going to add a **login** account to make our web application able to connect.

Adding the WorldCities login

The database's security settings can be configured using two different approaches:

- **Using the SSMS GUI**, which is only available when the database is hosted on a local (or remote) SQL Server instance, such as *SQL Server Express* or *Developer*
- **Using raw SQL commands**, which is always available—as well as the only available option if we created our SQL database on MS Azure (or if we're using *Azure Data Studio* instead of SSMS)

Let's start with the first option, which allows us to add and configure login accounts without writing a single line of SQL code.

Using the SSMS GUI

From the SSMS Object Explorer, go back to the top root folder and expand the Security folder, which should be just below it. Once there, do the following:

- Right-click on the Logins subfolder and choose **New Login**
- In the modal window that appears, set the login name to WorldCities
- From the radio button list below the login name, select **SQL Server Authentication** and set a suitable password with decent strength (such as **MyVeryOwn$721**—we're going to use this one for the code samples and screenshots from now on)
- Be sure to disable the **User must change the password at next login** option (which is *checked* by default); otherwise, Entity Framework Core will be unable to perform the login later on
- Set the user's default database to WorldCities
- Review all of the options, then click on **OK** to create the WorldCities account

If we want a simpler password, such as WorldCities or Password, we might have to disable the **enforce password policy** option. However, we strongly advise against doing that: choosing a weak password is never a wise choice, especially if we do that in a production-ready environment. We suggest that you always use a strong password, even in testing and development environments. Just be sure not to forget it, as we're going to need it later on.

Using raw SQL commands

If we're dealing with a SQL database hosted on MS Azure, we're using *Azure Data Studio*, or we prefer to use raw SQL, here's the script that will create the above user:

```
CREATE LOGIN WorldCities
    WITH PASSWORD = 'MyVeryOwn$721'
GO
```

If we want to relax the password policy, we can add the CHECK_POLICY = OFF option to the above query; however, we strongly advise against doing this for the security reasons explained early on.

Mapping the login to the database

The next thing we need to do is properly map this login to the WorldCities database we added earlier.

Here's how to do that using the SSMS GUI:

1. Double-click the WorldCities login name from the Security folder to open the same model we used just a few seconds ago.
2. From the navigation menu to the left, switch to the **User Mapping** tab.
3. Click on the checkbox to the left of the WorldCities database: the **User** cell should be automatically filled with the WorldCities value. If it doesn't, we'll need to manually type WorldCities into it.
4. In the **Database role membership for** box in the bottom-right panel, assign the db_owner membership role.

All of the preceding steps are depicted in the following screenshot:

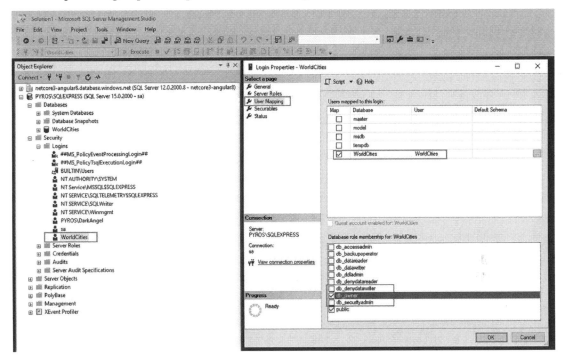

Figure 5.23: Mapping the login to the WorldCities database

Again, if we need (or prefer) to use raw SQL commands, here's the script to use (be sure to switch to the WorldCities database before launching it):

```
CREATE USER WorldCities
    FOR LOGIN WorldCities
    WITH DEFAULT_SCHEMA = dbo
GO
EXEC sp_addrolemember N'db_owner', N'WorldCities'
GO
```

That's it! Now, we can go back to our web application project, add the connection string, and create our tables (and data) using the Entity Framework Code-First approach.

Creating the database using Code-First

Before going further, let's do a quick checklist:

- Are we done with our entities? **Yes**
- Do we have a DBMS and a WorldCities database available? **Yes**
- Have we gone through all of the required steps we need to complete to actually create and fill in the aforementioned database using Code-First? **No**

As a matter of fact, we need to take care of two more things:

- Set up an appropriate **Database Context**
- Enable **Code-First Data Migrations support** within our project

Within the following sections, we're going to fill all of these gaps and eventually fill our WorldCities database.

Setting up the DbContext

To interact with data as objects/entity classes, Entity Framework Core uses the Microsoft. EntityFrameworkCore.DbContext class, also called DbContext or simply Context. This class is in charge of all of the entity objects during runtime, including populating them with data from the database, keeping track of changes, and persisting them to the database during CRUD operations.

We can easily create our very own DbContext class for our project—which we will call ApplicationDbContext—by doing the following:

1. From **Solution Explorer**, right-click on the /Data/ folder we created a while ago and add a new ApplicationDbContext.cs class file
2. Fill it with the following code:

```
using Microsoft.EntityFrameworkCore;
using WorldCitiesAPI.Data.Models;

namespace WorldCitiesAPI.Data
{
    public class ApplicationDbContext : DbContext
    {

        public ApplicationDbContext() : base()
        {
        }

        public ApplicationDbContext(DbContextOptions options)
         : base(options)
        {
        }

        public DbSet<City> Cities => Set<City>();
        public DbSet<Country> Countries => Set<Country>();

    }
}
```

As we can see, we took the chance to add a DbSet<T> property for each of our entities so that we can easily access them later on.

Entity type configuration methods

Since we chose to adopt the Code-First data modeling approach, we need to make sure that our entities are properly configured from within the code, so that the SQL scripts generated by Entity Framework Core will create the database using the names, database types, definitions, and rules that we want.

EF Core provides three available methods for configuring various aspects of your model:

- **Data Annotations**, through attributes applied directly on the entity types
- **Fluent API** (also known as *ModelBuilder API*), via custom rules applied by overriding the OnModelCreating method in DbContext
- **EntityTypeConfiguration classes**, via custom rules applied to separate configuration classes referenced in the DbContext OnModelCreating override method (by all means an alternative take on the **Fluent API** approach)

All of them are viable enough for most scenarios: however, in a real project, it is highly advisable to avoid mixing them and just pick one for the sake of consistency.

Let's briefly review all of them before choosing our pick.

Data Annotations

Data Annotations are dedicated attributes that can be applied to entity classes and properties to override the default Code-First conventions and/or to define new rules. The major advantage of Data Annotations is that they allow the developer to manage the data definition within the class code, which is great for code readability and maintainability.

As a matter of fact, we already used Data Annotations in our existing entity classes when we added the [Key], [Required], and [ForeignKey] attributes to their database-relevant properties. This means that, if we want to switch to another configuration method, we'll need to perform some minor refactoring on our code.

Data Annotations are great for applying simple configuration changes, which often makes them ideal for small projects; however, they don't support the whole set of configuration options made available by EF Core. Whenever we need to gain more control over our entity type settings, we might easily feel the urge to switch to a more powerful method.

Fluent API

In order to use the Fluent API, we need to override the OnModelCreating method in our derived context and use the ModelBuilder API to configure our model.

A great way to understand how we can use the Fluent API might be to see how we can convert our existing Data Annotations into ModelBuilder settings. Here's how we can do that:

```
[...]
```

```
protected override void OnModelCreating(ModelBuilder modelBuilder)
{
    base.OnModelCreating(modelBuilder);

    modelBuilder.Entity<City>().ToTable("Cities");
    modelBuilder.Entity<City>()
        .HasKey(x => x.Id);
    modelBuilder.Entity<City>()
        .Property(x => x.Id).IsRequired();
    modelBuilder.Entity<City>()
        .Property(x => x.Lat).HasColumnType("decimal(7,4)");
    modelBuilder.Entity<City>()
        .Property(x => x.Lon).HasColumnType("decimal(7,4)");

    modelBuilder.Entity<Country>().ToTable("Countries");
    modelBuilder.Entity<Country>()
        .HasKey(x => x.Id);
    modelBuilder.Entity<Country>()
        .Property(x => x.Id).IsRequired();
    modelBuilder.Entity<City>()
        .HasOne(x => x.Country)
        .WithMany(y => y.Cities)
        .HasForeignKey(x => x.CountryId);
}

[...]
```

 The preceding **override** method should be added to the **ApplicationDbContext** class right after the constructors: refer to the source code in the GitHub repository for details.

As we can see, for each data annotation that we've used so far there's a corresponding Fluent API method: ToTable() for [Table], HasKey() for [Key], IsRequired() for [Required], and so on.

The major advantage of the Fluent API is that such a method allows us to specify the entity configuration without modifying our entity classes; furthermore, Fluent API configurations have the highest precedence, meaning that they will override any existing EF Core convention and/or data annotation applied to entity classes and properties.

Their only real downside is that, despite being "fluid," they are quite verbose; in big projects and/or complex entity configuration scenarios, which is also when they really shine, the amount of code they require easily increases a lot as the required settings pile up, thus making the DbContext source code quite hard to read and maintain.

EntityTypeConfiguration classes

EntityTypeConfiguration classes are a pivotal aspect of an advanced coding pattern that aims to overcome the major issue of the Fluent API while retaining all their advantages.

In a nutshell, this technique leverages the ApplyConfigurationsFromAssembly Fluent API method, which allows the definition of external rules within separate configuration files, thus removing the need to stack up all of them within DbContext's OnModelCreating override method, and reduces the required amount of code to a single line.

Again, the best way to understand how this method works is to explain how we could convert our existing data annotation rules into configuration classes.

This time, we would need to create two additional files. The first one would be called /Data/Models/CityEntityTypeConfiguration.cs:

```
using Microsoft.EntityFrameworkCore;
using Microsoft.EntityFrameworkCore.Metadata.Builders;

namespace WorldCitiesAPI.Data.Models
{
    public class CityEntityTypeConfiguration
        : IEntityTypeConfiguration<City>
    {
        public void Configure(EntityTypeBuilder<City> builder)
        {
            builder.ToTable("Cities");
            builder.HasKey(x => x.Id);
            builder.Property(x => x.Id).IsRequired();
            builder
                .HasOne(x => x.Country)
                .WithMany(x => x.Cities)
                .HasForeignKey(x => x.CountryId);
            builder.Property(x => x.Lat).HasColumnType("decimal(7,4)");
            builder.Property(x => x.Lon).HasColumnType("decimal(7,4)");
        }
    }
}
```

And the second one would be called /Data/Models/CountryEntityTypeConfiguration.cs:

```
using Microsoft.EntityFrameworkCore;
using Microsoft.EntityFrameworkCore.Metadata.Builders;

namespace WorldCitiesAPI.Data.Models
{
    public class CountryEntityTypeConfiguration
        : IEntityTypeConfiguration<Country>
    {
        public void Configure(EntityTypeBuilder<Country> builder)
        {
            builder.ToTable("Countries");
            builder.HasKey(x => x.Id);
            builder.Property(x => x.Id).IsRequired();
        }
    }
}
```

Adding these configuration classes to our ApplicationDbContext would be as easy as adding this single line within the OnModelCreating method, which we added early on:

```
protected override void OnModelCreating(ModelBuilder modelBuilder)
{
    base.OnModelCreating(modelBuilder);

    // add the EntityTypeConfiguration classes
    modelBuilder.ApplyConfigurationsFromAssembly(
        typeof(ApplicationDbContext).Assembly
        );
}
```

Not bad, right?

Making a choice

Now that we've explored the three alternative ways to configure our entities offered by EF Core, we need to choose which one we use from now on.

It goes without saying that the EntityTypeConfiguration classes method is easily the most preferred approach for large projects because it gives us the chance to organize our settings in a consistent, structured, and readable way: however, since we'll be dealing with very simple database models that will require a minimal number of configuration settings throughout this book, we'll keep using the data annotation approach.

The basic implementation of the other two methods that we've discussed in this section early on is also available in this chapter's source code in the GitHub repository, so that readers who want to adopt a different approach can still review them. Both the `ApplicationDbContext`'s `OnModelCreating` method and the `EntityTypeConfiguration` classes have been documented with a `<summary>` explaining that this code is a redundant override of the data annotation rules and meant for educational purposes only: such redundant code will be removed in *Chapter 6, Fetching and Displaying Data*, and in the subsequent chapters, which will only feature the Data Annotations.

Database initialization strategies

Creating the database for the first time isn't the only thing we need to worry about; for example, how can we keep track of the changes that will definitely occur for our data model?

In previous, non-core versions of EF (up to 6.x), we could choose one of the database management patterns (known as **database initializers** or **DbInitializers**) offered by the *Code-First* approach, that is, by picking the appropriate database initialization strategy for our specific needs, out of:

- `CreateDatabaseIfNotExists`
- `DropCreateDatabaseIfModelChanges`
- `DropCreateDatabaseAlways`
- `MigrateDatabaseToLatestVersion`

Additionally, should we need to address specific requirements, we can also set up our own custom initializer by extending one of the preceding ones and overriding their core methods.

The major flaw of DbInitializers was them not being immediate and streamlined enough for the average developer. They were viable yet difficult to handle without extensive knowledge of Entity Framework's logic.

In Entity Framework Core, this pattern has been greatly simplified; there are no DbInitializers, and automatic data migrations have also been removed. The database initialization aspect is now entirely handled through PowerShell commands, with the sole exception of a small set of commands that can be placed directly on the `DbContext` implementation constructor to partially automatize the process; they are as follows:

- `Database.EnsureCreated()`
- `Database.EnsureDeleted()`
- `Database.Migrate()`

There's currently no way to create data migrations programmatically; they must be added via PowerShell, as we will see shortly.

Updating the appsettings.json file

From Solution Explorer, open the `appsettings.json` file and add a new `"ConnectionStrings"` JSON key section right below the `"Logging"` one with the following value (new lines are highlighted):

```
{
  "Logging": {
    "LogLevel": {
      "Default": "Warning"
    }
  },
  "AllowedHosts": "*",
  "ConnectionStrings": {
    "DefaultConnection": "Server=localhost\\SQLEXPRESS;
    Database=WorldCities;
    User Id=WorldCities;Password=MyVeryOwn$721;
    Integrated
Security=False;MultipleActiveResultSets=True;TrustServerCertificate=True"
  }
}
```

 Unfortunately, JSON doesn't support LF/CR, so we'll need to put the `DefaultConnection` value on a single line. If you copy and paste the preceding text, ensure that Visual Studio doesn't automatically add additional double quotes and/or escape characters to these lines; otherwise, your connection string won't work.

This is the connection string we'll be referencing in our project's `Program.cs` file later on.

IMPORTANT: As we can see, now our `appsettings.json` file contains our database `User Id` and `Password` in clear text, thus posing a non-trivial security issue. While this file currently resides solely on our development machine, it is possible that sooner or later it will be "accidentally" shared or published elsewhere, for example in a GitHub repository. For that very reason, do not check-in your project until you've read the next paragraph.

Securing the connection string

Being able to securely store the database password and API keys in web applications while maintaining full efficiency in terms of debugging and testing has always been a challenge for all developers.

Back in the ASP.NET pre-Core days, most ASP.NET developers used to store them in the `<connectionStrings>` and/or `<appSettings>` sections of their project's `Web.config` file in the following way:

```
<connectionStrings>
  <add name="DefaultConnection" connectionString="[MY CONNECTION STRING]"/>
</connectionStrings>
```

```
<appSettings>
  <add key="Google_ApiKey" value="[MY API KEY]"/>
  <add key="Facebook_Secret" value="[MY FB SECRET]"/>
</appSettings>
```

This practice is still in use nowadays, with the `Web.config` file being replaced by the `appsettings.json` file.

In terms of pure functionality, this behavior works very well, because when we launch our web applications, they will automatically fetch the required credentials whenever they need them even if we run them in *Debug* mode, just like they would do in a production environment.

This practice has always been very convenient because it also leverages the fact that ASP.NET allows us to define multiple files for different environments. More specifically:

- **The Web.config approach** can rely on multiple configuration files (`Web.Debug.config`, `Web.Release.config`, and so on) that could be easily "merged" during the publishing phase using a highly configurable XSD transformation feature
- **The appsettings.json approach** supports multiple configuration files as well (`appsettings.Development.json`, `appsettings.Production.json`, and so on) that can be used to add or override the default settings for specific runtime environments using a cascade logic

Unfortunately, none of these places are safe or secure: if we get used to putting our valuable credentials in those plain text files, there's a high risk that we'll end up "accidentally" pushing them in a GitHub repository, with all the other developers being able to see and use them. For that very reason, such a habit is widely considered a bad practice and—if we're still using it—we should definitely take the chance to get rid of it and start to handle our valuable secrets in a much better (and safer) way.

The question is: how we can do that without losing the effectiveness provided by the "good old" (and insecure) approach?

Introducing Secrets Storage

Starting with .NET Core 2.x and Visual Studio 2019, Microsoft provided their developers with a new feature that can be used to store any secret (database passwords, API keys, and so on) in a secure and effective way: this feature is called *Secrets Storage* and is well documented in Microsoft's *Safe storage of app secrets in development in ASP.NET Core* official guide, available at the following URL: `https://docs.microsoft.com/en-us/aspnet/core/security/app-secrets`.

In a nutshell, the new feature creates a `secrets.json` file in the development machine's user folder (in a typical Windows environment, the `\Users\UserName\AppData\Roaming\Microsoft\UserSecrets` directory), which can be used to add to or override elements of the standard `appsettings.json` files using the same syntax they already have.

This is good for a number of reasons, including:

- The `secrets.json` file cannot be accessed by remote users, such as those who could get the project from a GitHub repository, because it will be created in a local folder

- The `secrets.json` file cannot be accessed by local users, because it will be created in the developer's very own personal folder (which is inaccessible to other local users)
- The `secrets.json` file will work right out of the box, basically extending the `appsettings.json` file without forcing us to write any secrets there

This feature is a great alternative to the *environment variables* approach, which is another workaround suggested by Microsoft in the preceding guide that I personally don't like as much (at least for development environments) because it is much less flexible and straightforward.

Now that we've chosen our path, let's see how we can implement it.

Adding the secrets.json file

Among the greatest aspects of the *Secrets Storage* feature is the fact that it can be used from within the Visual Studio GUI, which is arguably the best way to do it.

All we need to do is to right-click the project's root folder from Solution Explorer and select the **Manage User Secrets** options, as shown in the following screenshot:

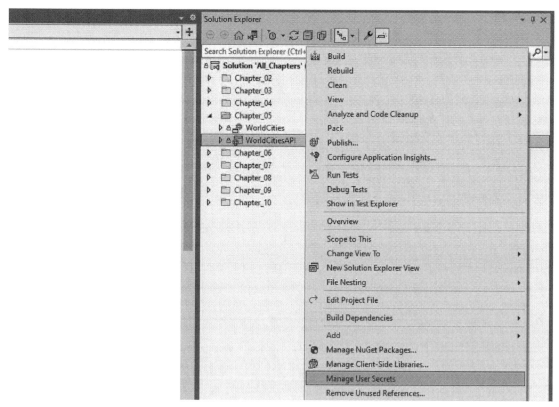

Figure 5.24: Adding the secrets.json file

As soon as we select that option, Visual Studio will add a `UserSecretsId` element within a `PropertyGroup` of the project's `.csproj` file, assigning a random GUID value to it:

```
<PropertyGroup>

    [...]

    <UserSecretsId>9430de8f-8575-4a47-9d22-a98e491af64c</UserSecretsId>
</PropertyGroup>
```

Such a random `UserSecretsId` value is then used by Visual Studio to generate an empty `secrets.json` file in the following folder:

```
\Users\UserName\AppData\Roaming\Microsoft\UserSecrets\
```

Right after that, Visual Studio will open that `secrets.json` file within the GUI in edit mode, so that we can use it to store our secrets.

Sharing the secrets.json file between multiple projects

By default, the inner text of `UserSecretsId` is a randomly generated GUID; however, this value is arbitrary and can be changed: using a (random) unique identifier will prevent different projects from having the same `secrets.json` file; at the same time, choosing the same identifier can be useful if we want to "share" the same secrets between multiple projects.

In this book's GitHub repository, we've taken advantage of this behavior by defining an arbitrary `UserSecretsId` for each different project—one for **HealthCheckAPI**, another one for **WorldCitiesAPI**, and so on—and "recycling" it through all the instances of these projects within the various chapters' folders. For example, here's the `UserSecretsId` value that we've used for all the instances of the current project:

```
<UserSecretsId>WorldCitiesAPI</UserSecretsId>
```

In order to manually set that value, we can use the **Edit Project File** option available from the Visual Studio GUI, which is accessible by right-clicking on Solutions Explorer's project root folder:

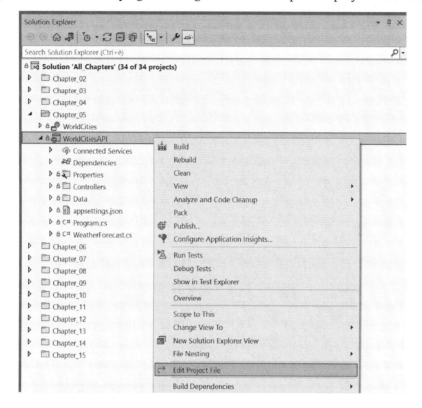

Figure 5.25: Manually setting the UserSecretsId value

Alternatively, we can also edit the WorldCities.csproj file in the project's root folder using a text editor of our choice (including the Windows **Notepad**) and find the relevant line/value to change.

Working with the secrets.json file

Now that we've created our secrets.json file, let's use it: open the appsettings.json file and cut out the whole ConnectionStrings block:

```
{
  "Logging": {
    "LogLevel": {
      "Default": "Warning"
    }
  },
  "AllowedHosts": "*"
}
```

And paste it within the `secrets.json` file in the following way:

```
{
  "ConnectionStrings": {
    "DefaultConnection": "Server=localhost\\SQLEXPRESS;
    Database=WorldCities;
    User Id=WorldCities;Password=MyVeryOwn$721;
    Integrated
Security=False;MultipleActiveResultSets=True;TrustServerCertificate=True"
  }
}
```

 NOTE: The "`DefaultConnection`" value must be specified over a single line, otherwise it won't work.

That's basically it: the JSON keys defined in the `secrets.json` file will be added to those already present in the `appsettings.json` file (replacing them if already present) in a seamless and transparent way, without us having to do anything else.

In the next section, we'll get a good chance to make use of such a handy feature.

Creating the database

Now that we have set up our own `DbContext` and defined a valid connection string pointing to our `WorldCities` database, we can easily add the initial migration and create our database.

Updating Program.cs

The first thing we have to do is add the `EntityFramework` support and our `ApplicationDbContext` implementation to our application startup class. Open the `Program.cs` file and add the following new lines right below the last service (it should be `SwaggerGen`):

```
// ...existing code...
builder.Services.AddSwaggerGen();

// Add ApplicationDbContext and SQL Server support
builder.Services.AddDbContext<ApplicationDbContext>(options =>
    options.UseSqlServer(
        builder.Configuration.GetConnectionString("DefaultConnection")
    )
);

// ...existing code...
```

The new code will also require the following namespace references:

```
using Microsoft.EntityFrameworkCore;
using WorldCitiesAPI.Data;
```

As we can see, we've used the `GetConnectionString("DefaultConnection")` extension method—provided by the `IConfiguration` interface—which can be used to retrieve the `ConnectionStrings:Defa ultConnection` JSON key from the `appsettings.json` file.

However, in our specific scenario, this value will be fetched from the `secrets.json` file, since we moved the whole `ConnectionStrings` block there a short while ago.

> The `GetConnectionString("DefaultConnection")` method is basically a shortcut for the `Configuration["ConnectionStrings:DefaultConnection"]` command: both of them will return the same JSON key value, as long as those keys exist, from the `appsettings.json` and/or `secrets.json` files.

Adding the initial migration

To add the initial migration we can either use the dotnet CLI (from the command line) or the Package Manager Console (from within the Visual Studio GUI).

> Based on reader feedback, if your development environment went through a number of .NET Core SDK subsequent updates, the Package Manager Console might pick the wrong tooling and fail. With that in mind, I suggest trying the CLI first, then switching to the Package Manager Console in case of issues: if both approaches fail, it might be advisable to uninstall some of the old .NET Core SDKs and try again.

Using the dotnet CLI

Open PowerShell Command Prompt and navigate through the project's root folder, which is as follows in our example:

```
C:\ThisBook\Chapter_05\WorldCities\WorldCitiesAPI\
```

Once there, type the following command to globally install the `dotnet-ef` command-line tool:

```
dotnet tool install --global dotnet-ef
```

Wait until the installation is complete. When we receive the *green* message output, type in the following command to add the first migration:

```
dotnet ef migrations add "Initial" -o "Data/Migrations"
```

 The optional -o parameter can be used to change the location where the migration code-generated files will be created; if we don't specify it, a root-level /Migrations/ folder will be created and used by default. Since we put all of the EntityFrameworkCore classes into the /Data/ folder, it's advisable to store migrations there as well.

The preceding command will produce the following output:

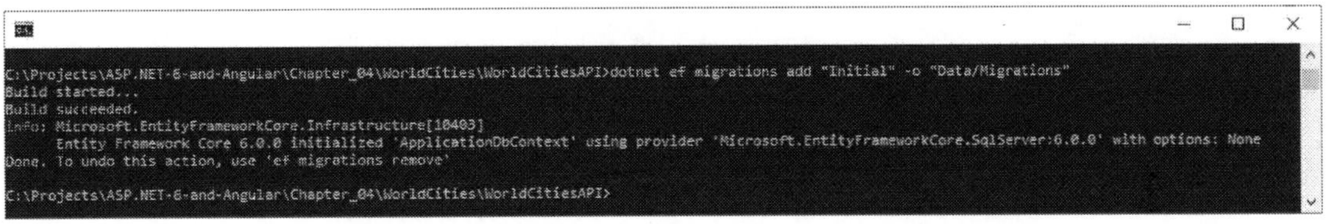

Figure 5.26: Command-line output after adding the first migration

If we see a "green" light, it means that everything went OK: the initial migration has been set up and we're ready to apply it.

 If we go back to Visual Studio and take a look at our project's **Solution Explorer**, we will see that there's a new /Data/Migrations/ folder containing a bunch of code-generated files. Those files contain the actual low-level SQL commands that will be used by Entity Framework Core to create and/or update the database schema.

Updating the Database

Applying a data migration basically means creating (or updating) the database in order to synchronize its contents (tables structure, constraints, and so on) with the rules that are defined by the overall patterns and definitions within the DbContext, and by the Data Annotations within the various Entity classes. More specifically, the first data migration creates the whole database from scratch, while the subsequent ones will update it (creating tables, adding/modifying/removing table fields, and so on).

In our specific scenario, we're about to execute our first migration. Here's the one-liner we need to type from the command line (within the project root folder, just like before) to do that:

```
dotnet ef database update
```

Once we hit *Enter*, a bunch of SQL statements will fill the output of our command-line terminal window. When done, if everything is looking good, we can go back to the SSMS tool, refresh the **Server Object Explorer** tree view, and verify that the WorldCities database has been created, along with all of the relevant tables:

Figure 5.27: Checking the Object Explorer

The "No executable found matching command dotnet-ef" error

At the time of writing, there's a nasty issue affecting most .NET-based Visual Studio projects that can prevent the dotnet ef command from working properly. More specifically, we may be prompted by the following error message when trying to execute any dotnet ef-based command:

```
No executable found matching command "dotnet-ef"
```

If we happen to experience this issue, we can try to check out the following:

- Double-check that we added the `Microsoft.EntityFrameworkCore.Tools` package library (as explained earlier) properly, as it's required for the command to work.
- Ensure that we're issuing the `dotnet ef` command in the project's root folder—the same one that also contains the `<ProjectName>.csproj` file; it won't work anywhere else.

 A lot more can be said regarding this issue but doing so is outside the scope of this book. Those of you who want to know more can take a look at this article I wrote about it while working on my *ASP.NET Core 2 and Angular 5* book at `https://goo.gl/Ki6mdb`.

Using the Package Manager Console

If we get issues while using the dotnet CLI, we can often avoid nasty headaches by switching to the Package Manager Console provided by the Visual Studio GUI. To activate it, select **View** > **Other Windows** > **Package Manager Console** from Visual Studio's main topmost menu.

Here's the full set of PMC commands that can be used to replace the previously mentioned dotnet ef ones:

```
Add-Migration Initial -OutputDir "Data/Migrations"
Update-Database
```

 To know more about the dotnet CLI commands and their corresponding Package Manager Console alternatives, check out the following official guides:

- **EF Core .NET CLI reference:** `https://docs.microsoft.com/en-us/ef/core/miscellaneous/cli/dotnet`
- **EF Core PMC / PowerShell reference:** `https://docs.microsoft.com/en-us/ef/core/miscellaneous/cli/powershell`

Checking the autogenerated DB tables

Regardless of the tool used (*dotnet CLI* or *Package Manager Console*), our `WorldCities` database should now have a couple of autogenerated tables ready to contain our `Cities` and `Countries` data: let's quickly check them out before proceeding.

Open the SSMS tool and connect to SQL Server like we did a while ago, and open the WorldCities database that we created early on: the Cities and Countries tables generated by the dotnet-ef tool should indeed be there with their columns and keys, as shown in the following screenshot:

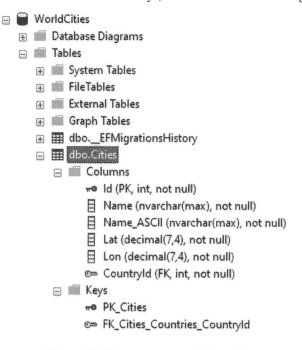

Figure 5.28: The autogenerated Cities table

Before we move on, it would be useful to say a few words explaining what *Code-First migrations* actually are, and the advantages we gain by using them.

Understanding migrations

Whenever we're developing an application and defining a data model, we can be sure that it will change a number of times for many good reasons: new requirements from the product owner, optimization processes, consolidation phases, and so on. A bunch of properties will be added, deleted, or have their types changed. Chances are, sooner or later, we'll be adding new entities as well and/or changing their relation pattern according to our ever-changing needs.

Each time we do something like that, we'll also put our data model out of sync with its underlying, Code-First-generated database. This won't be a problem when we're debugging our app within a development environment because that scenario usually allows us to recreate the database from scratch whenever the project changes.

Upon deploying the application into production, we'll be facing a whole different story: as long as we're handling real data, dropping and recreating our database won't be an option anymore. This is what the Code-First migrations feature is meant to address: giving the developer a chance to alter the database schema without having to drop/recreate the whole thing.

We won't dig deeper into this topic; Entity Framework Core is a world of its own and addressing it in detail is out of the scope of this book. If you want to learn more, we suggest that you start with the official Entity Framework Core MS documentation at the following link:

https://docs.microsoft.com/en-us/ef/core/

Is data migration required?

Data migration can be very useful, but it's not a required feature and we are definitely not forced to use it if we don't want to. As a matter of fact, it can be quite a difficult concept to understand for a lot of developers, especially for those who aren't much into DBMS design and/or scripting. It can also be very complex to manage in most scenarios, such as in companies where the DBA role is covered by someone who is below the IT development team (such as an external IT consultant or specialist).

Whenever we don't want to use data migration from the beginning—or we get to a point where we don't want to use it anymore—we can switch to a Database-First approach and start to manually design, create, and/or modify our tables: Entity Framework Core will work great, as long as the property types that are defined in the entities 100% match the corresponding database table fields. This can definitely be done, including when we put the project samples presented in this book into practice (this also applies to the WorldCities project), as long as we feel that data migration is not needed.

Alternatively, we can give it a try and see how it goes. The choice, as always, is yours.

Populating the database

Now that we have a SQL database available and a DbContext that we can use to read from and write to it, we are finally ready to populate those tables with our world cities data.

To do that, we need to implement a **data seeding** strategy. We can do this using one of the various Entity Framework Core-supported approaches:

- Model data seed
- Manual migration customization
- Custom initialization logic

These three methods are well explained in the following article, along with their very own sets of pros and cons: https://docs.microsoft.com/en-us/ef/core/modeling/data-seeding.

Since we have to handle a relatively big Excel file, we're going to adopt the most customizable pattern we can make use of: some *custom initialization logic* relying upon a dedicated .NET controller that we can execute—manually or even automatically—whenever we need to seed our database.

Implement SeedController

Our *custom initialization logic* implementation will rely upon a brand-new dedicated controller, which will be called SeedController.

From our project's **Solution Explorer**, do the following:

1. Open the /Controllers/ folder
2. If the WeatherForecastController is still there, remove it
3. Right-click on the /Controllers/ folder
4. Click on **Add | Controller**
5. Choose the **API Controller – Empty** option
6. Give the controller the **SeedController** name and click **Add** to create it

Once done, open the newly created /Controllers/SeedController.cs file and take a look at the source code: you'll see that there's just an empty class, just as expected for an empty controller! This is great since we need to understand some key concepts and—most importantly—learn how to properly translate them into source code.

Do you remember when we added our ApplicationDbContext class to the Program.cs file? As we should already know from *Chapter 2*, *Getting Ready*, this means that we've registered the Entity Framework Core-related services and our ApplicationDbContext in the DI container: this means that we can now leverage the dependency injection loading feature provided by the .NET architecture to inject an instance of that DbContext class within our controllers.

Here's how we can translate such a concept into source code (the new lines are highlighted):

```
using Microsoft.AspNetCore.Http;
using Microsoft.AspNetCore.Mvc;
using WorldCitiesAPI.Data;


namespace WorldCitiesAPI.Controllers
{
    [Route("api/[controller]")]
    [ApiController]
    public class SeedController : ControllerBase
    {
        private readonly ApplicationDbContext _context;

        public SeedController(ApplicationDbContext context)
        {
            _context = context;
        }
    }
}
```

As we can see, we've added a _context private variable and used it to store an object instance of the ApplicationDbContext class within the constructor.

Such an instance will be provided by the framework—through its dependency injection feature—within the constructor method of `SeedController`.

Before making good use of that `DbContext` instance to insert a bunch of entities into our database, we need to find a way to read those world cities values from the Excel file. How can we do that?

Import the Excel file

Luckily enough, there's a great third-party library that does precisely what we need: reading (and even writing!) Excel files using the Office Open XML format (`xlsx`), hence making their content available within any .NET-based application.

The name of this great tool is `EPPlus`. Its author, Jan Källman, made it freely available on GitHub and NuGet at the following URLs:

- **GitHub (source code)**: `https://github.com/JanKallman/EPPlus`
- **NuGet (.NET package)**: `https://www.nuget.org/packages/EPPlus`

As we can see, the project recently changed its licensing model:

- Until version 4.x, it was licensed under the GNU **Library General Public License (LGPL)** v3.0, meaning that we were allowed to integrate it into our software without limitations, as long as we didn't modify it.
- From version 5.x and below, it uses a *PolyForm Noncommercial* and *Commercial* dual license, which basically means that we can use it only for non-commercial purposes.

For that very reason, in order to avoid any possible license infringement, we're going to use the (now-deprecated) **4.5.3.3**, it being the latest GNU-LGPL version available.

That said, those who want to use the latest `EPPlus` version with the *Noncommercial* license can do that by adding the following line in the `Program.cs` file:

```
ExcelPackage.LicenseContext = LicenseContext.NonCommercial;
```

However, v4.x is still viable enough for the purposes of our sample.

 For additional info about the new `EPPlus` *PolyForm Noncommercial* license, check out the following URL:

`https://polyformproject.org/licenses/noncommercial/1.0.0/`

To find out more about the `EPPlus` licensing change, read this: `https://www.epplussoftware.com/Home/LgplToPolyform`.

The best way to install `EPPlus` in our `WorldCitiesAPI` project is to add the NuGet package using the NuGet Package Manager GUI:

1. From the project's Solution Explorer, right-click on the `WorldCitiesAPI` project
2. Select **Manage NuGet Packages...**

3. Use the **Browse** tab to search for the EPPlus package, choose the version you want to install (4.5.3.3 in our case), and then initiate the task by clicking the **Install** button at the top right:

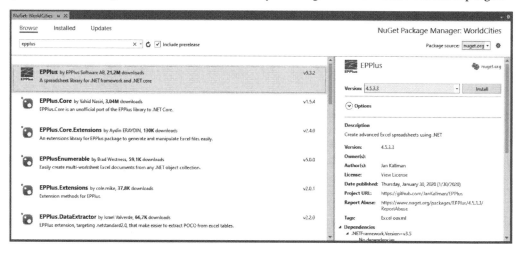

Figure 5.29: Adding the NuGet package using the NuGet Package Manager

Alternatively, type the following command from Visual Studio's Package Manager Console:

```
> Install-Package EPPlus -Version 4.5.3.3
```

Once done, we can go back to the SeedController.cs file and use the awesome features of EPPlus to read the worldcities.xlsx Excel file.

However, before doing that, it could be wise to move that file so that it's within our sample project's /Data/ folder so that we'll be able to read it using the .NET filesystem capabilities provided by the System.IO namespace. While we're there, let's create a /Data/Source/ subfolder and put it there to separate it from the other Entity Framework Core files:

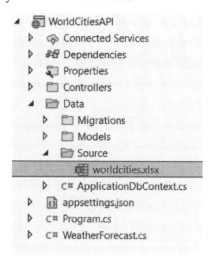

Figure 5.30: Creating a separate Source subfolder for the worldcities.xlsx file

Here's the source code that we need to add to our `SeedController.cs` file to read the `worldcities.xlsx` file and store all of the rows in a list of `City` entities:

```csharp
using System.Security;
using Microsoft.AspNetCore.Mvc;
using Microsoft.EntityFrameworkCore;
using OfficeOpenXml;
using WorldCitiesAPI.Data;
using WorldCitiesAPI.Data.Models;

namespace WorldCitiesAPI.Controllers
{
    [Route("api/[controller]/[action]")]
    [ApiController]
    public class SeedController : ControllerBase
    {
        private readonly ApplicationDbContext _context;
        private readonly IWebHostEnvironment _env;

        public SeedController(
            ApplicationDbContext context,
            IWebHostEnvironment env)
        {
            _context = context;
            _env = env;
        }

        [HttpGet]
        public async Task<ActionResult> Import()
        {
            // prevents non-development environments from running this method
            if (!_env.IsDevelopment())
                    throw new SecurityException("Not allowed");

            var path = Path.Combine(
                _env.ContentRootPath,
                "Data/Source/worldcities.xlsx");

            using var stream = System.IO.File.OpenRead(path);
            using var excelPackage = new ExcelPackage(stream);
```

```csharp
// get the first worksheet
var worksheet = excelPackage.Workbook.Worksheets[0];

// define how many rows we want to process
var nEndRow = worksheet.Dimension.End.Row;

// initialize the record counters
var numberOfCountriesAdded = 0;
var numberOfCitiesAdded = 0;

// create a lookup dictionary
// containing all the countries already existing
// into the Database (it will be empty on first run).
var countriesByName = _context.Countries
    .AsNoTracking()
    .ToDictionary(x => x.Name, StringComparer.OrdinalIgnoreCase);

// iterates through all rows, skipping the first one
for (int nRow = 2; nRow <= nEndRow; nRow++)
{
    var row = worksheet.Cells[
        nRow, 1, nRow, worksheet.Dimension.End.Column];

    var countryName = row[nRow, 5].GetValue<string>();
    var iso2 = row[nRow, 6].GetValue<string>();
    var iso3 = row[nRow, 7].GetValue<string>();

    // skip this country if it already exists in the database
    if (countriesByName.ContainsKey(countryName))
        continue;

    // create the Country entity and fill it with xlsx data
    var country = new Country
    {
        Name = countryName,
        ISO2 = iso2,
        ISO3 = iso3
    };

    // add the new country to the DB context
```

```
        await _context.Countries.AddAsync(country);

        // store the country in our lookup to retrieve its Id later on
        countriesByName.Add(countryName, country);

        // increment the counter
        numberOfCountriesAdded++;
    }


    // save all the countries into the Database
    if (numberOfCountriesAdded > 0)
        await _context.SaveChangesAsync();

    // create a lookup dictionary
    // containing all the cities already existing
    // into the Database (it will be empty on first run).
    var cities = _context.Cities
        .AsNoTracking()
        .ToDictionary(x => (
            Name: x.Name,
            Lat: x.Lat,
            Lon: x.Lon,
            CountryId: x.CountryId));

    // iterates through all rows, skipping the first one
    for (int nRow = 2; nRow <= nEndRow; nRow++)
    {
        var row = worksheet.Cells[
            nRow, 1, nRow, worksheet.Dimension.End.Column];

        var name = row[nRow, 1].GetValue<string>();
        var nameAscii = row[nRow, 2].GetValue<string>();
        var lat = row[nRow, 3].GetValue<decimal>();
        var lon = row[nRow, 4].GetValue<decimal>();
        var countryName = row[nRow, 5].GetValue<string>();

        // retrieve country Id by countryName
        var countryId = countriesByName[countryName].Id;

        // skip this city if it already exists in the database
        if (cities.ContainsKey((
```

```
                    Name: name,
                    Lat: lat,
                    Lon: lon,
                    CountryId: countryId)))
                    continue;

                // create the City entity and fill it with xlsx data
                var city = new City
                {
                    Name = name,
                    Lat = lat,
                    Lon = lon,
                    CountryId = countryId
                };

                // add the new city to the DB context
                _context.Cities.Add(city);

                // increment the counter
                numberOfCitiesAdded++;
            }

            // save all the cities into the Database
            if (numberOfCitiesAdded > 0)
                await _context.SaveChangesAsync();

            return new JsonResult(new
            {
                Cities = numberOfCitiesAdded,
                Countries = numberOfCountriesAdded
            });
        }
    }
}
```

As we can see, we're doing a lot of interesting things here. The preceding code features a lot of comments and should be very readable; however, it could be useful to briefly enumerate the most relevant parts:

- We injected an `IWebHostEnvironment` instance through dependency injection, just like we did for `ApplicationDbContext`, so that we can retrieve the web application path and be able to read the Excel file.

- We added an `Import` action method that will use `ApplicationDbContext` and the `EPPlus` package to read the Excel file and add `Countries` and `Cities`.

- At the start of the `Import` method's implementation, we used the `IWebHostEnvironment` instance to determine if we're running in a development environment or not: if we aren't, the code will throw a `SecurityException`. By acting that way we'll prevent anyone—including our users—from calling this method in production, thus restricting the whole importing task to developers only.

- `Countries` are imported first because the `City` entities require the `CountryId` foreign key value, which will be returned when the corresponding `Country` is created in the database as a new record.

- We defined a `Dictionary` container object to store all existing countries (plus each new `Country` right after we create it) so that we can query that list using LINQ to retrieve the `CountryId` instead of performing a lot of `SELECT` queries: this logic will also prevent the method from inserting the same country multiple times, should we happen to execute it more than once.

- We defined another `Dictionary` container object to prevent the insertion of duplicate cities as well.

- Last but not least, we created a JSON object to show the overall results on the screen.

It's worth noting that we've issued our queries using EF Core's `AsNoTracking` extension method, which returns a new query where the entities returned will not be cached in the `DbContext` or `ObjectContext` if they are modified within the code: this basically means that less data will be cached and tracked, with obvious benefits in terms of memory usage.

For additional info on the `AsNoTracking` extension method, check out the following URL:

`https://docs.microsoft.com/en-us/dotnet/api/system.data.entity.dbextensions.asnotracking`

If we want to get a closer look at how the whole importing procedure works, we can put some breakpoints inside the `if` loops to check it out while it's running.

To execute the action method, hit *F5* to launch the web application in debug mode and then type the following URL into the browser's address bar: `https://localhost:40443/api/Seed/Import`.

Be aware that the `Import` method is designed to import 230+ countries and 12,000+ cities, so this task will likely require some time—between about 10 and 30 seconds on an average development machine, depending on the amount of available RAM, CPU performance, and database connection speed. It's definitely a major data seed! We're kind of stressing out the framework here.

If we don't want to wait, we can always give the `nEndRow` internal variable a fixed value, such as 1,000, to limit the total number of cities (and countries) that will be read and therefore loaded into the database.

Eventually, we should be able to see the following response in our browser window:

Figure 5.31: Inspecting the data import

The preceding output means that the import has been performed successfully: we did it! Our database is now filled with 41001 cities and 237 countries for us to play with.

> Those numbers might slightly change depending on the *WorldCities* database version: at the time of writing we're using v1.74, which was updated on July 2021, but any subsequent version should work as well—as long as the MS Excel file structure doesn't change. If you want to use the same exact MS Excel file that was used to write this book, you can find it in the GitHub project's `/Data/Source/` folder.

In the next section, we're going to learn how we can read this data as well so that we'll be able to bring Angular into the loop.

Entity controllers

Now that we have thousands of cities and hundreds of countries in our database, we need to find a way to bring this data to Angular and vice versa. As we already know from *Chapter 2, Getting Ready*, this role is played by the .NET controllers, so we're going to create two of them:

- `CitiesController`, to serve (and receive) the cities' data
- `CountriesController`, to do the same with the countries

Let's get started.

CitiesController

Let's start with the cities. Remember what we did when we created `SeedController`? What we're going to do now is rather similar, but this time we'll make good use of Visual Studio's code-generation features.

From our project's **Solution Explorer**, follow these steps:

1. Right-click on the `/Controllers/` folder.
2. Click on **Add | Controller**.
3. Choose the **Add API Controller with actions, using Entity Framework** option (the last one from the top, at the time of writing).

4. In the model window that appears, choose the `City` model class and the `ApplicationDbContext`
    data context class, as shown in the following screenshot. Name the controller `CitiesController`
    and click **Add** to create it:

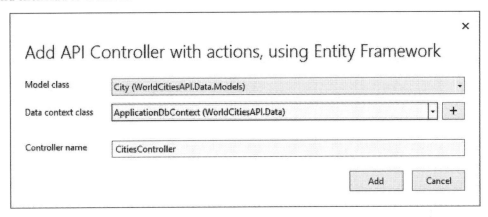

Figure 5.32: Creating CitiesController

The settings we specified during this phase will be used by Visual Studio to analyze our entities (and
our `DbContext`) and autogenerate a whole API controller stuffed with useful methods.

After the `CitiesController.cs` file has been generated we can open it and see how the code generator did a lot of useful work, while sticking to a pattern that's similar to the one we followed for our
`SeedController` class.

 You can see the generated code in the book's GitHub repository for this chapter.

Here's a breakdown of the relevant methods, in order of appearance:

*   `GetCities()` returns a JSON array containing all of the cities in the database
*   `GetCity(id)` returns a JSON object containing a single `City`
*   `PutCity(id, city)` allows us to modify an existing `City`
*   `PostCity(city)` allows us to add a new `City`
*   `DeleteCity(id)` allows us to delete an existing `City`

It definitely seems that we do have everything we need for our *front-end*. Before moving on to Angular,
let's do the same for our `Countries`.

CountriesController

From Solution Explorer, right-click the `/Controllers/` folder and perform the same set of tasks we performed to add `CitiesController`—except for the name, which will obviously be `CountriesController`.

At the end of the code-generation process, we'll end up with a `CountriesController.cs` file stuffed with the `Get`, `Put`, `Post`, and `Delete` action methods that we need to handle the `Countries`.

 Again, the generated code is available in the book's GitHub repository for this chapter.

Before going further, let's spend a couple of minutes examining some methodological considerations regarding using entities in controllers the way we just did.

Should we really use Entities?

When we created our `CitiesController` and `CountriesController` a short while ago, we selected our existing `City` and `Country` as our model classes. From a point of view, this seems like the most logical thing to do: those classes already contain everything we need to receive from the client, thus they are ideal for use as input parameters for the `Put()` and `Post()` action methods that we need.

However, using a model class to return results or accept parameters from the client is hardly a good practice: these model classes are meant to be a full representation of our database tables, not the interface to use to exchange data with the client. A much better approach is to keep the model entities that communicate with the database separated from the **Data Transfer Objects (DTOs)** that we use for **GET**, **POST**, and **PUT** methods. We'll talk more about that in *Chapter 8, Code Tweaks and Data Services*, when we'll refactor those action methods, replacing those model entities with DTOs, thus enforcing the *single responsibility principle* between them; however, for the next few chapters, we can benefit from the simplicity resulting from such a "non-recommended approach" and go ahead.

That concludes our journey through Entity Framework. Now, we need to connect the dots and reap what we've sown using our favorite *front-end* framework.

Testing it out

Now that our controllers are ready, we can perform a quick test to see if they're working as expected.

Hit *F5* to launch our web application in debug mode, then copy the following URL into the browser's address bar: `https://localhost:40443/api/Cities/`.

If we made everything properly, we should see something like this:

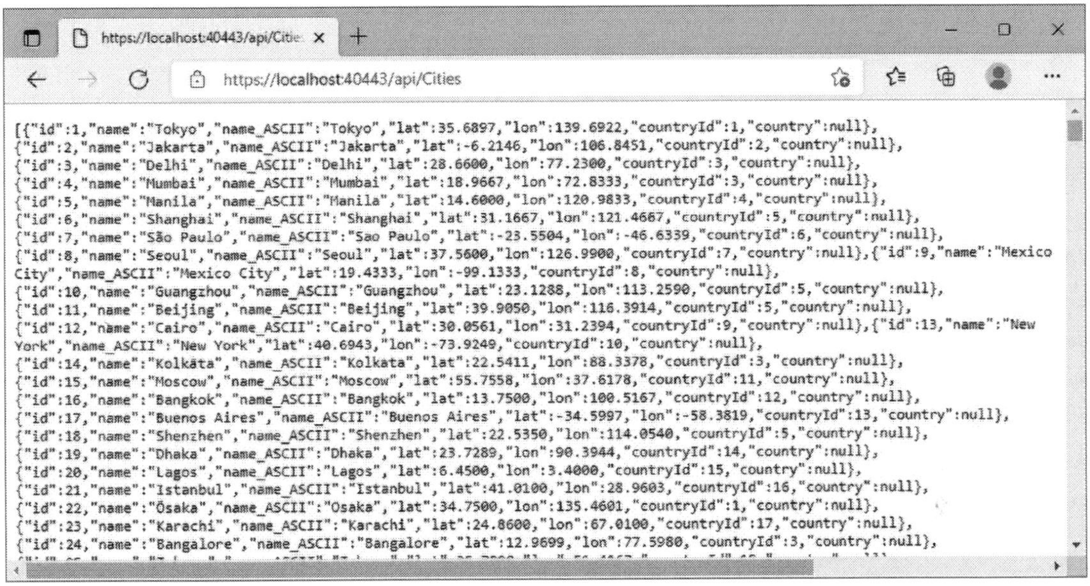

Figure 5.33: Testing CitiesController

Here come our cities!

While we're here, let's check the countries as well with the following URL: `https://localhost:40443/api/Countries/`.

This is what we should receive from our browser:

Figure 5.34: Testing CountriesController

Here they are.

Our job here is done: let's move on to the next chapter, where we'll see how to present this data to the *front-end*.

Summary

We started this chapter by enumerating a number of things that simply cannot be done without a proper data provider. To overcome these limitations, we decided to provide ourselves with a DBMS engine and a persistent database for reading and/or writing data. To avoid messing with what we did in the previous chapters, we created a brand-new web application project to deal with that, which we called `WorldCities`.

Then, we chose a suitable data source for our new project: a list of world cities and countries that we could download for free in a handy MS Excel file.

Right after that, we moved on to the data model: Entity Framework Core seemed an obvious choice to get what we wanted, so we added its relevant packages to our project. We briefly enumerated the available data modeling approaches and resorted to using Code-First due to its flexibility.

Once done, we created our two entities, `City` and `Country`, both of which are based on the data source values we had to store within our database, along with a set of Data Annotations and relationships taking advantage of the renowned Entity Framework Core's convention-over-configuration approach. Then, we built our `ApplicationDbContext` class accordingly.

After we created our data model, we evaluated the various options for configuring and deploying our DBMS engine: we reviewed the DMBS local instances and cloud-based solutions such as MS Azure, and we explained how to implement both of them.

Last but not least, we created our .NET controller classes to deal with the data: `SeedController` to read the Excel file and seed our database, `CitiesController` to deal with cities, and `CountriesController` to handle countries.

After completing all of these tasks, we ran our application in debug mode to verify that everything was still working as intended. Now, we're ready to mess with the *front-end* part of our app. In the next chapter, we'll learn how to properly fetch this data from the server and bring it to the user in a fashionable way.

Angular, here we come!

Suggested topics

For further information, we recommend the following topics: Web API, in-memory Web API, data source, data server, data model, data provider, ADO.NET, ORM, Entity Framework Core, Code-First, Database-First, Model-First, Entity class, Data Annotations, DbContext, CRUD operations, data migration, dependency injection, ORM mapping, JSON, ApiController.

References

- *Angular In-Memory Web API*: https://github.com/angular/in-memory-web-api/
- *Wikipedia: ISO 3166*: https://en.wikipedia.org/wiki/ISO_3166
- *Wikipedia: ISO 3166 alpha-2*: https://en.wikipedia.org/wiki/ISO_3166-1_alpha-2
- *Wikipedia: ISO 3166 alpha-3*: https://en.wikipedia.org/wiki/ISO_3166-1_alpha-3
- *ISO 3166 country codes*: https://www.iso.org/iso-3166-country-codes.html
- *SQL Server 2019 official page*: https://www.microsoft.com/en-us/sql-server/sql-server-2019
- *SQL Server 2019 – compare SQL Server versions*: https://www.microsoft.com/en-us/sql-server/sql-server-2019-comparison
- *SQL Server 2019 on Linux*: https://docs.microsoft.com/en-US/sql/linux/sql-server-linux-overview
- *Installing SQL Server on Windows*: https://docs.microsoft.com/en-US/sql/database-engine/install-windows/installation-for-sql-server
- *Installing SQL Server on Linux*: https://docs.microsoft.com/en-US/sql/linux/sql-server-linux-setup
- *Download SQL Server Management Studio (SSMS)*: https://docs.microsoft.com/en-us/sql/ssms/download-sql-server-management-studio-ssms
- *Create a SQL Server Database on Azure*: https://azure.microsoft.com/en-us/resources/videos/create-sql-database-on-azure/
- *Azure free account FAQ*: https://azure.microsoft.com/en-in/free/free-account-faq/
- *Azure SQL Server Managed Instance*: https://azure.microsoft.com/en-us/services/sql-database/
- *Use tags to organize your Azure resources*: https://docs.microsoft.com/en-us/azure/azure-resource-manager/management/tag-resources
- *Choose the right deployment option in Azure SQL*: https://docs.microsoft.com/en-US/azure/sql-database/sql-database-paas-vs-sql-server-iaas
- *Create an Azure SQL Database Managed Instance*: https://docs.microsoft.com/en-us/azure/sql-database/sql-database-managed-instance-get-started
- *Entity Framework Core: Loading Related Data*: https://docs.microsoft.com/en-US/ef/core/querying/related-data
- *Entity Framework Core: Modeling*: https://docs.microsoft.com/en-us/ef/core/modeling/
- *Entity Framework Core: Data Seeding*: https://docs.microsoft.com/en-us/ef/core/modeling/data-seeding
- *Entity Framework Core: DbContext*: https://www.entityframeworktutorial.net/efcore/entity-framework-core-dbcontext.aspx
- *EF Core .NET CLI reference*: https://docs.microsoft.com/en-us/ef/core/miscellaneous/cli/dotnet
- *EF Core PMC/PowerShell reference*: https://docs.microsoft.com/en-us/ef/core/miscellaneous/cli/powershell

- *#region (C# reference)*: `https://docs.microsoft.com/en-us/dotnet/csharp/language-reference/preprocessor-directives/preprocessor-region`
- *Are #regions an antipattern or code smell?*: `https://softwareengineering.stackexchange.com/questions/53086/are-regions-an-antipattern-or-code-smell`
- *PolyForm Noncommercial license*: `https://polyformproject.org/licenses/noncommercial/1.0.0/`
- *EPPlus library licensing change*: `https://www.epplussoftware.com/Home/LgplToPolyform`
- *DbExtensions.AsNoTracking Method*: `https://docs.microsoft.com/en-us/dotnet/api/system.data.entity.dbextensions.asnotracking`

6

Fetching and Displaying Data

In the previous chapter, we created a new `WorldCities` solution containing a `WorldCities` project (our Angular app) and a `WorldCitiesAPI` project (our ASP.NET Web API) and made a considerable effort to empower the latter with a DBMS-based data provider, built upon Entity Framework Core using the Code-First approach. Now that we have data persistence, we're ready to entrust our users with the ability to interact with our application; this means that we can switch to the Angular app and implement some much-needed stuff, such as the following:

- **Fetching data:** Querying the data provider from the client side using HTTP requests and getting structured results back from the server side
- **Displaying data:** Populating typical client-side components such as tables and lists, and thereby ensuring a good user experience for the end user
- **Adding countries to the loop:** For the sake of simplicity, we'll learn how to implement the *fetch* and *display* tasks by focusing on the **City** entity: in the last part of the chapter, we'll use the knowledge gained to apply the same techniques to the **Country** entity as well

In this chapter, we'll cover the *fetch* and *display* topics by adding several client-server interactions handled by standard HTTP request/response chains; it goes without saying that Angular will play a major role here, together with a couple of useful packages that will help us reach our goal.

Technical requirements

In this chapter, we're going to need all the technical requirements listed in the previous chapters, plus the following external library:

- `System.Linq.Dynamic.Core` (.NET Core NuGet package) for the `WorldCitiesAPI` ASP.NET app

As always, it's advisable to avoid installing them straight away; we're going to bring them in during this chapter to better contextualize their purpose within our project.

The code files for this chapter can be found at `https://github.com/PacktPublishing/ASP.NET-Core-6-and-Angular/tree/master/Chapter_06/`.

Fetching data

As we already know from *Chapter 2*, *Getting Ready*, reading data from the database is mostly a matter of having the Angular app (the *front-end*) send HTTP requests to the ASP.NET app (the *back-end*) and fetching the corresponding HTTP responses accordingly; these data transfers will be mostly implemented using **JavaScript Object Notation** (**JSON**), a lightweight data-interchange format that is natively supported by both frameworks.

In this section, we'll mostly talk about HTTP requests and responses, see how we can fetch data from the ASP.NET app, and lay out some raw UI examples using Angular components that will be further refined throughout the next sections.

Are we ready? Let's start!

Requests and responses

Let's start by taking a look at those HTTP requests and responses we'll be dealing with: hit *F5* to launch both `WorldCities` and `WorldCitiesAPI` projects in *debug* mode – or right-click the `WorldCitiesAPI` project and select **Debug** > **Start New Instance** to launch that project alone – and type the following URL in the browser's address bar: `https://localhost:40443/api/Cities/`.

If we did everything correctly, we should see a list of cities, each one with a unique `id`. From that list, we can easily pick the `id` of each city and add it to our URL to retrieve that specific city only: for example, we can choose to use `13`, which, in our specific scenario, corresponds to the city of New York.

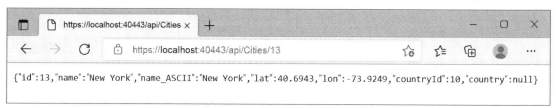

Figure 6.1: Entry for New York

   Important Note: The IDs of the various cities and countries referenced throughout the book might differ from those present in the reader's own database, depending on various factors: the world cities file version/progress, the starting auto-incrementing `id` of the `[Cities]` database table we used to store the data source, and so on. Don't mind that: all the code samples should still work, regardless of any difference in ID.

JSON conventions and defaults

As we can see, the JSON is basically a serialization of our `City` entity, with some built-in conventions such as the following:

- **camelCase instead of PascalCase:** We have `name` instead of `Name`, `countryId` instead of `CountryId`, and so on, meaning that all our PascalCase .NET class names and properties will be automatically converted into camelCase when they are serialized to JSON

- **No indentation and no line feed/carriage return (LF/CR):** Everything is stacked within a single line of text

These conventions are the default options set by ASP.NET when dealing with JSON outputs. Most of them can be changed by adding some customization options to the MVC middleware. However, we don't need to do that as they are perfectly supported by Angular, which is what we're going to use to deal with those strings; we'll just have to ensure that the Angular interfaces that we'll create to mirror the entity classes have their names and properties set to camelCase.

 Anyone who wants to know why they chose camelCase instead of PascalCase as the default serialization option should check out the following GitHub thread: `https://github.com/aspnet/Mvc/issues/4283`.

That said, if we want to increase the readability of our JSON output, we can add some indentation so that we'll be able to understand more of those outputs.

To do that, open the `Program.cs` file, and add the following options to the `builder.Services.AddControllers` method (new/updated lines highlighted):

```
builder.Services.AddControllers()
    .AddJsonOptions(options =>
    {
        options.JsonSerializerOptions.WriteIndented = true;
    });
```

Save the file, hit *F5*, and type the previous URL once more to see the following changes:

```
{
    "id": 13,
    "name": "New York",
    "name_ASCII": "New York",
    "lat": 40.6943,
    "lon": -73.9249,
    "countryId": 10,
    "country": null
}
```

Figure 6.2: New JSON file with camelCase and indentation changes

Here we go: as we can see, by enabling this option, the JSON becomes much more readable, with Angular still being able to properly access it. However, such a change will also have a (minor) impact on performance, since all those line feeds and space characters will slightly increase the overall size of all the HTTP responses returned by the server-side API.

If we wanted to switch from *camelCase* (default) to *PascalCase*, we could also add the following option:

```
options.JsonSerializerOptions.PropertyNamingPolicy = null;
```

That said, for the sake of these sample projects, we prefer to keep the default conventions (no indentation and *camelCase*): for that very reason, we'll comment out those two options.

 Those who want to uncomment those options are free to do that: just be aware that, if PascalCase is used instead of camelCase, the Angular code samples shown in this chapter – and in the following chapters – will need to be changed accordingly.

A (very) long list

Let's now move to our Angular app and create a sample component to show a list of Cities. We already created a component in *Chapter 4, Front-End and Back-End Interactions*, so we know what to do:

1. Open Command Prompt
2. Navigate to the /src/app/ folder of the *WorldCities* Angular project
3. Type ng generate component Cities --module=app --skip-tests to create the following new files using the Angular CLI:

    • /src/app/cities/cities.component.ts

    • /src/app/cities/cities.component.html

    • /src/app/cities/cities.component.scss

4. From Solution Explorer, create an additional city.ts file inside the /src/app/cities/ folder of the *WorldCities* Angular project

Once done, fill the new files with the following content.

city.ts

Open the /src/app/cities/city.ts file and add the following:

```
export interface City {
    id: number;
    name: string;
    lat: number;
    lon: number;
}
```

This small file contains our *city* interface, which we'll be using in our `CitiesComponent` class file. Since we're eventually going to use it in other components as well, it's better to create it within a separate file and decorate it with the `export` statement so that we'll be able to use it there as well when the time comes.

cities.component.ts

Open the `/src/app/cities/cities.component.ts` file and replace its content with the following:

```typescript
import { Component, OnInit } from '@angular/core';
import { HttpClient } from '@angular/common/http';
import { environment } from './../../environments/environment';

import { City } from './city';

@Component({
  selector: 'app-cities',
  templateUrl: './cities.component.html',
  styleUrls: ['./cities.component.scss']
})
export class CitiesComponent implements OnInit {
  public cities!: City[];

  constructor(private http: HttpClient) {
  }

  ngOnInit() {
    this.http.get<City[]>(environment.baseUrl + 'api/Cities')
      .subscribe(result => {
        this.cities = result;
      }, error => console.error(error));
  }
}
```

As we can see, we added an `import` reference to the `City` interface we created a short while ago. We also used the `ngOnInit()` life cycle hook method to perform the HTTP request that will retrieve the cities, just like we did in *Chapter 4, Front-End and Back-End Interactions*, for our previous `HealthCheck` app.

cities.component.html

Open the `/src/app/cities/cities.component.html` file and add the following:

```html
<h1>Cities</h1>

<p>Here's a list of cities: feel free to play with it.</p>
```

```
<p *ngIf="!cities"><em>Loading...</em></p>

<table class='table table-striped' aria-labelledby="tableLabel"
[hidden]="!cities">
  <thead>
    <tr>
      <th>ID</th>
      <th>Name</th>
      <th>Lat</th>
      <th>Lon</th>
    </tr>
  </thead>
  <tbody>
    <tr *ngFor="let city of cities">
      <td>{{ city.id }}</td>
      <td>{{ city.name }}</td>
      <td>{{ city.lat }}</td>
      <td>{{ city.lon }}</td>
    </tr>
  </tbody>
</table>
```

As we can see, the preceding HTML structure has nothing special: it's just a header, a paragraph, and a table with some standard loading logic to let the user know that we'll asynchronously load the data in a (hopefully) short while. However, there are at least two attributes that deserve a couple of words.

Basic table styling

If we take a look at the `<table>` HTML element, we can easily notice that we've applied a couple of CSS classes there: `table` and `table-striped`. These are two of the most widely used classes of the **Bootstrap** front-end framework when it comes to styling tables. In a nutshell, the former will apply some basic spacing and typography rules, while the latter will change the background color of the table's odd rows, thus reproducing a "striped" effect; both of them will greatly increase the table's readability.

 To read more about Bootstrap, its UI components, and its layout styling features, check out the official documentation at the following URL: `https://getbootstrap.com`.

Since we are not using Bootstrap for this project, we will have to create those classes by ourselves in the `cities.component.scss` file. However, before doing that, there's another thing worth focusing on.

The [hidden] attribute

If we keep looking at the `cities.component.html` file's HTML code, we can see that, shortly after the table's `class` definition, the `<table>` element features a strange `[hidden]` attribute. Why is it there, and why is it between square brackets?

As a matter of fact, the `hidden` attribute is an HTML5-valid content attribute that can be legitimately set on any HTML element. The role it's supposed to play is very similar to the CSS `display: none` setting: it indicates to the browser that the element and all of its descendants should not be visible or perceivable to any user. In other words, it's just another way to hide content from the user.

 For additional information regarding the `hidden` attribute, check out the following URL:

HTML Living Standard (last updated on November 26, 2019): `https://html.spec.whatwg.org/multipage/interaction.html#the-hidden-attribute`

As for the square brackets, that's just the Angular syntax used to define a property binding, that is, an HTML property or attribute within the component template (our `.html` file) that gets its value from a variable, property, or expression defined within the component class (our `.ts` file). It's worth noting that such a binding flows in one direction: from the component class (the source) to the HTML element within the component template (the target).

As a direct consequence of what we have just said, every time the source value evaluates to `true`, the HTML property (or attribute) between square brackets will be set to *true* as well (and vice versa); this is a great way to deal with a lot of HTML attributes that work with Boolean values because we can dynamically set them through the whole component's life cycle. That's precisely what we do with the `<table>` element in the preceding code block: its `hidden` attribute will evaluate to `false` until the `cities` component variable is filled by the actual *cities* fetched from the server, which will only happen when the `HttpClient` module finishes its request/response task. Not bad, right?

Wait a minute: isn't that the same behavior as the `*ngIf` *structural directive* that we already know from *Chapter 4*, *Front-End and Back-End Interactions*? Why are we using this `[hidden]` attribute instead?

This is a very good question that gives us the chance to clarify the difference between these two similar – yet not identical – approaches:

- The `*ngIf` structural directive adds or removes the element from the **Document Object Model (DOM)** based on its corresponding condition or expression; this means that the element will be initialized and/or disposed of (together with all its children, events, and so on) every time its status changes.
- The `hidden` attribute, much like the `display: none` CSS setting, will only instruct the browser to show the element to or hide the element from the user; this means that the element will still be there, thus being fully available and reachable (for example, by JavaScript or other DOM-manipulating actions).

As we can see by looking at the preceding HTML code, we're using both of them: the `*ngIf` structural directive adds or removes the *loading* `<p>` element, while the `[hidden]` *attribute binding* shows or hides the main `<table>`. We have chosen to do this for a reason: the `<p>` element won't have children or events depending on it, while the `<table>` attribute will soon become a complex object with a lot of features to initialize and preserve within the DOM. Using the `[hidden]` attribute for that will also grant better performance than `*ngIf` when we need to show/hide lots of DOM elements.

cities.component.scss

It's now time to add those table classes to our SCSS file, just like we planned to do a short while ago. Open the `/src/app/cities/cities.component.scss` file and add the following SASS code:

```scss
table.table {
  width: 100%;
  margin-bottom: 1rem;
  color: #212529;
  vertical-align: top;
  border-color: #dee2e6;

  &.table-striped > tbody > tr:nth-of-type(even) {
    background-color: rgba(0, 0, 0, 0.05);
    color: #212529;
  }

  &.table-hover > tbody > tr:hover {
    background-color: rgba(0, 0, 0, 0.075);
    color: #212529;
  }
}
```

That's it, at least for now. Our `CitiesComponent` is good enough to be shipped: we just need to integrate it within our Angular app.

app-routing.module.ts

As we already know, this component can only be loaded – and can only be reached by Angular client-side routing – if we add it to the `app-routing.module.ts` file in the following way (new lines are highlighted):

```typescript
import { NgModule } from '@angular/core';
import { Routes, RouterModule } from '@angular/router';
```

```
import { HomeComponent } from './home/home.component';
import { CitiesComponent } from './cities/cities.component';

const routes: Routes = [
  { path: '', component: HomeComponent, pathMatch: 'full' },
  { path: 'cities', component: CitiesComponent }
];

@NgModule({
  imports: [RouterModule.forRoot(routes)],
  exports: [RouterModule]
})
export class AppRoutingModule { }
```

Here we go: now we need to deal with the UI.

nav-component.html

More specifically, we need to add a reference to the new component route within the app navigator component; otherwise, the user won't be able to see (and thus reach) it using the UI.

To do that, open the `nav-menu-component.html` file and add the following (highlighted) lines:

```
<header>
  <mat-toolbar color="primary">
    <button mat-icon-button [routerLink]="['/']">
      <mat-icon>
        home
      </mat-icon>
    </button>
    <a mat-flat-button color="primary" [routerLink]="['/cities']">
      Cities
    </a>
  </mat-toolbar>
</header>
```

That's it. Now, we *could* launch our app, click on the **Cities** link that will appear in the top-right part of the screen, and experience the following outcome:

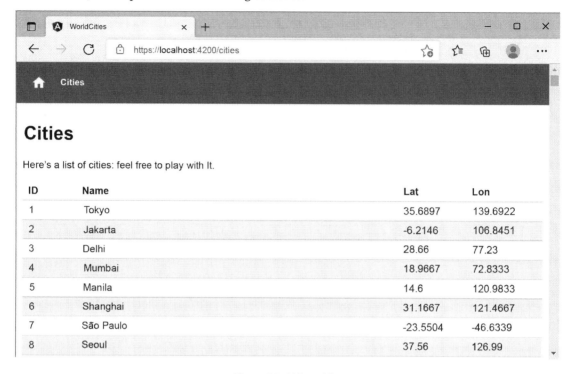

Figure 6.3: Cities table

As we can see by looking at the vertical scrollbar to the right, we would be overwhelmed by a huge HTML table consisting of more than 41,000 rows!

That's another huge performance stress for both ASP.NET and Angular – which should pass with flying colors on any average development machine since both frameworks can deal well with their respective tasks.

However, such a UI outcome is definitely a no-go in terms of user experience: we can't reasonably expect our end users to be happy if we force them to navigate through a ~41k-row HTML table with a browser. They would go mad trying to find the city they're looking for!

To fix these major usability issues, we need to implement a few important features that are frequently used to deal with fat HTML tables: **paging**, **sorting**, and **filtering**.

Serving data with Angular Material

To implement a table with paging, sorting, and filtering features, we're going to use **Angular Material**, the UI component library that we already introduced in *Chapter 4, Front-End and Back-End Interactions*.

However, before adding new Angular Material components, we'll take the chance to apply a bit of refactoring to the way we've implemented the existing ones.

Adding AngularMaterialModule

From Solution Explorer, navigate to the /src/app/ folder, create a new angular-material.module.
ts file, and fill it with the following content:

```
import { NgModule } from '@angular/core';
import { MatButtonModule } from '@angular/material/button';
import { MatIconModule } from '@angular/material/icon';
import { MatToolbarModule } from '@angular/material/toolbar';


@NgModule({
  imports: [
    MatButtonModule,
    MatIconModule,
    MatToolbarModule
  ],
  exports: [
    MatButtonModule,
    MatIconModule,
    MatToolbarModule
  ]
})
export class AngularMaterialModule { }
```

This is a brand-new module that we're going to use for all the Angular Material modules we want to implement within our app. As we can see by looking at the preceding code, we've already included every Angular Material component that we've learned to use so far. Putting them here instead of using the app.module.ts file will keep that file smaller, which is great for project manageability.

Needless to say, for this *module container* to work properly, we need to add it within our existing app.
module.ts file. Open that file, remove all references to Mat* modules in the import, imports[], and exports[] sections, and replace them with the following (highlighted) lines:

```
//.. existing code


import { BrowserAnimationsModule } from '@angular/platform-browser/animations';

import { AngularMaterialModule } from './angular-material.module';


//.. existing code

  imports: [
    BrowserModule,
    HttpClientModule,
```

```
    AppRoutingModule,
    BrowserAnimationsModule,
    AngularMaterialModule
  ],

//.. existing code
```

Here we go: now, everything we're going to put in the `angular-material.module.ts` file will also be referenced within our app.

Introducing MatTable

The Angular Material module we're going to use is `MatTable`, which provides a Material Design-styled HTML table that can be used to display rows of data. We briefly introduced it back in *Chapter 4, Front-End and Back-End Interactions*, when we revamped the UI of `FetchDataComponent` and `HealthCheckComponent` in our **HealthCheck** app. Now we'll learn how to use it properly to replace our plain HTML tables, which will allow us to take advantage of its unique and convenient features.

Updating AngularMaterialModule

Since we're planning to introduce a new Angular Material module, the first thing we need to do is add its references to our new `AngularMaterialModule`.

Open the `/src/app/angular-material.module.ts` file and add the following highlighted lines:

```
import { NgModule } from '@angular/core';
import { MatButtonModule } from '@angular/material/button';
import { MatIconModule } from '@angular/material/icon';
import { MatToolbarModule } from '@angular/material/toolbar';
import { MatTableModule } from '@angular/material/table';

@NgModule({
  imports: [
    MatButtonModule,
    MatIconModule,
    MatToolbarModule,
    MatTableModule
  ],
  exports: [
    MatButtonModule,
    MatIconModule,
    MatToolbarModule,
    MatTableModule
  ]
})
export class AngularMaterialModule { }
```

Now we can take advantage of the `MatTableModule` in all our Angular app's components.

Updating CitiesComponent

Let's start with `CitiesComponent`.

Open the `/src/app/cities/cities.component.ts` file and add the following (highlighted) lines:

```
// ...existing code...

export class CitiesComponent implements OnInit {
  public displayedColumns: string[] = ['id', 'name', 'lat', 'lon'];
  public cities!: City[];

  constructor(private http: HttpClient) {
  }
}

// ...existing code...
```

Right after that, open the `/src/app/cities/cities.component.html` file and replace our previous table implementation with the new `MatTableModule` in the following way (updated code is highlighted):

```
<h1>Cities</h1>

<p>Here's a list of cities: feel free to play with it.</p>

<p *ngIf="!cities"><em>Loading...</em></p>

<table mat-table [dataSource]="cities"
  class="mat-elevation-z8"
  [hidden]="!cities">
  <!-- Id Column -->
  <ng-container matColumnDef="id">
    <th mat-header-cell *matHeaderCellDef>ID</th>
    <td mat-cell *matCellDef="let city">{{city.id}}</td>
  </ng-container>

  <!-- Name Column -->
  <ng-container matColumnDef="name">
    <th mat-header-cell *matHeaderCellDef>Name</th>
    <td mat-cell *matCellDef="let city">{{city.name}}</td>
  </ng-container>
```

```
<!-- Lat Column -->
<ng-container matColumnDef="lat">
  <th mat-header-cell *matHeaderCellDef>Latitude</th>
  <td mat-cell *matCellDef="let city">{{city.lat}}</td>
</ng-container>

<!-- Lon Column -->
<ng-container matColumnDef="lon">
  <th mat-header-cell *matHeaderCellDef>Longitude</th>
  <td mat-cell *matCellDef="let city">{{city.lon}}</td>
</ng-container>

<tr mat-header-row *matHeaderRowDef="displayedColumns"></tr>
<tr mat-row *matRowDef="let row; columns: displayedColumns;"></tr>
</table>
```

As we can see, MatTableModule kind of mimics the behavior of a standard HTML table, but with a template-based approach for each column; the template features a series of auxiliary structural directives (applied using the *<directiveName> syntax) that can be used to mark certain template sections and define their template section's actual role. As we can see, all these directives end with the Def postfix.

Here are the most relevant ones among those used in the preceding code:

- The [hidden] attribute binding is not a surprise as it was already present in the previous table for the exact same purpose: keeping the table hidden until the *cities* have been loaded.
- The matColumnDef directive identifies a given column with a unique key.
- The matHeaderCellDef directive defines how to display the header for each column.
- The matCellDef directive defines how to display the data cells for each column.
- The matHeaderRowDef directive, which can be found near the end of the preceding code, identifies a configuration element for the table header row and the display order of the header columns. As we can see, we had this directive expression pointing to a component variable called displayedColumns, which we defined in the cities.component.ts file early on; this variable hosts an array containing all the column keys we want to show, which need to be identical to the names specified via the various matColumnDef directives.

Before testing our new MatTable-based implementation, we need to update our component's styling rules.

Open the /src/app/cities/cities.component.scss file and replace its content with the following:

```
table.mat-table {
    width: 100%;
}
```

As we can see, most of the previous CSS rules are gone, since we no longer need to style the HTML table element manually: Angular Material will do most of the styling job for us.

 For reference purposes, the previous TypeScript, HTML, and CSS implementation can be found in the GitHub repository – /Chapter_06/ folder, within the _cities.component_ v1.ts, _cities.component_v1.html, and _cities.component_v1.scss files.

Now we can hit *F5* and navigate to the **Cities** view to see what our brand-new table looks like. This can be seen in the following screenshot:

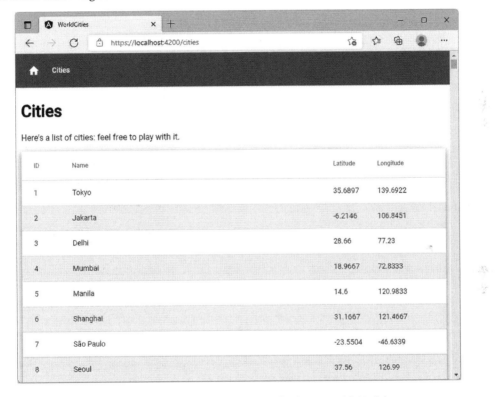

Figure 6.4: New Cities table implemented using MatTableModule

OK, Material Design is indeed there, but the table has the same UI/UX problems as before! For one, it's still very long; let's fix that by implementing the **paging** feature.

Adding pagination with MatPaginatorModule

Now that we are using Angular Material, implementing pagination is a rather easy task. The first thing we need to do is add a reference to MatPaginatorModule to the angular-material.module.ts file, just like we did with MatTableModule a short while ago.

Here's the `import` statement to add at the end of the already existing ones, right after `MatTableModule`:

```
import { MatPaginatorModule } from '@angular/material/paginator';
```

Remember to also add it to the `imports` and `exports` collections of `@NgModule`.

 For reasons of space, we're not going to show the resulting source code here: however, if you would like to, you can check out the updated `angular-material.module.ts` on GitHub.

Client-side paging

Now that we've referenced the new module, we can open the `cities.component.ts` file and import the `MatPaginator`, `MatTableDataSource`, and `ViewChild` services in the following way (new and updated lines are highlighted):

```
import { Component, OnInit, ViewChild } from '@angular/core';
import { HttpClient } from '@angular/common/http';
import { environment } from './../../environments/environment';
import { MatTableDataSource } from '@angular/material/table';
import { MatPaginator } from '@angular/material/paginator';

import { City } from './city';

@Component({
  selector: 'app-cities',
  templateUrl: './cities.component.html',
  styleUrls: ['./cities.component.scss']
})
export class CitiesComponent implements OnInit {
  public displayedColumns: string[] = ['id', 'name', 'lat', 'lon'];
  public cities!: MatTableDataSource<City>;

  @ViewChild(MatPaginator) paginator!: MatPaginator;

  constructor(private http: HttpClient) {
  }

  ngOnInit() {
    this.http.get<City[]>(environment.baseUrl + 'api/Cities')
      .subscribe(result => {
        this.cities = new MatTableDataSource<City>(result);
        this.cities.paginator = this.paginator;
```

```
        }, error => console.error(error));
    }
}
```

As we can see, we've used the `@ViewChild` decorator to set a static view query and store its result in the paginator variable; let's spend a couple of minutes on the purpose of such a decorator and why we need it.

In a nutshell, the `@ViewChild` decorator can be used to get a reference of a DOM template element from within the Angular component, thus making it a very useful feature whenever we need to manipulate the element's properties. As we can see from the preceding code, the decorator is defined using a *selector* parameter, which is required to access the DOM element: this *selector* can be a class name (if the class has either the `@Component` or `@Directive` decorator), a template reference variable, a provider defined in the child component tree, and so on.

In our specific scenario, we've used the `MatPaginator` class name, since it does have the `@Component` decorator.

> While we're at it, it can be useful to know that the `@ViewChild` decorator also accepts a second parameter, which was required until Angular 8 and became optional since Angular 9: a static flag, which can be either `true` or `false` (from Angular 9, it defaults to `false`). If this flag is explicitly set to `true`, `@ViewChild` is retrieved from the template before the change detection phase runs (that is, even before the `ngOnInit()` life cycle); conversely, the component/element retrieval task is resolved either after the change detection phase if the element is inside a nested view (for example, a view with a `*ngIf` conditional display directive), or before change detection if it isn't.
>
> Since we've used the `[hidden]` attribute binding in the template instead of the `*ngIf` directive, our `MatPaginator` won't run into initialization issues, even without having to set that flag to `true`.
>
> For additional information about the `@ViewChild` decorator, we suggest you take a look at the Angular docs: `https://angular.io/api/core/ViewChild`.

Once done, open the `cities.component.html` file and add the following pagination directive (highlighted) right after the `</table>` closing tag:

```html
<!-- ...existing code... -->

  <tr mat-header-row *matHeaderRowDef="displayedColumns"></tr>
  <tr mat-row *matRowDef="let row; columns: displayedColumns;"></tr>
</table>

<!-- Pagination directive -->
<mat-paginator [hidden]="!cities"
    [pageSize]="10"
```

```
     [pageSizeOptions]="[10, 20, 50]"
     showFirstLastButtons></mat-paginator>
```

As we can see, we used the [hidden] *attribute binding* again to keep the paginator hidden until the *cities* were loaded. The other properties that we can see on the <mat-paginator> element configure some of the MatPaginatorModule UI options, such as the default page size and an array of all the page size options that we want to make available to the users.

Now, we can hit *F5* and take a look at our efforts:

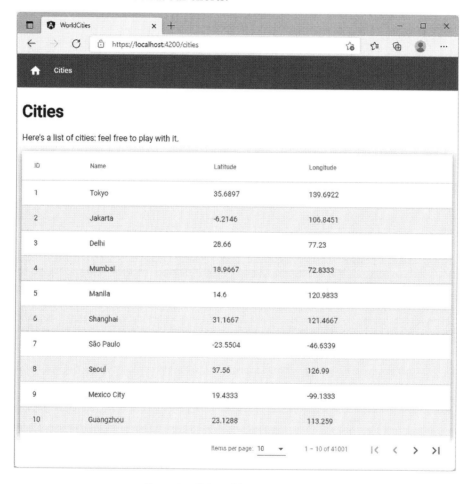

Figure 6.5: Cities table with pagination

Now, our table only shows the first 10 cities. It has also got a neat paginator at its bottom-right corner that can be used to navigate through the various pages using arrows. Our end user can even choose how many items per page to display using a neat drop-down list (10, 20, or 50 cities per page, as specified in the [pageSizeOptions] property). It definitely seems like we did it!

However, if we think about it, we can easily acknowledge that we're not quite there yet. Sure, now our users can browse the table nicely without having to scroll up and down for ages, but it doesn't take a genius to understand that all those rows are still being transferred to the client browser: we never told the server to actually support a paginated request, so we still fetch all of the cities from our data provider (and through the ASP.NET API Controller) just like before: as a matter of fact, they're just not rendered by the *front-end*.

This basically means that we still have the same performance impact that we had before on the server side (huge SQL query result, massive JSON) and only a partial performance improvement on the client side: even if fewer HTML elements are now added to the DOM, there are still lots of HTML rows to show/hide on each paginator action, leading to a page change.

In order to mitigate the aforementioned issues, we need to move from client-side paging to server-side paging – which is precisely what we'll do in the next section.

Server-side paging

Implementing server-side paging is a bit more complex than its client-side counterpart. Here's what we need to do (and where):

- **WorldCitiesAPI (ASP.NET project)**. Change our `CitiesController` class to make it support paged HTTP GET requests

- **WorldCitiesAPI (ASP.NET project)**. Create a new `ApiResult` class that we can use to improve the JSON response of our ASP.NET Controllers

- **WorldCities (Angular project)**. Change our `cities.controller.ts` Angular component – and the current `MatPaginatorModule` configuration – to make it able to issue the new GET request and deal with the new JSON response

Let's do this!

CitiesController

The `GetCities` method of our `CitiesController` returns a JSON array of all the ~41,000 cities in our database by default; that's definitely a no-go in terms of server-side performance, so we need to change it. Ideally, we would like to only return a small number of `Cities`, which is something we can easily pull off by adding some (required) variables to the method signature, such as `pageIndex` and `pageSize`.

Here's how we could change that to enforce such behavior (updated lines highlighted):

```
// ...existing code...


[HttpGet]
public async Task<ActionResult<IEnumerable<City>>> GetCities(
    int pageIndex = 0,
    int pageSize = 10)
{
```

```
        return await _context.Cities
                        .Skip(pageIndex * pageSize)
                        .Take(pageSize)
                        .ToListAsync();
}

// ...existing code...
```

That's it; we also specified some reasonable default values for those variables in order to avoid huge JSON responses *by default*.

Let's quickly test what we just did: hit *F5* and type the following URL in the browser's address bar: https://localhost:40443/api/Cities/?pageIndex=0&pageSize=10.

Here's what we should get:

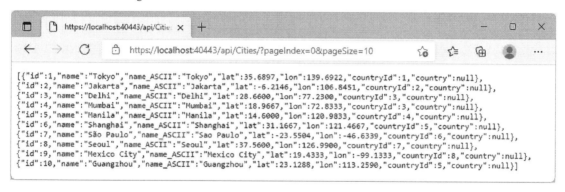

Figure 6.6: A snippet of the JSON array of 10 cities

It definitely seems that our plan is working!

However, there is a major issue we have to deal with: if we just return a JSON array of 10 cities, there will be no way for our Angular app to actually know how many cities are present in our database. Without that information, there is little chance that the paginator would reasonably work the way it did when we implemented the client-side pagination early on.

Long story short, we need to find a way to tell our Angular app some additional information, such as the following:

- The total number of pages (and/or records) available
- The current page
- The number of records on each page

Truth be told, the only required information is the first one as the Angular client would then be able to keep track of the other two; however, since we need to implement that one, we might as well return them all, thus making our *front-end* life a lot easier.

In order to do that, the best thing we can do is create a dedicated *response-type* class – which we're going to use a lot from now on.

ApiResult

From Solution Explorer, right-click the Data folder and add a new ApiResult.cs C# class file. Then, fill it up with the following content:

```
using Microsoft.EntityFrameworkCore;


namespace WorldCitiesAPI.Data
{
    public class ApiResult<T>
    {
        /// <summary>
        /// Private constructor called by the CreateAsync method.
        /// </summary>
        private ApiResult(
            List<T> data,
            int count,
            int pageIndex,
            int pageSize)
        {
            Data = data;
            PageIndex = pageIndex;
            PageSize = pageSize;
            TotalCount = count;
            TotalPages = (int)Math.Ceiling(count / (double)pageSize);
        }

        #region Methods
        /// <summary>
        /// Pages a IQueryable source.
        /// </summary>
        /// <param name="source">An IQueryable source of generic
        /// type</param>
        /// <param name="pageIndex">Zero-based current page index
        /// (0 = first page)</param>
        /// <param name="pageSize">The actual size of each
        /// page</param>
        /// <returns>
        /// A object containing the paged result
```

```csharp
/// and all the relevant paging navigation info.
/// </returns>
public static async Task<ApiResult<T>> CreateAsync(
    IQueryable<T> source,
    int pageIndex,
    int pageSize)
{
    var count = await source.CountAsync();
    source = source
        .Skip(pageIndex * pageSize)
        .Take(pageSize);

    var data = await source.ToListAsync();

    return new ApiResult<T>(
        data,
        count,
        pageIndex,
        pageSize);
}
#endregion

#region Properties
/// <summary>
/// The data result.
/// </summary>
public List<T> Data { get; private set; }

/// <summary>
/// Zero-based index of current page.
/// </summary>
public int PageIndex { get; private set; }

/// <summary>
/// Number of items contained in each page.
/// </summary>
public int PageSize { get; private set; }

/// <summary>
/// Total items count
/// </summary>
```

```
        public int TotalCount { get; private set; }


        /// <summary>
        /// Total pages count
        /// </summary>
        public int TotalPages { get; private set; }


        /// <summary>
        /// TRUE if the current page has a previous page,
        /// FALSE otherwise.
        /// </summary>
        public bool HasPreviousPage
        {
            get
            {
                return (PageIndex > 0);
            }
        }


        /// <summary>
        /// TRUE if the current page has a next page, FALSE otherwise.
        /// </summary>
        public bool HasNextPage
        {
            get
            {
                return ((PageIndex +1) < TotalPages);
            }
        }
        #endregion
    }
}
```

This `ApiResult` class contains some really interesting stuff. Let's try to summarize the most relevant things:

- `Data`: A property of the `List<T>` type that will be used to contain the paged data (it will be translated to a JSON array)
- `PageIndex`: Returns the zero-based index of the current page (0 for the first page, 1 for the second, and so on)
- `PageSize`: Returns the total page size (`TotalCount` / `PageSize`)
- `TotalCount`: Returns the total `Item` count number

- `TotalPages`: Returns the total number of pages taking into account the total `Items` count (`TotalCount` / `PageSize`)
- `HasPreviousPage`: Returns `True` if the current page has a previous page, otherwise `False`
- `HasNextPage`: Returns `True` if the current page has a next page, otherwise `False`

Those properties are precisely what we were looking for; the underlying logic to calculate their values should be quite easy to understand by looking at the preceding code.

Other than that, the class basically revolves around the static method `CreateAsync<T>(IQueryable<T>` `source, int pageIndex, int pageSize)`, which can be used to paginate an Entity Framework `IQueryable` object.

> It's worth noting that the `ApiResult` class cannot be instantiated from the outside since its constructor has been marked as `private`; the only way to create it is by using the static `CreateAsync` factory method. There are good reasons to do that: since it is not possible to define an `async` constructor, we have resorted to using a static `async` method that returns a class instance; the constructor has been set to `private` to prevent developers from directly using it instead of the factory method, since it's the only reasonable way to instantiate this class.

Here's how we can make use of our brand-new `ApiResult` class in the `GetCities` method of our `CitiesController`:

```
// ...existing code...


// GET: api/Cities
// GET: api/Cities/?pageIndex=0&pageSize=10
[HttpGet]
public async Task<ActionResult<ApiResult<City>>> GetCities(
        int pageIndex = 0,
        int pageSize = 10)
{
    return await ApiResult<City>.CreateAsync(
            _context.Cities.AsNoTracking(),
            pageIndex,
            pageSize
            );
}

// ...existing code...
```

Here we go! Now, we should have our 10 cities and all the information we were looking for.

It's worth nothing that, since we're performing a read-only task, we've used the `AsNoTracking()` extension method, which we introduced in *Chapter 5, Data Model with Entity Framework Core*, to prevent EF Core from tacking all the entities, thereby avoiding a non-trivial performance impact.

Let's hit *F5* and navigate to the same URL as before to see what's changed: `https://localhost:40443/api/Cities/?pageIndex=0&pageSize=10`.

Here's the updated JSON response:

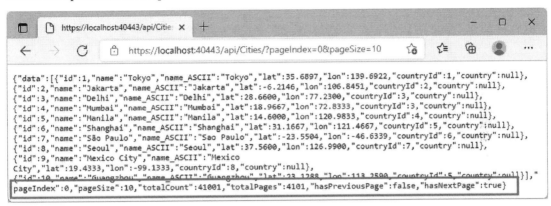

Figure 6.7: The updated JSON array containing extra page information

If we scroll down to the bottom of the result, we will see that the endpoint does not return a JSON *array* anymore; the new resulting content is a JSON *object* that contains our previous array (in the `data` property), as well as the new properties that we need to perform our pagination tasks.

Let's now move to our Angular's `CitiesComponent` and update it to use this new, optimized way of fetching our cities from the server.

CitiesComponent

The only Angular files we need to change are the following:

- The `CitiesComponent` TypeScript file, which is where we put all the data retrieval logic that we now need to update
- The `CitiesComponent` HTML file, to bind a specific event to our `MatPaginator` element

Let's do this.

Open the `cities.component.ts` file and perform the following changes (new/updated lines are highlighted):

```
import { Component, OnInit, ViewChild } from '@angular/core';
import { HttpClient, HttpParams } from '@angular/common/http';
import { environment } from './../../environments/environment';
```

```
import { MatTableDataSource } from '@angular/material/table';
import { MatPaginator, PageEvent } from '@angular/material/paginator';

import { City } from './city';

@Component({
  selector: 'app-cities',
  templateUrl: './cities.component.html',
  styleUrls: ['./cities.component.scss']
})
export class CitiesComponent implements OnInit {
  public displayedColumns: string[] = ['id', 'name', 'lat', 'lon'];
  public cities!: MatTableDataSource<City>;

  @ViewChild(MatPaginator) paginator!: MatPaginator;

  constructor(private http: HttpClient) {
  }

  ngOnInit() {
    var pageEvent = new PageEvent();
    pageEvent.pageIndex = 0;
    pageEvent.pageSize = 10;
    this.getData(pageEvent);
  }


  getData(event: PageEvent) {
    var url = environment.baseUrl + 'api/Cities';
    var params = new HttpParams()
      .set("pageIndex", event.pageIndex.toString())
      .set("pageSize", event.pageSize.toString());
    this.http.get<any>(url, { params })
      .subscribe(result => {
        this.paginator.length = result.totalCount;
```

```
            this.paginator.pageIndex = result.pageIndex;
            this.paginator.pageSize = result.pageSize;
            this.cities = new MatTableDataSource<City>(result.data);
        }, error => console.error(error));
    }
}
```

Let's try to summarize what we did here:

- We removed the HttpClient from the ngOnInit() life cycle hook method and placed the whole data retrieval login in a separate getData() method. In order to do this, we had to define a couple of internal class variables to host the HttpClient and the baseUrl to persist them so that we'll be able to use them multiple times (that is, on multiple getData() calls).
- We changed the data retrieval logic to match our new JSON response object.
- We modified our paginator configuration strategy to manually set the values we get from the server side instead of having it figure them out automatically; doing that is required, otherwise it would just take into account (and *paginate*) the small portion of cities we retrieve upon each HTTP request instead of the full batch.

As for the cities.component.html file, we just need to add a single line to the `<mat-paginator>` directive to bind the getData() event upon each paging event. Here's how to do that (the new line is highlighted):

```
<!-- ...existing code... -->

<!-- Pagination directive -->
<mat-paginator [hidden]="!cities"
    (page)="getData($event)"
    [pageSize]="10"
    [pageSizeOptions]="[10, 20, 50]"
    showFirstLastButtons></mat-paginator>
```

This simple binding plays a very important role: it ensures that the getData() event is called every time the user interacts with the paginator element to perform a page change, asking for the previous/next page, first/last page, changing the number of items to display, and so on. As we can easily understand, such a call is required for server-side pagination since we need to fetch the updated data from the server every time we have to display different rows.

Once done, let's try the new magic by hitting *F5* and then navigating to the **Cities** view. If we did everything properly, we should get the same UI that we could see before:

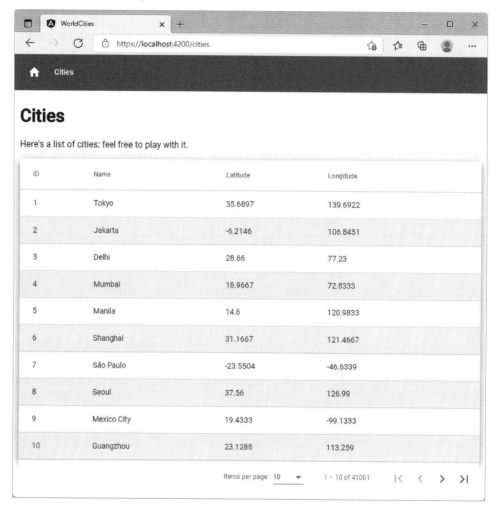

Figure 6.8: The same paginated Cities table with better performance

However, this time, we should experience better overall performance and faster response times for the initial page load. That's because we're not dealing with thousands of JSON items and HTML table rows under the hood; we're fetching only a few of them at a time (that is, those we get to see) using our improved server-side logic.

At the same time, navigating between pages can be a bit slower than before, since we are issuing a new HTTP request (and data fetch) for every page instead of getting the in-memory data. However, such a performance drawback is often preferable to downloading the entire dataset in one go, which is what happens when using client-side paging, unless we are working with a rather small dataset. As always when dealing with such performance issues, there is no "better approach": it all depends on the application requirements, the volume of affected data, and what we want to achieve.

Since we're done with paging, we can finally deal with **sorting**.

Adding sorting with MatSortModule

In order to implement sorting, we're going to use `MatSortModule`, which can be implemented just like the `paginator` module.

This time, we won't make client-side sorting experiments as we did with paging early on; we're going for the server-side pattern right from the start.

> In general terms, whenever we deal with paging and sorting, we should always take the server-side implementation into account, since it will likely improve the overall performance of our apps while often preventing the need to handle that kind of stuff using additional client-side code.

Extending ApiResult

Let's start with the ASP.NET *back-end* part – in other words, the **WorldCitiesAPI** project.

Do you remember the `ApiResult` class we created earlier? It's time to improve its source code to add sorting support.

From Solution Explorer, open the `/Data/ApiResult.cs` file and update its content accordingly (new/updated lines are highlighted):

```
using Microsoft.EntityFrameworkCore;
using System.Linq.Dynamic.Core;
using System.Reflection;

namespace WorldCitiesAPI.Data
{
    public class ApiResult<T>
    {
        /// <summary>
        /// Private constructor called by the CreateAsync method.
        /// </summary>
        private ApiResult(
            List<T> data,
            int count,
            int pageIndex,
            int pageSize,
            string? sortColumn,
            string? sortOrder)
        {
            Data = data;
```

```
        PageIndex = pageIndex;
        PageSize = pageSize;
        TotalCount = count;
        TotalPages = (int)Math.Ceiling(count / (double)pageSize);
        SortColumn = sortColumn;
        SortOrder = sortOrder;
    }

    #region Methods
    /// <summary>
    /// Pages and/or sorts a IQueryable source.
    /// </summary>
    /// <param name="source">An IQueryable source of generic
    /// type</param>
    /// <param name="pageIndex">Zero-based current page index
    /// (0 = first page)</param>
    /// <param name="pageSize">The actual size of each
    /// page</param>
    /// <param name="sortColumn">The sorting column name</param>
    /// <param name="sortOrder">The sorting order ("ASC" or
    /// "DESC")</param>
    /// <returns>
    /// A object containing the IQueryable paged/sorted result
    /// and all the relevant paging/sorting navigation info.
    /// </returns>
    public static async Task<ApiResult<T>> CreateAsync(
        IQueryable<T> source,
        int pageIndex,
        int pageSize,
        string? sortColumn = null,
        string? sortOrder = null)
    {
        var count = await source.CountAsync();

        if (!string.IsNullOrEmpty(sortColumn)
            && IsValidProperty(sortColumn))
        {
            sortOrder = !string.IsNullOrEmpty(sortOrder)
                && sortOrder.ToUpper() == "ASC"
                ? "ASC"
                : "DESC";
```

```
            source = source.OrderBy(
                string.Format(
                    "{0} {1}",
                    sortColumn,
                    sortOrder)
                );
        }

        source = source
            .Skip(pageIndex * pageSize)
            .Take(pageSize);

        var data = await source.ToListAsync();

        return new ApiResult<T>(
            data,
            count,
            pageIndex,
            pageSize,
            sortColumn,
            sortOrder);
    }
    #endregion

    #region Methods
    /// <summary>
    /// Checks if the given property name exists
    /// to protect against SQL injection attacks
    /// </summary>
    public static bool IsValidProperty(
        string propertyName,
        bool throwExceptionIfNotFound = true)
    {
        var prop = typeof(T).GetProperty(
            propertyName,
            BindingFlags.IgnoreCase |
            BindingFlags.Public |
            BindingFlags.Instance);
        if (prop == null && throwExceptionIfNotFound)
            throw new NotSupportedException(
                string.Format(
```

```
                    $"ERROR: Property '{propertyName}' does not exist.")
                );
        return prop != null;
    }
    #endregion

    #region Properties
    /// <summary>
    /// The data result.
    /// </summary>
    public List<T> Data { get; private set; }


    /// <summary>
    /// Zero-based index of current page.
    /// </summary>
    public int PageIndex { get; private set; }


    /// <summary>
    /// Number of items contained in each page.
    /// </summary>
    public int PageSize { get; private set; }


    /// <summary>
    /// Total items count
    /// </summary>
    public int TotalCount { get; private set; }


    /// <summary>
    /// Total pages count
    /// </summary>
    public int TotalPages { get; private set; }


    /// <summary>
    /// TRUE if the current page has a previous page,
    /// FALSE otherwise.
    /// </summary>
    public bool HasPreviousPage
    {
        get
        {
            return (PageIndex > 0);
```

```
        }
    }

    /// <summary>
    /// TRUE if the current page has a next page, FALSE otherwise.
    /// </summary>
    public bool HasNextPage
    {
        get
        {
            return ((PageIndex +1) < TotalPages);
        }
    }

    /// <summary>
    /// Sorting Column name (or null if none set)
    /// </summary>
    public string? SortColumn { get; set; }

    /// <summary>
    /// Sorting Order ("ASC", "DESC" or null if none set)
    /// </summary>
    public string? SortOrder { get; set; }
    #endregion
    }
}
```

What we did was add two new sortColumn and sortOrder attributes to the main class static method and implement them through the code; while we were there, we also took the opportunity to define two new properties with the same name (in uppercase) so that the sorting details will be part of the JSON response, just like the paging ones.

It's worth noting that since we're now assembling our **Language-Integrated Query** (LINQ)-to-SQL queries with literal data coming from the client, we also added a new IsValidProperty() method that will check that the sortColumn specified does actually exist as a typed property of the generic <T> entity we're dealing with; as the method comment clearly says, that's actually a security counter-measure against SQL injection attempts. This is a very important security issue that we'll be talking about in a short while.

 In the unlikely case that you've never heard of LINQ, don't worry: we'll get there soon.

If we try to build our project right after these changes, we'll most likely be greeted by some compiler errors, such as the following one:

```
Error CS0246: The type or namespace name System.Linq.Dynamic could not be found
(are you missing a using directive or an assembly reference?).
```

Don't worry, it's perfectly normal: we just need to add a new NuGet package to our project.

Installing System.Linq.Dynamic.Core

The `IQueryable<T>.OrderBy()` extension method that we used in the improved `ApiResult` source code to programmatically apply the column sorting is part of the `System.Linq.Dynamic.Core` namespace. Thanks to this library, it's possible to write Dynamic LINQ queries (string-based) on an `IQueryable`, which is just like what we did in the preceding code.

Unfortunately, `System.Linq.Dynamic.Core` is not part of the ASP.NET stock binaries; therefore, in order to use these features, we need to add them via NuGet.

The fastest way to do that is to open Visual Studio's **Package Manager Console** and issue the following command:

```
> Install-Package System.Linq.Dynamic.Core
```

IMPORTANT: Be sure to install `System.Linq.Dynamic.Core` and not `System.Linq.Dynamic`, which is its .NET Framework 4.0 counterpart; the latter won't work with our ASP.NET web application project. At the time of writing, the most recent version of the `System.Linq.Dynamic.Core` package is 1.2.14, which works absolutely fine for our purposes.

For those who want to retrieve additional information regarding this great package, we suggest you take a look at the following resources:

NuGet website: `https://www.nuget.org/packages/System.Linq.Dynamic.Core/`

GitHub project: `https://github.com/StefH/System.Linq.Dynamic.Core`

What is LINQ?

Before moving forward, let's spend a couple of minutes talking about LINQ in the unlikely case you have never heard anything about it.

Also known as Language-Integrated Query, LINQ is the code name of a Microsoft .NET Framework set of technologies that adds data query capabilities to .NET languages such as C# and VB.NET. LINQ was first released in 2007 and was one of the major new features of .NET Framework 3.5.

The main purpose of LINQ is to make the developer able to express structured queries against data using a first-class language construct without having to learn different query languages for each type of data source (collection types, SQL, XML, CSV, and so on). For each of these *major* data source types, there's a LINQ implementation that provides the same query experience for objects (*LINQ to Objects*), Entity Framework entities (*LINQ to Entities*), relational databases (*LINQ to SQL*), XML (*LINQ to XML*), and so on.

LINQ structured queries can be expressed using two alternative – yet also complementary – approaches:

- **Lambda expressions**, such as the following:

```
var city = _context.Cities.Where(c => c.Name == "New York").First();
```

- **Query expressions**, such as the following:

```
var city = (from c in _context.Cities where c.Name == "New York" select
c).First();
```

Both yield the same result with the same performance since query expressions are translated into their lambda expression equivalents before they're compiled.

> For additional information about LINQ, lambda expressions, and query expressions, check out the following links:
>
> LINQ: `https://docs.microsoft.com/en-us/dotnet/csharp/linq/`
>
> LINQ lambda expressions (C# programming guide): `https://docs.microsoft.com/en-us/dotnet/csharp/programming-guide/statements-expressions-operators/lambda-expressions`
>
> LINQ query expression basics: `https://docs.microsoft.com/en-us/dotnet/csharp/linq/query-expression-basics`

System.Linq.Dynamic.Core pros and cons

Now, since LINQ has been incorporated with .NET Framework since v3.5 and it's shipped with each subsequent ASP.NET version ever since, what does the System.Linq.Dynamic.Core package actually do and why are we using it?

As we can see from the two preceding examples, both lambda expressions and query expressions work with a strongly typed approach: whenever we *query* an object of any type using LINQ, the source type – together with all the properties we want our query to check for – must be known by the compiler. This means that we would be unable to use these techniques with generic objects (object) or types (<T>). That's where Linq.Dynamic comes to the rescue, allowing the developer to write lambda expressions and query expressions with literal strings and translate them into their strongly typed equivalents using **reflection**.

Here's the same query as before, written using System.Linq.Dynamic.Core:

```
var city = _context.Cities.Where("Name = @1", "New York").First();
```

We can immediately see the difference – and also the tremendous advantage we can get by using such an approach: we will be able to build our queries dynamically, regardless of whether we're dealing with strongly typed objects or generic types, just like we did within the source code of ApiResult a short while ago.

However, such an approach will also have a major downside: our code will be less testable and way too error-prone, for at least two important reasons:

- We'll be just *a literal string away* from query errors, which will almost always lead to major crashes

- The risk of unwanted queries (including SQL injection attacks) could increase exponentially, depending on how we build those queries and/or where we get our *dynamic* strings from

 Those who don't know what SQL injection is and/or why it is dangerous should definitely take a look at the following guide, written by Tim Sammut and Mike Schiffman from the Cisco Security Intelligence team:

Understanding SQL Injections: `https://tools.cisco.com/security/center/resources/sql_injection`

The former issue is bad, but the latter is even worse: being open to SQL injection attacks could be devastating and therefore is something we should avoid at any cost – including getting rid of the `System.Linq.Dynamic.Core` package.

Preventing SQL injection

Luckily enough, we don't need to do that; although we're getting *two* potentially harmful variable strings coming from the client – `sortColumn` and `sortOrder` – we have already put in place effective countermeasures for both of them in the preceding source code of `ApiResult`.

Here's what we did for `sortOrder`:

```
// ...existing code...

sortOrder = !string.IsNullOrEmpty(sortOrder)
    && sortOrder.ToUpper() == "ASC"
    ? "ASC"
    : "DESC";

// ...existing code...
```

As we can see, we'll convert it into either `"ASC"` or `"DESC"` before using it anywhere, thus leaving no openings to SQL injection.

The `sortColumn` parameter is way more complex to handle because it can theoretically contain any possible column name mapped to any of our entities: `id`, `name`, `lat`, `lon`, `iso2`, `iso3`... If we were to check them all, we would need a very long conditional block! Not to mention the fact that it would also be very hard to maintain whenever we added new entities and/or properties to our project.

For that very reason, we chose a completely different – and arguably better – approach, which relies upon the following `IsValidProperty` method:

```
// ...existing code...
```

```
public static bool IsValidProperty(
    string propertyName,
    bool throwExceptionIfNotFound = true)
{
    var prop = typeof(T).GetProperty(
        propertyName,
        BindingFlags.IgnoreCase |
        BindingFlags.Public |
        BindingFlags.Instance);
    if (prop == null && throwExceptionIfNotFound)
        throw new NotSupportedException($"ERROR: Property '{propertyName}' does
not exist.");
    return prop != null;
}

// ...existing code...
```

As we can see, this method checks that the given `propertyName` corresponds to an existing typed `Property` within our `<T>` generic entity class: if it does, it returns `True`; otherwise, it throws a `NotSupportedException` (or returns `False`, depending on how we call it). This is a great way to shield our code against SQL injection because there's absolutely no way that a harmful string would match one of our entity's properties.

The property name check has been implemented through `System.Reflection`, a technique that's used to inspect and/or retrieve metadata on types at runtime. To work with reflection, we need to include the `System.Reflection` namespace in our class – which is precisely what we did at the beginning of the source code of our improved `ApiResult`.

For additional information about `System.Reflection`, check out the following guide: `https://docs.microsoft.com/en-us/dotnet/csharp/programming-guide/concepts/reflection`.

As we can see by looking back at the `ApiResult` source code, such a method is being called in the following way:

```
if (!string.IsNullOrEmpty(sortColumn)
    && IsValidProperty(sortColumn))
{
    /// if we are here, sortColumn is safe to use
}
```

Those curly brackets define our SQL injection safety zone: as long as we deal with `sortColumn` within them, we have nothing to worry about.

Truth be told, even after implementing this defensive approach, there's still a minor threat we could be exposed to: if we have some reserved columns/properties that we don't want the client to interact with (system columns, for example), the preceding countermeasure won't block it from doing that; although being unable to acknowledge their existence or to read their data, an experienced user could still be able to "order" the table results by them – provided that the user knows their precise name somehow.

If we want to prevent this remote – yet theoretically possible – leak, we can set these properties to private (since we told our IsValidProperty method to only check for public properties) and/or rethink the whole method logic so that it better suits our security needs.

Updating CitiesController

Now that we have improved our ApiResult class, we can implement it within our CitiesController.

Open the /Controllers/CitiesController.cs file and change its contents accordingly (updated lines are highlighted):

```
// ...existing code...


// GET: api/Cities
// GET: api/Cities/?pageIndex=0&pageSize=10
// GET: api/Cities/?pageIndex=0&pageSize=10&sortColumn=name&
//    sortOrder=asc
[HttpGet]
public async Task<ActionResult<ApiResult<City>>> GetCities(
        int pageIndex = 0,
        int pageSize = 10,
        string? sortColumn = null,
        string? sortOrder = null)
{
    return await ApiResult<City>.CreateAsync(
            _context.Cities,
            pageIndex,
            pageSize,
            sortColumn,
            sortOrder);
}

// ...existing code...
```

Thanks to these two new parameters, our GetCities method will be able to sort the cities the way we want.

We're done with the *back-end* part; let's now move on to the *front-end*.

Updating the Angular app

As always, we need to change three files:

- The angular-material.module.ts file, where we need to add the new @angular/material module
- The cities.component.ts file, to implement the sorting business logic
- The cities.component.html file, to bind the new variables, methods, and references defined in the .ts file within the UI template

Let's do that.

angular-material.module.ts

Open the /src/app/angular-material.module.ts file and add the references to MatSortModule:

```
import { MatSortModule } from '@angular/material/sort';
```

Don't forget to update the imports and exports arrays of @NgModule as well.

From now on, we'll be able to import the MatSortModule-related classes in any Angular component.

cities.component.ts

Once done, open the cities.component.ts file and make the following modifications (updated lines are highlighted):

```
import { Component, OnInit, ViewChild } from '@angular/core';
import { HttpClient, HttpParams } from '@angular/common/http';
import { environment } from './../../environment';
import { MatTableDataSource } from '@angular/material/table';
import { MatPaginator, PageEvent } from '@angular/material/paginator';
import { MatSort } from '@angular/material/sort';

import { City } from './city';

@Component({
  selector: 'app-cities',
  templateUrl: './cities.component.html',
  styleUrls: ['./cities.component.scss']
})
export class CitiesComponent implements OnInit {
  public displayedColumns: string[] = ['id', 'name', 'lat', 'lon'];
  public cities!: MatTableDataSource<City>;

  defaultPageIndex: number = 0;
```

```
defaultPageSize: number = 10;
public defaultSortColumn: string = "name";
public defaultSortOrder: "asc" | "desc" = "asc";

@ViewChild(MatPaginator) paginator!: MatPaginator;
@ViewChild(MatSort) sort!: MatSort;

constructor(private http: HttpClient) {
}

ngOnInit() {
  this.loadData();
}

loadData() {
  var pageEvent = new PageEvent();
  pageEvent.pageIndex = this.defaultPageIndex;
  pageEvent.pageSize = this.defaultPageSize;
  this.getData(pageEvent);
}

getData(event: PageEvent) {
  var url = environment.baseUrl + 'api/Cities';
  var params = new HttpParams()
    .set("pageIndex", event.pageIndex.toString())
    .set("pageSize", event.pageSize.toString())
    .set("sortColumn", (this.sort)
      ? this.sort.active
      : this.defaultSortColumn)
    .set("sortOrder", (this.sort)
      ? this.sort.direction
      : this.defaultSortOrder);
    this.http.get<any>(url, { params })
      .subscribe(result => {
        console.log(result);
        this.paginator.length = result.totalCount;
        this.paginator.pageIndex = result.pageIndex;
        this.paginator.pageSize = result.pageSize;
        this.cities = new MatTableDataSource<City>(result.data);
      }, error => console.error(error));
```

```
        }
    }
```

Here's a breakdown of the most relevant changes:

- We imported the `MatSort` reference from the `@angular/material` package.
- We added four new class variables to set the paging and sorting default values: `defaultPageIndex`, `defaultPageSize`, `defaultSortColumn`, and `defaultSortOrder`. Two of them have been defined as `public` because we need to use them from the HTML template via two-way data binding.
- We moved the initial `getData()` call from the class constructor to a new centralized `loadData()` function so that we can bind it to the table (as we'll see in a short while).
- We added the `sortColumn` and `sortOrder` HTTP GET parameters to our `HttpParams` object so that we can send the sorting information to the server side.

Now we can move to the HTML template file.

cities.component.html

Open the `cities.component.html` file and make the following modifications (updated lines are highlighted):

```html
<!-- ...existing code... -->

<table mat-table [dataSource]="cities"
  class="mat-elevation-z8"
  [hidden]="!cities"
  matSort (matSortChange)="loadData()"
  [matSortActive]="defaultSortColumn"
  [matSortDirection]="defaultSortOrder">

  <!-- Id Column -->
  <ng-container matColumnDef="id">
    <th mat-header-cell *matHeaderCellDef mat-sort-header>ID</th>
    <td mat-cell *matCellDef="let city"> {{city.id}} </td>
  </ng-container>

  <!-- Name Column -->
  <ng-container matColumnDef="name">
    <th mat-header-cell *matHeaderCellDef mat-sort-header>Name</th>
    <td mat-cell *matCellDef="let city"> {{city.name}} </td>
  </ng-container>

  <!-- Lat Column -->
  <ng-container matColumnDef="lat">
```

```
    <th mat-header-cell *matHeaderCellDef mat-sort-header>Latitude
    </th>
    <td mat-cell *matCellDef="let city"> {{city.lat}} </td>
  </ng-container>

  <!-- Lon Column -->
  <ng-container matColumnDef="lon">
    <th mat-header-cell *matHeaderCellDef mat-sort-header>Longitude
    </th>
    <td mat-cell *matCellDef="let city"> {{city.lon}} </td>
  </ng-container>

  <tr mat-header-row *matHeaderRowDef="displayedColumns"></tr>
  <tr mat-row *matRowDef="let row; columns: displayedColumns;"></tr>
</table>

<!-- ...existing code... -->
```

Here's what we did in a nutshell:

- We added the following attributes to the `<table mat-table>` element:

    - `matSort`: A reference to the `matSort` local variable we added to the `cities.component.ts` file early on

    - `(matSortChange)`: An event binding that will execute the `sortData()` method (also defined in the `.ts` file earlier) upon each sorting attempt by the user

    - `matSortActive` and `matSortDirection`: Two data bindings to the `defaultSortColumn` and `defaultSortOrder` variables that we defined in the `.ts` file early on

- We added the `mat-sort-header` attribute to each `<th mat-header-cell>` element (one for each table column)

 Now we can see why we didn't use the sleek URL we defined early on in our ASP.NET `CitiesController` and opted for the standard GET parameters instead: this approach allows us to programmatically add an indefinite number of HTTP GET parameters to our request thanks to the `HttpParams` class from the `@angular/common/http` package.

Let's quickly test it out by hitting *F5* and navigating to the **Cities** view. Here's what we should be able to see:

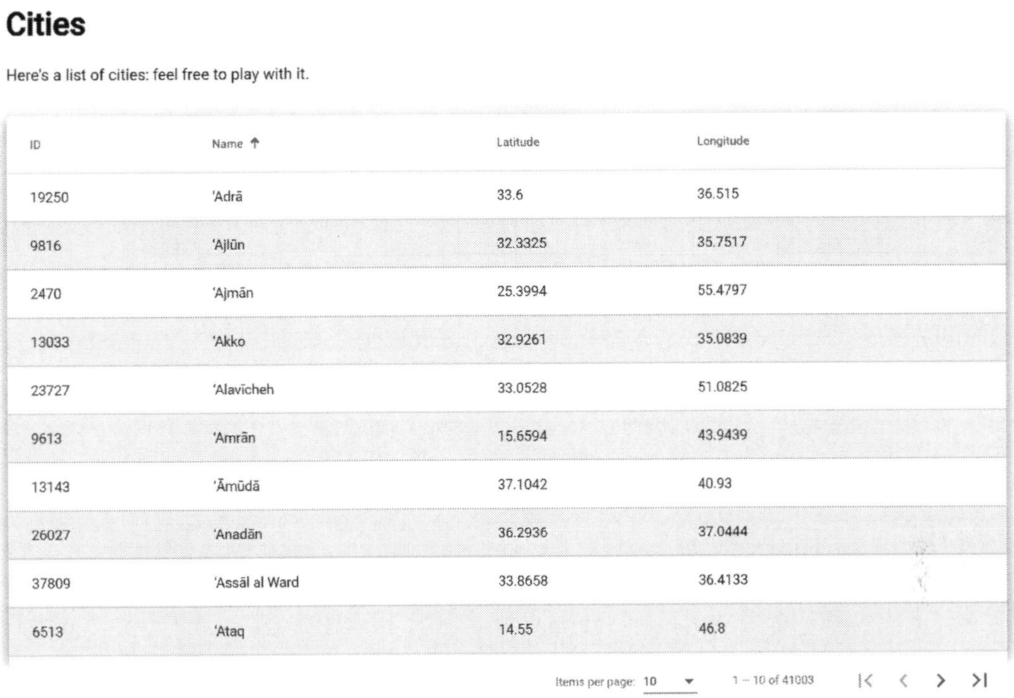

Cities

Here's a list of cities: feel free to play with it.

ID	Name ↑	Latitude	Longitude
19250	'Adrā	33.6	36.515
9816	'Ajlūn	32.3325	35.7517
2470	'Ajmān	25.3994	55.4797
13033	'Akko	32.9261	35.0839
23727	'Alavīcheh	33.0528	51.0825
9613	'Amrān	15.6594	43.9439
13143	'Āmūdā	37.1042	40.93
26027	'Anadān	36.2936	37.0444
37809	'Assāl al Ward	33.8658	36.4133
6513	'Ataq	14.55	46.8

Items per page: 10 ▾   1 – 10 of 41003 |< < > >|

Figure 6.9: Cities table with pagination and sorting

The cities are now sorted alphabetically in ascending order. If we click on the various column headers, we can change their order as we please: the first click will sort the content in ascending order, while the second will do the opposite.

> It's worth noting how the paging and sorting features are able to coexist without issues; needless to say, whenever we try to change the table sorting, the paging will just roll back to the first page.

Now that the sorting has been implemented, there's only one missing feature left: **filtering**.

Adding filtering

If we think that we'll be able to get away with another component, this time, we're going to be disappointed: Angular Material does not provide a specific module to be used for filtering purposes. This means that we cannot rely on a standard approach to add filtering to our table; we have to figure out a reasonable approach by ourselves.

In general terms, the best thing to do whenever we need to code a feature by ourselves is to start to visualize what we want it to look like: for example, we can imagine a **Search** input field lying on top of our table that would trigger our `CitiesComponent` to reload the cities data from the server – through its `getData()` method – whenever we type something in it. How does that sound?

Let's try to lay down an action plan:

1.   As always, we'll need to extend our `ApiResult` class to programmatically handle the filtering task on the server side

2.   We'll also need to change the signature of the `GetCities()` action method of our .NET `CitiesController` so we can get the additional information from the client

3.   Right after that, we'll have to implement the filtering logic within our Angular `CitiesComponent`

4.   Eventually, we'll need to add the input textbox in the `CitiesComponent` HTML template file and bind an event to it to trigger the data retrieval process upon typing something

5.   Before moving further, we'll take the chance to talk about the performance impact of our filtering feature and how we can address it

Now that we have made it, let's do our best to put this plan into action.

Extending ApiResult (again)

It seems like we need to perform another upgrade to our beloved `ApiResult` class to add filtering support to the already existing paging and sorting logic.

Truth be told, we're not forced to do everything within the `ApiResult` class: we could skip that part entirely and just add the following to our existing `CitiesController`:

```
// ...existing code...

[HttpGet]
public async Task<ActionResult<ApiResult<City>>> GetCities(
        int pageIndex = 0,
        int pageSize = 10,
        string? sortColumn = null,
        string? sortOrder = null,
        string? filterColumn = null,
        string? filterQuery = null)
{
    // first we perform the filtering...
    var cities = _context.Cities;
    if (!string.IsNullOrEmpty(filterColumn)
        && !string.IsNullOrEmpty(filterQuery))
    {
        cities= cities.Where(c => c.Name.StartsWith(filterQuery));
    }

    // ... and then we call the ApiResult
    return await ApiResult<City>.CreateAsync(
            cities,
```

```
                    pageIndex,
                    pageSize,
                   sortColumn,
                   sortOrder);
}


// ...existing code...
```

That's definitely a viable approach. As a matter of fact, if we weren't using the System.Linq.Dynamic.Core package library, this would most likely be the only possible approach; we would have no way to programmatically set a column filter using an external class that works with generic IQueryable<T> objects because such a class would be unaware of the entity type and property names.

Luckily enough, we do have that package, so we can avoid performing the preceding changes (or roll them back, if we have already done that) and modify our /Data/ApiResult.cs class file in the following way instead:

```
using Microsoft.EntityFrameworkCore;
using System.Linq.Dynamic.Core;
using System.Reflection;

namespace WorldCitiesAPI.Data
{
    public class ApiResult<T>
    {
        /// <summary>
        /// Private constructor called by the CreateAsync method.
        /// </summary>
        private ApiResult(
            List<T> data,
            int count,
            int pageIndex,
            int pageSize,
            string? sortColumn,
            string? sortOrder,
            string? filterColumn,
            string? filterQuery)
        {
            Data = data;
            PageIndex = pageIndex;
            PageSize = pageSize;
            TotalCount = count;
```

```
        TotalPages = (int)Math.Ceiling(count / (double)pageSize);
        SortColumn = sortColumn;
        SortOrder = sortOrder;
        FilterColumn = filterColumn;
        FilterQuery = filterQuery;
    }

    #region Methods
    /// <summary>
    /// Pages, sorts and/or filters a IQueryable source.
    /// </summary>
    /// <param name="source">An IQueryable source of generic
    /// type</param>
    /// <param name="pageIndex">Zero-based current page index
    /// (0 = first page)</param>
    /// <param name="pageSize">The actual size of
    /// each page</param>
    /// <param name="sortColumn">The sorting column name</param>
    /// <param name="sortOrder">The sorting order ("ASC" or
    /// "DESC")</param>
    /// <param name="filterColumn">The filtering column
    ///   name</param>
    /// <param name="filterQuery">The filtering query (value to
    /// lookup)</param>
    /// <returns>
    /// A object containing the IQueryable paged/sorted/filtered
    /// result
    /// and all the relevant paging/sorting/filtering navigation
    /// info.
    /// </returns>
    public static async Task<ApiResult<T>> CreateAsync(
        IQueryable<T> source,
        int pageIndex,
        int pageSize,
        string? sortColumn = null,
        string? sortOrder = null,
        string? filterColumn = null,
        string? filterQuery = null)
    {
        if (!string.IsNullOrEmpty(filterColumn)
            && !string.IsNullOrEmpty(filterQuery)
```

```
            && IsValidProperty(filterColumn))
    {
        source = source.Where(
            string.Format("{0}.StartsWith(@0)",
            filterColumn),
            filterQuery);
    }

    var count = await source.CountAsync();

    if (!string.IsNullOrEmpty(sortColumn)
        && IsValidProperty(sortColumn))
    {
        sortOrder = !string.IsNullOrEmpty(sortOrder)
            && sortOrder.ToUpper() == "ASC"
            ? "ASC"
            : "DESC";
        source = source.OrderBy(
            string.Format(
                "{0} {1}",
                sortColumn,
                sortOrder)
            );
    }

    source = source
        .Skip(pageIndex * pageSize)
        .Take(pageSize);

    var data = await source.ToListAsync();

    return new ApiResult<T>(
        data,
        count,
        pageIndex,
        pageSize,
        sortColumn,
        sortOrder,
        filterColumn,
        filterQuery);
}
```

```
/// <summary>
/// Checks if the given property name exists
/// to protect against SQL injection attacks
/// </summary>
public static bool IsValidProperty(
    string propertyName,
    bool throwExceptionIfNotFound = true)
{
    var prop = typeof(T).GetProperty(
        propertyName,
        BindingFlags.IgnoreCase |
        BindingFlags.Public |
        BindingFlags.Static |
        BindingFlags.Instance);
    if (prop == null && throwExceptionIfNotFound)
        throw new NotSupportedException($"ERROR: Property
'{propertyName}' does not exist.");
    return prop != null;
}
#endregion

#region Properties
/// <summary>
/// IQueryable data result to return.
/// </summary>
public List<T> Data { get; private set; }

/// <summary>
/// Zero-based index of current page.
/// </summary>
public int PageIndex { get; private set; }

/// <summary>
/// Number of items contained in each page.
/// </summary>
public int PageSize { get; private set; }

/// <summary>
/// Total items count
```

```csharp
/// </summary>
public int TotalCount { get; private set; }

/// <summary>
/// Total pages count
/// </summary>
public int TotalPages { get; private set; }

/// <summary>
/// TRUE if the current page has a previous page,
/// FALSE otherwise.
/// </summary>
public bool HasPreviousPage
{
    get
    {
        return (PageIndex > 0);
    }
}

/// <summary>
/// TRUE if the current page has a next page, FALSE otherwise.
/// </summary>
public bool HasNextPage
{
    get
    {
        return ((PageIndex +1) < TotalPages);
    }
}

/// <summary>
/// Sorting Column name (or null if none set)
/// </summary>
public string? SortColumn { get; set; }

/// <summary>
/// Sorting Order ("ASC", "DESC" or null if none set)
/// </summary>
public string? SortOrder { get; set; }
```

```
/// <summary>
/// Filter Column name (or null if none set)
/// </summary>
public string? FilterColumn { get; set; }


/// <summary>
/// Filter Query string
/// (to be used within the given FilterColumn)
/// </summary>
public string? FilterQuery { get; set; }
#endregion
    }
}
```

And that's it. As we can see, we were able to programmatically implement the IQueryable<T>.Where() method – which actually performs the filtering task – thanks to another useful extension method provided by the System.Linq.Dynamic.Core package.

Needless to say, we took the chance to use our IsValidProperty method again to shield our code against possible SQL injection attempts: the filtering-related logic (and dynamic LINQ query) will only be executed if it returns True, that is, if the filterColumn parameter value matches an existing entity's public property.

While we were there, we also added two additional properties (FilterColumn and FilterQuery), so that we'll have them on the JSON response object, and modified the constructor method signature accordingly.

CitiesController

Now, we can open our /Controllers/CitiesController.cs file and make the following changes:

```
[HttpGet]
public async Task<ActionResult<ApiResult<City>>> GetCities(
        int pageIndex = 0,
        int pageSize = 10,
        string? sortColumn = null,
        string? sortOrder = null,
        string? filterColumn = null,
        string? filterQuery = null)
{
    return await ApiResult<City>.CreateAsync(
            _context.Cities.AsNoTracking(),
            pageIndex,
            pageSize,
            sortColumn,
```

```
                sortOrder,
                filterColumn,
                filterQuery);
}
```

The preceding code is very similar to the alternative implementation that we assumed in the previous section; as we mentioned earlier, both approaches are viable, depending on our tastes. However, since we're going to use this same implementation for the *countries* in a short while, making good use of System.Linq.Dynamic.Core, and centralizing all the IQueryable logic, is arguably a better approach since it keeps our source code as DRY as possible.

 Don't Repeat Yourself (DRY) is a widely implemented principle of software development. Whenever we violate it, we fall into a **WET** approach, which could mean **Write Everything Twice**, **We Enjoy Typing**, or **Waste Everyone's Time**, depending on what we like the most.

The .NET part is done; let's move on to Angular.

CitiesComponent

Open the /src/app/cities/cities.component.ts file and update its content in the following way (modified lines are highlighted):

```
import { Component, OnInit, ViewChild } from '@angular/core';
import { HttpClient, HttpParams } from '@angular/common/http';
import { environment } from '../../environment';
import { MatTableDataSource } from '@angular/material/table';
import { MatPaginator, PageEvent } from '@angular/material/paginator';
import { MatSort } from '@angular/material/sort';


import { City } from './city';

@Component({
  selector: 'app-cities',
  templateUrl: './cities.component.html',
  styleUrls: ['./cities.component.scss']
})
export class CitiesComponent implements OnInit {
  public displayedColumns: string[] = ['id', 'name', 'lat', 'lon'];
  public cities!: MatTableDataSource<City>;

  defaultPageIndex: number = 0;
  defaultPageSize: number = 10;
  public defaultSortColumn: string = "name";
```

```
public defaultSortOrder: "asc" | "desc" = "asc";

defaultFilterColumn: string = "name";
filterQuery?:string;

@ViewChild(MatPaginator) paginator!: MatPaginator;
@ViewChild(MatSort) sort!: MatSort;

constructor(private http: HttpClient) {
}

ngOnInit() {
    this.loadData(null);
}

loadData(query?: string) {
  var pageEvent = new PageEvent();
  pageEvent.pageIndex = this.defaultPageIndex;
  pageEvent.pageSize = this.defaultPageSize;
  this.filterQuery = query;
  this.getData(pageEvent);
}

getData(event: PageEvent) {
  var url = environment.baseUrl + 'api/Cities';
  var params = new HttpParams()
    .set("pageIndex", event.pageIndex.toString())
    .set("pageSize", event.pageSize.toString())
    .set("sortColumn", (this.sort)
      ? this.sort.active
      : this.defaultSortColumn)
    .set("sortOrder", (this.sort)
      ? this.sort.direction
      : this.defaultSortOrder);

  if (this.filterQuery) {
      params = params
          .set("filterColumn", this.defaultFilterColumn)
          .set("filterQuery", this.filterQuery);
  }
```

```
      this.http.get<any>(url, { params })
        .subscribe(result => {
          this.paginator.length = result.totalCount;
          this.paginator.pageIndex = result.pageIndex;
          this.paginator.pageSize = result.pageSize;
          this.cities = new MatTableDataSource<City>(result.data);
      }, error => console.error(error));
   }
 }
```

This time, the new code only consists of a few additional lines; we've just changed the signature of the loadData() method (with a string? optional type, so that we won't break anything) and conditionally added a couple of parameters to our HTTP request – that's it.

CitiesComponent template (HTML) file

Let's see what we need to add to the /src/app/cities/cities.component.html template file:

```
<h1>Cities</h1>

<p>Here's a list of cities: feel free to play with it.</p>

<p *ngIf="!cities"><em>Loading...</em></p>

<mat-form-field [hidden]="!cities">
    <input matInput #filter (keyup)="loadData(filter.value)"
        placeholder="Filter by name (or part of it)...">
</mat-form-field>

<table mat-table [dataSource]="cities"
  class="mat-elevation-z8"
  [hidden]="!cities"
  matSort (matSortChange)="loadData()"
  [matSortActive]="defaultSortColumn"
  [matSortDirection]="defaultSortOrder">

<!-- ...existing code... -->
```

As we can see, we just added a <mat-form-field> element with the usual [hidden] attribute binding (to make it appear only after our cities have been loaded) and a (keyup) event binding that will trigger the loadData() method upon each keypress; this call will also contain the input value, which will be handled by our component class by the means we just implemented there.

The only thing worth noting is that we've introduced a new Angular feature in the above code: a *template reference variable* (`#filter`), which allows us to use data from a single element in another part of the template. We did that so that we could pass the updated value of the `MatInput` element to our `loadData()` method.

Theoretically speaking, we could have used `$event.target.value` instead of relying on a template reference variable: however, we'll make further use of that `#filter` in the following chapters, so we took the chance to introduce it now.

For additional info on Angular's template reference variables, check out the following URL: `https://angular.io/guide/template-reference-variables`.

CitiesComponent style (SCSS) file

Before testing it out, we need to make a minor change to the `/src/app/cities/cities.component.scss` file as well:

```scss
table.mat-table {
  width: 100%;
}


.mat-form-field {
  font-size: 14px;
  width: 100%;
}
```

This is required to make our new `MatInputModule` span through the entire available space (it's limited to `180px` by default).

AngularMaterialModule

Wait a minute: did we just say `MatInputModule`? That's correct: as a matter of fact, it seems like we have actually used an Angular Material module in our filtering implementation after all – and for good reason, since it looks much better than a vanilla HTML input textbox!

However, since we did that, we need to reference it within our `AngularMaterialModule` container or we'll get a compiler error. To do that, open the `/src/app/angular-material.module.ts` file and add the required `import` statement...

```typescript
import { MatInputModule } from '@angular/material/input';
```

... and the two references in the `imports` and `exports` arrays of `@NgModule`.

That's it: now, we can hit *F5* and navigate to the **Cities** view to test the new filtering feature. If we did everything properly, we should be able to see something similar to the following screenshot:

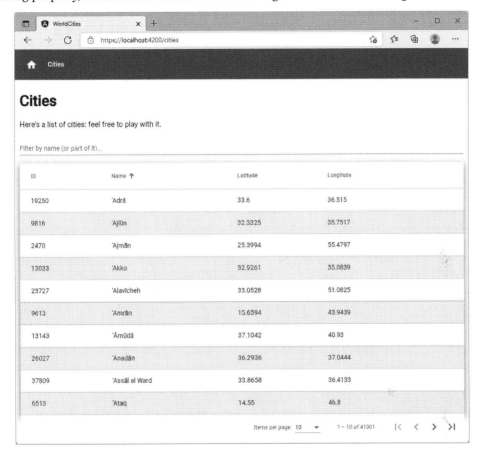

Figure 6.10: Cities table with pagination, sorting, and filtering

Looks pretty good, right?

If we try to type something into the filter textbox, we should see the table and the paginator update accordingly in real time. Look at what happens if we type **New York** in the filter textbox:

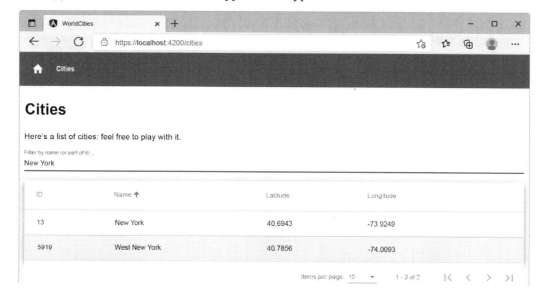

Figure 6.11: Cities table filtered for "New York"

That's definitely a good real-time filtering feature.

Performance considerations

Before moving further, it would be wise to spend a few minutes talking about the performance impact of the filter we've just implemented.

As we can see, the call to the loadData method is directly bound to the HTML input's *keyup* event, meaning that will fire upon each user's keystroke. This is great in terms of user experience because our users will immediately get filtered data as they type; however, this real-time filter also has a serious downside in terms of performance impact: every time the filter text changes (that is, upon each keystroke), Angular fires an HTTP request to the back-end to retrieve the updated list of results. Such behavior is intrinsically resource-intensive and can easily become a huge performance issue, especially if we're dealing with large tables and/or non-indexed columns.

Are there ways to improve this approach without compromising the results obtained in terms of user experience? As a matter of fact, the answer is yes, but we won't do that now: we'll talk more about it in *Chapter 7, Forms and Data Validation*, when we introduce the concepts of *debouncing* and *throttling*.

Adding countries to the loop

Before moving on, how about getting the countries up to speed? Yeah, it would mean redoing everything that we just did a second time; however, now that we know how to do this, we'll arguably be able to do it in a flash... or maybe not.

Nonetheless, we should definitely spend a reasonable amount of time doing that now because it would be a great way to plant everything we have learned so far in our muscle memory.

Let's do this now so that we can move on to trying something else. To avoid wasting pages, we'll just focus on the most relevant steps here, leaving everything else to what we just did with the cities – and to our GitHub repository, which hosts the full source code of what we need to do.

ASP.NET

Let's start with the ASP.NET part.

CountriesController

We should already have our `CountriesController` ready from *Chapter 5, Data Model with Entity Framework Core*, right? Open that file and replace the `GetCountries()` default action method with the following code:

```
// ...existing code...

[HttpGet]
public async Task<ActionResult<ApiResult<Country>>> GetCountries(
        int pageIndex = 0,
        int pageSize = 10,
        string? sortColumn = null,
        string? sortOrder = null,
        string? filterColumn = null,
        string? filterQuery = null)
{
    return await ApiResult<Country>.CreateAsync(
            _context.Countries.AsNoTracking(),
            pageIndex,
            pageSize,
            sortColumn,
            sortOrder,
            filterColumn,
            filterQuery);
}

// ...existing code...
```

Luckily enough, our `ApiResult` class is type-agnostic; therefore, we can use it there with no issues. Also, since we have centralized all the hard work there, the .NET server-side part is already done.

An odd JSON naming issue

Before moving on, let's quickly test the component: hit *F5* and type the following URL into the browser's address bar: `https://localhost:40443/api/Countries/?pageIndex=0&pageSize=5`.

As soon as we hit *Enter*, we should be able to see the following interface:

Figure 6.12: JSON array for the countries

It seems like it's all g... Hey, wait a minute: what's up with those `isO2` and `isO3` property names? They shouldn't be capitalized like that!

In order to understand what happened there, we need to take a step back and acknowledge something we might have underestimated so far: the camelCase conversion that the brand-new `System.Text.Json` API (introduced with .NET Core 3) automatically does when serializing all our .NET classes to JSON. We already talked about this issue early on in this chapter, when we saw the .NET `CitiesController` JSON output for the first time, and we said that it wasn't a big deal since Angular is also camelCase-oriented – we would just have to define the various interfaces using camelCase as well.

Unfortunately, such automatic camelCase conversion might cause unwanted side effects when dealing with all-uppercase properties such as those two; whenever this happens, we need to adapt our source code to properly deal with that:

- The most obvious thing to do would be to just define them in our Angular interface in the exact same way, that is, using that exact casing; however, this would mean dealing with those `isO2` and `isO3` variable names throughout our whole Angular code, which is rather ugly and might also be quite misleading.
- If we don't want to adopt those hideous property names, there is an alternative – and arguably better – workaround we can use: we can decorate our offending properties with the `[JsonPropertyName]` data annotation, which allows us to force a JSON property name, regardless of the default casing convention (be it camelCase or PascalCase) specified within the `Startup` class.

The `[JsonPropertyName]` workaround seems the most reasonable fix we can apply to our specific scenario; let's just go with it and get rid of this problem for good!

Open the `/Data/Models/Country.cs` file and add the following lines to the existing code (new lines are highlighted):

```
// ...existing code...
```

```
/// <summary>
/// Country code (in ISO 3166-1 ALPHA-2 format)
/// </summary>
[JsonPropertyName("iso2")]
public string ISO2 { get; set; }


/// <summary>
/// Country code (in ISO 3166-1 ALPHA-3 format)
/// </summary>
[JsonPropertyName("iso3")]
public string ISO3 { get; set; }


// ...existing code...
```

The [JsonPropertyName] attribute requires the following reference at the top of the file:

```
using System.Text.Json.Serialization;
```

Now, we can see whether those properties will respect this behavior by hitting *F5* and typing the same URL as before into the browser's address bar: `https://localhost:40443/api/Countries/?pageIndex=0&pageSize=5`

Figure 6.13: Amended JSON array for countries

It definitely seems like they do; thanks to this unexpected issue, we had the chance to add a powerful new weapon to our ASP.NET arsenal.

Now, we just need to create and configure the Angular component.

Angular

The Angular implementation will be less straightforward than the ASP.NET one since we'll have to deal with multiple aspects:

- Creating a new CountriesComponent
- Implementing the Countries table, as well as the paging, sorting, and filtering features as we did with the cities
- Updating NavComponent to add the navigation link

We already know what we need to do since we just did that with our `CitiesComponent`.

1. Open Command Prompt
2. Navigate to the `/src/app/` folder
3. Type `ng generate component Countries --module=app --skip-tests` to create the `ts`, `html`, and `scss` files, as well as a new `/src/app/countries/` folder
4. From Solution Explorer, create an additional `country.ts` file inside the `/src/app/countries/` folder of the **WorldCities** project

Once done, fill the new files with the following content.

country.ts

Here's the source code for the `/src/app/countries/country.ts` interface file:

```
export interface Country {
    id: number;
    name: string;
    iso2: string;
    iso3: string;
}
```

Nothing new here – the code is very similar to what we did when we created the `city.ts` interface file.

countries.component.ts

Here's the source code for the `/src/app/countries/countries.component.ts` file:

```
import { Component, OnInit, ViewChild } from '@angular/core';
import { HttpClient, HttpParams } from '@angular/common/http';
import { environment } from './../../environments/environment';
import { MatTableDataSource } from '@angular/material/table';
import { MatPaginator, PageEvent } from '@angular/material/paginator';
import { MatSort } from '@angular/material/sort';

import { Country } from './country';

@Component({
  selector: 'app-countries',
  templateUrl: './countries.component.html',
  styleUrls: ['./countries.component.scss']
})
export class CountriesComponent implements OnInit {
  public displayedColumns: string[] = ['id', 'name', 'iso2', 'iso3'];
  public countries!: MatTableDataSource<Country>;
```

```
defaultPageIndex: number = 0;
defaultPageSize: number = 10;
public defaultSortColumn: string = "name";
public defaultSortOrder: "asc" | "desc" = "asc";

defaultFilterColumn: string = "name";
filterQuery?: string;

@ViewChild(MatPaginator) paginator!: MatPaginator;
@ViewChild(MatSort) sort!: MatSort;

constructor(private http: HttpClient) {
}

ngOnInit() {
    this.loadData();
}

loadData(query?: string) {
    var pageEvent = new PageEvent();
    pageEvent.pageIndex = this.defaultPageIndex;
    pageEvent.pageSize = this.defaultPageSize;
    this.filterQuery = query;
    this.getData(pageEvent);
}

getData(event: PageEvent) {
    var url = environment.baseUrl + 'api/Countries';
    var params = new HttpParams()
        .set("pageIndex", event.pageIndex.toString())
        .set("pageSize", event.pageSize.toString())
        .set("sortColumn", (this.sort)
            ? this.sort.active
            : this.defaultSortColumn)
        .set("sortOrder", (this.sort)
            ? this.sort.direction
            : this.defaultSortOrder);
    if (this.filterQuery) {
        params = params
            .set("filterColumn", this.defaultFilterColumn)
            .set("filterQuery", this.filterQuery);
```

```
        }

        this.http.get<any>(url, { params })
            .subscribe(result => {
                this.paginator.length = result.totalCount;
                this.paginator.pageIndex = result.pageIndex;
                this.paginator.pageSize = result.pageSize;
                this.countries = new MatTableDataSource<Country>(result.data);
            }, error => console.error(error));
    }
}
```

Again, this is basically a mirror of the `cities.component.ts` file.

countries.component.html

Here's the source code for the `/src/app/countries/countries.component.html` file:

```
<h1>Countries</h1>

<p>Here's a list of countries: feel free to play with it.</p>

<p *ngIf="!countries"><em>Loading...</em></p>

<mat-form-field [hidden]="!countries">
  <input matInput #filter (keyup)="loadData(filter.value)"
      placeholder="Filter by name (or part of it)...">
</mat-form-field>

<table mat-table [dataSource]="countries"
  class="mat-elevation-z8"
  [hidden]="!countries"
  matSort (matSortChange)="loadData()"
  [matSortActive]="defaultSortColumn"
  [matSortDirection]="defaultSortOrder">

  <!-- Id Column -->
  <ng-container matColumnDef="id">
    <th mat-header-cell *matHeaderCellDef mat-sort-header>ID</th>
    <td mat-cell *matCellDef="let country"> {{country.id}} </td>
  </ng-container>

  <!-- Name Column -->
```

```
  <ng-container matColumnDef="name">
    <th mat-header-cell *matHeaderCellDef mat-sort-header>Name</th>
    <td mat-cell *matCellDef="let country"> {{country.name}} </td>
  </ng-container>

  <!-- ISO2 Column -->
  <ng-container matColumnDef="iso2">
    <th mat-header-cell *matHeaderCellDef mat-sort-header>ISO 2</th>
    <td mat-cell *matCellDef="let country"> {{country.iso2}} </td>
  </ng-container>

  <!-- ISO3 Column -->
  <ng-container matColumnDef="iso3">
    <th mat-header-cell *matHeaderCellDef mat-sort-header>ISO 3</th>
    <td mat-cell *matCellDef="let country"> {{country.iso3}} </td>
  </ng-container>

  <tr mat-header-row *matHeaderRowDef="displayedColumns"></tr>
  <tr mat-row *matRowDef="let row; columns: displayedColumns;"></tr>
</table>

<!-- Pagination directive -->
<mat-paginator [hidden]="!countries"
    (page)="getData($event)"
    [pageSize]="10"
    [pageSizeOptions]="[10, 20, 50]"
    showFirstLastButtons></mat-paginator>
```

The template, just as expected, is almost identical to the cities.component.html template file.

countries.component.scss

Here's the source code for the /src/app/countries/countries.component.scss file:

```
table.mat-table {
  width: 100%;
}


.mat-form-field {
  font-size: 14px;
  width: 100%;
}
```

The preceding file is so similar to the `cities.component.scss` file that we could even reference it instead of creating a new one; however, dealing with separate files is almost always a better choice, considering that we might need to apply different changes to the `Cities` and `Countries` tables later on.

AppModule

Since we've created our component using the Angular CLI, we don't need to perform any change to the `AppModule` configuration file, since the new component should have been registered automatically: all we need to do is to update the routing module and the navigation component.

AppRoutingModule

The routing rule that we need to add is very similar to the one we added to `CitiesComponent` a while ago:

```
import { NgModule } from '@angular/core';
import { Routes, RouterModule } from '@angular/router';
import { HomeComponent } from './home/home.component';
import { CitiesComponent } from './cities/cities.component';
import { CountriesComponent } from './countries/countries.component';


const routes: Routes = [
  { path: '', component: HomeComponent, pathMatch: 'full' },
  { path: 'cities', component: CitiesComponent },
  { path: 'countries', component: CountriesComponent }
];


@NgModule({
  imports: [RouterModule.forRoot(routes)],
  exports: [RouterModule]
})
export class AppRoutingModule { }
```

The new routing rule will make our new `CountriesComponent` get served by Angular when the client browser points to the `/countries` dedicated route. However, our users won't know that such a route exists if we don't add a visible link to it within our `NavComponent` menu; that's precisely why we're going to add it next.

NavComponent

Open the `/src/app/nav-menu/nav-menu.component.html` file and add the following highlighted lines to the existing code:

```
<header>
  <mat-toolbar color="primary">
    <button mat-icon-button [routerLink]="['/']">
      <mat-icon>
```

```
      home
    </mat-icon>
  </button>
  <a mat-flat-button color="primary" [routerLink]="['/cities']">
    Cities
  </a>
  <a mat-flat-button color="primary" [routerLink]="['/countries']">
    Countries
  </a>
  </mat-toolbar>
</header>
```

... and that's it!

Our CountriesComponent is done, and – if we didn't make mistakes – it should work in about the same way as our beloved CitiesComponent that took so much time to finalize.

Testing CountriesComponent

It's time to see the results of our hard work: hit *F5*, navigate to the **Countries** view, and expect to see the following:

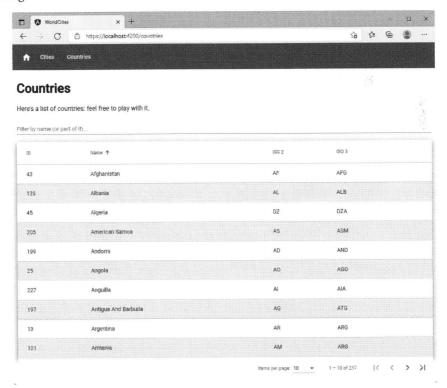

Figure 6.14: Countries table with pagination, sorting, and filtering

If you were able to get this same output on your first attempt, it definitely means that you have learned what to do; if you didn't, don't worry: you'll just have to check what you did wrong and fix it. Practice makes perfect.

IMPORTANT: Don't be fooled by appearances; be sure to check that paging, sorting, and filtering are working properly before going any further.

> The browser's console log can be a very useful tool for debugging server-side and client-side errors; most Angular errors come with well-documented exception text and a contextual link to the corresponding file and source code line, thus making it quite easy for the developer to understand what happens under the hood.

Summary

This chapter was all about reading data from the ASP.NET *back-end* and finding a way to properly show it to the browser with the Angular *front-end*.

We started by using our existing `CitiesController` to fetch a large number of cities with Angular components; although both frameworks are perfectly able to deal with massive data, we quickly understood that we need to improve the whole data request, response, and render flow process to grant our users a decent user experience.

For this very reason, we chose to adopt the `System.Linq.Dynamic.Core` .NET package to revamp our server-side business logic and the Angular Material npm package to greatly improve our client-side UI. By combining the powerful features of these two packages, we managed to pull off a bunch of interesting features: paging, sorting, and filtering. During our development journey, we also took the chance to identify, address, and mitigate some important security issues, such as a harmful SQL injection risk.

Right after finishing our work with `Cities`, we moved on to `Countries`, taking the chance to retrace our steps and cement what we just learned into our muscle memory.

After all our hard work, we can definitely say that we did a great job and fulfilled our goal: being able to read our data from the .NET *back-end* and gracefully present it through the *front-end* with Angular, thus making end users fully able to see and interact with it.

We're now ready to add another layer of complexity to our application: give our users the chance to modify the existing data and/or add new data using HTML forms; these features are a must-have for most interactive web applications such as CMSes, forums, social networks, chat rooms, and the like. In the next chapter, *Chapter 7, Forms and Data Validation*, we'll see how we can deal with such tasks using reactive forms, a pivotal Angular module that provides a model-driven approach to handling form inputs whose values change over time.

Suggested topics

For further information, we recommend the following topics: JSON, RESTful conventions, HTTP verbs, HTTP status, life cycle hooks, client-side paging, server-side paging, sorting, filtering, dependency injection, and SQL injection.

ASP.NET

System.Linq, System.Linq.Dynamic.Core, IQueryable, and Entity Framework Core.

Angular

Components, routing, modules, AppModule, HttpClient, ngIf, hidden, data binding, property binding, attribute binding, ngFor, directives, structural directives, interpolations, templates, and template reference variables.

References

- *Add sorting, filtering, and paging – ASP.NET MVC with EF Core*: `https://docs.microsoft.com/en-us/aspnet/core/data/ef-mvc/sort-filter-page`
- *Bootstrap official website*: `https://getbootstrap.com`
- *Angular Material official website*: `https://material.angular.io/`
- *Angular Material GitHub repository*: `https://github.com/angular/components`
- *Angular Material typography*: `https://material.angular.io/guide/typography`
- *Angular BrowserAnimationsModule*: `https://angular.io/api/platform-browser/animations/BrowserAnimationsModule`
- *Angular animation system*: `https://angular.io/guide/animations`
- *Angular Material – table overview*: `https://material.angular.io/components/table/overview`
- *Angular – ViewChild*: `https://angular.io/api/core/ViewChild`
- *System.Linq.Dynamic.Core project page on GitHub*: `https://github.com/StefH/System.Linq.Dynamic.Core`
- *LINQ overview*: `https://docs.microsoft.com/en-us/dotnet/csharp/linq/`
- *LINQ (Language Integrated Query)*: `https://docs.microsoft.com/en-us/dotnet/csharp/programming-guide/concepts/linq/`
- *LINQ lambda expressions (C# programming guide)*: `https://docs.microsoft.com/en-us/dotnet/csharp/programming-guide/statements-expressions-operators/lambda-expressions`
- *LINQ Query expression basics*: `https://docs.microsoft.com/en-us/dotnet/csharp/linq/query-expression-basics`
- *Reflection (C#)*: `https://docs.microsoft.com/en-us/dotnet/csharp/programming-guide/concepts/reflection`
- *.NET Core and Entity Framework – set IQueryable<T> Column Names programmatically with Dynamic LINQ*: `https://www.ryadel.com/en/asp-net-core-set-column-name-programmatically-dynamic-linq-where-iqueryable/`
- *Understanding SQL injection*: `https://tools.cisco.com/security/center/resources/sql_injection.html`
- *Angular's template reference variables*: `https://angular.io/guide/template-reference-variables`

7

Forms and Data Validation

In this chapter, we'll mostly deal with forms, data input, and validation techniques. As we already know, HTML forms are one of the most important and delicate aspects of any business application. Nowadays, forms are used to fulfill almost any task involving user-submitted data, such as registering or logging in to a website, issuing a payment, reserving a hotel room, ordering a product, performing and retrieving search results, and more.

If we were asked to define a form from a developer's perspective, we would come out with the statement that *a form is a UI-based interface that allows authorized users to enter data that will be sent to a server for processing*. The moment we accept this definition, two additional considerations should come to mind:

1. Each form should provide a data entry experience good enough to efficiently guide our users through the expected workflow; otherwise, they won't be able to use it properly.

2. Each form, as long as it brings potentially insecure data to the server, could have a major security impact in terms of data integrity, data security, and system security, unless the developer possesses the required *know-how* to adopt and implement the appropriate countermeasures.

These two considerations provide a good summary of what we'll do in this chapter: we'll do our best to guide our users into submitting data in the most appropriate way, and we'll also learn how to check these input values properly to prevent, avoid, and/or minimize a wide spectrum of integrity and security threats. It's also important to understand that these two considerations are frequently intertwined with each other; hence, we'll often deal with them at the same time.

In this chapter, we'll cover the following topics:

- **Exploring Angular forms**, where we'll deal with **Template-Driven Forms** as well as **Reactive Forms**, all while understanding the pros and cons of both approaches and looking at which is the most suitable to use in various common scenarios
- **Building our first Reactive Form**, where we'll use the gained knowledge to create a Reactive Form to edit our existing cities, as well as adding new ones
- **Adding a new city**, using our brand-new Reactive Form

- **Understanding data validation**, where we'll learn how to double-check our users' input data in the *front-end* and also from the *back-end*, as well as the various techniques to give visual feedback when they send incorrect or invalid values

- **Introducing the FormBuilder**, where we'll implement another Reactive Form for our countries using some factory methods instead of manually instantiating the various form model elements

- **Improving the filter behavior**, where we'll introduce some *throttling* and *debouncing* techniques to improve the overall performance and reduce server load

At the end of each task, we'll also take some time to verify the result of our work using our web browser.

Technical requirements

In this chapter, we're going to need all the technical requirements that we mentioned in the previous chapters, with no additional resources, libraries, or packages.

The code files for this chapter can be found at https://github.com/PacktPublishing/ASP.NET-Core-6-and-Angular/tree/main/Chapter_07.

Exploring Angular forms

If we take a look at our current .NET Core with Angular projects, we will see how none of them allow our users to *interact* with the data:

- For the HealthCheck app, this is expected since there's simply no data to deal with: this is a monitor app that doesn't store anything and requires no input from the user

- The WorldCities app, however, tells a whole different story: we do have a database that we use to return results to our users, who could — at least theoretically— be allowed to make changes

It goes without saying that the WorldCities app would be our best candidate for implementing our forms. In the following sections, we'll do just that, starting with the Angular project (the front-end) and then moving to the ASP.NET Core Web API project (the back-end).

Forms in Angular

Let's take a minute to briefly review our WorldCities app in the state we left it in at the end of *Chapter 6, Fetching and Displaying Data*. If we take a look at the CitiesComponent and CountriesComponent templates, we will see that we actually already have a data input element of some sort: we're clearly talking about <mat-form-field>, which is the *selector* of Angular Material's MatInputModule, which we added to the loop during *Chapter 6, Fetching and Displaying Data*, to let our users filter the cities and countries by their names.

Here's the relevant code snippet:

```
<mat-form-field [hidden]="!cities">
    <input matInput #filter (keyup)="loadData(filter.value)"
        placeholder="Filter by name (or part of it)...">
</mat-form-field>
```

This means that we are already accepting some kind of user action – consisting of a single input string – and reacting to it accordingly: such an action + reaction chain is the basis of an interaction between the user and the app, which is basically what the vast majority of forms are all about.

However, if we look at the generated HTML code, we can clearly see that we do not have any actual <form> element. We can test it by right-clicking that view's input element from our browser window and selecting **Inspect element**, as shown in the following screenshot:

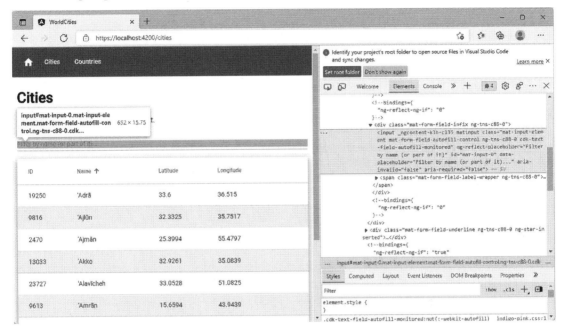

Figure 7.1: Inspecting the HTML of the input element

As we can see, there is no main form, only a single input field that perfectly handles the task we've assigned to it. The absence of the form is not missed because we're not submitting anything using FormData we're performing our data fetching using the Angular HttpClient module, which technically does this using an asynchronous **XMLHttpRequest** (**XHR**) through JavaScript – in one word, AJAX.

Such an approach does not require a <form> container element and is capable of handling the data encoding and transmission tasks using the following supported methods:

- application/x-www-form-urlencoded
- multipart/form-data
- text/plain

It only needs the actual input elements to get the required values from the user.

For further details regarding the encoding method supported by the HTML `<form>` element, take a look at the following specifications:

- *URL Living Standard – URL-encoded Form Data*: `https://url.spec.whatwg.org/#concept-urlencoded`
- *HTML Living Standard, section 4.10.21.7 – Multipart Form Data*: `https://html.spec.whatwg.org/multipage/form-control-infrastructure.html#multipart-form-data`
- *HTML Living Standard, section 4.10.21.8 – Plain Text Form Data*: `https://html.spec.whatwg.org/multipage/form-control-infrastructure.html#plain-text-form-data`

Although not required, a `form` element – or any HTML container for our input elements – might be very useful for a number of important tasks that don't fall into the data encoding and transmission subjects. Let's see what they are and why we may need them.

Reasons to use forms

Let's try to summarize the most blatant shortcomings of our current formless approach:

- We cannot keep track of the global form state since there's no way we can tell whether the input text is valid or not
- We have no easy way to display an error message to the users to let them know what they have to do to make the form valid
- We don't verify the input data in any way; we just collect and toss it to the server without thinking twice

That's absolutely fine in our specific scenario since we're only dealing with a single text string and we don't care too much about its length, the input text, and so on. However, if we have to deal with multiple input elements and several value types, such limitations could seriously hinder our work – in terms of either data flow control, data validation, or user experience.

Sure, we could easily work around most of the aforementioned issues by implementing some custom methods within our form-based *components*; we could throw some errors such as `isValid()`, `isNumber()`, and so on here and there, and then hook them up to our template syntax and show/hide the validation messages with the help of structural directives such as `*ngIf`, `*ngFor`, and the like. However, it would definitely be a horrible way to address our problem; we didn't choose a feature-rich client-side framework such as Angular to work that way.

Luckily enough, we have no reason to do that since Angular provides us with a couple of alternative strategies to deal with these common form-related scenarios:

- **Template-Driven Forms**
- **Model-Driven Forms**, also known as **Reactive Forms**

Both of them are highly coupled with the framework and thus extremely viable; they both belong to the @angular/forms library and also share a common set of form control classes. However, they also have their own specific sets of features, along with their pros and cons, which could ultimately lead to us choosing one of them.

Let's try to quickly summarize these differences.

Template-Driven Forms

If you've come from AngularJS, there's a high chance that the Template-Driven approach will ring a bell or two. As the name implies, Template-Driven Forms host most of the logic in the template code; working with a Template-Driven Form means:

- Building the form in the .html template file
- Binding data to the various input fields using an ngModel instance
- Using a dedicated ngForm object related to the whole form and containing all the inputs, with each being accessible through their name

These things need to be done in order to perform the required validity checks.

To understand this, here's what a Template-Driven Form looks like:

```html
<form novalidate autocomplete="off" #form="ngForm"
    (ngSubmit)="onSubmit(form)">


    <input type="text" name="name" value="" required
        placeholder="Insert the city name..."
        [(ngModel)]="city.Name" #title="ngModel"
        />


    <button type="submit" name="btnSubmit"
      [disabled]="form.invalid">
      Submit
    </button>


</form>
```

As we can see, we can access any element, including the form itself, using some convenient *template reference variables* – the attributes with the # sign, which we've already seen in *Chapter 6, Fetching and Displaying Data* – and check for their current states to create our own validation workflow. We'll talk more about these states later on, when we dive into form validation techniques.

This is Template-Driven Forms in a nutshell; now that we've had an overall look at them, let's try to summarize the pros and cons of this approach.

The pros

Here are the main advantages of Template-Driven Forms:

- **Template-Driven Forms are very easy to write.** We can recycle most of our HTML knowledge (assuming that we have any). On top of that, if we came from AngularJS, we already know how well we can make them work once we've mastered the technique.

- **They are rather easy to read and understand**, at least from an HTML point of view; we have a plain, understandable HTML structure containing all the input fields and validators, one after another. Each element will have a name, a two-way binding with the underlying ngModel, and (possibly) Template-Driven logic built upon aliases that have been hooked to other elements that we can also see, or to the form itself.

The cons

Here are their weaknesses:

- **Template-Driven Forms require a lot of HTML code**, which can be rather difficult to maintain and is generally more error-prone than pure TypeScript.

- For the same reason, **these forms cannot be unit tested.** We have no way to test their validators or to ensure that the logic we implemented will work, other than running an end-to-end test with our browser, which is hardly ideal for complex forms.

- **Their readability will quickly drop** as we add more and more validators and input tags. Keeping all their logic within the template might be fine for small forms, but it doesn't scale well when dealing with complex data items.

Ultimately, we can say that Template-Driven Forms might be the way to go when we need to build small forms with simple data validation rules, where we can benefit more from their simplicity. On top of that, they are quite similar to the typical HTML code we're already used to (assuming that we do have a plain HTML development background); we just need to learn how to decorate the standard `<form>` and `<input>` elements with aliases and throw in some validators handled by structural directives such as the ones we've already seen, and we'll be set in (almost) no time.

 For additional information on Template-Driven Forms, we highly recommend that you read the official Angular documentation at `https://angular.io/guide/forms`.

That being said, the lack of unit testing, the HTML code bloat that they will eventually produce, and the scaling difficulties will eventually lead us toward an alternative approach for any non-trivial form.

Model-Driven/Reactive Forms

The Model-Driven approach was specifically added in Angular 2+ to address the known limitations of Template-Driven Forms. The forms that are implemented with this alternative method are known as **Model-Driven Forms** or Reactive Forms, which are the exact same thing.

The main difference here is that (almost) nothing happens in the template, which acts as a mere reference to a more complex TypeScript object that gets defined, instantiated, and configured programmatically within the component class: the form **model**.

To understand the overall concept, let's try to rewrite the previous form in a Model-Driven/Reactive way (the relevant parts are highlighted). The outcome of doing this is as follows:

```html
<form [formGroup]="form" (ngSubmit)="onSubmit()">

    <input formControlName="name" required />

    <button type="submit" name="btnSubmit"
        [disabled]="form.invalid">
        Submit
    </button>

</form>
```

As we can see, the required amount of code is less and more readable.

Here's the underlying form model that we will define in the component class file (the relevant parts are highlighted in the following code):

```typescript
import { FormGroup, FormControl } from '@angular/forms';

class ModelFormComponent implements OnInit {
    form: FormGroup;

    ngOnInit() {
        this.form = new FormGroup({
            name: new FormControl()
        });
    }
}
```

Let's try to understand what's happening here:

- The form property is an instance of FormGroup and represents the form itself.
- FormGroup, as the name suggests, is a container of form controls sharing the same purpose. As we can see, the form itself acts as a FormGroup, which means that we can nest FormGroup objects inside other FormGroup objects (we didn't do that in our sample, though).
- Each data input element in the form template – in the preceding code, name – is represented by an instance of FormControl.
- Each FormGroup instance encapsulates the state of each child control, meaning that it will only be valid if/when all its children are also valid.

Also, note that we have no way of accessing the `FormControl` objects directly like we were doing in Template-Driven Forms; we have to retrieve them using the `.get()` method of the main `FormGroup`, which is the form itself.

At first glance, the Model-Driven template doesn't seem too different from the Template-Driven one; we still have a `<form>` element, an `<input>` element hooked to a `<span>` validator, and a `submit` button; on top of that, checking the state of the input elements takes a greater amount of source code since they have no aliases we can use. What's the real deal, then?

To help us visualize the difference, let's look at the following diagrams. Here's a schema depicting how **Template-Driven Forms** work:

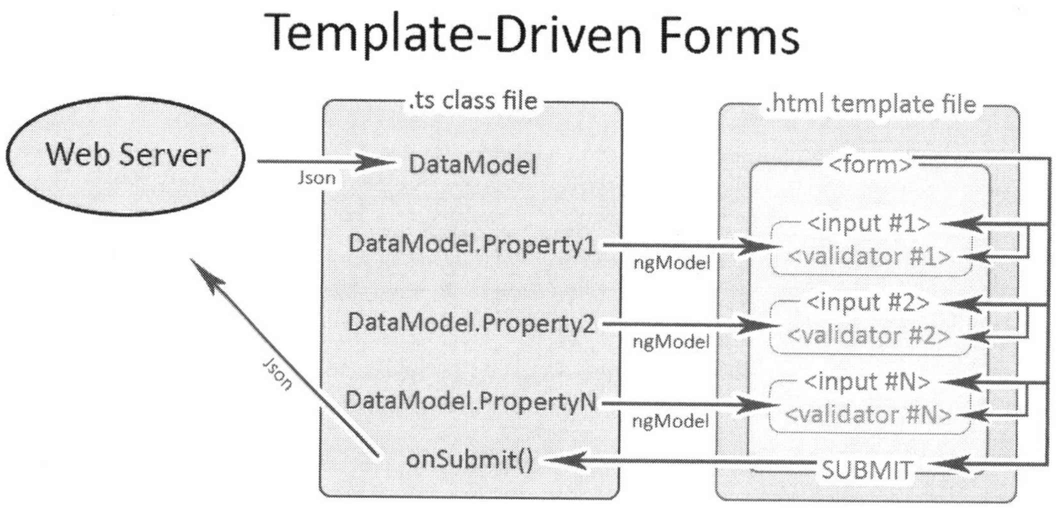

Template-Driven Forms

Figure 7.2: Template-Driven Forms schematic

By looking at the arrows, we can easily see that, in **Template-Driven Forms**, everything happens in the template; the HTML form elements are directly bound to the **DataModel** component represented by a property filled with an asynchronous HTML request to the **Web Server**, much like we did with our cities and country table. That **DataModel** will be updated as soon as the user changes something, that is, unless a validator prevents them from doing that. If we think about it, we can easily understand how there isn't a single part of the whole workflow that happens to be under our control; Angular handles everything by itself using the information in the data bindings defined within our template. This is what *Template-Driven* actually means: the template is calling the shots.

Now, let's take a look at the **Model-Driven Forms** (or Reactive Forms) approach:

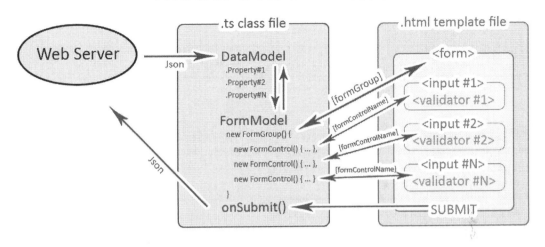

Figure 7.3: Model-Driven/Reactive Forms schematic

As we can see, the arrows depicting the **Model-Driven Forms** workflow tell a whole different story. They show how the data flows between the **DataModel** component – which we get from the **Web Server** – and a UI-oriented form model that retains the states and the values of the HTML form (and its children input elements) that are presented to the user. This means that we'll be able to get in between the data and the form control objects and perform a number of tasks firsthand: push and pull data, detect and react to user changes, implement our own validation logic, perform unit tests, and so on.

Instead of being superseded by a template that's not under our control, we can track and influence the workflow programmatically, since the form model that calls the shots is also a TypeScript class; that's what Model-Driven Forms are about. This also explains why they are also called **Reactive Forms** – an explicit reference to the Reactive programming style that favors explicit data handling and change management throughout the workflow.

 For additional information on Model-Driven/Reactive Forms, we highly recommend reading the official Angular documentation at https://angular.io/guide/reactive-forms.

Enough with the theory; it's time to empower our components with some Reactive Forms.

Building our first Reactive Form

In this section, we'll create our first Reactive Form. More specifically, we're going to build a CityEditComponent that will give our users the chance to edit an existing *city* record.

To do that, we'll do the following:

- Add a reference to the ReactiveFormsModule to our AppModule class
- Create the CityEditComponent TypeScript and template files

Let's get started.

ReactiveFormsModule

The first thing we have to do to start working with Reactive Forms is to add a reference to the ReactiveFormsModule in the AppModule class.

From Solution Explorer, open the /src/app/app.module.ts file and add the following import statement right after the BrowserModule:

```
import { ReactiveFormsModule } from '@angular/forms';
```

As always, remember to also add the ReactiveFormsModule to @NgModule's imports collection.

Now that we've added a reference to the ReactiveFormsModule in our app's AppModule file, we can implement the Angular component that will host the actual form.

CityEditComponent

Since our CityEditComponent is meant to allow our users to modify a city, we'll need to let it know which city it has to fetch from (and send to) the server.

To do that, we need to pass the city id from the city listing to that component: the most effective way to do that is by using a GET parameter, such as the city id, which can then be used by the component to retrieve the city info from the server and show it to the user.

Therefore, we're going to implement a standard **Master/Detail** UI pattern, much like the following one:

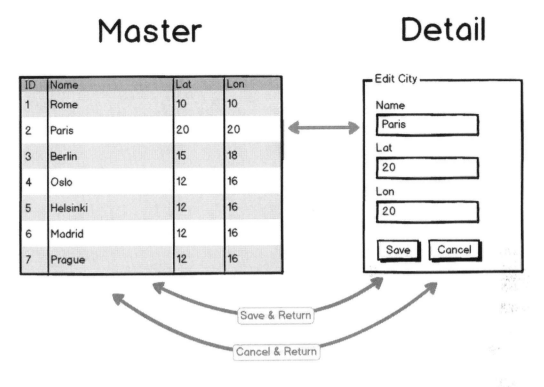

Figure 7.4: A Master/Detail UI pattern

This editing pattern, other than being the most used in the world when dealing with a list of items, is a perfect fit for our scenario. Sounds like a plan: let's do it!

Let's start with creating a new CityEditComponent using the Angular CLI. However, this time we'll run the ng generate component command in the /src/app/cities/ folder, since we want the new component to be generated within that folder – together with the existing CitiesComponents and the City.ts interface.

To do that, we also need to use the --flat option, which tells the CLI to generate the new files in the current folder instead of creating a new one. Here's the command we need to execute:

```
ng generate component CityEdit --flat --module=app --skip-tests
```

Once done, we can start updating the new component's ts, html, and scss files.

city-edit.component.ts

Open the three new (and empty) files and fill them with the following, the source code for the /src/
app/cities/city-edit.component.ts file:

```
import { Component, OnInit } from '@angular/core';
import { HttpClient } from '@angular/common/http';
import { ActivatedRoute, Router } from '@angular/router';
import { FormGroup, FormControl } from '@angular/forms';

import { environment } from './../../environments/environment';
import { City } from './city';

@Component({
  selector: 'app-city-edit',
  templateUrl: './city-edit.component.html',
  styleUrls: ['./city-edit.component.scss']
})
export class CityEditComponent implements OnInit {

  // the view title
  title?: string;

  // the form model
  form!: FormGroup;

  // the city object to edit
  city?: City;

  constructor(
    private activatedRoute: ActivatedRoute,
    private router: Router,
    private http: HttpClient) {
  }

  ngOnInit() {
    this.form = new FormGroup({
      name: new FormControl(''),
      lat: new FormControl(''),
      lon: new FormControl('')
    });
```

```
      this.loadData();
  }


  loadData() {

    // retrieve the ID from the 'id' parameter
    var idParam = this.activatedRoute.snapshot.paramMap.get('id');
    var id = idParam ? +idParam : 0;


    // fetch the city from the server
    var url = environment.baseUrl + 'api/Cities/' + id;
    this.http.get<City>(url).subscribe(result => {
      this.city = result;
      this.title = "Edit - " + this.city.name;


      // update the form with the city value
      this.form.patchValue(this.city);
    }, error => console.error(error));
  }


  onSubmit() {
    var city = this.city;
    if (city) {
      city.name = this.form.controls['name'].value;
      city.lat = +this.form.controls['lat'].value;
      city.lon = +this.form.controls['lon'].value;


      var url = environment.baseUrl + 'api/Cities/' + city.id;
      this.http
        .put<City>(url, city)
        .subscribe(result => {

          console.log("City " + city!.id + " has been updated.");


          // go back to cities view
          this.router.navigate(['/cities']);
        }, error => console.error(error));
    }
  }
}
```

This is a fair amount of source code: luckily enough, there are a lot of comments that should help us understand the purpose of each relevant step.

WARNING: the above can raise a TypeScript compilation error, such as:

`Property 'name' comes from an index signature, so it must be accessed by ['name'].`

This can happen when using an old version of TypeScript, where *direct property access* for dictionary members wasn't allowed. This restriction has been relaxed in TypeScript 2.2 and now it can be done, with great benefits in terms of code readability and ergonomics. This means that the above issue can be fixed by either updating its TypeScript version or switching to the *bracket notation property access*, following the advice given by the error message.

The whole topic is summarized in the following *Stack Overflow* answer: `https://stackoverflow.com/a/39768162/1233379`.

And here's the official announcement from the TypeScript development team: `https://devblogs.microsoft.com/typescript/announcing-typescript-2-2/`.

Let's try to summarize what we did here:

- We added some `import` references to the modules we're about to use within this class. Among them, we can see a couple of new kids on the block: `@angular/router` and `@angular/form`. The former is required to define some internal routing patterns, while the latter contains the `FormGroup` and `FormControl` classes that we need in order to build our form.

- Right below the class definition, we created a `FormGroup` instance within a `form` variable: that's our form model.

- The `form` variable instance contains three `FormControl` objects that will store the *city* values we want to allow our users to change: `name`, `lat`, and `lon`. We don't want to make them change the `Id` or the `CountryId` – at least, not for now.

- Right below the `form` variable, we defined a `city` variable that will host the actual city when we retrieve it from the database.

- The city retrieval task is handled by the `loadData()` method, which is rather similar to the one we implemented in the `cities.component.ts` file: a standard data-fetching task handled by an `HttpClient` module that's injected (as usual) through the `constructor()`. The most relevant difference here is that the method, right after the HTTP request/response cycle, proactively loads the retrieved city data within the form model (by using the form's `patchValue()` method) instead of relying on the Angular data-binding feature: that's hardly a surprise since we're using the Model-Driven/Reactive approach and not the Template-Driven one.

- The `onSubmit()` method is where the update magic takes place: `HttpClient` plays a major role here as well by issuing a `PUT` request to the server, sending the `city` variable properly. Once the *Observable* subscription has been processed, we use the `router` instance to redirect the user back to the `CitiesComponent` (the *Master* view).

Before moving further, it could be wise to spend a couple of words talking about the `patchValue()` method that we used in the preceding code.

The `@angular/forms` package gives us two ways to update a Reactive Form's model: the `setValue()` method, which sets a new value for each individual control, and the `patchValue()` method, which will replace any properties that have been defined in the object that have changed in the form model.

The main difference between them is that `setValue()` performs a strict check of the source object and will throw errors if it doesn't fully adhere to the model structure (including all nested `FormControl` elements), while `patchValue()` will silently fail on those errors.

Therefore, we can say that the former method might be a better choice for complex forms and/or whenever we need to catch nesting errors, while the latter is the way to go when things are simple enough – like in our current samples.

The `@angular/router` package deserves a special mention because it's the first time we have seen it in a component TypeScript file, and we've only used it twice before:

- In the `app-routing.module.ts` file, to define our client-side routing rules
- In the `nav.component.html` file, to implement the aforementioned routing rules and make them appear as navigation links within the web application's main menu

This time, we had to `import` it because we needed a way to retrieve the *City* id parameter from the URL. To do this, we used the `ActivatedRoute` interface, which allows us to retrieve information about the currently active route, as well as the GET parameter we were looking for.

city-edit.component.html

Here's the content for the `/src/app/cities/city-edit.component.html` template file:

```html
<div class="city-edit">
  <h1>{{title}}</h1>
  <p *ngIf="!city"><em>Loading...</em></p>
  <div [formGroup]="form" (ngSubmit)="onSubmit()">

    <!-- Name -->
    <mat-form-field>
      <mat-label>Name:</mat-label>
      <input matInput formControlName="name" required
             placeholder="Type a name">
    </mat-form-field>

    <!-- Lat -->
    <mat-form-field>
      <mat-label>Latitude:</mat-label>
```

```
        <input matInput formControlName="lat" required
              placeholder="Insert latitude">
      </mat-form-field>

      <!-- Lon -->
      <mat-form-field>
        <mat-label>Longitude:</mat-label>
        <input matInput formControlName="lon" required
              placeholder="Insert longitude">
      </mat-form-field>
      <div>
        <button mat-flat-button color="primary"
          type="submit" (click)="onSubmit()">
          Save
        </button>
        <button mat-flat-button color="secondary"
          [routerLink]="['/cities']">
          Cancel
        </button>
      </div>
    </div>
  </div>
```

Wait a minute: where's our <form> HTML element? Didn't we say that we were working with form-based approaches because they are way better than placing a bunch of separate <input> fields here and there?

As a matter of fact, we **do** have a form: we just used a <div> rather than the classic <form> element. As you may have guessed at this point, forms in Angular don't necessarily have to be created using the <form> HTML element, since we won't be using its distinctive features. For that very reason, we are free to define them using <div>, <p>, or any HTML block-level element that could reasonably contain <input> fields.

However, using the <form> HTML element has some advantages that we might want to consider, such as:

- We won't need to explicitly bind the onSubmit() handler to the submit button's click event, since the form will be automatically submitted when the users click on it
- If our app includes the FormsModule – which is required for the *Template-Driven Forms* approach – Angular will automatically apply the NgForm directive to every <form> HTML template element
- Using a <form> element to contain a sequence of <input> elements will make our HTML code compliant with the W3C standards and recommendations

For all these reasons, it might be wise to replace that <div> element with a <form> element in the following way:

```
<form [formGroup]="form" (ngSubmit)="onSubmit()">
```

```
<!-- ...existing code... -->

</form>
```

While not being strictly required, such changes will make our HTML code more readable and easier to understand by other developers.

Right after that, we should also remove the (now redundant) manual bind to the onSubmit() event handler that we have on the submit button:

```
<button mat-flat-button color="primary"
  type="submit">
  Save
</button>
```

If we don't do that, the onSubmit() method would be called twice, which is something that we should definitely avoid.

city-edit.component.scss

Last but not least, here's our /src/app/cities/city-edit.component.scss content:

```
mat-form-field {
  display: block;
  margin: 10px 0;
}
```

Again, nothing fancy here: just the minimum amount of styles to override Angular Material's form fields default behavior – inline-block, which allows them to stack horizontally – and force a vertical layout instead, with a minimum amount of spacing between fields.

Adding the navigation link

Now that our CityEditComponent is ready, we need to enforce our master/detail pattern by adding a navigation link that will allow our users to navigate from our city listing (master) to the city edit form (detail).

To do that, we need to perform the following tasks:

- Create a new route within the app-routing.module.ts file
- Implement the preceding route in the template code of CitiesComponent

As always, we shouldn't need to add the references for the city-edit.component.ts file in the app.module.ts file, since the Angular CLI should've automatically done that when we generated the component.

Let's do this!

app-routing.module.ts

The first thing to do is to add a new route to the app-routing.module.ts file with the following source code (new lines are highlighted):

```ts
import { NgModule } from '@angular/core';
import { Routes, RouterModule } from '@angular/router';
import { HomeComponent } from './home/home.component';
import { CitiesComponent } from './cities/cities.component';
import { CityEditComponent } from './cities/city-edit.component';
import { CountriesComponent } from './countries/countries.component';

const routes: Routes = [
  { path: '', component: HomeComponent, pathMatch: 'full' },
  { path: 'cities', component: CitiesComponent },
  { path: 'city/:id', component: CityEditComponent },
  { path: 'countries', component: CountriesComponent },
];

@NgModule({
  imports: [RouterModule.forRoot(routes)],
  exports: [RouterModule]
})
export class AppRoutingModule { }
```

As we can see, we imported the CityEditComponent and defined a new city/:id corresponding to the route. The syntax we used will route any URL composed by city and a parameter that will be registered with the id name.

cities.component.html

Now that we have the navigation route, we need to implement it within the *Master* view so that the *Detail* view can be reached.

Open the /src/app/cities/cities.component.html file and change the HTML template code for the city's Name column in the following way:

```html
<!-- ...existing code... -->

<!-- Name Column -->
```

```
<ng-container matColumnDef="name">
  <th mat-header-cell *matHeaderCellDef mat-sort-header>Name</th>
  <td mat-cell *matCellDef="let city">
    <a [routerLink]="['/city', city.id]">{{city.name}}</a>
  </td>
</ng-container>

<!-- ...existing code... -->
```

Once you're done, test it out by hitting *F5* and navigating to the **Cities** view. As shown in the following screenshot, the city names are now clickable links:

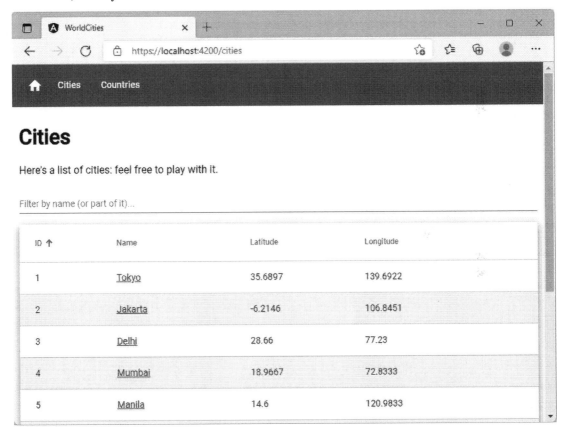

Figure 7.5: Cities table with clickable links

From there, filter the table for Paris and click on the first result to access the CityEditComponent, which we'll finally be able to see (as shown in the following screenshot):

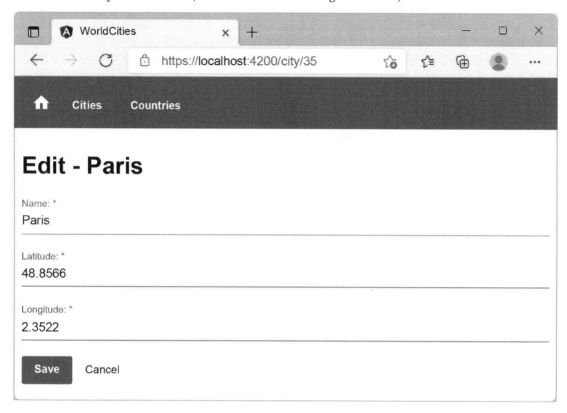

Figure 7.6: The CityEditComponent

As we can see, everything is much as we would expect it to be. We have three textboxes, as well as a **Save** button and a **Cancel** button, both of which are ready to perform the task they have been assigned. The **Save** button will send the modified text to the server for the update and then redirect the user to the *Master* view, while the **Cancel** button will redirect the user without performing any changes.

That's definitely a good start! However, we're far from done: we still have to add validators, implement error handling, and write a couple of unit tests for the client side and the server side. Let's get started.

Adding a new city

Before going any further, let's spend a couple more minutes adding a very useful feature to our CityEditComponent: the chance to add a brand-new City. This is a rather classic requirement of a *Detail* view with editing capabilities, which can be handled with the same component – as long as we perform some small modifications to enable it to handle a new feature (adding a new city) as well as the existing one (editing an existing city) in a seamless way.

To do that, we'll have to perform the following steps:

1. **Extend the functionalities of CityEditComponent** to make it able to add new cities, as well as editing existing ones
2. **Add a new Add City button** to our component's template file and bind it to a new client-side route
3. Implement the required functionalities to **select a country** for the newly added city, which will also be useful in edit mode (it will allow users to change the country for existing cities)

Let's get to work!

Extending the CityEditComponent

Open the /src/app/cities/city-edit.component.ts file and add the following code (the new/updated lines are highlighted):

```
import { Component, OnInit } from '@angular/core';
import { HttpClient } from '@angular/common/http';
import { ActivatedRoute, Router } from '@angular/router';
import { FormGroup, FormControl } from '@angular/forms';

import { environment } from './../../environments/environment';
import { City } from './city';

@Component({
  selector: 'app-city-edit',
  templateUrl: './city-edit.component.html',
  styleUrls: ['./city-edit.component.scss']
})
export class CityEditComponent implements OnInit {
  // the view title
  title?: string;

  // the form model
  form!: FormGroup;

  // the city object to edit or create
  city?: City;

  // the city object id, as fetched from the active route:
  // It's NULL when we're adding a new city,
  // and not NULL when we're editing an existing one.
  id?: number;
```

```
constructor(
  private activatedRoute: ActivatedRoute,
  private router: Router,
  private http: HttpClient) {
}

ngOnInit() {
  this.form = new FormGroup({
    name: new FormControl(''),
    lat: new FormControl(''),
    lon: new FormControl('')
  });

  this.loadData();
}

loadData() {

  // retrieve the ID from the 'id' parameter
  var idParam = this.activatedRoute.snapshot.paramMap.get('id');
  this.id = idParam ? +idParam : 0;
  if (this.id) {
    // EDIT MODE

    // fetch the city from the server
    var url = environment.baseUrl + 'api/Cities/' + this.id;
    this.http.get<City>(url).subscribe(result => {
      this.city = result;
      this.title = "Edit - " + this.city.name;

      // update the form with the city value
      this.form.patchValue(this.city);
    }, error => console.error(error));
  }
  else {
    // ADD NEW MODE

    this.title = "Create a new City";
  }
}
```

```
onSubmit() {
  var city = (this.id) ? this.city : <City>{};
  if (city) {
    city.name = this.form.controls['name'].value;
    city.lat = +this.form.controls['lat'].value;
    city.lon = +this.form.controls['lon'].value;

    if (this.id) {
      // EDIT mode

      var url = environment.baseUrl + 'api/Cities/' + city.id;
      this.http
        .put<City>(url, city)
        .subscribe(result => {

          console.log("City " + city!.id + " has been updated.");

          // go back to cities view
          this.router.navigate(['/cities']);
        }, error => console.error(error));
    }
    else {
      // ADD NEW mode
      var url = environment.baseUrl + 'api/Cities';
      this.http
        .post<City>(url, city)
        .subscribe(result => {

          console.log("City " + result.id + " has been created.");

          // go back to cities view
          this.router.navigate(['/cities']);
        }, error => console.error(error));
    }
  }
}
```

Thanks to these modifications, our code will now be able to distinguish between the two different user actions (adding a new city or editing an existing one) and properly deal with both of them.

The HTML template file may also perform a minor update to notify the user of the new feature.

Open the `/src/app/cities/cities-edit.component.html` file and modify it in the following way (the new/updated lines are highlighted).

Add the following highlighted code near the beginning of the file:

```
<!-- ... existing code ... -->

<p *ngIf="this.id && !city"><em>Loading...</em></p>

<!-- ... existing code ... -->
```

With such an improvement, we'll ensure that the `"Loading..."` message won't appear when we're adding a new city since the `city` variable will be empty.

Finally, change the **Save** button's fixed text with a dynamic value using Angular's *string interpolation* feature, which we've already seen various times:

```
<button mat-flat-button color="primary"
        type="submit">
  {{ this.id ? "Save" : "Create" }}
</button>
```

This minor yet useful addition will let us know if the form is working as expected: whenever we add a new city (and `this.id` evaluates to `false`), we will see a more appropriate **Create** button instead of the **Save** one, which will still be visible in edit mode.

Now, we need to do two things:

1. Find a nice way to let our users know that they can add new cities, as well as modifying the existing ones
2. Make them able to access this new feature

A simple **Add a new City** button will fix both these issues at once: let's add it to our `CitiesComponent`.

Adding the "Add a new City" button

Open the `/src/app/cities/cities.component.html` file and add the following code right after the `Loading...` paragraph:

```
<!-- ... existing code ... -->

<p *ngIf="!cities"><em>Loading...</em></p>

<button mat-flat-button color="primary"
  class="btn-add" *ngIf="cities" [routerLink]="['/city']">
```

```
    Add a new City
  </button>

  <!-- ... existing code ... -->
```

There's nothing new here; we've added the usual *route*-based button within a container and an *ngIf *structural directive* to make it appear after the Cities array becomes available.

Since we've given that button a new .btn-add CSS class, we can take the chance to decorate it with some minimal UI styling by opening the /src/app/cities/cities.component.scss file and adding something like this:

```
.btn-add {
    float: right;
}
```

This way, the button will be aligned to the right of the screen.

Adding a new route

Now, we need to define the new route that we referenced for the **Add a new City** button.

To do that, open the /src/app/app-routing.module.ts file and update the code, as follows:

```
// ...existing code...

const routes: Routes = [
  { path: '', component: HomeComponent, pathMatch: 'full' },
  { path: 'cities', component: CitiesComponent },
  { path: 'city/:id', component: CityEditComponent },
  { path: 'city', component: CityEditComponent },
  { path: 'countries', component: CountriesComponent },
]),

// ...existing code...
```

As we can see, the (new) route to add a new city and the (existing) route to edit an existing city are very similar since they both redirect the user to the same component; the only difference is that the latter doesn't have the id parameter, which is the technique we used to make our component aware of which task it has been called for. If the id is present, the user is editing an existing city; otherwise, they're adding a new one.

We are doing well... but we're not quite there yet. If we were to test what we've done so far by hitting *F5* and trying to add a new city, our `HttpClient` module would be greeted by an `HTTP 500 - Internal Server Error` from the server, similar to the one shown in the following screenshot:

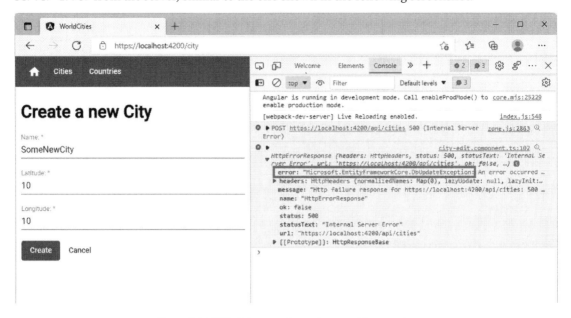

Figure 7.7: HTTP 500 error after trying to add a new city

Here's the full error text (with the relevant parts highlighted):

```
---> Microsoft.Data.SqlClient.SqlException (0x80131904): The INSERT statement
conflicted with the FOREIGN KEY constraint "FK_Cities_Countries_CountryId".
The conflict occurred in database "WorldCities", table "dbo.Countries", column
'Id'.
The statement has been terminated.
```

It definitely seems like we forgot the `CountryId` property of the `City` entity: we did that on purpose when we had to define the Angular city interface because we didn't need it at that time. We didn't suffer from its absence when we implemented the city edit mode because that property was *silently* fetched from the server and then stored within our Angular local variable, which we were sending back to the server while the HTTP `PUT` request was performing the update. However, now that we do want to create a new city from scratch, such a missing property will eventually take its toll.

To fix this, we need to add the `countryId` property to the `/src/app/cities/city.ts` file in the following way (the new lines are highlighted):

```
export interface City {
    id: number;
    name: string;
    lat: number;
    lon: number;
```

```
    countryId: number;
}
```

However, this won't be enough: we also need to give our users the chance to assign a specific Country to the new city; otherwise, the countryId property will never see an actual value – unless we define it programmatically with a fixed value, which would be a rather ugly workaround (to say the least).

Let's fix this in a decent way by adding a list of countries to CityEditComponent so that the user will be able to select one before hitting the **Create** button. Such a new feature will be very useful – even when the component runs in edit mode – since it will allow our users to change the country for existing cities.

HTML select

The easiest way to allow our users to pick a country from a list of countries would be to use a <select> element and populate it by fetching our data from the .NET back-end via the CountriesController GetCountries() method. Let's do that now.

Open the /src/app/cities/city-edit.component.ts file and add the following code (the new and updated lines are highlighted):

```typescript
import { Component, OnInit } from '@angular/core';
import { HttpClient, HttpParams } from '@angular/common/http';
import { ActivatedRoute, Router } from '@angular/router';
import { FormGroup, FormControl } from '@angular/forms';

import { environment } from './../../environments/environment';
import { City } from './city';
import { Country } from './../countries/country';

@Component({
  selector: 'app-city-edit',
  templateUrl: './city-edit.component.html',
  styleUrls: ['./city-edit.component.scss']
})
export class CityEditComponent implements OnInit {

  // the view title
  title?: string;

  // the form model
  form!: FormGroup;

  // the city object to edit or create
  city?: City;

  // the city object id, as fetched from the active route:
```

```
// It's NULL when we're adding a new city,
// and not NULL when we're editing an existing one.
id?: number;

// the countries array for the select
countries?: Country[];

constructor(
  private activatedRoute: ActivatedRoute,
  private router: Router,
  private http: HttpClient) {
}

ngOnInit() {
  this.form = new FormGroup({
    name: new FormControl(''),
    lat: new FormControl(''),
    lon: new FormControl(''),
    countryId: new FormControl('')
  });

  this.loadData();
}

loadData() {

  // load countries
  this.loadCountries();

  // retrieve the ID from the 'id' parameter
  var idParam = this.activatedRoute.snapshot.paramMap.get('id');
  this.id = idParam ? +idParam : 0;
  if (this.id) {
    // EDIT MODE

    // fetch the city from the server
    var url = environment.baseUrl + 'api/Cities/' + this.id;
    this.http.get<City>(url).subscribe(result => {
      this.city = result;
      this.title = "Edit - " + this.city.name;

      // update the form with the city value
      this.form.patchValue(this.city);
```

```
    }, error => console.error(error));
  }
  else {
    // ADD NEW MODE

    this.title = "Create a new City";
  }
}


loadCountries() {
  // fetch all the countries from the server
  var url = environment.baseUrl + 'api/Countries';
  var params = new HttpParams()
    .set("pageIndex", "0")
    .set("pageSize", "9999")
    .set("sortColumn", "name");

  this.http.get<any>(url, { params }).subscribe(result => {
    this.countries = result.data;
  }, error => console.error(error));
}

onSubmit() {
  var city = (this.id) ? this.city : <City>{};
  if (city) {
    city.name = this.form.controls['name'].value;
    city.lat = +this.form.controls['lat'].value;
    city.lon = +this.form.controls['lon'].value;
    city.countryId = +this.form.controls['countryId'].value;

    if (this.id) {
      // EDIT mode

      var url = environment.baseUrl + 'api/Cities/' + city.id;
      this.http
        .put<City>(url, city)
        .subscribe(result => {

          console.log("City " + city!.id + " has been updated.");

          // go back to cities view
          this.router.navigate(['/cities']);
        }, error => console.error(error));
```

```
        }
        else {
          // ADD NEW mode
          var url = environment.baseUrl + 'api/Cities';
          this.http
            .post<City>(url, city)
            .subscribe(result => {

              console.log("City " + result.id + " has been created.");

              // go back to cities view
              this.router.navigate(['/cities']);
            }, error => console.error(error));
        }
      }
    }
  }
```

What did we do here?

- We added the HttpParams module to the import list of @angular/common/http
- We added a reference to our Country interface since we need to handle countries as well
- We added a countries variable to store our countries
- We added a countryId form control (with a required validator, since it's a required value) to our form
- We added a loadCountries() method to fetch the countries from the server
- We added a call to the loadCountries() method from the loadData() method so that we'll asynchronously fetch the countries while we do the rest of the loadData() stuff (such as loading the city and/or setting up the form)
- We updated the city's countryId so that it matches the one that's selected in the form in the onSubmit() method; this means that it will be sent to the server for the insert or update task

It's worth noting how, in the `loadCountries()` method, we had to set up some `GET` parameters for the `/api/Countries` URL to comply with the strict default values that we set in *Chapter 6, Fetching and Displaying Data*: we don't need paging here since we need to fetch the entire countries list to populate our select list. More specifically, we set a `pageSize` of `9999` to ensure that we get all our countries, as well as an appropriate `sortColumn` to have them ordered by their name.

Now, we can use our brand-new `countries` variable on our HTML template.

Open the `/src/app/cities/city-edit.component.html` file and add the following code right below the longitude `mat-form-field` (the new lines are highlighted):

```html
<!-- ...existing code... -->

<!-- Lon -->
<mat-form-field>
  <mat-label>Longitude:</mat-label>
  <input matInput formControlName="lon" required
         placeholder="Insert longitude">
</mat-form-field>

<!-- Country -->
<p *ngIf="countries">
  <select id="countryId" formControlName="countryId">
    <option value="">--- Select a country ---</option>
    <option *ngFor="let country of countries" [value]="country.id">
      {{country.name}}
    </option>
  </select>
</p>

<!-- ...existing code... -->
```

If we press *F5* to test our code and navigate to the **Add a new City** or **Edit City** view, we'll see the following output:

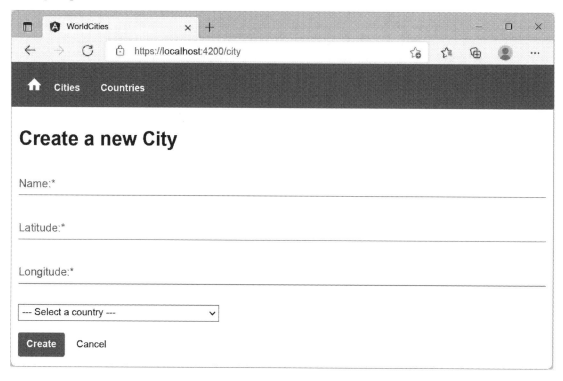

Figure 7.8: The CityEditComponent with a country drop-down list

Now, by clicking the --- **Select a country** --- drop-down list, our users will be able to pick a country from the ones that are available. That's not bad, right? However, the layout is not that great: the default, unstyled `<select>` HTML element does not fill well with Angular Material's UI.

Luckily enough, we can definitely improve this aspect by replacing our standard HTML `select` with a more powerful component from the **Angular Material** package library: `MatSelectModule`.

Angular Material select (MatSelectModule)

Since we've never used `MatSelectModule` before, we need to add it to the `/src/app/angular-material.module.ts` file.

Here's the `using` reference to add:

```
import { MatSelectModule } from '@angular/material/select';
```

As always, remember to also add the module in `@NgModule`'s `imports` and `exports` collections.

Right after that, we can replace the `<select>` HTML element we added to the `/src/app/cities/city-edit.component.html` file a short while ago in the following way:

```
<!-- ...existing code... -->

<!-- Country -->
<mat-form-field *ngIf="countries">
  <mat-label>Select a Country...</mat-label>
  <mat-select id="countryId" formControlName="countryId">
    <mat-option *ngFor="let country of countries"
      [value]="country.id">
      {{country.name}}
    </mat-option>
  </mat-select>
</mat-form-field>

<!-- ...existing code... -->
```

And that's it! We can see the updated result by hitting *F5* (see the following screenshot for the output):

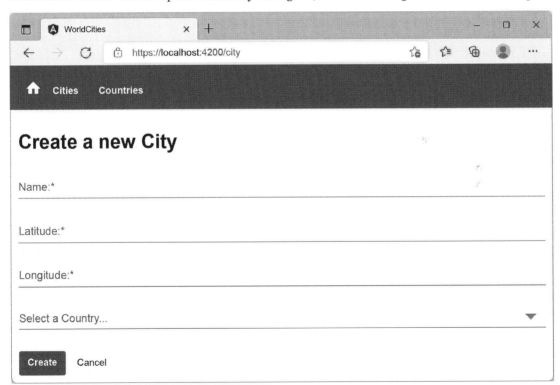

Figure 7.9: The CityEditComponent using MatSelectModule for the country dropdown

The MatSelectModule is definitely prettier than the stock <select> HTML element, all while retaining the same features: we don't even need to change the underlying component class file since it uses the same binding interface.

Now, we can add our brand-new city to our database. Let's do this using the following data:

- **Name:** New Tokyo
- **Latitude:** 35.685
- **Longitude:** 139.7514
- **Country:** Japan

Fill in our **Create a new City** form with these values and click the **Create** button. If everything went well, we should be brought back to the **Cities** view, where we'll be able to find our New Tokyo city using the filter (see the following screenshot):

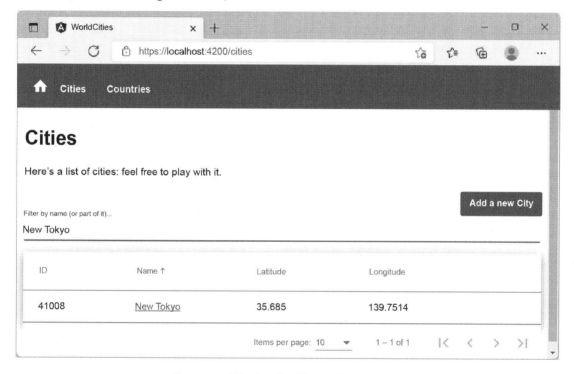

Figure 7.10: Cities list after filtering for New Tokyo

Here we go: we successfully added our first city!

Now that our *Reactive Form* is working properly and we have decent know-how about how it works, we're ready to spend some time tweaking it by adding something that could be very useful in a production scenario: some error-handling capabilities. We'll obtain these capabilities

Understanding data validation

Adding data validation to a form is hardly an option: it's a required feature to check the user input in terms of accuracy and completeness to improve the overall data quality by validating the data we want – or need – to collect. It's also very useful in terms of user experience because the error-handling capabilities it comes with will make our users able to understand why the form doesn't work and what they can do to fix the issues preventing them from submitting their data.

To understand such a concept, let's take our current `CityEditComponent` Reactive Form: it works fine if our users fill out all the required fields; however, there's no way for them to understand what the required values actually are, or what happens if they forget to fill all of them out... except for a console error message, which is what our source code currently displays whenever our `PUT` and `POST` requests end up with a back-end error of any sort.

In this section, we'll learn how we can validate user input from the front-end UI and display useful validation messages using our current Reactive Form. While we're there, we'll also take the chance to create an **Edit Country/Add new Country** form and learn something new in the process.

Template-Driven validation

For the sake of simplicity, we've chosen to not mess around with Template-Driven Forms and bring our focus to Model-Driven/Reactive Forms instead. However, it might be wise to spend a couple of minutes understanding how we can add validation to a Template-Driven Forms as well.

The good news about this is that we can use the same standard validation attributes that we would normally use to validate a native HTML form: the Angular framework uses directives to match them with validator functions internally and in a fully transparent way. More specifically, every time the value of a form control changes, Angular will run these functions and generate either a list of validation errors, thus resulting in an invalid status, or `null`, meaning that the form is valid.

The form's state – as well as each form control's state – can be checked/inspected by exporting `ngModel` to a local template variable. Here's an example that can help clarify this:

```
<input id="name" name="name" required minlength="4"
    [(ngModel)]="city.name" #name="ngModel">


<div *ngIf="name.invalid && (name.dirty || name.touched)">
    <div *ngIf="name.errors?.required">Name is required.</div>
    <div *ngIf="name.errors?.minlength">Name must be at least 4
      characters long.</div>
</div>
```

The *data validation directives* are highlighted in bold. As we can see, the preceding form will raise an error – and show a `<div>` element with an alert style to the user – whenever the city's name is not present or its character count is smaller than 4, since this is the minimum allowed length for the name input.

It's worth noting that we're checking two properties that might sound rather odd: `name.dirty` and `name.touched`. Here's a brief explanation of what they mean and why it's wise to check for their status:

- The `dirty` property starts as being `false` and becomes `true` whenever the user changes its starting values
- The `touched` property starts as being `false` and becomes `true` whenever the user blurs the form control element, that is, clicks (or taps, or "tabs") away from it after having it in focus

Now that we know how these properties work, we should be able to understand why we are checking them: we want our data validator error to only be seen if/when the user goes away from the control, leaving it with an invalid value – or no value at all.

 That's it for Template-Driven validation, at least for the purposes of this book. Those who need additional information should check out the following guide at https://angular. io/guide/forms#template-driven-forms.

Model-Driven validation

When dealing with Reactive Forms, the whole validation approach is rather different. In a nutshell, we could say that most of this job has to be done within the component class: instead of adding validators using HTML attributes in the template, we'll have to add validator functions directly to the form control model in the component class so that Angular will be able to call them whenever the value of the control changes.

Since we'll mostly be dealing with functions, we'll also get the option to make them sync or async, thus getting the chance to add synchronous and/or asynchronous validators:

- **Sync validators** immediately return either a set of validation errors or null. They can be set up using the second argument when we instantiate the FormControl they need to check (the first one being the default value).

- **Async validators** return a *Promise* or *Observable* that's been configured to emit a set of validation errors or null. They can be set up using the third argument when we instantiate the FormControl they need to check.

 It's important to know that async validators will only be executed/checked after the sync validators, and only if all of them successfully pass. Such an architectural choice has been made for performance reasons.

In the upcoming sections, we'll create both of them and add them to our form.

Our first validators

Enough with the theory: let's add our first set of validators in our CityEditComponent form.

Open the /src/app/cities/city-edit.component.ts file and add the following code:

```
import { Component, OnInit } from '@angular/core';
import { HttpClient, HttpParams } from '@angular/common/http';
import { ActivatedRoute, Router } from '@angular/router';
import { FormGroup, FormControl, Validators } from '@angular/forms';

// ...existing code...
```

```
' ' ' ' ' ' ' ' ' ' ' ' ' ' ' ' '
  ngOnInit() {
    this.form = new FormGroup({
      name: new FormControl('', Validators.required),
      lat: new FormControl('', Validators.required),
      lon: new FormControl('', Validators.required),
      countryId: new FormControl('', Validators.required)
    });

    this.loadData();
  }

// ...existing code...
```

As we can see, we added the following:

- An import reference to the Validators class from the @angular/forms package.
- A Validators.required to each of our FormControl elements. As the name suggests, this validator expects a non-null value for these fields; otherwise, it will return an invalid status.

 Validators.required is a built-in sync validator among those available from the Validators class. Other built-in validators provided by this class include min, max, requiredTrue, email, minLength, maxLength, pattern, nullValidator, compose, and composeAsync.

For more information regarding Angular's built-in validators, take a look at the following URL: https://angular.io/api/forms/Validators.

Once you're done, open the /src/app/cities/city-edit.component.html file and append the following <mat-error> elements at the end of each corresponding mat-form-field existing element, before that element's closing tag:

```
<!-- ...existing code... --!/>


<mat-error *ngIf="this.form.controls['name'].errors?.['required']">
  Name is required.
</mat-error>


<!-- ...existing code... --!/>


<mat-error *ngIf="this.form.controls['lat'].errors?.['required']">
  Latitude is required.
</mat-error>
```

```
<!-- ....existing code... --!/>

<mat-error *ngIf="this.form.controls['lon'].errors?.['required']">
  Longitude is required.
</mat-error>

<!-- ...existing code... --!/>

<mat-error *ngIf="this.form.controls['countryId'].errors?.['required']">
  Please select a Country.
</mat-error>

<!-- ...existing code... --!/>
```

Each one of these new `<mat-error>` elements will check the corresponding `input` or `select` value and return an error if one (or more) of the configured validators fails to validate it.

As we can see, all `mat-error` elements share the same underlying logic: they will be shown only when `FormControl`'s `error.required` property is set to `true`, which happens when the corresponding field's value is empty (since the required validator has been set for all of them).

It's worth noting that the `mat-error`, as per its default behavior, will only be shown when the control is invalid and either the user has interacted with the element (`touched`) or the parent form has been submitted. This is great for our purposes, since it means that we don't have to add additional checks to the `*ngIf` directive to handle the `touched` status like we did early on in this chapter. Furthermore, it's important to remember that each `mat-error` element needs to be placed within its corresponding `mat-form-field` element in order to work.

For additional info on the `mat-error` default behavior (and how to change it), see the following URL from the Angular Material docs:

`https://material.angular.io/components/input/overview#changing-when-error-messages-are-shown`

All we need to do now is to properly test these validators. However, before doing that, let's spend a couple of minutes explaining the meaning of the `?` question mark that we've used within the `*ngIf` directives in the TypeScript code above.

The Safe Navigation Operator

Let's take another look at that code:

```
*ngIf="this.form.controls['lon'].errors?.['required']"
```

That question mark is TypeScript's *Safe Navigation Operator*, also known as the **Elvis Operator**, and is very useful for protecting against null and undefined values in property paths. When the Safe Navigation Operator is present, TypeScript stops evaluating the expression when it hits the first null value. In the preceding code, if the errors nullable property happens to be null (which happens whenever the FormControl has no errors), the whole expression would return false without checking the required property, thus avoiding one of the following null-reference errors:

```
TypeError: Cannot read property 'required' of null.
Error TS2531: Object is possibly 'null'
```

In more general terms, the *Safe Navigation Operator* makes us able to navigate an object path – even when we are not aware of whether such a path exists or not – by returning either the value of the object path (if it exists) or null. Such behavior is very convenient whenever we need to check for the value of any nullable object: FormControl errors, GET or POST parameters, and a lot of other common scenarios. For this very reason, we're going to use it a lot from now on.

> It's worth noting that the *Safe Navigation Operator* has been part of the Angular HTML template language since Angular 2 and was only recently added to TypeScript. This much-needed addition occurred in November 2019, with the release of TypeScript v3.7:
>
> `https://www.typescriptlang.org/docs/handbook/release-notes/typescript-3-7.html`

For more information about the Safe Navigation Operator, check out the following URL: `https://angular.io/guide/template-expression-operators#safe-navigation-operator`.

Testing the validators

Let's quickly check everything we've done so far: hit *F5*, navigate to the **Cities** view, click on the **Add a new City** button, and play with the form while trying to trigger the validators.

Here's what happens when we cycle through the various input values without typing anything:

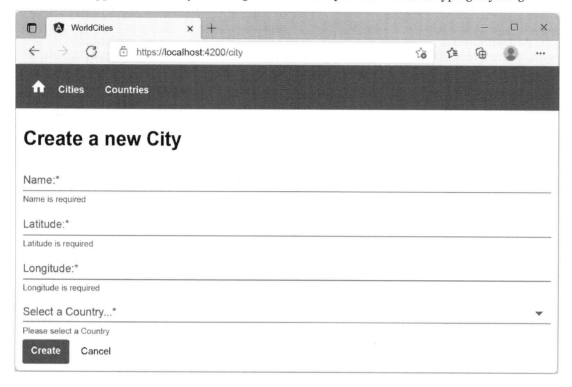

Figure 7.11: Testing the CityEditComponent form validators

Not bad, right? The input errors couldn't be more visible, and the **Create** button will stay disabled until they are all fixed, thus preventing accidental submits. All of these colored warnings should help our users understand what they're doing wrong and fix these issues.

Before ending our data validation journey, there's still one topic we need to cover: server-side validation, which can often be the only reasonable way to prevent some complex errors.

Server-side validation

Server-side validation is the process of checking for errors (and handling them accordingly) on the server side, that is, after the data has been sent to the back-end. This is a whole different approach from **client-side validation**, where the data is checked by the front-end, that is, before the data is sent to the server.

Handling errors on the *client side* has a lot of advantages in terms of speed and performance because the user immediately knows whether the input data is valid or not without having to query the server. However, *server-side* validation is a required feature of any decent web application because it prevents a lot of potentially harmful scenarios, such as the following:

- **Implementation errors** of the *client-side validation* process, which can fail to block badly formatted data
- **Client-side hacks** performed by experienced users, browser extensions, or plugins that might want to allow the user to send unsupported input values to the back-end
- **Request forgery**, that is, false HTTP requests containing incorrect or malicious data

All of these techniques are based upon circumventing the *client-side validators*, which is always possible because we have no way to prevent our users (or hackers) from skipping, altering, or eliminating them; conversely, *server-side validators* cannot be avoided because they will be performed by the same back-end that will process the input data.

Therefore, in a nutshell, we could reasonably say that *client-side validation* is an optional and convenient feature, while *server-side validation* is a requirement for any decent web application that cares about the quality of the input data.

 To avoid confusion, it is important to understand that server-side validation, although being implemented on the back-end, also requires a front-end implementation, such as calling the back-end and then showing the validation results to the user. The main difference between client-side validation and server-side validation is that the former only exists on the client side and never calls the back-end, while the latter relies upon a front-end and back-end coordinated effort, thus being more complex to implement and test.

Moreover, there are some scenarios where server-side validation is the only possible way to check for certain conditions or requirements that cannot be verified by *client-side* validation alone. To explain this concept, let's look at a quick example.

Launch our `WorldCities` app in *debug* mode by hitting *F5*, go to our **Cities** view, and type `paris` into the filter textbox.

You should see the following output:

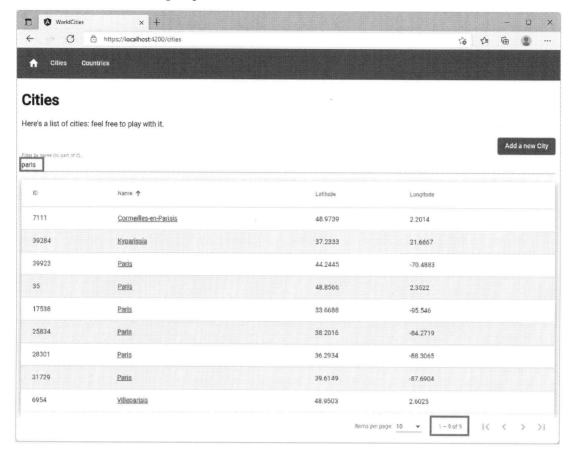

Figure 7.12: Cities list after filtering for "paris"

The preceding screenshot tells us the following things:

- There are at least *nine* cities whose name contains the word "paris" all over the world... and *six* of them are actually called Paris (!)
- Multiple cities can have the same name

That's not surprising: when we created our database using Entity Framework with *code-first*, we didn't make the name field *unique* since we knew that there was a high chance of *homonymous* cities. Luckily enough, this isn't an issue since we can still distinguish between them by looking at the lat, lon, and country values.

 If we check some of these cities on *Google Maps*, we will see that one of them is in *France*, another one is in *Texas* (US), a third one is in *Tennessee* (US), and so on: same name, different cities.

Now, what about adding a *validator* that could check if the city we are trying to add has the same name, lat, and lon values as a city already present in our database? Such a feature would block our users from inserting the same city multiple times, thus avoiding real duplicates, without blocking the *homonyms* that have different coordinates.

Unfortunately, there's no way to do that on the *client side* only. To fulfill this task, we would need to create an Angular *custom validator* that could *asynchronously* check these values against the *server* and then return an *OK* (*valid*) or *KO* (*invalid*) result: in other words, a *server-side validation* task.

Let's try to do that now.

DupeCityValidator

In this section, we'll create a custom validator that will perform an asynchronous call to our .NET Core back-end to ensure that the city we're trying to add doesn't have the same name, lat, lon, and country as an existing one.

city-edit.component.ts

The first thing we have to do is create the validator itself and bind it to our Reactive Form. To do that, open the /src/app/cities/city-edit.component.ts file and change its contents accordingly (the new/updated lines are highlighted):

```
// ...existing code...

import { FormGroup, FormControl, Validators, AbstractControl, AsyncValidatorFn
} from '@angular/forms';
import { Observable } from 'rxjs';
import { map } from 'rxjs/operators';

// ...existing code...

  ngOnInit() {
    this.form = new FormGroup({
      name: new FormControl('', Validators.required),
      lat: new FormControl('', Validators.required),
      lon: new FormControl('', Validators.required),
      countryId: new FormControl('', Validators.required)
    }, null, this.isDupeCity());

    this.loadData();
  }

// ...existing code...
```

```
isDupeCity(): AsyncValidatorFn {
  return (control: AbstractControl): Observable<{ [key: string]: any } |
null> => {

    var city = <City>{};
    city.id = (this.id) ? this.id : 0;
    city.name = this.form.controls['name'].value;
    city.lat = +this.form.controls['lat'].value;
    city.lon = +this.form.controls['lon'].value;
    city.countryId = +this.form.controls['countryId'].value;

    var url = environment.baseUrl + 'api/Cities/IsDupeCity';
    return this.http.post<boolean>(url, city).pipe(map(result => {

      return (result ? { isDupeCity: true } : null);
    }));
  }
}
```

As we can see, we've made some important changes in the preceding code:

- We added some import references (AbstractControl, AsyncValidatorFn, Observable, and map) that we used to implement our new async custom validator. If you don't get what we need them for, don't worry: we'll be talking about this topic later on.
- We created a new isDupeCity() method, which contains the whole implementation of our async custom validator.
- We configured the new validator to be used by the main FormGroup (the one related to the whole form).

As for our custom validator, it seems way more complex than it actually is. Let's try to summarize what it does:

- The first thing worth mentioning is that the isDupeCity() method returns an AsyncValidatorFn that, in turn, returns an Observable: this means that we're not returning a value, but a *subscriber function instance* that will eventually return a value – which will be either a *key/value* object or null. This value will only be *emitted* when the Observable is executed.
- The *inner function* creates a temporary city object, fills it with the real-time form data, calls an IsDupeCity *back-end* URL that we don't know yet (but we will soon enough), and eventually returns either true or null, depending on the result. It's worth noting that we're not *subscribing* to the HttpClient this time, as we often did in the past: we're manipulating it using the pipe and map *ReactJS (RxJS)* operators, which we'll be talking about in a short while.

For more information regarding custom async validators, read the following guide: https://angular.io/guide/form-validation#implementing-a-custom-async-validator.

Since our custom validator relies on an HTTP request being sent to our .NET Core *back-end*, we need to implement that method as well.

CitiesController

Switch to the **WorldCityAPI** project, then open the /Controllers/CitiesController.cs file and add the following method at the bottom of the file:

```
// ...existing code...

private bool CityExists(int id)
{
    return _context.Cities.Any(e => e.Id == id);
}

[HttpPost]
[Route("IsDupeCity")]
public bool IsDupeCity(City city)
{
    return _context.Cities.Any(
        e => e.Name == city.Name
        && e.Lat == city.Lat
        && e.Lon == city.Lon
        && e.CountryId == city.CountryId
        && e.Id != city.Id
    );
}

// ...existing code...
```

The .NET method is very straightforward: it checks the data model for a City that has the same Name, Lat, Lon, and CountryId as the one provided by the front-end (as well as a different Id) and returns true or false as the result. The Id check has been added to conditionally disable the *dupe check* when the user is editing an existing city. If that's the case, using the *same* Name, Lat, Lon, and CountryId would be allowed since we're basically overwriting the same city and not creating a new one. When the user adds a new city, that Id value will always be set to *zero*, preventing the *dupe check* from being disabled.

city-edit.component.html

Now that the *back-end* code is ready, we need to create a suitable error message from the UI. Open the `/src/app/cities/city-edit.component.html` file and update its content in the following way (the new lines are highlighted):

```html
<div class="city-edit">
  <h1>{{title}}</h1>
  <p *ngIf="this.id && !city"><em>Loading...</em></p>
  <form [formGroup]="form" (ngSubmit)="onSubmit()">

    <p>
      <mat-error *ngIf="form.invalid && form.hasError('isDupeCity')">
        <strong>ERROR</strong>:
        A city with the same <i>name</i>, <i>lat</i>,
        <i>lon</i> and <i>country</i> already exists.
      </mat-error>
    </p>

<!-- ...existing code... -->
```

As shown in the preceding code, the alert `<div>` we added will only be shown if the following three conditions are met:

- The form is invalid
- There are errors that are strictly related to the form itself
- The `isDupeCity` error is returning `true`

It's very important to check all of them, otherwise we risk showing such an alert even when it doesn't have to be shown.

Testing it out

Now that the component HTML template has been set up, we can test the result of our hard work. Press *F5*, navigate to the **Cities** view, click the **Add a new City** button, and insert the following values:

- **Name:** `New Tokyo`
- **Latitude:** `35.685`
- **Longitude:** `139.7514`
- **Country:** `Japan`

If we did everything properly, we should be greeted by the following error message:

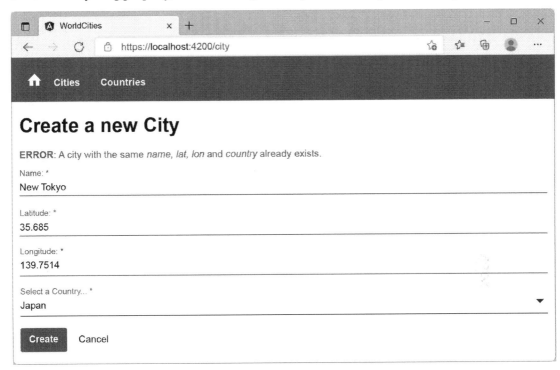

Figure 7.13: Testing the duplicate city validator

That's great! Our custom *async* validator is working fine and triggers both the front-end and the back-end validation logic.

Observables and RxJS operators

The *async* logic that's used to perform the call makes use of the Observable/RxJS pattern: this time, though, instead of relying on the subscribe() method we've already used a number of times, we opted for a pipe + map approach. These are two very important RxJS operators that allow us to perform our data manipulation tasks while retaining the Observable status of the returned value, while subscriptions will *execute* the Observable and return actual data instead.

This concept might be quite difficult to understand. Let's try to put it in other words:

- We should use the subscribe() method when we want to execute the Observable and get its actual result; for example, a JSON structured response. Such a method returns a *Subscription* that can be canceled but **can't be subscribed** to anymore.

- We should use the map() operator when we want to transform/manipulate the data events of the Observable without executing it so that it can be passed to other *async* actors that will also manipulate (and eventually execute) it. Such a method returns an Observable that **can be subscribed to**.

As for the `pipe()`, it's just an RxJS operator that composes/chains other operators (such as `map`, `filter`, and so on).

The most important difference between Observable methods and RxJS operators is that the latter always returns Observables, while the former returns a different (and mostly final) object type. Does this ring a bell?

If we think about what we learned back in *Chapter 6*, *Fetching and Displaying Data*, when dealing with .NET Entity Framework, it should definitely sound familiar. Remember when we were playing around with the `IQueryable<T>` interface? The various `Where`, `OrderBy`, and `CountAsync` `IQueryable` methods that we used when we built our `ApiResult` class are quite similar to what we can do in Angular by chaining multiple `map` functions with the `pipe` operator. Conversely, the `subscribe()` method strictly resembles the various `ToListAsync()`/`ToArrayAsync()` methods that we used in .NET to execute the `IQueryable` and retrieve its result in a usable object.

Performance issues

Before moving on, let's try to answer the following question: *when will this validator be checked?* In other words, can we reasonably expect performance issues, considering the fact it performs a *server-side* API call upon each check?

If we recall what we said earlier, the *asynchronous* validators will only be checked when all the *synchronous* validators return `true`. Since `isDupeCity` is *async*, it won't be called until all the `Validators.required` that we previously set up in all the `FormControl` elements return `true`. That's a piece of great news indeed, since there would be no sense in checking for an existing city with `name`, `lat`, `lon`, and/or `countryId` being `null` or empty.

Based on what we have just said, we can reasonably expect the `isDupeCity` validator to be called once or twice for each form submission, which is perfectly fine in terms of performance impact. Everything is fine, then. Let's move on.

Introducing the FormBuilder

Now that our `CityEditComponent` has been set up, we might be tempted to reuse the same techniques to create a `CountryEditComponent` and get the job done, just like we did in *Chapter 6*, *Fetching and Displaying Data* with our `CitiesComponent` and `CountryComponent` files. However, we won't be doing this. Instead, we'll take the chance to introduce a new tool to our shed that can be very useful when dealing with multiple forms: the `FormBuilder` service.

In the following sections, we'll do the following:

* Create our `CountryEditComponent` with all the required TypeScript, HTML, and SCSS files
* Learn how to use the `FormBuilder` service to generate form controls in a better way
* Add a new set of `Validators` (including a brand-new `isDupeCountry` custom validator) to the new form implementation
* Test our new `FormBuilder`-based implementation to check that everything works

By the end of this section, we'll have a fully functional `CountryEditComponent` that will work in the same way that `CityEditComponent` does, except it will be based on a slightly different approach.

Creating the CountryEditComponent

Let's start by creating the Angular component, just like we did with the `CityEditComponent` early on.

Open a command-line prompt, navigate to our `WorldCities` project's `/src/app/countries/` folder, and then execute the following command:

```
ng generate component CountryEdit --flat --module=app --skip-tests
```

Once you're done, fill the newly created component files with the following content.

country-edit.component.ts

Open the `/src/app/countries/country-edit.component.ts` file and fill it with the following code. Watch out for the highlighted parts, which are rather different from the previous `CityEditComponent`; other minor differences, such as country instead of city, countries instead cities, and the like, are not highlighted, since they're more than expected:

```typescript
import { Component, OnInit } from '@angular/core';
import { HttpClient, HttpParams } from '@angular/common/http';
import { ActivatedRoute, Router } from '@angular/router';
import { FormGroup, FormBuilder, Validators, AbstractControl, AsyncValidatorFn
} from '@angular/forms';
import { Observable } from 'rxjs';
import { map } from 'rxjs/operators';

import { environment } from './../../environments/environment';
import { Country } from './country';

@Component({
  selector: 'app-country-edit',
  templateUrl: './country-edit.component.html',
  styleUrls: ['./country-edit.component.scss']
})
export class CountryEditComponent implements OnInit {

  // the view title
  title?: string;

  // the form model
  form!: FormGroup;
```

```
  // the country object to edit or create
  country?: Country;

  // the country object id, as fetched from the active route:
  // It's NULL when we're adding a new country,
  // and not NULL when we're editing an existing one.
  id?: number;

  // the countries array for the select
  countries?: Country[];

  constructor(
    private fb: FormBuilder,
    private activatedRoute: ActivatedRoute,
    private router: Router,
    private http: HttpClient) {
  }

  ngOnInit() {
    this.form = this.fb.group({
      name: ['',
        Validators.required,
        this.isDupeField("name")
      ],
      iso2: ['',
        [
          Validators.required,
          Validators.pattern(/^[a-zA-Z]{2}$/)
        ],
        this.isDupeField("iso2")
      ],
      iso3: ['',
        [
          Validators.required,
          Validators.pattern(/^[a-zA-Z]{3}$/)
        ],
        this.isDupeField("iso3")
      ]
    });

    this.loadData();
```

```
    }

    loadData() {

      // retrieve the ID from the 'id' parameter
      var idParam = this.activatedRoute.snapshot.paramMap.get('id');
      this.id = idParam ? +idParam : 0;
      if (this.id) {
        // EDIT MODE

        // fetch the country from the server
        var url = environment.baseUrl + "api/Countries/" + this.id;
        this.http.get<Country>(url).subscribe(result => {
          this.country = result;
          this.title = "Edit - " + this.country.name;

          // update the form with the country value
          this.form.patchValue(this.country);
        }, error => console.error(error));
      }
      else {
        // ADD NEW MODE

        this.title = "Create a new Country";
      }
    }

    onSubmit() {
      var country = (this.id) ? this.country : <Country>{};
      if (country) {
        country.name = this.form.controls['name'].value;
        country.iso2 = this.form.controls['iso2'].value;
        country.iso3 = this.form.controls['iso3'].value;

        if (this.id) {
          // EDIT mode

          var url = environment.baseUrl + 'api/Countries/' + country.id;
          this.http
            .put<Country>(url, country)
            .subscribe(result => {
```

```
          console.log("Country " + country!.id + " has been updated.");

          // go back to countries view
          this.router.navigate(['/countries']);
        }, error => console.error(error));
    }
    else {
      // ADD NEW mode
      var url = environment.baseUrl + 'api/Countries';
      this.http
        .post<Country>(url, country)
        .subscribe(result => {

          console.log("Country " + result.id + " has been created.");

          // go back to countries view
          this.router.navigate(['/countries']);
        }, error => console.error(error));
    }
  }
}

isDupeField(fieldName: string): AsyncValidatorFn {
  return (control: AbstractControl): Observable<{
    [key: string]: any
  } | null> => {

    var params = new HttpParams()
      .set("countryId", (this.id) ? this.id.toString() : "0")
      .set("fieldName", fieldName)
      .set("fieldValue", control.value);
    var url = environment.baseUrl + 'api/Countries/IsDupeField';
    return this.http.post<boolean>(url, null, { params })
      .pipe(map(result => {
        return (result ? { isDupeField: true } : null);
      }));
    }
  }
}
```

As we can see, the component's source code is quite similar to `CityEditComponent`, except for some limited yet important differences that we're going to summarize here:

- The `FormBuilder` service has been added to the `@angular/forms` import list, replacing the `FormControl` reference that we don't need anymore. As a matter of fact, we're still creating form controls, but we'll do that via the `FormBuilder` instead of manually instantiating them, which means we don't need to *explicitly reference* them.

- The `form` variable is now instantiated using a different approach that strongly relies upon the new `FormBuilder` service.

- The various `FormControl` elements that get instantiated within the `form` feature are some *validators* that we have never seen before.

The `FormBuilder` service gives us three *factory methods* so that we can create our form structure: `control()`, `group()`, and `array()`. Each generates an instance of the corresponding `FormControl`, `FormGroup`, and `FormArray` class. In our example, we're creating a single containing group with three controls, each with its own set of *validators*.

As for the *validators*, we can see two new entries:

- `Validators.pattern`: A built-in *validator* that requires the control's *value* to match a given regular expression (*regex*) pattern. Since our `ISO2` and `ISO3` country fields are defined using a strict format, we're going to use them to ensure that the user will input correct values.

- `isDupeField`: This is a custom async validator that we implemented here for the first time. It's similar to the `isDupeCity` validator we created for our `CityEditComponent` but with some key differences that we're going to summarize in the next section.

 Those who don't know much about regular expressions (or regex for short) and want to use the `Validators.pattern` to its full extent should definitely visit the following website, which contains a good number of resources regarding regex and a great online builder and tester with full JavaScript and PHP/PCRE regex support: `https://regexr.com/`.

The `pattern` validator is quite self-explanatory, while the `isDupeField` custom validator deserves some additional explanation.

The isDupeField validator

As we can see by looking at the preceding component's source code, the `isDupeField` custom validator is not assigned to the main `FormGroup` like `isDupeCity` is; instead, it's set three times: once for each `FormControl` it needs to check. The reason for this is simple: compared to `isDupeCity`, which was meant to check for duplicate cities using a four-field dupe key, `isDupeField` needs to **individually check** each field it's assigned to. We need to do that because we don't want more than one country having the same `name`, **or** the same `iso2`, **or** the same `iso3`.

This also explains why we need to specify a `fieldname` and a corresponding `fieldValue` instead of passing a `Country` interface: the `isDupeField` *server-side* API will have to perform a different check for each `fieldName` we're going to pass, instead of relying on a single general-purpose check like the `isDupeCity` API does.

As for the `countryId` parameter, it's required to prevent the *dupe check* from raising a validation error when editing an existing *country*. In the `isDupeCity` validator, it was passed as a property of the `city` class. Now, we need to explicitly add it to the POST parameters.

The IsDupeField server-side API

Now, we need to implement our custom validator's *back-end* API, just like we did with `IsDupeCity()` early on. Switch to the **WorldCitiesAPI** project, then open the `/Controllers/CountriesController.cs` file and add the following method at the bottom of the file:

```
// ...existing code...

private bool CountryExists(int id)
{
    return _context.Countries.Any(e => e.Id == id);
}


[HttpPost]
[Route("IsDupeField")]
public bool IsDupeField(
    int countryId,
    string fieldName,
    string fieldValue)
{
    switch (fieldName)
    {
        case "name":
            return _context.Countries.Any(
                c => c.Name == fieldValue && c.Id != countryId);
        case "iso2":
            return _context.Countries.Any(
                c => c.ISO2 == fieldValue && c.Id != countryId);
        case "iso3":
            return _context.Countries.Any(
                c => c.ISO3 == fieldValue && c.Id != countryId);
        default:
            return false;
    }
}
```

Although the code resembles the IsDupeCity *server-side* API, we're switching the fieldName parameter and performing a different *dupe check* depending on its value; such logic is implemented with a
standard switch/case conditional block with *strongly typed* LINQ lambda expressions for each field
we can reasonably expect. Again, we're also checking that the countryId is different so that our users
can *edit* an existing country.

If the fieldName that's received from the client differs from the three supported values, our API will
respond with false.

An alternative approach using Linq.Dynamic

Before moving on, we may want to ask ourselves why we've implemented the IsDupeField API using
strongly typed lambda expressions inside a switch...case block, instead of relying on the System.
Linq.Dynamic.Core library.

As a matter of fact, we did that for the sake of simplicity, since the *dynamic* approach would require us
to have to write additional code to protect our method from *SQL injection* attacks. However, since we
already implemented such a task in the IsValidProperty() method of our ApiResult class, maybe
we can use it and shrink the preceding code down: after all, we've made it *public* and *static* so that we
can use it anywhere.

Here's an alternative implementation using the aforementioned tools (the old code is commented,
while the new code is highlighted):

```
using System.Linq.Dynamic.Core;

// ...existing code...

[HttpPost]
[Route("IsDupeField")]
public bool IsDupeField(
    int countryId,
    string fieldName,
    string fieldValue)
{

    // Default approach (using strongly-typed LAMBA expressions)
    //switch (fieldName)
    //{
    // case "name":
    // return _context.Countries.Any(c => c.Name == fieldValue);
    // case "iso2":
    // return _context.Countries.Any(c => c.ISO2 == fieldValue);
    // case "iso3":
    // return _context.Countries.Any(c => c.ISO3 == fieldValue);
    // default:
```

```
    // return false;
    //}

    // Alternative approach (using System.Linq.Dynamic.Core)
    return (ApiResult<Country>.IsValidProperty(fieldName, true))
        ? _context.Countries.Any(
            string.Format("{0} == @0 && Id != @1", fieldName),
            fieldValue,
            countryId)
        : false;
}
```

Not bad, right?

The *alternative dynamic* approach definitely looks more DRY and versatile than the *default* one, all while retaining the same security level against *SQL injection* attacks. The only downside may be due to the additional overhead brought by the System.Linq.Dynamics.Core library, which will likely have some minor performance impact. Although this shouldn't be an issue in most scenarios, whenever we want our APIs to respond to HTTP requests as quickly as possible, we should arguably favor the default approach.

country-edit.component.html

It's time to implement the template of our CountryEditComponent.

Open the /src/app/countries/country-edit.component.html file and fill it with the following code. Once again, pay attention to the highlighted parts, which are rather different from the template of CityEditComponent; other minor differences, such as country instead of city, are not highlighted since they're more than expected:

```html
<div class="country-edit">
  <h1>{{title}}</h1>
  <p *ngIf="this.id && !country"><em>Loading...</em></p>
  <form [formGroup]="form" (ngSubmit)="onSubmit()">

    <!-- Name -->
    <mat-form-field>
      <mat-label>Name:</mat-label>
      <input matInput formControlName="name" required
            placeholder="Type a name">
      <mat-error *ngIf="this.form.controls['name'].errors?.['required']">
        Name is required.
      </mat-error>
      <mat-error *ngIf="this.form.controls['name'].errors?.['isDupeField']">
        Name already exists: please choose another.
```

```html
      </mat-error>
    </mat-form-field>


    <!-- ISO2 -->
    <mat-form-field>
      <mat-label>
        ISO 3166-1 ALPHA-2 Country code (2 letters)
      </mat-label>
      <input matInput formControlName="iso2" required
              placeholder="Insert the ISO2 Country code">
      <mat-error *ngIf="this.form.controls['iso2'].errors?.['required']">
        ISO 3166-1 ALPHA-2 Country code is required.
      </mat-error>
      <mat-error *ngIf="this.form.controls['iso2'].errors?.['pattern']">
        ISO 3166-1 ALPHA-2 Country code requires 2 letters.
      </mat-error>
      <mat-error *ngIf="this.form.controls['iso2'].errors?.['isDupeField']">
        This code already exists: please choose another.
      </mat-error>
    </mat-form-field>


    <!-- ISO3 -->
    <mat-form-field>
      <mat-label>
        ISO 3166-1 ALPHA-3 Country code (3 letters)
      </mat-label>
      <input matInput formControlName="iso3" required
              placeholder="Insert the ISO3 Country code">
      <mat-error *ngIf="this.form.controls['iso3'].errors?.['required']">
        ISO 3166-1 ALPHA-3 Country code is required.
      </mat-error>
      <mat-error *ngIf="this.form.controls['iso3'].errors?.['pattern']">
        ISO 3166-1 ALPHA-3 Country code requires 3 letters.
      </mat-error>
      <mat-error *ngIf="this.form.controls['iso3'].errors?.['isDupeField']">
        This code already exists: please choose another.
      </mat-error>
    </mat-form-field>


    <div>
      <button mat-flat-button color="primary"
```

```
            type="submit">
        {{ this.id ? "Save" : "Create" }}
      </button>
      <button mat-flat-button color="secondary"
              [routerLink]="['/countries']">
        Cancel
      </button>
    </div>
  </form>
</div>
```

As we can see, the most relevant differences are all related to the HTML code that's required to show the new *pattern* and isDupeField validators. Now, we have as many as *three* different validators for our fields, which is pretty awesome: our users won't be given a chance to input wrong values!

country-edit.component.scss

Last but not least, let's apply the UI styling.

Open the /src/app/countries/country-edit.component.scss file and fill it with the following code:

```
mat-form-field {
    display: block;
    margin: 10px 0;
}
```

No surprises here; the preceding stylesheet code is identical to the one we used for CityEditComponent.

Our component is finally done! Now we just need to reference it in the AppRoutingModule file to implement the client-side navigation routes.

AppRoutingModule

By now, we should know what to do. Open the app-routing.module.ts file and add the following routing rules (new lines are highlighted):

```
// ...existing code...

import { CountryEditComponent } from './countries/country-edit.component';

// existing code...

{ path: 'countries', component: CountriesComponent },
{ path: 'country/:id', component: CountryEditComponent },
```

```
{ path: 'country', component: CountryEditComponent }

// ...existing code...
```

Now that we've laid down the two routes so that we can edit and add countries, we just need to implement them in the CountriesComponent template file by adding the route link in the **Name** column and the **Add new Country** button, just like we did with the cities.

CountriesComponent

Open the /src/app/countries/countries.component.html file and add the following code (the new and updated lines are highlighted):

```
<!-- ...existing code... -->

<p *ngIf="!countries"><em>Loading…</em></p>

<button mat-flat-button color="primary"
        class="btn-add" [routerLink]="['/country']">
  Add a new Country
</button>

<!-- ...existing code... -->

<!--Name Column -->
<ng-container matColumnDef="name">
  <th mat-header-cell *matHeaderCellDef mat-sort-header>Name</th>
  <td mat-cell *matCellDef="let country">
    <a [routerLink]="['/country', country.id]">{{country.name}}</a>
  </td>
</ng-container>

<!-- ...existing code... -->
```

We're almost done: we just need to add the .add-btn CSS class to the countries.component.scss file, so that the **Add new Country** button will be aligned to the right...

```
.btn-add {
    float: right;
}
```

... And that's it! Now, we're ready to test everything out.

Testing the CountryEditComponent

Now, it's time to press *F5* and admire the result of our hard work.

Once the app has been launched in *debug* mode, navigate to the **Countries** view to see the **Add a new Country** button and the edit links on the various country names, as shown in the following screenshot:

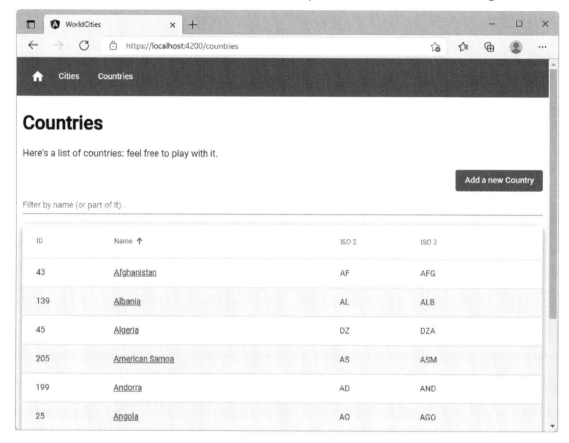

Figure 7.14: Countries list with the Add a new Country button and edit links

Now, let's search for Denmark using our filter and click on the name to enter the CountryEditComponent in *edit mode*. If everything works fine, the name, iso2, and iso3 fields should all be green, meaning that our isDupeField custom validator(s) are not raising errors:

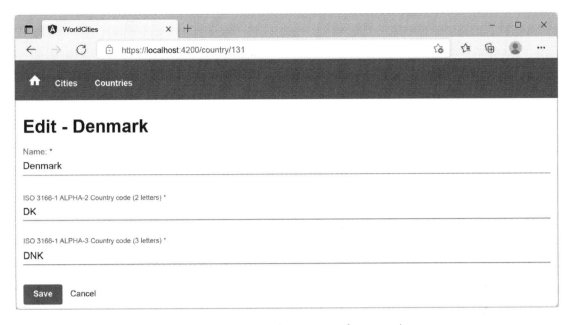

Figure 7.15: CountryEditComponent for Denmark

Now, let's try to change the country name to Japan and the **ISO 3166-1 ALPHA-2 Country code** to IT and see what happens:

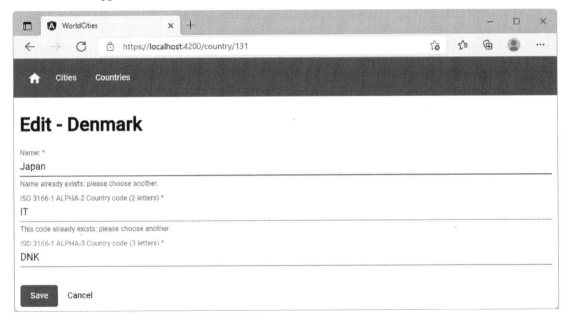

Figure 7.16: Duplicate error messages when trying to edit Denmark

This is a great result: this means that our custom validators are doing their job, positively raising some dupe errors since these values have been reserved for other existing countries (Japan and Italy, respectively).

Now, let's hit the **Cancel** button and go back to the **Countries** view. From there, click the **Add a new Country** button and try to insert a country with the following values:

- **Name:** New Japan
- **ISO 3166-1 ALPHA-2 Country code:** JP
- **ISO 3166-1 ALPHA-3 Country code:** NJ2

If everything is working fine, we should raise two more validation errors, as shown in the following screenshot:

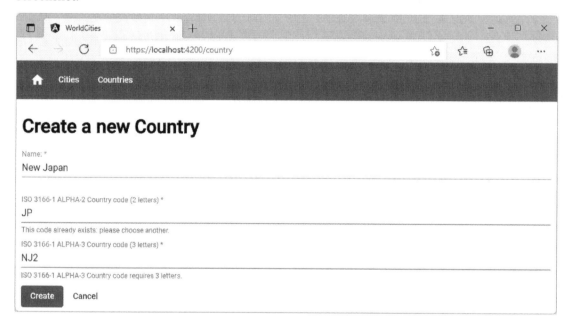

Figure 7.17: Duplicate errors while trying to add a new country

The former error is raised by our isDupeField custom validator and is due to the fact that the ALPHA-2 country code already belongs to an existing country (Japan); the latter one is raised by the built-in Validators.pattern, which we configured with a *regular expression*, /^[a-zA-Z]{3}$/, that doesn't allow digits.

Let's fix these errors by typing in the following values:

- **Name:** New Japan
- **ISO 3166-1 ALPHA-2 Country code:** NJ
- **ISO 3166-1 ALPHA-3 Country code:** NJP

Once you're done, click **Create** to create the new country. If everything is working as expected, the view should redirect us to the main **Countries** view.

From there, we can type New Japan into our text filter to ensure that our brand-new country is actually there:

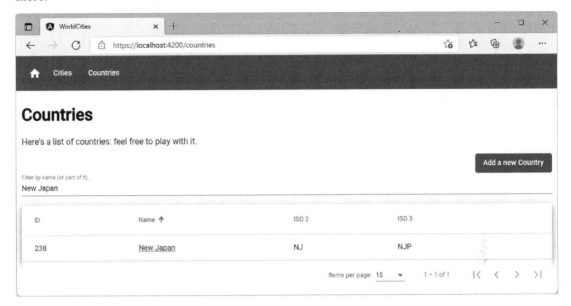

Figure 7.18: Countries list after filtering for New Japan

Here it is! This means that we're finally done with CountryEditComponent and ready to move on to new, exciting tasks.

Improving the filter behavior

The real-time filter that we've implemented in our Cities and Countries listing views works well and should be very helpful for our users: however, every time the filter text changes (that is, upon each keystroke), Angular fires an HTTP request to the back-end to retrieve the updated list of results. Such behavior is intrinsically resource-intensive and can easily become a huge performance issue, especially if we're dealing with large tables and/or non-indexed columns.

Are there ways to improve this approach without compromising the results obtained in terms of user experience? As a matter of fact, the answer is yes, as long as we're willing to implement a couple of widely used techniques specifically meant to improve the performance of code that gets executed repeatedly within a short period of time.

Throttling and debouncing

If we think about it, our everyday life is full of situations where we are forced to do something while our attention is captured by something else: social networks like Twitter and instant messaging apps such as WhatsApp are a perfect example of that, since they flood us with notifications regardless of what we're doing.

What do we usually do in these cases? Let's consider the following alternatives:

- **Respond to all notifications in real time**, which would be great for the requesting party but would compromise what we're doing
- **Take no immediate action** and check our messages only once every, let's say, five minutes
- **Take no immediate action** and check our messages only when no new notifications have come in for the last five minutes

The first approach is what our app is currently doing; the second is called *throttling*, while the third is called *debouncing*. Let's try to better understand what these terms actually mean.

Definitions

In software development, **throttling** is used to define a behavior that enforces a maximum number of times a function can be called over time. To put it in other words, it's a way to say, *"let's execute this function at most once every N milliseconds."* No matter how many times the user fires the event, that function will be executed only once in a given time interval.

The term **debouncing** is used to define a technique that prevents a function from being called until a certain amount of time has passed without it being called: in other words, it's a way to say, *"let's execute this function only if N milliseconds have passed without it being called."* The concept has some similarities with the throttling technique, with an important difference: no matter how many times the user fires the event, the attached function will be executed only after the specified time once the user stops firing the event.

In a nutshell, we can say that the main difference between throttling and debouncing is that throttling executes the function at a regular interval, while debouncing executes the function only after a cooling period.

Why would we want to throttle or debounce our code?

Let's cut it short – in information technology, throttling and debouncing are mostly useful for two main reasons: optimization and performance. They are widely used in JavaScript because they can be very helpful to efficiently handle some resource-intensive DOM-related tasks, such as scrolling and resizing HTML components, as well as retrieving data from the server.

In our given scenario, we can think of them as two ways to optimize event handling, thus lifting some work from our server (controller and database): more specifically, we want to find a way to reduce the HTTP requests that Angular currently makes to our server upon each keystroke.

Shall we do that using throttling or debouncing?

If we think about how the filter function works in terms of user experience, we can easily determine the correct answer. Since we're talking about a textbox that can be used to filter the listing results to those that contain one or more characters typed by the user, we can reasonably conclude that we could defer the HTTP request until the user stops typing, as long as we process it right after it does. Such behavior won't hinder the user experience granted by the current filter while preventing a good number of unnecessary HTTP calls.

In other words, we need to *debounce* our calls to the back-end: let's see how we can do that.

Debouncing calls to the back-end

An easy approach to debouncing with Angular is given by RxJS, the Reactive Extensions for JavaScript library, which allows us to use Observables, which we introduced in *Chapter 4, Front-End and Back-End Interactions*. Since we're using an Observable to perform the HTTP call, we're halfway there: we just need to make use of the handy debounceTime RxJS operator, which will emit a value from the source Observable only after a particular time span has passed without another source emission. While we are there, we can also take the chance to add the distinctUntilChanged operator as well, which emits a value only if it's different from the last one inserted by the user: this will prevent any HTTP call identical to the previous one, which could happen – for example – if the user writes a sentence, then adds a letter and immediately deletes it.

Updating the CitiesComponent

To implement such logic, open the /src/app/cities/cities.component.ts file and perform the following changes:

```
// [...]

import { MatSort } from '@angular/material/sort';

import { Subject } from 'rxjs';
import { debounceTime, distinctUntilChanged } from 'rxjs/operators';

// ...existing code...

  @ViewChild(MatPaginator) paginator!: MatPaginator;
  @ViewChild(MatSort) sort!: MatSort;

  filterTextChanged: Subject<string> = new Subject<string>();

// ...existing code...

  ngOnInit() {
    this.loadData();
  }

  // debounce filter text changes
  onFilterTextChanged(filterText: string) {
    if (this.filterTextChanged.observers.length === 0) {
      this.filterTextChanged
        .pipe(debounceTime(1000), distinctUntilChanged())
```

```
        .subscribe(query => {
            this.loadData(query);
        });
    }
    this.filterTextChanged.next(filterText);
}

// ...existing code...
```

As we can see, we haven't touched the loadData method at all, so that we won't mess up anything that we've done up to now; we added a new onFilterTextChanged method instead, which will be called by the filter's input and will transparently handle the debouncing task.

If we take a closer look at the onFilterTextChanged method, we can see that it works with a new filterTextChanged variable that we've also added to our component class: this variable hosts a *Subject*, a special type of Observable that allows values to be multi-casted to many Observers.

In a nutshell, here's what this new method does every time it gets called by the filter's input method:

- Checks the filterTextChanged *Subject* to see if there are *Observers* listening; if there are no *Observers* yet, pipes the debounceTime and distinctUntilChanged operators and adds a new subscription for the loadData method
- Feeds a new value to the *Subject*, which will be multi-casted to the *Observers* registered to listen to it

 For space reasons, we won't say any more about *Subjects* here, but the topic can be further studied by taking a look at the following page from the RxJS official guide: https://rxjs-dev.firebaseapp.com/guide/subject#.

Although we've already explained what these operators do, let's quickly recap their role again:

- debounceTime will emit the value after 1,000 milliseconds of no source input coming from the user
- distinctUntilChanged will emit the value only if it's different from the last inserted one

Now that we've implemented the debouncing logic in the Angular class, we just need to update the component's template file to make the filter's input call the new onFilterTextChanged method instead of loadData.

Open the /src/app/cities/cities.component.html file and apply the following changes:

```
<mat-form-field [hidden]="!cities">
  <input matInput #filter (keyup)="onFilterTextChanged(filter.value)"
         placeholder="Filter by name (or part of it)...">
</mat-form-field>
```

That's it.

Updating the CountriesComponent

Before going further, let's update the `CountriesComponent` in the exact same way. This can be done by opening the following files:

- `/src/app/countries/countries.component.ts`
- `/src/app/countries/countries.component.html`

and applying the same changes that we did on the `CitiesComponent` files.

 For space reasons, we won't demonstrate how to perform these changes here; however, the updated `CountriesComponent` source code can be found in the GitHub repository.

Delaying these HTTP requests in these two components will shut out most unnecessary HTTP requests coming from our Angular app, thus preventing our database from being called over and over rapidly.

What about throttling?

As a matter of fact, our `WorldCities` Angular app doesn't have tasks or features that could benefit from throttling. However, it's worth noting that such a technique can be implemented using the same approach that we've used for debouncing, replacing the `debounceTime` RxJS operator with `throttleTime`.

 For additional info regarding these RxJS operators, refer to the following pages from the RxJS official guide:

`https://rxjs-dev.firebaseapp.com/api/operators/debounceTime`

`https://rxjs-dev.firebaseapp.com/api/operators/throttleTime`

Summary

This chapter was entirely dedicated to Angular forms. We started by clarifying what a form actually is and enumerated the features it needs to have in order to fulfill its duties, grouping them into two main requirements: providing a good user experience and properly handling the submitted data.

Then, we turned our focus to the Angular framework and to the two form design models it offers: the *Template-Driven* approach, mostly inherited from AngularJS, and the *Model-Driven* or *Reactive* alternative. We took some valuable time to analyze the pros and cons provided by both of them, and then we performed a detailed comparison of the underlying logic and workflow. At the end of the day, we chose to embrace the *Reactive* way of doing things, as it gives the developer more control and enforces a more consistent separation of duties between the *data model* and the *form model*.

Right after that, we went from theory to practice by creating a `CityEditComponent` and used it to implement a fully featured *Reactive Form*; we also added the *client-side* and *server-side* data validation logic by making good use of the *Angular template syntax* in conjunction with the classes and directives granted by Angular's `ReactiveFormsModule`.

Once done, we did the same with `CountryEditComponent`, where we took the chance to try and use a `FormBuilder` instead of the `FormGroup`/`FormControl` instances we used previously.

Once done, we performed a surface test with our browser to check all the *built-in* and *custom* validators, ensuring that they worked properly on the front-end as well as on their back-end APIs.

Last but not least, we spent some valuable time analyzing some performance issues of our filter feature and found a way to mitigate them by implementing a debouncing technique: this allowed us to learn how to use some very useful features from the RxJS library: `Subject`, `debounceTime`, and `distinctUntilChanged`.

In the next chapter, we're going to refine what we've done so far by refactoring some rough aspects of our Angular components in a better way. By doing so, we'll learn how to post-process the data, add decent error handling, implement some retry logic to deal with connection issues, debug our form using the Visual Studio *client-side* debugger, and – most importantly – perform some *unit tests*.

Suggested topics

For further information, we recommend the following topics: Template-Driven Forms, Model-Driven Forms, Reactive Forms, JSON, RFC 7578, RFC 1341, URL Living Standard, HTML Living Standard, data validation, Angular validators, custom validators, asynchronous validators, regular expressions (regex), Angular pipes, FormBuilder, RxJS, Observables, Safe Navigation Operator (Elvis Operator), RxJS operators, Subject, debounceTime, throttleTime.

References

- *The application/www-form-urlencoded format draft-hoehrmann-urlencoded-01*: `https://tools.ietf.org/html/draft-hoehrmann-urlencoded-01`
- *RFC 7578 – Returning Values from Forms: multipart/form-data*: `https://tools.ietf.org/html/rfc7578`
- *RFC 1341, section 7.2 – The Multipart Content-Type*: `https://www.w3.org/Protocols/rfc1341/7_2_Multipart.html`
- *URL Living Standard – URL-encoded Form Data*: `https://url.spec.whatwg.org/#concept-urlencoded`
- *HTML Living Standard, section 4.10.21.7 – Multipart form data*: `https://html.spec.whatwg.org/multipage/form-control-infrastructure.html#multipart-form-data`
- *HTML Living Standard, section 4.10.21.8 – Plain Text Form Data*: `https://html.spec.whatwg.org/multipage/form-control-infrastructure.html#plain-text-form-data`
- *Angular: Template-driven forms*: `https://angular.io/guide/forms#template-driven-forms`
- *Angular: Reactive forms*: `https://angular.io/guide/reactive-forms`
- *Angular: Form validation*: `https://angular.io/guide/form-validation`
- *Angular: Validators*: `https://angular.io/api/forms/Validators`

- *Angular: Custom Async Validators*: https://angular.io/guide/form-validation#implementing-a-custom-async-validator
- *RegExr: Learn, Build, and Test RegEx*: https://regexr.com/
- *Angular Material input error messages*: https://material.angular.io/components/input/overview#changing-when-error-messages-are-shown
- *TypeScript 3.7 Release Notes*: https://www.typescriptlang.org/docs/handbook/release-notes/typescript-3-7.html
- *Angular Template expression operators*: https://angular.io/guide/template-expression-operators#safe-navigation-operator
- *RxJS Subject*: https://rxjs-dev.firebaseapp.com/guide/subject#
- *RxJS debounceTime operator*: https://rxjs-dev.firebaseapp.com/api/operators/debounceTime
- *RxJS throttleTime operator*: https://rxjs-dev.firebaseapp.com/api/operators/throttleTime

8
Code Tweaks and Data Services

Our WorldCities web application is now a full-fledged project providing a number of interesting features: we can **retrieve a list** of all the *cities* and *countries* available in our DBMS and browse them through paged tables that we can *order* and *filter*; thanks to our *master/detail* UI pattern, we can also access a detailed view of each *city* and *country*, where we can **read** and/or **edit** the most relevant fields for both of them; and last, but not least, we can **create** new *cities* and *countries* thanks to the "add new" capabilities of the aforementioned *Detail* view.

Now, before going further, it could be wise to spend some time consolidating what we've learned so far and improve the basic patterns we have followed. After all, refining our *front-end* and *back-end* and the overall logic they're currently relying upon will definitely make them more *versatile* and *fail-proof* for what is yet to come.

This chapter is entirely dedicated to those tasks. Here's what we're going to do through the various sections that we're about to face:

- **Optimizations and tweaks**, where we'll implement some high-level source code and UI refinements
- **Bug fixes and improvements**, where we'll leverage the preceding tweaks to enhance our app's consistency and add some new features
- **Data services**, where we'll learn how to migrate from our current simplified implementation – where we used the raw HttpClient service directly inside the components – to a more versatile approach that allows us to add features such as post-processing, error handling, retry logic, and more

All these changes will be worth their time because they'll strengthen our app's source code and prepare it for the *debugging* and *testing* phase that will appear in the next chapter.

All right, then...let's get to work.

Technical requirements

In this chapter, we're going to need all the technical requirements that were listed in all the previous chapters, with no additional resources, libraries, or packages.

The code files for this chapter can be found at `https://github.com/PacktPublishing/ASP.NET-Core-6-and-Angular/tree/master/Chapter_08/`.

Optimizations and tweaks

In computer programming, the term **code bloat** is commonly used to describe an unnecessarily long, slow, or wasteful amount of source code. Such code is hardly desirable because it inevitably makes our app more vulnerable to human error, regression bugs, logical inconsistencies, wasted resources, and so on. It also makes *debugging* and *testing* a lot more difficult and stressful; for all of the aforementioned reasons, we should try to prevent that from happening as much as we can.

The most effective way to counter code bloat is to adopt and adhere to the **Don't Repeat Yourself (DRY)** principle, which is something that any developer should try to follow whenever they can. As already stated in *Chapter 6, Fetching and Displaying Data*, DRY is a widely achieved principle of software development: whenever we violate it, we fall into a *WET* approach, which could mean *Write Everything Twice*, *We Enjoy Typing*, or *Waste Everyone's Time*, depending on what we like the most.

In this section, we'll try to address some rather *WET* parts of our current code and see how we can make them more *DRY*: doing that will greatly help our *debugging* and *testing* sessions later on.

Template improvements

If we take another look at our `CityEditComponent` and `CountryEditComponent` template files, we can definitely see a certain amount of code bloat. More specifically, we have a lot of `mat-error` elements, sometimes as many as three of them (!) for a single `input` – such as those for ISO 3166-1 ALPHA-2 and ALPHA-3 country codes; furthermore, most of these elements are redundant, meaning that they check the same error status for different inputs and – when triggered – return a very similar error text.

This approach can have some advantages, especially in small forms: for example, it provides a good level of readability, since those `mat-error` elements allow us to immediately understand what happens for each specific error. However, when dealing with big forms – or with an app with a lot of forms – this approach will eventually produce a considerable amount of source code, which could become hard to maintain: that's even more true for multi-language apps, where the effort required to handle literal strings grows exponentially with the number of strings. What do we do in those cases? Is there a 'better' or 'smarter' way to address that?

As a matter of fact, there is: whenever we feel like we're writing too much code or repeating a complex task too many times, we can create one or more helper methods within our component class in order to centralize the underlying logic. These helper methods will act as *shortcuts* that we can call instead of repeating the whole validation logic. Let's try to add them to our *form*-related Angular Components.

Form validation shortcuts

Let's see how to add form validation shortcuts in the CountryEditComponent class, which ended up with a lot of redundant mat-error elements since we had to check a lot of possible error statuses for the two ISO 3166-1 country codes.

Open the /src/app/countries/country-edit.component.ts file and add the following code right after the class declaration (new lines are highlighted):

```
// ... existing code...

export class CountryEditComponent implements OnInit {

getErrors(
  control: AbstractControl,
  displayName: string,
  ): string[] {
  var errors: string[] = [];
  Object.keys(control.errors || {}).forEach((key) => {
    switch (key) {
      case 'required':
        errors.push('${displayName} is required.');
        break;
      case 'pattern':
        errors.push('${displayName} contains invalid characters.');
        break;
      case 'isDupeField':
        errors.push('${displayName} already exists: please choose another.');
        break;
      default:
        errors.push('${displayName} is invalid.');
        break;
    }
  });
  return errors;
}

// ... existing code...
```

As we can see, we added a simple getErrors() function that returns an array of error messages corresponding to all the active errors for any given control, or an empty array if there are none; these errors will also be prepended with the displayName parameter, which can be set by the caller to ensure that each control will have its own personalized set of error messages.

The switch statement we've set up contains all the validators that we currently use and might want to centralize, including the custom isDupeField validator that we implemented back in *Chapter 7, Forms and Data Validation*; we've even included a default case returning a generic error, which will act as a catch-all for all the non-supported validators.

That's precisely what we need: a centralized "shortcut" method that allows us to shrink the HTML template and – most importantly – remove some mat-error elements and redundant literal text.

Let's see how we can refactor the existing ISO2 mat-form-field component in the country-edit. component.html file, which currently contains three mat-error elements, to take advantage of our new getErrors() function:

```html
<!-- existing code -->

<!-- ISO2 -->
<mat-form-field>
  <mat-label>
    ISO 3166-1 ALPHA-2 Country code (2 letters)
  </mat-label>
  <input matInput formControlName="iso2" required
         placeholder="Insert the ISO2 Country code">
  <mat-error *ngFor="let error of getErrors(form.get('iso2')!,
              'ISO 3166-1 ALPHA 2 Country code')">
    {{error}}
  </mat-error>
</mat-form-field>

<!-- ...existing code... -->
```

Much better, right? If we test the component now, we can see that its behavior is still the same, meaning that we have found a way to optimize the template without losing anything.

All we need to do now is to refactor all the other mat-form-field components in the CountryEditComponent template, then switch to CityEditComponent and perform the same optimization trick there...

... Or not.

Wait a minute: didn't we just say we would adhere to the DRY pattern as much as we can? How can we reasonably expect to do that if we're about to *copy and paste* the same identical variables and methods throughout different classes? What if we had 10 form-based components to patch instead of just 2? That doesn't sound anything but *WET*. Now that we've found a good way to shrink our template code, we also need to find a decent way to implement those form-related methods without spawning clones everywhere.

Luckily enough, TypeScript provides a great way to handle these kinds of scenarios: **class inheritance**. Let's see how we can use these features to our advantage.

Class inheritance

Object-oriented programming (OOP) is usually defined by two core concepts: *polymorphism* and *inheritance*. Although both concepts are related, they are not the same. Here's what they mean in a nutshell:

- **Polymorphism** allows us to assign multiple interfaces on the same *entity* (such as a *variable*, *function*, *object*, or *type*) and/or to assign the same interface on different *entities*. In other words, it allows *entities* to have more than one form.

- **Inheritance** allows us to *extend* an object or class by *deriving* it from another object (*prototype-based inheritance*) or class (*class-based inheritance*) while retaining a similar implementation; the extended class is commonly called a **subclass** or **child class**, while the inherited class takes the name of *superclass* or *base class*.

Let's now focus on **inheritance**: in TypeScript, as in most class-based, object-oriented languages, a type created through *inheritance* (a *child* class) acquires all the properties and behaviors of the parent type, except constructors, destructors, overloaded operators, and *private* members of the *base class*.

If we think about it, it's just what we need in our scenario: if we create a base class and implement all our form-related methods there, we'll just need to *extend* our current component class without having to write it more than once.

Let's see how we can pull this off.

Implementing a BaseFormComponent

We've used the ng generate CLI command several times to generate *components*, but Command Prompt the first time we're going to use it to generate a *class*.

Open a Command Prompt, navigate to the /src/app/ folder, and then type the following command:

```
ng generate component BaseForm --skip-import --skip-tests --inline-template
--inline-style --flat
```

These settings will prevent the Angular CLI from creating anything other than the TypeScript file, since the component that we want to generate doesn't need HMTL, tests, and (S)CSS files, and doesn't require to be referenced in the AppModule: the preceding command will just create the /src/app/ base-form.component.ts file and nothing else.

 This also means that we could even manually create that file instead of using the Angular CLI, should we prefer to do that.

Once the file has been created, open it and replace the existing content with the following code:

```
import { Component } from '@angular/core';
import { FormGroup, AbstractControl } from '@angular/forms';


@Component({
```

```
    template: ''
})
export abstract class BaseFormComponent {

    // the form model
    form!: FormGroup;

    getErrors(
        control: AbstractControl,
        displayName: string,
    ): string[] {
        var errors: string[] = [];
        Object.keys(control.errors || {}).forEach((key) => {
            switch (key) {
                case 'required':
                    errors.push('${displayName} is required.');
                    break;
                case 'pattern':
                    errors.push('${displayName} contains invalid characters.');
                    break;
                case 'isDupeField':
                    errors.push('${displayName} already exists: please choose another.');
                    break;
                default:
                    errors.push('${displayName} is invalid.');
                    break;
            }
        });
        return errors;
    }

    constructor() { }

}
```

As we can see, there's nothing much there, only the getError() method that we saw a short while ago, and the form variable itself: these two members can be moved (and centralized) here instead of declaring them in any controller that needs to deal with a form. Also, we've purposely added the abstract modifier since we don't plan to ever instantiate this class; we only want other classes to derive from it.

From now on, we'll take it for granted that we've got the logic behind our code samples; consequently, we're going to present them in a more succinct way to avoid wasting more pages by saying the obvious: please bear with it! After all, whenever we need to see the full file, we can always find it in the book's online source code repository on GitHub.

Now, we do have a `BaseFormComponent` *superclass* that we can use to *extend* our subclasses; this means that we can update our current `CityEditComponent` and `CountryEditComponent` TypeScript files in order to extend its class accordingly.

Extending CountryEditComponent

Open the `/src/app/countries/country-edit.component.ts` file, then add the `BaseFormComponent` *superclass* at the end of the `import` list to the beginning of the file:

```
// ...existing code...

import { Country } from './country';
import { BaseFormComponent } from '../base-form.component';

// ...existing code...
```

Now, we need to implement the class inheritance using the `extends` modifier that is right after the class declaration:

```
// ...existing code...

export class CountryEditComponent
    extends BaseFormComponent implements OnInit {

// ...existing code...
```

That's it: `CountryEditComponent` has now officially become a *child class* of the `BaseFormComponent` *superclass*.

Last but not least, we need to invoke the *superclass* constructor by calling super() inside the *child class* constructor's implementation:

```
// ...existing code...

constructor(
    private fb: FormBuilder,
    private activatedRoute: ActivatedRoute,
    private router: Router,
```

```
    private http: HttpClient) {
    super();
}

// ...existing code...
```

Before closing the TypeScript file, we should take the chance to remove the `form` variable, as well as the `getErrors()` method, since we have chosen to centralize them in the *superclass*.

Now we can finally refactor the remaining `mat-form-field` components included in the `CountryEditComponent`'s HTML template (`name` and `iso3`) using the `getErrors()` method defined in the base class, since our *child class* will transparently *inherit* it from its *superclass*.

 For reasons of space, we don't show how to refactor them: just keep what we did with the `iso2` field early on for reference, changing the `form.get` and `displayName` parameters accordingly, or look at the GitHub code for this chapter for the fully updated source code.

Let's now test what we did by hitting *F5* and navigating through `CountryEditComponent` in both the *edit* and *add new* modes. If we did everything correctly, we should see no issues: everything should work just like it was, with a considerably smaller amount of source code.

 When performing the test, be sure to check out all the validators, since what we did affects them the most: if the form validators are still working and show their errors when triggered, this means that the child class is able to inherit and use the required method for its base class, thereby proving that our brand-new superclass/subclass implementation is working fine.

As soon as we're sure that everything is working fine, we can finally switch to the `CityEditComponent` and perform the same optimization tweak there.

Extending CityEditComponent

`CityEditComponent` can be extended just like we did with the TypeScript file for `CountryEditComponent`: adding the `import` statement for the `BaseFormComponent` class, using the `extends` keyword in the class declaration, and finally, adding the `super()` function within the constructor.

 We're not going to show the source code changes here because the required steps are almost identical to what we've just seen; if you've got any doubts, you can refer to this chapter's source code on the GitHub repository.

Once this is done, we can remove the now-redundant `form` variable, just like we did with the `CountryEditComponent` class a minute ago.

Right after that, we can move to the CityEditComponent's HTML template and refactor all the mat-form-field components so that each one of them will have a single mat-error element using the getErrors() method.

At the end of the day, the only mat-error element that won't be touched by our refactoring task will be the one triggered by isDupeCity validator (the first one in order of appearance); as a matter of fact, centralizing this code doesn't make much sense, since we will hardly ever (re)use it outside CityEditComponent.

 That's a perfect example of context-specific, non-reusable code that should just be kept there, as moving it to a *superclass* won't make our code base any *DRY*er.

Now that we've optimized and refactored our components' TypeScript and HTML code, let's see what we can do to improve our app's user experience.

Bug fixes and improvements

Let's be honest: although we made a decent job of building up our *master/detail* UI pattern, and we assembled both views using the most relevant *city* and *country* fields, our app is still lacking something that our users might want to see. More specifically, the following detail is missing:

- **Our City Detail view doesn't validate the lat and lon input values properly:** For example, we are allowed to type letters instead of numbers, which utterly crashes the form
- **Our Countries view doesn't show the number of cities** that each *country* actually contains
- **Our Cities view doesn't show the country name** for each listed city

Let's do our best to fix all of these issues for good.

Validating lat and lon

Let's start with the only real *bug*: a form that can be broken from the *front-end* is something that we should always avoid, even if those input types are implicitly checked in the *back-end* by our ASP.NET Core API.

Luckily enough, we already know how to fix those kinds of errors: we need to add some *pattern-based validators* to the lat and lon *FormControls* for CityEditComponent, just like we did with the iso2 and iso3 controls in the CountryEditComponent files. As we already know, we'll need to update the CityEditComponent *class* file in order to implement the validators and define a *validation pattern* based upon a *regex*.

city-edit.component.ts

Open the /src/app/cities/city-edit.component.ts file and update its content accordingly (new/updated lines are highlighted):

```
// ...existing code...

  ngOnInit() {
    this.form = new FormGroup({
      name: new FormControl('', Validators.required),
      lat: new FormControl('', [
        Validators.required,
        Validators.pattern(/^[-]?[0-9]+(\.[0-9]{1,4})?$/)
      ]),
      lon: new FormControl('', [
        Validators.required,
        Validators.pattern(/^[-]?[0-9]+(\.[0-9]{1,4})?$/)
      ]),
      countryId: new FormControl('', Validators.required)
    }, null, this.isDupeCity());
    this.loadData();
  }

// ...existing code...
```

Here we go. As we already know from *Chapter 7, Forms and Data Validation*, this form's implementation is still based on the manually instantiated FormGroup and FormControl objects instead of using FormBuilder; however, there's no reason to change it now, since we were still able to implement Validators.pattern without any issues.

Let's spend a couple of minutes explaining the *regex* that we've used there:

- ^ defines the start of the *user input* string that we need to check
- [-]? allows the presence of an *optional* minus sign, which is required when dealing with negative coordinates
- [0-9]+ asks for *one or more* numbers between 0 and 9
- (\.[0-9]{1,4})? defines an *optional group* (thanks to ? at the end), which, if present, needs to respect the following rules:
    - \.: requires the input to start with *a single dot* (the decimal sign). The dot is escaped because it's a reserved *regex* character, which, when unescaped, means *any character*.
    - [0-9]{1,4} asks for *one to four* numbers between 0 and 9 (since we do want *between 1 and 4 decimal values* after the dot).
- $ defines the end of the *user input* string

We could've used \d (any digit) as an alternative to [0-9], which is a slightly more succinct syntax; however, we have chosen to stick with [0-9] for better readability. Feel free to replace it with \d at any time.

Now that the pattern validators have been set in place, everything should automatically work: the corresponding error message will already be handled by our centralized getError() function, which already contains a proper message to return when the pattern validator raises an error.

However, the message is still rather generic:

```
{displayName} contains invalid characters.
```

This warning will make our users aware of the fact that they have typed something wrong, but it won't tell them what characters they should use instead. What if we want to provide them with these additional details? We can hardly fix that by simply rewriting it, since this message is used for ISO2 and ISO3, which require only *letters*, as well as for LAT and LON, which only want *numbers*.

As a matter of fact, we only have two options:

- Avoid using the getError() centralized function for these fields, and use some manual mat-error elements instead
- Improve the getError() centralized function so that it can (optionally) accept custom messages for one (or more) validator error types

Both approaches are viable. However, since we don't want to discard the hard work we just did, we might as well go for the latter and improve our getError() method.

Luckily enough, that won't be hard.

base-form.component.ts

Open the /src/app/base-form.component.ts file and change the existing code of the getError() function in the following way (updated code has been highlighted):

```
// ... existing code...

getErrors(
  control: AbstractControl,
  displayName: string,
  customMessages: { [key: string] : string } | null = null
): string[] {
  var errors: string[] = [];
  Object.keys(control.errors || {}).forEach((key) => {
    switch (key) {
      case 'required':
```

```
          errors.push('${displayName} ${customMessages?.[key] ?? "is
required."}');
        break;
      case 'pattern':
          errors.push('${displayName} ${customMessages?.[key] ?? "contains
invalid characters."}');
        break;
      case 'isDupeField':
          errors.push('${displayName} ${customMessages?.[key] ?? "already exists:
please choose another."}');
        break;
      default:
        errors.push('${displayName} is invalid.');
        break;
    }
  });
  return errors;
}

// ... existing code...
```

Here we go. As we can see, we've added an optional third parameter that we can now use to specify optional `customMessages` whenever we don't want to use the generic message, and we can do that for *any* validator, not just for the pattern one.

 It's worth noting that since the new `customMessages` parameter is optional, the `getErrors()` refactoring that we just did is backward-compatible, meaning that our existing code will still work – even if we don't implement the new feature in any of our HTML templates.

Let's see how we can implement the new feature, starting with the HTML template file of `CityEditComponent`.

city-edit.component.html

Open the `/src/app/cities/city-edit.component.html` file and change the existing implementation for the LAT and LON fields in the following way (updates have been highlighted):

```html
<!-- ... existing code... -->

<!--Lat -->
<mat-form-field>
```

```
      <mat-label>Latitude:</mat-label>
      <input matInput formControlName="lat" required
            placeholder="Insert latitude">
      <mat-error *ngFor="let error of getErrors(form.get('lat')!,
        'Latitude',
          { 'pattern' : 'requires a positive or negative number with 0-4 decimal
values' })">
        {{error}}
      </mat-error>
    </mat-form-field>

    <!--Lon -->
    <mat-form-field>
      <mat-label>Longitude:</mat-label>
      <input matInput formControlName="lon" required
            placeholder="Insert longitude">
      <mat-error *ngFor="let error of getErrors(form.get('lon')!,
        'Longitude',
          { 'pattern' : 'requires a positive or negative number with 0-4 decimal
values' })">
        {{error}}
      </mat-error>
    </mat-form-field>

    <!-- ... existing code... -->
```

Once this is done, do the same in the ISO2 and ISO3 fields of the /src/app/country-edit.component.html file, using a slightly different custom error message for ISO2:

```
{ 'pattern' : 'requires 2 letters' }
```

... And for ISO3:

```
{ 'pattern' : 'requires 3 letters' }
```

Let's quickly test what we have done so far:

1. Hit *F5* to start the app in *debug* mode
2. Navigate through the **Cities** view
3. Filter the list to find **Madrid**
4. Type some invalid characters in the **City latitude** and **City longitude** input fields

If the new feature has been implemented properly, we should see our error messages appear in all their glory and the **Save** button disabled, just like in the following screenshot:

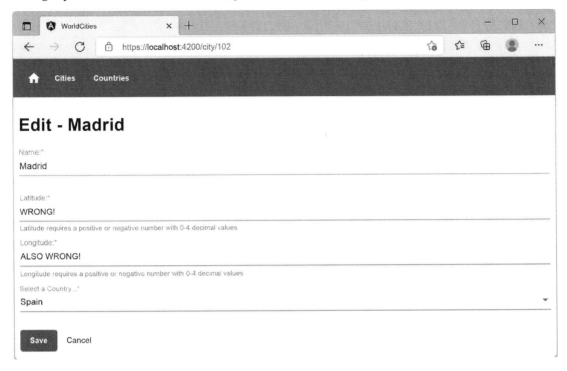

Figure 8.1: Error messages when inputting invalid latitude and longitude

That's it. Now we can repeat the same test for CountryEditController to ensure that everything is working there as well.

Now that we have fixed our first UI bug, let's move on to the next task.

Adding the number of cities

What we need to do now is find a way to show an additional column in the **Countries** view that will allow users to instantly see the *number of cities* for each listed *country*. In order to do that, we definitely need to improve our *back-end* web API because we know that there's currently no way to retrieve such info from the server.

Well, technically speaking, there is a way: we could use the GetCities() method of CitiesController with a huge pageSize parameter (99,999 or so) and a suitable filter to retrieve the whole set of cities for each country, and then count that collection and output the number.

However, doing this would indeed have a *huge* performance impact: not only would we have to retrieve all the cities for all the listed *countries*, but we would have to do that by issuing a separate HTTP request for each table row. That's definitely not what we want if we are aiming to fulfill our task smartly and efficiently.

Here's what we're going to do instead:

- Find a smart and efficient way to count the number of cities for each listed country from the *back-end*
- Add a TotCities property to our Country Angular *interface* to store that same number on the *client*

Let's do this.

CountriesController

Let's start with the *back-end* part. Finding a smart and efficient way to count the number of cities for each country might be harder than it seems.

If we want to retrieve this value in a single shot, that is, without making additional API requests with Angular, there's no doubt that we need to improve our current GetCountries() method of CountriesController, which is what we're currently using to fetch the *countries* data.

Let's open our /Controllers/CountriesController.cs file and see how ASP.NET Core and **Entity Framework Core (EF Core)** can help us to do what we want.

Here's the GetCountries() method that we need to update:

```
public async Task<ActionResult<ApiResult<Country>>> GetCountries(
        int pageIndex = 0,
        int pageSize = 10,
        string? sortColumn = null,
        string? sortOrder = null,
        string? filterColumn = null,
        string? filterQuery = null)
{
    return await ApiResult<Country>.CreateAsync(
            _context.Countries.AsNoTracking(),
            pageIndex,
            pageSize,
            sortColumn,
            sortOrder,
            filterColumn,
            filterQuery);
}
```

As we can see, there's no trace of Cities. Although we know that our Country entity contains a Cities property that is meant to store a list of *cities*, we also remember (from *Chapter 5*, *Data Model with Entity Framework Core*) that this property is set to null, since we've never told EF Core to load the entity's related data.

What if we do it now? We could be tempted to solve our issue by activating the *Eager Loading* ORM pattern (as discussed in *Chapter 5, Data Model with Entity Framework Core*) and filling our `Cities` property with actual values with which to feed our Angular client. Here's how we could do that:

```
return await ApiResult<Country>.CreateAsync(
            _context.Countries.AsNoTracking()
                    .Include(c => c.Cities),
            pageIndex,
            pageSize,
            sortColumn,
            sortOrder,
            filterColumn,
            filterQuery);
```

However, it doesn't take a genius to understand that such a workaround is hardly smart and efficient: a *country* entity might have lots of cities, sometimes *hundreds* of them. Do we really think it would be acceptable for our *back-end* to retrieve them all from the DBMS? Are we really going to flood our Angular *front-end* with those huge JSON arrays?

That's definitely a no-go: we can do better than that, especially considering that, after all, we don't need to retrieve all the city data for each country to fulfill our goal: we just need to know the *number* of cities.

Here's how we can do that (updated code is highlighted):

```
[HttpGet]
public async Task<ActionResult<ApiResult<CountryDTO>>> GetCountries(
        int pageIndex = 0,
        int pageSize = 10,
        string? sortColumn = null,
        string? sortOrder = null,
        string? filterColumn = null,
        string? filterQuery = null)
{
    return await ApiResult<CountryDTO>.CreateAsync(
            _context.Countries.AsNoTracking()
                    .Select(c => new CountryDTO()
                    {
                        Id = c.Id,
                        Name = c.Name,
                        ISO2 = c.ISO2,
                        ISO3 = c.ISO3,
                        TotCities = c.Cities!.Count
                    }),
            pageIndex,
            pageSize,
```

```
                    sortColumn,
                    sortOrder,
                    filterColumn,
                    filterQuery);
    }
```

As we can see, we went for a totally different approach: the `Include()` method is out of the way; now, instead of eagerly loading the cities, we're using the `Select()` method to *project* our resulting *countries* into a brand-new `CountryDTO` object that contains exactly the same properties as its source, plus a new `TotCities` variable. That way, we never get the cities; we only fetch their number.

 It's also worth noting that since we switched out our **Country** *entity class* for a new **CountryDTO** class, we had to change the `ApiResult` generic type (from `ApiResult<Country>` to `ApiResult<CountryDTO>`) in the method's return type.

Although this method is a bit more complex to pull off, it's definitely a *smart and efficient* way to deal with our task; the only downside is that we need to create the `CountryDTO` class, which doesn't exist yet.

Creating the CountryDTO class

From Solution Explorer, right-click on the /Data/ folder, then add a new `CountryDTO.cs` file, open it, and fill it with the following content:

```
using System.Text.Json.Serialization;

namespace WorldCitiesAPI.Data
{
    public class CountryDTO
    {
        #region Properties
        public int Id { get; set; }

        public string Name { get; set; } = null!;

        [JsonPropertyName("iso2")]
        public string ISO2 { get; set; } = null!;

        [JsonPropertyName("iso3")]
        public string ISO3 { get; set; } = null!;

        public int? TotCities { get; set; } = null!;
        #endregion
    }
}
```

As we can see, the `CountryDTO` class contains most of the properties that are already provided by the `Country` *entity class*, without the `Cities` property – which we know we won't need here – and a single, additional `TotCities` property: it's a **Data Transfer Object** (**DTO**) class that only serves the purpose of feeding the client with (just) the data that we need to send.

> As the name implies, a DTO is an object that carries data between processes. It's a widely used concept when developing web services and microservices, where each HTTP call is an expensive operation that should always be cut to the bare minimum amount of required data.
>
> The difference between DTOs and business objects and/or data access objects (such as DataSets, DataTables, DataRows, IQueryables, and Entities) is that a DTO should only store, serialize, and deserialize its own data.

It's worth noting that we had to use the `[JsonPropertyName]` attributes here as well, since this class will be converted to JSON and the `ISO2` and `ISO3` properties won't be converted in the way that we expect (as we saw in *Chapter 6, Fetching and Displaying Data*).

Angular front-end updates

It is time to switch to Angular and update the *front-end* accordingly, with the new changes applied to the *back-end*.

Follow these steps:

1. Open the `/src/app/countries/country.ts` file to add the `TotCities` property to the `Country` interface in the following way:

    ```
    export interface Country {
        id: number;
        name: string;
        iso2: string;
        iso3: string;
        totCities: number;
    }
    ```

2. Right after that, open the `/src/app/countries/countries.component.ts` file and update the `displayedColumns` inner variable in the following way:

    ```
    // ...existing code...

    public displayedColumns: string[] = ['id', 'name', 'iso2',
      'iso3', 'totCities'];

    // ...existing code...
    ```

3. Once done, open the `/src/app/countries/countries.component.html` file and add the `TotCities` column to Angular Material's `MatTable` template in the following way (updated lines are highlighted):

```html
<!-- ...existing code... -->

<!-- ISO3 Column -->
<ng-container matColumnDef="iso3">
  <th mat-header-cell *matHeaderCellDef mat-sort-header>ISO 3</th>
  <td mat-cell *matCellDef="let country"> {{country.iso3}} </td>
</ng-container>

<!-- TotCities Column -->
<ng-container matColumnDef="totCities">
  <th mat-header-cell *matHeaderCellDef mat-sort-header>Tot. Cities</th>
  <td mat-cell *matCellDef="let country"> {{country.totCities}} </td>
</ng-container>

<!-- ...existing code... -->
```

4. Now, we can finally hit *F5* and see the results of our hard work. If we did everything correctly, we should be able to see the new **Tot. Cities** column, as shown in the following screenshot:

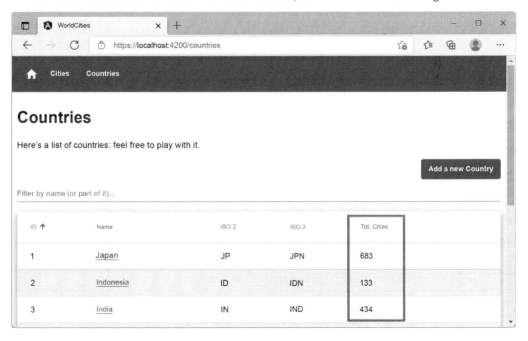

Figure 8.2: Countries table with the total cities column

Not bad at all: on top of that, the new column will also be *sortable*, meaning that we can order our countries by the number of listed cities in *ascending* or *descending* order using one or two clicks. Thanks to this new feature, we can learn that the United States is the country that has the most listed cities (7,824), while New Japan, the imaginary country that we created back in *Chapter 7, Forms and Data Validation*, still has *zero*.

While we're here, let's quickly fix this by going to the **Cities** view, using it to edit **New Tokyo**, and changing its *country* to **New Japan**.

After hitting the **Save** button to apply the changes, go to the **Countries** view and search for **New Japan**: that country should now show a single city in the **Tot. Cities** column, as shown in the following screenshot:

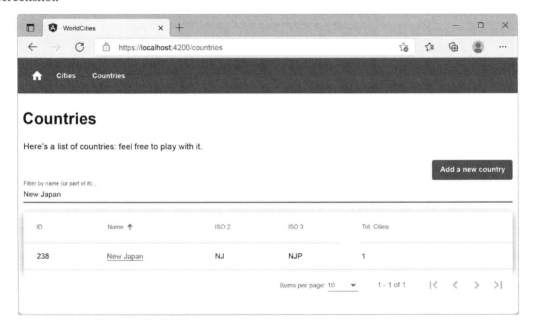

Figure 8.3: Filtering the Countries list for New Japan

Now that we've successfully shown the number of cities for each *country* in our **Countries** views – and bound **New Japan** together with **New Tokyo** in the process – we're ready to move on to the third improvement.

However, before doing that, it could be useful to spend some time thinking about that *DTO class* that we had to create to fulfill our latest task.

DTO classes – should we really use them?

Now that we've seen how similar the Country *entity class* and the CountryDTO *class* actually are, we should be asking ourselves whether we could do something better than that. For example, we could inherit the Country *entity class* in the CountryDTO class, thus preventing the repetition of four properties; or we could entirely omit the CountryDTO class, and just add the TotCities property to the Country entity instead.

Well, the answer is **yes**: we definitely could've used those workarounds, thereby obviating the need to create additional properties (or classes) and keeping the code undeniably more *DRY*. Why didn't we do that?

The answer is rather simple: because both of the previous workarounds come with some relevant design and security flaws. Let's do our best to address them and understand why they should be avoided whenever we can.

Separation of concerns

As a general rule of thumb, *entity classes* shouldn't be burdened with properties that only exist to fulfill our *client-side* needs: whenever we need to create them, it's wise to create an intermediate class, and then separate the *entity* from the output object that we send to the client through the web APIs.

 If you've worked with the ASP.NET MVC framework, you can relate this separation of concerns with the one that distinguishes the **Model** from the **ViewModel** in the **Model-View-ViewModel** (**MVVM**) presentation pattern. The scenario is basically the same: both are simple classes with attributes, but they do have different audiences – the controller and the view. In our scenario, the view is our Angular client.

Now, it goes without saying that putting a `TotCities` property within an *entity class* would break that *separation of concerns*. There's no `TotCities` column in our `Countries` database table; that property would only be there to send some additional data to the *front-end*.

On top of that, there would be no relations between the `TotCities` property and the already existing `Cities` property: if we do activate the EF Core *Eager Loading* pattern and fill the `Cities` property, the `TotCities` property will still be set to zero (and vice versa); such misleading behavior would be a bad design choice and could even result in implementation errors for those who reasonably expect our *entity classes* to be a C# version of our data source.

Security considerations

Keeping *entity classes* separate from the *client-side* API output classes is often a good choice, even for security purposes. Now that we're dealing with *cities* and *countries*, we don't really suffer from it, but what if we were to handle a *users* table with personal and/or login data? If we think about it, there are a lot of possible scenarios where it wouldn't be wise to just pull all the fields from the database and send them to the client in JSON format. The default methods created by ASP.NET Core Web API Controllers when we add them from the Visual Studio interface – which is what we did in *Chapter 5, Data Model with Entity Framework Core* – don't care about that, which is perfectly fine for code samples and even simple API-based projects. However, when things become more complex, it's recommended to feed the client with limited data and in a controlled way.

That said, the most effective way to do that in .NET is to create and serve thinner, and more secure, *DTO classes* instead of the main *Entities*: this is precisely what we have done with the `CountryDTO` class in the preceding sections.

DTO classes versus anonymous types

The only acceptable alternative to the aforementioned *DTO classes* would be using the Select() method to *project* the main *entity classes* to *anonymous types*, and serve them, instead.

Here's another version of the previous GetCountries() method of CountriesController, using an *anonymous type* instead of the CountryDTO *class* (relevant changes are highlighted in the following code):

```
[HttpGet]
public async Task<ActionResult<ApiResult<object>>> GetCountries(
    int pageIndex = 0,
    int pageSize = 10,
    string? sortColumn = null,
    string? sortOrder = null,
    string? filterColumn = null,
    string? filterQuery = null)
{

    return await ApiResult<object>.CreateAsync(
            _context.Countries.AsNoTracking()
                .Select(c => new
                {
                    id = c.Id,
                    name = c.Name,
                    iso2 = c.ISO2,
                    iso3 = c.ISO3,
                    totCities = c.Cities!.Count
                }),
            pageIndex,
            pageSize,
            sortColumn,
            sortOrder,
            filterColumn,
            filterQuery);
}
```

As expected, we had to change our ApiResult generic type to object in the code, and also in the method's *return value*; other than that, the preceding method seems to be fine and it will definitely work just like the previous one.

For additional info on the anonymous types in C#, read the following document: https://docs.microsoft.com/en-us/dotnet/csharp/programming-guide/classes-and-structs/anonymous-types.

What should we use, then? *DTO classes* or *anonymous types*?

Truth be told, both methods are perfectly fine. *Anonymous types* can often be a great option, especially when we need to quickly define JSON return types; however, there are some specific scenarios (such as *unit testing*, as we're going to see later on) where we would prefer to deal with *named types* instead. The choice, as always, depends on the situation. In our current scenario, we'll stick to the CountryDTO class, but we're going to use *anonymous types* as well in the near future.

Securing entities

If we don't want to use *DTO classes*, and *anonymous types* aren't our cup of tea, there's a third viable alternative that we might want to consider: securing our *entities* to prevent them from either giving incorrect instructions (such as creating wrong columns) to EF Core, or sending too much data through our RESTful APIs. If we manage to do that, we could just continue to use them and keep our web API code DRY.

We can achieve this result by decorating our entities' properties with some specific *Data Annotation attributes*, such as the following:

- [NotMapped]: Prevents EF Core from creating a *database column* for that property
- [JsonIgnore]: Prevents a property from being serialized or deserialized
- [JsonPropertyName("name")]: Allows us to override the property name upon the JSON class serialization and deserialization, overriding the property name and any naming policy that is specified by the JsonNamingPolicy settings within the Program.cs file

The first attribute requires the Microsoft.EntityFrameworkCore namespace, while the others are part of the System.Text.Json.Serialization namespace.

We've already used the [JsonPropertyName] *attribute* back in *Chapter 6, Fetching and Displaying Data*, where we had to specify a JSON property name for the ISO2 and ISO3 properties of the Country *entity*. Let's now implement the other two as well.

[NotMapped] and [JsonIgnore] attributes

Open the /Data/Models/Country.cs file and update the existing code at the end of the file as follows (new/updated lines are highlighted):

```
#region Client-side properties
/// <summary>
/// The number of cities related to this country.
/// </summary>
[NotMapped]
public int TotCities
{
    get
    {
        return (Cities != null)
```

```
                ? Cities.Count
                : _TotCities;
        }
    set { _TotCities = value; }
}

private int _TotCities = 0;
#endregion

#region Navigation Properties
/// <summary>
/// A list containing all the cities related to this country.
/// </summary>
[JsonIgnore]
public ICollection<City>? Cities { get; set; } = null!;
#endregion
```

Here's what we've done, in a nutshell:

- We have implemented the TotCities property in the *Entity* code and decorated it with the [NotMapped] attribute so that EF Core won't create its corresponding database column upon any *migration* and/or *update* task.
- While we were there, we took the chance to write some additional logic to *link* this property to the Cities property value (only when it's not null). That way, our *Entity* won't give misleading info, such as having 20+ cities in the Cities list property and a TotCities value of zero at the same time.
- Last but not least, we added the [JsonIgnore] attribute to the Cities properties, thus preventing this info from being sent to the client (regardless of its value, even when null).

The [NotMapped] attribute, which we've never used before, helps mitigate the fact that we're using an entity to store the properties that are required by the front-end, and are therefore completely unrelated to the data model. In a nutshell, this attribute will tell EF Core that we do not want to create a database column for that property in the database.

Since we've created our database using EF Core's code-first approach (see *Chapter 5, Data Model with Entity Framework Core*), and we're using migrations to keep the database structure updated, we need to use that attribute each and every time we want to create an extra property on our *entity classes*. Whenever we forget to do that, we will definitely end up with unwanted database fields.

Using [JsonIgnore] to prevent the server from sending away the Cities property might seem like overkill: why would we even want to skip this value, since it's currently null?

As a matter of fact, we've taken this decision as a precaution. Since we're using *entities* directly, instead of relying upon *DTO classes* or *anonymous types*, we want to implement a restrictive approach with our data. Whenever we don't need it, it's wise to apply [JsonIgnore] to be sure we won't be disclosing anything more than we need to; we could call it a *Data Protection by Default* approach, which will hopefully help us to keep our web API under control and prevent it from sharing too much. After all, we can always remove that attribute whenever we need to.

It goes without saying that, if we want to adopt the *Secured Entities* approach, we won't need the CountryDTO.cs class anymore; therefore, we could *revert* the changes we recently made to the /Controllers/CountriesController.cs file's GetCountries() method and put the Country reference back where it was:

```
return await ApiResult<Country>.CreateAsync(
        _context.Countries.AsNoTracking()
            .Include(c => c.Cities)
            .Select(c => new Country()
            {
                Id = c.Id,
                Name = c.Name,
                ISO2 = c.ISO2,
                ISO3 = c.ISO3,
                TotCities = c.Cities!.Count
            }),
        pageIndex,
        pageSize,
        sortColumn,
        sortOrder,
        filterColumn,
        filterQuery);
```

However, before doing all that, we should spend a couple of minutes carefully evaluating the downsides of this *Securing Entities* approach.

The downsides of Swiss Army knives

The *Securing Entities* approach that we've just discussed might sound like a valid DTO alternative: it gives us the chance to write less code by "shrinking" all the logic within the *entity class*, which will become a "jack of all trades." But is it really as good as it looks?

Unfortunately, the answer is no. Although this method will work, it exposes our code base to several downsides that we should want to avoid.

Here's a list of reasons that should lead us to avoid this method:

- *Entity classes* are meant to be object wrappers for database tables and views; directly using them to "configure" the JSON data output for our client-side app will break the **Single Responsibility Principle** (SRP), which states that every module, class, or function in a computer program should be responsible for a single part of that program's functionality.

- Entities can contain a lot of data that the user and/or the client-side app should never be able to see, such as password hashes and personal data. Hiding these properties with [JsonIgnore] attributes will continuously force the developer to over-complicate their source code, which will eventually lead to a confusing code base.

- *Entity classes* will likely evolve over the course of time. For example, in the database table, they are meant to "wrap" changes; all developers working on the project will have to be aware of the fact that all new properties will be served by the API response, unless it's properly "secured": a single missing [JsonIgnore] attribute could cause a dangerous leak.

- Last but not least, populating the TotCities field forced us to load the whole Cities property using the Include(c => c.Cities) method, which means transferring a lot of data from the DBMS to the back-end. This behavior, known as *over-fetching*, would have a significant performance impact, is widely considered a bad practice, and hence should be avoided at any cost.

All considered, this approach will eventually expose our database's data to potential leaks due to an increased chance of developer mistakes, with the only real advantage being having fewer (useful) classes to deal with. Is it worth it?

Honestly, we don't think so: we don't need a few *Swiss Army knives*, but several well-made and readable classes that can deal with their required tasks in the best (and most efficient) possible way.

A **Swiss Army knife**, sometimes also known as a **kitchen sink**, is a name that most developers give to excessively complex class interfaces explicitly designed to meet all possible needs; this approach often overcomplicates things instead of simplifying them, thus ending up in a futile attempt that negates most of their premises. For this very reason, it is almost always considered a bad practice.

Enough with theorycrafting: it's now time to draw our conclusions.

Final thoughts

All three alternative implementations of the GetCountries() method that have been discussed in this section – CountryDTO, *anonymous types*, and Country – are available in the /Controllers/CountriesController.cs file in the GitHub source code for this chapter. The first is what we'll be using for this book's samples, while the other two have been commented out and put there for reference only. Readers are encouraged to switch them at will in order to find the most suitable approach for their programming style. That said, we strongly suggest taking our advice into consideration in order to make the most responsible choice.

That's it. Now we can finally move on to our third and final task.

Adding the country name

Now, we need to find a way to add a Country column to the **Cities** view so that our users will be able to see the *country* name for each listed city. Considering what we just did with the *countries*, this should be a rather straightforward task.

CitiesController

As always, let's start with the web API. Follow these steps:

1. Open the /Controllers/CitiesController.cs file and change the GetCities() method in the following way:

```
// ...existing code...

[HttpGet]
public async Task<ActionResult<ApiResult<CityDTO>>> GetCities(
        int pageIndex = 0,
        int pageSize = 10,
        string? sortColumn = null,
        string? sortOrder = null,
        string? filterColumn = null,
        string? filterQuery = null)
{
    return await ApiResult<CityDTO>.CreateAsync(
            _context.Cities.AsNoTracking()
                .Select(c => new CityDTO()
                {
                    Id = c.Id,
                    Name = c.Name,
                    Lat = c.Lat,
                    Lon = c.Lon,
                    CountryId = c.Country!.Id,
                    CountryName = c.Country!.Name
                }),
            pageIndex,
            pageSize,
            sortColumn,
            sortOrder,
            filterColumn,
            filterQuery);
}

// ...existing code...
```

As we can see, we're sticking to the DTO-based pattern, meaning that we'll have to create an additional `CityDTO` class.

2. Use the Visual Studio Solution Explorer to add a new `/Data/CityDTO.cs` file and fill it with the following content:

```
namespace WorldCitiesAPI.Data
{
    public class CityDTO
    {
        public int Id { get; set; }

        public string Name { get; set; } = null!;

        public decimal Lat { get; set; }

        public decimal Lon { get; set; }

        public int CountryId { get; set; }

        public string? CountryName { get; set; } = null!;
    }
}
```

That's it. It goes without saying that, as we saw when working with the `GetCountries()` method of `CountriesController` early on, we could have implemented the web API by using anonymous types, or with a secured `City` entity, thus avoiding having to write the `CityDTO` class. However, we intentionally went for the DTO approach because of the security considerations that we mentioned earlier on.

Our web API is ready, so let's move to Angular.

Angular front-end updates

Let's start with the `/src/app/cities/city.ts` interface, where we need to add the `countryName` property. Open that file and update its content as follows:

```
export interface City {
    id: number;
    name: string;
    lat: number;
    lon: number;
    countryId: number;
    countryName: string;
}
```

Once done, open the `/src/app/cities/cities.component.ts` class, where we need to add the countryName column definition:

```
// ...existing code...

public displayedColumns: string[] = ['id', 'name', 'lat', 'lon',
'countryName'];

// ...existing code...
```

Then, open the `/src/app/cities/cities.component.html` class and add a new `<ng-container>` accordingly:

```
<!-- ...existing code... -->

<!-- Lon Column -->
<ng-container matColumnDef="lon">
  <th mat-header-cell *matHeaderCellDef mat-sort-header>Longitude</th>
  <td mat-cell *matCellDef="let city">{{city.lon}}</td>
</ng-container>

<!-- CountryName Column -->
<ng-container matColumnDef="countryName">
  <th mat-header-cell *matHeaderCellDef mat-sort-header>Country</th>
  <td mat-cell *matCellDef="let city">
    <a [routerLink]="['/country', city.countryId]">{{city.countryName}}</a>
  </td>
</ng-container>

<!-- ...existing code... -->
```

As we can see, we wrapped countryName within routerLink, pointing to the *Edit Country* view, so that our users will be able to use it as a navigation element.

Let's test what we've done. Hit *F5* to launch the app in *debug* mode, then go to the **Cities** view. If we did everything properly, we should be welcomed by the following result:

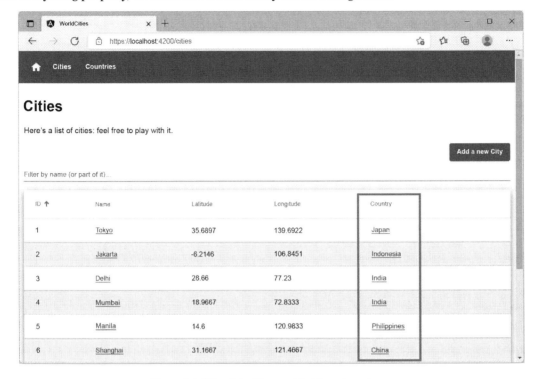

Figure 8.4: Cities list with an added Country column

Not bad, right?

From there, if we click on a *country* name, we should be brought to the *Edit Country* view. That's awesome, right?

This brings us to the end of the *minor* code improvements and UI tweaks. In the next section, we'll face a more demanding task, which will require a *code refactoring* of all the Angular Components that we've created so far.

In software development, code refactoring is the process of restructuring existing source code without changing its external behavior. There could be multiple reasons to perform refactoring activities, such as improving the code's readability, extensibility, or performance, making it more secure, or reducing its complexity.

For additional information regarding the high-level concept of code refactoring, check out the following URL: `https://docs.microsoft.com/en-us/visualstudio/ide/refactoring-in-visual-studio`.

It's now time to move to a whole different topic, which will make another major improvement to our Angular app.

Data services

The two web applications that we have created so far – HealthCheck and WorldCities – both feature *front-end* to *back-end* communication between their two projects over the HTTP(S) protocol, and in order to establish such communication, we made good use of the HttpClient class, a built-in Angular HTTP API client shipped with the @angular/common/http package that rests on the XMLHttpRequest interface.

Angular's HttpClient class has a lot of benefits, including testability features, *request* and *response* typed objects, *request* and *response* interception, *Observable* APIs, and streamlined error handling. It can even be used without a *data server* thanks to the *in-memory web API package*, which emulates CRUD operations over a RESTful API. We briefly talked about that at the beginning of *Chapter 5*, *Data Model with Entity Framework Core*, when we were asking ourselves if we really needed a *data server* or not (the answer was no, therefore we didn't use it).

For all of these reasons, making good use of the HttpClient class is arguably the most logical choice for anyone who wants to develop a *front-end* web app using the Angular framework; that said, there are multiple ways to implement it, depending on how much we want to take advantage of its valuable features.

In this section, after a brief look at the alternatives, we'll see how to refactor our app in order to replace our current HttpClient implementation with a more versatile approach, based upon a dedicated *HTTP data service*.

XMLHttpRequest versus Fetch (versus HttpClient)

As we said a moment ago, Angular's HttpClient class is based on **XMLHttpRequest** (XHR), an API consisting of an object that is provided by the browser through its JavaScript engine, which can be used to transfer data between a web browser and a web server *asynchronously*, and without having to reload the whole page. This technique, which recently celebrated its 20-year anniversary, was basically the only option until 2017, when the **Fetch API** eventually came out.

The Fetch API is another interface for fetching resources that aims to be a modern alternative to the XMLHttpRequest API, providing a more powerful and flexible feature set; in the next section, we'll quickly review both of them and discuss their pros and cons.

XMLHttpRequest

The concept behind this made its first appearance back in 1999, when Microsoft released the first version of **Outlook Web Access (OWA)** for Exchange Server 2000.

Here's an excerpt of a very old post written by Alex Hopmann, one of the developers who gave birth to it:

> *"XMLHTTP actually began its life out of the Exchange 2000 team. I had joined Micro-soft in November 1996 and moved to Redmond in the spring of 1997, working initially on some internet Standards stuff as related to the future of Outlook. I was specifically doing some work on meta-data for websites including an early proposal called "Web Collections". During this time period, Thomas Reardon one day dragged me down the hall to introduce me to this guy named Jean Paoli that had just joined the company. Jean was working on this new thing called XML that some people suspected would be very big someday (for some unclear reason at the time)."*
>
> *– Alex Hopmann, The Story of XMLHTTP.*

The quote comes from a post on his blog, which unfortunately doesn't seem to be online anymore: `http://www.alexhopmann.com/xmlhttp.htm`.

However, there's an archived copy here: `http://archive.is/7i5l`.

Alex was right: a few months later, his team released an interface called `IXMLHTTPRequest`, which was implemented in the second version of the **Microsoft XML Core Services** (**MSXML**) library. That version was then shipped with Internet Explorer 5.0 in March 1999, which arguably was the first browser that was able to access that interface (through ActiveX).

Soon after that, the Mozilla project developed an interface called `nsIXMLHttpRequest` and implemented it in their Gecko layout engine. This was very similar to the Microsoft interface, but it also came with a wrapper that allowed it to be used through JavaScript, thanks to an object that was returned by the browser. The object, which was made accessible on Gecko v0.6 on December 6, 2000, was called `XMLHttpRequest`.

In the following years, the `XMLHttpRequest` object became a de facto standard in all major browsers, being implemented in *Safari 1.2* (February 2004), *Opera 8.0* (April 2005), *iCab 3.0b352* (September 2005), and *Internet Explorer 7* (October 2006). These early adoptions allowed Google engineers to develop and release *Gmail* (2004) and *Google Maps* (2005), two pioneering web applications, which were entirely based upon the `XMLHttpRequest` API. A single look at these apps was enough to demonstrate that web development had entered a new era.

The only thing missing for this exciting technology was a name, which was found on February 18, 2005, when *Jesse James Garrett* wrote an iconic article called *AJAX: A New Approach to Web Applications*.

This was the first known **appearance of the term AJAX**, the acronym for **Asynchronous JavaScript + XML**, a set of web development techniques that can be used to create asynchronous web applications from the *client side*, where the `XMLHttpRequest` object played a pivotal role.

On April 5, 2006, the **World Wide Web Consortium** (W3C) released the first draft specification for the XMLHttpRequest object in an attempt to create an official web standard.

 The latest draft of the XMLHttpRequest object was published on October 6, 2016, and is available at the following URL: https://www.w3.org/TR/2016/NOTE-XMLHttpRequest-20161006/.

The W3C draft paved the way to the wide adoption of AJAX development. However, the first implementations were rather difficult for most web developers due to some differences between the various browsers' implementation of the involved APIs. Luckily enough, things became a lot easier thanks to the many cross-browser JavaScript libraries – such as *jQuery*, *Axios*, and *MooTools* – that were smart enough to add it to their available set of tools. This allowed developers to use the underlying XMLHttpRequest object functionality indirectly, through a standardized set of high-level methods.

Over time, the XHR data format quickly switched from XML to *JSON*, *HTML*, and *plain text*, which were more suited to work with the DOM page, without changing the overall approach. Also, when the **Reactive Extensions for JavaScript** (RxJS) library came out, the XMLHttpRequest object could be easily put behind Observable, thus gaining a lot of advantages (such as being able to mix and match it with other *Observables*, *subscribe/unsubscribe*, and *pipe/map*).

This is the main idea behind Angular's HttpClient class, which can be described as *the Angular way to deal with XMLHttpRequest*: a very convenient wrapper that allows developers to effectively use it through the Observable pattern.

Fetch

During its early years, using the raw XMLHttpRequest object was rather difficult for most web developers, and could easily lead to a large amount of JavaScript source code that was often difficult to read and understand; these issues were eventually solved by the *superstructures* that were provided by libraries such as *jQuery*, but at the cost of some inevitable code (and resource) overheads.

The Fetch API was released to address such issues more cleanly, using a *built-in*, *Promise-based* approach, which could be used to perform the same *asynchronous* server requests easily, without requiring third-party libraries.

Here's an example of an HTTP request using *XHR*:

```
var oReq = new XMLHttpRequest();
oReq.onload = function() {
  // success
  var jsonData = JSON.parse(this.responseText);
};
oReq.onerror = function() {
  // error
```

```
    console.error(err);
};
oReq.open('get', './api/myCmd', true);
oReq.send();
```

And here's the same request performed using `fetch`:

```
fetch('./api/myCmd')
  .then((response) => {
    response.json().then((jsonData) => {
      // success
    });
  })
  .catch((err) => {
    // error
    console.error(err);
  });
```

As we can see, the `fetch`-based code is definitely more readable. Its generic interfaces provide better consistency, the native JSON capabilities make the code more DRY, and the *Promises* it returns permit easier *chaining* and *async/await* tasks without having to define callbacks.

Long story short, it doesn't take a genius to see that if we compare the raw XHR implementation with the brand-new `fetch()` API, the latter clearly wins.

HttpClient

Thanks to Angular's `HttpClient` class, using raw XHR is out of the question; what we'll use is the built-in abstraction that is provided by the client, which allows us to write the previous code in the following way:

```
this.http.get('./api/myCmd')
  .subscribe(jsonData => {
    // success
  },
  error => {
    // error
    console.error(error));
  };
```

As we can see, the *Observable*-based code of `HttpClient` in the previous code provides similar benefits to the `fetch`-based code that we saw before: we get a consistent interface, native JSON capabilities, *chaining*, and *async/await* tasks.

On top of that, *Observables* can also be converted into *Promises*, meaning that we could even do the following:

```
this.http.get('./api/myCmd')
  .toPromise()
  .then((response) => {
    response.json().then((jsonData) => {
      // success
    });
  })
  .catch((err) => {
    // error
    console.error(err);
  });
```

 At the same time, it's true that *Promises* can also be converted to *Observables* using the RxJS library.

All in all, both the *JavaScript-native* Fetch API and the *Angular-native* HttpClient class are perfectly viable and either of them can be effectively used in an Angular app.

Here are the major advantages of using Fetch:

- It's the *newest* industry standard that can be used to handle HTTP *requests* and *responses*
- It's *JavaScript-native*; therefore, it can be used not only on *Angular*, but also on any other JavaScript-based *front-end* framework (such as *React* and *Vue*)
- It simplifies working with *service workers*, as the *request* and *response* objects are the same as the ones we are using in our normal code
- It's built around the *norm* that HTTP requests have *single return values*, thus returning a *Promise* instead of a stream-like type, like the *Observer* is (this can be an advantage in most scenarios, but it can also become a disadvantage)

And here are the most relevant advantages of using HttpClient:

- It's *Angular-native*, and therefore widely supported and constantly updated by the framework (and will most likely be in the future as well)
- It allows easy mixing and matching of multiple *Observables*
- Its abstraction level allows us to easily implement some *HTTP magic* (such as defining *auto-retry* attempts in case of request failures)
- *Observers* are arguably more versatile and feature-rich than *Promises*, which can be useful in some complex scenarios, such as performing *sequencing calls* and being able to cancel HTTP *requests* after they have been sent

- It can be *injected*, and therefore used to write *unit tests* for various scenarios

- It allows us to use *HttpInterceptors* to transparently handle HTTP headers, bearer tokens, and more HTTP-based tasks, as we'll see in *Chapter 11, Authentication and Authorization*

For all of these reasons, after careful consideration, we genuinely think that adopting `HttpClient` in Angular might be a better choice, and therefore we'll be sticking to it for the rest of the book. That said, since the Fetch API is almost as viable in most scenarios, readers can definitely try both approaches and see which one is the most fitting for any given task.

For the sake of simplicity, we're not going any further with these topics. Those who want to know more about `XMLHttpRequest`, the Fetch API, *Observables*, and *Promises* are encouraged to check out the following URIs:

XMLHttpRequest Living Standard (September 24, 2019): `https://xhr.spec.whatwg.org/`

Fetch API – Concepts and usage: `https://developer.mozilla.org/en-US/docs/Web/API/Fetch_API`

RxJS – Observable: `https://angular.io/guide/observables`

MDN – Promise: `https://developer.mozilla.org/en-US/docs/Web/JavaScript/Reference/Global_Objects/Promise`

Now that we know the advantage of the Angular `HttpClient`, we can see how to further improve the way we use it in our code.

Building a data service

Since we've chosen to stick with Angular's `HttpClient` class, which we've already used everywhere, this means we're good, right?

Well, as a matter of fact, no. Although using `HttpClient` is definitely a good choice, we have implemented it using an oversimplified approach. If we look at our Angular source code, we can see how the actual HTTP calls are placed inside the *components*, which could be acceptable for small-scale sample apps, but it's definitely not the best way of doing it in real-life scenarios. What if we want to handle the HTTP errors in a more complex way (for example, sending them all to a remote server for statistical purposes)? What if we need to *cache* and/or *post-process* the data that we fetch through the *back-end* API? Not to mention the fact that we would definitely implement some retry logic in order to deal with potential connectivity issues, which is a typical requirement of any *Progressive Web App*.

Shall we implement all of the previous stuff within each *component's* set of methods? That's definitely not an option if we want to stick to the DRY pattern; maybe we could define a *superclass*, provide it with HTTP capabilities, and adapt our *subclasses'* source code to perform everything by calling the *super* methods with a bunch of highly customized parameters. Such a workaround could work for small tasks, but it could easily become a mess once things become more complex.

As a general rule, we should try our best to prevent our *TypeScript* classes – be they *standard*, *super*, or *sub* – from being cluttered with huge amounts of data access code. As soon as we fall into that pit, our components will become much more difficult to understand, and we will have a hard time whenever we want to upgrade, standardize, and/or test them. In order to avoid such an outcome, it's highly advisable to separate the *data access layer* from the *data presentation logic*, which can be done by encapsulating the former in a separate service and then *injecting* that service into the component itself.

This is precisely what we're about to do.

Creating the BaseService

Since we're dealing with multiple component classes that handle different tasks depending on their *context* (that is, the data source that they need to access), it's highly advisable to create multiple services, one for each *context*.

More specifically, we'll need the following:

- CityService, to deal with the *city-related* Angular Components and ASP.NET Core web APIs
- CountryService, to deal with the *country-related* Angular Components and ASP.NET Core web APIs

Also, assuming that they will most likely have some relevant things in common, it might be useful to provide them each of them with a *superclass* that will act as a *common interface*. Let's do it.

> Using an abstract superclass as a common interface might seem a bit counter-intuitive: why don't we just create an interface? We already have two of them, for cities (/cities/ city.ts) and countries (/countries/country.ts).
>
> As a matter of fact, we did that for a good reason: *Angular does not allow us to provide interfaces as providers* because interfaces aren't compiled in the JavaScript output of TypeScript. Therefore, in order to create an interface for a service to an interface, the most effective way to do that is to use an abstract class.

To create the BaseService, we can either run the following CLI command from the /src/app/ folder of our Angular project:

```
ng generate service Base --flat --skip-tests
```

Or we can simply create a new /src/app/base.service.ts file using the Visual Studio's Solution Explorer.

Once the new file has been created, open it and fill it with the following code:

```
import { HttpClient } from '@angular/common/http';


export abstract class BaseService {
  constructor(
```

```
        protected http: HttpClient) {
   }
}
```

The preceding source code (minus the abstract and protected highlighted modifiers) is also the *core* of a typical HTTP data service: we're going to use it as a *base class* with which to extend our service classes; more precisely, we'll have a single *superclass* (BaseService) containing a *common interface* for the two different *subclasses* (CityService and CountryService) that will be injected in to our *components*.

As for the two highlighted modifiers, let's try to shed some light on them:

- abstract: We used this modifier in the BaseFormComponent class earlier on. While we're here, let's talk a bit more about it. In TypeScript, an abstract class is a class that may have some unimplemented methods: these methods are called **abstract methods**. Abstract classes can't be created as instances, but other classes can extend the abstract class, and therefore reuse its constructor and members.

- protected: The HttpClient class will be required by all the service *subclasses*. Therefore, it's the first member that we're going to make available to them (and also the only one, at least for now). In order to do that, we need to use an *access modifier* that allows the subclasses to use it. In our sample, we've used *protected*, but we could have used *public* as well.

Before going any further, it might be useful to briefly recap how many *access modifiers* are supported by TypeScript and how they actually work. If we already know them from C# or other object-oriented programming languages, it'll be a familiar story for the most part.

TypeScript access modifiers

Access modifiers are a TypeScript concept that allows developers to declare methods and properties as public, private, protected, or read-only. If no modifier is provided, then the method or property is assumed to be public, meaning that it can be accessed internally and externally without issues. Conversely, if it is marked as private, that method or property will only be accessible within the class, *not including its subclasses* (if any). protected implies that the method or property is accessible only internally *within the class and all its subclasses*, that is, any class that extends it, but not externally. Finally, read-only will cause the TypeScript compiler to throw an error if the value of the property is changed after its initial assignment in the class constructor.

 For the sake of completeness, it's worth noting that *access modifiers* work in a slightly different way when assigned to constructor parameters. If no modifier is provided there, the variable will only be available within the constructor's scope; conversely, if we assign a modifier to that variable, it will be accessible within the whole class following the modifier rules that we described earlier on, just like it was declared as a separate member.

However, it's important to keep in mind that *these access modifiers will be enforced only at compile time*. The TypeScript transpiler will warn us about all inappropriate uses, but it won't be able to stop inappropriate usage at runtime.

Adding the common interface methods

Let's now expand our `BaseService` *common interface* with some high-level methods that correspond to what we'll need to do in our subclasses. Since the *components* we're refactoring are already there, the best way to define these *common interface methods* is by reviewing their source code and acting accordingly.

Here's a good start:

```typescript
import { HttpClient } from '@angular/common/http';
import { Observable } from 'rxjs';
import { environment } from '../environments/environment';

export abstract class BaseService<T> {
  constructor(
    protected http: HttpClient) {
  }

  abstract getData(
    pageIndex: number,
    pageSize: number,
    sortColumn: string,
    sortOrder: string,
    filterColumn: string | null,
    filterQuery: string | null): Observable<ApiResult<T>>;

  abstract get(id: number): Observable<T>;
  abstract put(item: T): Observable<T>;
  abstract post(item: T): Observable<T>;

  protected getUrl(url: string) {
    return environment.baseUrl + url;
  }
}

export interface ApiResult<T> {
  data: T[];
  pageIndex: number;
  pageSize: number;
  totalCount: number;
  totalPages: number;
  sortColumn: string;
  sortOrder: string;
  filterColumn: string;
  filterQuery: string;
}
```

Let's briefly review each one of the preceding abstract methods:

- `getData()`: The updates are meant to replace our current implementation for methods in our `CitiesComponent` and `CountriesComponent` TypeScript files to retrieve the *cities* and *countries* lists. As we can see, we took the chance to specify a new *strongly typed* interface – `ApiResult<T>` – that will be populated with the structured JSON output that we already receive from the `GetCities` and `GetCountries` ASP.NET Core web APIs.
- `get()`: This will replace our current implementation for the `loadData()` methods of our `CityEditComponent` and `CountryEditComponent` TypeScript files.
- `put()` and `post()`: These methods will replace our current implementations for the `submit()` methods of our `CityEditComponent` and `CountryEditComponent` TypeScript files.
- `getUrl()`: This helper method will centralize the required tasks to build the URL for the API endpoints, thus avoiding the compulsive usage of the `environment.baseUrl` property for each HTTP request.

Since we're using a good number of generic-type variables, it may be useful to briefly recap what they are and how they can help us to define our common interfaces.

Type variables and generic types – <T> and <any>

It's worth noting that for the *get*, *put*, and *post* methods, we didn't use a *strongly typed* interface, but we went for a *type variable* instead. We were kind of forced to do that because these methods will return either a `City` or a `Country` interface, depending on the *derived* class that will implement them.

Taking that into account, we will choose to use <T> instead of <any> so that we won't lose the information about what that type was when the function returns. The <T> generic type allows us to defer the specification of the returned variable type until the class or method is declared and instantiated by the client code, meaning that *we'll be able to capture the type of the given argument whenever we implement the method in the derived class* (that is, when we know what is being returned).

 The type <T> variable is a great way to deal with unknown types in an interface, to the point that we've also used it in the preceding `ApiResult` Angular interface, just like we did in the `/Data/ApiResult.cs` C# file in the .NET back-end.

These concepts are nothing new, since we've already used them in our *back-end* code: it's just great that we can also use them on the Angular *front-end*, thanks to the TypeScript programming language.

Why return Observables and not JSON?

Before moving on, it could be wise to briefly explain why we've chosen to return `Observable` types instead of the actual *JSON-based interfaces* that we already have, such as `City`, `Country`, and `ApiResult`. Wouldn't it be a more practical choice?

As a matter of fact, it's the exact opposite: our *interface* types have extremely limited options if we compare them to the feature-rich `Observable` collections that we've talked about a number of times since *Chapter 4, Front-End and Back-End Interactions*.

Why would we want to limit ourselves and the components that will call these methods? Even if we wanted (or needed) to actually execute the HTTP call and retrieve the data from within it, we could always recreate Observable and return it after this task. We'll talk about this more in the next chapters.

Creating CityService

Let's now create our first derived service, that is, the first *derived* class (or *subclass*) of BaseService.

From Solution Explorer, browse to the /src/app/cities/ folder, *right-click* to create a new city. service.ts file, and fill it with the following code:

```
import { Injectable} from '@angular/core';
import { HttpClient, HttpParams } from '@angular/common/http';
import { BaseService, ApiResult } from '../base.service';
import { Observable } from 'rxjs';

import { City } from './city';

@Injectable({
  providedIn: 'root',
})
export class CityService
  extends BaseService<City> {
  constructor(
    http: HttpClient) {
      super(http);
  }

  getData(
    pageIndex: number,
    pageSize: number,
    sortColumn: string,
    sortOrder: string,
    filterColumn: string | null,
    filterQuery: string | null
    ): Observable<ApiResult<City>> {
    var url = this.getUrl("api/Cities");
    var params = new HttpParams()
      .set("pageIndex", pageIndex.toString())
      .set("pageSize", pageSize.toString())
      .set("sortColumn", sortColumn)
```

```
        .set("sortOrder", sortOrder);

    if (filterColumn && filterQuery) {
      params = params
        .set("filterColumn", filterColumn)
        .set("filterQuery", filterQuery);
    }

    return this.http.get<ApiResult<City>>(url, { params });
  }

  get(id: number): Observable<City> {
    var url = this.getUrl("api/Cities/" + id);
    return this.http.get<City>(url);
  }

  put(item: City): Observable<City> {
    var url = this.getUrl("api/Cities/" + item.id);
    return this.http.put<City>(url, item);
  }

  post(item: City): Observable<City> {
    var url = this.getUrl("api/Cities");
    return this.http.post<City>(url, item);
  }
}
```

The most relevant aspect of the preceding source code is the providedIn property in the service's @
Injectable() decorator, which we've set to root. This will tell Angular to provide this injectable in
the application root, thus making it a *singleton* service.

A singleton service is a service for which only one instance exists in an app. In other words,
Angular will create only one instance of that service, which will be shared with all the
components that will use it (through dependency injection) in our application. Although
Angular services are not required to be singletons, this technique makes efficient use of
memory and provides good performance, thereby making it the most frequently used
implementation approach.

For additional info about singleton services, check out the following URL: https://
angular.io/guide/singleton-services.

Other than that, there's nothing new in the preceding code: we just copied (and slightly adapted) the implementation that already exists in our `CitiesComponent` and `CityEditComponent` TypeScript files. The main difference is that we're now using `HttpClient` here, meaning that we can remove it from the component classes and abstract its usage with `CityService` instead.

Implementing CityService

Let's now refactor our Angular Components to use our brand-new `CityService` instead of the raw `HttpClient`. As we'll be able to see in a short while, the new singleton services pattern that we used (and talked about) earlier will make things slightly easier than before.

AppModule

In Angular versions prior to 6.0, the only way to make a *singleton* service available throughout the app would have been to reference it within the `AppModule` file in the following way:

```
// ...existing code...

import { CityService } from './cities/city.service';

// ...existing code...

  providers: [ CityService ],

// ...existing code...
```

As we can see, we should have added the `import` statement for the new service at the beginning of the `AppModule` file, and also registered the service itself in the existing (albeit still empty) `providers: [ ]` section.

Luckily enough, since we've used the `providedIn: root` approach that was introduced with Angular 6.0, the previous technique is no longer required – although it is still supported as a viable alternative.

> As a matter of fact, the `providedIn: root` approach is preferable because it makes our service tree-shakable. **Tree shaking** is a method of optimizing the JavaScript-compiled code bundles by eliminating any code from the final file that isn't actually being used.
>
> For additional info about tree shaking in JavaScript, take a look at the following URL: https://developer.mozilla.org/en-US/docs/Glossary/Tree_shaking.

Long story short, thanks to the new approach, we no longer have to update the `AppModule` file: we just need to refactor the components that will use the service.

CitiesComponent

From Solution Explorer, open the /src/app/cities/cities.component.ts file and update its content as follows:

```typescript
import { Component, OnInit, ViewChild } from '@angular/core';
// import { HttpClient, HttpParams } from '@angular/common/http';
import { MatTableDataSource } from '@angular/material/table';
import { MatPaginator, PageEvent } from '@angular/material/paginator';
import { MatSort } from '@angular/material/sort';

import { Subject } from 'rxjs';
import { debounceTime, distinctUntilChanged } from 'rxjs/operators';

import { City } from './city';
import { CityService } from './city.service';
import { ApiResult } from '../base.service';

@Component({
  selector: 'app-cities',
  templateUrl: './cities.component.html',
  styleUrls: ['./cities.component.scss']
})
export class CitiesComponent implements OnInit {

// ...existing code...

  constructor(
    private cityService: CityService) {
  }

// ...existing code...

  getData(event: PageEvent) {

    var sortColumn = (this.sort)
        ? this.sort.active
        : this.defaultSortColumn;

    var sortOrder = (this.sort)
        ? this.sort.direction
        : this.defaultSortOrder;
```

```
            var filterColumn = (this.filterQuery)
                ? this.defaultFilterColumn
                : null;

            var filterQuery = (this.filterQuery)
                ? this.filterQuery
                : null;

            this.cityService.getData(
                event.pageIndex,
                event.pageSize,
                sortColumn,
                sortOrder,
                filterColumn,
                filterQuery)
                .subscribe(result => {
                    this.paginator.length = result.totalCount;
                    this.paginator.pageIndex = result.pageIndex;
                    this.paginator.pageSize = result.pageSize;
                    this.cities = new MatTableDataSource<City>(result.data);
                }, error => console.error(error));
        }
    }
```

As we can see, we just had to perform some minor updates:

- In the import section, we added some references to our new files
- In the constructor, we switched the existing http variable of the HttpClient type with a brand-new cityService variable of the CityService type
- Last but not least, we changed the getData() method's existing implementation—based upon the HttpClient—for a new one that relies upon the new CityService

It's worth noting that we have commented out all the import references from the @angular/common/http package simply because we no longer need them now that we're not directly using that stuff in this class.

CityEditComponent

Implementing CityService in CityEditComponent is going to be just as easy as it was for CitiesComponents.

From Solution Explorer, open the /src/app/cities/city-edit.component.ts file and update its content as follows:

```typescript
import { Component, OnInit } from '@angular/core';
import { HttpClient, HttpParams } from '@angular/common/http';
import { ActivatedRoute, Router } from '@angular/router';
import { FormGroup, FormControl, Validators, AbstractControl, AsyncValidatorFn
} from '@angular/forms';
import { Observable } from 'rxjs';
import { map } from 'rxjs/operators';

import { City } from './city';
import { Country } from './../countries/country';
import { BaseFormComponent } from '../base-form.component';
import { CityService } from './city.service';
import { ApiResult } from '../base.service';

// ...existing code...

  constructor(
    private activatedRoute: ActivatedRoute,
    private router: Router,
    private http: HttpClient,
    private cityService: CityService) {
      super();
  }

// ...existing code...

  onSubmit() {

    // ...existing code...

    if (this.id) {
      // EDIT mode
      this.cityService
        .put(city)
        .subscribe(result => {

          console.log("City " + city!.id + " has been updated.");

          // go back to cities view
          this.router.navigate(['/cities']);
```

```
            }, error => console.error(error));
        }
        else {
            // ADD NEW mode
            this.cityService
                .post(city)
                .subscribe(result => {

                    console.log("City " + result.id + " has been created.");

                    // go back to cities view
                    this.router.navigate(['/cities']);
                }, error => console.error(error));
        }
    }

    // ...existing code...
```

As we can see, this time we weren't able to get rid of the @angular/common/http package reference because we still need HttpClient to perform some specific tasks – loadCountries() and isDupeCity() – that we can't handle with our current service. In order to fix these issues, it definitely seems like we need to implement two more methods in CityService.

Let's do this!

Implementing loadCountries and isDupeCity in CityService

From Solution Explorer, open the /src/app/cities/city.service.ts file and add the following methods at the end of the file, just before the last curly bracket:

```
// ...existing code...

getCountries(
  pageIndex: number,
  pageSize: number,
  sortColumn: string,
  sortOrder: string,
  filterColumn: string | null,
  filterQuery: string | null
): Observable<ApiResult<Country>> {
  var url = this.getUrl("api/Countries");
  var params = new HttpParams()
    .set("pageIndex", pageIndex.toString())
    .set("pageSize", pageSize.toString())
```

```
    .set("sortColumn", sortColumn)
    .set("sortOrder", sortOrder);

  if (filterColumn && filterQuery) {
    params = params
      .set("filterColumn", filterColumn)
      .set("filterQuery", filterQuery);
  }

  return this.http.get<ApiResult<Country>>(url, { params });
}

isDupeCity(item: City): Observable<boolean> {
  var url = this.getUrl("api/Cities/isDupeCity");
  return this.http.post<boolean>(url, item);
}
```

Since this code contains a reference to the Country interface, we also need to add the following import statement (we can put that right below the City interface):

```
import { Country } from './../countries/country';
```

Now that we have these methods, we can patch our CityEditComponent class file as follows:

```
import { Component, OnInit } from '@angular/core';
// import { HttpClient, HttpParams } from '@angular/common/http';

// ...existing code...

  constructor(
    private activatedRoute: ActivatedRoute,
    private router: Router,
    private cityService: CityService) {
    super();
  }

// ...existing code...

  loadData() {

    // ...existing code...

    // fetch the city from the server
```

```
      this.cityService.get(this.id).subscribe(result => {

    // ...existing code...
  }


  loadCountries() {
    // fetch all the countries from the server
    this.cityService.getCountries(
      0,
      9999,
      "name",
      "asc",
      null,
      null,
      ).subscribe(result => {
        this.countries = result.data;
      }, error => console.error(error));
  }

// ...existing code...

  isDupeCity(): AsyncValidatorFn {
    return (control: AbstractControl): Observable<{ [key: string]:
    any } | null> => {

      var city = <City>{};
      city.id = (this.id) ? this.id : 0;
      city.name = this.form.controls['name'].value;
      city.lat = +this.form.controls['lat'].value;
      city.lon = +this.form.controls['lon'].value;
      city.countryId = +this.form.controls['countryId'].value;


      return this.cityService.isDupeCity(city)
        .pipe(map(result => {
          return (result ? { isDupeCity: true } : null);
        }));
    }
  }
}
```

And that's it! Now, we can remove the @angular/common/http references and HttpClient from our CityEditComponent code.

 Before going further, it would be wise to check what we have done so far by hitting *F5* and ensuring that everything is still working as before. If we did everything correctly, we should see no differences: our new CityService should be able to transparently perform all the tasks that were previously handled by HttpClient. That's expected, since we're still using it under the hood!

In the next section, we'll do the same with the *country-related* components.

Creating CountryService

It's now time to create CountryService, which will be the second – and last – *derived* class (or *subclass*) of BaseService.

Just like we did with CityService early on, create a new /src/app/countries/country.service.ts file using the ng generate Angular CLI command (or Solution Explorer) and fill it with the following code:

```
import { Injectable } from '@angular/core';
import { HttpClient, HttpParams } from '@angular/common/http';
import { BaseService, ApiResult } from '../base.service';
import { Observable } from 'rxjs';

import { Country } from './country';

@Injectable({
  providedIn: 'root',
})
export class CountryService
  extends BaseService<Country> {
  constructor(
    http: HttpClient) {
    super(http);
  }

  getData (
    pageIndex: number,
    pageSize: number,
    sortColumn: string,
    sortOrder: string,
    filterColumn: string | null,
    filterQuery: string | null
  ): Observable<ApiResult<Country>> {
```

```
      var url = this.getUrl("api/Countries");
      var params = new HttpParams()
        .set("pageIndex", pageIndex.toString())
        .set("pageSize", pageSize.toString())
        .set("sortColumn", sortColumn)
        .set("sortOrder", sortOrder);

      if (filterColumn && filterQuery) {
        params = params
        .set("filterColumn", filterColumn)
        .set("filterQuery", filterQuery);
      }

        return this.http.get<ApiResult<Country>>(url, { params });
    }

  get(id: number): Observable<Country> {
    var url = this.getUrl("api/Countries/" + id);
    return this.http.get<Country>(url);
  }

  put(item: Country): Observable<Country> {
    var url = this.getUrl("api/Countries/" + item.id);
    return this.http.put<Country>(url, item);
  }

  post(item: Country): Observable<Country> {
    var url = this.getUrl("api/Countries");
    return this.http.post<Country>(url, item);
  }

  isDupeField(countryId: number, fieldName: string, fieldValue: string):
Observable<boolean> {
    var params = new HttpParams()
      .set("countryId", countryId)
      .set("fieldName", fieldName)
      .set("fieldValue", fieldValue);
    var url = this.getUrl("api/Countries/IsDupeField");
    return this.http.post<boolean>(url, null, { params });
  }
}
```

As we can see, this time we went ahead of time and took the chance to directly add the isDupeField() method, since we're definitely going to need it to refactor the validator of our CountryEditComponent in a short while.

As always, now that we have created the service, we need to implement it within our app. Luckily enough, as we explained earlier on, we don't have to reference it in our AppModule file; we just need to properly implement it in our country-related components.

CountriesComponent

From Solution Explorer, open the /src/app/countries/countries.component.ts file and update its content as follows:

```typescript
import { Component, OnInit, ViewChild } from '@angular/core';
// import { HttpClient, HttpParams } from '@angular/common/http';
import { MatTableDataSource } from '@angular/material/table';
import { MatPaginator, PageEvent } from '@angular/material/paginator';
import { MatSort } from '@angular/material/sort';

import { Subject } from 'rxjs';
import { debounceTime, distinctUntilChanged } from 'rxjs/operators';

import { Country } from './country';
import { CountryService } from './country.service';
import { ApiResult } from '../base.service';

  // ...existing code...

  constructor(
    private countryService: CountryService) {
  }

  // ...existing code...

  getData(event: PageEvent) {

    var sortColumn = (this.sort)
      ? this.sort.active
      : this.defaultSortColumn;

    var sortOrder = (this.sort)
      ? this.sort.direction
      : this.defaultSortOrder;
```

```
    var filterColumn = (this.filterQuery)
      ? this.defaultFilterColumn
      : null;

    var filterQuery = (this.filterQuery)
      ? this.filterQuery
      : null;

    this.countryService.getData(
      event.pageIndex,
      event.pageSize,
      sortColumn,
      sortOrder,
      filterColumn,
      filterQuery)
      .subscribe(result => {
        this.paginator.length = result.totalCount;
        this.paginator.pageIndex = result.pageIndex;
        this.paginator.pageSize = result.pageSize;
        this.countries = new MatTableDataSource<Country>(result.data);
      }, error => console.error(error));
  }
}
```

Nothing new here; we just repeated what we did with CitiesComponent a short while ago.

CountryEditComponent

From Solution Explorer, open the /src/app/countries/country-edit.component.ts file and change its content as follows:

```
import { Component, OnInit } from '@angular/core';
// import { HttpClient, HttpParams } from '@angular/common/http';
import { ActivatedRoute, Router } from '@angular/router';
import { FormGroup, FormBuilder, Validators, AbstractControl, AsyncValidatorFn
} from '@angular/forms';
import { map } from 'rxjs/operators';
import { Observable } from 'rxjs';

import { Country } from './country';
import { BaseFormComponent } from '../base-form.component';
import { CountryService } from './country.service';
```

```
// ...existing code...

  constructor(
    private fb: FormBuilder,
    private activatedRoute: ActivatedRoute,
    private router: Router,
    private countryService: CountryService) {
    super();
  }

// ...existing code...

  loadData() {

    // ...existing code...

      // fetch the country from the server
      this.countryService.get(this.id)
        .subscribe(result => {
          this.country = result;
          this.title = "Edit - " + this.country.name;

          // update the form with the country value
          this.form.patchValue(this.country);
        }, error => console.error(error));
    }
    else {
      // ADD NEW MODE

      this.title = "Create a new Country";
    }
  }

  onSubmit() {

    // ...existing code...

    if (this.id) {
      // EDIT mode
      this.countryService
```

```
            .put(country)
        .subscribe(result => {

            console.log("Country " + country!.id + " has been updated.");

            // go back to countries view
            this.router.navigate(['/countries']);
        }, error => console.error(error));
    }
    else {
      // ADD NEW mode
      this.countryService
        .post(country)
        .subscribe(result => {

            console.log("Country " + result.id + " has been created.");

            // go back to countries view
            this.router.navigate(['/countries']);
        }, error => console.error(error));
    }
  }

  isDupeField(fieldName: string): AsyncValidatorFn {
    return (control: AbstractControl): Observable<{ [key: string]:
      any } | null> => {

      return this.countryService.isDupeField(
        this.id ?? 0,
        fieldName,
        control.value)
        .pipe(map(result => {
          return (result ? { isDupeField: true } : null);
      }));
    }
  }
}
```

As we can see, the code changes that we applied here are very similar to what we did in `CityEditComponent`. Since we took the chance to preventively add the `isDupeField()` method in our `CountryService` class, this time we were able to get rid of the `@angular/common/http` package in a single shot.

That's it, at least for now. In the next chapter, we'll make good use of these new services. However, before going further, you are strongly advised to perform some debug runs (by hitting *F5*) in order to ensure that everything is still working.

In case it isn't, refer to the *Bug fixes and improvements* section earlier in this chapter.

Summary

In this chapter, we have spent some valuable time consolidating the existing source code of our World-Cities Angular app. We successfully implemented some optimizations and tweaks by making good use of the TypeScript class inheritance features, and we learned how to create base classes (*superclasses*) and derived classes (*subclasses*), thus making our source code more maintainable and DRY. At the same time, we took the chance to perform some bug fixing and add a couple of new features to our app's UI.

Right after that, we refined the data fetching capabilities of our Angular app by switching from direct usage of Angular's `HttpClient` class in our components to a more versatile *service-based* approach. Eventually, we created `CityService` and `CountryService` – both extending a `BaseService` abstract class – to deal with all the HTTP requests, thus paving the way for post-processing, error handling, retry logic, and more interesting stuff that will be introduced in the upcoming chapter.

Suggested topics

For further information, we recommend the following topics: object-oriented programming, polymorphism, inheritance, AJAX, XMLHttpRequest, Fetch API, Angular HttpClient, Angular services, RxJS, Observables, Promises, tree shaking, singleton services, TypeScript access modifiers, TypeScript generic types, base classes and derived classes, superclasses and subclasses, access modifiers.

References

- *Jesse James Garrett – AJAX: A New Approach to Web Applications*: `https://web.archive.org/web/20061107032631/http://www.adaptivepath.com/publications/essays/archives/000385.php`

- *The XMLHttpRequest Object – W3C First Working Draft (April 5, 2006)*: `https://www.w3.org/TR/2006/WD-XMLHttpRequest-20060405/`

- *Alex Hopmann talks about XMLHttpRequest (currently offline)*: `http://www.alexhopmann.com/xmlhttp.htm`

- *Alex Hopmann talks about XMLHttpRequest (archived copy)*: `http://archive.is/7i5l`

- *XMLHttpRequest Level 1 – W3C Latest Draft (October 6, 2016)*: `https://www.w3.org/TR/2016/NOTE-XMLHttpRequest-20161006/`

- *XMLHttpRequest Living Standard (September 24, 2019)*: `https://xhr.spec.whatwg.org/`

- *Fetch API – Concepts and usage*: `https://developer.mozilla.org/en-US/docs/Web/API/Fetch_API`

- *RxJS – Observables*: `https://angular.io/guide/observables`

- *MDN – Promises*: https://developer.mozilla.org/en-US/docs/Web/JavaScript/Reference/Global_Objects/Promise

- *Angular – Singleton services*: https://angular.io/guide/singleton-services

- *Tree shaking in JavaScript*: https://developer.mozilla.org/en-US/docs/Glossary/Tree_shaking

- *TypeScript: Access Modifiers*: http://www.typescriptlang.org/docs/handbook/classes.html#public-private-and-protected-modifiers

- *TypeScript: Generic Types*: https://www.typescriptlang.org/docs/handbook/generics.html

- *Anonymous Types in C#*: https://docs.microsoft.com/en-us/dotnet/csharp/programming-guide/classes-and-structs/anonymous-types

- *Create Data Transfer Objects (DTOs)*: https://docs.microsoft.com/en-us/aspnet/web-api/overview/data/using-web-api-with-entity-framework/part-5

- *Pros and Cons of Data Transfer Objects*: https://docs.microsoft.com/en-us/archive/msdn-magazine/2009/brownfield/pros-and-cons-of-data-transfer-objects

- *Microsoft.EntityFrameworkCore Namespace*: https://docs.microsoft.com/en-us/dotnet/api/microsoft.entityframeworkcore

- *System.Text.Json.Serialization Namespace*: https://docs.microsoft.com/en-us/dotnet/api/system.text.json.serialization

- *Refactoring code*: https://docs.microsoft.com/en-us/visualstudio/ide/refactoring-in-visual-studio

9

Back-End and Front-End Debugging

One of the most relevant features of all *programming* languages (such as C#), and most *scripting* languages (such as JavaScript), is the debugging capabilities they offer to developers.

> *"If debugging is the process of removing software bugs, then programming must be the process of putting them in."*
>
> — *E. W. Dijkstra*

The term debugging universally refers to the process of finding and resolving the issues and/or problems, commonly called **bugs**, that prevent a program or an application from working as expected. In a nutshell, we can say that the debugging process allows the developer to better understand how the source code is being executed under the hood and why it produces the result that it does.

Debugging is a very important skill for any developer, arguably as much as programming itself; it's a skill that all developers have to learn with theory, practice, and experience, just like coding.

The best way to fulfill these tasks is by making use of a debugger—a tool that allows running the target program under controlled conditions. This enables the developer to track its operations in real time, halting them using breakpoints, executing them step by step, viewing the values of the underlying type, and so on. Advanced debugger features also allow the developer to access the memory contents, CPU registers, storage device activities, and so on, viewing or altering their values to reproduce specific conditions that might be causing the addressed issues.

Luckily enough, **Visual Studio** provides a set of debuggers that can be used to track any .NET application. Although most of its features have been designed to debug the managed code portion of our app (for example, our C# files), some of them—when configured properly—can be very useful to track the client-side code as well.

Throughout this chapter, we'll learn how to use them, as well as the various debugging tools built into some web browsers such as Chrome, Firefox, and Edge to constantly monitor and keep under control the whole HTTP workflow of our *WorldCities* app.

For practical reasons, the debugging process has been split into two separate sections:

- The back-end, where the debug tasks are mostly being handled using the Visual Studio and .NET Core tools
- The front-end, where both Visual Studio and the web browser play a major role

The last section of the chapter is dedicated to back-end logging using the .NET logging API and a third-party logging provider (Serilog).

By the end of this chapter, we'll have learned how to properly debug our web application's Web API, as well as our Angular components, using the various debugging and logging tools provided by Visual Studio and ASP.NET Core to their full extent.

Technical requirements

In this chapter, we're going to need all the technical requirements listed in the previous chapters, plus the following external libraries:

- The `EFCore.BulkExtensions` NuGet package
- The `Serilog.AspNetCore` NuGet package
- The `Serilog.Settings.Configuration` NuGet package
- The `Serilog.Sinks.MSSqlServer` NuGet package

The code files for this chapter can be found here: `https://github.com/PacktPublishing/ASP.NET-Core-6-and-Angular/tree/master/Chapter_09/`.

Back-end debugging

In this section, we'll learn how to make use of the debug features offered by the Visual Studio environment to take a look at the server-side life cycle of our web application and understand how we can properly troubleshoot some potential flaws.

However, before doing that, let's spend a couple of minutes seeing how it works for the various operating systems available.

Windows or Linux?

For the sake of simplicity, we'll take for granted that we're using the Visual Studio Community, Professional, or Enterprise edition for Windows operating systems. However, since .NET and .NET Core have been designed to be cross-platform, there are at least two options for those who want to debug in other environments, such as Linux or macOS:

- Using Visual Studio Code, a lightweight and open source alternative to Visual Studio available for Windows, Linux, and macOS with full debug support

- Using Visual Studio, thanks to the Docker container tools available since Visual Studio 2017 and built into Visual Studio since version 2019 (16.3)

Visual Studio Code can be downloaded for free (under the MIT license) from the following URL: `https://code.visualstudio.com/download`.

Visual Studio Docker container tools require Docker Desktop, which can be installed from the following URL: `https://docs.docker.com/desktop/windows/install/`.

The container tools usage information is available here: `https://docs.microsoft.com/en-us/aspnet/core/host-and-deploy/docker/visual-studio-tools-for-docker`.

For additional information about the .NET Core debugging features under Linux and macOS, check out the following URL: `https://github.com/Microsoft/MIEngine/wiki/Offroad-Debugging-of-.NET-Core-on-Linux---OSX-from-Visual-Studio`.

In this book, for the sake of simplicity, we'll stick to the Windows environment, thus making use of the Visual Studio set of debuggers available for Windows.

The basics

We'll take for granted that everyone who is reading this book already knows all the basic debugging features offered by Visual Studio, such as the following:

- Debug versus Release build configuration modes
- Breakpoints and how to set and use them
- Stepping in and out of a program
- The *Watch*, *Call Stack*, *Locals*, and *Immediate* windows

For those who don't know (or remember) them well enough, here's a great tutorial that can be useful if you want a quick recap: `https://docs.microsoft.com/en-US/dotnet/core/tutorials/debugging-with-visual-studio?tabs=csharp`.

In the following section, we'll briefly introduce some advanced debug options that can be useful in our specific scenarios.

Conditional breakpoints

The conditional breakpoint is a useful debugging feature that is often unknown to (or underutilized by) most developers; it acts just like a normal breakpoint, but it only triggers when certain conditions are met.

To set a conditional breakpoint, just click on the *Settings* contextual icon (the one with a cogwheel) that appears when we create a standard breakpoint, as shown in the following screenshot:

```
54
55        // GET: api/Cities/5
56        [HttpGet("{id}")]
          0 references | - changes | -authors, -changes
57        public async Task<ActionResult<City>> GetCity(int id)
58        {
59            var city = await _context.Cities.FindAsync(id);
60
61            if (city == null)
62            {
63                return NotFound();
64            }

66            return city;
67        }
68
```

Figure 9.1: Creating a conditional breakpoint

As soon as we do that, a panel will appear at the bottom of the window showing a number of possible conditional settings that we can configure for that breakpoint:

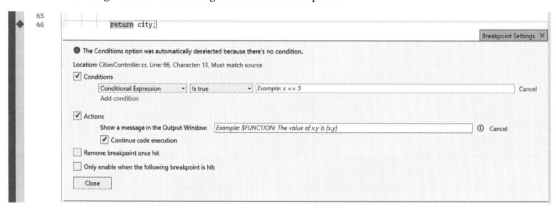

Figure 9.2: Conditional breakpoint settings panel

As we can see, there are a number of possible settings available (**Conditions**, **Actions**, and so on). Let's see how we can use them.

Conditions

If we check the **Conditions** checkbox, we'll be able to define the code condition that will trigger the breakpoint.

To better explain how it works, let's perform a quick debugging test:

1. From **Solution Explorer**, choose the **WorldCitiesAPI** project and open the /Controllers/ CitiesController.cs file.

2. Set a breakpoint on the last line of the GetCity() method (the one that returns the city to the client once it has been found—see the following screenshot for details).

3. Click the **Settings** icon to access the **Breakpoint Settings** panel.

4. Activate the **Conditions** checkbox.

5. Select **Conditional Expression** and **Is true** in the two drop-down lists.

6. Type the following condition into the textbox to the right: city.Name == "Moscow".

Once done, our **Breakpoint Settings** panel should look like the following screenshot:

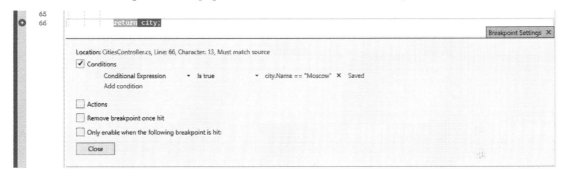

Figure 9.3: Activating the Conditions checkbox

As we can see, our condition has been created; the interface lets us add other conditions, as well as perform certain **Actions** by activating the checkbox below it.

Actions

The **Actions** feature can be used to show a custom message in the **Output** window (such as, **Hey, we're currently editing Moscow from our Angular app!**) and/or choose whether the code execution should continue or not. If no **Action** is specified, the breakpoint will behave normally, without emitting messages and halting the code execution.

While we're here, let's take the chance to test the **Actions** feature as well. Activate the checkbox, then type the message in the previous paragraph into the rightmost textbox. Once done, our **Breakpoint Settings** panel should look like the following screenshot:

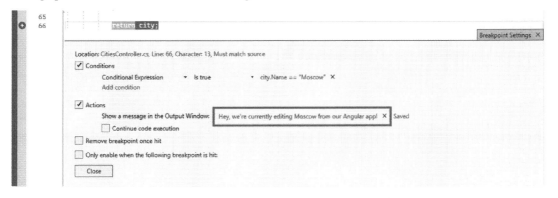

Figure 9.4: Activating the Actions checkbox

We've just created our first conditional breakpoint; let's quickly test it to see how it works.

Testing the conditional breakpoint

To test what happens when the breakpoint is hit, run the **WorldCities** app in debug mode (by hitting *F5*), navigate to the **Cities** view, filter the table to locate the city of **Moscow**, and click on its name to enter edit mode.

If everything has been done properly, our conditional breakpoint should trigger and behave in the following way:

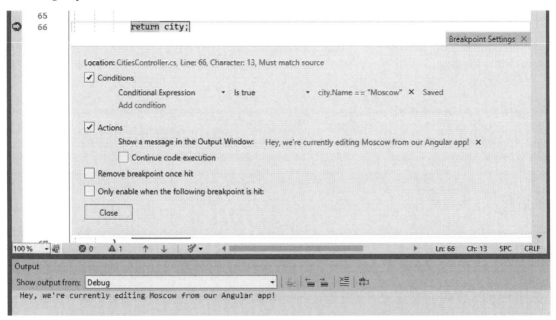

Figure 9.5: Outcome after triggering the conditional breakpoint

As we can see, the **Output** window has been populated with our custom message as well. If we now repeat the same test with any other city with a different name (for example, Rome, Prague, or New York), that same breakpoint won't trigger at all; nothing will happen.

> It's worth mentioning that there are two cities called Moscow in our WorldCities database: the Russian capital city and a city in Idaho, USA. It goes without saying that our conditional breakpoint will trigger on both of them because it only checks for the `Name` property. If we wanted to limit its scope to the Russian city only, we should refine the conditional expression to also match `CityId`, `CountryId`, or any other suitable property.

All good so far; let's move on.

The Output window

In the previous section, we talked about the Visual Studio **Output** window, which we used to write a custom message whenever our conditional breakpoint was hit.

If you have some experience with the Visual Studio debugger, you'll know about the utmost importance of this window for understanding what happens behind the curtain. The **Output** window shows the status messages for various features in the IDE, meaning that most .NET middlewares, libraries, and packages write their relevant information there, just like we did with our conditional breakpoint.

> To open the **Output** window, either choose **View** | **Output** from the main menu bar or press *Ctrl + Alt + O*.

If we take a look at what happened in the **Output** window during the test we have just performed, we can see some interesting stuff:

```
Output                                                                                    ▼ □ ×
Show output from: Debug                          ▼  │ ≧ │ ╘ ≧ │ ⚍ │ ♣
SELECT CASE
    WHEN EXISTS (
        SELECT 1
        FROM [Cities] AS [c]
        WHERE ((([c].[Name] = @__city_Name_0) AND ([c].[Lat] = @__city_Lat_1)) AND ([c].[Lon] = @__city_Lon_2)) AND ([c].[CountryId] = @__city_Count
    ELSE CAST(0 AS bit)
END
Microsoft.EntityFrameworkCore.Infrastructure: Information: Entity Framework Core 6.0.0 initialized 'ApplicationDbContext' using provider 'Microsoft.F
Microsoft.EntityFrameworkCore.Database.Command: Information: Executed DbCommand (5ms) [Parameters=[@__city_Name_0='?' (Size = 4000), @__city_Lat_1='?
SELECT CASE
    WHEN EXISTS (
        SELECT 1
        FROM [Cities] AS [c]
        WHERE ((([c].[Name] = @__city_Name_0) AND ([c].[Lat] = @__city_Lat_1)) AND ([c].[Lon] = @__city_Lon_2)) AND ([c].[CountryId] = @__city_Count
    ELSE CAST(0 AS bit)
END
Angular is running in development mode. Call enableProdMode() to enable production mode.
[webpack-dev-server] Live Reloading enabled.
Microsoft.EntityFrameworkCore.Infrastructure: Information: Entity Framework Core 6.0.0 initialized 'ApplicationDbContext' using provider 'Microsoft.F
Microsoft.EntityFrameworkCore.Infrastructure: Information: Entity Framework Core 6.0.0 initialized 'ApplicationDbContext' using provider 'Microsoft.F
Microsoft.EntityFrameworkCore.Database.Command: Information: Executed DbCommand (4ms) [Parameters=[], CommandType='Text', CommandTimeout='30']
SELECT COUNT(*)
FROM [Countries] AS [c]
Microsoft.EntityFrameworkCore.Database.Command: Information: Executed DbCommand (4ms) [Parameters=[@__p_0='?' (DbType = Int32)], CommandType='Text',
SELECT TOP(1) [c].[Id], [c].[CountryId], [c].[Lat], [c].[Lon], [c].[Name]
FROM [Cities] AS [c]
WHERE [c].[Id] = @__p_0
Hey, we're currently editing Moscow from our Angular app!
Immediate Window   Exception Settings   Call Stack   Error List   Output   Locals   Watch 1
```

Figure 9.6: The Visual Studio Output window

The **Output** window is full of info coming from *EntityFrameworkCore*, including the actual SQL queries used to map the `City` entity properties and the database content; however, we don't have info from any other source. Why are we only tracking the status messages coming from the `Microsoft.EntityFrameworkCore` namespace?

The reason for such behavior is pretty simple: it all depends on the `LogLevel` that we've set for the various namespaces (or namespace prefixes) in the `appsettings.json` file.

If we open the `appsettings.Development.json` files of our **WorldCitiesAPI** project, we can see that our current `LogLevel` settings for the `Microsoft.AspNetCore` namespace prefix is currently set to *Warning*:

```
"Logging": {
  "LogLevel": {
    "Default": "Information",
```

```
        "Microsoft.AspNetCore": "Warning"
    }
}
```

We've briefly seen those LogLevel settings back in *Chapter 3*, *Looking Around*, when we talked about the appsettings.json and appsettings.<Environment>.json files. However, we haven't spent time explaining how such settings actually work and how can we use them to influence the **Output** window – and any other logging provider we might want to use: let's do it now.

LogLevel types

The LogLevel settings specify the minimum level to log for any given namespace (or namespace prefix). This level corresponds to one of the seven possible values supported by the framework, each one having a distinctive name and a corresponding incremental number: *Trace* (0), *Debug* (1), *Information* (2), *Warning* (3), *Error* (4), *Critical* (5), and *None* (6).

Here's a quick breakdown for each one of them:

- **Trace**: The application's internal activities and values – typically useful only for debugging low-level operations. It is a rarely used LogLevel because it often contains confidential data, such as the control of encryption keys or other "sensitive" information that should not be memorized or viewed: for that reason, using it in production is highly discouraged and might lead to severe security issues.
- **Debug**: Interactive analysis and debugging info. These are logs that should be disabled in production environments as they may contain information that should not be disclosed.
- **Information**: Information messages, that is, they describe events relating to the normal behavior of the system.
- **Warning**: Abnormal or unexpected behaviors, but ones that do not cause the application to stop running.
- **Error**: Info captured when the current execution flow is interrupted due to an error: this means that they are error messages related to the current activity, not to be confused with application-wide runtime errors (see *Critical*).
- **Critical**: Events that describe an irreversible application crash.
- **None**: A placeholder value that we can use if we want to entirely disable logging ("don't log anything").

All events and/or status messages produced by any ASP.NET Core library fall in one of the seven categories above: the LogLevel settings allow us to choose what to "capture" and what to ignore.

 It's important to understand that the value present in the *LogLevel* setting specifies the minimum level to log: for example, if we set the LogLevel to Warning, the system will log *Warning*, *Error*, and *Critical* events and status messages.

Now that we understand how the LogLevel settings work, let's take another look at our appsettings. Development.json's LogLevel settings and give meaning to these values:

- The **Default** namespace is set to Information, meaning that we want to see all Information, Warning, Error, and Critical events and status messages for all namespaces that don't have more specific rules.

- The **Microsoft.AspNetCore** namespace is set to Warning, meaning that we want to see all Warning, Error, and Critical events and status messages for everything related to a namespace that starts with Microsoft.AspNetCore.

It's worth noting that the specialized Microsoft.AspNetCore key will override the value of the generic Default key, which acts as a catch-all for any unspecified namespace: if we consider that we've almost only used built-in middlewares and services that belong to the Microsoft.AspNetCore namespace, we can now easily understand why we don't see any of them in the **Output** window: we have explicitly told our app to not show them.

At the same time, the Microsoft.EntityFrameworkCore namespaces start with a different prefix: for this very reason they will fall back to the Default behavior and therefore get the Information settings, and this is why we do see them and all their informative events and status messages (in addition to the Warning, Error, and Critical ones).

Testing the LogLevel

To quickly demonstrate how the LogLevel settings work, let's perform a quick test.

Open the appsettings.Development.json file and add Microsoft.EntityFrameworkCore to the LogLevel JSON key using the same settings of the Microsoft.AspNetCore namespace, in the following way:

```
"Logging": {
  "LogLevel": {
    "Default": "Debug",
    "Microsoft.AspNetCore": "Warning",
    "Microsoft.EntityFrameworkCore": "Warning"
  }
}
```

Right after that, launch our project(s) again and perform the same identical steps until they trigger the "Moscow" conditional breakpoint that we set earlier.

This time the **Output** window will be more succinct than before, as shown in the following screenshot:

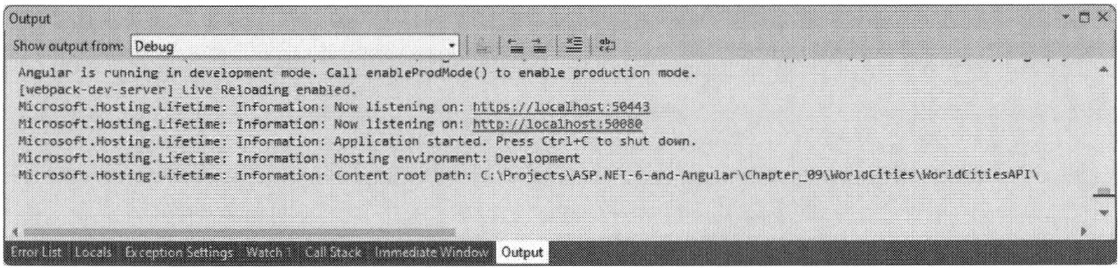

Figure 9.7: The Visual Studio Output window with the Microsoft.EntityFrameworkCore's new LogLevel settings

Now, let's configure all `LogLevel` settings to `Information` in the following way:

```
"Logging": {
  "LogLevel": {
    "Default": "Information",
    "Microsoft.AspNetCore": "Information"
  }
}
```

Once done, run the project again and perform another test up to the "Moscow" conditional breakpoint, then take another look at the **Output** window:

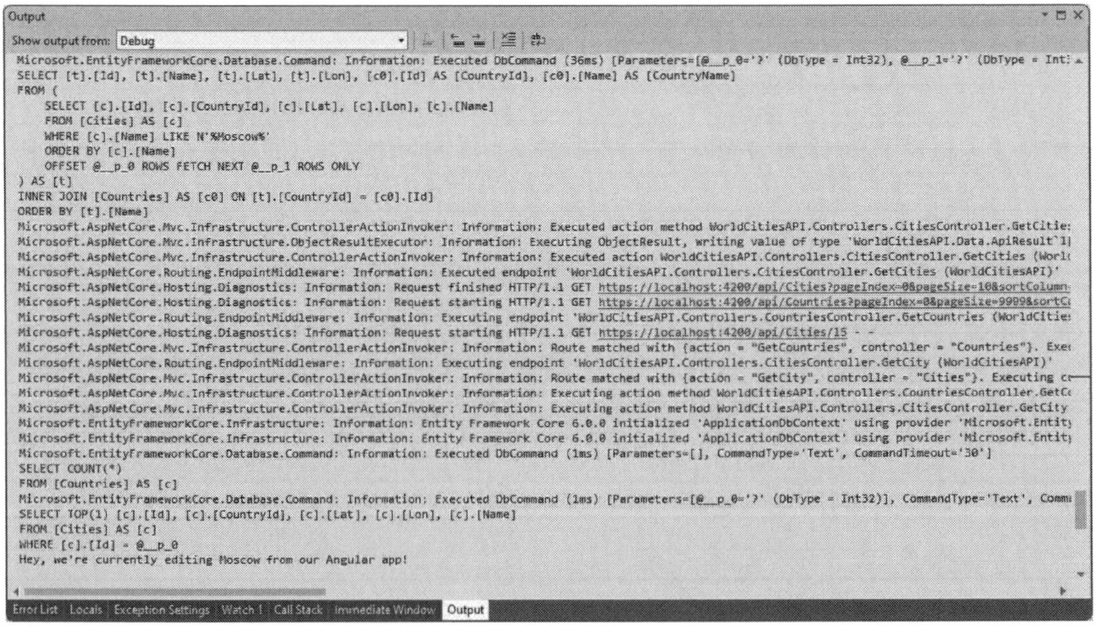

Figure 9.8: Visual Studio Output window

As we can see, now there are pieces of information coming out from a number of different sources, including the following:

- `Microsoft.AspNetCore.Hosting.Diagnostics`: The ASP.NET Core middleware dedicated to exception handling, exception display pages, and diagnostics information. It handles developer exception page middleware, exception handler middleware, runtime information middleware, status code page middleware, and welcome page middleware. In a nutshell, it's the king of the **Output** window when debugging web applications.

- `Microsoft.AspNetCore.Mvc.Infrastructure`: The namespace that handles (and tracks) the controller's actions and responds to the .NET Core MVC middleware.

- `Microsoft.AspNetCore.Routing`: The ASP.NET Core middleware that handles static and dynamic routing, such as all our web application's URI endpoints.

- `Microsoft.EntityFrameworkCore`: The ASP.NET Core middleware that handles the connections to the data source; for example, our SQL server, which we extensively talked about in *Chapter 5, Data Model with Entity Framework Core*.

All this information is basically a sequential log of everything that happens during our web application's execution. We can learn a lot from the ASP.NET Core life cycle just by performing a user-driven action and reading it.

Configuring the Output window

Needless to say, the Visual Studio interface allows us to filter the output and/or choose the level of detail of the captured information.

To configure what to show and what to hide, select **Debug | Options** from the main menu, then navigate to **Output Window** from the tree menu item to the right. From that panel, we can select (or deselect) a number of output messages: **Exception Messages**, **Module Load Messages/Module Unload Messages**, **Process Exit Messages**, **Step Filtering Messages**, and so on:

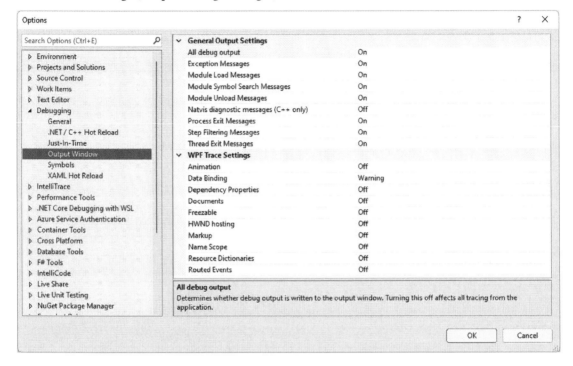

Figure 9.9: Output window configuration

Now that we've got the gist of the back-end debugging output, let's move our focus to one of the middlewares that arguably requires special attention: **Entity Framework (EF) Core**.

Debugging EF Core

If we take a look at the **Output** window right after one of our web application's runs in debug mode, we should be able to see a bunch of SQL queries written in plain text. These are the SQL queries generated by EF Core from our lambda expressions, query expressions, `IQueryable` objects, and expression trees into valid T-SQL queries.

Here's the output information line emitted by the `Microsoft.EntityFrameworkCore` middleware containing the SQL query used to retrieve the city of Moscow (the actual SQL query is highlighted):

```
Microsoft.EntityFrameworkCore.Database.Command: Information: Executed DbCommand
(36ms) [Parameters=[@__p_0='?' (DbType = Int32), @__p_1='?' (DbType = Int32)],
CommandType='Text', CommandTimeout='30']
SELECT [t].[Id], [t].[Name], [t].[Lat], [t].[Lon], [c0].[Id] AS [CountryId],
[c0].[Name] AS [CountryName]
FROM (
```

```
    SELECT [c].[Id], [c].[CountryId], [c].[Lat], [c].[Lon], [c].[Name]
    FROM [Cities] AS [c]
    WHERE [c].[Name] LIKE N'Moscow%'
    ORDER BY [c].[Name]
    OFFSET @__p_0 ROWS FETCH NEXT @__p_1 ROWS ONLY
) AS [t]
INNER JOIN [Countries] AS [c0] ON [t].[CountryId] = [c0].[Id]
ORDER BY [t].[Name]
```

Not bad, right? These SQL queries in clear text might be very useful to determine whether EF Core does a good job or not when converting our lambda or LINQ query expressions to SQL in terms of performance.

The GetCountries() SQL query

Let's try to use this same technique to retrieve the SQL query that corresponds to the CountriesController's GetCountries() method implementation, which we refined during *Chapter 8, Code Tweaks and Data Services*, to include the cities count.

Here's the source code snippet:

```
return await ApiResult<CountryDTO>.CreateAsync(
        _context.Countries.AsNoTracking()
            .Select(c => new CountryDTO()
            {
                Id = c.Id,
                Name = c.Name,
                ISO2 = c.ISO2,
                ISO3 = c.ISO3,
                TotCities = c.Cities!.Count
            }),
        pageIndex,
        pageSize,
        sortColumn,
        sortOrder,
        filterColumn,
        filterQuery);
```

To see how it was converted into T-SQL, do the following:

1. Hit *F5* to run the web app in debug mode.
2. Navigate to the **Countries** view.
3. Take a look at the resulting **Output** window (searching for TotCities will help there).

Here's the SQL query that we should find there:

```sql
SELECT [c].[Id], [c].[Name], [c].[ISO2], [c].[ISO3], (
    SELECT COUNT(*)
    FROM [Cities] AS [c0]
    WHERE [c].[Id] = [c0].[CountryId]) AS [TotCities]
FROM [Countries] AS [c]
ORDER BY [c].[Name]
OFFSET @__p_0 ROWS FETCH NEXT @__p_1 ROWS ONLY
```

That's not bad; EF Core converted our LINQ expression to SQL using a subquery, which is a good choice in terms of performance. The OFFSET part of the SQL query, together with the DBCommand parameters mentioned in the preceding code snippet, handles the pagination and ensures that we're only getting the rows we've been asking for.

However, the Visual Studio **Output** window is not the only way to take a look at those SQL queries—we can provide ourselves with an even better alternative by adding another great third-party NuGet package, as we're going to see in the following sections.

Getting the SQL code programmatically

The **Output** window is good enough for most scenarios, but what if we want to retrieve the SQL code from an IQueryable<T> programmatically? Such an option might be very useful to debug (or conditionally debug) some parts of our app, especially if we want to automatically save these SQL queries outside the **Output** window (for example, a log file or a log aggregator service).

To achieve such a result we can do one of the following:

- Create a dedicated function that will be able to do that using System.Reflection, the .NET namespace containing types that can be used to retrieve information about assemblies, modules, members, parameters, and other entities in managed code by examining their metadata
- Install a third-party NuGet package that already does that

Sometimes it can be useful (and instructive) to manually code something instead of relying on an existing library; however, when it comes to System.Reflection tasks that's often not the case, since the practice of extracting info from non-public members can easily lead to unstable code workarounds, which is often also very hard to maintain.

For that very reason, instead of reinventing the wheel, let's install the EFCore.BulkExtensions NuGet package to our **WorldCitiesAPI** project. As always, we can do that using Visual Studio's GUI (**Manage NuGet Packages**) or the Package Manager Console interface in the following way:

```
PM> Install-Package EFCore.BulkExtensions
```

In this book we're going to use version **6.2.3**, which is the latest at the time of writing and provides full support for *Entity Framework Core 6*.

Once the package has been installed, we'll be able to use the new `ToParametrizedSql()` extension method from any of our existing `IQueryable<T>` objects, simply by adding a reference to the `EFCore.BulkExtensions.IqueryableExtensions` namespace to the class.

Such a namespace provides several extensions method for the `IQueryable<T>` type: a very convenient approach to extend the functionality of that type without creating a new derived type, modifying the original type, or creating a static function that will explicitly require it as a reference parameter.

> For those who have never heard of them, C# extension methods are static methods that can be called as if they were instance methods on the extended type. For further information, take a look at the following URL from the Microsoft C# programming guide: `https://docs.microsoft.com/en-us/dotnet/csharp/programming-guide/classes-and-structs/extension-methods`.

Let's see how we can implement the `ToParametrizedSql()` extension method in our `ApiResult.cs` class, which is the place where most of our `IQueryable<T>` objects get executed.

Implementing the ToParametrizedSql() method

From Solution Explorer, select the `/Data/ApiResult.cs` file, open it for editing, and add the following lines to the existing `CreateAsync` method implementation (the new lines are highlighted):

```
using Microsoft.EntityFrameworkCore;
using System.Linq.Dynamic.Core;
using System.Reflection;
using EFCore.BulkExtensions;

// ...existing code...

    source = source
        .Skip(pageIndex * pageSize)
        .Take(pageSize);

    // retrieve the SQL query (for debug purposes)
    var sql = source.ToParametrizedSql();

    var data = await source.ToListAsync();

// ...existing code...
```

As we can see, we added a single variable to store the results of the `ToParametrizedSql` method immediately before calling the `ToListAsync()` method, which requires the execution of the resulting SQL query.

Let's quickly test it out to see how it works. Put a breakpoint on the line of the `ApiResult.cs` class, immediately below the new lines we added earlier on. Once done, hit *F5* to run the web application in debug mode, then navigate to the **Countries** view. Wait for the breakpoint to hit, then move the mouse cursor over the `sql` variable and click the magnifier lens icon.

After doing all that, we should be able to see the SQL query in the **Text Visualizer** window, as shown in the following screenshot.

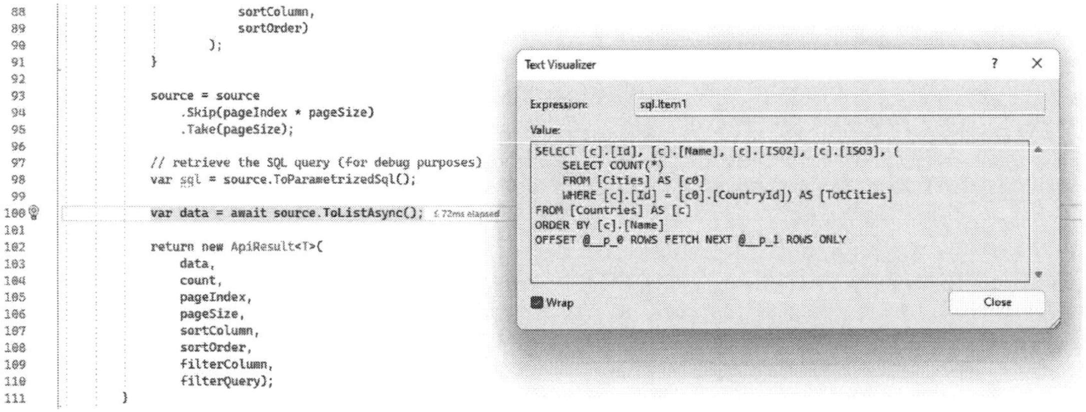

Figure 9.10: Seeing the SQL query when the breakpoint is triggered

Now we know how to quickly view the SQL queries produced by EF Core from our `IQueryable<T>` objects.

Using the #if preprocessor directive

If we are worried about the performance hit of the `ToParametrizedSql()` method task, we can definitely tweak the previous code using the `#if` preprocessor directive in the following way:

```
#if DEBUG
    // retrieve the SQL query (for debug purposes)
    var sql = source.ToParametrizedSql();
    // TODO: do something with the sql string
#endif
```

As we can see, we have wrapped the `ToParametrizedSql()` method call in an `#if` *preprocessor directive* block: when the C# compiler encounters these directives, it will compile the code between them only if the specified symbol is defined. More specifically, the `DEBUG` symbol that we used in the previous code will prevent that wrapped code from being compiled unless the web application is being run in debug mode, thus avoiding any performance loss in release/production builds.

For additional information regarding the C# preprocessor directives, take a look at the following URLs:

C# preprocessor directives: `https://docs.microsoft.com/en-us/dotnet/csharp/language-reference/preprocessor-directives/`

`#if` preprocessor directives: `https://docs.microsoft.com/en-us/dotnet/csharp/language-reference/preprocessor-directives/preprocessor-if`

There is still a lot to say about the back-end debugging features offered by Visual Studio and .NET; however, for our purposes, it's better to stop here for the time being and move on to the front-end.

Front-end debugging

In this section, we'll briefly review the various front-end debugging options we have available (Visual Studio or the browser's developer tools). Right after that, we'll take a look at some Angular features that we can leverage to increase our awareness of the various tasks performed by our client-side application under the hood and debug them.

Visual Studio JavaScript debugging

Front-end debugging works just like back-end debugging, thanks to the **JavaScript debugging** feature of Visual Studio. The JavaScript debugger is not enabled by default, but the Visual Studio IDE will automatically ask whether to activate it or not the first time we put a breakpoint on a JavaScript (or TypeScript) file and run our app in debug mode.

As of the time of writing, client-side debugging support is only provided for Chrome and Microsoft Edge. On top of that, since we're using TypeScript and not JavaScript directly, the use of source maps is required if we want to set and hit breakpoints in the TypeScript file (our Angular component class file) and not in the JavaScript-transpiled file.

Luckily enough, the Angular template we're using already provides source map support, as we can see by taking a look at the `sourceMap` parameter value in the `/tsconfig.json` file of our **WorldCities** Angular project:

```
[ ... ]

"sourceMap": true

[ ... ]
```

This means that we can do the following:

1. Open the `/src/app/countries/countries.component.ts` file.
2. Place a breakpoint inside the subscription to the `Observable` returned by the `countryService` (see the following screenshot for details).
3. Hit *F5* to launch the web application in debug mode.

If we did everything correctly, the runtime environment will stop the program execution as soon as we navigate to the **Countries** view.

> Since this is likely the first time we're using the JavaScript debugging feature for this project, Visual Studio could ask us whether we want to enable the JavaScript debugging feature: if it does, be sure to enable it.

Once the breakpoint is hit, we'll be able to inspect the various members of the Angular component class, such as the `result` object returned by the `getData()` method and containing the countries data, as shown in the following screenshot:

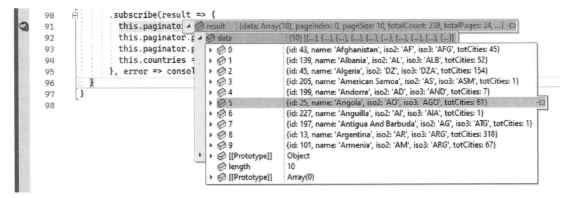

Figure 9.11: Inspecting the Angular Component class

That's pretty cool, right? We can even define conditional breakpoints and use the *Watch, Call Stack, Locals,* and *Immediate* windows without significant flaws.

> For additional information about debugging a TypeScript or JavaScript app in Visual Studio, take a look at the following URL: `https://docs.microsoft.com/en-US/visualstudio/javascript/debug-nodejs`.

In the next section, we're going to introduce another important front-end debugging resource: JavaScript source maps.

JavaScript source maps

For those who don't know what source maps actually are, let's try to briefly summarize the concept.

Technically speaking, a source map is a file that maps the code within a compressed, combined, minified, and/or transpiled file back to its original position in a source file. Thanks to these mappings, we can debug our applications even after our assets have been optimized.

Minification, also known as **minimisation** or **minimization,** is the process of removing all unnecessary characters from the source code of interpreted programming languages or markup languages without changing its functionality; this includes white spaces, new line/carriage returns, comments, and everything that is not required for the code to be executed. Minification is good for a production environment because it will reduce the size of the source code, thus making its transmission more efficient in terms of bandwidth.

As we saw a moment ago, source maps are extensively used by the Visual Studio JavaScript debugger to enable us to set breakpoints within the TypeScript source code, and they are also supported by the Google Chrome, Mozilla Firefox, and Microsoft Edge developer tools, thus allowing these browsers' built-in debuggers to display the unminified and uncombined source to the developer, even when dealing with compressed and minified files.

For additional information about JavaScript source maps, check out the following URLs:

Introduction to JavaScript Source Maps, Ryan Seddon: `https://www.html5rocks.com/en/tutorials/developertools/sourcemaps/`

An Introduction to Source Maps, Matt West: `https://blog.teamtreehouse.com/introduction-source-maps`

However, given our specific scenario, the debugging capabilities of the aforementioned browsers might not be ideal; in the next section, we'll do our best to explain why.

Browser developer tools

As we can easily guess, the Visual Studio JavaScript debugging feature is not the only way we can debug a client-side script. However, since we're dealing with a TypeScript application, it's arguably the best available option due to the fact that it allows the debugging of the `.ts` files through the autogenerated source maps.

Although the browser's built-in debugging tools can definitely use the source maps to make us deal with the unminified and uncombined files, they cannot do anything to revert these transpiled files back into their former TypeScript classes—because they have never seen them to begin with.

For that very reason, if we try to activate, for example, the Chrome developer tools to debug our CountriesComponent Angular class, we'll experience something like this:

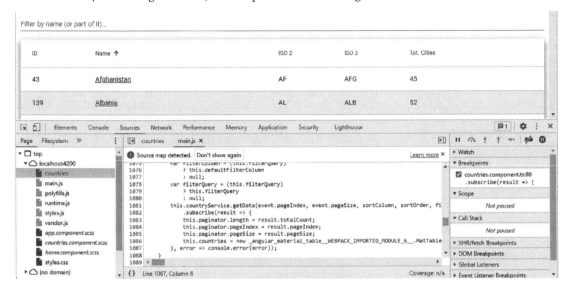

Figure 9.12: Chrome developer tools

As we can see, the TypeScript file is not there. The browser is dealing with a huge main.js transpiled file, which basically contains all the Angular components. In that file, the CountriesComponent class (which is currently less that 100 lines long) corresponds to line 888 of that main.js file (the actual line number might vary).

However, there's an informative alert at the top of the window showing the JavaScript code that informs us that a source map has been detected: thanks to its presence, the browser will be able to identify the original file using the info contained in the source map. To quickly demonstrate this, let's see what happens if we place a breakpoint in the same source code line as before – inside the subscription returned by the countryService.

As soon as we click on that line to set a breakpoint there, the corresponding TypeScript file will also become accessible, just like in Visual Studio:

Figure 9.13: Seeing the countries.components.ts file after setting a breakpoint

How is such a thing possible? Didn't we just say that the browser doesn't know anything about the TypeScript class?

If we read the informative line placed at the bottom of the development window, we can see that the browser gives us the answer: the TypeScript source is mapped from the `main.js` file. Now, since we're running the app in an *Angular Live Development Server* (as explained in *Chapter 2*, *Getting Ready*), the browser, although receiving only the `main.js` JavaScript transpiled file, can follow the source map to reach the underlying TypeScript files.

If we set the breakpoint on the TypeScript page, as soon as we make it trigger, we should be brought back to Visual Studio, where we can debug the `CountriesComponent` TypeScript file just like we did when we put the breakpoint there.

Angular form debugging

In this section, we're going to spend some valuable time understanding some key concepts related to form debugging.

As we mentioned in *Chapter 7*, *Forms and Data Validation*, one of the advantages granted by the model-driven approach is the fact that it allows us to have granular control over our form elements. How can we use these features to our advantage and translate them into writing more robust code?

In the following sections, we'll try to address this question by showing some useful techniques that can be used to gain more control over our forms.

A look at the Form Model

We talked a lot about the Form Model in *Chapter 7*, *Forms and Data Validation*, yet we've never seen it up close. It would greatly help to have it on screen while developing the form templates, especially if it can be updated in real time as we play with the form inputs and controls.

Here's a convenient HTML snippet containing the template syntax required to let it happen:

```
<!-- Form debug info panel -->
<div class="info">
  <div class="info-header">Form Debug Info</div>
  <div class="info-body">
    <div class="info-label">
      Form Value:
    </div>
    <div class="info-value">
      {{ form.value | json }}
    </div>
    <hr />
    <div class="info-label">
      Form Status:
    </div>
    <div class="info-value">
      {{ form.status | json }}
    </div>
  </div>
</div>
```

And here's its SCSS styling:

```
.info {
  margin-top: 20px;
  background-color: #efefef;
  border: 1px solid #cdcdcd;
  border-radius: 10px;

  .info-header {
    font-weight: 500;
    padding: 10px 20px;
    border-bottom: 1px solid #cdcdcd;
  }
```

```scss
.info-body {
  background-color: #fafafa;
  padding: 10px 20px;
  border-radius: 0 0 10px 10px;

  .info-label {
  }

  .info-value {
    padding: 2px 0;
    font-size: 0.8em;
  }

  hr {
    border: 0;
    border-top: 1px solid #cdcdcd;
  }
}
}
```

Append the first snippet to the `CityEditComponent` HTML file and the second to the `CityEditComponent` SCSS file to obtain the following result:

Figure 9.14: The Form Debug Info window while editing Tokyo

Pretty useful, right? If we play with the form a bit, we can see how the values contained in the **Form Debug Info** panel will change as we change the input controls; something like that will definitely come in handy when dealing with complex forms.

The pipe operator

By looking at the highlighted lines of the preceding source code, we can see how we used the pipe operator (|), which is another useful tool coming from the Angular template syntax.

To quickly summarize what it does, we can say the following: the pipe operator allows the use of some transformation functions that can be used to perform various tasks such as format strings, join array elements into a string, uppercase/lowercase text, and sort a list.

Here are the pipes built into Angular:

- `DatePipe`
- `UpperCasePipe`
- `LowerCasePipe`
- `CurrencyPipe`
- `PercentPipe`
- `JsonPipe`

These are all pipe operators available for use in any template. Needless to say, we used the last pipe in the preceding script to transform the `form.value` and `form.status` objects into readable JSON strings.

 It's worth noting that we can also chain multiple pipes and define custom pipes; however, we don't need to do that for the time being, and talking about such a topic would take us far away from the scope of this chapter. Those who want to know more about pipes should take a look at the official Angular documentation at: `https://angular.io/guide/pipes`.

Reacting to changes

One of the reasons we chose the Reactive approach was to be able to react to the changes issued by the user. We can do that by subscribing to the `valueChanges` property exposed by the `FormGroup` and `FormControl` classes, which returns an *RxJS Observable* that emits the latest values.

We've been using Observables since *Chapter 4, Front-End and Back-End Interactions*, when we subscribed to the `get()` method of `HttpClient` to handle the `HTTP` response received by the web server for the first time. We used them again in *Chapter 7, Forms and Data Validation*, when we had to implement support for the `put()` and `post()` methods as well.

Last but not least, we extensively talked about them in *Chapter 8, Code Tweaks and Data Services*, when we explained their pros and cons against Promises, learned about some of their most relevant features, and integrated them into our `CityService` and `CountryService`. As a matter of fact, we'll likely keep using them wherever and whenever we need to fetch the JSON data that feeds our Data Model interfaces and Form Model objects.

In the following section, we're going to use them to demonstrate how we can perform some arbitrary operations whenever the user changes something within a form. More precisely, we'll try to observe the observable by implementing a custom activity log.

The activity log

Once again, `CityEditComponent` will be our lab rat.

Open the `/src/app/cities/city-edit.component.ts` class file and update its code with the following highlighted lines:

```
// ...existing code...


// Activity Log (for debugging purposes)
activityLog: string = '';

constructor(
  private activatedRoute: ActivatedRoute,
  private router: Router,
  private cityService: CityService) {
    super();
  }

ngOnInit() {
  this.form = new FormGroup({
    name: new FormControl('', Validators.required),
    lat: new FormControl('', [
      Validators.required,
      Validators.pattern(/^[-]?[0-9]+(\.[0-9]{1,4})?$/)
    ]),
    lon: new FormControl('', [
      Validators.required,
      Validators.pattern(/^[-]?[0-9]+(\.[0-9]{1,4})?$/)
    ]),
    countryId: new FormControl('', Validators.required)
  }, null, this.isDupeCity());

  // react to form changes
  this.form.valueChanges
    .subscribe(() => {
      if (!this.form.dirty) {
        this.log("Form Model has been loaded.");
      }
```

```
        else {
            this.log("Form was updated by the user.");
        }
    });

    this.loadData();
}

log(str: string) {
    this.activityLog += "["
        + new Date().toLocaleString()
        + "] " + str + "<br />";
}

// ...existing code...
```

In the preceding code, we provided our Form Model with a simple, yet effective, logging feature that will register any change activity performed by the framework and/or by the user.

As we can see, all the logic has been put within the ngOnInit because this is where the component class gets initialized, along with the observable we need to monitor. The log() function is just a shortcut to append a basic timestamp to the log activity string and add it to the activityLog local variable in a centralized way.

In order to enjoy our new logging feature to the fullest, we have to find a way to put the activityLog on screen.

To do that, open the /src/app/cities/city-edit.component.html template file and append the following HTML code snippet at the end of the file, right below the previous **Form Debug Info** panel:

```
<!-- Form activity log panel -->
<div class="info">
  <div class="info-header">Form Activity Log</div>
  <div class="info-body">
    <div class="info-value">
      <span *ngIf="activityLog"
            [innerHTML]="activityLog">
      </span>
    </div>
  </div>
</div>
```

That's it; now, the activity log will be shown in real time, meaning in a truly reactive way.

It's worth noting that we didn't use the double curly braces of interpolation here—we went straight for the [innerHTML] directive instead. The reason for that is very simple. The interpolation strips the HTML tags from the source string; hence, we would've lost the <br /> tag that we used in the log() function to separate all log lines with a line feed. If not for that, we would have used the {{ activityLog }} syntax instead.

Testing the activity log

All we need to do now is test our new activity log.

To do so, run the project in debug mode, go straight to CityEditComponent by editing an already-existing city (for example, **Prague**), play with the form fields, and see what happens in the **Form Activity Log** panel:

> **Form Activity Log**
>
> [8/12/2021, 23:34:39] Form Model has been loaded.
> [8/12/2021, 23:34:41] Form was updated by the user.
> [8/12/2021, 23:34:41] Form was updated by the user.

Figure 9.15: Testing the activity log

The first log line should trigger automatically as soon as the HttpClient retrieves the city JSON from the back-end Web API and the Form Model gets updated. Then, the form will log any updates performed by the user; all we can do is change the various input fields, yet that's more than enough for our humble reactivity test to complete successfully.

Extending the activity log

Reacting to the Form Model changes is not the only thing we can do; we can extend our subscriptions to observe any form control as well. Let's perform a further upgrade on our current activity log implementation to demonstrate that.

Open the /src/app/cities/city-edit.component.ts class file and update the code in the ngOnInit method with the following highlighted lines:

```
// ...existing code...

// react to form changes
this.form.valueChanges
  .subscribe(val => {
    if (!this.form.dirty) {
      this.log("Form Model has been loaded.");
    }
    else {
```

```
      this.log("Form was updated by the user.");
  }
});

// react to changes in the form.name control
this.form.get("name")!.valueChanges
  .subscribe(() => {
    if (!this.form.dirty) {
      this.log("Name has been loaded with initial values.");
    }
    else {
      this.log("Name was updated by the user.");
    }
  });

// ...existing code...
```

The preceding code will add further log lines within the **Form Activity Log**, all related to the changes occurring in the name form control, which contains the city name, as follows:

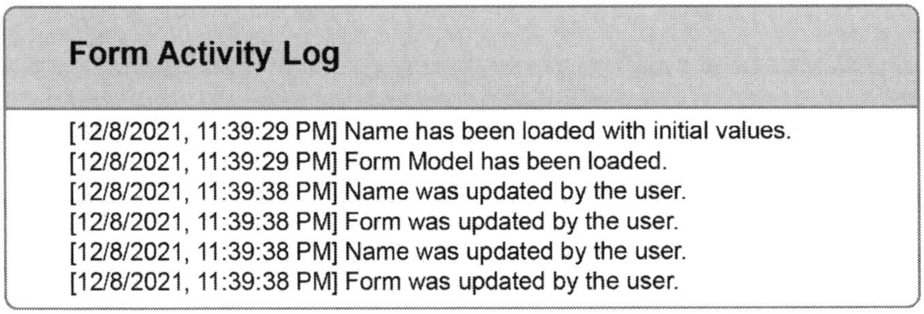

Form Activity Log

[12/8/2021, 11:39:29 PM] Name has been loaded with initial values.
[12/8/2021, 11:39:29 PM] Form Model has been loaded.
[12/8/2021, 11:39:38 PM] Name was updated by the user.
[12/8/2021, 11:39:38 PM] Form was updated by the user.
[12/8/2021, 11:39:38 PM] Name was updated by the user.
[12/8/2021, 11:39:38 PM] Form was updated by the user.

Figure 9.16: Inspecting the Form Activity Log for changes in the name form control

What we just did here is more than enough to demonstrate the wonders of the valueChanges observable property; let's move on to the next topic.

> We can definitely keep the **Form Debug Info** and **Form Activity Log** panels in the CityEditComponent template for further reference, yet there's no need to copy/paste it within the other form-based components' templates or anywhere else: after all, this logging info will be unnecessary for the average user and shouldn't be visible in the application user interface, for demonstration purposes.

Client-side debugging

Another great advantage of Observables is that we can use them to debug a good part of the whole Reactive workflow by placing breakpoints within our subscription source code. To quickly demonstrate this, just add a Visual Studio breakpoint to our latest subscription, as follows:

```
71      // react to changes in the form.name control
72      this.form.get("name")!.valueChanges
73        .subscribe(() => {
74          if (!this.form.dirty) {
75            this.log("Name has been loaded with initial values.");
76          }
77          else {
78            this.log("Name was updated by the user.");
79          }
80        });
81
82      this.loadData();
83    }
84
```

Figure 9.17: Adding a Visual Studio breakpoint

Once done, run the project in debug mode and navigate to CityEditComponent; the breakpoint will be hit as soon as the Form Model is loaded, since the name control will be updated as well, and also every time we make a change to that control. Whenever this happens, we'll be able to use all the Visual Studio JavaScript debugging tools and features that are available on client-side debugging, such as *Watch*, *Locals*, *Autos*, *Immediate*, *Call Stack*, and more.

For additional information about client-side debugging with Google Chrome, we strongly suggest reading the following post on the official MSDN blog: https://blogs. msdn.microsoft.com/webdev/2016/11/21/client-side-debugging-of-asp-net-projects-in-google-chrome/.

Unsubscribing the Observables

Observables are a great way to monitor our client-side app's behavior: once we subscribe to them, we can be sure that our event handlers will be called when a new value is emitted. However, with great power comes great responsibility: whenever we subscribe to an *Observable*, such subscription will live until that *Observable* completes its job, unless we proactively unsubscribe. However, most *Observables* (such as our valueChanges mentioned above) are not meant to complete: if we subscribe to those "infinite *Observables*" and don't unsubscribe from them, those subscriptions will live on indefinitely, even when the component that originated them is destroyed, thus ending up with a memory leak until the whole Angular app is removed from memory—such as when we navigate away to a different site.

In order to avoid such behavior, we need to learn how to properly deal with them: in a word, **unsubscribe**. Let's briefly introduce some ways to do that using imperative, declarative, and automatic approaches.

The unsubscribe() method

The first approach we should consider is to collect all the subscriptions that we can declare within our CityEditComponent class in a single Subscription instance in the following way:

```
// ... existing code...

import { Observable, Subscription } from 'rxjs';

// ... existing code...

private subscriptions: Subscription = new Subscription();
```

And then use it to store all our existing subscriptions:

```
// ...existing code...

// react to form changes
this.subscriptions.add(this.form.valueChanges
  .subscribe(val => {
    if (!this.form.dirty) {
      this.log("Form Model has been loaded.");
    }
    else {
      this.log("Form was updated by the user.");
    }
  }));

// react to changes in the form.name control
this.subscriptions.add(this.form.get("name")!.valueChanges
  .subscribe(() => {
    if (!this.form.dirty) {
      this.log("Name has been loaded with initial values.");
    }
    else {
      this.log("Name was updated by the user.");
    }
  }));

// ...existing code...
```

If we do that, we can then unsubscribe all the "collected" subscriptions in the ngOnDestroy lifecycle hook, which gets called when the component is destroyed:

```
ngOnDestroy() {
    this.subscriptions.unsubscribe();
}
```

That's it: in the preceding code, we make good use of a neat built-in mechanism provided by the Subscription class that does most of the unsubscribe job for us; we just have to "wrap up" all the subscriptions that we want to get rid of and implement the ngOnDestroy method above.

The takeUntil() operator

If we prefer to use a declarative approach, we can use another fancy mechanism provided by the RxJS library: the takeUntil operator.

Here's how we can implement it in the CityEditComponent class, replacing the previous unsubscribe() approach (new/updated lines are highlighted):

```
// ...existing code...

import { Observable, Subject } from 'rxjs';
import { map, takeUntil } from 'rxjs/operators';

// ...existing code...

private destroySubject = new Subject();

// ...existing code...

    // react to form changes
    this.form.valueChanges
      .pipe(takeUntil(this.destroySubject))
      .subscribe(() => {
        if (!this.form.dirty) {
          this.log("Form Model has been loaded.");
        }
        else {
          this.log("Form was updated by the user.");
        }
      });
```

```
    // react to changes in the form.name control
    this.form.get("name")!.valueChanges
      .pipe(takeUntil(this.destroySubject))
      .subscribe(() => {
        if (!this.form.dirty) {
          this.log("Name has been loaded with initial values.");
        }
        else {
          this.log("Name was updated by the user.");
        }
      });


// ...existing code...


ngOnDestroy() {
    // emit a value with the takeUntil notifier
    this.destroySubject.next(true);
    // complete the subject
    this.destroySubject.complete();
}
```

In a nutshell, here's what we've done:

- We've added a destroySubject internal variable of type Subject, a special type of Observable introduced in *Chapter 8, Code Tweaks and Data Services*, that allows values to be multi-casted to many observers
- We've piped the takeUntil() operator to all our observable chains; the operator will register destroySubject as a notifier, meaning that it will emit the values emitted by the source observable until destroySubject emits
- We've implemented the ngOnDestroy life cycle hook where our notifier emits a value (thus stopping all the subscriptions) and marks itself as completed: by completing the subject, all existing subscriptions will be unsubscribed

As we can see, this method allows us to declare our observable chain beforehand with everything that it needs to accommodate for the whole life cycle from start to end: a viable alternative to the unsubscribe() method... as long as we don't forget to implement the ngOnDestroy interface! To help us remember it, we could acquire the (good) habit of explicitly declaring the OnDestroy interface in all our component classes:

```
import { Component, OnInit, OnDestroy } from '@angular/core';

// ... existing code...
```

```
export class CityEditComponent
  extends BaseFormComponent implements OnInit, OnDestroy {
```

For the time being, let's do this in our `CityEditComponent` and move on.

In order to give a proper source code reference to the reader, we've implemented the `takeUntil()` method—as well as the `OnDestroy` explicit declaration—in `CityEditComponent`: the code can be found in the book's GitHub repository for this chapter.

Other viable alternatives

There are many other ways of unsubscribing from Observables, most of them being even more efficient and concise for some specific scenarios.

For example, if we only need a single result to be emitted, we can use the `first()` or `take(1)` operators: these operators can be "piped" before the subscription just like the `takeUntil()` operator and will automatically complete after receiving the first result, without having to create a `destroySubject` notifier; if we want to unsubscribe from the source stream once the emitted value no longer matches a certain condition, we can use the `takeWhile()` operator.

 A great advantage of all these RxJS operators is that they will automatically unsubscribe, without having to perform it manually (thus removing the risk of forgetting about it). However, if not used correctly they could still cause memory leaks: for example, if we use a `first()` operator and the component is destroyed before the source observable emits for the first time, that operator won't come into play and the subscription will keep on living. For that very reason, even when using those operators, it's highly recommended to adopt some disposal techniques such as the `takeUntil(destroy)` pattern or the subscription object explained above.

Furthermore, whenever we use a subscription to feed data to our templates, we can use the Angular `async pipe`, which subscribes and unsubscribes automatically when the component is destroyed. This basically means that, in our `CityEditComponent` TypeScript class file, instead of doing this:

```
// ...

// the countries array for the select
countries?: Country[];

// ...

loadCountries() {
  // fetch all the countries from the server
  this.cityService.getCountries(
    0,
    9999,
    "name",
```

```
      null,
      null,
      null,
  ).subscribe(result => {
    this.countries = result.data;
  }, error => console.error(error));
}
```

We could do this:

```
// ...

// the countries observable for the select (using async pipe)
countries?: Observable<Country[]>;

// ...

loadCountries() {
  // fetch all the countries from the server
  this.countries = this.cityService
    .getCountries(
      0,
      9999,
      "name",
      "asc",
      null,
      null,
    ).pipe(map(x => x.data));
}
```

And then handle the updated countries variable (which is now an *observable*) by modifying the city-edit.component.html template file in the following way:

```
<!-- ... -->

<mat-form-field *ngIf="countries | async as result">
  <mat-label>Select a Country...</mat-label>
  <mat-select formControlName="countryId">
    <mat-option *ngFor="let country of result" [value]="country.id">
      {{country.name}}
    </mat-option>
```

```
    </mat-select>
  </mat-form-field>

  <!-- ... -->
```

Now the `async` pipe will automatically subscribe to the observable, return the latest value, and then unsubscribe from it when the component is destroyed, thus avoiding memory leaks.

Let's quickly implement this valuable sample in our `CityEditComponent` (TypeScript and HTML files) and move on; as always, those who encounter issues while trying to do that can find the full source code reference in the GitHub repository.

> For reasons of space, we won't have the chance to talk much more about these techniques within this book; however, the reader can learn how to use them by taking a look at the following posts:
>
> **No need to unsubscribe - RxJS operators will help you out**, by *Wojciech Trawiński*: `https://medium.com/javascript-everyday/no-need-to-unsubscribe-rxjs-operators-will-help-you-out-f8b8ce7bf26a`
>
> **Async Pipe all the Things!**, by *Joaquin Cid*: `https://medium.com/@joaqcid/async-pipe-all-the-things-2607a7bc6732`

Should we always unsubscribe?

As a matter of fact, no; however, in order to determine when we should unsubscribe, we need to understand where our "enemy" actually hides.

In a nutshell, the memory leaks that we would like to avoid occur when we destroy and recreate our components without cleaning up existing subscriptions: if those components are re-created, which will likely happen if the user keeps browsing around the app, they will spawn more and more sub-scriptions, and so on, thus producing the leak.

This brief analysis should be more than enough to help you understand when we should use the un-subscribe method(s) explained previously: as a general rule, we should do it for the Observables that get subscribed in components that are meant to be instantiated and destroyed multiple times, such as the components hosting the views.

Conversely, any component that gets instantiated only once during the application startup won't have the chance to generate multiple "endless subscriptions" and therefore doesn't require any "unsub-scription" logic. `AppComponent`, as well as most of the services, are good examples: they are meant to live for the whole duration of the application lifetime and won't produce any memory leaks while the app is running.

For additional info regarding this topic, we strongly suggest reading the following articles by Tomas Trajan and Maciej Treder:

```
https://medium.com/angular-in-depth/the-best-way-to-unsubscribe-rxjs-
observable-in-the-angular-applications-d8f9aa42f6a0
```

```
https://www.twilio.com/blog/prevent-memory-leaks-angular-observable-
ngondestroy
```

Now that we've dealt with unsubscribing and we know how to properly debug our back-end code, let's switch to a slightly different topic.

Application logging

As all developers most likely know, the term logging—when used in any IT context, from programming languages to computer science—is mostly used to define the process of recording application actions and state to a *secondary* channel. To better understand this definition, we need to grasp the difference between a *primary* and *secondary* channel.

All applications are meant to communicate with their users through a dedicated interface, which is often called the **user interface**, or **UI**:

- **Desktop applications,** for example, use the **Graphical User Interface (GUI)** provided by the Windows (or other operating systems) libraries
- **Console applications** rely upon the operating system terminal
- **Web applications** display their data through the web browser

... and so on. In all the preceding examples, the *user interface* is the main output mechanism used by the software to communicate with users, thus being the application's *primary* channel.

At the same time, it's often very useful for an application to keep track of the various actions it performs while it works: state changes, access to internal resources, event handlers that trigger in response to user interactions, and so on. We made something like that in Angular early on in this chapter, when we implemented the activity log.

Now, that level of info is often neglectable for the average user, as long as the application works as expected; not to mention the fact that such low-level details could easily disclose some internal mechanics and/or behaviors of our web application that shouldn't be made available to the public for obvious security reasons.

At the same time, these logs might become extremely useful for developers and system administrators whenever the app hangs or behaves in an unexpected way, because they could greatly help them to understand what is going wrong and how to fix it. Truth be told, any experienced developer knows that logging is a must-have feature for any application, as it is necessary for detecting, investigating, and debugging issues.

Which brings us to the main question: if the *primary* channel is not an option, where should we put such info? The answer lies in the definition of logging that we stated a short while ago: in a *secondary* channel that only developers, system administrators, and other interested (and authorized) parties will be able to access.

If we think of a client-side framework, such as Angular, the best *secondary* channel we have available is the browser's console log, which can be accessed using the `console.log` and/or `debug.log` JavaScript commands; ideally, that's the place where we should move all our activity log's output, thus keeping the user interface—the *primary* channel—as clear as possible.

Doing this would be simple, and we should just change a couple of things:

- Remove the **Form Activity Log** panel (up to the root `<div>` element)
- Remove the `this.activityLog` variable (in the `city-edit.component.ts` file)
- Modify the `CityEditComponent`'s `log` method in the following way:

```
log(str: string) {
  console.log("["
    + new Date().toLocaleString()
    + "] " + str);
}
```

That's it for the client side.

> The previous "on-screen" implementation will be kept in the book's GitHub source code for reference purposes; however, the reader is strongly encouraged to rely upon `console.log` for most real-case scenarios.

What about server-side logging? We've previously seen that we have the **Output** window, but that's only available when we're running our app from Visual Studio, right?

Or not?

Introducing ASP.NET Core logging

.NET provides support for a standardized, general-purpose logging API through the `Microsoft.Extensions.Logging` NuGet package, which is implicitly included when building an ASP.NET Core application; this API can be used to collect, display, and/or store logs using a default interface (`ILogger`) that has been implemented by a variety of built-in and third-party logging providers.

In a typical ASP.NET Core web application, the built-in logging providers are automatically added to our web application by the `Program.cs` file's `CreateDefaultBuilder` helper method, which we saw back in *Chapter 3, Looking Around*. More precisely, the following providers are enabled:

- **Console**, which logs output to the console
- **Debug**, which writes log output by using the `System.Diagnostics.Debug` class

- **Event Source**, which writes to a cross-platform event source with the name `Microsoft-Extensions-Logging`
- **EventLog**, which sends log output to the Windows event log (Windows operating system only)

As a matter of fact, the content that we see within Visual Studio's **Output** window entirely comes from the **Debug** built-in provider. This also means that, if we want to add additional logging features, all we need to do is to find more providers that can write these logs whenever we want to.

DBMS structured logging with Serilog

As we can see, there are no native logging providers that can be used to have these logs stored within a **Database Management System** (**DBMS**), which would certainly be very useful as it would allow us to review our logs using a *structured* approach. As a matter of fact, structured logging would definitely be a great way to produce readable, filterable, indexed, and exportable logs.

Luckily enough, we can achieve this using one of the many third-party logging providers that implement the `ILogger` interface available on NuGet: its name is **Serilog** and it's pretty awesome.

In the following sections, we'll see how we can implement it within our **WorldCitiesAPI** project to save its logs in a dedicated SQL Server database in a structured way.

Installing the NuGet packages

The first thing we must do is add the following NuGet packages to our **WorldCitiesAPI** project:

- `Serilog.AspNetCore`
- `Serilog.Settings.Configuration`
- `Serilog.Sinks.MSSqlServer`

As always, these packages can be installed using Visual Studio's GUI (**Manage NuGet Packages**) or the Package Manager Console interface in the following way:

```
PM> Install-Package Serilog.AspNetCore
PM> Install-Package Serilog.Settings.Configuration
PM> Install-Package Serilog.Sinks.MSSqlServer
```

`Serilog.Sinks.MSSqlServer` is required in our scenario since we're using an MS SQL Server; however, there are many other connectors ("sinks") available for MySQL, MariaDB, PostgreSQL, and even NoSQL databases, such as RavenDB and MongoDB.

Configuring Serilog

Once the required NuGet packages have been installed, we can configure Serilog using our web application's configuration files. More precisely, we're going to update the `Program.cs` file, where the `IHostBuilder` is created with its set of built-in logging providers.

From **Solution Explorer**, open the `Program.cs` file and add the following code (new lines highlighted):

```
using Microsoft.EntityFrameworkCore;
using WorldCitiesAPI.Data;
```

```
using Serilog;
using Serilog.Events;
using Serilog.Sinks.MSSqlServer;

var builder = WebApplication.CreateBuilder(args);

// Adds Serilog support
builder.Host.UseSerilog((ctx, lc) => lc
    .ReadFrom.Configuration(ctx.Configuration)
    .WriteTo.MSSqlServer(connectionString:
            ctx.Configuration.GetConnectionString("DefaultConnection"),
        restrictedToMinimumLevel: LogEventLevel.Information,
        sinkOptions: new MSSqlServerSinkOptions
        {
            TableName = "LogEvents",
            AutoCreateSqlTable = true
        }
    )
    .WriteTo.Console()
    );

// ...existing code...
```

As we can see, we've performed several different tasks here:

1. We added the required references to the various Serilog namespaces.
2. We added Serilog support to the IHostBuilder that will be eventually used to build the ASP. NET Core app.
3. We told Serilog to read its configuration settings from the context's IConfiguration, which stores the values declared and/or overridden in the appsettings.json, appsettings.<Environment>. json, and secrets.json combined files.
4. We configured Serilog to write logs to SQL Server, using our existing connection string, and to the console.

The Serilog SQL Server sink that we are using here writes the logs to a dedicated [LogEvents] table, creating that table if it doesn't exist already. Now, since we've used the same connection string that we used to instantiate our ApplicationDbContext in *Chapter 5, Data Model with Entity Framework Core*, such a table will be created within our existing **WorldCities** database.

Automatically creating the [LogEvents] table is OK in our scenario, since we don't have an existing [LogEvents] table that we want to preserve: if we had that, we could either change the Serilog default log table name or disable the "create if it not exists" default behavior of the MSSQLServer sink using the TableName and AutoCreateSqlTable options above.

All the Serilog configuration settings that we've added from within the code could've been defined in the `appsettings.json` file(s) within a `"Serilog"` key.

For additional info on how to do that and regarding the settings syntax, read the MSSqlServer sink official docs on GitHub: `https://github.com/serilog/serilog-sinks-mssqlserver`.

Before we test our implementation, let's spend a minute adding another useful logging feature to our application: the `SerilogRequestLogging` middleware.

Logging HTTP requests

Another great feature of Serilog is that we can use it to log the incoming HTTP requests. Once implemented, this feature will produce the following log message:

```
HTTP GET /cities responded 200 in 1348.6188 ms
```

In order to do that, we need to add the `UseSerilogRequestLogging` middleware to our `Program.cs` file in the following way:

```
// ... existing code...


var app = builder.Build();


app.UseSerilogRequestLogging();


// ... existing code...
```

Let's do that.

Now that everything is set, we just have to perform a quick test to confirm that our new Serilog-based logging provider actually works.

Accessing the logs

Since we've told **Serilog** to auto-create the *LogEvents* table if it doesn't exist yet, we just have to launch our project in debug mode by hitting *F5* and see what happens to the database.

As soon as the web app is fully loaded, open SQL Server Management Studio and access the **World-Cities** database following the instructions given in *Chapter 5, Data Model with Entity Framework Core*.

If we did everything as expected, we should be able to see the new *LogEvents* table and a bunch of initialization logs, just as shown in the following screenshot:

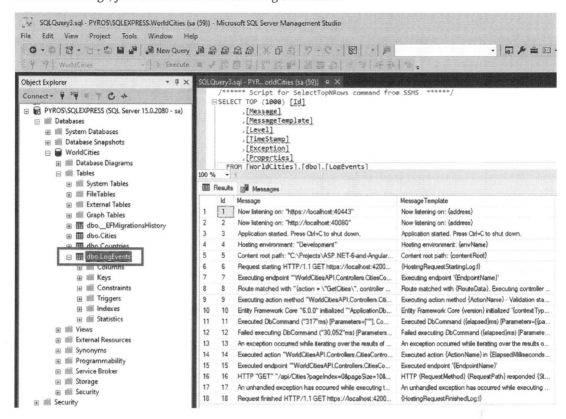

Figure 9.18: Viewing our new LogEvents table

Now we can conveniently access our log in a structured way using SQL queries.

Furthermore, we can use this new feature to log whatever we want using the convenient `Serilog.Log` static entry point provided by the library.

Here's how we can do that from a controller:

```
public class SampleController : Controller
{
    public SampleController()
    {
        Serilog.Log.Information("SampleController initialized.");
    }
}
```

And here's how to call it within a view:

```
@Serilog.Log.Information("SampleView shown to the user");
```

If we don't like the Serilog.Log static entry point, we can still use the standard ILogger interface using *dependency injection* and achieve the same result, since it will also use the new Serilog outputs/sinks.

Here's how to implement the ILogger interface in a controller:

```
using  Microsoft.Extensions.Logging;

[...]

public class SampleController : Controller
{
    public ILogger<SampleController> Logger { get; set; }

    public SampleController(ILogger<SampleController> logger)
    {
        Logger = logger;
        Logger.LogInformation("SampleController initialized.");
    }
}
```

And here's the same approach within a view:

```
@using Microsoft.Extensions.Logging
@inject ILogger<_Views_Dress_Edit> logger

@logger.LogInformation("SampleView shown to the user");
```

The Serilog.Log static entry point is great and provides a lot of additional features; that said, the standard ILogger interface is often the most advisable approach because it will make it easier to connect our app with other MS-based telemetry and monitoring tools (such as Application Insights on MS Azure).

 Those who want to know more about Serilog and all the available settings can check out the following URL: https://serilog.net/.

It's important to understand that we've only scratched the surface of *Serilog* here, just to demonstrate how easy it is to set it up to write logs to a DBMS of our choice; for example, we could've used a different database within the same SQL Server instance—or even a different DBMS engine; we could've modified the default EventLog table name and/or column names, as well as adding additional columns; and so on.

Summary

Throughout this chapter, we talked about a number of debugging features and techniques that can be very useful during development. Let's try to quickly summarize what we've learned so far.

We started our journey with the Visual Studio server-side debugging features. These are a set of run-time debugging features that can be used to prevent most compiler errors on our Web API and allow us to track the whole back-end application life cycle: from the middleware initialization, through to the whole HTTP request/response pipeline, down to the controllers, entities, and IQueryable objects.

Right after that, we moved to the Visual Studio client-side debugging feature. This is a neat JavaScript debugger that, thanks to the source maps created by the TypeScript transpiler, allows us to directly debug our TypeScript classes and access variables, subscriptions, and initializers in a truly efficient way.

Furthermore, we designed and implemented a real-time activity log. This is a quick and effective way to exploit the Reactive features of the various Observables exposed by the Angular modules to keep track of what happens to our components; not to mention the fact that the Visual Studio TypeScript transpiler (and IntelliSense) will hopefully shield us from most syntax, semantic, and logical programming errors, freeing us from the pests of script-based programming, at least for the most part.

Last but not least, we saw how to implement a handy third-party library (*Serilog*) to store our application logs in the database, so that we'll be able to access them in a structured way.

However, what if we want to test our forms against some specific use cases? Is there a way we can mock our back-end ASP.NET Core controllers' behaviors, as well as those of our front-end Angular components, and perform unit tests?

The answer is yes. As a matter of fact, our two frameworks of choice provide various open source testing tools to perform unit tests. In the next chapter, we'll learn how to use them to improve the quality of our code and prevent bugs during refactoring, regression, and new implementation processes.

Suggested topics

For further information, we recommend the following topics: Visual Studio Code, debugger, server-side debugging, client-side debugging, extension methods, C# preprocessor directives, JavaScript source maps, Angular pipes, Observable, Subject, unsubscribe, RxJS operators, async pipe, ILogger, and Serilog.

References

- *Visual Studio Code*: https://code.visualstudio.com/
- *Visual Studio Container Tools with ASP.NET Core*: https://docs.microsoft.com/en-us/aspnet/core/host-and-deploy/docker/visual-studio-tools-for-docker
- *Offroad Debugging of .NET Core on Linux OSX from Visual Studio*: https://github.com/Microsoft/MIEngine/wiki/Offroad-Debugging-of-.NET-Core-on-Linux---OSX-from-Visual-Studio
- *Debug an application using Visual Studio*: https://docs.microsoft.com/en-US/dotnet/core/tutorials/debugging-with-visual-studio?tabs=csharp

- *Extension Methods*: https://docs.microsoft.com/en-us/dotnet/csharp/programming-guide/classes-and-structs/extension-methods

- *Microsoft.EntityFrameworkCore Namespace*: https://docs.microsoft.com/en-us/dotnet/api/microsoft.entityframeworkcore

- *C# Preprocessor Directives*: https://docs.microsoft.com/en-us/dotnet/csharp/language-reference/preprocessor-directives/

- *The #IF preprocessor directive in C#*: https://docs.microsoft.com/en-us/dotnet/csharp/language-reference/preprocessor-directives/preprocessor-if

- *Debug a JavaScript or TypeScript app in Visual Studio*: https://docs.microsoft.com/en-US/visualstudio/javascript/debug-nodejs

- *Introduction to JavaScript Source Maps*: https://www.html5rocks.com/en/tutorials/developertools/sourcemaps/

- *An Introduction to Source Maps*: https://blog.teamtreehouse.com/introduction-source-maps

- *Angular Pipes*: https://angular.io/guide/pipes

- *No need to unsubscribe – RxJS operators will help you out*: https://medium.com/javascript-everyday/no-need-to-unsubscribe-rxjs-operators-will-help-you-out-f8b8ce7bf26a

- *Async Pipe all the Things!*: https://medium.com/@joaqcid/async-pipe-all-the-things-2607a7bc6732

- *Client-side debugging of ASP.NET projects in Google Chrome*: https://blogs.msdn.microsoft.com/webdev/2016/11/21/client-side-debugging-of-asp-net-projects-in-google-chrome/

- *Angular Debugging*: https://blog.angular-university.io/angular-debugging/

- *The best way to unsubscribe RxJS Observables in Angular*: https://medium.com/angular-in-depth/the-best-way-to-unsubscribe-rxjs-observable-in-the-angular-applications-d8f9aa42f6a0

- *Preventing Memory Leaks in Angular Observables with ngOnDestroy*: https://www.twilio.com/blog/prevent-memory-leaks-angular-observable-ngondestroy

- *Serilog*: https://serilog.net

- *Serilog MSSqlServer sink*: https://github.com/serilog/serilog-sinks-mssqlserver

10

ASP.NET Core and Angular Unit Testing

Unit testing is the name given to a method of software testing that helps to determine whether the isolated modules of a program (units) are working correctly. After the various units have been verified, they can be merged together and tested as a whole (integration testing and system testing) and/or released in production.

Given this definition, it's pretty easy to understand the importance of properly defining and isolating the various units. These are the smallest testable parts of our software, featuring a few inputs and a single output. In **Object-Oriented Programming** (OOP), where the program's source code is split into classes, a unit is often a method of a super, abstract, or derived class, yet it can also be a static function of a helper class.

Although they've become a *de facto* standard for high-quality projects, unit tests are often underestimated by most developers and project managers who are eager to speed up the whole development process and therefore reduce its overall cost. As a matter of fact, creating several unit tests alongside development might become a hindrance for small-scale projects with low profit margins, since such an approach undeniably requires some additional work. However, it's very important to understand their huge benefits for medium-to-big projects and enterprise solutions, especially if they require the coordinated effort of a large number of developers.

This chapter is entirely dedicated to unit tests. More precisely, we'll learn how to define, implement, and perform the following:

- **Back-end unit tests in ASP.NET Core**, using the **xUnit.net** testing tool
- **Front-end unit tests in Angular**, using the **Jasmine** testing framework and the **Karma** test runner that we briefly saw in *Chapter 3*, *Looking Around*

We'll also get the opportunity to briefly introduce some widely used testing practices that can help us to get the most out of our tests, such as **Test-Driven Development** (TDD) and **Behavior-Driven Development** (BDD).

By the end of this chapter, we'll have learned how to properly design and implement *back-end* and *front-end* unit tests following these practices.

For the sake of simplicity, we're going to perform our unit test in our existing WorldCities Angular app. However, to do this, we're going to add some new packages to our project.

Technical requirements

In this chapter, we're going to need all of the technical requirements listed in previous chapters, with the following additional packages:

- Microsoft.NET.Test.Sdk
- xunit
- xunit.runner.visualstudio
- Moq
- Microsoft.EntityFrameworkCore.InMemory

As always, it's advisable to avoid installing them straight away. We're going to bring them in during this chapter to better contextualize their purpose within our project.

The code files for this chapter can be found here: https://github.com/PacktPublishing/ASP.NET-Core-6-and-Angular/tree/main/Chapter_10/.

ASP.NET Core unit tests

In this section, we'll learn how to build an ASP.NET Core unit test project using xUnit.net, a free, open-source, community-focused unit testing tool for .NET created by Brad Wilson, who also developed NUnit v2. We've chosen this tool because it's arguably one of the most powerful and easy-to-use unit testing tools available today. It's part of the .NET Foundation, hence operating under their code of conduct, and is licensed under the Apache License, version 2.

Before moving on, we'll also take the opportunity to talk about TDD and BDD in the following sections. These are two widely used testing approaches that have a number of similarities and differences that are worth exploring.

Creating the WorldCitiesAPI.Tests project

The first thing to do is to add a *third* project to our WorldCities solution, which currently hosts the WorldCities Angular app and the WorldCitiesAPI ASP.NET Core Web API.

If you created the solution in a dedicated folder, as we suggested in *Chapter 2, Getting Ready* —leaving the flag **Place solution and project in the same directory** set to OFF—the task is rather easy: just open a command-line prompt, navigate to the solution folder—such as C:/Projects/WorldCities/—and type the following command:

```
> dotnet new xunit -o WorldCitiesAPI.Tests
```

The .NET CLI should create a new project for us and process some post-creation actions. Once done, a message will inform us that the restore task has been completed (**Restore succeeded**). If we have done everything correctly, a new WorldCitiesAPI.Tests project should be present at the same folder level as the existing WorldCities and WorldCitiesAPI projects.

Immediately after this, we can add our new WorldCitiesAPI.Tests project to our main solution in the following way:

1. From **Solution Explorer**, right-click on the root solution's node and select **Add Existing Project**
2. Navigate inside the **/WorldCitiesAPI.Tests/** folder and select the WorldCitiesAPI.Tests.proj file

The new WorldCitiesAPI.Tests project will be loaded in the existing solution, right below the existing WorlCitiesAPI project, as shown in the following screenshot:

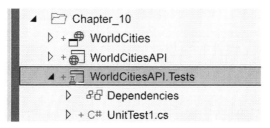

Figure 10.1: The new WorldCitiesAPI.Tests project

 Alternatively, we could add the new project to the solution file directly from the CLI with the following command: dotnet sln add WorldCitiesAPI.Tests.

Let's delete the existing UnitTest1.cs file, since we won't need it. We'll create our own unit testing classes in a short while.

The new WorldCitiesAPI.Tests project should already have the following NuGet package references:

• **Microsoft.NET.Test.Sdk** (version 16.11 or later)
• **xunit** (version 2.4.1 or later)
• **xunit.runner.visualstudio** (version 2.4.3 or later)

 The preceding packages' version numbers are the latest at the time of writing, and the ones that we're going to use in this book.

The first thing to do is to upgrade the `Microsoft.NET.Test.Sdk` package to version **17.0.0** (the latest at the time of writing). Furthermore, we need to install two additional NuGet packages: `Moq` and `Microsoft.EntityFrameworkCore.InMemory`. Let's see what they are meant for and how to add them in the following sections.

Moq

`Moq` is arguably the most popular and friendly mocking framework for .NET. To better understand why we need it, we need to introduce the concept of mocking.

Mocking is a convenient feature that we can use in unit testing whenever the unit that we want to test has external dependencies that cannot be easily created within the testing project. The main purpose of a mocking framework is to create replacement objects that simulate the behavior of real ones. `Moq` is a minimalistic framework that will do just that.

To install it, do the following:

1. From Solution Explorer, right-click on the `WorldCitiesAPI.Tests` project and choose **Manage NuGet Packages**
2. Search for the `Moq` keyword
3. Find and install the `Moq` NuGet package

Alternatively, just type the following command in Visual Studio's Package Manager Console (setting `WorldCitiesAPI.Tests` as the default project):

```
> Install-Package Moq
```

At the time of writing, we're using `Moq` **4.16.1**, this being the latest stable version. To be sure that you are using this version as well, just add `-version 4.16.1` to the preceding command.

The latest `Moq` `NuGet` package, as well as all of the previous versions, are available here: `https://www.nuget.org/packages/moq/`.

That's it! We now need to install another NuGet package.

Microsoft.EntityFrameworkCore.InMemory

`Microsoft.EntityFrameworkCore.InMemory` is an in-memory database provider for Entity Framework Core that can be used for testing purposes. This is basically the same concept as the Angular in-memory Web API that we talked about in *Chapter 5, Data Model with Entity Framework Core*. In a nutshell, we can think of it as a convenient database mock.

To install it, do the following:

1. From Solution Explorer, right-click on the `WorldCitiesAPI.Tests` project and choose **Manage NuGet Packages**
2. Search for the `Microsoft.EntityFrameworkCore.InMemory` keyword

3. Find and install the `Microsoft.EntityFrameworkCore.InMemory` NuGet package

Alternatively, just type the following command in Visual Studio's Package Manager Console:

```
> Install-Package Microsoft.EntityFrameworkCore.InMemory
```

At the time of writing, we're using `Microsoft.EntityFrameworkCore.InMemory 6.0.1`, this being the latest stable version. To be sure that you are using this version as well, just add `-version 6.0.1` to the preceding command.

The latest `Microsoft.EntityFrameworkCore.InMemory` NuGet package, as well as all of the previous versions, are available here: `https://www.nuget.org/packages/Microsoft.EntityFrameworkCore.InMemory/`.

With this we're done with the external packages.

Adding the WorldCities dependency reference

The next thing we need to do is to add a reference to the API project in our new `WorldCitiesAPI.Tests` project's dependencies so that we'll be able to import the required classes and types.

To do that, right-click on the **Dependencies** node of the new project to add a new `Project Reference` to the `WorldCitiesAPI` project, as shown in the following screenshot, and press **OK**:

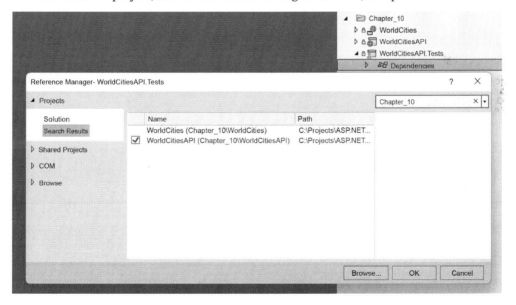

Figure 10.2: Adding a new Project Reference

By doing this, our test project will be able to access (and hence test) the whole `WorldCitiesAPI` code.

We're now ready to learn how `xUnit` actually works. As always, the best way to do this is to create our first unit test.

Our first test

In **Standard Testing Development** practice, which we're going to call **STD** from now on, unit tests are often used to ensure that our existing code is working properly. Once ready, those units will be protected against regression bugs and breaking changes.

Since our *back-end* code is a Web API, the first thing we cover with our unit tests should be the individual controllers' methods. However, instantiating our controllers outside our web application's lifecycle is not that simple, since they have at least two important dependencies: HttpContext and ApplicationDbContext. Is there a way to instantiate them too in our WorldCitiesAPI.Tests project?

Thanks to Microsoft.EntityFrameworkCore.InMemory, this can be a rather easy task... as soon as we understand how to use it.

From Solution Explorer, open the WorldCitiesAPI.Tests project. Create a new CitiesController_Test.cs file in the project's root and fill it with the following content:

```
using Microsoft.EntityFrameworkCore;
using System.Threading.Tasks;
using WorldCitiesAPI.Controllers;
using WorldCitiesAPI.Data;
using WorldCitiesAPI.Data.Models;
using Xunit;

namespace WorldCitiesAPI.Tests
{
    public class CitiesController_Tests
    {
        /// <summary>
        /// Test the GetCity() method
        /// </summary>
        [Fact]
        public async Task GetCity()
        {
            // Arrange
            // todo: define the required assets

            // Act
            // todo: invoke the test

            // Assert
            // todo: verify that conditions are met.
        }
    }
}
```

As we can see by looking at the highlighted comments, we have split the unit test into three code blocks, or phases:

- **Arrange**: Defines the assets required to run the test
- **Act**: Invokes the testing subject's behavior
- **Assert**: Verifies that the expected conditions are met by evaluating the behavior's return value, or measuring it against some user-defined rules

Such an approach is known as the **Arrange, Act, Assert** pattern. This is a typical way to describe the various phases of software testing in TDD. However, there are also alternative names used to describe these same test phases; for example, BDD frameworks usually refer to them as *Given*, *When*, and *Then*.

TDD and BDD are two development practices that enforce a different coding approach when compared to STD. We'll talk more about these soon enough.

Regardless of the names, the important thing here is to understand the following key concepts:

- Separating the three phases increases the readability of the test
- Executing the three phases in the proper order makes the test easier to understand

Let's now take a look at how we have implemented the three phases.

Arrange

The `Arrange` phase is the place where we define the assets required to run the test. In our scenario, since we're going to test the functionality of the `GetCity()` method of `CitiesController`, we need to provide our controller with a suitable `ApplicationDbContext`.

However, since we're not testing `ApplicationDbContext` itself, instantiating the real thing wouldn't be advisable, at least for now. We don't want our test to fail just because the database is unavailable, or the database connection is incorrect, because these are different units and therefore should be checked by different unit tests. Moreover, we definitely can't allow our unit tests to operate against our actual data source: what if we want to test an update or a delete task?

The best thing we can do to test our Web API controllers is to find a way to provide them with a replacement object that can behave just like our real `ApplicationDbContext`; in other words, a mock. This is where the `Microsoft.EntityFrameworkCore.InMemory` NuGet package that we installed earlier on might come in handy.

Here's how we can use it to properly implement the `Arrange` phase:

```
// ...existing code...

// Arrange
var options = new DbContextOptionsBuilder<ApplicationDbContext>()
    .UseInMemoryDatabase(databaseName: "WorldCities")
    .Options;
using var context = new ApplicationDbContext(options);
```

```
context.Add(new City()
{
    Id = 1,
    CountryId = 1,
    Lat = 1,
    Lon = 1,
    Name = "TestCity1"
});
context.SaveChanges();


var controller = new CitiesController(context);
City? city_existing = null;
City? city_notExisting = null;

// ...existing code...
```

As we can see, we've used the UseInMemoryDatabase extension method provided by the Microsoft.
EntityFrameworkCore.InMemory package to create a suitable DbContextOptionsBuilder. Once we
have it, we can use it to instantiate an ApplicationDbContext session with an in-memory database,
instead of the SQL server used by the WorldCities project: it's worth noting that we've instantiated it
using a using statement, so that the ApplicationDbContext will be automatically disposed of at the
end of the test method.

> Starting from C# 8, the using statement can be used without setting an explicit scope, thus
> allowing for a more convenient syntax as we did in the above code. For additional info
> about such a convenient feature, read the official docs at the following URL:
>
> https://docs.microsoft.com/en-us/dotnet/csharp/language-reference/
> keywords/using-statement

Once created, that context can be populated by creating new cities, which is what we did in the preceding code, creating TestCity1 with some random data. This will allow our GetCity() method of
CitiesController to actually retrieve something, provided that we pass a city id.

Other than that, we have created a CitiesController instance using the *in-memory* context and defined two City objects that will contain the two specimens for this test.

Act

The Act phase is where the test takes place. It often consists of a single instruction that corresponds
to the behavior of the unit that we want to check.

Here's the Act phase implementation:

```
// ...existing code...
```

```
// Act
city_existing = (await controller.GetCity(1)).Value;
city_notExisting = (await controller.GetCity(2)).Value;

// ...existing code...
```

The above code is quite self-explanatory. We are using the previously created `controller` instance to execute the `GetCity()` method two times:

- The first occasion is to retrieve an existing city (using the same `Id` that we used to populate our in-memory database)
- The second occasion is to retrieve a non-existing city (using a different `Id`)

The two return values are then stored in the `city_existing` and `city_notExisting` variables. Ideally, the first one should contain `TestCity1`, which we created in the `Arrange` phase, while the latter should be `null`.

Assert

The purpose of the `Assert` phase is to verify that the conditions that we expect are properly met by the values retrieved by the `Act` phase. To do this, we'll make use of the `Assert` class provided by **xUnit**, which contains various static methods that can be used to verify that these conditions are met.

Here's the `Assert` phase implementation:

```
// ...existing code...

// Assert
Assert.NotNull(city_existing);
Assert.Null(city_notExisting);

// ...existing code...
```

As we can see, we're just checking the values of the two variables that contain the return values of the two `GetCity()` method calls of `CitiesController` made in the `Act` phase. We reasonably expect `city_existing` not to be null, while `city_notExisting` should definitely be `null`.

Our test is now ready, so let's see how we can execute it.

Executing the test

Each unit test can be executed in two ways:

- **From the command line**, using the .NET CLI
- **From the Visual Studio GUI**, using Visual Studio's built-in test runner (Test Explorer)

Let's quickly try both of these approaches.

Using the CLI

To execute our test unit(s) by using the .NET CLI, perform the following steps:

1. Open Command Prompt
2. Navigate to the `WorldCitiesAPI.Tests` project root folder
3. Execute the following command:

```
> dotnet test
```

If we have done everything correctly, we should see something like this:

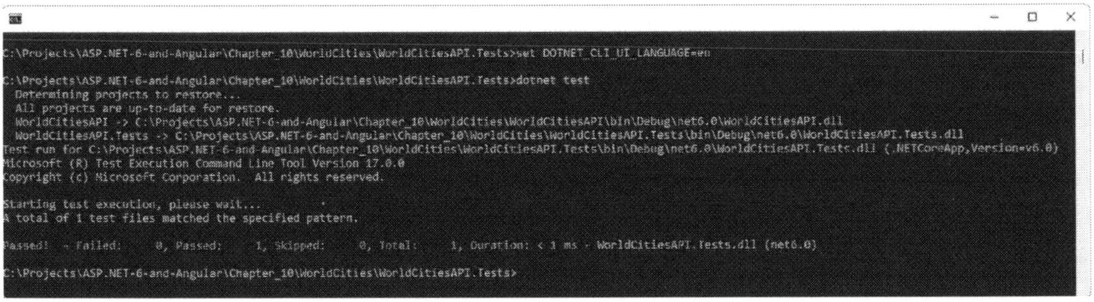

Figure 10.3: Command Prompt output after executing the test

That's it. Our test is working and it passes, meaning that the `GetCity()` method of `CitiesController` is behaving as expected.

Using the Visual Studio Test Explorer

Being able to run our tests from the command line can be a great feature if we want to automate these kinds of tasks. However, in most cases, we'll instead want to be able to run these tests directly from within the Visual Studio GUI.

Luckily enough, this is definitely possible thanks to the Test Explorer window, which can be activated by pressing *Ctrl* + *E*, *T*, or from **Menu** | **View**, as shown in the following screenshot:

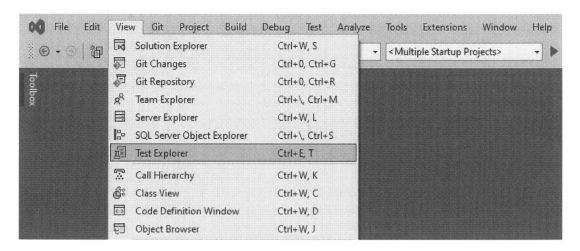

Figure 10.4: Navigating to Test Explorer in Visual Studio

Once activated, the **Test Explorer** window should appear, either undocked in the middle of the screen or in the rightmost part of the Visual Studio GUI, just below the **Solution Explorer** window. From there, we can either run all tests or just the current test by pressing the first two green *play* icons placed in the top-left part of the panel, called **Run All** and **Run**, respectively (refer to the following screenshot):

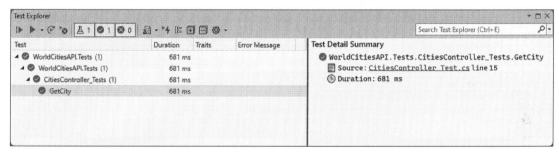

Figure 10.5: The Test Explorer window

Since we only have a single test, for now, either command will do the same thing: run our unit test and show the results using either a green check (success) or a red cross (failure).

As we can see in the preceding screenshot, those green and/or red icons will be used to determine the combined results of the testing class, the namespace, and the whole assembly.

Before moving further, we should spend another couple of minutes learning how to debug these unit tests.

Debugging tests

If we click on the *arrow handle* next to the second *Run* icon in the top-left part of the **Test Explorer** window, we can see that there are a number of other possible commands we can give to our tests, including **Debug**, **Debug All Tests In View**, and **Debug Last Run** (refer to the following screenshot):

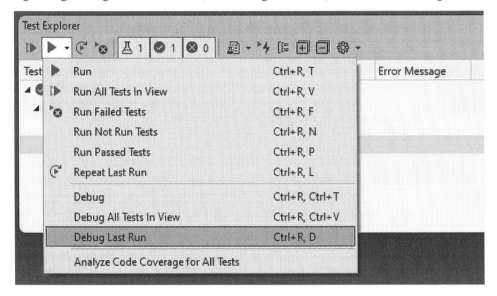

Figure 10.6: Viewing the test run and debug options

Alternatively, we can use the **Debug Tests** command that is shown when we right-click on the `WorldCitiesAPI.Tests` project node from the **Solution Explorer** window:

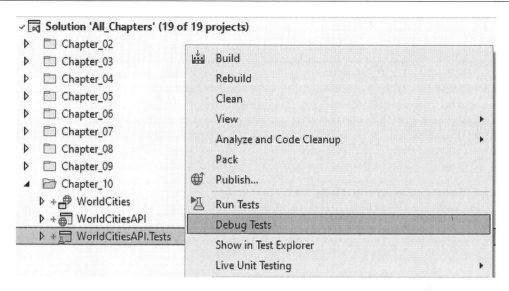

Figure 10.7: Viewing the Debug Tests option

Both commands will execute our test in debug mode, meaning that we can set breakpoints (or conditional breakpoints) and evaluate the results.

To quickly test it, set a breakpoint on the first line of the Assert region, then execute the preceding **Debug Tests** command, and wait for the hit:

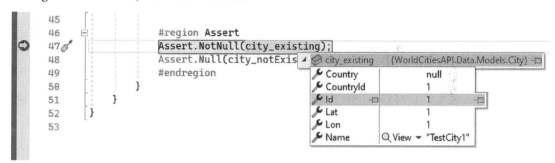

Figure 10.8: Hitting the breakpoint

There we go. Now, we know how to debug our unit tests. This can be very useful during the adoption phase when we still don't know how to properly use them and/or we're still learning the various xUnit. net commands.

Those readers who want to know more about xUnit.net for .NET and the unique unit test classes and methods provided by this package are strongly encouraged to check out the following URL: https://xunit.net/docs/getting-started/netcore/cmdline.

Before switching to the *front-end*, it is worth spending a couple of minutes familiarizing ourselves with the concepts of TDD and BDD, since this is something that could greatly help us to create useful and relevant tests.

Test-driven development

TDD is more of a programming practice than a testing approach, and it can be a very good practice, at least for certain scenarios.

In a nutshell, a software developer that adopts the TDD methodology will convert all of the software requirements into specific test cases, and then write the new code, or improve the existing code, so that the tests will pass.

Let's try to visualize the actual life cycle of these programming practices with the help of a small diagram:

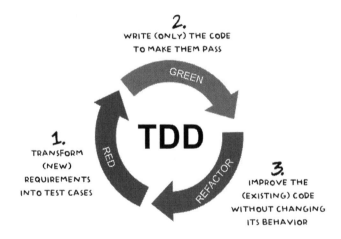

Figure 10.9: Test-driven development life cycle

As we can see, TDD is mostly a way of designing the code that requires developers to **start writing test cases that express what they intend the code to do before writing any actual code (RED)**. Once done, it asks them to **only write the code required to make the test cases pass (GREEN)**.

Eventually, **when all of the test cases pass, the existing code can be improved (REFACTOR)**, until more test cases appear. This short development cycle is conventionally called **RED-GREEN-REFACTOR** and is the backbone of the TDD practice. It's worth noting that **RED** is always the initial step of any cycle since the tests will always fail at the start because the code that could allow them to pass is yet to be written.

Such a practice is very different from the STD practice, where we first generate the code and then (maybe) the tests. In other words, our source code can be (and therefore usually is) written before (or even without) test cases. The main difference between the two approaches is that, in TDD, tests are the requirement conditions that we need to fulfill, while in STD, as we have already said a short while ago, they are mostly the proof that our existing code is working.

In the next chapter, when dealing with authentication and authorization, we'll try to create a couple of *back-end* unit tests using the TDD approach; after all, since the TDD practice requires the creation of test cases only when we have to implement additional requirements, the best way to use it is when we have some new features to add.

Behavior-driven development

BDD is an Agile software development process that shares the same test-first approach as TDD but **emphasizes results from the end-user's perspective instead of focusing on implementation.**

To better understand the key differences between TDD and BDD, we can ask ourselves the following question:

What are we testing for?

That's a great question to ask when we're about to write some unit tests.

If we want to test the actual implementation of our methods/units, TDD might be the proper way to go. However, if we aim to figure out the end-user behavior of our application under specific circumstances, TDD might give us false positives, especially if the system evolves (as Agile-driven projects often do). More specifically, we could encounter a scenario where one or more units are passing their tests despite failing to deliver the expected end-user outcome.

In more general terms, we can say the following:

- TDD is meant to **enforce developers' control over the source code they write**
- BDD aims to **satisfy both the developer** *and* **the end-user** (or customer)

Therefore, we can easily see how BDD supersedes TDD instead of replacing it.

Let's try to wrap up these concepts in a diagram:

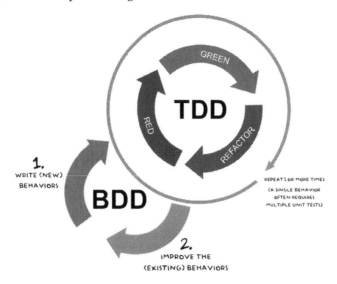

Figure 10.10: Behavior-driven development life cycle

As we can see, BDD acts just like an extension to TDD. Instead of writing the test cases, we start by writing a behavior. As soon as we do that, we will develop the required code for our application to be able to perform it (arguably using TDD), and then move on to define additional behaviors or refactor existing ones.

Since these behaviors are aimed at the end-user, they must also be written using understandable terms. For that very reason, BDD tests are usually defined using a semi-formal format that is borrowed from Agile's user stories, with a strong narrative and explicit contextualization. These user stories are generally meant to comply with the following structure:

- **Title**: An explicit title, such as *Editing an Existing City*
- **Narrative**: A descriptive section that uses the *Role / Feature / Benefit* pattern from Agile user stories, such as *As a user, I want to edit an existing City, so that I can change its values*
- **Acceptance criteria**: A description of the three test phases, using the *Given / When / Then* model, which is basically a more understandable version of the *Arrange / Act / Assert* cycle used in TDD, such as **Given** *a world cities database containing one or more cities*; **When** *the user selects a City*; **Then** *the app must retrieve it from the DB and display it on the front-end*

As we can see, we just tried to describe the unit test we created a while ago using a typical BDD approach. Although it mostly works, it's evident that a single behavior might require multiple *back-end* and *front-end* unit tests. This lets us understand another distinctive feature of the BDD practice. Emphasizing the utmost importance of the *front-end* testing phase is the best way to test user behavior rather than an implementation spec.

All in all, BDD can be a great way to extend a standard TDD approach to design our tests in a way that means their results can address a wider audience—provided we're able to properly design not only the required *back-end* test (using ASP.NET Core) but also the *front-end* tests (using Angular).

In this section, we've learned how to handle the *back-end* part of the story; in the next section, we're going to expand our knowledge to the *front-end*.

Angular unit tests

Luckily enough, this time, we won't need to install anything since the ASP.NET Core and Angular Visual Studio template that we've used to create our WorldCities project already contains everything we need to write app tests for our Angular application.

More specifically, we can already count on the following packages, which we briefly introduced in *Chapter 3*, *Looking Around*:

- **Jasmine:** A JavaScript testing framework that fully supports the BDD approach that we talked about earlier
- **Karma:** A tool that lets us spawn browsers and run our Jasmine tests inside them (and show their results) from the command line
- **Protractor:** An end-to-end test framework that runs tests against Angular applications from within a real browser, interacting with it as if it were a real user

 For additional information regarding Jasmine and Karma, check out the following guides:

Karma: https://karma-runner.github.io/

Jasmine: https://jasmine.github.io/

Protractor: https://www.protractortest.org/

Angular unit test: https://angular.io/guide/testing

In the following sections, we're going to do the following:

- **Review the testing configuration files** still present in our WorldCities Angular app
- **Introduce the TestBed interface,** one of the most important concepts of Angular testing
- **Explore Jasmine and Karma** to understand how they actually work
- **Create some .spec.ts files** to test our existing components
- **Set up and configure some tests** for our Angular app

Let's get started!

General concepts

In contrast to what we did in ASP.NET Core, where we created our unit tests in separate WorldCitiesAPI. Tests projects, all our *front-end* tests will be written in the same project that hosts our Angular app.

As a matter of fact, we've already seen one of these tests in *Chapter 3, Looking Around*, when we explored the /src/app/ Angular folder of our **HealthCheck** app for the first time. The test was written in the app.component.spec.ts file, and we played with it just before refactoring that component.

Now we've switched to the **WorldCities** app, however we should still have the following test-related files in our Angular project:

- /karma.conf.js: The application-specific Karma configuration file, containing information about the reporters, the browser to use, the TCP port, and so on
- /src/test.ts: The Angular entry point for the project's unit test; this is where Angular initializes the testing environment, configures the .spec.ts extensions to identify the test files, and loads the required modules from the @angular/core/testing and @angular/platform-browser-dynamic/testing packages

Since we've created all our components using the Angular CLI's ng generate command with the --skip-tests option, we should only have a single .spec.ts file in our Angular project: the app. component.spec.ts file. This means that if we want to create some tests for our components, we need to manually create them.

However, before doing that, it would be wise to spend a bit longer explaining how Angular testing actually works.

Introducing the TestBed interface

The **TestBed** interface is one of the most important concepts of the Angular testing approach. In a nutshell, TestBed is a dynamically constructed Angular test module that emulates the behavior of an Angular @NgModule.

The TestBed concept was first introduced with Angular 2 as a convenient way to test a component with a real DOM behind it. The TestBed interface significantly assists in this regard thanks to its support for injecting services (either real or mock) into our components, as well as automatically binding components and templates.

To better understand how TestBed actually works and how we can use it, let's take a look at the TestBed implementation of the app.component.spec.ts file that we modified back in *Chapter 3, Looking Around*:

```
await TestBed.configureTestingModule({
  imports: [
    HttpClientTestingModule
  ],
  declarations: [
    AppComponent
  ],
}).compileComponents();
```

In the preceding code, we can see how TestBed reproduces the behavior of a minimalistic `AppModule` file—the bootstrap `@NgModule` of an Angular app—with the sole purpose of compiling the components that we need to test: more specifically, it uses the Angular module system to declare and compile the `AppComponent` so that we can use its source code in our tests.

Testing with Jasmine

Jasmine tests are usually constructed using the following three main APIs:

- `describe()`: A wrapping context used to create a group of tests (also called a *test suite*)
- `it()`: The declaration of a single test
- `expect()`: The expected result of a test

These APIs are already available within the `*.spec.ts` files generated by the Angular CLI, thanks to the built-in Angular integration with the Jasmine testing framework: if we quickly check our `app.component.spec.ts` file, we can easily confirm that.

Keeping this in mind, let's create our first testing class file for our Angular app.

Our first Angular test suite

Let's now create our own test suite, and a corresponding TestBed, for one of our existing Angular components. We'll use `CitiesComponent` since we know it very well.

> Unfortunately, the Angular CLI doesn't (yet) provide a way to automatically generate `spec.ts` files for existing component classes. However, there are a number of third-party libraries that generate specs based on Angular CLI spec presets.
>
> The most popular (and widely used) package that does that is called `ngx-spec` and is available on GitHub at the following URL: `https://github.com/smnbbrv/ngx-spec`.
>
> However, we're not going to use it in our specific scenario: we'll create and implement our `spec.ts` files manually so that we can better understand how they work.

From **Solution Explorer**, create a new `/src/app/cities/cities.component.spec.ts` file and open it. Since we're going to write a fair amount of source code, it would be wise to separate it into multiple blocks.

The import section

Let's start by defining the required `import` statements:

```
import { ComponentFixture, TestBed } from '@angular/core/testing';
import { BrowserAnimationsModule } from '@angular/platform-browser/animations';
import { AngularMaterialModule } from '../angular-material.module';
import { RouterTestingModule } from '@angular/router/testing';
import { of } from 'rxjs';
```

```
import { CitiesComponent } from './cities.component';
import { City } from './city';
import { CityService } from './city.service';
import { ApiResult } from '../base.service';

// ... to be continued ...
```

As we can see, we added a bunch of modules that we already used in our `AppModule` and `CitiesComponent` classes. This is certainly anticipated since our TestBed will need to reproduce a suitable `@NgModule` for our tests to run.

The describe and beforeEach sections

Now that we have got all of our required references, let's see how we can use the `describe()` API to lay out our testing suite:

```
// ...existing code...

describe('CitiesComponent', () => {
  let component: CitiesComponent;
  let fixture: ComponentFixture<CitiesComponent>;

  beforeEach(async () => {

    // TODO: declare & initialize required providers

    await TestBed.configureTestingModule({
      declarations: [CitiesComponent],
      imports: [
        BrowserAnimationsModule,
        AngularMaterialModule,
        RouterTestingModule
      ],
      providers: [

        // TODO: reference required providers

      ]
    })
    .compileComponents();
  });
```

```
  beforeEach(() => {
    fixture = TestBed.createComponent(CitiesComponent);
    component = fixture.componentInstance;

    // TODO: configure fixture/component/children/etc.

    fixture.detectChanges();
  });

  it('should create', () => {
    expect(component).toBeTruthy();
  });

  // TODO: implement some other tests

});
```

As we can see by looking at the preceding code, everything happens within a single `describe()` wrapping context, which represents our `CitiesComponent` test suite. All of the tests related to our `CitiesComponent` class will be implemented inside this suite.

 It's worth noting that the above `cities.component.spec.ts` source code is almost identical to the one generated by the Angular CLI when running the `ng generate component` command without using the `--skip-tests` option: such boilerplate is a great way to start writing tests, since it already contains the TestBed, the component references, and a basic sample test.

The first thing we have done in the test suite is defined two important variables that will play a pivotal role in all tests:

- `fixture`: This property hosts a fixed state of `CitiesComponent` for running tests; we can use this fixture to interact with the instantiated component and its child elements
- `component`: This property contains the `CitiesComponent` instance created from the preceding fixture

Immediately after this we have two consecutive `beforeEach()` method calls:

- An asynchronous `beforeEach()`, where TestBed is created and initialized
- A synchronous `beforeEach()`, where fixtures and components are instantiated and configured

Inside the first (asynchronous) beforeEach() we have defined a TestBed for our CitiesComponent, which imports the required modules for the tests we want to add: BrowserAnimationModule, AngularMaterialModule, and RouterTestingModule. As we can see from the two *todo* comments we've placed here, this is also the place where we're going to declare, initialize, and reference our providers (such as CityService), otherwise, CitiesComponent won't be able to inject them; we'll do that in a short while.

Inside the second (synchronous) beforeEach(), we have instantiated our fixture and component variables. Since we'll likely have to properly set them up and / or configure some of our component's child elements, we've left a third *todo* comment there as well.

At the end of the file we can find our first test, which basically checks that the component has been created without errors: such a test mimics the "default" test created by the Angular CLI when using the ng generate component command without the --skip-tests option.

That first test is followed by a fourth *todo* comment: this is where we'll get to implement our additional tests using the it() and expect() APIs provided by the Jasmine framework.

Adding a mock CityService

Now, we're going to replace our first and second *todos* by implementing a *mock* CityService so that we can reference it within our TestBed.

 As we already know from back-end testing using .NET and xUnit, a mock is a replacement object that simulates the behavior of a real one.

Just like ASP.NET Core and xUnit, Jasmine provides multiple ways to set up mock objects. In the following sections, we'll briefly review some of the most frequently used approaches.

Fake service class

We can create a fake CityService, which just returns whatever we want for our test. Once done, we can import it in the .spec.ts class and add it to TestBed's providers list so that it will be called by our component just like the real one.

Extending and overriding

Instead of creating a whole double class, we can just extend the real service and then override the methods we need in order to perform our tests. Once done, we can set up an instance of the extended class in our TestBed using @NgModule's useValue feature.

Interface instance

Instead of creating a new double or extended class, we can just instantiate the interface of our service, implementing just the method that we need for our tests. Once done, we can set up that instance in our TestBed using @NgModule's useValue feature.

Spy

This approach relies upon a Jasmine-specific feature called a *spy*, which lets us take an existing class, function, or object and mock it so that we can control its return values. Since the real method won't be executed, a spy method will work just like an override, without having to create an extended class.

We can use such a feature to create a real instance of our service, spy the method that we want to override, and then set up that specific instance in our TestBed using @NgModule's useValue feature. Alternatively, we can use the jasmine.createSpyObj() static function to create a mock object with multiple spy methods that we can then configure in various ways.

Implementing the mock CityService

Which route should we take? Unfortunately, there's no one best answer for all scenarios, since the best approach often depends on the complexity of the features we want to test and/or how we want to structure our test suite.

Theoretically speaking, creating a whole **fake service class** is arguably the safest and most versatile choice since we can fully customize our mock service return values. However, it can also be time-consuming and often unnecessary, when we're dealing with simple services and/or small-scale tests. Conversely, the **extend and override**, **interface**, and **spy** approaches are often a great way to address the basic requirements of most tests, yet they might give unexpected results in complex testing scenarios, unless we pay close attention to overriding/spying all of the required methods.

Everything considered, since our CityService is quite small and features a simple implementation with a small number of methods, we're going to use the spy approach, which seems to be the aptest for our given scenario.

Let's go back to the /src/cities/cities.components.spec.ts file. Once there, the following line of code needs to be replaced:

```
// TODO: declare & initialize required providers
```

The preceding line of code has to be replaced with the following code:

```
// Create a mock cityService object with a mock 'getData' method
let cityService = jasmine.createSpyObj<CityService>('CityService',
['getData']);

// Configure the 'getData' spy method
cityService.getData.and.returnValue(
  // return an Observable with some test data
  of<ApiResult<City>>(<ApiResult<City>>{
    data: [
      <City>{
        name: 'TestCity1',
        id: 1, lat: 1, lon: 1,
```

```
      countryId: 1, countryName: 'TestCountry1'
    },
    <City>{
      name: 'TestCity2',
      id: 2, lat: 1, lon: 1,
      countryId: 1, countryName: 'TestCountry1'
    },
    <City>{
      name: 'TestCity3',
      id: 3, lat: 1, lon: 1,
      countryId: 1, countryName: 'TestCountry1'
    }
  ],
  totalCount: 3,
  pageIndex: 0,
  pageSize: 10
}));
```

That's it. Now, we can add our new mock `CityService` to the TestBed configuration, replacing the second *todo*:

```
// TODO: reference required providers
```

This is replaced with the highlighted lines of the following code:

```
// ...existing code...

await TestBed.configureTestingModule({
  declarations: [CitiesComponent],
  imports: [
    BrowserAnimationsModule,
    AngularMaterialModule,
    RouterTestingModule
  ],
  providers: [
    {
      provide: CityService,
      useValue: cityService
    }
  ]
})
  .compileComponents();
```

```
// ...existing code...
```

That mock `CityService` will now be injected into `CitiesComponent`, thereby making us able to control the data returned for each test.

Alternative implementation using the interface approach

Here's how we could have implemented the mock `CityService` using the interface approach:

```
// Create a mock cityService object with a mock 'getData' method
let cityService = <CityService>{
  put: (): Observable<City>  => { /* todo */ },
  post: (): Observable<City> => { /* todo */ },
  // todo
};
```

As we can see, implementing the interface would require a lot of additional code if we want to maintain the `<CityService>` type assertion. That's why we've used the **spy** approach instead.

Configuring the fixture and the component

It's now time to remove the third *todo* in our `/src/cities/cities.components.spec.ts` class:

```
// todo: configure fixture/component/children/etc.
```

This needs to be replaced with the following highlighted lines:

```
// ...existing code...

beforeEach(() => {
    fixture = TestBed.createComponent(CitiesComponent);
    component = fixture.componentInstance;

    component.paginator = jasmine.createSpyObj(
      "MatPaginator", ["length", "pageIndex", "pageSize"]
    );

    fixture.detectChanges();
  });

// ...existing code...
```

The preceding code will perform the following steps directly before each test:

- Create a mock `MatPaginator` object instance
- Trigger a change detection run on our component

As we might easily surmise, change detection isn't done automatically there: it must be triggered by calling the detectChanges method on our **fixture**. Such a call will make our ngOnInit() method fire and populate the table with the cities. Since we're testing the component behavior, that's definitely something to do before running our tests.

Now we're finally ready to create our first test.

Creating the title test

The last remaining *todo* line in our /src/cities/cities.components.spec.ts class needs to be replaced:

```
// TODO: implement some other tests
```

The preceding line of code needs to be replaced as follows:

```
it('should display a "Cities" title', () => {
  let title = fixture.nativeElement
    .querySelector('h1');
  expect(title.textContent).toEqual('Cities');
});
```

As we can see, we're finally using the it() and expect() Jasmine methods. The former declares the meaning of our test, while the latter evaluates the component's behavior against the expected one and determines the test result.

In this first test, we want to check that the component displays a Cities title to the user. Since we know that our component's template holds the title inside an <H1> HTML element, we can check it by performing a DOM query against fixture.nativeElement, the root component element that contains all of the rendered HTML content.

Once we get the title element, we check its textContent property to see whether it's what we expect (Cities). This is what will make the test pass or fail.

Creating the cities tests

Before running our test suite, let's add another test.

Open the /src/cities/cities.components.spec.ts file again and add the following lines right below the previous test:

```
// ...existing code...

it('should contain a table with a list of one or more cities', () => {
  let table = fixture.nativeElement
    .querySelector('table.mat-table');
  let tableRows = table
    .querySelectorAll('tr.mat-row');
```

```
    expect(tableRows.length).toBeGreaterThan(0);
});


// ...existing code...
```

This time, we're checking the table that contains the list of cities. More precisely, we're counting the table body rows to ensure that the resulting number is greater than zero, meaning that the table has been filled with at least one city. To perform such a count, we're using the CSS classes that Angular Material assigns to its `MatTable` component by default.

To better understand this, take a look at the following screenshot:

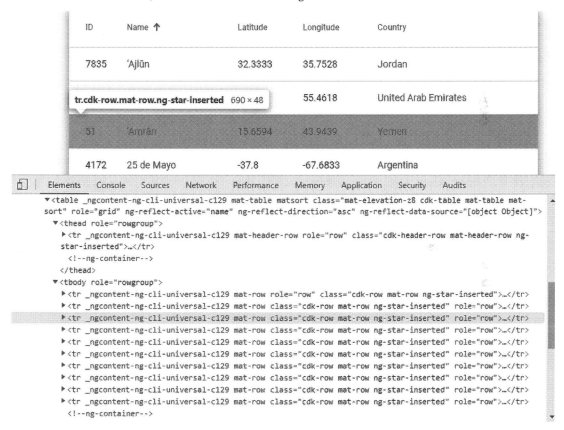

Figure 10.11: Inspecting rows of our Cities list

As we can see, the `mat-row` CSS class is only applied to the table body rows, while the table header rows have the `mat-header-row` class. Therefore, if the test passes, it definitely means that the component created at least one row within the table.

It goes without saying that relying upon CSS classes applied by a third-party package to define our tests is not a good practice. We're doing this just to demonstrate what we can do with our current implementation. A safer approach for such DOM-based tests would arguably require defining custom CSS classes and checking for their presence instead.

Running the test suite

It's now time to run our test suite and see what we've got.

To do this, perform the following steps:

1. Open Command Prompt
2. Navigate to the root folder of the `WorldCities` Angular project
3. Execute the following command:

```
> ng test
```

This will launch the Karma test runner, which will open a dedicated browser to run the tests in. If we have done everything correctly, we should be able to see the following results:

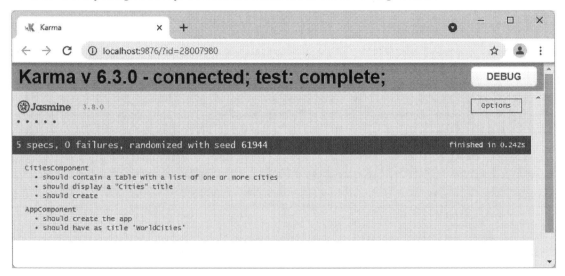

Figure 10.12: Results of our test

That's it; all three tests designed for `CitiesComponent` have passed. To be 100% certain that we did everything properly, let's now try to make them fail.

Open the `/src/cities/cities.components.spec.ts` file again and modify the test's source code in the following way (the updated lines are highlighted):

```
it('should display a "Cities" title', () => {
  let title = fixture.nativeElement
    .querySelector('h1');
  expect(title.textContent).toEqual('Cities!!!');
});

it('should contain a table with a list of one or more cities', () => {
  let table = fixture.nativeElement
    .querySelector('table.mat-table');
```

```
   let tableRows = table
     .querySelectorAll('tr.mat-row');
   expect(tableRows.length).toBeGreaterThan(3);
 });
```

Now, our first test will expect an incorrect title value, and the second is looking for more than three rows, which won't be the case since our mock `CityService` has been configured to serve three of them.

As soon as we save the file, the Karma test runner should automatically reload the testing page and show the updated results (refer to the following screenshot):

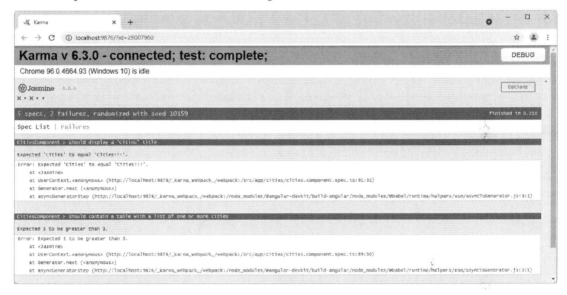

Figure 10.13: Results showing the test has failed

There we go. Now, we are experiencing two failures, just as expected. The Jasmine framework is also telling us what's wrong so that we can address the issues promptly.

Let's do this. Open the `/src/cities/cities.components.spec.ts` file and revert the test's source code back to how it was before:

```
it('should display a "Cities" title', () => {
  let title = fixture.nativeElement
    .querySelector('h1');
  expect(title.textContent).toEqual('Cities');
});


it('should contain a table with a list of one or more cities', () => {
  let table = fixture.nativeElement
    .querySelector('table.mat-table');
  let tableRows = table
```

```
    .querySelectorAll('tr.mat-row');
  expect(tableRows.length).toBeGreaterThan(0);
});
```

That's it. Now that we have *tested* our test suite, we can close the test runner by pressing *Ctrl* + *C* on the ng test terminal window and then choosing *Y* (and hitting *Enter*) to terminate the batch job.

With this, we've concluded our learning journey through *front-end* testing.

Summary

This chapter was entirely dedicated to the concepts of testing and unit testing. After a brief introduction, where we explained the meaning of these concepts and the various testing practices available, we spent some valuable time learning how to implement them properly.

We started focusing on *back-end* testing with the help of the xUnit.net testing tool. Such an approach required us to create a new test project, where we implemented our first *back-end* unit tests. While working at it, we learned the importance of some test-related concepts, such as mocking, which we used to emulate the behavior of our ApplicationDbContext class to provide some in-memory data instead of using our SQL Server data source.

The *back-end* testing approach greatly helped us to understand the meaning of TDD and its similarities and differences vis-à-vis the BDD approach, which is a distinctive *front-end* testing practice.

Such a comparison guided us to Angular, where we used the **Jasmine** testing framework and the **Karma** test runner to develop some *front-end* tests. Here, we got the opportunity to learn some good testing practices as well as other important concepts strictly related to the Jasmine framework, such as Test-Bed, test suites, and spies. Eventually, we successfully saw our tests in action in our WorldCities app.

In the next chapter, we'll try to design some more tests when dealing with the authorization and authentication topics. The concepts that we learned here will definitely be very useful when having to implement the registration and login workflows.

Suggested topics

For further information, we recommend the following topics: Unit Testing, xUnit, Moq, TDD, BDD, Mock, Stub, Fixture, Jasmine, Karma, Protractor, Spy, test suite, TestBed.

References

- *Getting Started with xUnit.net*: https://xunit.net/docs/getting-started/netcore/cmdline
- *Unit testing in .NET*: https://docs.microsoft.com/en-US/dotnet/core/testing/
- *Unit test controller logic in ASP.NET Core*: https://docs.microsoft.com/en-us/aspnet/core/mvc/controllers/testing
- *The using statement (C#)*: https://docs.microsoft.com/en-US/dotnet/csharp/language-reference/keywords/using-statement

- *xUnit.net – Using ASP.NET Core with the .NET SDK command line*: `https://xunit.net/docs/getting-started/netcore/cmdline`
- *Angular – Testing*: `https://angular.io/guide/testing`
- *Protractor: End-to-end testing for Angular*: `https://www.protractortest.org/`
- *Jasmine: Behavior-Driven JavaScript*: `https://jasmine.github.io/`
- *Karma: Spectacular Test Runner for JavaScript*: `https://karma-runner.github.io/latest/index.html`
- *Angular Testing: ComponentFixture*: `https://angular.io/api/core/testing/ComponentFixture`
- *Angular References: ngAfterViewInit*: `https://ngrefs.com/latest/core/ng-after-view-init`

11

Authentication and Authorization

Generally speaking, the term *authentication* refers to any process of verification that determines whether someone, be it a human being or an automated system, is who (or what) they claim to be. This is also true within the context of the **World Wide Web** (**WWW**), where that same word is mostly used to denote any technique used by a website or service to collect a set of login information from a user agent, typically a web browser, and authenticate them using a membership and/or identity service.

Authentication should never be confused with *authorization*, as this is a different process and is in charge of a very different task. To give a quick definition, we can say that the purpose of authorization is to confirm that the requesting user is allowed to have access to the action they want to perform. In other words, while authentication is about who they are, authorization is about what they're allowed to do.

To better understand the difference between these two, apparently, similar concepts, we can think of two real-world scenarios:

1. A free, yet registered, account trying to gain access to a paid or premium-only service or feature. This is a common example of authenticated, yet not authorized, access; we know who they are, yet they're not allowed to go there.

2. An anonymous user trying to gain access to a publicly available page or file; this is an example of non-authenticated, yet authorized, access; we don't know who they are, yet they can access public resources just like everyone else.

Authentication and authorization will be the main topics of this chapter, which we'll try to address from both theoretical and practical points of view, as well as showing some possible implementation approaches, for demonstration purposes only.

More precisely, we're going to talk about the following topics:

- **To auth, or not to auth?** Here, we discuss some typical scenarios where authentication and authorization could either be required or not, ensuring we properly understand the meaning of such terms and how they can be implemented in a typical web application context.

- **Proprietary auth with .NET Core.** Introduces ASP.NET Core Identity, a modern membership system that allows developers to add login functionality to their applications, as well as JwtBearerMiddleware, a middleware designed to add **JWT authentication** support to any ASP.NET Core application; furthermore, we'll implement *ASP.NET Core Identity* and *JwtBearerMiddleware* to add login functionalities to our existing *WorldCities* app.

- **Updating the Database.** Focuses on updating our existing WorldCities database to create the auth-related tables and add a couple of test users to test the login.

- **Implementing authentication in Angular.** This is where we'll refactor our Angular app to make it able to interact with the ASP.NET Core Identity system, introducing some new Angular features, such as *HTTP interceptors* and *Route Guards*, that will handle the whole authentication and authorization flow.

Let's do our best!

Technical requirements

In this chapter, we're going to need all the technical requirements listed in the previous chapters, with the following additional packages:

- Microsoft.AspNetCore.Identity.EntityFrameworkCore
- Microsoft.AspNetCore.Authentication.JwtBearer

As always, it's advisable to avoid installing them straight away; we're going to bring them in during the chapter to better contextualize their purposes within our project.

The code files for this chapter can be found at https://github.com/PacktPublishing/ASP.NET-Core-6-and-Angular/tree/master/Chapter_11/.

To auth, or not to auth

As a matter of fact, implementing authentication and/or authorization logic isn't mandatory for most web-based applications or services; there are a number of websites that still don't do that, mostly because they serve content that can be accessed by anyone at any time. This used to be pretty common among most corporate, marketing, and informative websites until some years ago; that was before their owners learned how important it is to build a network of registered users and how much these "loyal" contacts are worth nowadays.

We don't need to be experienced developers to acknowledge how much the WWW has changed in the last few years; each and every website, regardless of its purpose, has an increasing and more or less legitimate interest in tracking its users nowadays, giving users the chance to customize their navigation experience, interact with their social networks, collect email addresses, and so on. None of the preceding can be done without an authentication mechanism of some sort.

There are billions of websites and services that require authentication to work properly, as most of their content and/or intentions depend upon the actions of registered users: forums, blogs, shopping carts, subscription-based services, and even collaborative tools such as wikis.

Long story short, the answer is yes; as long as we want to have users performing **Create, Read, Update, and Delete (CRUD)** operations within our client app, there is no doubt that we should implement some kind of authentication and authorization procedure. If we're aiming for a production-ready **Single-Page Application (SPA)** featuring some user interactions of any kind, we definitely want to know who our users are in terms of names and email addresses. It is the only way to determine who will be able to view, add, update, or delete our records, not to mention perform administrative-level tasks, keep track of our users, and so on.

Authentication

Since the origin of the WWW, the vast majority of authentication techniques rely upon **HTTP/HTTPS implementation standards**, and all of them work more or less in the following way:

1. A non-authenticated user agent asks for content that cannot be accessed without some kind of permission.
2. The web application returns an authentication request, usually in the form of an HTML page containing an empty web form to complete.
3. The user agent fills in the web form with their credentials, usually a username and a password, and then sends it back with a POST command, which is most likely issued by a click on a **Submit** button.
4. The web application receives the POST data and calls the aforementioned server-side implementation, which will try to authenticate the user with the given input and return an appropriate result.
5. If the result is successful, the web application will authenticate the user and store the relevant data somewhere, depending on the chosen authentication method; this may include sessions/cookies, tokens, signatures, and so on (we'll talk about these later on). Conversely, the result will be presented to the user as a readable outcome inside an error page, possibly asking them to try again, contact an administrator, or something else.

This is still the most common approach nowadays. Almost all websites we can think of are using it, albeit with a number of big or small differences regarding security layers, state management, **JSON Web Tokens (JWTs)** or other RESTful tokens, basic or digest access, single sign-on properties, and more. Before moving forward, let's spend a bit of time explaining the most relevant of them.

Authentication methods

As we most certainly know, the HTTP protocol is *stateless*, meaning that whatever we do during a request/response cycle will be lost before the subsequent request, including the authentication result. The only way we have to overcome this is to store that result somewhere, along with all its relevant data, such as user ID, login date/time, and last request time. In the following sections, we'll briefly discuss some methods for storing that data.

Sessions/cookies

Up until a few years ago, the most common and traditional method to do this was to store that data on the server using either a memory-based, disk-based, or external session manager.

Each session could be retrieved using a unique ID that the client received with the authentication response, usually inside a session cookie, which was transmitted to the server on each subsequent request.

Here's a brief diagram outlining the **Session-Based Authentication Flow:**

Session-Based Authentication Flow

Authentication Request

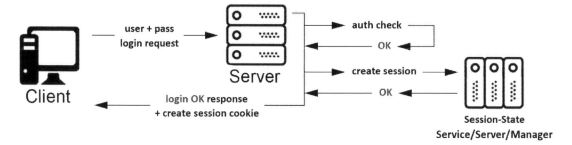

Subsequent Requests

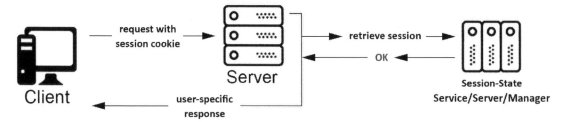

Figure 11.1: Session-based authentication flow

This is still a very common technique used by most web applications. There's nothing wrong with adopting this approach, as long as we are okay with its widely acknowledged downsides, such as the following:

- **Memory issues:** Whenever there are many authenticated users, the web server will consume more and more memory. Even if we use a file-based or external session provider, there will nonetheless be an intensive I/O, TCP, or socket overhead.

- **Scalability issues:** Replicating a session provider in a scalable architecture (*IIS web farm, load-balanced cluster,* and the like) might not be an easy task, and will often lead to bottlenecks or wasted resources.

- **Cross-domain issues:** Session cookies behave just like standard cookies, so they cannot be easily shared between different origins/domains. These kinds of problems can often be solved with some workarounds, yet they will often lead to insecure scenarios to make things work.

- **Security issues:** There is a wide range of detailed literature on security-related issues involving sessions and session cookies: for instance, **Cross-Site Request Forgery (CSRF)** attacks, and a number of other threats that won't be covered here for the sake of simplicity. Most of them can be mitigated by some countermeasures, yet they can be difficult to handle for junior or novice developers.

As these issues have arisen over the years, there's no doubt that most analysts and developers have put a lot of effort into figuring out different approaches, as well as mitigating them.

A pivotal improvement regarding mitigation was achieved in 2016 with the *SameSite cookies* draft, which suggested an HTTP security policy that was then improved by the *Cookies HTTP State Management Mechanism* (April 2019) and the *Incrementally Better Cookies* (May 2019) drafts.

These drafts are linked here, should you wish to read them yourself:

https://tools.ietf.org/html/draft-west-first-party-cookies-07

https://tools.ietf.org/html/draft-west-cookie-incrementalism-00

https://tools.ietf.org/html/draft-west-first-party-cookies-07

Now that most browsers have adopted the **SameSite** cookie specification, cookie-based authentication is a lot safer than before.

Tokens

Token-based authentication has been increasingly adopted by **Single-Page Applications (SPAs)** and mobile apps in the last few years for a number of undeniably good reasons that we'll try to briefly summarize here.

The most important difference between session-based authentication and token-based authentication is that the latter is *stateless*, meaning that we won't be storing any user-specific information on the server memory, database, session provider, or other data containers of any sort.

This single aspect solves most of the downsides that we pointed out earlier for session-based authentication. We won't have sessions, so there won't be an increasing overhead; we won't need a session provider, so scaling will be much easier. Also, for browsers supporting LocalStorage, we won't even be using cookies, so we won't get blocked by *cross-origin* restrictive policies and, hopefully, we'll get around most security issues.

Here's a typical **Token-Based Authentication Flow:**

Token-Based Authentication Flow

Authentication Request

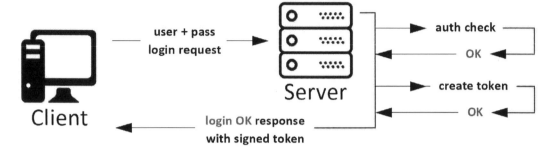

Subsequent Requests

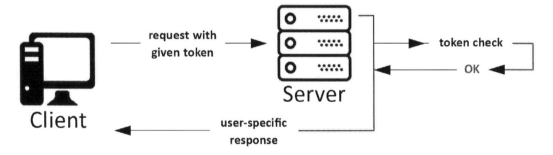

Figure 11.2: Token-based authentication flow

In terms of client-server interaction, these steps don't seem that different from the session-based authentication flow diagram; apparently, the only difference is that we'll be issuing and checking tokens instead of creating and retrieving sessions. However, the real deal is happening (or not happening) on the server side. We can immediately see that the token-based auth flow does not rely on a stateful session-state server, service, or manager. This will easily translate into a considerable boost in terms of performance and scalability.

Signatures

This is a method used by most modern API-based cloud computing and storage services, including **Microsoft Azure** and **Amazon Web Services (AWS)**.

In contrast to session-based and token-based approaches, which rely on a transport layer that can theoretically be accessed by or exposed to a third-party attacker, signature-based authentication performs a hash of the whole request using a previously shared private key. This ensures that no intruder or man-in-the-middle can ever act as the requesting user, as they won't be able to sign the request.

Two-factor

This is the standard authentication method used by most banking and financial accounts, being arguably the most secure one.

The implementation may vary, but it always relies on the following base workflow:

- The user performs a standard login with a username and password
- The server identifies the user and prompts them with an additional, user-specific request that can only be satisfied by something obtained or obtainable through a different channel; for example, an OTP password sent by SMS, a unique authentication card with a number of answer codes, or a dynamic PIN generated by a proprietary device or a mobile app
- If the user gives the correct answer, they are authenticated using a standard session-based or token-based method

Two-Factor Authentication (2FA) has been supported by ASP.NET Core since its 1.0 release, which implemented it using SMS verification (SMS 2FA). However, starting with ASP.NET Core 2, the SMS 2FA approach was deprecated in favor of a **Time-Based One-Time Password (TOTP) algorithm**, which became the industry-recommended approach to implement 2FA in web applications.

> For additional information about SMS 2FA, check out the following URL:
>
> `https://docs.microsoft.com/en-us/aspnet/core/security/authentication/2fa`
>
> For additional information about TOTP 2FA, take a look at the following URL:
>
> `https://docs.microsoft.com/en-us/aspnet/core/security/authentication/identity-enable-qrcodes`

After reviewing all these authentication methods, we can definitely say that the token-based authentication approach seems to be a viable choice for our specific scenario: for that very reason, in the upcoming sections, we're going to follow this route.

Third-party authentication

Regardless of the authentication method that a web application chooses to adopt, being forced to have a potentially different username and password for each website visit can be frustrating, and can also require users to develop custom password storage techniques that might lead to security risks. In order to overcome this issue, a large number of IT developers started to look around for an alternative way to authenticate users who could replace the standard authentication technique, based on usernames and passwords, with an authentication protocol based on trusted third-party providers.

The rise and fall of OpenID

Among the first successful attempts to implement a third-party authentication mechanism was the first release of **OpenID**, an open and decentralized authentication protocol promoted by the non-profit OpenID Foundation. Available since 2005, it was quickly and enthusiastically adopted by some big players such as Google and Stack Overflow, who originally based their authentication providers on it.

Here's how it works in a few words:

- Whenever our application receives an OpenID authentication request, it opens a transparent connection interface through the requesting user and a trusted third-party authentication provider (for example, the **Google identity provider**); the interface can be a popup, an AJAX-populated modal window, populated modal windows, or an API call, depending on the implementation
- The user sends their username and password to the aforementioned third-party provider, who performs the authentication accordingly and communicates the result to our application by redirecting the user to where they came from, along with a security token that can be used to retrieve the authentication result
- Our application consumes the token to check the authentication result, authenticating the user in the event of success or sending an error response in the event of failure

Despite the great enthusiasm for OpenID between 2005 and 2009, with a good number of relevant companies publicly declaring their support for OpenID and even joining the foundation, including PayPal and Facebook, the original protocol didn't live up to its great expectations. Legal controversies, security issues, and, most importantly, the massive popularity surge of the social networks with their improper—yet working—**OAuth-based** social logins in the 2009–2012 period basically killed it.

 Those who don't know what OAuth is, have patience; we'll get there soon enough.

OpenID Connect

In a desperate attempt to keep their flag flying after the takeover of the **OAuth/OAuth 2** social logins, the OpenID Foundation released the third generation of the OpenID technology in February 2014; this was called **OpenID Connect (OIDC)**.

Despite the name, the new installment of OIDC has little to nothing to do with its ancestor; it's merely an authentication layer built upon the OAuth 2 authorization protocol. In other words, it's little more than a standardized interface to help developers use OAuth 2 as an authentication framework in a less improper way, which is kind of funny, considering that OAuth 2 played a major role in taking out OpenID 2.0 in the first place.

The choice of giving up on OpenID in favor of OIDC was highly criticized in 2014; however, after all these years, we can definitely say that OIDC can still provide a useful, standardized way to obtain user identities.

It allows developers to request and receive information about authenticated users and sessions using a convenient, RESTful-based JSON interface; it features an extensible specification that also supports some promising optional features such as encryption of identity data, auto-discovery of OpenID providers, and even session management. In short, it's still useful enough to be used instead of relying on pure OAuth 2.

> For additional information about OpenID, we strongly suggest reading the following specifications from the OpenID Foundation official website:
>
> **OpenID Connect:** `http://openid.net/specs/openid-connect-core-1_0.html`
>
> **OpenID 2.0 to OIDC migration guide:** `http://openid.net/specs/openid-connect-migration-1_0.html`

Authorization

In most standard implementations, including those featured by ASP.NET, the authorization phase kicks in right after authentication, and it's mostly based on permissions or roles; any authenticated user might have their own set of permissions and/or belong to one or more roles and thus be granted access to a specific set of resources. These *role-based* checks are usually set by the developer in a declarative fashion within the application source code and/or configuration files.

Authorization, as we said, shouldn't be confused with authentication, despite the fact that it can be easily exploited to perform an implicit authentication as well, especially when it's delegated to a third-party actor.

Proprietary authorization

Most development frameworks provide a built-in authorization model, which can be used to implement permission-based, role-based, and/or claims-based policies. ASP.NET Core makes no exception since it ships with a simple, declarative API: in a nutshell, authorization is expressed in *requirements*, intended as required claims to access a given resource or perform a specific task; these requirements are checked by *handlers* that evaluate the user's claims against them.

Using a proprietary authorization model is often a good choice, providing that the developers have the required skills and know-how to properly implement it and handle the level of complexity inevitably bound to such an approach.

Third-party authorization

The best-known third-party authorization protocol nowadays is the 2.0 release of OAuth, also known as OAuth 2, which supersedes the former release (OAuth 1, or simply OAuth) originally developed by Blaine Cook and Chris Messina in 2006.

We have already talked about it a lot for good reason: OAuth 2 has quickly become the industry-standard protocol for authorization and is currently used by a gigantic number of community-based websites and social networks, including Google, Facebook, and Twitter.

It basically works like this:

- Whenever an existing user requests a set of permissions to our application via OAuth, we open a transparent connection interface between them and a third-party authorization provider that is trusted by our application (for example, Facebook)
- The provider acknowledges the user and, if they have the proper rights, responds by entrusting them with a temporary, specific access key
- The user presents the access key to our application and will be granted access

We can clearly see how easy it is to exploit this authorization logic for authentication purposes as well; after all, if Facebook says I can do something, shouldn't it also imply that I am who I claim to be? Isn't that enough?

The short answer is no. It might be the case for Facebook because their OAuth 2 implementation implies that subscribers receiving the authorization must have authenticated themselves to Facebook first; however, this assurance is not written anywhere. Considering how many websites are using it for authentication purposes, we can assume that Facebook won't likely change their actual behavior, yet we have no guarantees of this.

Theoretically speaking, these websites can split their authorization system from their authentication protocol at any time, thus leading our application's authentication logic to an unrecoverable state of inconsistency. More generally, we can say that presuming something from something else is almost always a bad practice, unless that assumption lies upon very solid, well-documented, and (most importantly) highly guaranteed grounds.

Proprietary versus third-party

Theoretically speaking, it's possible to entirely delegate the authentication and/or authorization tasks to existing external, third-party providers such as those we mentioned before; there are a lot of web and mobile applications that proudly follow this route nowadays. There are a number of undeniable advantages to using such an approach, including the following:

- **No user-specific database tables/data models,** just some provider-based identifiers to use here and there as reference keys
- **Immediate registration,** since there's no need to fill in a registration form and wait for a confirmation email—no username, no password. This will be appreciated by most users and will probably increase our conversion rates as well
- **Few or no privacy issues,** as there's no personal or sensitive data on the application server
- **No need to handle usernames and passwords** and implement automatic recovery processes
- **Fewer security-related issues** such as form-based hacking attempts or brute-force login attempts

Of course, there are also some downsides:

- **There won't be an actual user base,** so it will be difficult to get an overview of active users, get their email addresses, analyze statistics, and so on

- **The login phase might be resource-intensive**, since it will always require an external, back-and-forth secure connection with a third-party server
- **All users will need to have (or open) an account with the chosen third-party provider(s)** in order to log in
- **All users will need to trust our application** because the third-party provider will ask them to authorize it to access their data
- **We will have to register our application with the provider** in order to be able to perform a number of required or optional tasks, such as receiving our public and secret keys, authorizing one or more URI initiators, and choosing the information we want to collect

Taking all these pros and cons into account, we can say that relying on third-party providers might be a great time-saving choice for small-scale apps, including ours; however, building our own account management system seems to be the only way to overcome the aforementioned governance and control-based flaws undeniably brought by that approach.

Therefore, in this chapter, we'll explore the *proprietary* option: more specifically, we'll create an **internal membership provider** that will handle authentication and provide its very own set of authorization rules.

Proprietary auth with .NET Core

The authentication patterns made available by ASP.NET Core are basically the same as those supported by the previous versions of ASP.NET:

- **No authentication**, if we don't feel like implementing anything or if we want to use (or develop) a self-made auth interface without relying upon the ASP.NET Core Identity system
- **Individual user accounts**, when we set up an internal database to store user data using the standard ASP.NET Core Identity interface
- **Azure Active Directory** (AD), which implies using a token-based set of API calls handled by the **Azure AD Authentication Library** (**ADAL**)
- **Windows authentication**, which is only viable for local-scope applications within Windows domains or AD trees

However, the implementation patterns introduced by the ASP.NET Core team over the past few years are constantly evolving in order to match the latest security practices available.

All the aforementioned approaches—excluding the first one—are handled by the **ASP.NET Core Identity system**, a membership system that allows us to add authentication and authorization functionalities to our application.

For additional info about the ASP.NET Core Identity APIs, check out the following URL:

https://docs.microsoft.com/en-us/aspnet/core/security/authentication/
identity

Starting with .NET Core 3.0, ASP.NET Core Identity has been integrated with a third-party authorization mechanism to handle authentication in SPAs; this new feature is based on *IdentityServer*, a piece of open source OIDC and OAuth 2.0 middleware that has been part of the .NET Foundation since .NET Core 3.0.

Further information about *IdentityServer* can be retrieved from the official documentation website, which is available at the following URLs:

`https://identityserver.io/`

`http://docs.identityserver.io/en/latest/`

However, on October 1, 2020, the *IdentityServer* team made an announcement saying that the license model would be changed to a reciprocal public license: in a nutshell, this means that the product will be still open source for testing, learning, and non-commercial use, but if used for commercial purposes and the organization makes more than 1M USD/year, then a paid license must be purchased.

The full *IdentityServer* team announcement can be read at the following URL: `https://leastprivilege.com/2020/10/01/the-future-of-identityserver/`

Following this change in the *IdentityServer* license model, the ASP.NET development team made its own announcement on May 7, 2021, saying that they will continue to ship *IdentityServer* in .NET 6 templates, but they will be looking for an alternative for .NET 7 and beyond since they want to provide a built-in identity system for any purpose.

The full ASP.NET development team announcement can be read at the following URL: `https://devblogs.microsoft.com/dotnet/asp-net-core-6-and-authentication-servers/`

Therefore, for the purposes of this book, we're not going to use *IdentityServer*: we'll implement a login mechanism that will allow our users to create an account and log in with a username and a password using the services and middlewares natively provided by ASP.NET Core.

More specifically, we'll implement an authentication mechanism based upon **JSON Web Tokens (JWTs)**, a JSON-based open standard explicitly designed for native web applications, available in multiple languages, such as .NET, Python, Java, PHP, Ruby, JavaScript/Node.js, and Perl. We've chosen it because it's becoming a de facto standard for token authentication, as it's natively supported by most technologies.

For additional information about JSON web tokens, check out the following URL: `https://jwt.io/`

In this section, we're going to do the following:

- **Introduce the ASP.NET Core Identity model**, the framework provided by ASP.NET Core to manage and store user accounts
- **Set up an ASP.NET Core Identity implementation** by installing the required NuGet packages in our existing WorldCities app

Setting up ASP.NET Core Identity will require the following steps:

- **Add the required NuGet packages** for the services and middlewares we're going to use
- **Create the ApplicationUser** entity to handle registered users
- **Extend the ApplicationDbContext** using the *Individual User Accounts* authentication type
- **Configure** the ASP.NET Core Identity Service in our application's Program class based upon the ApplicationUser and ApplicationDbContext classes
- **Implement a new AccountController** with a Login action method to validate login attempts from the Angular client and return a valid JWT token in case of success
- **Configure the JwtBearerMiddleware** in our application's Program class to validate the JWT tokens that will be sent by the Angular client within the HTTP requests (when we'll implement this feature)
- **Update the existing SeedController** by adding a method to create our default users with the .NET Identity API providers
- **Secure the Action Methods** with the [Authorize] attribute whenever we want to restrict their usage to authorized users only

Right after that, we'll take the opportunity to say a couple of words about the ASP.NET Core **Task Asynchronous Programming (TAP)** model, and then we'll switch to Angular to implement the *client-side* part of the job.

The ASP.NET Core Identity model

ASP.NET Core provides a unified framework to manage and store user accounts that can be easily used in any .NET application (even non-web ones); this framework is called **ASP.NET Core Identity** and provides a set of APIs that allows developers to handle the following tasks:

- Design, set up, and implement user registration and login functionalities
- Manage users, passwords, profile data, roles, claims, tokens, email confirmations, and so on
- Support external (third-party) login providers such as Facebook, Google, Microsoft account, Twitter, and more

The ASP.NET Core Identity source code is open source and available on GitHub at https://github.com/aspnet/AspNetCore/tree/master/src/Identity.

It goes without saying that ASP.NET Core Identity requires a persistent data source to store (and retrieve) the identity data (usernames, passwords, and profile data), such as a SQL Server database; for that very reason, it features built-in integration mechanisms with Entity Framework Core.

This means that, in order to implement our very own identity system, we'll basically extend what we did in *Chapter 5, Data Model with Entity Framework Core*; more specifically, we'll update our existing `ApplicationDbContext` to support the additional entity classes required to handle users, roles, and so on.

Entity types

The ASP.NET Core Identity platform strongly relies upon the following entity types, each one of them representing a specific set of records:

- `User`: The users of our application
- `Role`: The roles that we can assign to each user
- `UserClaim`: The claims that a user possesses
- `UserToken`: The authentication token that a user might use to perform auth-based tasks (such as logging in)
- `UserLogin`: The login account associated with each user
- `RoleClaim`: The claims that are granted to all users within a given role
- `UserRole`: The lookup table to store the relationship between users and their assigned roles

These entity types are related to each other in the following ways:

- Each `User` can have many `UserClaim`, `UserLogin`, and `UserToken` entities (*one-to-many*)
- Each `Role` can have many associated `RoleClaim` entities (*one-to-many*)
- Each `User` can have many associated `Role` entities, and each `Role` can be associated with many `User` entities (*many-to-many*)

The many-to-many relationship requires a join table in the database, which is represented by the `UserRole` entity.

Luckily enough, we won't have to manually implement all these entities from scratch because ASP.NET Core Identity provides some default **Common Language Runtime** (**CLR**) types for each one of them:

- `IdentityUser`
- `IdentityRole`
- `IdentityUserClaim`
- `IdentityUserToken`
- `IdentityUserLogin`
- `IdentityRoleClaim`
- `IdentityUserRole`

These types can be used as *base classes* for our own implementation, whenever we need to explicitly define an identity-related entity model. Moreover, most of them don't have to be implemented in most common authentication scenarios, since their functionalities can be handled at a higher level thanks to the ASP.NET Core Identity sets of APIs, which can be accessed from the following classes:

- `RoleManager<TRole>`: Provides the APIs for managing roles

- SignInManager<TUser>: Provides the APIs for signing users in and out (login and logout)
- UserManager<TUser>: Provides the APIs for managing users

Once the ASP.NET Core Identity service has been properly configured and set up, these providers can be injected into our ASP.NET Core controllers using **Dependency Injection** (**DI**), just like we did with ApplicationDbContext; in the following section, we'll see how we can do that.

Setting up ASP.NET Core Identity

In *Chapter 2*, *Getting Ready* and *Chapter 5*, *Data Model with Entity Framework Core*, when we created our HealthCheckAPI and WorldCitiesAPI .NET Core projects, we always chose to go with an empty project featuring no authentication. That was because we didn't want Visual Studio to install **ASP.NET Core Identity** within our application's start up files right from the start. However, now that we're using it, we need to manually perform the required setup steps.

Adding the NuGet packages

Enough with the theory, let's put the plan into action.

From Solution Explorer, right-click on the *WorldCitiesAPI* tree node, then select **Manage NuGet Packages**. Look for the following two packages and install them:

- Microsoft.AspNetCore.Identity.EntityFrameworkCore
- Microsoft.AspNetCore.Authentication.JwtBearer

Alternatively, open **Package Manager Console** and install them with the following commands:

```
> Install-Package Microsoft.AspNetCore.Identity.EntityFrameworkCore
> Install-Package Microsoft.AspNetCore.Authentication.JwtBearer
```

At the time of writing, the latest version for both of them is **6.0.1**; as always, we are free to install a newer version, as long as we know how to adapt our code accordingly to fix potential compatibility issues.

Creating ApplicationUser

Now that we have installed the required identity libraries, we need to create a new ApplicationUser entity class with all the features required by the ASP.NET Core Identity service to use it for auth purposes. Luckily enough, the package comes with a built-in IdentityUser base class that can be used to extend our own implementation, thus granting it everything that we need.

From Solution Explorer, navigate to the /Data/Models/ folder and then create a new ApplicationUser. cs class and fill its content with the following code:

```
using Microsoft.AspNetCore.Identity;

namespace WorldCitiesAPI.Data.Models
{
```

```
    public class ApplicationUser : IdentityUser
    {
    }
}
```

As we can see, we don't need to implement anything there, at least not for the time being; we'll just extend the IdentityUser base class, which already contains everything we need for now.

Extending ApplicationDbContext

In order to support the .NET Core authentication mechanism, our existing ApplicationDbContext needs to be extended from a different database abstraction base class that supports ASP.NET Core Identity.

Open the /Data/ApplicationDbContext.cs file and update its contents accordingly (updated lines are highlighted):

```
using Microsoft.AspNetCore.Identity.EntityFrameworkCore;
using Microsoft.EntityFrameworkCore;
using Microsoft.Extensions.Options;
using WorldCitiesAPI.Data.Models;

namespace WorldCitiesAPI.Data
{
    public class ApplicationDbContext
        : IdentityDbContext<ApplicationUser>
    {

// ... existing code...
```

As we can see from the preceding code, we replaced the current DbContext base class with the new IdentityDbContext base class; the new class strongly relies on the ASP.NET Core Identity service we're about to add.

Configuring the ASP.NET Core Identity service

Now that we're done with all the prerequisites, we can open the Program.cs file and add the following highlighted lines to set up the services required by the ASP.NET Core Identity system:

```
// ...existing code...

using WorldCitiesAPI.Data.Models;
using Microsoft.AspNetCore.Identity;

// ...existing code...
```

```
// Add ApplicationDbContext and SQL Server support
builder.Services.AddDbContext<ApplicationDbContext>(options =>
    options.UseSqlServer(
        builder.Configuration.GetConnectionString("DefaultConnection")
        )
);

// ...existing code...

// Add ASP.NET Core Identity support
builder.Services.AddIdentity<ApplicationUser, IdentityRole>(options =>
{
    options.SignIn.RequireConfirmedAccount = true;
    options.Password.RequireDigit = true;
    options.Password.RequireLowercase = true;
    options.Password.RequireUppercase = true;
    options.Password.RequireNonAlphanumeric = true;
    options.Password.RequiredLength = 8;
})
    .AddEntityFrameworkStores<ApplicationDbContext>();

// ...existing code...
```

The preceding code loosely resembles the default ASP.NET Core Identity implementation used by most Visual Studio ASP.NET Core templates: in a nutshell, we're adding the ASP.NET Identify service for the specified User and Role types. While there, we took the chance to override some of the default password policy settings to demonstrate how we can configure the Identity service to better suit our needs.

Let's take another look at the preceding code, emphasizing the changes (highlighted lines):

```
options.SignIn.RequireConfirmedAccount = true;
options.Password.RequireLowercase = true;
options.Password.RequireUppercase = true;
options.Password.RequireDigit = true;
options.Password.RequireNonAlphanumeric = true;
options.Password.RequiredLength = 8;
```

These changes don't alter the RequireConfirmedAccount default settings, which would require a confirmed user account (verified through email) to sign in. What we did instead was explicitly set our password strength requirements so that all our users' passwords would need to have the following:

- At least one lowercase letter
- At least one uppercase letter

- At least one digit character
- At least one non-alphanumeric character
- A minimum length of eight characters

That will grant our app a decent level of authentication security, should we ever want to make it publicly accessible on the web. Needless to say, we can change these settings depending on our specific needs; a development sample could probably live with more relaxed settings, as long as we don't make it available to the public.

 It's worth noting that the preceding code will also require some using references to the new identity-related packages that we installed a moment ago, and to the namespace that we used for our data models, since we're now referencing the `ApplicationUser` class.

Now that we have properly set up the ASP.NET Core Identity service in our `Program` class, we can add the required code to deal with actual login attempts coming from our Angular client.

Implementing AccountController

Based on what we've learned in the previous chapters, we already know that our Angular app will handle the end user authentication attempts using a *login form*; such form will likely issue an HTTP POST request to our ASP.NET Core Web API containing the end user's **username** and **password**. Since we are implementing a JWT-based authentication mechanism, we need to perform the following *server-side* steps:

- **Validate that username and password** against the internal user database
- **Create a JSON Web Token** (referred to as JWT from here on) if the given credentials are valid
- **Return a JSON result** containing the JWT or a client-readable error depending on the login attempt result

These tasks can be done with a dedicated controller that we need to add to our current **WorldCitiesAPI** project. However, before adding that controller, we need to create some utility classes that will serve as prerequisites for those tasks.

LoginRequest

The first class we're going to add is a DTO that we will use to receive the user's credentials from the client. We already know why we need a DTO to better deal with this kind of task from *Chapter 9, Back-End and Front-End Debugging*, right? We already did that for our `City` and `Country` entities, and now `ApplicationUser` needs it as well. However, since we're only going to use this class to handle login requests, calling it `ApplicationUserDTO` would be rather confusing: for that very reason, we'll just call it `LoginRequest`, which best represents our limited purpose.

Create a new file in the /Data/ folder, call it `LoginRequest.cs`, and fill it with the following code:

```
using System.ComponentModel.DataAnnotations;
```

```
namespace WorldCitiesAPI.Data
{
    public class LoginRequest
    {
        [Required(ErrorMessage = "Email is required.")]
        public string Email { get; set; } = null!;

        [Required(ErrorMessage = "Password is required.")]
        public string Password { get; set; } = null!;
    }
}
```

The preceding code should be self-explanatory at this point: let's move on.

LoginResult

The next thing to do is to create a strongly typed result class to inform our client of the login attempt result, and send it the JWT in the event of success: we'll call it LoginResult, since that's precisely what it is.

It's worth noting that we can't use our existing **ApiResult** class for this purpose since it's meant to store an array of results.

Create a new file in the /Data/ folder, call it LoginResult.cs, and fill it with the following code:

```
namespace WorldCitiesAPI.Data
{
    public class LoginResult
    {
        /// <summary>
        /// TRUE if the login attempt is successful, FALSE otherwise.
        /// </summary>
        public bool Success { get; set; }

        /// <summary>
        /// Login attempt result message
        /// </summary>
        public string Message { get; set; } = null!;

        /// <summary>
        /// The JWT token if the login attempt is successful, or NULL if not
        /// </summary>
        public string? Token { get; set; }
    }
}
```

Again, there's not much to say about this class: the comments provided should explain everything.

Now we just need to generate our JWT.

JwtSettings

To securely generate a JWT, we need to know some information in advance, such as:

- The security key for creating the token
- The identity of the issuer (the server that generates the token) and the audience (the clients who will receive and use it)
- The token expiration time

Most of these settings must be configured at runtime: however, since they contain some security-sensitive information, instead of hardcoding them in our source code, we should define them in the appsettings.json configuration file(s), just like we did with our database connection strings back in *Chapter 5*, *Data Model with Entity Framework Core*. Such good practice will also allow us to define environment-specific settings, as well as protect that data using the *User Secrets* technique that we explained in that same chapter.

For the sake of simplicity, for now, let's just add some sample settings at the end of our appsettings.json file:

```
// ...existing code...

"JwtSettings": {
    "SecurityKey": "MyVeryOwnSecurityKey",
    "Issuer": "MyVeryOwnIssuer",
    "Audience": "https://localhost:4200",
    "ExpirationTimeInMinutes": 30
  },

// ...existing code...
```

It's worth noting that we're going to use these settings not only to generate the JWT, but also to validate them.

JwtHandler

Now we can finally create the service class that will generate the JWT.

Create a new file in the /Data/ folder, call it JwtHandler.cs and fill it with the following code:

```
using Microsoft.AspNetCore.Identity;
using Microsoft.IdentityModel.Tokens;
using System.IdentityModel.Tokens.Jwt;
using System.Security.Claims;
using System.Text;
```

```csharp
using WorldCitiesAPI.Data.Models;

namespace WorldCitiesAPI.Data
{
    public class JwtHandler
    {
        private readonly IConfiguration _configuration;
        private readonly UserManager<ApplicationUser> _userManager;

        public JwtHandler(
            IConfiguration configuration,
            UserManager<ApplicationUser> userManager
            )
        {
            _configuration = configuration;
            _userManager = userManager;
        }

        public async Task<JwtSecurityToken> GetTokenAsync(ApplicationUser user)
        {
            var jwtOptions = new JwtSecurityToken(
                issuer: _configuration["JwtSettings:Issuer"],
                audience: _configuration["JwtSettings:Audience"],
                claims: await GetClaimsAsync(user),
                expires: DateTime.Now.AddMinutes(Convert.ToDouble(
                    _configuration["JwtSettings:ExpirationTimeInMinutes"])),
                signingCredentials: GetSigningCredentials());
            return jwtOptions;
        }

        private SigningCredentials GetSigningCredentials()
        {
            var key = Encoding.UTF8.GetBytes(
                _configuration["JwtSettings:SecurityKey"]);
            var secret = new SymmetricSecurityKey(key);
            return new SigningCredentials(secret,
                SecurityAlgorithms.HmacSha256);
        }

        private async Task<List<Claim>> GetClaimsAsync(
          ApplicationUser user)
```

```
        {
            var claims = new List<Claim>
            {
                new Claim(ClaimTypes.Name, user.Email)
            };

            foreach (var role in await _userManager.GetRolesAsync(user))
            {
                claims.Add(new Claim(ClaimTypes.Role, role));
            }
            return claims;
        }
    }
}
```

As we can see, this class hosts a public GetTokenAsync method, which can be used to generate the JWT, and a couple of private methods used internally to retrieve the security key, algorithm, and digest to digitally sign the token, as well as the claims to add – the user's Name, Email, and all their Roles.

It's worth noting that, to retrieve the app's configuration settings and the user's roles, we've injected the IConfiguration object that hosts the appsettings.json values and the UserManager<TUser> provider that we talked about early on; we did that using *Dependency Injection*, just like we did with ApplicationDbContext and IWebHostEnvironment back in *Chapter 5, Data Model with Entity Framework Core*.

The JwtHandler class is the first ASP.NET Core service that we create: since we're going to use it through dependency injection, we need to add it to the app's DI container by adding the following highlighted line to the Program.cs file, just before building the app:

```
// ...existing code...

builder.Services.AddScoped<JwtHandler>();

var app = builder.Build();

// ...existing code...
```

As we can see, we're adding it using the AddScoped method, meaning that the service will be registered with the Scoped registration option. Before going further, it might be worth taking a few words to explain what these registration options are and how they impact the service's lifetime.

Dependency injection registration options

We already know from *Chapter 2, Getting Ready* that ASP.NET Core supports the **dependency injection (DI)** software design pattern, a technique for achieving **Inversion of Control (IoC)** between classes and their dependencies.

In a typical ASP.NET Core app, such dependencies are registered in the built-in service container (IServiceProvider) within the Program.cs file. Whenever we register a service in the DI container, we can choose a registration option, which will determine how that service's instances will be provided during the app and/or the request life cycle.

The following registration options are available:

- **Transient.** A new instance of the service is provided every time it's requested, regardless of the HTTP scope. This basically means that we'll always have a brand-new object, thus without the risk of having concurrency issues.
- **Scoped.** A new instance of the service is provided for each different HTTP request. However, the same instance is provided within the scope of any single HTTP request.
- **Singleton.** A single instance of the service will be created upon the first request and then provided to all subsequent requests until the application stops.

The *Transient* option is great for lightweight services with little or no state; however, it uses more memory and resources, thus having a negative impact on performance, especially if the website must deal with a lot of simultaneous HTTP requests.

The *Scoped* option is the framework default and is often the best approach whenever we need to maintain state within HTTP requests, assuming that we don't need to recreate the service every time we inject it.

The *Singleton* option is the most efficient in terms of memory and performance since the service is created once and reused everywhere within the app's life cycle; on top of that, it can also be useful to preserve a "global", request-independent state. However, the fact that the service (and its state) is shared with all requests strongly limits its scope and, if used improperly, might lead to vulnerabilities, memory leaks, or other security or performance issues.

Since our JwtHandler service is very lightweight and doesn't have specific state requirements, any registration option would work without issues. That said, we've opted for the *Scoped* approach so that each instance will follow the same life cycle of the login HTTP request that makes use of it.

Now we're finally ready to implement our AccountController.

AccountController

Create a new file in the /Controllers/ folder, call it AccountController.cs, and fill it with the following code:

```
using System.IdentityModel.Tokens.Jwt;
using Microsoft.AspNetCore.Identity;
using Microsoft.AspNetCore.Mvc;
using WorldCitiesAPI.Data;
using WorldCitiesAPI.Data.Models;

namespace WorldCitiesAPI.Controllers
{
    [Route("api/[controller]")]
```

```
[ApiController]
public class AccountController : ControllerBase
{
    private readonly ApplicationDbContext _context;
    private readonly UserManager<ApplicationUser> _userManager;
    private readonly JwtHandler _jwtHandler;

    public AccountController(
        ApplicationDbContext context,
        UserManager<ApplicationUser> userManager,
        JwtHandler jwtHandler)
    {
        _context = context;
        _userManager = userManager;
        _jwtHandler = jwtHandler;
    }

    [HttpPost("Login")]
    public async Task<IActionResult> Login(LoginRequest loginRequest)
    {
        var user = await _userManager.FindByNameAsync(loginRequest.Email);
        if (user == null
            || !await _userManager.CheckPasswordAsync(user, loginRequest.
Password))
                return Unauthorized(new LoginResult() {
                    Success = false,
                    Message = "Invalid Email or Password."
                });
        var secToken = await _jwtHandler.GetTokenAsync(user);
        var jwt = new JwtSecurityTokenHandler().WriteToken(secToken);
        return Ok(new LoginResult() {
            Success = true, Message = "Login successful", Token = jwt
        });
    }
}
```

As we can see, the Login action method makes good use of all the classes we've implemented so far. More specifically, it does the following:

- Accepts the LoginRequest object containing the user's credentials

- Validates them using the UserManager API that we've injected in the controller using dependency injection
- Creates a JWT using our JwtHandler class if the given credentials are valid, otherwise, it emits an error message
- Sends the overall result to the client using the LoginResult POCO class we've added a short while ago

Now our ASP.NET Core Web API can authenticate a login request and return a JWT. However, we're still unable to properly verify those tokens and confirm they're valid. To do that, we need to set up JwtBearerMiddleware with the same configuration settings we're using to generate them.

Configuring JwtBearerMiddleware

To properly set up the JwtBearerMiddleware, we need to append the following lines to the Program. cs file, just below the ASP.NET Core Identity settings that we've added a while ago:

```
// ...existing code...

// Add Authentication services & middlewares
builder.Services.AddAuthentication(opt =>
{
    opt.DefaultAuthenticateScheme = JwtBearerDefaults.AuthenticationScheme;
    opt.DefaultChallengeScheme = JwtBearerDefaults.AuthenticationScheme;
}).AddJwtBearer(options =>
{
    options.TokenValidationParameters = new TokenValidationParameters
    {
        RequireExpirationTime = true,
        ValidateIssuer = true,
        ValidateAudience = true,
        ValidateLifetime = true,
        ValidateIssuerSigningKey = true,
        ValidIssuer = builder.Configuration["JwtSettings:Issuer"],
        ValidAudience = builder.Configuration["JwtSettings:Audience"],
        IssuerSigningKey = new SymmetricSecurityKey(System.Text.Encoding.UTF8.
GetBytes(builder.Configuration["JwtSettings:SecurityKey"]))
    };
});

// ...existing code...
```

The preceding code will register JwtBearerMiddleware, which will extract any JWT from the Authorization request header and validate it using the configuration settings defined in the appsettings.json file.

It's worth noting that, since we're now using the authentication services, we also need to add `AuthenticationMiddleware` to the request pipeline in the `Program.cs` file. We can do that just before `AuthorizationMiddleware`, in the following way (the new line is highlighted):

```
// ...existing code...

app.UseAuthentication();
app.UseAuthorization();

// ...existing code...
```

All we need to do now is to create some users to authenticate.

Updating SeedController

The best way to create a new user from scratch would be from `SeedController`, which implements the *seeding mechanism* that we set up in *Chapter 5*, *Data Model with Entity Framework Core*; however, in order to interact with the ASP.NET Core Identity APIs required to do that, we need to inject them using DI, just like we already did with `ApplicationDbContext`.

Adding RoleManager and UserManager through DI

From Solution Explorer, open the `/Controllers/SeedController.cs` file of the `WorldCities` project and update its content accordingly with the following code (new/updated lines are highlighted):

```
using Microsoft.AspNetCore.Identity;

// ...existing code...

public class SeedController : ControllerBase
{
    private readonly ApplicationDbContext _context;
    private readonly RoleManager<IdentityRole> _roleManager;
    private readonly UserManager<ApplicationUser> _userManager;
    private readonly IWebHostEnvironment _env;
    private readonly IConfiguration _configuration;

    public SeedController(
        ApplicationDbContext context,
        RoleManager<IdentityRole> roleManager,
        UserManager<ApplicationUser> userManager,
        IWebHostEnvironment env,
        IConfiguration configuration)
```

```
    {
        _context = context;
        _roleManager = roleManager;
        _userManager = userManager;
        _env = env;
        _configuration = configuration;
    }

// ...existing code...
```

Again, we added the `RoleManager<TRole>` and `UserManager<TUser>` providers using DI. We'll see how we can use these providers to create our users and roles soon enough.

While we were there, we also took the opportunity to inject a `IConfiguration` instance that we're going to use to retrieve the default passwords for our users. We can define these passwords in our `secrets.json` file in the following way:

```
{
    "ConnectionStrings": {
        // ...
    },
    "DefaultPasswords": {
        "RegisteredUser": "Sampl3Pa$$_User",
        "Administrator": "Sampl3Pa$$_Admin"
    },
    // ...
```

Let's do this now so that we'll have them ready later.

Now, let's define the following method at the end of the `/Controllers/SeedController.cs` file, right below the existing `Import()` method:

```
// ...existing code...

[HttpGet]
public async Task<ActionResult> CreateDefaultUsers()
{
    throw new NotImplementedException();
}

// ...existing code...
```

In a typical `ApiController`, adding another action method with the `[HttpGet]` attribute would create an ambiguous route that will conflict with the original method accepting HTTP GET requests (the `Import()` method): this code will not run when you hit the endpoint. However, since our `SeedController` has been configured to take the action names into account thanks to the `[Route("api/[controller]/[action]")]` routing rule that we placed above the class constructor back in *Chapter 5, Data Model with Entity Framework Core*, we're entitled to add this method without creating a conflict.

Opposite to what we usually do, we're not going to implement this method straight away; we'll take this chance to embrace the **Test-Driven Development** (**TDD**) approach, which means that we'll start with creating a (failing) unit test.

Defining the CreateDefaultUsers() unit test

If we want to emulate the "add new user" process within a test, we're going to need a `UserManager` instance (to add users) and a `RoleManager` instance (to give them a role). For that very reason, before creating the actual test method, it could be useful to provide our `WorldCitiesAPI.Tests` project with a helper class that we can use to create these instances. Let's do this.

Adding the IdentityHelper static class

From Solution Explorer, create a new `IdentityHelper.cs` file in the `WorldCitiesAPI.Tests` project. Once done, fill its content with the following code:

```
using Microsoft.AspNetCore.Identity;
using Microsoft.Extensions.Logging;
using Microsoft.Extensions.Options;
using Moq;
using System;
using System.Collections.Generic;
using System.Text;

namespace WorldCitiesAPI.Tests
{
    public static class IdentityHelper
    {
        public static RoleManager<TIdentityRole>
        GetRoleManager<TIdentityRole>(
            IRoleStore<TIdentityRole> roleStore) where TIdentityRole :
            IdentityRole
        {
```

```
            return new RoleManager<TIdentityRole>(
                    roleStore,
                    new IRoleValidator<TIdentityRole>[0],
                    new UpperInvariantLookupNormalizer(),
                    new Mock<IdentityErrorDescriber>().Object,
                    new Mock<ILogger<RoleManager<TIdentityRole>>>(
                    ).Object);
        }

        public static UserManager<TIDentityUser>
         GetUserManager<TIDentityUser>(
            IUserStore<TIDentityUser> userStore) where TIDentityUser :
             IdentityUser
        {
            return new UserManager<TIDentityUser>(
                    userStore,
                    new Mock<IOptions<IdentityOptions>>().Object,
                    new Mock<IPasswordHasher<TIDentityUser>>().Object,
                    new IUserValidator<TIDentityUser>[0],
                    new IPasswordValidator<TIDentityUser>[0],
                    new UpperInvariantLookupNormalizer(),
                    new Mock<IdentityErrorDescriber>().Object,
                    new Mock<IServiceProvider>().Object,
                    new Mock<ILogger<UserManager<TIDentityUser>>>(
                    ).Object);
        }
    }
}
```

As we can see, we created two methods—GetRoleManager and GetUserManager—which we can use to create these providers for other tests. It's worth noting that we are creating *real instances* (not *mocks*) of the RoleManager and UserManager providers since we'll need them to perform some read/write operations to the *in-memory* database that we will provide to the ApplicationDbContext that will be instantiated for the test. This basically means that these providers will perform their job for real, but everything will be done on the in-memory database instead of the SQL Server data source, just like we did with our previous tests.

That said, we still made good use of the Moq package library to create a number of *mocks* to emulate a number of parameters required to instantiate RoleManager and UserManager. Luckily enough, most of them are internal objects that won't be needed to perform our current tests; for those that are required, we had to create a real instance.

For example, for both providers, we were forced to create a real instance of `UpperInvariantLookupNormalizer`—which implements the `ILookupNormalizer` interface—because it's being used internally by `RoleManager` (to look up existing roles) as well as `UserManager` (to look up existing usernames); if we had mocked it instead, we would've hit some nasty runtime errors while trying to make these tests pass.

Now that we have these two helper methods, we can create the test that will make good use of them.

Adding the SeedController_Test class

From Solution Explorer, create a new /SeedController_Tests.cs file in the `WorldCitiesAPI.Tests` project. Once done, fill its content with the following code:

```
using Microsoft.AspNetCore.Hosting;
using Microsoft.AspNetCore.Identity;
using Microsoft.AspNetCore.Identity.EntityFrameworkCore;
using Microsoft.EntityFrameworkCore;
using Microsoft.Extensions.Configuration;
using Moq;
using System.Threading.Tasks;
using WorldCitiesAPI.Controllers;
using WorldCitiesAPI.Data;
using WorldCitiesAPI.Data.Models;
using Xunit;

namespace WorldCitiesAPI.Tests
{
    public class SeedController_Tests
    {
        /// <summary>
        /// Test the CreateDefaultUsers() method
        /// </summary>
        [Fact]
        public async Task CreateDefaultUsers()
        {
            // Arrange
            // create the option instances required by the
            // ApplicationDbContext
            var options = new
              DbContextOptionsBuilder<ApplicationDbContext>()
                .UseInMemoryDatabase(databaseName: "WorldCities")
                .Options;
```

```
            // create a IWebHost environment mock instance
            var mockEnv = Mock.Of<IWebHostEnvironment>();

            // create a IConfiguration mock instance
            var mockConfiguration = new Mock<IConfiguration>();
            mockConfiguration.SetupGet(x => x[It.Is<string>(s => s ==
"DefaultPasswords:RegisteredUser")]).Returns("M0ckP$$word");
            mockConfiguration.SetupGet(x => x[It.Is<string>(s => s ==
"DefaultPasswords:Administrator")]).Returns("M0ckP$$word");


            // create a ApplicationDbContext instance using the
            // in-memory DB
            using var context = new ApplicationDbContext(options);

            // create a RoleManager instance
            var roleManager = IdentityHelper.GetRoleManager(
                new RoleStore<IdentityRole>(context));

            // create a UserManager instance
            var userManager = IdentityHelper.GetUserManager(
                new UserStore<ApplicationUser>(context));

            // create a SeedController instance
            var controller = new SeedController(
                context,
                roleManager,
                userManager,
                mockEnv,
                mockConfiguration.Object
                );

            // define the variables for the users we want to test
            ApplicationUser user_Admin = null!;
            ApplicationUser user_User = null!;
            ApplicationUser user_NotExisting = null!;

            // Act
            // execute the SeedController's CreateDefaultUsers()
            // method to create the default users (and roles)
            await controller.CreateDefaultUsers();
```

```
        // retrieve the users
        user_Admin = await userManager.FindByEmailAsync(
            "admin@email.com");
        user_User = await userManager.FindByEmailAsync(
            "user@email.com");
        user_NotExisting = await userManager.FindByEmailAsync(
            "notexisting@email.com");

        // Assert
        Assert.NotNull(user_Admin);
        Assert.NotNull(user_User);
        Assert.Null(user_NotExisting);
    }
  }
}
```

The above code is quite long but should be easily understandable by now. Here, in a nutshell, is what we are doing there:

- In the **Arrange** phase, we create the mock (and non-mock) instances required to perform the actual test
- In the **Act** phase, we execute the test and attempt to retrieve the resulting (created) users to confirm the result
- In the **Assert** phase, we evaluate the expected outcome

With this, our unit test is ready; we just need to execute it to see it fail.

To do that, right-click the WorldCitiesAPI.Test node from Solution Explorer and select **Run Tests**.

 Alternatively, just switch to the **Test Explorer** window and use the topmost buttons to run the tests from there.

If we did everything correctly, we should be able to see our CreateDefaultUsers() test failing, just like in the following screenshot:

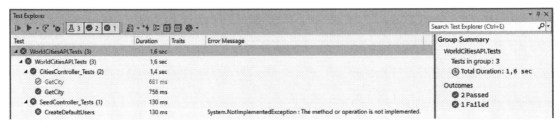

Figure 11.3: Failure of our CreateDefaultUsers() test

That's it; all we have to do now is to implement the `CreateDefaultUsers()` method in our `SeedController` to make the preceding test pass.

Implementing the CreateDefaultUsers() method

Open the `/Controllers/SeedController.cs` file again, scroll down to the `CreateDefaultUsers` action method, and replace `NotImplementedException` with the following code:

```
// ...existing code...

[HttpGet]
public async Task<ActionResult> CreateDefaultUsers()
{
    // setup the default role names
    string role_RegisteredUser = "RegisteredUser";
    string role_Administrator = "Administrator";

    // create the default roles (if they don't exist yet)
    if (await _roleManager.FindByNameAsync(role_RegisteredUser) ==
     null)
        await _roleManager.CreateAsync(new
         IdentityRole(role_RegisteredUser));

    if (await _roleManager.FindByNameAsync(role_Administrator) ==
     null)
        await _roleManager.CreateAsync(new
         IdentityRole(role_Administrator));

    // create a list to track the newly added users
    var addedUserList = new List<ApplicationUser>();

    // check if the admin user already exists
    var email_Admin = "admin@email.com";
    if (await _userManager.FindByNameAsync(email_Admin) == null)
    {
        // create a new admin ApplicationUser account
        var user_Admin = new ApplicationUser()
        {
            SecurityStamp = Guid.NewGuid().ToString(),
            UserName = email_Admin,
            Email = email_Admin,
        };
```

```csharp
        // insert the admin user into the DB
        await _userManager.CreateAsync(user_Admin, _
    configuration["DefaultPasswords:Administrator"]);

        // assign the "RegisteredUser" and "Administrator" roles
        await _userManager.AddToRoleAsync(user_Admin,
         role_RegisteredUser);
        await _userManager.AddToRoleAsync(user_Admin,
         role_Administrator);

        // confirm the e-mail and remove lockout
        user_Admin.EmailConfirmed = true;
        user_Admin.LockoutEnabled = false;

        // add the admin user to the added users list
        addedUserList.Add(user_Admin);
    }

    // check if the standard user already exists
    var email_User = "user@email.com";
    if (await _userManager.FindByNameAsync(email_User) == null)
    {
        // create a new standard ApplicationUser account
        var user_User = new ApplicationUser()
        {
            SecurityStamp = Guid.NewGuid().ToString(),
            UserName = email_User,
            Email = email_User
        };

        // insert the standard user into the DB
        await _userManager.CreateAsync(user_User, _
    configuration["DefaultPasswords:RegisteredUser"]);

        // assign the "RegisteredUser" role
        await _userManager.AddToRoleAsync(user_User,
         role_RegisteredUser);

        // confirm the e-mail and remove lockout
        user_User.EmailConfirmed = true;
        user_User.LockoutEnabled = false;
```

```
            // add the standard user to the added users list
            addedUserList.Add(user_User);
    }

    // if we added at least one user, persist the changes into the DB
    if (addedUserList.Count > 0)
        await _context.SaveChangesAsync();

    return new JsonResult(new
    {
        Count = addedUserList.Count,
        Users = addedUserList
    });
}


// ...existing code...
```

The code is quite self-explanatory, and it has a lot of comments explaining the various steps; however, here's a convenient summary of what we just did:

- We started by defining some default role names (`RegisteredUsers` for the standard registered users, `Administrator` for the administrative-level ones).
- We created a logic to check whether these roles already exist. If they don't exist, we create them. As expected, both tasks have been performed using `RoleManager`.
- We defined a user list local variable to track the newly added users so that we can output it to the user in the JSON object we'll return at the end of the action method.
- We created a logic to check whether a user with the `admin@email.com` username already exists. If it doesn't, we create it and assign it both the `RegisteredUser` and `Administrator` roles, since it will be a standard user *and also* the administrative account of our app.
- We created a logic to check whether a user with the `user@email.com` username already exists; if it doesn't, we create it and assign it the `RegisteredUser` role.
- At the end of the action method, we configured the JSON object that we'll return to the caller; this object contains a count of the added users and a list containing them, which will be serialized into a JSON object that will show their entity values.

The `Administrator` and `RegisteredUser` roles we just implemented here will be the core of our authorization mechanism; all of our users will be assigned to at least one of them. Note how we assigned both of them to the **Admin** user to make them able to do everything a standard user can do, plus more: all the other users only have the latter role, so they'll be unable to perform any administrative-level tasks—as long as they're not provided with the `Administrator` role.

Before moving on, it's worth noting that we're using the user's email address for both the Email and UserName fields. We did that on purpose because those two fields in the ASP.NET Core Identity system are used interchangeably by default; whenever we add a user using the default APIs, the Email provided is saved in the UserName field as well, even if they are two separate fields in the AspNetUsers database table. Although this behavior can be changed, we're going to stick to the default settings so that we'll be able to use the default settings without changing them throughout the whole ASP.NET Core Identity system.

Rerunning the unit test

Now that we have implemented the test, we can rerun the CreateDefaultUsers() test and see whether it passes. As usual, we can do that by right-clicking the WorldCitiesAPI.Test root node from Solution Explorer and selecting **Run Tests**, or from within the **Test Explorer** panel.

If we did everything correctly, we should see something like this:

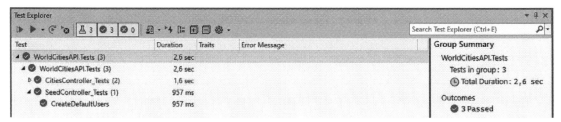

Figure 11.4: CreateDefaultUsers() test passed

Now that our unit test has passed, we can move to the next topic.

Securing the action methods

The main purpose of what we're doing in this chapter is to restrict the usage of some of our Web API to authorized users only. That's the reason we're adding the ASP.NET Identity system, creating a couple of registered users and roles, and implementing a process to authenticate them.

However, we still have to tell our ASP.NET Core app what we want to restrict to registered users only: as a matter of fact, all our controllers and action methods are currently available to everyone, regardless of the HTTP request coming from a registered user – determined by the presence of a valid JWT – or not. What's the point of authenticating these requests if we don't "close" some of these doors?

To perform such a task, we can use AuthorizeAttribute, included with the Microsoft.AspNetCore. Authorization namespace. This attribute can be used to restrict access to controllers and/or action methods to authorized users only; on top of that, it also allows us to specify one or more Roles to authorize, which is precisely what we need to implement a granular authorization scheme.

The first thing we must do is to identify the action methods we want to protect: in our current scenario, it can be wise to restrict the access to all the PUT and POST methods of CitiesController and CountriesController to *registered users* only, meaning that anonymous users won't be able to perform updates to our database.

An even more restrictive policy should be applied to the DELETE methods of those controllers and to the whole SeedController, since they are meant to perform critical changes to our data. Those actions should be accessible to *administrators* only.

Let's see how we can use AuthorizeAttribute to do this.

Securing CitiesController

Open the /Controllers/CitiesController.cs file and add the following using statement to the top of the file:

```
using Microsoft.AspNetCore.Authorization;
```

Once done, add the following attribute above the PutCity and PostCity methods:

```
[Authorize(Roles = "RegisteredUser")]
```

Last but not least, add the following attribute above the DeleteCity method:

```
[Authorize(Roles = "Administrator")]
```

That's it. Let's do the same with CountriesController.

Securing CountriesController

Open the /Controllers/CountriesController.cs file and add the following using statement to the top of the file:

```
using Microsoft.AspNetCore.Authorization;
```

Once done, add the following attribute above the PutCountry and PostCountry methods:

```
[Authorize(Roles = "RegisteredUser")]
```

Last but not least, add the following attribute above the DeleteCountry method:

```
[Authorize(Roles = "Administrator")]
```

Now we can switch to SeedController.

Securing SeedController

SeedController requires a more radical approach, since we want to secure *all* of its action methods, and not just some of them.

To do that, after adding the usual using reference to the Microsoft.AspNetCore.Authorization namespace to the top of the file, put the following attribute above the SeedController constructor:

```
[Authorize(Roles = "Administrator")]
```

When placed at the constructor level, AuthorizeAttribute will be applied to all the controller's action methods, which is precisely what we want.

Now, all these action methods are protected against unauthorized access, as they will accept only requests coming from registered and logged-in users; those who don't have access will receive a `401 Unauthorized` HTTP error response.

That's it; now we're finally done updating our project's classes. However, before switching to Angular, let's take a couple of minutes to better understand a fundamental ASP.NET Core architectural concept that we've been using for quite a while.

A word on async tasks, awaits, and deadlocks

As we can see by looking at what we did so far, all the ASP.NET Core Identity system API's relevant methods are *asynchronous*, meaning that they return an *async task* rather than a given return value. For that very reason, since we need to execute these various tasks one after another, we had to prepend all of them with the `await` keyword.

Here's an example of await usage taken from the preceding code:

```
await _userManager.AddToRoleAsync(user_Admin, role_RegisteredUser);
```

The `await` keyword, as the name implies, awaits the completion of the async task before going forward. It's worth noting that such an expression does not block the thread on which it is executing; instead, it causes the compiler to sign up the rest of the `async` method as a continuation of the awaited task, thus returning the thread control to the caller. Eventually, when the task completes, it invokes its continuation, thus resuming the execution of the `async` method where it left off.

 That's the reason why the `await` keyword can only be used within `async` methods; as a matter of fact, the preceding logic requires the caller to be `async` as well, otherwise, it wouldn't work.

Alternatively, we could have used the `Wait()` method, in the following way:

```
_userManager.AddToRoleAsync(user_Admin, role_RegisteredUser).Wait();
```

However, we didn't do that for good reason. In the opposite way to the `await` keyword, which tells the compiler to *asynchronously wait* for the async task to complete, the parameterless `Wait()` method will *block the calling thread* until the async task has been completed. Therefore, the calling thread will unconditionally wait until the task completes.

To better explain how such techniques impact our ASP.NET Core application, we should spend a little time better understanding the concept of async tasks as they are a pivotal part of the ASP.NET Core TAP model.

One of the first things we should learn when working with sync methods invoking async tasks in ASP. NET is that when the top-level method awaits a task, its current execution context gets blocked until the task completes. This won't be a problem unless that context allows only one thread to run at a time, which is precisely the case with `AspNetSynchronizationContext`.

Chapter 11   527

If we combine these two things, we can easily see that *blocking* an `async` method (that is, a method returning an async task) will expose our application to a high risk of *deadlock*.

A *deadlock*, from a software development perspective, is a dreadful situation that occurs whenever a process or thread enters a waiting state indefinitely, usually because the resource it's waiting for is held by another waiting process. In any legacy ASP.NET web application, we would face a deadlock every time we're blocking a task, simply because that task, in order to complete, will require the same execution context as the invoking method, which is kept blocked by that method until the task completes!

Luckily enough, we're not using legacy ASP.NET here; we're using ASP.NET Core, where the legacy ASP.NET pattern based upon `SynchronizationContext` has been replaced by a *contextless* approach layered upon a versatile, deadlock-resilient thread pool.

This basically means that *blocking the calling thread* using the `Wait()` method is no longer that problematic. Therefore, if we switched our `await` keywords with it, our method would still run and complete just fine. However, by doing so, we would basically use synchronous code to perform asynchronous operations, which is generally considered a bad practice; moreover, we would lose all the benefits brought by asynchronous programming, such as performance and scalability.

For all those reasons, the `await` approach is definitely the way to go there.

For additional information regarding threads, async task awaits, and asynchronous programming in ASP.NET, we highly recommend checking out the outstanding articles written by *Stephen Cleary* on the topic, which will greatly help in understanding some of the most tricky and complex scenarios that we could face when developing with these technologies. Some of them were written a while ago, yet they never really age:

https://blog.stephencleary.com/2012/02/async-and-await.html

https://blogs.msdn.microsoft.com/pfxteam/2012/04/12/asyncawait-faq/

http://blog.stephencleary.com/2012/07/dont-block-on-async-code.html

https://msdn.microsoft.com/en-us/magazine/jj991977.aspx

https://blog.stephencleary.com/2017/03/aspnetcore-synchronization-context.html

Also, we strongly suggest checking out this excellent article about asynchronous programming with async and await at the following link:

https://docs.microsoft.com/en-us/dotnet/csharp/programming-guide/concepts/async/index

Now that we've updated our project's classes and acknowledged the importance of `async` tasks, we can switch to our database and do what it takes to bring it up to speed with our brand-new, identity-powered *Data Model*.

Updating the database

It's now time to create a new migration, and reflect the code changes to the database, by taking advantage of the code-first approach we adopted in *Chapter 5, Data Model with Entity Framework Core*.

Here's a list of what we're going to do in this section:

- **Add the identity migration** using the dotnet-ef command, just like we did in *Chapter 5, Data Model with Entity Framework Core*
- **Apply the migration to the database**, updating it without altering the existing data or performing a drop and recreate
- **Seed the data** using the CreateDefaultUsers() method of SeedController that we implemented earlier on

Let's get to work.

Adding identity migration

The first thing we need to do is to add a new migration to our data model to reflect the changes that we have implemented by extending the ApplicationDbContext class.

To do that, open a command line or PowerShell prompt, go to our WorldCitiesAPI project's root folder, and then write the following:

```
dotnet ef migrations add "Identity" -o "Data/Migrations"
```

A new migration should then be added to the project, as shown in the following screenshot:

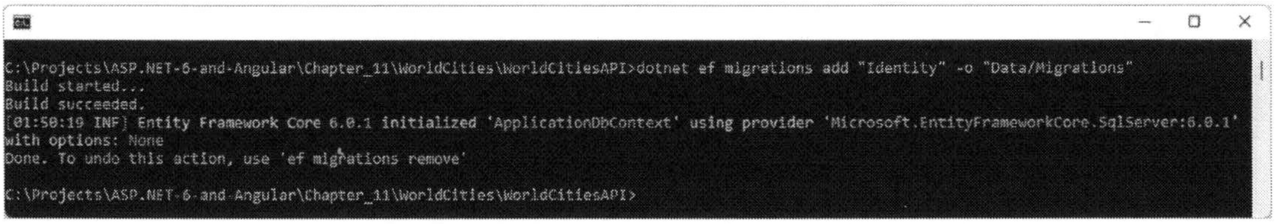

Figure 11.5: Adding a new migration

The new migration files will be autogenerated in the \Data\Migrations\ folder.

> Those who experience issues while creating migrations can try to clear the `\Data\`
> `Migrations\` folder before running the preceding `dotnet-ef` command.
>
> For additional information regarding Entity Framework Core migrations, and how to
> troubleshoot them, check out the following guide:
>
> `https://docs.microsoft.com/en-us/ef/core/managing-schemas/migrations/`

Applying the migration

The next thing to do is to apply the new migration to our database. We can choose between two options:

- **Updating the existing data model schema** while keeping all its data as it is
- **Dropping and recreating the database** from scratch

As a matter of fact, the whole purpose of the EF Core migration feature is to provide a way to incrementally update the database schema while preserving existing data in the database; for that very reason, we're going to follow the former path.

> Before applying migrations, it's always advisable to perform a full database backup; this
> advice is particularly important when dealing with production environments. For small
> databases such as the one currently used by our `WorldCitiesAPI` web app, it would take
> a few seconds.
>
> For additional information about how to perform a full backup of a SQL Server database,
> read the following guide:
>
> `https://docs.microsoft.com/en-us/sql/relational-databases/backup-restore/`
> `create-a-full-database-backup-sql-server`

Updating the existing data model

To apply the migration to the existing database schema without losing the existing data, run the following command from our `WorldCitiesAPI` project's root folder:

```
dotnet ef database update
```

The dotnet ef tool will then apply the necessary updates to our SQL database schema and output the relevant information, as well as the actual SQL queries, in the console buffer.

Once the task has been completed, we should connect to our database using the **SQL Server Management Studio** tool that we installed back in *Chapter 5, Data Model with Entity Framework Core*, and check for the presence of the new identity-related tables.

If everything went well, we should be able to see the new identity tables together with our existing Cities and Countries tables:

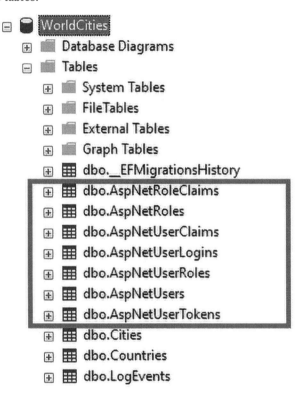

Figure 11.6: Viewing the new identity tables in SSMS Object Explorer

As we can easily guess, these tables are still empty. To populate them, we'll have to run the CreateDefaultUsers() method of SeedController, which is something that we're going to do in a short while.

Dropping and recreating the data model from scratch

For completeness, let's spend a little time looking at how to recreate our data model and **database schema (DB schema)** from scratch. Needless to say, if we opt for that route, we will lose all our existing data. However, we could always reload everything using the Import() method of SeedController, hence it wouldn't be a great loss.

As a matter of fact, we would only lose what we did during our CRUD-based tests in *Chapter 5, Data Model with Entity Framework Core*.

Although performing a database drop and recreate is not the suggested approach, especially considering that we've adopted the *migration* pattern precisely to avoid such a scenario, it can be a decent workaround whenever we lose control of our migrations, provided that we entirely back up the data before doing that and, most importantly, know how to restore everything afterward.

 Although it might seem like a horrible way to fix things, that's definitely not the case; we're still in the development phase, hence we can definitely allow a full database refresh.

Should we choose to take this route, here are the **dotnet-ef** console commands to use:

```
> dotnet ef database drop
> dotnet ef database update
```

The drop command should ask for a Y/N confirmation before proceeding. When it does, hit the *Y* key and let it happen. When the drop and update tasks are both done, we can run our project in *Debug* mode and pay a visit to the Import() method of SeedController. Once done, we should have an updated database with ASP.NET Core Identity support.

Seeding the data

Regardless of the option we chose to update the database, we now have to repopulate it.

To do that, open the /Controllers/SeedController.cs file and (temporarily) comment out the AuthorizeAttribute that we've added a moment ago to restrict its usage to *Administrators*, so that we'll (temporarily) be able to use it.

As a matter of fact, we need to do that because we currently have no way to authenticate ourselves as administrators since our Angular app doesn't have a login form (yet). Don't worry, though: we'll close this gap soon enough!

Once done, hit *F5* to run the project in *Debug* mode, and then manually input the following URL in the browser's address bar: https://localhost:40443/api/Seed/CreateDefaultUsers.

Then, let the CreateDefaultUsers() method of SeedController work its magic.

We should then be able to see the following JSON response:

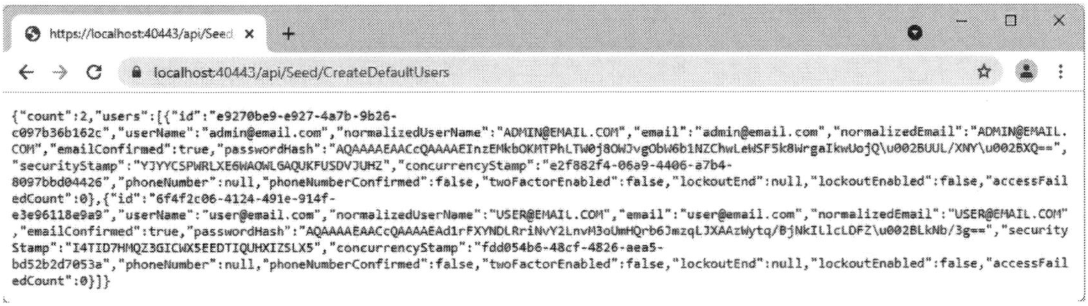

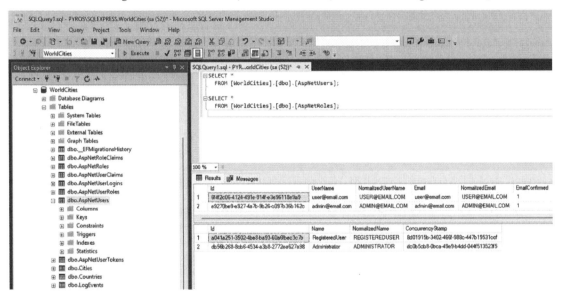

Figure 11.7: The CreateDefaultUsers() JSON response

This output already tells us that our first two users have been created and stored in our data model. However, we can also confirm that by connecting to our database using the SQL Server Management Studio tool and taking a look at the dbo.AspNetUsers table (see the following screenshot):

Figure 11.8: Querying dbo.AspNetUsers

As we can see, we used the following T-SQL queries to check for the existing users and roles:

```sql
SELECT *
  FROM [WorldCities].[dbo].[AspNetUsers];


SELECT *
  FROM [WorldCities].[dbo].[AspNetRoles];
```

Now that we've confirmed that the users and roles are there, we can uncomment the AuthorizeAttribute of SeedController to protect it from unauthorized access.

We're finally done with the *back-end* part. Our ASP.NET Core Identity system implementation is up, running, and fully integrated with our data model and database; now we just need to implement it within our controllers and hook it up with our Angular client app.

Implementing authentication in Angular

In order to handle JWT-based token authentication, we need to set up our ASP.NET *back-end* and our Angular *front-end* to handle all the required tasks.

In the previous sections, we spent a good amount of time configuring the .NET Core Identity services and middlewares, meaning that we're halfway done; as a matter of fact, we're almost done with the *server-side* tasks. At the same time, we did nothing at the *front-end* level: the sample users that we created in the previous section—admin@email.com and user@email.com—have no way to log in, and there isn't a registration form for creating new users.

However, if we think about what we did during the previous chapters, we should already know what to do to fill such gap: implementing an interactive *login* (and possibly a *registration*) form, using the same techniques adopted for CityEditComponent and CountryEditComponent.

More specifically, here's a list of our upcoming tasks:

- **Add the LoginRequest and LoginResult interfaces** to communicate with the ASP.NET Core Web API
- **Implement a new AuthService** that will perform the HTTP requests and receive the login challenge result
- **Create a LoginComponent** that will host the login form and allow the users that own an account to initiate the login attempt
- **Update the NavMenuComponent** to allow users to access the LoginComponent, make them aware of their logged-in status, and perform the logout
- **Add some additional control mechanisms** to better deal with the authentication status and authorization permissions, such as *HttpInterceptor* and *Route Guards*
- **Test the new implementation** to see if everything works up to this point

By the end of the section, we should be able to log in and log out using the users that we created with SeedController earlier on.

Adding the LoginRequest interface

Let's start by creating a new /src/app/auth/ folder in our WorldCities angular project, where we'll put everything that we're going to add.

Once done, create a new login-request.ts file in that folder and fill it with the following content:

```
export interface LoginRequest {
  email: string;
  password: string;
}
```

As we can see, the interface strictly resembles the `LoginRequest` class used by our ASP.NET Core Web API. That shouldn't be a surprise, since it will be used by the HTTP request that will call the `Login` action method of `AccountController`.

Adding the LoginResult interface

Now we need the interface that will handle the login action method's JSON response.

Create a new `login-result.ts` file in the `/src/app/auth/` folder and fill it with the following content:

```
export interface LoginResult {
  success: boolean;
  message: string;
  token?: string;
}
```

Again, the interface strictly resembles the `LoginResult` POCO class of our ASP.NET Core Web API.

Implementing AuthService

Now that we have the required interfaces to initiate our requests (and receive the responses), we can implement the Angular service that will perform them.

Create a new `auth.service.ts` file in the `/src/app/auth/` folder and fill it with the following content:

```
import { Injectable } from '@angular/core';
import { HttpClient } from '@angular/common/http';
import { Observable } from 'rxjs';

import { environment } from './../../environments/environment';
import { LoginRequest } from './login-request';
import { LoginResult } from './login-result';

@Injectable({
  providedIn: 'root',
})
export class AuthService {
  constructor(
    protected http: HttpClient) {
  }

  public tokenKey: string = "token";

  isAuthenticated() : boolean {
    return this.getToken() !== null;
  }
```

```
    getToken() : string | null {
      return localStorage.getItem(this.tokenKey);
    }

    login(item: LoginRequest): Observable<LoginResult> {
      var url = environment.baseUrl + "api/Account/Login";
      return this.http.post<LoginResult>(url, item);
    }
  }
```

The preceding code shouldn't be a surprise. We're just doing the same tasks we already did in the previous Angular services we've implemented back in *Chapter 8, Code Tweaks and Data Services*. The only notable difference is that we're not extending the `BaseService` superclass here. We don't need to do that, at least for now.

Creating LoginComponent

Let's now create the `LoginComponent` file, which will allow our users to perform the login attempt.

Open **Command Prompt**, navigate up to the `WorldCities` Angular project's `/src/app/auth/` folder, and type the following:

```
> ng generate component Login --flat --module=app --skip-tests
```

The above command will create the `LoginComponent` files within the current folder.

login.component.ts

Once done, open the `login.component.ts` file and update its content in the following way:

```
import { Component, OnInit } from '@angular/core';
import { ActivatedRoute, Router } from '@angular/router';
import { FormGroup, FormControl, Validators, AbstractControl, AsyncValidatorFn
} from '@angular/forms';

import { BaseFormComponent } from '../base-form.component';
import { AuthService } from './auth.service';
import { LoginRequest } from './login-request';
import { LoginResult } from './login-result';

@Component({
  selector: 'app-login',
  templateUrl: './login.component.html',
  styleUrls: ['./login.component.scss']
})
```

```
export class LoginComponent
  extends BaseFormComponent implements OnInit {

  title?: string;
  loginResult?: LoginResult;

  constructor(
    private activatedRoute: ActivatedRoute,
    private router: Router,
    private authService: AuthService) {
    super();
  }

  ngOnInit() {
    this.form = new FormGroup({
      email: new FormControl('', Validators.required),
      password: new FormControl('', Validators.required)
      });
  }

  onSubmit() {
    var loginRequest = <LoginRequest>{};
    loginRequest.email = this.form.controls['email'].value;
    loginRequest.password = this.form.controls['password'].value;

    this.authService
      .login(loginRequest)
      .subscribe(result => {
        console.log(result);
        this.loginResult = result;
        if (result.success && result.token) {
          localStorage.setItem(this.authService.tokenKey, result.token);
        }
      }, error => {
        console.log(error);
        if (error.status == 401) {
          this.loginResult = error.error;
        }
      });
  }
}
```

For the sake of simplicity, we'll not review the preceding code, since we should already be able to fully understand everything it does. The only new concept there is introduced by the following line, when the successful token is stored in localStorage:

```
localStorage.setItem(this.authService.tokenKey, result.token);
```

The above line makes use of the *Web Storage API*, a JavaScript feature that provides a storage mechanism that browsers can use to securely store key/value pairs. The API provides two mechanisms to store data:

- **sessionStorage**, which is available for the duration of the page session as long as the browser is open (including page reloads and restores)
- **localStorage**, which persists even when the browser is closed and then reopened: the data stored that way has no expiration date and must be manually cleared (through JavaScript or by clearing the browser's cache or *Locally Stored Data*)

In our code sample, we're using localStorage because we want to keep the JWT token until we manually invalidate it when it expires. However, both mechanisms are viable enough, depending on the given usage scenario and desired outcome.

login.component.html

Let's now open the login.component.html file and provide our LoginComponent with a suitable UI:

```html
<div class="login">
  <h1>Login</h1>
  <form [formGroup]="form" (ngSubmit)="onSubmit()">

    <p>
      <mat-error *ngIf="loginResult && !loginResult.success">
        <strong>ERROR</strong>: {{loginResult.message}}
      </mat-error>
    </p>

    <!-- Name -->
    <mat-form-field>
      <mat-label>Email:</mat-label>
      <input matInput formControlName="email" required
             placeholder="Insert email">
      <mat-error *ngFor="let error of getErrors(form.get('email')!,
          'Email')">
        {{error}}
      </mat-error>
    </mat-form-field>

    <!-- Lat -->
```

```
    <mat-form-field>
      <mat-label>Password:</mat-label>
      <input matInput type="password" formControlName="password" required
             placeholder="Insert Password">
      <mat-error *ngFor="let error of getErrors(form.get('password')!,
      'Password')">
        {{error}}
      </mat-error>
    </mat-form-field>

    <div>
      <button mat-flat-button color="primary"
              type="submit">
        Login
      </button>
      <button mat-flat-button color="secondary"
              [routerLink]="['/']">
        Cancel
      </button>
    </div>
  </form>
</div>
```

Again, nothing new here: just a plain *Reactive Form* featuring *Angular Material* components, created using the same techniques of our good old `CityEditComponent`. The only real difference is `type="password"`, which we used in `matInput` used for the password field, which will mask the input text when we type it.

As we can see, we've used a global `mat-error` component to handle the error message of `LoginResult` coming with a failed login attempt, and added the usual required validator checks to the two form fields we need to use: `email` and `password`.

login.component.scss

Last but not least, let's insert some minimal content in the `login.component.scss` file:

```
mat-form-field {
  display: block;
  margin: 10px 0;
}
```

And that's it! Our `LoginComponent` is ready; we just need to add the client-side route and update our `NavMenuComponent` so that our users will be able to reach it.

Updating AppRoutingModule

Open the `app-routing.module.ts` file and add the following line after the last `import` statement:

```
import { LoginComponent } from './auth/login.component';
```

And the following line after the last route:

```
    { path: 'login', component: LoginComponent }
```

Now, our users will be able to access `LoginComponent` using the `/login` route.

Updating NavMenuComponent

However, we definitely don't want them having to manually type it in their browser's address bar.

For that very reason, open the `nav-menu.component.html` file and add the following highlighted lines to the existing **Countries** button:

```
<!-- ...existing code... -->
<a mat-flat-button color="primary" [routerLink]="['/countries']">
  Countries
</a>
<span class="separator"></span>
<a mat-flat-button color="primary" [routerLink]="['/login']">
  Login
</a>

<!-- ...existing code... -->
```

As we can see, this time we didn't just add a new **Login** button: we also took the chance to add a separator element between the new button and the previous ones to enforce a different UI behavior. More precisely, we want our login button to be aligned to the right side of our navigation menu instead of being stacked on the left with the other ones.

To make this happen, we need to open the `nav-menu.component.scss` file and add the following class:

```
.separator {
    flex: 1 1 auto;
}
```

That's it. Now we can finally test what we have done so far.

Testing LoginComponent

To test our new `LoginComponent`, hit *F5* to run the projects in *Debug* mode, and then click on the **Login** navigation link that should appear to the right side of our top menu. If we did everything properly, we should see the login form.

Let's test the error message first. Fill the form with invalid data and press the **Login** button. If we did everything properly, we should see mat-error displaying the error message, as shown in the following screenshot:

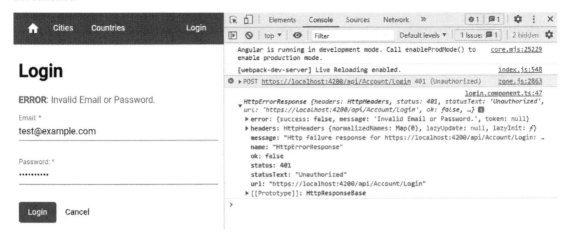

Figure 11.9: Angular LoginComponent showing an error

Now we can test the actual login using the user@email.com address that we created with our SeedController early on (and its password). If everything works as it should, we should be able to receive a valid token in the browser's console log, as shown in the following screenshot:

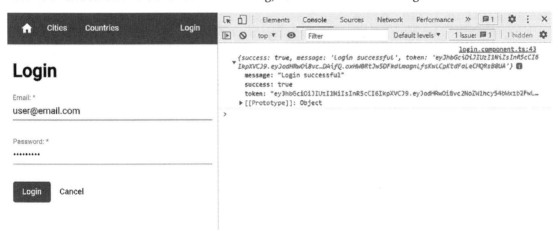

Figure 11.10: Angular LoginComponent performing a successful login

Not bad. Furthermore, if we check our browser's *Local Storage* (**Application** > **Local Storage** for chromium-based browsers), we should also find our token stored there.

Now we need to update our app's UI to let our users know that they are logged in, as well as perform a logout. Let's do this.

Adding the authStatus observable

A great way to let our Angular app know that a valid token has been retrieved, and therefore the user has been successfully authenticated, is to set up a dedicated Observable in AuthService.

Open the auth.service.ts file and add the following highlighted lines to the existing code:

```typescript
import { Injectable } from '@angular/core';
import { HttpClient } from '@angular/common/http';
import { Observable, Subject, tap } from 'rxjs';

import { LoginRequest } from './login-request';
import { LoginResult } from './login-result';
import { environment } from './../../environments/environment';

@Injectable({
  providedIn: 'root',
})
export class AuthService {

  private tokenKey: string = "token";

  private _authStatus = new Subject<boolean>();
  public authStatus = this._authStatus.asObservable();

  constructor(
    protected http: HttpClient) {
  }

  isAuthenticated() : boolean {
    return this.getToken() !== null;
  }

  getToken() : string | null {
    return localStorage.getItem(this.tokenKey);
  }

  init() : void {
    if (this.isAuthenticated())
      this.setAuthStatus(true);
  }

  login(item: LoginRequest): Observable<LoginResult> {
    var url = environment.baseUrl + "api/Account/Login";
```

```
        return this.http.post<LoginResult>(url, item)
          .pipe(tap(loginResult => {
            if (loginResult.success && loginResult.token) {
              localStorage.setItem(this.tokenKey, loginResult.token);
              this.setAuthStatus(true);
            }
          }));
    }


    logout() {
        localStorage.removeItem(this.tokenKey);
        this.setAuthStatus(false);
    }


    private setAuthStatus(isAuthenticated: boolean): void {
        this._authStatus.next(isAuthenticated);
    }
}
```

The authStatus observable we've just added to the AuthService class will notify all the subscribed components regarding the authentication status (true or false, depending on the login challenge result). The status can be updated using the setAuthStatus method, which we'll have to call two times:

- **When the user logs in,** passing a true parameter
- **When the user logs out,** passing a false parameter
- **When the app starts,** passing a true parameter if the user is already authenticated

We've already implemented the second case in the new logout() method, where we've also removed the token from localStorage; as for the first one, we have to implement it within LoginComponent, as the login process happens there; the third and last one can be implemented in the AppComponent class.

Let's start with LoginComponent. Open the login.component.ts file and update the existing onSubmit() method in the following way (new/updated lines are highlighted):

```
// ...existing code...


if (result.success) {
  this.router.navigate(["/"]);
}


// ...existing code...
```

While we were there, we took the chance to call the router.navigate method to bring the authorized user back to the home view.

It's also worth noting that, since we've encapsulated all the token's read and write tasks in AuthService, we've changed the access modifier of the tokenKey variable from public to private.

Now we just need to subscribe to the authStatus observable wherever we need it.

Updating the UI

The first component that comes to mind is NavMenuComponent, since we want to update the app's top navigation menu according to the user login status.

However, since we've used localStorage and therefore we plan to preserve the token between browser sessions, we also need to update the **AppComponent** to notify the authStatus subscribers of the token presence when the app starts up.

NavMenuComponent

Let's start with NavMenuComponent. Open the nav-menu.component.ts file and add the following high-lighted lines:

```
import { Component, OnInit, OnDestroy } from '@angular/core';
import { Router } from '@angular/router';
import { Subject, takeUntil } from 'rxjs';
import { AuthService } from '../auth/auth.service';


@Component({
  selector: 'app-nav-menu',
  templateUrl: './nav-menu.component.html',
  styleUrls: ['./nav-menu.component.scss']
})
export class NavMenuComponent implements OnInit, OnDestroy {

  private destroySubject = new Subject();
  isLoggedIn: boolean = false;

  constructor(private authService: AuthService,
    private router: Router) {
    this.authService.authStatus
      .pipe(takeUntil(this.destroySubject))
      .subscribe(result => {
        this.isLoggedIn = result;
      })
  }
```

```
onLogout(): void {
    this.authService.logout();
    this.router.navigate(["/"]);
}

ngOnInit(): void {
    this.isLoggedIn = this.authService.isAuthenticated();
}

ngOnDestroy() {
    this.destroySubject.next(true);
    this.destroySubject.complete();
}
}
```

As we can see, we subscribed to the authStatus observable to change the value of our isLoggedIn variable, which we can use to update the UI.

We've also added a local onLogout() method that we can use to handle a **Logout** action: when the user performs a logout, that method will call the logout() method of AuthService that will remove the token and notify the subscribers. Right after that, the onLogout() method will bring the user back to the home view using the Router service that we've injected into the constructor.

While we were there, we also took the opportunity to implement the takeUntil() method that we've seen in *Chapter 9, Back-End and Front-End Debugging* to unsubscribe it when the component is destroyed. This measure wasn't strictly necessary in this specific case, as NavMenuComponent is typically meant to be instantiated once, but getting used to it won't hurt.

Let's now make use of these new local members. Open the nav-menu.component.html file and update its content by adding the following highlighted lines:

```
<!-- ...existing code... -->

<span class="separator"></span>
<a *ngIf="!isLoggedIn" mat-flat-button color="primary"
    [routerLink]="['/login']">
  Login
```

```
</a>
<a *ngIf="isLoggedIn" mat-flat-button color="primary"
    (click)="onLogout()">
  Logout
</a>

<!-- ...existing code... -->
```

That's it.

AppComponent

Let's now move on to AppComponent. Open the app.component.ts file and change the existing code accordingly with the following highlighted lines:

```
import { Component, OnInit } from '@angular/core';
import { AuthService } from './auth/auth.service';

@Component({
  selector: 'app-root',
  templateUrl: './app.component.html',
  styleUrls: ['./app.component.scss']
})

export class AppComponent implements OnInit {
  title = 'WorldCities';

  constructor(private authService: AuthService) { }

  ngOnInit(): void {
    this.authService.init();
  }
}
```

Now, the authStatus subscribers will be notified of the token presence when the app starts up and act accordingly. In our scenario, this will allow NavMenuComponent to show a **Login** or **Logout** link according to the user's status.

Testing the observable

Now we can run the same test we did a short while ago again and see the result of our work. If we did everything correctly, we should be able to see the **Logout** button in the navigation menu (as shown in the following screenshot), which can be used to bring the user back to the initial, non-logged-in status:

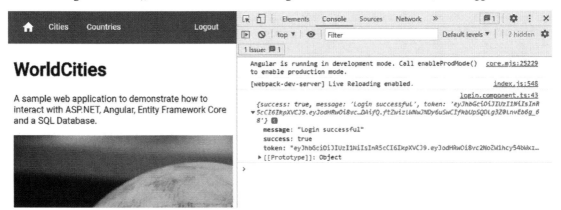

Figure 11.11: Angular LoginComponent with the Logout button

That's great, right? However, our authentication puzzle still has two very important missing pieces:

- We need to add that token to the header of all our HTTP requests so that the Web API will be able to check it and authenticate our calls
- We need to restrict some routes of our Angular app so that unauthorized users won't be able to navigate to the components they're not allowed to reach, see, and/or interact with

Luckily enough, the Angular framework provides two powerful interfaces that allow us to do all that: *HttpInterceptors* and *Route Guards*. In the next section, we'll learn what they are meant for and how we can use them to fulfill our tasks.

HttpInterceptors

The Angular HttpInterceptor interface provides a standardized mechanism to intercept and/or transform outgoing HTTP requests and/or incoming HTTP responses. Interceptors are quite similar to the ASP.NET middlewares that we introduced in *Chapter 3*, *Looking Around* and then played with up to this chapter, except that they work at the front-end level.

Interceptors are a major feature of Angular since they can be used for a number of different tasks: they can inspect and/or log our app's HTTP traffic, modify the requests, cache the responses, and so on; they are a convenient way to centralize all these tasks so that we don't have to implement them explicitly on our data services and/or within the various HttpClient-based method calls. Moreover, they can also be chained, meaning that we can have multiple interceptors working together in a forward-and-backward chain of request/response handlers.

For additional information about HTTP interceptors, take a look at the following URLs:

https://angular.io/api/common/http/HttpInterceptor

https://angular.io/api/common/http/HTTP_INTERCEPTORS

The best way to understand how an HttpInterceptor works is to implement one.

Implementing AuthInterceptor

Create a new auth.interceptor.ts file in the /src/app/auth/ folder and fill its content in the following way:

```
import { Injectable } from '@angular/core';
import { HttpInterceptor, HttpRequest, HttpHandler, HttpEvent,
HttpErrorResponse } from '@angular/common/http';
import { Router } from '@angular/router';
import { catchError, Observable, throwError } from 'rxjs';
import { AuthService } from './auth.service';

@Injectable({
  providedIn: 'root'
})
export class AuthInterceptor implements HttpInterceptor {
  constructor(
    private authService: AuthService,
    private router: Router) { }


  intercept(req: HttpRequest<any>, next: HttpHandler):
Observable<HttpEvent<any>> {
    // get the auth token
    var token = this.authService.getToken();

    // if the token is present, clone the request
    // replacing the original headers with the authorization
    if (token) {
      req = req.clone({
        setHeaders: {
          Authorization: 'Bearer ${token}'
        }
      });
    }
```

```
    // send the request to the next handler
    return next.handle(req).pipe(
      catchError((error) => {
        // Perform logout on 401 - Unauthorized HTTP response errors
        if (error instanceof HttpErrorResponse && error.status === 401) {
          this.authService.logout();
          this.router.navigate(['login']);
        }
        return throwError(error);
      })
    );
  }
}
```

As we can see, `AuthInterceptor` implements the `HttpInterceptor` interface by defining an `intercept()` method. This method carries out two main tasks:

- Intercepting all the outgoing HTTP requests and adding the JWT bearer token to their HTTP headers (if present), so that the ASP.NET Core's `JwtBearerMiddleware` will be able to validate it and authenticate our calls
- Intercepting all HTTP errors and, in case of a `401 - Unauthorized` response status code, performing the `logout()` method of `AuthService` and bringing the user back to the `Login` view

Calling the `logout()` method after a `401` error will ensure that the token will be removed from `localStorage` whenever the *back-end* discovers it is no longer valid (such as when it expires), thus allowing our users to log in again.

 Removing the JWT token when it expires – and consequently logging out our users – is an implementation choice that we made to keep things simple: most production apps provide a better alternative by adopting a *refresh token mechanism,* which can be rather complex to implement within the scope of this book. See the **Finishing touches** section at the end of this chapter for further details on that.

Now we have an `AuthInterceptor` that can make good use of our JWT token throughout the whole HTTP request/response cycle: we just need to tell our Angular app to use it.

Updating AppModule

Just like any other Angular class, `AuthInterceptor` needs to be properly configured within the root-level `AppModule`. This requires the addition of the following highlighted references:

```
import { HttpClientModule, HTTP_INTERCEPTORS } from '@angular/common/http';
import { AuthInterceptor } from './auth/auth.interceptor';
```

And add the `AuthInterceptor` in the `providers` collection, in the following way:

```
providers: [
    { provide: HTTP_INTERCEPTORS,
      useClass: AuthInterceptor,
      multi: true }
]
```

`AuthInterceptor` is now ready to "intercept" all the outgoing HTTP requests and add the token (if present) so that our ASP.NET Core Web API will be able to fetch it and authorize us accordingly.

 The `multi: true` property that we can see in the preceding code is a required setting because `HTTP_INTERCEPTORS` is a multi-provider token that is expecting to inject an array of multiple values, rather than a single one.

Before moving on to the next topic, let's spend a moment checking that `AuthInterceptor` is working fine.

Testing HttpInterceptor

Hit *F5* to run our app in *Debug* mode. Click the **Login** link on the navigation menu and perform the login using one of our test users, just like we did for our previous tests.

Once logged in, navigate to the **Countries** view and then click to a country of our choice to access the **Edit Country** view; once there, try to edit the country and save our work. If the `HttpInterceptor` is working properly, we should be brought back to the **Countries** view and see the updated country's data because the HTTP request was sent to the Web API with a valid token.

Right after that, click the **Logout** link on the navigation menu and try to perform the same identical steps. If `HttpInterceptor` is working properly, we should now see a *401 – Unauthorized* HTTP error message in the browser's console log when trying to save our country. That's the expected behavior since the JWT token was removed from `localStorage` right after the logout, and therefore the HTTP request was sent without a valid authorization header, thus being blocked by the Web API's `AuthorizeAttribute`.

Let's now move to the next feature: *Route Guards*.

Route Guards

As we learned in *Chapter 3, Looking Around*, the Angular router is the service that allows our users to navigate through the various *views* of our app; each view updates the *front-end* and (possibly) calls the *back-end* to retrieve content.

If we think about it, we can see how the Angular router is the *front-end* counterpart of the ASP.NET Core routing interface, which is responsible for mapping request URIs to *back-end* endpoints and dispatching incoming requests to those endpoints. Since both of these modules share the same behavior, they also have similar requirements that we have to take care of when we implement an authentication and authorization mechanism in our app.

Throughout the previous chapters, we've defined a lot of routes on the *back-end* as well as on the *front-end* to grant our users access to the various ASP.NET Core action methods and Angular views that we've implemented. If we think about it, we can see how all of these routes share a common feature: *anyone can access them*. To put it in other words, *any user is free to go anywhere within our web app*. They can edit cities and countries, to say one... Or at least they will *think* they can, until the AuthorizeAttribute that we implemented on our back-end controllers early on prevents them from doing that. The fact that the Web API will actively block their attempt is great for protecting our data, and we should never get rid of such a feature, but it's not that great in terms of user experience since it will still leave our users in the dark:

Why does the app tell me I can edit such an item if I am not allowed to?

It goes without saying that such behavior, although acceptable in development, is highly undesirable in any production scenario; when the app goes live, we would definitely want to protect some of these routes by restricting them to authorized users only—in other words, to *guard* them.

Route Guards are a mechanism to properly enforce such a requirement; they can be added to our route configuration to return values that can control the router's behavior in the following way:

- If a Route Guard returns true, the navigation process continues
- If it returns false, the navigation process stops
- If it returns UrlTree, the navigation process is canceled and replaced by a new navigation to the given UrlTree

When implemented properly, *Route Guards* will prevent our users from seeing odd client-side behaviors and asking questions like the one above.

Available guards

The following Route Guards are currently available in Angular:

- CanActivate: Mediates navigation to a given *route*
- CanActivateChild: Mediates navigation to a given *child route*
- CanDeactivate: Mediates navigation away from the current *route*
- Resolve: Performs some arbitrary operations (such as custom data retrieval tasks) before activating the *route*
- CanLoad: Mediates navigation to a given asynchronous *module*

Each one of them is available through a *superclass* that acts as a *common interface*. Whenever we want to create our own guard, we'll just have to extend the corresponding superclass and implement the relevant method(s).

Any route can be configured with multiple guards: CanDeactivate and CanActivateChild guards will be checked first, from the deepest child route to the top; right after that, the router will check CanActivate guards from the top down to the deepest child route. Once done, CanLoad routes will be checked for asynchronous modules. If any of these guards returns false, the navigation will be stopped and all pending guards will be canceled.

For further information about Route Guards and their role in the Angular routing work-flow, check out the following link: https://angular.io/guide/router#preventing-unauthorized-access

Enough with the theory: let's add our own `AuthGuard`.

Implementing AuthGuard

Create a new auth.guard.ts file in the /src/app/auth/ folder and fill its content in the following way:

```
import { Injectable } from '@angular/core';
import { CanActivate, ActivatedRouteSnapshot, RouterStateSnapshot, Router,
UrlTree } from '@angular/router';
import { Observable } from 'rxjs';
import { AuthService } from './auth.service';


@Injectable({
  providedIn: 'root'
})
export class AuthGuard implements CanActivate {
  constructor(
    private authService: AuthService,
    private router: Router
  ) {
  }

  canActivate(route: ActivatedRouteSnapshot, state: RouterStateSnapshot):
    Observable<boolean | UrlTree> | Promise<boolean | UrlTree> | boolean |
UrlTree {
    if (this.authService.isAuthenticated()) {
      return true;
    }
    this.router.navigate(['/login'], { queryParams: { returnUrl: state.url }
});
    return false;
  }
}
```

As we can see, our guard extends the `CanActivate` interface, returning `true` or `false` depending on the return value of the `isAuthenticated()` method of `AuthService` (which is *injected* into the constructor through DI), thus conditionally allowing or blocking the navigation based on it; no wonder its name is `AuthGuard`.

Once they have been created, guards can be bound to the various routes from within the route configuration itself, which provides a property for each guard type. Let's add the `canActivate` property to the relevant routes within our `AppRoutingModule`.

Updating AppRoutingModule

Open the `app-routing.module.ts` file and updates its content accordingly with the following highlighted lines:

```
// ...existing code...

import { AuthGuard } from './auth/auth.guard';

const routes: Routes = [
  { path: '', component: HomeComponent, pathMatch: 'full' },
  { path: 'cities', component: CitiesComponent },
  { path: 'city/:id', component: CityEditComponent, canActivate: [AuthGuard] },
  { path: 'city', component: CityEditComponent, canActivate: [AuthGuard] },
  { path: 'countries', component: CountriesComponent },
  { path: 'country/:id', component: CountryEditComponent, canActivate:
[AuthGuard] },
  { path: 'country', component: CountryEditComponent, canActivate: [AuthGuard]
},
  { path: 'login', component: LoginComponent }
];

// ...existing code...
```

That's it. Our `AuthGuard` will now prevent non-registered users from accessing `CityEditComponent` and `CountryEditComponent`.

Testing AuthGuard

Let's now test our `AuthGuard` to see whether it returns the expected results.

Hit *F5* to run our app in *Debug* mode. Click the **Login** link on the navigation menu and perform the login using one of our test users, just like we did for our previous tests.

Once logged in, navigate to the **Countries** view and then click to a country of our choice to access the **Edit Country** view. If `AuthGuard` is working properly, we should be able to reach the view, since our *logged-in* status allows us to activate that route.

Once done, click the **Logout** link on the navigation menu and try to perform the same identical steps. If `AuthGuard` is working properly, clicking on the country name or the **Add new country** button should bring us to the **Login** view, since our *not logged in* status prevents unregistered users from activating those routes.

That's it. Now, our Angular app's behavior will be consistent with the auth policies that we've set up in our Web API.

Finishing touches

Our hard work has finally come to an end. However, our app still lacks some additional finishing touches that would further improve what we did so far.

More specifically, here's a list of "minor" and major UI, UX, and functional issues that we should address if we aim to release our app in production:

- **Hide the "Add New City" and "Add new Country" buttons** to unregistered users, using the `*ngIf` preprocessor directive and the `isAuthenticated()` method of `AuthService`.

- **Implement a RegisterComponent** to allow users to create an account. Needless to say, this feature will also require the addition of new client-side routes, new interfaces, new validators for email addresses and passwords, new action methods in `AccountController`, and so on.

- **Add a refresh token mechanism** to allow the client to automatically retrieve a new token after the previous one expires instead of deleting the expired one and redirecting our users to the login page. Implementing this feature will require a refactor of our `AuthInterceptor` class, a dedicated DB table to store the refresh tokens (the `AspNetUserTokens` created by our *Identity* migration can be used to do that, at least to some extent), additional back-end endpoints, and more.

The first two features can be easily implemented with what we've learned so far; however, the refresh token mechanism can be rather complex to implement and goes way beyond the sample implementation that we've pulled off in this chapter, which is intended to be for demonstration purposes only.

Luckily enough, there are many third-party packages, including, but not yet limited to, the *IdentityServer* that we've talked about at the start of this chapter, that will allow us to skip most of the heavy lifting.

Summary

At the start of this chapter, we introduced the concepts of authentication and authorization, acknowledging the fact that most applications, including ours, do require a mechanism to properly handle authenticated and non-authenticated clients as well as authorized and unauthorized requests.

We took some time to properly understand the similarities and differences between authentication and authorization as well as the pros and cons of handling these tasks using our own internal provider or delegating them to third-party providers such as Google, Facebook, and Twitter. Right after that, we briefly enumerated the various web-based authentication methods available nowadays: sessions, tokens, signatures, and two-factor strategies of various sorts. After careful consideration, we chose to stick with the token-based approach using JWT, this being a solid and well-known standard for any *front-end* framework.

To be able to use it, we added the required packages to our project and did what was needed to properly configure them, such as performing some updates in our `Program` and `ApplicationDbContext` classes and creating a new `ApplicationUser` entity. After implementing all the required *back-end* changes, as well as adding some new controllers and services, we created a new Entity Framework Core migration to update our database accordingly.

Right after that, we switched to our Angular project, where we had to deal with the *front-end* part of the job. While doing that, we spent some valuable time reviewing the new Angular features we were using to perform the various tasks, such as *HTTP interceptors* and *Route Guards*, and learning how to use them to protect some of our application views, routes, and APIs from unauthorized access.

We're now ready to switch to the next topic, **progressive web apps**, which will keep us busy throughout the next chapter.

Suggested topics

For further information, we recommend the following topics: Authentication, authorization, HTTP protocol, secure socket layer, session state management, indirection, single sign-on, Azure AD Authentication Library (ADAL), ASP.NET Core Identity, IdentityServer, OpenID, Open ID Connect (OIDC), OAuth, OAuth 2, Two-Factor Authentication (2FA), SMS 2FA, Time-Based One-Time Password Algorithm (TOTP), TOTP 2FA, IdentityUser, stateless, Cross-Site Scripting (XSS), Cross-Site Request Forgery (CSRF), Angular HttpClient, Route Guard, Http Interceptor, LocalStorage, Web Storage API, server-side prerendering, Angular Universal, browser types, Generic Types, JWTs, Claims, and AuthorizeAttribute.

References

- *Introduction to Identity on ASP.NET Core*: `https://docs.microsoft.com/en-us/aspnet/core/security/authentication/identity`

- *Authentication and authorization for SPAs*: `https://docs.microsoft.com/en-us/aspnet/core/security/authentication/identity-api-authorization`

- *RoleManager<TRole> Class*: `https://docs.microsoft.com/en-us/dotnet/api/microsoft.aspnetcore.identity.rolemanager-1`

- *Identity model customization in ASP.NET Core*: `https://docs.microsoft.com/en-US/aspnet/core/security/authentication/customize-identity-model`

- *Overview of ASP.NET Core security*: `https://docs.microsoft.com/en-us/aspnet/core/security/`

- *Async and await*: `https://blog.stephencleary.com/2012/02/async-and-await.html`

- *Async/await FAQ*: `https://blogs.msdn.microsoft.com/pfxteam/2012/04/12/asyncawait-faq/`

- *Don't Block on Async Code*: `http://blog.stephencleary.com/2012/07/dont-block-on-async-code.html`

- *Async/await – Best practices in asynchronous programming*: `https://msdn.microsoft.com/en-us/magazine/jj991977.aspx`

- *ASP.NET Core SynchronizationContext*: `https://blog.stephencleary.com/2017/03/aspnetcore-synchronization-context.html`

- *Asynchronous programming with async and await*: `https://docs.microsoft.com/en-us/dotnet/csharp/programming-guide/concepts/async/index`
- *EF Core migrations*: `https://docs.microsoft.com/en-us/ef/core/managing-schemas/migrations/`
- *SQL Server: Create a full database backup*: `https://docs.microsoft.com/en-us/sql/relational-databases/backup-restore/create-a-full-database-backup-sql-server`
- *Two-factor authentication with SMS in ASP.NET Core*: `https://docs.microsoft.com/en-us/aspnet/core/security/authentication/2fa`
- *Enable QR code generation for TOTP authenticator apps in ASP.NET Core*: `https://docs.microsoft.com/en-us/aspnet/core/security/authentication/identity-enable-qrcodes`
- *Angular: Router guards*: `https://angular.io/guide/router#preventing-unauthorized-access`
- *Routing in ASP.NET Core*: `https://docs.microsoft.com/en-us/aspnet/core/fundamentals/routing`
- *Introduction to authorization in ASP.NET Core*: `https://docs.microsoft.com/en-us/aspnet/core/security/authorization/introduction`
- *Simple authorization in ASP.NET Core*: `https://docs.microsoft.com/en-us/aspnet/core/security/authorization/simple`
- *Authorize with a specific scheme in ASP.NET Core*: `https://docs.microsoft.com/en-us/aspnet/core/security/authorization/limitingidentitybyscheme`
- *Scaffold identity in ASP.NET Core projects*: `https://docs.microsoft.com/en-us/aspnet/core/security/authentication/scaffold-identity`
- *ASP.NET Core Identity: Create a full identity UI source*: `https://docs.microsoft.com/en-us/aspnet/core/security/authentication/scaffold-identity#full`
- *Create reusable UI using the Razor class library project in ASP.NET Core*: `https://docs.microsoft.com/en-us/aspnet/core/razor-pages/ui-class`
- *Angular: HttpInterceptor*: `https://angular.io/api/common/http/HttpInterceptor`
- *Role-based authorization in ASP.NET Core*: `https://docs.microsoft.com/en-us/aspnet/core/security/authorization/roles`
- *Account confirmation and password recovery in ASP.NET Core*: `https://docs.microsoft.com/en-us/aspnet/core/security/authentication/accconfirm`

12

Progressive Web Apps

In this chapter, we'll focus on a topic that we just briefly mentioned back in *Chapter 2*, *Getting Ready*, when we first talked about the different development patterns for web applications available nowadays: **Progressive Web Apps (PWAs)**.

As a matter of fact, both our HealthCheck and WorldCities apps currently stick to the **Single-Page Application (SPA)** model, at least for the most part; in the following sections, we'll see how we can turn them into PWAs by implementing several well-established capabilities required by such a development approach.

As we learned in *Chapter 2*, *Getting Ready*, a PWA is a web application that uses a modern web browser's capabilities to deliver an app-like experience to users. To achieve this, the PWA needs to meet some technical requirements, including (yet not limited to) a *Web App Manifest file* and a service worker to allow it to work in *offline mode* and behave just like a mobile app.

More precisely, here's what we're going to talk about:

- **PWA distinctive features, where we'll summarize the main characteristics of a PWA and identify the technical requirements** of a PWA by following its known specifications
- **Implementing the PWA requirements** on our existing HealthCheck and WorldCities apps to turn them into PWAs. More precisely, we'll do that using two different approaches: manually performing all the required steps for the HealthCheck app, and then using the *PWA automatic setup* offered by the Angular CLI for the WorldCities app
- **Handling the offline status**, where we'll update our components to behave differently when the app is offline – such as limiting their features and/or showing an offline status informative message
- **Testing the new PWA capabilities**, where we'll ensure that our implementation will properly work with both of our apps

By the end of this chapter, we'll have learned how to successfully convert an existing SPA into a PWA.

Technical requirements

In this chapter, we're going to need all previous technical requirements listed in previous chapters, with the following additional packages:

- `@angular/service-worker` (npm package)
- `angular-connection-service` (npm package)
- `Microsoft.AspNetCore.Cors` (NuGet package)
- `WebEssentials.AspNetCore.ServiceWorker` (NuGet package, *optional*)
- `http-server` (npm package)

As always, it's advisable to avoid installing them straight away; we're going to bring them in during this chapter to better contextualize their purposes within our project.

The code files for this chapter can be found at `https://github.com/PacktPublishing/ASP.NET-Core-6-and-Angular/tree/master/Chapter_12/`.

PWA distinctive features

Let's start by summarizing the main distinctive characteristics of a PWA:

- **Progressive**: A PWA should work for every user, regardless of the platform and/or browser used.
- **Responsive**: They must adapt well to any form factor: desktop, mobile, tablet, and so on.
- **Connectivity-independent**: They must be able to work offline—at least to some extent, such as informing the user that some features might not work in *offline mode*—or on low-quality networks.
- **App-like**: They need to provide the same navigation and interaction mechanics as mobile apps. This includes tap support, gesture-based scrolling, and so on.
- **Safe**: They must provide HTTPS support for better security, such as preventing snooping and ensuring that their content has not been tampered with.
- **Discoverable**: They have to be identifiable as *web applications* using a W3C manifest file and a service worker registration scope so that search engines will be able to find, identify, and categorize them.
- **Re-engageable**: They should make re-engagement easy through features such as *push notifications*.
- **Installable**: They should allow users to install and keep them on their desktop and/or mobile home screen, just like any standard mobile app, yet without the hassle of having to download and install them from an app store.
- **Linkable**: They should be easily shared through a URL, without requiring complex installation.

The preceding characteristics can be inferred from the following articles written by the Google developers and engineers who spent their efforts on introducing the PWA concept and defining its core specs:

`https://developers.google.com/web/progressive-web-apps`

`https://developers.google.com/web/fundamentals`

`https://infrequently.org/2015/06/progressive-apps-escaping-tabs-without-losing-our-soul/`

These high-level requirements can be translated into specific technical tasks that we have to implement. The best way to do that is by starting with the technical baseline criteria described by Alex Russell, the Google Chrome engineer who coined the term PWA together with the designer Frances Berriman back in 2015:

- **Originate from a secure origin**: In other words, there's full HTTPS support with no mixed content (*green padlock* display)
- **Load while offline**, even if it's just an *offline* information page: This clearly implies that we need to implement a service worker
- **Reference a Web App Manifest** with at least the four key properties: `name`, `short_name`, `stat_url`, and `display` (with either a *standalone* or *fullscreen* value)
- **A 144 × 144 icon** in PNG format: Other sizes are supported, but the 144 x 144 one is the minimum requirement
- **Use vector graphics**, as they can scale indefinitely and require smaller file sizes

Each one of these technical requirements can be translated into a specific technical task that we have to implement. In the following sections, we'll see how we can implement them.

Secure origin

Implementing the **secure origin** feature basically means serving our app through an HTTPS certificate. Such a requirement is rather easy to fulfill nowadays: TLS certificates are quite cheap thanks to the many resellers available. A PositiveSSL certificate issued by Comodo Inc. can be purchased online for $10/year or so and is immediately available for download.

If we don't want to spend money, there's also a free alternative provided by **Let's Encrypt**: a free, automated, open Certificate Authority that can be used to obtain a TLS certificate without costs. However, the method they use to release the certificate requires shell access (also known as **SSH access**) to the deployment web host.

For additional information about **Let's Encrypt** and how to obtain an HTTPS certificate for free, check out the official site: `https://letsencrypt.org/`.

For the sake of simplicity, we'll not cover the HTTPS certificate release and installation part; we'll take for granted that the reader will be able to properly install it, thanks to the many how-to guides available from the various resellers' websites (including **Let's Encrypt**).

Offline loading

Connection independency is one of the most important capabilities of PWAs; to properly implement it, we need to introduce—and implement—a concept that we've just barely mentioned until now: service workers. What are they, and how can they help our app to work while offline?

The best way to figure out what a service worker is would be to think of it as a *script that runs inside the web browser* and handles a specific task for the application that registered it: such tasks can include *caching support* and *push notifications*.

When properly implemented and registered, service workers will enhance the **user experience** (**UX**) provided by standard websites by delivering a UX similar to what can be achieved by native mobile apps; technically, their role is to intercept any ongoing HTTP request made by the user and—whenever it's directed to the web application they are registered for—check for the web application's availability and act accordingly. To put it in other words, we could say that they act as an HTTP proxy with fallback capabilities when the application is unable to handle the request.

Such a *fallback* can be configured by the developer to behave in many ways, such as the following:

- **Caching service** (also known as **offline mode**): The service worker will deliver a cached response by querying an internal (local) cache previously built from the app (when it was online)
- **Offline warning**: Whenever no cached content is available (or if we didn't implement a caching mechanism), the service worker can serve an *offline status* informative text, warning the user that the app is unable to work

Those who are familiar with forward cache services might prefer to imagine service workers as reverse proxies (or CDN edges) installed in the end user's web browser instead.

The *caching service* feature is great for web applications that provide static content, such as HTML5-based gaming apps and Angular apps that don't require any *back-end* interaction. Unfortunately, it's not ideal for our two apps: both `HealthCheck` and `WorldCities` strongly rely upon the *back-end* Web API provided by ASP.NET. Conversely, these apps can definitely benefit from an *offline warning*, so that their users will be informed that an internet connection is required—instead of getting a *connection error*, a `404 - Not Found` message, or any other message.

Service workers versus HttpInterceptors

If we remember the various Angular features that we introduced in *Chapter 11, Authentication and Authorization*, we can see how the aforementioned behavior reminds us of the role performed by `HttpInterceptors`.

However, since *interceptors* are part of the Angular app script bundle, they always cease to work whenever the user closes the browser tab that contains the web app.

Furthermore, interceptors are only able to intercept calls made with Angular's HttpClient: they won't be able to handle browser requests issued to load scripts, stylesheets, images, and so on.

Conversely, service workers need to be preserved after the user closes the tab so that they can intercept the browser requests *before* connecting to the app.

Enough with the theory, let's now see how we can implement an *offline mode*, *Web App Manifest*, and *PNG icons* in our existing apps.

Introducing @angular/service-worker

Starting with version 5.0.0, Angular provides a fully featured service worker implementation that can be easily integrated into any app without needing to code against low-level APIs. Such an implementation is handled by the @angular/service-worker npm package and relies upon a manifest file that is loaded from the server that describes the resources to cache and will be used as an index by the service worker, which behaves in the following way:

- **When the app is online**, each indexed resource will be checked to detect changes; if the source has changed, the service worker will update or rebuild the cache
- **When the app is offline**, the cached version will be served instead

The aforementioned manifest file is generated from a CLI-generated configuration file called ngsw-config.json, which we'll have to create and set up accordingly.

 It's worth mentioning that web browsers will always ignore service workers if the website that tries to register them is served over an unsecured (non-HTTPS) connection. The reason for that is quite simple to understand: since service workers' defining role is to proxy their source web application and potentially serve alternative content, malicious parties could be interested in tampering with them; therefore, allowing their registration to secure websites only will provide an additional security layer to the whole mechanism.

Here's an example of a manifest file similar to the one we need (and that we'll add in a short while):

```
{
    "name": "My Sample App",
    "short_name": " MySampleApp ",
    "start_url": ".",
    "display": "standalone",
    "background_color": "#fff",
    "description": "A simply readable Hacker News app.",
    "icons": [{
        "src": "images/touch/homescreen48.png",
        "sizes": "48x48",
        "type": "image/png"
    }, {
        "src": "images/touch/homescreen72.png",
```

```
      "sizes": "72x72",
      "type": "image/png"
   }, {

... multiple icon definitions ...

   }],
   "related_applications": [{
     "platform": "play",
     "url": "https://play.google.com/store/apps/details?id=my.sample.app "
   }]
}
```

It's worth noting that `@angular/service-worker` isn't the only available approach we could adopt to implement the service worker and *Web App Manifest* file's PWA capabilities. As a matter of fact, ASP.NET Core provides its own way to deal with these requirements with a set of middleware that can be easily installed and integrated into our project's HTTP stack.

The ASP.NET Core PWA middleware alternative

Among the various solutions provided, the most interesting one—at least in our opinion—is the `WebEssentials.AspNetCore.ServiceWorker` NuGet package developed by Mads Kristensen, a prolific author of Visual Studio extensions and ASP.NET Core libraries; the package provides fully featured ASP.NET Core PWA middleware that comes with full *Web App Manifest* support and pre-built service workers and is a valid *back-end* and *front-end* alternative to the pure *front-end* solution provided by the `@angular/service-worker` npm package.

To get additional information about the `WebEssentials.AspNetCore.ServiceWorker` NuGet package, check out the following URLs:

`https://github.com/madskristensen/WebEssentials.AspNetCore.ServiceWorker`

`https://www.nuget.org/packages/WebEssentials.AspNetCore.ServiceWorker/`

All in all, it seems that we have two convenient ways to fulfill our PWA-related tasks: which one should we choose?

Ideally, we would have loved to implement both of them; however, for reasons of space, we'll just use the `@angular/service-worker` npm package, leaving the ASP.NET Core PWA middleware alternative for another time.

Choosing the Angular service worker will also give us some advantages: since it's specifically designed for Angular, it will definitely help us to fix some common issues.

In the following section, we'll learn how to implement the @angular/service-worker package in our existing Angular apps following two very different—yet equally rewarding—approaches.

Implementing the PWA requirements

To perform the required implementation steps that we've focused on in the previous section, we have two choices:

- **Perform a manual update** of our app's source code
- **Use the automatic installation feature** provided by the Angular CLI

To learn the most from the experience, both of these paths should be taken at least once. Luckily enough, we have two existing Angular apps to experiment with. Therefore, we'll take the manual route for our HealthCheck app first, then we'll experience the automatic CLI setup for the WorldCities app.

Manual installation

In this section, we'll see how to manually implement the required technical steps we're still missing to make our HealthCheck app fully compliant with the PWA requirements.

Let's briefly recap them:

- Add the @angular/service-worker npm package (package.json)
- Enable service worker support in the Angular CLI configuration file (angular.json)
- Import and register ServiceWorkerModule in the AppModule class (app.module.ts)
- Update the main app's HTML template file (index.html)
- Add a suitable icon file (favicon.ico)
- Add the manifest file (manifest.webmanifest)
- Add the service worker configuration file (ngsw-config.json)

For each step, we've mentioned the relevant file that we'll have to update in parentheses.

Adding the @angular/service-worker npm package

The first thing to do is to add the @angular/service-worker npm package to our package.json file. As we can easily guess, such a package contains Angular's service worker implementation that we were talking about a moment ago.

Open the package.json file and add the following package reference to the "dependencies" section, right below the @angular/router package:

```
// ...

"@angular/router": "13.0.1",
"@angular/service-worker": "13.0.1",

// ...
```

As soon as we save the file, the npm package should be downloaded and installed automatically by Visual Studio; if that's not the case, run `npm install` manually to force the packages to update.

Updating the angular.json file

Open the `angular.json` configuration file and add the `"serviceWorker"` and `"ngswConfigPath"` keys to the end of the **projects | HealthCheck | architect | build | options** section:

```
// ...

"scripts": [],
"serviceWorker": true,
"ngswConfigPath": "ngsw-config.json"

// ...
```

 As always, whenever we have issues while applying these changes, we can check out the source code available from this book's GitHub repository.

The `"serviceWorker"` flag that we've just set up will cause the production build to include a couple of extra files in the output folder:

- `ngsw-worker.js`: The main service worker file
- `ngsw.json`: The Angular service worker's runtime configuration

Both of these files are required for our service worker to perform its job.

Importing ServiceWorkerModule

`ServiceWorkerModule` provided by the `@angular/service-worker` npm package library will take care of registering the service worker as well as providing a few services we can use to interact with it.

To install it on our `HealthCheck` app, open the `/src/app/app.module.ts` file and add the following lines (the new lines are highlighted):

```
// ...

import { ServiceWorkerModule } from '@angular/service-worker';
import { environment } from '../environments/environment';

// ...

imports: [
  // ...
```

```
    ServiceWorkerModule.register('ngsw-worker.js', {
        enabled: environment.production,
        // Register the ServiceWorker as soon as the app is stable
        // or after 30 seconds (whichever comes first).
        registrationStrategy: 'registerWhenStable:30000'
    })
],

// ...
```

As we said earlier, the `ngsw-worker.js` file referenced in the preceding code is the main service worker file, which will be auto-generated by the Angular CLI when building the app.

When implemented in this way, the service worker will be enabled only when our Angular app runs in a production environment, which is precisely what we want.

 For additional information regarding the service worker registration options and the various `registrationStrategy` settings, visit the following URL: `https://angular.io/api/service-worker/SwRegistrationOptions`.

Updating the index.html file

The `/src/index.html` file is the main entry point for our Angular app(s). It contains the `<app-root>` element, which will be replaced by our app's GUI at the end of the bootstrap phase, as well as some resource references and meta tags that describe our application's behavior and configuration settings.

Open that file and add the following code at the end of the `<head>` element (the updated lines are highlighted):

```
<!doctype html>
<html lang="en">
<head>
  <meta charset="utf-8">
  <title>HealthCheck</title>
  <base href="/">
  <meta name="viewport" content="width=device-width, initial-scale=1">
  <link rel="icon" type="image/x-icon" href="favicon.ico">
  <link rel="preconnect" href="https://fonts.gstatic.com">
  <link href="https://fonts.googleapis.com/
css2?family=Roboto:wght@300;400;500&display=swap" rel="stylesheet">
  <link href="https://fonts.googleapis.com/icon?family=Material+Icons"
rel="stylesheet">
  <!-- PWA required files -->
  <link rel="manifest" href="manifest.webmanifest">
```

```
    <meta name="theme-color" content="#1976d2">
</head>
<body class="mat-typography">
  <app-root></app-root>
</body>
</html>
```

The highlighted lines configure the app's theme-color, and—most importantly—the link to the manifest.webmanifest file, which—as its name clearly implies—is the app's manifest file, one of the key requirements for any PWA.

That's great to hear, except it doesn't exist in our app yet: let's fix this gap now.

Adding the Web App Manifest file

Instead of manually creating a *Web App Manifest* file from scratch, we can generate it automatically using one of the various Web App Manifest generators available online.

For the purpose of this book we're going to use the *Web App Manifest Generator* by Samson Amaugo: https://github.com/sammychinedu2ky/Web-App-Manifest-Generator

And more specifically, we'll use the instance hosted by Netlify at the following URL: https://manifest-gen.netlify.app/.

This handy tool will also generate all of the required PNG icon files for us, hence saving us a lot of time. However, we'll require a 512 x 512 image source. If we don't have one, we can easily create one using the *DummyImage* website, another useful free tool that can be used to generate placeholder images of any size, which is available at https://dummyimage.com/.

Here's a generated PNG file that we can use to feed the preceding Firebase *Web App Manifest Generator* tool:

Figure 12.1: PNG file generated by DummyImage

As we can easily guess, **HC** stands for **HealthCheck**; we won't likely win a graphic design contest with this image, but it will work just fine for our current task.

The preceding PNG file can be downloaded from: `https://dummyimage.com/512x512/361f47/fff.png&text=HC`.

The reader is free to either use it, create another file using that same tool, or provide another image.

The 512 x 512 icon will be used by the Web App Manifest Generator online tool to create all the required icons for our PWA.

As per Google's recommendations, a valid PWA manifest file will need at least two icons with a respective size of 192 x 192 and 512 x 512 pixels: `https://web.dev/installable-manifest/#recommendations`.

The online generator will vastly exceed the minimum requirements by creating eight different icons to accommodate most of the major formats used by different devices.

Once done, go back to the Web App Manifest Generator online tool and configure it using the following parameters:

- **App Name:** `HealthCheck`
- **Short Name:** `HealthCheck`
- **Theme Color:** `#2196f3`
- **Background Color:** `#2196f3`
- **Display Mode:** `Standalone`
- **Orientation:** `Any`
- **Application Scope:** `/`
- **Start Url:** `/`

Then, click to the right of the **UPLOAD** button below the **Upload via Graphql** option and select the HC image that we generated a moment ago, as shown in the following screenshot:

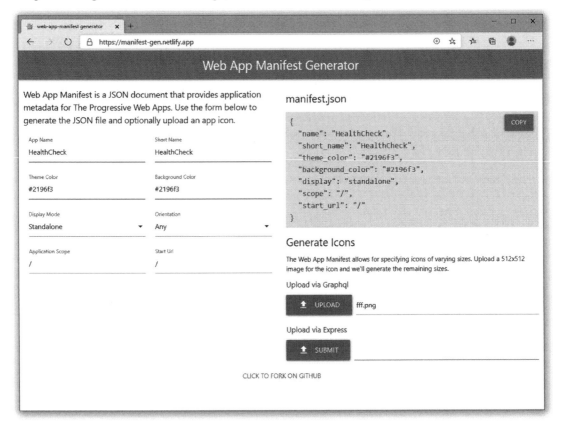

Figure 12.2: Web App Manifest Generator

Generate the archive file by clicking on the **UPLOAD** button, unpack it, and copy the included files in the following way:

- The manifest.json file in the /src/ folder
- The /icons/ folder, with all of its content, in the /src/assets/ folder, so that the actual PNG files will be placed in the /src/assets/icons/ folder

Once done, we need to perform the following changes to the manifest.json file:

- Change all of the icon starting paths from images/icons/ to assets/icons/
- Rename it from manifest.json to manifest.webmanifest, since that's the name defined by the Web App Manifest W3C specs

As a matter of fact, the .json and .webmanifest extensions will both work; however, since most web servers do not natively support the .webmanifest extension, opting for the .json choice would arguably make things easier.

That said, since we do want our PWAs to adhere to the Web App Manifest W3C specs, we're going to perform the above renaming and use the .webmanifest extension for our sample apps. This decision will require us to perform some additional tasks when we deploy our PWAs in production, such as manually adding that extension (and its application/manifest+json MIME type) to the list of supported file types in several web servers – as we'll see in *Chapter 15, Windows, Linux, and Azure Deployment*.

Those who want to take a look at the Web App Manifest W3C Working Draft 09 December 2019 can visit the following URL: https://www.w3.org/TR/appmanifest/.

To know more about the .json versus .webmanifest extension debate, take a look at this interesting discussion in the Web App Manifest GitHub repository: https://github.com/w3c/manifest/issues/689.

Now that we have made the necessary changes to the manifest.json file, we need to ensure it will be included in the Angular publishing bundle.

Publishing the Web App Manifest file

To have our /src/manifest.webmanifest file published together with the rest of our HealthCheck Angular app files, we need to add it to the /angular.json CLI configuration file.

Open that file and locate all of the following entries:

```
"assets": [
  "src/favicon.ico",
  "src/assets"
],
```

Replace them with the following updated value:

```
"assets": [
  "src/favicon.ico",
  "src/assets",
  "src/manifest.webmanifest"
],
```

There should be two "asset" key entries in the angular.json file:

*   projects > health_check > architect > build > options
*   projects > health_check > architect > test > options

Both of them need to be modified as explained in the preceding code.

With this update, the manifest.webmanifest file will be published to the output folder whenever we build the Angular app.

Adding the favicon

A *favicon* (also known as a favorite icon, shortcut icon, website icon, tab icon, URL icon, or bookmark icon) is a file containing one or more small icons that can be used to identify a specific website; whenever we see a small icon in a browser's address bar, history, and/or tab containing a given website, we're looking at that website's *favicon*.

Favicons can be generated manually, but if we're not graphic designers, we might want to use one of the various *favicon generators* available online, especially considering that most of them are entirely free to use; the only thing that we need is a suitable image, which needs to be provided manually (and uploaded to the service).

Here's a couple of recommended favicon online generators available nowadays:

favicon.io (`https://favicon.io/`)

Real Favicon Generator (`https://realfavicongenerator.net/`)

Alternatively, we can download one of the many *royalty-free* favicon sets available online.

Here are some websites that offer free favicons to download:

Icons8 (`https://icons8.com/icons/set/favicon`)

FreeFavicon (`https://www.freefavicon.com/freefavicons/icons/`)

As a matter of fact, the ASP.NET Core and Angular Visual Studio template that we used to create our HealthCheck project already provided us with a *favicon*: we can find it in our project's /wwwroot/ folder.

Honestly speaking, this *favicon* is not that bad, as we can see from the following screenshot:

Figure 12.3: The default favicon provided by our template

Keeping the above favicon won't prevent our app from becoming a PWA; that said, if we want to replace it with a custom one, we're free to do that using one of the aforementioned websites.

Adding the ngsw-config.json file

From Solution Explorer, create a new ngsw-config.json file in the HealthCheck project's root folder, and replace the content with the following:

```
{
  "$schema": "./node_modules/@angular/service-worker/config/schema.json",
```

```
    "index": "/index.html",
    "assetGroups": [
      {
        "name": "app",
        "installMode": "prefetch",
        "resources": {
          "files": [
            "/favicon.ico",
            "/index.html",
            "/manifest.webmanifest",
            "/*.css",
            "/*.js"
          ]
        }
      },
      {
        "name": "assets",
        "installMode": "lazy",
        "updateMode": "prefetch",
        "resources": {
          "files": [
            "/assets/**",
            "/*.(eot|svg|cur|jpg|png|webp|gif|otf|ttf|woff|woff2|ani)"
          ]
        }
      }
    ]
  }
```

As we can see by looking at the assetGroups > app section, the preceding file tells Angular to cache the favicon.ico file and the manifest.webmanifest file, which we created a short while ago, as well as the main index.html file and all of the CSS and JS bundles—in other words, our application's static asset files. Right after that, there is an additional assetGroup > assets section, which defines the image files to cache.

The main difference between these two sections is the installMode parameter value, which determines how these resources are initially cached:

- prefetch tells the service worker to fetch those resources while it's caching the current version of the app; in other words, it will put all of those contents in the cache as soon as they become available, that is, the first time the browser visits the online app. We might call this an **up-front caching strategy**.

- lazy tells the service worker to only cache those resources when the browsers explicitly request them for the first time. This could be called an **on-demand caching strategy**.

The preceding settings can be good for generic Angular apps that only rely on the *front-end* (no *back-end* required calls) since *these files basically contain the whole app*; more specifically, an Angular app hosting an HTML5 game—which arguably relies upon a lot of image files—might think about moving some of its image files (or even all of them) from the assets section to the app section, so that the whole application—including the icons, the sprites, and all of the image resources—will be cached upfront and be entirely available even when the app is offline.

However, such a caching strategy would not be enough for our HealthCheck and WorldCities apps; even if we tell our service worker to cache the whole app files, all of our apps' HTTP calls would still fail whenever the browser is offline, without letting the user know anything about it. As a matter of fact, our *back-end* availability requirement forces us to do some additional work for both of our apps.

However, before doing that, let's bring our WorldCities app up to speed.

Automatic installation

All of the steps that we performed manually in the previous section to enable *Service Worker* support for our HealthCheck app can be done automatically by using the following CLI command:

```
> ng add @angular/pwa@13.0.1
```

Let's adopt this alternative technique for our WorldCities app.

Open Command Prompt and navigate to the WorldCities app's root folder, then execute the preceding command; the Angular CLI will automatically configure our app by adding the @angular/service-worker package and performing the other required steps.

The most relevant information for the whole operation will be written in the console output, as shown in the following screenshot:

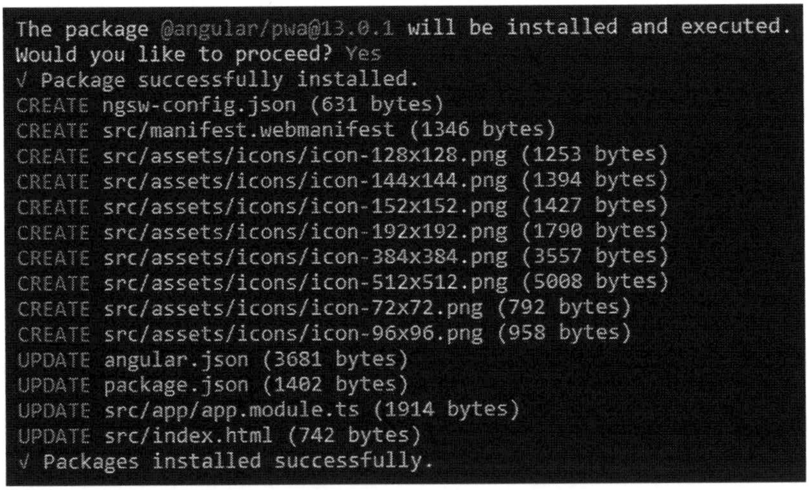

```
The package @angular/pwa@13.0.1 will be installed and executed.
Would you like to proceed? Yes
√ Package successfully installed.
CREATE ngsw-config.json (631 bytes)
CREATE src/manifest.webmanifest (1346 bytes)
CREATE src/assets/icons/icon-128x128.png (1253 bytes)
CREATE src/assets/icons/icon-144x144.png (1394 bytes)
CREATE src/assets/icons/icon-152x152.png (1427 bytes)
CREATE src/assets/icons/icon-192x192.png (1790 bytes)
CREATE src/assets/icons/icon-384x384.png (3557 bytes)
CREATE src/assets/icons/icon-512x512.png (5008 bytes)
CREATE src/assets/icons/icon-72x72.png (792 bytes)
CREATE src/assets/icons/icon-96x96.png (958 bytes)
UPDATE angular.json (3681 bytes)
UPDATE package.json (1402 bytes)
UPDATE src/app/app.module.ts (1914 bytes)
UPDATE src/index.html (742 bytes)
√ Packages installed successfully.
```

Figure 12.4: Enabling service worker support via Command Prompt

As we can see from the logs, the automatic process performs the same steps that we just applied to the `HealthCheck` app.

The Angular PNG icon set

The PWA automatic setup feature will also provide some PNG icons of various sizes in the `/src/assets/icons/` folder. If we open them with a graphics application, we can see that they all reproduce the Angular logo, as shown in the following figure:

Figure 12.5: The Angular logo provided by the PWA automatic setup

Whenever we want to make our app available to the public, we will likely want to change these icons. However, they are more than enough, at least for the time being; let's keep these files as they are and move on to the last remaining task to transform our SPAs into PWAs.

Handling the offline status

Now that we have configured a service worker in both of our apps, we can think of a way to handle the *offline status* message, so that each one of our components will be able to behave in a different way when the app is offline—such as limiting their features and showing an *offline status* informative message to our users.

To implement these conditional behaviors, we need to find a way to properly determine the browser connectivity status, that is, whether it's online or not; in the following sections, we'll briefly review several different approaches that we can use to do that to make the (arguably) best possible choice. These approaches are:

- The window's `ononline`/`onoffline` event
- The `Navigator.onLine` property
- A third-party package that determines the online/offline status in Angular

We will go into each of these in the following sections.

Option 1 – the window's ononline/onoffline event

If we're willing to accept a pure JavaScript way to handle this, such a task can be easily achieved using the `window.ononline` and `window.onoffline` JavaScript events, which are directly accessible from any Angular class.

Here's how we can use them:

```
window.addEventListener("online", function(e) {
  alert("online");
}, false);

window.addEventListener("offline", function(e) {
  alert("offline");
}, false);
```

However, if we're willing to adopt a pure JavaScript approach, there's an even better way to implement it.

Option 2 – the Navigator.onLine property

Since we don't want to track the network status changes and are just looking for a simple way to determine whether the browser is online or not, we can make things even simpler by just checking the `window.navigator.onLine` property:

```
if (navigator.onLine) {
  alert("online");
}
else {
  alert("offline");
}
```

As we can easily guess from its name, this property returns the online status of the browser. The property returns a Boolean value, with `true` meaning online and `false` meaning offline, and is updated whenever the browser's ability to connect to the network changes.

Thanks to this property, our Angular implementation could be reduced to this:

```
ngOnInit() {
  this.isOnline = navigator.onLine;
}
```

Then, we can use the `isOnline` local variable within our component's template file so that we can show different content to our users using the `ngIf` structural directive. That would be pretty easy, right?

Unfortunately, things are never that simple; let's try to understand why.

Downsides of the JavaScript approaches

Both of the JavaScript-based approaches we've mentioned suffer from a serious drawback caused by the fact that modern browsers implement the `navigator.onLine` property (as well as the `window.ononline` and `window.onoffline` events) in different ways.

More specifically, Chrome and Safari – as well as the new Chromium-based Microsoft Edge – will set that property to `true` whenever the browser can connect to a LAN or a router.

This can easily produce a false positive since most home and business connections are connected to the internet through a LAN, which will probably stay up even when the actual internet access is down.

> For additional information regarding the `Navigator.onLine` property and its drawbacks, check out the following URL: `https://developer.mozilla.org/en-US/docs/Web/API/NavigatorOnLine/onLine`.

All things considered, this basically means that we cannot use the convenient approaches described earlier to check our browser's online status, so in order to seriously deal with this matter, we need to find a better way to do it.

Option 3 – the angular-connection-service npm package

Luckily enough, there's a neat npm package that does precisely what we need: its name is `ng-online-status` and it's basically an *internet connection monitoring service* that can detect whether the browser has an active internet connection or not.

The online detection task is performed using a (configurable) *heartbeat* mechanism, which will periodically issue HTTP *head* requests to a (configurable) URL to determine the internet connection status.

Unfortunately, the `ng-connection-service` latest version—which introduced the heartbeat feature —is not available on npm as of the time of writing: the last updated version is **1.0.4**, which was developed for Angular 6 some years ago and was still based upon the `window.ononline` and `window.onoffline` events that we talked about earlier.

At the time of writing, I don't know why the author hasn't updated the npm package yet; however, since he made the latest version's source code available on GitHub under an **MIT** license, a lot of developers forked its original work, updated it for Angular's newer versions, and published the resulting packages to npm under that same license. For that very reason, we're going to use one of these forks, which is called `angular-connection-service`.

Here are the package default values:

- `enableHeartbeat: true`
- `heartbeatUrl: //httpstat.us/200`
- `heartbeatInterval: 3000` (milliseconds)
- `heartbeatRetryInterval: 1000`
- `requestMethod: head`

> For additional information about the `ng-connection-service` npm package, check out the following URL: `https://github.com/ultrasonicsoft/ng-connection-service`.

Most of them are good, except for `heartbeatUrl`—for various reasons that we'll explain later on.

Needless to say, with it being an Angular service, we'll be able to configure it in a centralized way and then inject it whenever we need to without having to manually configure it every time: that almost seems too good to be true!

Let's see how we can implement it.

Installing the service

To do that, open the package.json file of the HealthCheck project and add the following line right below the @angular/service-worker package that we added a moment ago:

```
// ...

"@angular/service-worker": "13.0.1",
"angular-connection-service": "13.0.1",

// ...
```

Be sure to use a version compatible with the Angular version we're currently using.

Version 13.0.1, the latest at the time of writing, is meant to work with the version of Angular recommended by this book.

Once done, open Command Prompt and execute npm install to update the packages: right after that, we can implement the service within our app(s).

Updating the AppModule file

The first thing to do is to add the package module to our AppModule file. To do that, open the *Health-Check* project's app.module.ts file and add the following highlighted lines:

```
// ...

import { environment } from '../environments/environment';
import { ConnectionServiceModule, ConnectionServiceOptions,
ConnectionServiceOptionsToken } from 'angular-connection-service';

@NgModule({
// ...

  imports: [

// ...
```

```
      ConnectionServiceModule
    ],
    providers: [
      {
        provide: ConnectionServiceOptionsToken,
        useValue: <ConnectionServiceOptions>{
          heartbeatUrl: environment.baseUrl + 'api/heartbeat',
        }
      }
    ],

    // ...
```

As we can see, we took the chance to modify the heartbeatUrl value; instead of querying the default httpstat.us third-party website, we're going to check a dedicated api/heartbeat endpoint that we'll make available within our Web API project. We've opted for that choice for several good reasons, the most important of them being the following:

- **To avoid being a nuisance** to those third-party hosts
- **To receive a more relevant result**, since we need to know if our app can reach our specific Web API domain
- **To avoid Cross-Origin Resource Sharing (CORS) issues** against third-party resources (more on that later)

Before switching to ASP.NET Core and creating that api/endpoint endpoint, let's finish the Angular part of the job.

Updating the AppComponent

The whole point of what we're doing right now is to make our users aware of the app being offline with an *offline status* informative message. To be effective, this message should be displayed:

- **As soon as possible**, so that our users will know the app's connectivity status before navigating somewhere
- **Everywhere**, so that they will be warned about it even if they're visiting some internal views

Therefore, a good place to implement it would be the AppComponent class, which contains all of our components, regardless of the *front-end* route picked by the user.

app.component.ts

Let's start with the TypeScript file.

Open the /src/app/app.component.ts file and modify its class file accordingly (the updated lines are highlighted):

```
import { Component } from '@angular/core';
```

```
import { ConnectionService } from 'angular-connection-service';

@Component({
  selector: 'app-root',
  templateUrl: './app.component.html',
  styleUrls: ['./app.component.scss']
})

export class AppComponent {
  title = 'HealthCheck';

  hasNetworkConnection: boolean = true;
  hasInternetAccess: boolean = true;

  constructor(private connectionService: ConnectionService) {
    this.connectionService.monitor().subscribe((currentState: any) => {
      this.hasNetworkConnection = currentState.hasNetworkConnection;
      this.hasInternetAccess = currentState.hasInternetAccess;
    });
  }

  public isOnline() {
    return this.hasNetworkConnection && this.hasInternetAccess;
  }
}
```

The above code should be quite easy to understand at this point: we've set up some local variables and subscribed to the connectionService – instantiated in the component's constructor using DI – to periodically update them. Last but not least, we've added an isOnline() method that can be used to determine the app's online status.

app.component.html

Now that we have the isOnline() method, we can modify the template file of AppComponent to show the informative "offline status" message to our users whenever it returns false.

Open the /src/app/app.component.html file and update its content with the following highlighted lines:

```
<app-nav-menu></app-nav-menu>

<div class="alert alert-warning" *ngIf="!this.isOnline()">
  <strong>WARNING</strong>: the app is currently <i>offline</i>:
  some features that rely upon the back-end might not work as
```

```
    expected. This message will automatically disappear as soon
    as the internet connection becomes available again.
</div>

<div class="container">
  <router-outlet></router-outlet>
</div>
```

That's it: since our app's *Home view* doesn't directly require a *back-end* HTTP request, we've chosen to just show a warning message to inform the user that some of our app's features might not work while offline. Conversely, we could've entirely shut down the app by putting an additional `ngIf="!this.isOnline()"` structural directive to the other elements, so that the *offline status* message would be the only visible output.

app.component.scss

Now we just need to style our new *offline status* alert.

Open the `/src/app/app.component.scss` file and append the following lines to the existing content:

```scss
.alert {
  position: relative;
  padding: .75rem 1.25rem;
  margin-bottom: 1rem;
  border: 1px solid transparent;
  border-radius: .25rem;

  &.alert-warning {
    color: #856404;
    background-color: #fff3cd;
    border-color: #ffeeba;
  }
}
```

That's it: with this we're done with our Angular tasks.

Before switching to ASP.NET Core, let's perform a quick test of what we did so far: hit *F5* to run the project in *Debug* mode and press *CTRL + SHIFT + J* to show the console window.

If we did everything correctly, the `AppComponent` should subscribe to the new service, which should hit an HTTP 404 while trying to check for the `api/heartbeat` endpoint, which doesn't exist yet.

As a result, the `isOnline()` method should return `false`, thus causing the alert to show up, as in the following screenshot:

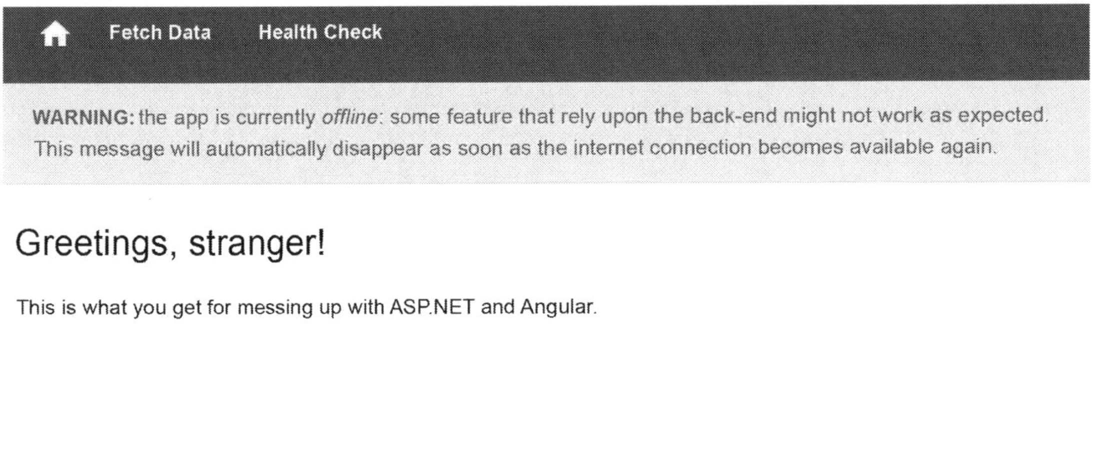

> **WARNING:** the app is currently *offline*: some feature that rely upon the back-end might not work as expected. This message will automatically disappear as soon as the internet connection becomes available again.

Greetings, stranger!

This is what you get for messing up with ASP.NET and Angular.

Figure 12.6: The offline alert message showing up

Now we need to ensure that the `api/heartbeat` endpoint will be found: to do that, we need to switch to the `HealthCheckAPI` project and perform some updates there as well.

However, before switching to the ASP.NET Core Web API project, let's take the chance to apply all the Angular changes to the *WorldCities* project as well. The GitHub project repository for this chapter contains all the required updates for both projects and is a good reference for those who need help.

Adding the api/heartbeat endpoint

To create a new API endpoint in our ASP.NET Core app we might be tempted to add a new `Controller`, just like we did in all previous chapters: or maybe we can create a new action method in an existing controller?

As a matter of fact, both options would work just fine: however, the `HealthCheckAPI` project doesn't have any controller yet, and creating a new one just to handle a *heartbeat* HEAD request might be over-kill. As for the `WorldCitiesAPI` project, the existing controllers are meant to serve a specific purpose: what would a `heartbeat` action method have to do with controllers returning cities and countries data?

If controllers were the only way to handle such a task, we would definitely have to create a new controller in both of our Web API projects. However, we can take this chance to introduce an alternative method to deal with HTTP requests that we've never used until now; this method is called **Minimal APIs** and it was introduced with *ASP.NET Core 6*.

Introducing Minimal APIs

Explaining Minimal APIs in few words is not an easy task: however, for the sake of simplicity, let's try to briefly summarize the concepts of this new ASP.NET Core feature.

In a nutshell, Minimal APIs are a set of helper methods introduced to allow developers to handle HTTP requests with minimal dependencies, files, and source code.

This new approach can be used together with standard controllers, as well as to entirely replace them, depending on the given scenario: ideally, they are best suited for microservices and lightweight APIs, or to handle very simple requests – just like the `api/heartbeat` endpoint that we need to add.

Without further ado, let's open the `Program.cs` file and implement our very first Minimal API, right below the existing `app.MapControllers()` method:

```
//...

app.MapControllers();

app.MapMethods("/api/heartbeat", new[] { "HEAD" },
    () => Results.Ok());

//...
```

As we can see, the newly added method is rather minimalistic, yet very readable: we are handling incoming HTTP requests pointing to the `api/heartbeat` endpoint (HEAD requests only), returning a standard *200 – OK* HTTP response without content. That's a lot swifter than creating a dedicated controller, right?

As for the empty content, we just did that because we don't need any: the content for a HEAD request is quite irrelevant, the `angular-connection-service` just needs to check the status code of our response to determine our app's online status.

To test what we just did, we can run our `HealthCheck` project again: this time the alert shouldn't be visible anymore, meaning that our new `api/heartbeat` endpoint can be reached by the Angular app and causing the `AppComponent`'s `isOnline()` method to return `true`.

Now we just need to perform the same tasks in our `WorldCitiesAPI` project, then we can move to the next step.

Cross-Origin Resource Sharing

Now that we've added the `api/heartbeat` endpoint to our ASP.NET Web API project, let's spend some valuable time understanding the concept of *Cross-Request Resource Sharing*, better known as CORS.

As we said earlier, the latest version of `angular-connection-service` allows us to perform a HEAD request over a defined amount of time ("heartbeat") to determine whether we're online or not. However, we have chosen to change the third-party website that was set in the service's default values (`// httpstat.us/200`) to a dedicated Web API endpoint under our control (`api/heartbeat`) that we've just added for that specific purpose.

Why did we do that? What's wrong with periodically issuing a HEAD request against a third-party website?

The first reason is rather simple to understand: we don't want to be a nuisance to those websites since they're definitely not meant for us to check their online status.

If their system administrators see our requests in their log, they could ban us or take some counter-measures that could prevent our heartbeat check from working or—even worse—compromise its reliability status.

Another reason is because the reliability of a third-party site like httpstat.us could be very different from our Web API: what if such a website is reachable while the production environment of our WorldCitiesAPI project is not? It's rather obvious that we should check *our* heartbeat, not a different website's one.

However, there's yet another important reason for avoiding such a practice.

Allowing our app to issue HTTP requests to *external* websites might violate the default CORS policy settings of those websites; while we're here, it could be useful to take a bit of time to better understand this concept.

As we might already know, modern browsers have built-in security settings that prevent a web page from making JavaScript requests to a different domain than the one that served the web page: such a restriction is called a **same-origin policy** and is introduced to prevent a malicious third-party website from reading data from another site.

However, most websites might want (or need) to issue some external requests to other websites: for example, the default heartbeatUrl configured in angular-connection-service would have told our app to issue a HEAD request to the //httpstat.us external website to check its online status.

These requirements, which are rather common in most apps, are called **CORS**: to allow them, the browser expects to receive from the receiving server—the one that hosts the required resources—a suitable **CORS policy** that will allow them to pass. If this policy doesn't come—or doesn't include the requesting origin—the HTTP request will be blocked. Since this *heartbeat-based* mechanism is now a critical part of our app, we can't take the risk of being blocked by third-party CORS restrictions: therefore, we've replaced that troublesome *external* reference with a more secure URL pointing to an *internal* resource under our control.

At the time of writing, all httpstat.us endpoints have been configured to allow all origins, headers, and HTTP methods, thus posing no CORS issues: however, we have no guarantees that such a "no-restrictions" approach will be maintained in the future.

That said, since our Web API is playing the role of the *external* server, we might still want to configure such a policy to allow our app to be able to call the api/heartbeat endpoint – as well as any other endpoint – even from a *non-local* origin. This is not required now that we're testing our app in our localhost environment, but could definitely be the case when we publish our project in production.

For additional information about CORS and its settings, visit the following URL: https://developer.mozilla.org/en-US/docs/Web/HTTP/CORS.

Enough with the theory: let's see how we can implement CORS in our `HealthCheckAPI` project and allow all of its endpoints – including, yet not limited to, the `api/heartbeat` one – to be called from external servers.

Implementing CORS

Configuring CORS in ASP.NET Core requires adding the *CORS services* and the *CORS middleware*, part of the `Microsoft.AspNetCore.Cors` namespace, to the `Program.cs` file.

However, before doing that, we need to provide our app with a configuration setting that we can use to specify the origin that we want to allow: a suitable place to do that is the `appsettings.json` file.

Adding the AllowedCORS configuration setting

Open the *HealthCheckAPI's* `appsettings.json` file and add a new `AllowedCORS` key right below the `AllowedHosts` key, as shown below:

```
// ...

"AllowedHosts": "*",
"AllowedCORS": "*"

// ...
```

The `"*"` wildcard value will relax the CORS policy for any endpoint, which can be good for our testing purposes: we'll restrict such permissive behavior in *Chapter 15, Windows, Linux, and Azure Deployment,* when we'll deploy our app(s) in production.

> As we can see, we didn't use the existing `AllowedHosts` key because it serves a different purpose – which we will not deal with for reasons of space. Those interested to know more about it can check out the following URL: https://docs.microsoft.com/en-us/aspnet/core/fundamentals/servers/kestrel/host-filtering.

Right after saving the *HealthCheckAPI's* `appsettings.json` file, open the *WorldCitiesAPI's* `appsettings.json` file and add the `AllowedCORS` key there as well before moving on.

Now that we have the `AllowedCORS` configuration setting available, we can update our `Program.cs` file.

Updating the Program.cs file

Open the *HealthCheckAPI's* `Program.cs` file and add the required highlighted lines of code:

```
using Microsoft.AspNetCore.Cors;

// ...

builder.Services.AddSwaggerGen();
```

```
builder.Services.AddCors(options =>
    options.AddPolicy(name: "AngularPolicy",
        cfg => {
            cfg.AllowAnyHeader();
            cfg.AllowAnyMethod();
            cfg.WithOrigins(builder.Configuration["AllowedCORS"]);
        }));

// ...


app.UseAuthorization();

app.UseCors("AngularPolicy");

// ...
```

The above code shouldn't be too hard to understand:

- We've added the CORS services (`AddCors`) and configured a CORS policy that – when applied – relaxes CORS for any HTTP header and method for the `AllowedCORS` endpoints specified in the `appsettings.json` file.
- Down below, we added the CORS middleware (`UseCors`) just below the `UseAuthorization()` method: it's very important to place it *before* the middlewares that handle the various endpoints (Controllers, HealthChecks, Minimal APIs, and so on), so that our CORS policy will be applied to all of them.

With this, we've successfully implemented all the required PWA features. Again, be sure to also apply the above CORS settings to the *WorldCitiesAPI* project before moving on.

Let's now find a way to properly test out what we did; it won't be easy to do that from within Visual Studio due to the distinctive features of PWAs, but there are some workarounds we can use to pull it off.

Testing the PWA capabilities

In this section, we'll try to test the service worker registration for our `HealthCheck` app. Unfortunately, doing it from a Visual Studio development environment is a rather complex task for several reasons, including the following:

- `ng serve`, the Angular CLI command that pre-installs the packages and starts the app whenever we run our app in *debug* mode, doesn't support service workers
- The service worker registration tasks that we put in the `AppModule` class a while ago only register it when the app is running in a *production* environment

- The required static files generated by the Angular CLI using the `angular.json` configuration file that we modified earlier on will only be available in *production* environments

However, we can easily work around these limitations by compiling our Angular app for production and then running the generated files with a separate, dedicated HTTP server.

In the following sections, we are going to see how we can do all that.

Compiling the app

Here's how we can publish our app using the Angular CLI. Open the Command Prompt, navigate to the project's root folder, and type the following command:

```
ng build
```

The CLI will compile our Angular app within a new `/dist/` folder that will contain all the generated files. It's worth noting that we are going to use this folder (and all its content) to test our service worker only, deleting it afterward.

 As an alternative, we could also exclude it from version control by adding the folder path to the `.gitignore` file – which is what we did in the GitHub repository for this book.

Now we just need to install a separate HTTP server that can support our service worker. To this end, we're going to use the `http-server` npm package: a simple, zero-configuration command-line static HTTP server that is also recommended by the official Angular documentation for service workers.

It's important to understand that `http-service` is not meant to be used for production usage: however, its overall simplicity makes it perfect to use for testing, local development, and learning.

Installing http-server

`http-server` can be either installed using `npm` or directly launched using `npx`, a tool shipped with Node.js that can be used to execute `npm` package binaries without installing them.

If we want to globally install it before launching it, we can do so with the following commands:

```
> npm install http-server -g
> http-server -p 8080 -c-1 dist/HealthCheck/
```

If we just want to test out our service worker, we can use the following command instead:

```
> npx http-server -p 8080 -c-1 dist/HealthCheck/
```

Both commands will launch `http-server` and serve our `HealthCheck` app to the local 8080 TCP port, as shown in the following screenshot:

Figure 12.7: Launching http-server and serving the HealthCheck app

As soon as we do that, we can connect to it by opening a browser and typing the following URL in the address bar: `http://localhost:8080`.

We can check out the PWA capabilities of our apps just like we did with Visual Studio and IIS Express earlier; however, we won't be able to test the *back-end* HTTP requests since `http-server` doesn't natively support ASP.NET Core. Luckily enough, we don't need the back-end to run these tests.

Testing out our PWAs

For the sake of simplicity, the following screenshots will be all related to `HealthCheck`, but the same checks could be applied to the `WorldCities` app as well since we configured it using the same implementation patterns.

> It's strongly advisable to perform the following tests with a Chromium-based browser, such as Google Chrome or Microsoft Edge, since such engines come with some neat built-in tools to check for Web App Manifest and service worker presence. Also, it's strongly advisable to use the browser's *incognito mode* to ensure that the service worker will always start from scratch, without reading previously built caches or states.

Let's start our test by stopping all our projects and closing all the windows to ensure we have no running or active processes. Right after that, launch the `http-server` – as explained in the previous section – and open a browser to the following URL: `http://localhost:8080`.

If we did everything correctly we should see the app's **Home** view with the yellow *offline alert* visible on screen. The reason for that is quite simple: our Web API is not launched (yet), hence the Angular app is unable to reach the `api/heartbeat` endpoint.

We can easily check out this behavior by pressing *Shift + Ctrl + J* to open the *Chrome Developer Tools* and then look at the **Console** tab, as shown in the following screenshot:

Figure 12.8: Chrome Developer Tools

Now we can hit *F5* to start our **HealthCheck** and **HealthCheckAPI** projects, which should make the offline alert message disappear within a few seconds: once done, we can proceed with the following test.

Keeping the *Chrome Developer Tools* window open, navigate to the **Application** tab where we can see that our *Web App Manifest* file has been properly loaded. If we scroll down the **Application | Manifest** panel, we'll be able to see our PNG icons as well.

 NOTE: It can take a while (10–20 seconds on a typical development machine) before the service worker actually shows up on the first installation.

The next thing we can check is the **Application | Service Workers** panel, which should strongly resemble the one shown in the following screenshot:

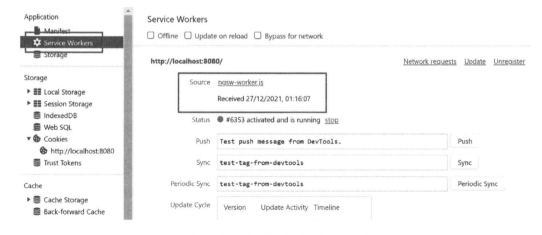

Figure 12.9: The Service Workers panel

The *service worker* JavaScript file should be clearly visible, as well as its registration date and current *up-and-running* status.

Let's now try to put our web browser offline. To do that, activate the **Offline** checkbox in the top-left section of the Chrome Developer Tools' **Application** tab and see what happens:

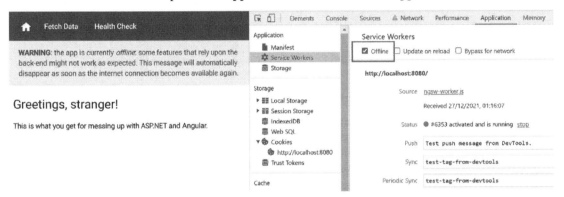

Figure 12.10: View after putting the web browser offline

Our *offline warning* info message should immediately kick in, thanks to our `angular-connected-service` implementation. If we move to the **Network** tab, we can see that the `api/heartbeat` endpoint isn't reachable anymore, meaning that the `isOnline()` method of `AppComponent` is now returning `false`.

Now, we can resume the connectivity (by de-selecting the **Offline** checkbox) and check out two more things: the *linkable* and *installable* PWA capabilities. Both of them are clearly shown on the rightmost part of the browser's address bar, as we can see in the following screenshot:

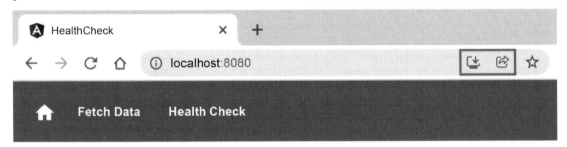

Figure 12.11: Checking the linkable and installable icons

If we go there with the mouse pointer, we should be able to see the contextual messages asking us to send the app's URL to other devices (left) and install it to the desktop (right).

Installing the PWA

Let's now click the **install** button (the one with the *plus* sign inscribed in a circle) and confirm that we want to locally install the `HealthCheck` PWA.

Within seconds, we should be able to see the Home view of our newly installed app in a *desktop app-like* window, as shown in the following screenshot:

Health Check

Here are the results of our health check:

Name	Response Time	Status	Description
ICMP_01	163.9788	Healthy	ICNIP to www.ryadel.com took 14 ms.
ICMP_02	175.4264	Healthy	ICMP to www.google.com took 13 ms.
ICMP_03	4713.6076	Unhealthy	ICMP to 10.0.0.0 failed: TimedOut

Figure 12.12: HealthCheck PWA in a desktop app-like window

From there, do the following:

1. Press *Shift + Ctrl + J* to open the Google Chrome **Developer Tools** again
2. Navigate to the **Application | Service Workers** panel
3. Click on the **Offline** checkbox to check/activate it again

The app should, again, show the *offline warning* information message.

Needless to say, we won't be able to see our health check results table while our app is offline, since that data is fetched in real time and we currently have no offline caching mechanism that will save it in local storage and make it available when the internet connection is unavailable; however, the *offline warning* information message is enough to make our users aware of the fact that the app is offline.

That's it: we have successfully turned our SPAs into PWAs. As a matter of fact, we have just scratched the surface of the many possibilities offered by such a promising deployment approach; however, we've successfully demonstrated that our *front-end* and *back-end* frameworks are fully able to handle their main requirements properly and consistently.

Summary

This chapter was all about PWAs: we spent some valuable time better understanding the high-level distinctive features of this modern web development pattern and how to translate them into technical specifications. Right after that, we started implementing them, taking into account the various available options offered by our *front-end* and *back-end* frameworks.

Since the PWA concept is closely related to the *front-end* aspects of our app, we chose to adopt the Angular way of implementing their required capabilities; with that in mind, we chose to take the manual route for our HealthCheck app first, then to experience the automatic installation feature powered by the Angular CLI for the WorldCities app. In both scenarios, we made good use of the @angular/service-worker npm package, a module available since Angular 5 that provides a fully featured service worker implementation that can be easily integrated into our apps.

Once done, we took some time to understand how we could handle the offline status of our app, evaluating various strategies and eventually choosing a heartbeat-based solution using the angular-connection-service npm package and a dedicated Web API endpoint. While dealing with these tasks, we took the chance to learn and implement some convenient ASP.NET Core features, such as *Minimal APIs* and *Cross-Origin Resource Sharing*.

After we did that, we manually ran some consistency tests to check the brand-new PWA capabilities of our apps using Google Chrome and its developer tools.

At the end of this chapter, we finally saw our service worker in action, as well as the *Web App Manifest* file being able to serve the PNG icons and provide the installing and linking features to our apps.

The various concepts that we learned throughout this chapter have also helped us to focus on some very important issues regarding the differences between *development* and *production* environments, hence making us ready to properly face the final part of our journey: Windows, Linux, and Azure deployment, which will be the main topics of *Chapter 15, Windows, Linux, and Azure Deployment*. However, before we get to that point, there are still a couple of topics that we need to address in the next two chapters.

Suggested topics

For further information, we recommend the following topics: Progressive Web Apps (PWAs), @angular/service-worker, secure origin, HTTPS, TLS, Let's Encrypt, service workers, HTTPInterceptors, favicons, Web App Manifest file, Microsoft.AspNetCore.Cors, Cross-Origin Resource Sharing (CORS), offline status, window.navigator, ng-connection-service, IIS Express, and http-server.

References

- *Progressive Web Apps*: https://developers.google.com/web/progressive-web-apps
- *Web Fundamentals*: https://developers.google.com/web/fundamentals
- *Progressive Web Apps: Escaping Tabs Without Losing Our Soul*: https://infrequently.org/2015/06/progressive-apps-escaping-tabs-without-losing-our-soul/
- *Let's Encrypt*: https://letsencrypt.org/
- *The Web App Manifest*: https://developers.google.com/web/fundamentals/web-app-manifest
- *Angular Service Workers*: https://angular.io/guide/service-worker-getting-started
- *Service worker configuration*: https://angular.io/guide/service-worker-config
- *Service Workers – Practical Guided Introduction (several examples)*: https://blog.angular-university.io/service-workers/

- *Angular University: Service Worker step-by-step guide*: `https://blog.angular-university.io/angular-service-worker/`

- *favicon.io*: `https://favicon.io/`

- *Real Favicon Generator*: `https://realfavicongenerator.net/`

- *Icons8*: `https://icons8.com/icons/set/favicon`

- *FreeFavicon*: `https://www.freefavicon.com/freefavicons/icons/`

- *Firebase Web App Manifest Generator*: `https://app-manifest.firebaseapp.com`

- *DummyImage – Placeholder Image Generator*: `https://dummyimage.com/`

- *Google Developers recommendation for installability requirements*: `https://web.dev/installable-manifest/#recommendations`

- *Web App Manifest – W3C Working Draft 09 December 2019*: `https://www.w3.org/TR/appmanifest/`

- *Enable Cross-Origin Requests (CORS) in ASP.NET Core*: `https://docs.microsoft.com/en-us/aspnet/core/security/cors`

- *http-server*: `https://www.npmjs.com/package/http-server`

- *npx - execute npm package binaries*: `https://www.npmjs.com/package/npx`

- *ng-serve*: `https://angular.io/cli/serve`

- *angular-connection-service*: `https://github.com/Ryadel/angular-connection-service`

- *Visual Studio publish profiles (.pubxml) for ASP.NET Core app deployment*: `https://docs.microsoft.com/en-us/aspnet/core/host-and-deploy/visual-studio-publish-profiles`

- *Angular – Service Worker registration options*: `https://angular.io/api/service-worker/SwRegistrationOptions`

13

Beyond REST – Web API with GraphQL

Up until this point, we have always assumed that the ASP.NET Web APIs used to feed data to our Angular app would do their job using the **Representational State Transfer** (**REST**) architectural style. Such an assumption is fully justified by the fact that REST has been the most popular option for accessing web services for decades, having imposed itself on all previous alternatives (such as SOAP) thanks to its undeniable advantages in terms of reliability, performance, and bandwidth usage.

However, despite having become the *de facto* standard for most data retrieval tasks, the REST approach is not always ideal in all circumstances and might suffer from some undeniable shortcomings, such as being unable to keep up with the rapidly changing requirements of the clients.

In this chapter, we're going to introduce a modern query language created with the specific aim of providing a more efficient and flexible alternative to the traditional REST API architecture: the name of this language is **GraphQL** and it's reportedly already used by thousands of companies in their tech stacks, including Facebook, Shopify, Instagram, GitHub, Twitter, PayPal, Airbnb, Atlassian, Pinterest, and many more.

More specifically, here's what we'll do:

- **Introduce GraphQL**, explaining its distinctive features and its advantages over a traditional REST architecture
- **Add GraphQL support to our ASP.NET Core Web API** using a third-party NuGet package
- **Add GraphQL support to our Angular app** using a third-party GraphQL client
- **Perform some integration tests** to see how the new GraphQL architecture works and how we can use it to improve our existing app

Are we ready? Let's start!

Technical requirements

In this chapter, we're going to need all the previous technical requirements listed in previous chapters, along with the following additional ASP.NET Core NuGet packages:

- `HotChocolate.AspNetCore`
- `HotChocolate.Data.EntityFramework`

And the following Angular **npm** packages:

- `@apollo/client`
- `apollo-angular`
- `graphql`

As always, it's advisable to avoid installing them straight away; we're going to bring them in during this chapter to better contextualize their purpose within our project.

The code files for this chapter can be found at `https://github.com/PacktPublishing/ASP.NET-Core-6-and-Angular/tree/main/Chapter_13/`.

GraphQL versus REST

As we said early on, GraphQL is an open source data query and manipulation language that provides a set of rules and standards to create efficient and flexible Web APIs. The language was developed by Facebook in 2012 as an internal project, before being released to the public in 2015, immediately getting the attention of many developers due to its innovative approach.

Comparing GraphQL with REST is almost inevitable since the former has been developed with the precise goal of solving some of the most notable REST drawbacks: for that very reason, the best thing we can do to understand the pros and cons of these two approaches is to briefly summarize the distinctive features of each one of them, starting with the technology that came first.

REST

Representational State Transfer, better known as REST, is an architectural style specifically designed for network-based applications that use the standard HTTP `get` `post` `put` and `delete` request methods to access and manipulate data.

> Those HTTP methods have been defined in RFC 2616 (June 1999), which contains the specifications for the HTTP/1.1 protocol: `https://www.w3.org/Protocols/rfc2616/rfc2616.html`.

The REST concept was first introduced and defined in 2000 by *Roy Thomas Fielding*, co-founder of the *Apache HTTP Server project* and one of the principal authors of the HTTP specification, in his doctoral dissertation *Architectural Styles and the Design of Network-based Software Architectures*.

As opposed to what many believe, in that dissertation, Fielding didn't introduce a new set of methodologies to build Web APIs: he mostly summarized the core architectural principles used to design the HTTP protocol and specifications, which he had contributed to (HTTP/1.0) and co-authored (HTTP/1.1). As a matter of fact, the REST architectural style is nothing more than the distillation of these principles, which (he thought) could be used as guidelines to implement any distributed application over the web, including, but not limited to, those services specifically built to exchange data between clients and servers that we now call Web APIs.

The fact that Fielding's intuition was right is proven by the millions of RESTful web services created in the last 20 years to handle a wide variety of tasks: websites, desktop and mobile apps, online games, operating systems, IoT devices, and so on.

 Our `HealthCheckAPI` and `WorldCitiesAPI` ASP.NET Core apps are also part of that list since they have been developed with a REST-based approach.

If we consider that one of the most important functions of the internet is to exchange data, then we can acknowledge the importance of this architecture, since most of the information is currently transmitted using REST.

Guiding constraints

The HTTP core architectural principles identified by Fielding define six REST guiding constraints that, when properly implemented, provide the system with a set of desirable non-functional properties, including *performance*, *scalability*, *simplicity*, *modifiability*, *visibility*, *portability*, and *reliability*.

Here's a brief list of these six guiding constraints and the properties they allow us to achieve:

1. **Client-server architecture.** RESTful APIs should enforce the *Separation of Concerns* principle, thus separating the *UI* from *Data Storage*. Keeping these concerns apart improves the API's *portability*, as well as the *simplicity*, *scalability*, and *modifiability* of the whole system.

2. **Statelessness.** The server should handle all communications between clients without retaining data from previous calls. This basically means that the server shouldn't keep a session state containing context-related info (such as authentication keys). This implies that, if clients need to authenticate and/or authorize themselves, the server should provide them with the means to do that upon each call. A perfect example of that would be the JWT that we talked about in *Chapter 11, Authentication and Authorization*, which is stored in the client's local storage and authenticated by the server without the need to retain any additional info. The *statelessness* approach helps to reduce the overhead of each request on the server, which can significantly improve the *performance* and *scalability* of the whole system, especially under heavy load.

3. **Cacheability.** Servers and clients should make use of the caching capabilities natively provided by the HTTP protocol. This basically means that all HTTP responses should include the appropriate caching (or non-caching) headers to reduce the size of the data being transferred, as well as minimize the risk of serving stale or outdated content.

A good caching strategy can have a huge impact on the *scalability* and *performance* of the whole system.

4. **Layered system.** The server, instead of being accessed directly, should be put behind one or more intermediary HTTP services or filters (NATs, proxies, load balancers, and the like). Intermediating the incoming calls will not only improve the overall security aspects of a Web API, but also strengthen its *performance*, *scalability*, and *reliability* properties.

5. **Code on Demand.** The server should provide the clients with executable code or scripts that can be used to adopt custom behavior. This is the only REST optional constraint and is rarely used nowadays since it poses obvious security issues, if not implemented properly. Furthermore, the usage scenario is kind of limited: one possible application example might be distributed computing, where the server might want to delegate to its clients part of its job, or remote evaluation techniques, where the server needs the client to perform some local checks, such as verifying whether some applications or drivers are installed. In these edge case scenarios *Code on Demand* will likely improve the *performance* and *scalability* of the system: however, it might also reduce its overall *visibility*.

6. **Uniform interface.** This constraint defines four fundamental requirements that a RESTful interface needs to implement to decouple the client requirements (data exchange) from the underlying implementation (such as data retrieval, update, and delete). These features are:

    1. **Identification of resources.** Each resource must be univocally identified through a unique URI.

    2. **Manipulation of resources through representations.** Clients must be able to perform basic operations on resources using the resource URI and the corresponding HTTP method without the need for additional info.

    3. **Self-descriptive messages.** Each sender's message must include all the information required by the recipient to properly understand and process it. Such a requirement is easy to implement with the HTTP protocol thanks to the HTTP headers that can be included in both requests and responses.

    4. **Hypermedia As The Engine Of Application State (HATEOAS).** The server should provide clients with usage information through a standardized set of hyperlinks and URIs. Such a requirement decouples the server from its clients and allows the server to evolve independently, reducing the risks of creating backward-compatibility issues.

When a web service implements all the above constraints, it's conventionally called *RESTful*.

Drawbacks

Despite its undeniable success, the REST approach is intrinsically affected by some known limitations that might have little or no impact in most scenarios but can become troublesome when dealing with non-trivial data retrieval tasks. Let's try to acknowledge them by looking at the REST API provided by our `WorldCitiesAPI` app and used by our current Angular client to interact with the underlying *WorldCities* database.

Whenever our client wants to retrieve a `Country`, it must call the following API endpoint: `/api/Countries/{id}`.

That call also allows the client to retrieve the number of cities, thanks to the TotCities property that we added back in *Chapter 8, Code Tweaks and Data Services*.

However, we are currently unable to retrieve some properties of these cities, such as their *name* or *id*. That endpoint is unable to do that. Moreover, we don't currently have any endpoint returning a list of Cities for a given CountryId. The only endpoint that returns a list of Cities, /api/Cities, won't accept such a filter.

This basically means that, if we wanted to do that, we should do one of the following things:

- Update the existing /api/Countries/{id} endpoint, adding an additional Cities property to the resulting CountryDTO containing a list of all the cities belonging to that country, with all the properties we might possibly need
- Update the existing /api/Cities endpoint, making it accept a CountryId parameter (or filter)
- Implement a new endpoint, such as /api/Countries/{countryId}/Cities or something similar

We can easily see how all the above alternatives have their drawbacks:

- Updating the /api/Countries/{id} endpoint to make it return a list of cities will greatly increase the size of the HTTP response, which could have non-trivial performance impacts; moreover, the update might produce some unexpected *regression bugs* and/or could require changing its interface, thus forcing us to update the Angular app. Furthermore, we'll ultimately end up with a lot of Cities data that we don't need for our purposes – an undesirable phenomenon commonly known as *over-fetching*, or the *N+1 problem*.
- Updating the existing /api/Cities method might mitigate the *over-fetching* issue, but won't minimize the risks of *regression bugs*; furthermore, it will force us to perform an additional *roundtrip* (a new HTTP request) to retrieve the data we need.
- Adding an additional endpoint would preserve us from *regression bugs*, but will still require the additional *roundtrip*. Furthermore, it would likely impact the back-end development time and add complexity to our API.

The above example allows us to identify some important shortcomings of the REST architectural style: the risk of *over-fetching* and the frequent need for *multiple roundtrips*, both due to the lack of flexibility of such approaches. As for *regression bugs*, although they aren't a drawback specific to REST, the risk of hitting them is often increased by the inevitable refactoring required whenever a new change request arises: what if we need to only retrieve Cities within a certain lat/lon range? Or, Countries with more (or less) than N cities? And so on.

As we can easily understand, overcoming such issues might be not that simple, especially if we need a high level of versatility in terms of client-side data fetching requirements.

GraphQL

After 15 years of undisputed supremacy – and millions of *RESTful* web services developed around the world – the REST architectural style was challenged by a newcomer.

On September 14, 2015, Facebook decided to release the specifications of its internal query language to the public, followed by a wide set of implementation tools for most popular programming languages, including JavaScript, Go, PHP, Java, Python, Ruby, and more.

The GraphQL release allowed the developer community to take advantage of the distinctive features of the new language, which allowed clients to send and retrieve data in a very different way than REST. More precisely, instead of having to perform multiple HTTP requests to different endpoints and receive multiple HTTP responses containing different datasets, clients could ask for what they needed with a single request to a single endpoint and receive precisely what they need with a single, dynamically structured response.

Advantages over REST

The main differences between REST and GraphQL can be visualized by looking at the following schema:

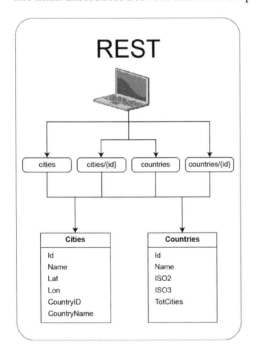 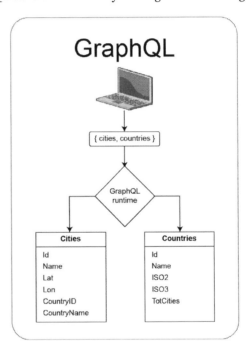

Figure 13.1: REST versus GraphQL

As we can see, with **REST**, we have to deal with multiple API endpoints, each one of them retrieving data from our DBMS using its own implementation strategy (which might be standardized, specific, or a mix of both). Adding more endpoints will reduce the risks of *over-fetching* and *regression bugs*, but will inevitably require *multiple roundtrips*, as well as adding *complexity* and increasing the development time.

Conversely, **GraphQL** gives us the chance to deal with a single endpoint that will accept our data retrieval query, execute it against the DBMS, and return a "merged" set of JSON data, without *over-fetching* and avoiding *multiple roundtrips*. It's worth noting that both the query and the resulting data will have the same JSON structure, built using the standards given by the GraphQL specs, that will be processed by a dedicated server-side runtime.

Limitations

While GraphQL has some undeniable advantages over traditional REST APIs, it comes with several key disadvantages as well. Let's briefly discuss the most relevant ones:

- GraphQL requires a *client-side* module to build queries and a *server-side* runtime to execute those queries (or make a compatible ORM able to process them). These requirements will inevitably add some complexity to client and servers and/or increase the development time.

- GraphQL queries often return an HTTP status code of 200, regardless of whether that query was successful. More precisely, if the query failed, the JSON response will have a top-level `errors` key with the error message(s). This will make error handling more difficult for the client and might also lead to additional complexity for logging and monitoring tasks. However, such a limitation is mostly due to the fact that the tools we typically use for these tasks are meant to receive and process HTTP-based responses, while GraphQL has been designed to sit on top of that protocol.

- GraphQL comes with no built-in caching support. As opposed to REST APIs, which can leverage native HTTP caching thanks to their multiple endpoints returning the same data for the same requests, GraphQL requires the developer to implement custom (and often non-RESTful) caching support, or to adopt a client library supporting such a feature.

- GraphQL queries are definitely more complex to implement than REST endpoints. This is true at the client level, when we need to assemble the query, and even more true on the server side, where we have to execute the query against the DBMS.

The above limitations are the main reason why **GraphQL** is currently unable to defeat **REST**, at least as of today. As a matter of fact, whenever we have to deal with simple datasets and/or with data that is relatively consistent over time, the REST approach is still the most effective and convenient way to go. Conversely, if we need to handle complex scenarios with rapidly changing data, GraphQL might solve some painful REST drawbacks and help us create a more robust, efficient, and maintainable app.

For the purpose of this book, considering the overall simplicity of our sample `HealthCheckAPI` and `WorldCitiesAPI` projects (and the underlying DBMS), we can say that REST APIs are definitely the way to go. That said, in the next section, we'll briefly see how we can implement a fully featured GraphQL API on top of our existing **WorldCities** code base.

Implementing GraphQL

Providing **GraphQL** support to the **WorldCities** app requires some *back-end* and *front-end* level work. Here are the tasks we're going to address in this section:

- **Add GraphQL support to ASP.NET Core** with the *HotChocolate* third-party library
- **Add GraphQL support to Angular** using the *Apollo Angular* GraphQL client
- **Test the server-side and client-side integration** with Visual Studio

Let's put this plan into action.

Adding GraphQL to ASP.NET Core

If we want to provide our existing ASP.NET Core app with GraphQL support, we need to add a GraphQL layer to the HTTP pipeline that can perform the following tasks:

- **Expose an API endpoint** that clients will use to send their GraphQL queries
- **Process the incoming queries** using our existing data model
- **Retrieve the requested data** from the underlying DBMS
- **Provide the response** with the resulting data in JSON format

Implementing these features from scratch would require a considerable amount of work, even for our limited database schema.

Luckily enough, we don't need to do that thanks to the existence of several ASP.NET Core client libraries designed to do most of the job for us, such as `GraphQL.NET` and `HotChocolate`, both available on GitHub under the MIT license.

GraphQL.NET is available at the following URL: `https://github.com/graphql-dotnet/graphql-dotnet/`.

And here's the URL for `HotChocolate`: `https://github.com/ChilliCream/hotchocolate`.

In this chapter, we're going to use `HotChocolate`, a comprehensive .NET GraphQL platform that can help us to achieve the above goal with minimal effort.

Installing HotChocolate

The `HotChocolate` components that we need are available in two convenient NuGet packages, which we can install from the Visual Studio GUI (using the NuGet Package Manager) or using the Package Manager console with the following command:

```
PM> Install-Package HotChocolate.AspNetCore -Version 12.6.0
PM> Install-Package HotChocolate.AspNetCore.Authorization -Version 12.6.0
PM> Install-Package HotChocolate.Data.EntityFramework -Version 12.6.0
```

The suggested version, the latest at the time of writing, is fully compatible with our `WorldCitiesAPI` project.

As always, we're free to opt for a different version if we think we're able to deal with the required updates.

The first NuGet package contains `HotChocolate`'s GraphQL services and middlewares and is the only one required.

The second and third packages contain some useful (yet optional) extensions that will allow us to seamlessly integrate the ASP.NET Core authorization model and *Entity Framework Core* into HotChocolate, which will greatly speed up our development time: that's the reason why we're going to use this library.

Right after installing HotChocolate, we can start to set up the *GraphQL schema*, which defines how we want to expose data to our client and the CRUD operations we want to allow. Such a schema can be configured using three root types:

- **Query**, which exposes all the possible queries clients can use, thereby allowing them to retrieve data in a *read-only* manner. We can think of it as a centralized view of all our entities, with a number of methods corresponding to the various ways to retrieve them.
- **Mutation**, which can be used by clients to perform *write* operations such as inserting, updating, and deleting entities.
- **Subscription**, which allows clients to subscribe to events and be notified in real time of their occurrence.

In the following sub-sections, we're going to implement the *Query* and *Mutation* types, which will allow our clients to perform the same *read*, *add*, *update*, and *delete* operations that we've implemented over the preceding chapters using REST.

Query

Using Solution Explorer, create a new /Data/GraphQL/ folder in the WorldCitiesAPI project. Once done, add a new Query.cs file within it and fill its content with the following lines:

```
using Microsoft.EntityFrameworkCore;
using WorldCitiesAPI.Data.Models;

namespace WorldCitiesAPI.Data.GraphQL
{
    public class Query
    {
        /// <summary>
        /// Gets all Cities.
        /// </summary>
        [Serial]
        [UsePaging]
        [UseFiltering]
        [UseSorting]
        public IQueryable<City> GetCities(
            [Service] ApplicationDbContext context)
            => context.Cities;

        /// <summary>
        /// Gets all Countries.
```

```
        /// </summary>
        [Serial]
        [UsePaging]
        [UseFiltering]
        [UseSorting]
        public IQueryable<Country> GetCountries(
            [Service] ApplicationDbContext context)
            => context.Countries;
    }
}
```

As we can see, the preceding `Query` type features two methods that use *Entity Framework* to return `IQueryable` objects.

The most important thing worth noting here is those *Data Annotation Attributes* that we've added above the two methods to enable *paging*, *filtering*, and *sorting*. As we can easily guess, those attributes allow us to transparently use some powerful built-in features of `HotChocolate`.

More specifically:

- **Serial**. This attribute will tell `HotChocolate` to execute certain tasks in serial rather than parallel mode, thus making it compatible with our current `ApplicationDbContext` implementation. It's worth noting that this option will have a non-trivial impact on performances; however, we're going to use that – at least for this sample scenario – to avoid refactoring our app (see below for additional info).

- **UsePaging**. This attribute will add a *Pagination Middleware* that allows GraphQL clients to paginate results using the *Cursor Connections Specification*, a standardized way to allow clients to consistently handle pagination best practices with support for related metadata.

- **UseFiltering**. This attribute will add a *Filtering Middleware* that allows GraphQL clients to use filters, which will be translated to native database queries. The available filters will be automatically inferred by `HotChocolate` by looking at the `IQueryable` entity types.

- **UseSorting**. This attribute will add a *Sorting Middleware* that allows GraphQL clients to sort results using a sorting argument, which will be translated by `HotChocolate` to a LINQ query, and eventually, thanks to *EF Core*, to native database queries.

The *Serial* attribute, and the reason why we're using it, is a rather complex topic that deserves some additional explanation. When we use `services.AddDbContext<T>` to register a `DbContext` as a scoped service, one instance of this `DbContext` is created and used for the entirety of a GraphQL request. This is an issue since `HotChocolate` executes the query resolvers in parallel for performance reasons. If two resolvers are executed in parallel and both try to perform an operation using the same `DbContext`, we might see one of the following exceptions being thrown:

- A second operation started in this context before a previous operation was completed
- Cannot access a disposed object

Both of them are *concurrency* exceptions caused by the fact that, in a nutshell, our DbContext is not thread-safe. This issue can be fixed by either using the Serial attribute, thus forcing HotChocolate to work in serial mode, or by implementing the AddDbContextFactory extension method – first introduced in .NET 5 – that allows us to register a factory instead of a single DbContext instance.

To keep things simple, we're going to use the [Serial] attribute workaround for our current implementation scenario. That said, the AddDbContextFactory approach is the way to go for production-level apps.

Let's switch to the other attributes: UsePaging, UseFiltering, and UseSorting. If we think about that for a second, we can see how they handle the same requirements that we've implemented in *Chapter 6, Fetching and Displaying Data*, with our ApiResult class, without the need to write a single line of code. These powerful built-in features are part of the reason why we're using HotChocolate with the integration package for *EF Core*.

To learn more about the above concepts, take a look at the following links from the Graph-QL official docs:

https://chillicream.com/docs/hotchocolate/integrations/entity-framework#serial-execution

https://chillicream.com/docs/hotchocolate/fetching-data/pagination

https://chillicream.com/docs/hotchocolate/fetching-data/filtering

https://chillicream.com/docs/hotchocolate/fetching-data/sorting

This minimal Query type is all that we need to fulfill our *read-only* requirements. Let's now move to the *writing* part of the story.

Mutation

Add a new Mutation.cs file within it and fill its content with the following lines:

```
using HotChocolate.AspNetCore.Authorization;
using Microsoft.EntityFrameworkCore;
using WorldCitiesAPI.Data.Models;

namespace WorldCitiesAPI.Data.GraphQL
{
    public class Mutation
    {
        /// <summary>
        /// Add a new City
        /// </summary>
```

```
[Serial]
[Authorize(Roles = new[] { "RegisteredUser" })]
public async Task<City> AddCity(
    [Service] ApplicationDbContext context, CityDTO cityDTO)
{
    var city = new City() {
        Name = cityDTO.Name,
        Lat = cityDTO.Lat,
        Lon = cityDTO.Lon,
        CountryId = cityDTO.CountryId
    };
    context.Cities.Add(city);
    await context.SaveChangesAsync();
    return city;
}


/// <summary>
/// Update an existing City
/// </summary>
[Serial]
[Authorize(Roles = new[] { "RegisteredUser" })]
public async Task<City> UpdateCity(
    [Service] ApplicationDbContext context, CityDTO cityDTO)
{
    var city = await context.Cities
        .Where(c => c.Id == cityDTO.Id)
        .FirstOrDefaultAsync();
    if (city == null)
        // todo: handle errors
        throw new NotSupportedException();
    city.Name = cityDTO.Name;
    city.Lat = cityDTO.Lat;
    city.Lon = cityDTO.Lon;
    city.CountryId = cityDTO.CountryId;
    context.Cities.Update(city);
    await context.SaveChangesAsync();
    return city;
}


/// <summary>
/// Delete a City
```

```
/// </summary>
[Serial]
[Authorize(Roles = new[] { "Administrator" })]
public async Task DeleteCity(
    [Service] ApplicationDbContext context, int id)
{
    var city = await context.Cities
        .Where(c => c.Id == id)
        .FirstOrDefaultAsync();
    if (city != null)
    {
        context.Cities.Remove(city);
        await context.SaveChangesAsync();
    }
}


/// <summary>
/// Add a new Country
/// </summary>
[Serial]
[Authorize(Roles = new[] { "RegisteredUser" })]
public async Task<Country> AddCountry(
    [Service] ApplicationDbContext context, CountryDTO countryDTO)
{
    var country = new Country() {
        Name = countryDTO.Name,
        ISO2 = countryDTO.ISO2,
        ISO3 = countryDTO.ISO3
    };
    context.Countries.Add(country);
    await context.SaveChangesAsync();
    return country;
}


/// <summary>
/// Update an existing Country
/// </summary>
[Serial]
[Authorize(Roles = new[] { "RegisteredUser" })]
public async Task<Country> UpdateCountry(
    [Service] ApplicationDbContext context, CountryDTO countryDTO)
```

```
{
    var country = await context.Countries
        .Where(c => c.Id == countryDTO.Id)
        .FirstOrDefaultAsync();
    if (country == null)
        // todo: handle errors
        throw new NotSupportedException();
    country.Name = countryDTO.Name;
    country.ISO2 = countryDTO.ISO2;
    country.ISO3 = countryDTO.ISO3;
    context.Countries.Update(country);
    await context.SaveChangesAsync();
    return country;
}


/// <summary>
/// Delete a Country
/// </summary>
[Serial]
[Authorize(Roles = new[] { "Administrator" })]
public async Task DeleteCountry(
    [Service] ApplicationDbContext context, int id)
{
    var country = await context.Countries
        .Where(c => c.Id == id)
        .FirstOrDefaultAsync();
    if (country != null)
    {
        context.Countries.Remove(country);
        await context.SaveChangesAsync();
    }
}
}
}
```

As we can see, we've set up six methods that will allow clients to *add*, *update*, and *delete* our Cities and Countries entities using *Entity Framework*.

It's worth noting that, in the *add* and *update* methods implementation, we've used the CityDTO and CountryDTO *Data Transfer Object* classes that we have set up in *Chapter 8, Code Tweaks and Data Services*, mapping them to the corresponding City and Country entities.

We've also applied the [Authorize] attribute provided by the HotChocolate.AspNetCore.Authorization package to those methods to restrict access to authorized users (roles) only. This is basically the same approach we've used in CitiesController and CountriesController, with one important difference: that time we made use of a different [Authorize] attribute, provided by the Microsoft.AspNetCore. Authorization namespace, which won't work here.

> The two attributes share the same name, but luckily enough they accept a different Roles parameter type. Microsoft's attribute wants a string, while HotChocolate's requires a string array. This difference can help us to distinguish between them.

Be sure to add the correct namespace reference on the top of the file, just like we did in the preceding code.

Program.cs

Now that our GraphQL schema is ready, we just need to add the required services and middlewares to our Program.cs file.

Let's start with the service. Open the Program.cs file and add the following highlighted lines right below the JwtHandler service that we added in *Chapter 11, Authentication and Authorization*:

```
// ...

using WorldCitiesAPI.Data.GraphQL;

// ...

builder.Services.AddScoped<JwtHandler>();

builder.Services.AddGraphQLServer()
    .AddAuthorization()
    .AddQueryType<Query>()
    .AddMutationType<Mutation>()
    .AddFiltering()
    .AddSorting();

// ...
```

The service comes with a lot of helper methods that can be used to configure its various settings. However, we don't need to do anything now, since the default values are good enough for us. We just need to add the Query and Mutation types that we've implemented early on and enable *filtering* and *sorting*.

Let's now switch to middleware. Scroll down a bit and add the following highlighted lines right below the MapControllers() method:

```
// ...

app.MapControllers();

app.MapGraphQL("/api/graphql");

// ...
```

Again, the middleware accepts various configuration settings. In our scenario, we just had to configure the GraphQL endpoint (default is "/graphql") to make it compatible with the Angular Proxy rule that we already have in the proxy.conf.js file of our Angular app.

Now we can finally test what we have done so far.

Testing the GraphQL schema

Another great feature of HotChocolate is that it comes with a built-in GraphQL web-based client that can be used to test our GraphQL service using a convenient visual interface. That's great for our purposes since we still have to deal with our Angular app.

The name of this client is **Banana Cake Pop** (BCP), and it can be accessed using the default endpoint (/api/graphql). To access it, launch the app by hitting *F5* and then navigate to the following URL: https://localhost:40443/api/graphql.

If we did everything correctly, we should be able to see the BCP welcome screen, as shown in the following screenshot:

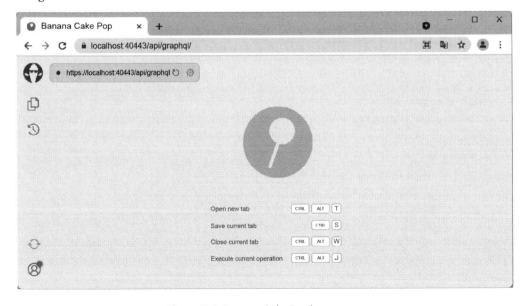

Figure 13.2: Banana Cake Pop home page

From there, hit *CTRL* + *ALT* + *T* to open a new tab and then type the following sample query:

```
query {
  cities(order: { id: ASC }, first:3 ) {
    nodes {
      id
      name
    }
  }
}
```

To receive the following result:

```
{
  "data": {
    "cities": {
      "nodes": [
        {
          "id": 1,
          "name": "Tokyo"
        },
        {
          "id": 2,
          "name": "Jakarta"
        },
        {
          "id": 3,
          "name": "Delhi"
        }
      ]
    }
  }
}
```

If we can see the above results, this means that our *server-side* implementation using HotChocolate works!

With this first query, we've already tested the sorting middleware. To test the filter middleware, we can alter the query in the following way:

```
query {
  cities(
    order: { id: ASC }
    first:3
```

```
      where: { name: { endsWith: "kyo" } }
  )
    {
    nodes {
      id
      name
    }
  }
}
```

This restricts our results to the only two cities ending with "kyo", *Tokyo* and *New Tokyo*, the city that we added back in *Chapter 7, Forms and Data Validation*.

GraphQL naming issues

Everything is looking good while querying Cities. However, if we try to retrieve some Countries, we will likely face the resurgence of odd behavior that we've already addressed in the past.

For example, if we try to execute this query:

```
query {
  countries(order: { id: ASC }, first:3 ) {
    nodes {
      name
      iso2
      iso3
    }
  }
}
```

We'll receive the following error in the BCP response window:

```
"The field 'iso2' does not exist on the type 'Country'."
```

We already know the reason for such an error. It's the same "naming issue" that we stumbled upon in *Chapter 6, Fetching and Displaying Data*, due to the automatic camelCase conversion of the System. Text.Json API, which we fixed using the [JsonPropertyName] data annotation attribute in our Country and CountryDTO classes.

As a matter of fact, HotChocolate enforces that same behavior, automatically converting our object's properties to camelCase, and the [JsonPropertyName] attribute means nothing to it.

Luckily enough, the package provides a dedicated [GraphQLName] attribute that can be used to obtain the same result. This basically means that, to fix our issue, we just need to add such an attribute to our Country and CountryDTO classes in the following way:

```
        [JsonPropertyName("iso2")]
        [GraphQLName("iso2")]
```

```
            public string ISO2 { get; set; } = null!;


            [JsonPropertyName("iso3")]
            [GraphQLName("iso3")]
            public string ISO3 { get; set; } = null!;
```

As soon as we do that, the above query should work without any issues.

 Be sure to apply the `[GraphQLName]` attribute to the ISO2 and ISO3 properties of both the Country and CountryDTO classes, otherwise this chapter's sample code won't work.

All good so far. Now is the time to switch to Angular and connect to our new *server-side* GraphQL service with our client.

Adding GraphQL to Angular

To consume our new GraphQL endpoint in Angular, we have two options:

- **Manually implement a GraphQL client**, taking care of the underlying HTTP connection as well as the various fetching, caching, and optimization tasks
- **Add a third-party package** that (hopefully) already does all that

As odd as it might sound, implementing a minimal GraphQL client wouldn't be that hard. Now that we know how Angular's HttpClient works, we can put that knowledge into action and implement an observable-based service using the superclass/subclass pattern we've used back in *Chapter 8*, *Code Tweaks and Data Services*, with our existing BaseService, CountryService, and CityService types.

However, for the sake of simplicity, we'll opt for the third-party package. More specifically, we're going to use **Apollo Angular**, a flexible, community-driven GraphQL client for Angular, JavaScript, and native platforms. The main advantage of such a client is given by the fact that it is incredibly easy to configure and set up, which allows us to just drop it into our existing Angular app within minutes.

Here's what we'll do in the upcoming sections:

- **Install Apollo Angular** in our *WorldCities* project, together with all its dependencies
- **Update our CityService** by refactoring a sample method so that it will use GraphQL instead of the existing REST endpoints
- **Test it** to see whether the new implementation works as expected
- **Improve the implementation** by refactoring other REST methods
- **Extend the changes** by applying them to CountryService as well

Are we ready? Let's go!

Installing Apollo Angular

Starting from version 2, *Apollo Angular* supports the ng-add command, meaning that we can install it with a one-line command from the Angular CLI in the following way:

```
> ng add apollo-angular
```

However, at least at the time of writing, this approach fails due to some typing errors that can only be fixed by installing other NPM packages or altering our existing TypeScript configuration, which is something we don't want to do. For that very reason, we'll just install the required packages using NPM.

Adding the NPM packages

Open a command-line console, navigate to the WorldCities app's root folder, and type the following commands:

```
> npm install @apollo/client@3.5.6
> npm install apollo-angular@2.6.0
> npm install graphql@15.8.0
```

Or, if you prefer, just add a reference for each of the preceding packages in the project's package.json file and then perform an npm install.

 As always, the suggested versions are fully compatible with the current book's code base. Those who want to change/update them are free to do that, assuming they will be able to handle any compatibility issue with other packages/dependencies that such a choice might entail.

The apollo/client package is the core GraphQL client, while apollo-angular is just a bridge to make it compatible with Angular. Similar bridges are available for *React*, *Vue*, *Svelte*, and many other frameworks. The graphql package is the official JS implementation for GraphQL.

As soon as the npm packages have been installed, we can start to configure the client within our app.

Updating AppModule

Open the app.module.ts file and add the following highlighted lines:

```
// ...

import {APOLLO_OPTIONS} from 'apollo-angular';
import {HttpLink} from 'apollo-angular/http';
import {InMemoryCache} from '@apollo/client/core';

// ...

  providers: [
```

```
// ...

  {
    provide: APOLLO_OPTIONS,
    useFactory: (httpLink: HttpLink) => {
      return {
        cache: new InMemoryCache({
          addTypename: false
        }),
        link: httpLink.create({
          uri: environment.baseUrl + 'api/graphql',
        }),
        defaultOptions: {
          watchQuery: { fetchPolicy: 'no-cache' },
          query: { fetchPolicy: 'no-cache' }
        }
      };
    },
    deps: [HttpLink],
  }
],

// ...
```

As we can see, all we had to do was include the required `import` references and add a new provider with the configuration settings we need, such as the GraphQL endpoint that we've set on our ASP.NET Core application.

It's worth noting that Apollo Angular natively supports a convenient *in-memory* cache built-in feature, which allows the convenient storage of temporary data. However, since using the caching store will pose some non-trivial issues on the retrieved data, for the sake of simplicity, we're not going to use it within our code samples. That's the reason why we've explicitly disabled it using the `fetchPolicy` configuration setting.

 Those who want to know more about this can read the following URL from the Apollo Angular official docs:

https://apollo-angular.com/docs/caching/configuration/

Now we're ready to replace our existing REST implementation with GraphQL.

Refactoring CityService

Let's start with a simple drop-in replacement of the get(id) method of CityService, which we currently use to retrieve a single City.

Here's the existing REST-based code:

```
get(id: number): Observable<City> {
  var url = this.getUrl("api/Cities/" + id);
  return this.http.get<City>(url);
}
```

And here's the replacement code for GraphQL:

```
// ...

import { Observable, map } from 'rxjs';
import { Apollo, gql } from 'apollo-angular';

// ...

  constructor(
    http: HttpClient,
    private apollo: Apollo) {
    super(http);
  }

// ...

  get(id: number): Observable<City> {
    return this.apollo
      .query({
        query: gql`
          query GetCityById($id: Int!) {
            cities(where: { id: { eq: $id } }) {
              nodes {
                id
                name
                lat
                lon
                countryId
              }
            }
          }
```

```
            ,
        variables: {
            id
        }
    })
    .pipe(map((result: any) =>
        result.data.cities.nodes[0]));
    }

// ...
```

Here we go. Take a closer look at what we did there:

- We've replaced our `HttpClient` with the `Apollo` client, thus adding the required import references.

- We've used the `query` method to send a GraphQL query not much different from those we've used to test the GraphQL *server-side* implementation early on in this chapter. This time, instead of returning a collection of cities, we're getting just one of them – the one corresponding to the `id` variable we're using inside the query.

- We've mapped the `query` method return type to the resulting `node` that contains the properties of the resulting `City`.

Here's the underlying GraphQL query that the above method will use to retrieve a given `City`, let's say with an `id` value of 1:

```
query {
  cities(where: { id: { eq: 1 } })
  {
    nodes {
        id
        name
        lat
        lon
        countryId
    }
  }
}
```

And here's the corresponding GraphQL *server-side* JSON response:

```
{
    "data": {
        "cities": {
            "nodes": [
                {
```

```
        "id": 1,
        "name": "Tokyo",
        "lat": 35.6897,
        "lon": 139.6922,
        "countryId": 1
      }
    ]
  }
  }
}
```

If we want to perform a quick test now, we can run our WorldCities and WorldCitiesAPI apps and check whether we can still edit a City without issues. If we did everything correctly, we should see no issues – everything should be working as it was before, when we had the REST implementation up. This means that the drop-in replacement of the get(id) method went fine.

Let's do the same with the getData<ApiResult> method, which poses some additional issues. This method returns an ApiResult, the POCO class that we added back in *Chapter 6*, *Fetching and Displaying Data* to support features such as *sorting*, *filtering*, and *paging*.

As a matter of fact, we know that the HotChocolate and *Entity Framework Core* implementation that we set up early on natively support these features; however, the HotChocolate paging – which follows the *GraphQL Cursor Connections Specification* – works in a rather different way, and refactoring our app to comply with those specs will require a lot of frontend work, as well as some non-straightforward changes to our UI.

 To learn more about *GraphQL Cursor Connections Specification*, visit the following URL: https://relay.dev/graphql/connections.htm.

For that very reason, in order to preserve our existing work, we'll approach it from the other direction; work at the server-side level to make the GraphQL query return the same object (and data) that we're already set up to receive.

Improving the GraphQL query

Let's switch back to our ASP.NET Core's WorldCitiesAPI project. Open the /Data/GraphQL/Query.cs file and add the following GetCitiesApiResult method, right below the existing ones:

```
/// <summary>
/// Gets all Cities (with ApiResult and DTO support).
/// </summary>
[Serial]
public async Task<ApiResult<CityDTO>> GetCitiesApiResult(
    [Service] ApplicationDbContext context,
```

```
        int pageIndex = 0,
        int pageSize = 10,
        string? sortColumn = null,
        string? sortOrder = null,
        string? filterColumn = null,
        string? filterQuery = null)
{
    return await ApiResult<CityDTO>.CreateAsync(
            context.Cities.AsNoTracking()
                .Select(c => new CityDTO()
                {
                    Id = c.Id,
                    Name = c.Name,
                    Lat = c.Lat,
                    Lon = c.Lon,
                    CountryId = c.Country!.Id,
                    CountryName = c.Country!.Name
                }),
            pageIndex,
            pageSize,
            sortColumn,
            sortOrder,
            filterColumn,
            filterQuery);
}
```

As we can see, there's nothing new here; it's the same approach that we've used in our `CitiesController` to receive the *paging, filtering,* and *sorting* parameters from the client and return `ApiResult` objects containing the resulting data. This workaround is hardly the best GraphQL approach we can take, but it's a great way to show how versatile it can be when we need to comply with an existing scenario.

> If we had more time (and pages), we might as well take the other route, replacing our existing client-side pagination (and UI components) to implement the cursor-based GraphQL pagination, which would allow us to use the `GetCities` method of `Query` instead of the newly added one.

Now that we can conveniently count on the new `GetCitiesApiResult` method, we just need to consume it from our client.

Back to Angular

Switch back to the *WorldCities* Angular app, open the `city.service.ts` file, and replace the existing
`GetData` method with the following:

```
getData(
  pageIndex: number,
  pageSize: number,
  sortColumn: string,
  sortOrder: string,
  filterColumn: string | null,
  filterQuery: string | null
): Observable<ApiResult<City>> {
  return this.apollo
    .query({
      query: gql'
        query GetCitiesApiResult(
            $pageIndex: Int!,
            $pageSize: Int!,
            $sortColumn: String,
            $sortOrder: String,
            $filterColumn: String,
            $filterQuery: String) {
          citiesApiResult(
            pageIndex: $pageIndex
            pageSize: $pageSize
            sortColumn: $sortColumn
            sortOrder: $sortOrder
            filterColumn: $filterColumn
            filterQuery: $filterQuery
          ) {
            data {
              id
              name
              lat
              lon
              countryId
              countryName
            },
            pageIndex
            pageSize
            totalCount
```

```
                    totalPages
                    sortColumn
                    sortOrder
                    filterColumn
                    filterQuery
                }
            }
        ',
        variables: {
          pageIndex,
          pageSize,
          sortColumn,
          sortOrder,
          filterColumn,
          filterQuery
        }
      })
      .pipe(map((result: any) =>
          result.data.citiesApiResult));
  }
```

As we can see, we wrote a long, parametrized GraphQL query using the various values fetched from the UI, and then used the new `GetCitiesApiResult` server-side method (and mapped its result) to return the same `Observable<ApiResult>` as before.

To test what we did, we can launch our two projects and navigate to the `Cities` list. If we did everything correctly, we should see no differences.

Now we just need to replace the `put`, `post`, `getCountries`, and `isDupeCity` methods. The last two methods are quite straightforward, now that we know how to read GraphQL data. The actual challenge comes with the first two since they perform write operations to the server-side data.

Querying the mutation

Refactoring the `put` and `post` methods of `CityService` means that we'll finally have to use ASP.NET Core's `Mutation.cs` file, which we implemented a while ago and haven't used hitherto.

Before getting back to Angular, it might be useful to launch our `WorldCitiesAPI` project and navigate to the *Banana Cake Pop* UI of `HotChocolate` to see what our `Mutation` type looks like.

Open the browser and navigate to the following URL:

```
https://localhost:40443/api/graphql/
```

Once there, select **Schema Reference** from the drop-down list below the server URL and then click on **Mutation** from the **Types** menu located to the far right, as shown in the following screenshot:

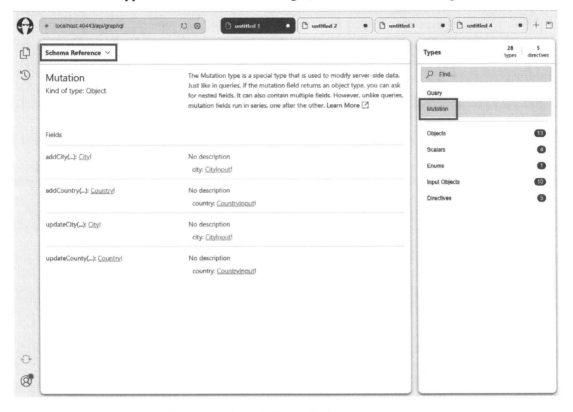

Figure 13.3: Schema Reference for the mutation type

As we can see, we have four mutations that we can use to do what we need to do.

With that knowledge, we can now open the `city.service.ts` file and replace the existing put and post methods with the following code:

```
put(input: City): Observable<City> {
  return this.apollo
    .mutate({
      mutation: gql'
        mutation UpdateCity($city: CityDTOInput!) {
          updateCity(cityDTO: $city) {
            id
            name
            lat
            lon
            countryId
          }
```

```
          }
        ',
      variables: {
        city: input
      }
    }).pipe(map((result: any) =>
      result.data.updateCity));
}

post(item: City): Observable<City> {
  return this.apollo
    .mutate({
      mutation: gql'
        mutation AddCity($city: CityDTOInput!) {
          addCity(cityDTO: $city) {
            id
            name
            lat
            lon
            countryId
          }
        }
      ',
      variables: {
        city: item
      }
    }).pipe(map((result: any) =>
      result.data.addCity));
}
```

That's it. The preceding code should be quite easy to understand since we're just executing the GraphQL method specified in the `Mutation.cs` class. The only new concept there is the use of the `variables` parameter, a JSON object that can be used to send one or more variables to the GraphQL engine. Those variables can be used in the preceding query parameter, prepending them with the `$` character, just like we did.

> Using variables is often a convenient way to put dynamic data in the GraphQL query without having to resort to JS or TS string manipulation techniques or other not-so-clean workarounds.

As always, we can test the new implementation by launching our apps and trying to update an existing city and/or add a new city. If we did everything correctly, we should still be able to do that without issues.

With that, we're done with `CityService`.

Refactoring CountryService

In this section, we'll quickly recap what we need to do to refactor `CountryService` to use GraphQL instead of REST for its most relevant data retrieval and update methods, just like we did for `CityService`.

For reasons of space, we're not going to show all the source code updates. They can be found in the GitHub repository for this chapter. However, trying to carry out updates to `CountryService` without looking at the GitHub code might be a great exercise for the reader, who is strongly encouraged to do that.

Here's a list of the relevant steps:

- Refactor the `get(id)` method, which is the easiest to update since we can use the default `GetCountries()` method of the GraphQL `Query` type
- Refactor the `getData` method, which will be slightly more complex since it will also require adding a new `GetCountriesApiResult` method in the `Country.cs` file of the ASP.NET Core app (which can be found in the GitHub repository for reference)
- Refactor the `put` and `post` methods, which will leverage the existing `updateCountry` and `addCountry` methods of the `Mutation` type

`CityService` can be a great reference for all the above tasks since the underlying entities are quite similar. It all comes down to replacing some class and property names.

Summary

This chapter was entirely dedicated to GraphQL, an open source data query and manipulation language aiming to be a great alternative to the REST architectural style for some specific scenarios, as it allows the mitigation of some known REST limitations, such as *over-fetching* and the risks of *regression bugs*.

Following a quick review of the pros and cons of both approaches, we started to implement GraphQL in our *WorldCities* ASP.NET Core project. We did that using `HotChocolate`, a comprehensive third-party .NET GraphQL platform that helped us to do that with minimal effort, mostly thanks to the fact that it provides great support to *Entity Framework Core* through its extension package.

Installing and configuring `HotChocolate` gave us the chance to familiarize ourselves with several GraphQL-related concepts such as *queries*, *mutations*, and *subscriptions*, all part of the overall *GraphQL schema*. Upon completing the setup, we also took the opportunity to practice with some actual queries during the first *server-side* tests.

Then we switched to Angular. Again, we have chosen to use a third-party package to lift most of the hard work. The choice fell on **Apollo Angular**, a flexible, community-driven GraphQL client for Angular that could be used as a drop-in replacement for our existing REST implementation with minimal changes to the code base.

After installing *Apollo Angular*, we spent some valuable time refactoring most of the data retrieval and update methods of our existing `CityService` to use GraphQL instead of the REST endpoints. Then we tested the knowledge acquired by performing the same changes on the `CountryService` class.

Suggested topics

For further information, we recommend the following topics: GraphQL, REST, GraphQL Schema, Query, Mutation, Subscription, HotChocolate, Banana Cake Pop, and Apollo Angular.

References

- *GraphQL adopters*: `https://graphql.org/users/`
- *RFC 2616 (HTTP/1.1)*: `https://www.w3.org/Protocols/rfc2616/rfc2616.html`
- *Architectural Styles and the Design of Network-based Software Architectures (Roy Thomas Fielding)*: `https://www.ics.uci.edu/~fielding/pubs/dissertation/top.htm`
- *GraphQL specifications*: `https://github.com/graphql/graphql-spec`
- *HotChocolate – Entity Framework integration*: `https://chillicream.com/docs/hotchocolate/integrations/entity-framework`
- *HotChocolate – Pagination*: `https://chillicream.com/docs/hotchocolate/fetching-data/pagination`
- *HotChocolate – Filtering*: `https://chillicream.com/docs/hotchocolate/fetching-data/filtering`
- *HotChocolate – Sorting*: `https://chillicream.com/docs/hotchocolate/fetching-data/sorting`
- *Apollo Angular*: `https://apollo-angular.com/`
- *Apollo Angular Caching*: `https://apollo-angular.com/docs/caching/configuration/`
- *GraphQL Cursor Connections specification*: `https://relay.dev/graphql/connections.htm`

14

Real-Time Updates with SignalR

In this chapter, we'll talk about **ASP.NET Core SignalR**, an open-source library that allows us to add real-time functionality to web applications by enabling server-side code to push content to clients instantly.

Such a requirement might have little or no use in most general-purpose apps, including the WorldCities app we've been working on since *Chapter 5, Data Model with Entity Framework Core*; however, it can be very useful for some specific scenarios, such as:

- Online games, especially if they need to support multiple players acting simultaneously in a common or shared environment
- Social networks, assuming they need some kind of notification system
- Collaborative apps such as blogs, CMSes, whiteboards, team meetings, file-sharing services, and the like
- Dashboard and monitoring apps, including our HealthCheck app

As we can easily guess, the HealthCheck app will be the perfect candidate to explore such a topic. With that in mind, here's what we'll do in the following sections:

- **Review the various techniques** and workarounds to implement real-time capabilities in web applications using *server push technologies* since the introduction of HTTP/1.0
- **Introduce SignalR**, an open-source library that allows us to add real-time web functionality to apps leveraging the above techniques
- **Implement SignalR** at the server-side level in our HealthCheckAPI ASP.NET Core app
- **Add SignalR capabilities** at the client-side level to our Angular app

Are we ready? Let's go!

Technical requirements

In this chapter, we're going to need all the technical requirements listed in previous chapters, with the following additional packages:

- `Microsoft.AspNetCore.SignalR`
- `@microsoft/signalr`

The `Microsoft.AspNetCore.SignalR` package comes with the `Microsoft.AspNetCore.App` framework, meaning that our ASP.NET Core apps already have it.

As always, it's advisable to avoid installing them straight away; we're going to bring them in during this chapter to better contextualize their purpose within our project.

The code files for this chapter can be found at `https://github.com/PacktPublishing/ASP.NET-Core-6-and-Angular/tree/master/Chapter_14/`.

Real-time HTTP and Server Push

Providing real-time functionalities to a web application was a very complex task for the first two decades of the Internet, mostly due to the fact that the HTTP protocol was never meant for that. As we learned in *Chapter 13, Beyond REST – Web API and GraphQL*, when we briefly reviewed the REST principles and constraints distilled from the HTTP/1.0 and 1.1 specifications, there were no references to real-time communications, streaming protocols, server-initiated calls, or any other technique that might lead to something different from the *pull-based* request/response cycle initiated by a client request and handled by the server with a corresponding (and terminating) response.

For that very reason, for most of the '90s, the most effective ways to implement real-time behaviors in a web application were:

- Using Java, Flash/ActionScript, or other "embeddable" content that could (A) support a suitable technology to achieve such behavior (socket, streaming, push/pub) and (B) interact with the DOM via JavaScript, a browser plug-in, a VM, a runtime component, or any other viable technique
- "Emulating" real-time behavior, performing frequent content updates via full-page refresh, iframe-based refresh, Ajax-based (`XMLHttpRequest`) polls, or other workarounds that could be used to keep the data up to date

The above techniques were rather common in stock exchange and chat-based websites: however, they weren't widely used since they were difficult to maintain and often led to compatibility issues among the various browsers—it was the "cross-browser compatibility hell" period, after all.

However, RFC 2616 (HTTP/1.1, 1999) introduced a significant difference promoting persistent connections to the default behavior of any HTTP connection; this basically meant that, unless otherwise indicated, the client SHOULD assume that the server will maintain a persistent connection, even after error responses from the server.

Such a statement, although not strictly related to streaming or real-time communication, has led many developers to look for an alternative way to establish a connection between the client and server that could allow the two-way exchange of information in real time. Such experiments, over the course of almost 20 years, led to **pushlets**, **long polling**, **Server-Sent Events (SSE)**, and—eventually—HTTP/2-based alternatives such as **Web Push**, **gRPC**, and **WebRTC**: however, it was only after the introduction and adoption of the **WebSocket** protocol (RFC 6455, December 2011) that the presence of real-time capabilities in web applications began to spread widely.

Introducing SignalR

What does all this have to do with *SignalR*? As a matter of fact, the ASP.NET Core approach to handle real-time requirements for web applications is an *abstraction* of most of the techniques we've just mentioned.

More specifically, SignalR takes advantage of the following transport methods (in order of fallback):

- WebSockets
- SSE
- HTTP long polling

The best technology supported by the client and server is used by SignalR to initiate the connection and fulfill its tasks, which are mostly handled through *hubs* and data exchange *protocols*.

Hubs

Hubs are a pivotal concept in SignalR, as they are used to communicate between clients and servers: the Hub type is defined within the `Microsoft.AspNetCore.SignalR` namespace and is part of the `Microsoft.AspNetCore.SignalR` NuGet package.

We can think of hubs as high-level dispatchers that allow the client and the server to call methods on each other using a standardized API—the *SignalR Hubs API*.

Protocols

The data between the client and the server is transmitted using serialization and deserialization techniques based upon two data exchange protocols: a *JSON*-based text protocol and a binary protocol based on *MessagePack*, a lesser-known data interchange format.

 As a matter of fact, there's a third protocol named *BlazorPack* that is used exclusively with Blazor Server applications since it requires the Blazor Server hosting model. For more information, see the official docs at the following URL:

```
https://github.com/dotnet/aspnetcore/blob/068797e16a1bfe66461e15c8a2ffa
864369d384d/src/SignalR/docs/specs/HubProtocol.md
```

A Hub is exposed by the server through a dedicated route, which can be used by clients to *connect* and receive events in the form of messages, which are dispatched to the subscribed *users* and *groups*.

Connections, Users, and Groups

Connections, users, and groups are the three fundamental concepts used by the server to transmit real-time messages to clients using SignalR. Each of them has peculiar characteristics and serves a specific purpose:

- **Connections**. In SignalR, each client has a unique connection to the server: when a client connects to a hub, SignalR generates a unique identifier that is known only by the interested parties, meaning that each client connection has its own identifier.

- **Users**. A user is seen by SignalR as a subscribed individual, which is handled as part of a group. Users shouldn't be confused with connections or clients, since a single user can connect from multiple client applications: for example, the same user might connect from a web browser and a mobile phone at the same time, thus receiving messages on both of them.

- **Groups**. Groups are collections of one or more connections and are the main mechanism used by SignalR to transmit real-time data to clients. Any group has a given name that acts as its unique identifier; this name will be used by SignalR to send real-time messages. When these messages are dispatched to a group, all the group members (the connections that are part of that group) are notified.

Enough with the theory: the best way to understand these concepts is to see SignalR in action, which is what we're going to do in the upcoming sections.

Implementing SignalR

Let's briefly recap how our `HealthCheck` and `HealthCheckAPI` projects currently work:

- The `HealthCheck` Angular app features a component—the `HealthCheckComponent`—that, right after being loaded, performs a call to the *server-side* `/health` endpoint.

- The above endpoint is handled by the `HealthCheckMiddleware`: when called, the `HealthCheckAPI` ASP.NET Core Web API is configured to launch various ICMP health checks, each one configured to ping a hostname or IP address and return its status (*healthy* or *unhealthy*).

- The health checks' statuses are wrapped together by the `HealthCheckMiddleware` and sent in a single JSON response.

- The `HealthCheck` Angular app fetches the JSON response and uses it to create an HTML table, thus showing the result in a readable format.

As we can see, the only interaction between the two projects is a single HTTP call issued to the `/health` endpoint: right after the first health check result is received, the on-screen result will not change unless we manually refresh the browser's page, thus "rebooting" the `HealthCheckComponent` and forcing a new HTTP call. Until we do that, the data shown by the HTML table is nothing more than a static, possibly outdated, snapshot from the past.

Rest assured, we could easily implement a timer (using a JS interval function or something like that) to automatically force a page refresh every few minutes or seconds, thus ensuring that the HTML data will always be fresh: that's the "real-time emulation" strategy we talked about at the beginning of the chapter, where a frequent polling technique is used to work around the fact that the data-update task is always initiated by the client (*pull*) and never by the server (*push*).

However, such a workaround would have a lot of disadvantages:

- **Performance impact.** A lot of potentially unnecessary (and non-cached) HTTP requests, not to mention the ICMP calls issued by the server each time it's asked to show the updated result.
- **Over-fetching.** Frequently polling the health check will inevitably lead to a lot of useless calls: more precisely, any HTTP request receiving a JSON response with the same result as the previous one can be considered "wasted."
- **Inefficient.** No matter how frequently we configure the polling, there will always be a certain amount of "lag" between a health check change and the corresponding UI update: if we plan to use that HTML table as a monitor to promptly react whenever a check fails, our reaction time would be hindered by that lag.
- **Self-limited.** Whenever the data-update task can only be initiated at the client level, each client will always work as a separate, independent peer. This means that there will be no way to update that data from a different source, such as the server, a third-party service, another client, and so on.

SignalR can help us to improve the current behavior of the HealthCheck app without hitting the above downsides: more precisely, we can use it to implement a data-update strategy initiated by the server using a broadcast message simultaneously sent to all connected clients, which will trigger a refresh.

Here's a breakdown of the required tasks to achieve such a result:

- **Set up and configure SignalR in ASP.NET Core** using the required services and middleware, as well as the required CORS configuration settings to allow connections from external sources
- **Update the HealthCheckAPI project** to implement SignalR at the server-side level
- **Install and configure SignalR in Angular** using the @microsoft/signalr npm package
- **Update the HealthCheck project** to implement SignalR in our Angular app
- **Test everything** to ensure that our implementation is working as expected

As always, let's start with the *server-side* tasks.

Setting up SignalR in ASP.NET Core

To enable the SignalR services in the *HealthCheckAPI* project, the first thing we need to do is to create a hub: then we will set up the required services and middleware, and finally, we'll implement the broadcast message to issue the client update.

Creating the HealthCheckHub

Create a new `HealthCheckHub.cs` file in the `HealthCheckAPI` project's root folder and fill it with the following content:

```
using Microsoft.AspNetCore.SignalR;

namespace HealthCheckAPI
{
    public class HealthCheckHub : Hub
    {
    }
}
```

The class is intentionally empty since we don't need to add any method (yet): however, the important thing was to have it derived from the Hub base class, which is a requirement for any SignalR hub.

Setting up services and middleware

Now that we have a hub, we can add the SignalR services and middleware in our app's configuration class. Open the `Program.cs` file and add the following line right below the CORS settings:

```
// ...

builder.Services.AddCors(options =>
    options.AddPolicy(name: "AngularPolicy",
        cfg => {
            cfg.AllowAnyHeader();
            cfg.AllowAnyMethod();
            cfg.WithOrigins(builder.Configuration["AllowedCORS"]);
        }));

builder.Services.AddSignalR();

// ...
```

Once done, scroll down to the end of the file and add the following line right below the Minimal API that handles the heartbeat that we added back in *Chapter 12, Progressive Web Apps*:

```
// ...

app.MapMethods("/api/heartbeat", new[] { "HEAD" },
    () => Results.Ok());

app.MapHub<HealthCheckHub>("/api/health-hub");
```

```
// ...
```

The `/api/health-hub` endpoint will allow our client to connect to the hub and receive the broadcast message: now we just need to find a way to send it.

Adding the Broadcast Message

The best thing we can do to implement a SignalR broadcast message in a way that we can send it on-demand is to add a dedicated route that does just that: this will allow us to issue the message by executing a given URL, which is great for testing since it allows us to emulate not only a server-side task but also something initiated by a third party.

Using a Controller

If we want to handle such a route using a `Controller`, we can do that by adding a new `BroadcastController.cs` file in the `/Controllers/` folder and filling it with the following code:

```csharp
using Microsoft.AspNetCore.Mvc;
using Microsoft.AspNetCore.SignalR;

namespace HealthCheckAPI.Controllers
{
    [ApiController]
    [Route("api/[controller]/[action]")]
    public class BroadcastController : ControllerBase
    {
        private IHubContext<HealthCheckHub> _hub;

        public BroadcastController(
            IHubContext<HealthCheckHub> hub
            )
        {
            _hub = hub;
        }

        [HttpGet]
        public async Task<IActionResult> Update()
        {
            await _hub.Clients.All.SendAsync("Update", "test");
            return Ok("Update message sent.");
        }
    }
}
```

The above code should be quite easy to understand: we've just injected our Hub in the controller's constructor using DI, and then used it within the Update action method to broadcast an "Update" message to all connected clients.

This basically means that the broadcast message will be fired upon executing the /api/broadcast/ update endpoint.

Using the Minimal API

However, using a controller is not the only way to fulfill our task: since .NET 6, we can also opt for a Minimal API to achieve the same result with a considerably smaller amount of source code.

Let's take the chance to implement this alternative as well. Open the Program.cs file and add the following highlighted lines right below the SignalR middleware:

```
using Microsoft.AspNetCore.SignalR;

// ...

app.MapHub<HealthCheckHub>("/api/health-hub");

app.MapGet("/api/broadcast/update2", async (IHubContext<HealthCheckHub> hub) =>
{
    await hub.Clients.All.SendAsync("Update", "test");
    return Results.Text("Update message sent.");
});

// ...
```

As we can see, we've used a different route to distinguish the two approaches, since we want to support both of them: now the broadcast message will be fired upon executing either the /api/broadcast/ update endpoint (handled by the BroadcastController) or the /api/broadcast/update2 endpoint (handled by the Minimal API method above).

 It's worth noting that having a *controller* and a *Minimal API* method performing the same task is something we should always avoid in real-world apps: we're doing this here for sample purposes only. The important thing to understand here is how these two approaches can be used together in the same web application, ideally to handle different tasks.

Now we can finally switch to Angular.

Installing SignalR in Angular

To install SignalR in Angular we're going to use @microsoft/signalr, an npm package released by Microsoft containing the required JavaScript and TypeScript clients. Once done, we will create a HealthCheckService to perform the required tasks and replace the current HttpClient implementation within the HealthCheckComponent.

Adding the npm package

Let's start with the @microsoft/signalr npm package. Open a command-line console, navigate to the HealthCheck app's root folder, and type the following command:

```
> npm install @microsoft/signalr@6.0.1
```

Or, if you prefer, just add the package reference in the project's package.json file and then perform an npm install.

> As always, the suggested version is fully compatible with the current book's codebase: those who want to change/update it are free to do that, assuming they will be able to handle any compatibility issues with other packages/dependencies that such a choice might cause.

Now we can create our new service.

Implementing the HealthCheckService

The HealthCheck app doesn't have any services yet: as a matter of fact, we never felt the urge to create one, since it performs a minimal amount of HTTP calls. However, now that we need to add some SignalR-related tasks, it's better to refactor the whole HTTP connection and retrieval logic in a dedicated class.

From Visual Studio's **Solution Explorer**, navigate to the /src/app/health-check/ folder, create a new health-check.service.ts file, and fill it with the following code:

```
import { Injectable } from '@angular/core';
import { HttpClient } from '@angular/common/http';


import * as signalR from "@microsoft/signalr";


import { environment } from './../../environments/environment';
import { Observable, Subject, tap } from 'rxjs';

@Injectable({
  providedIn: 'root'
})
export class HealthCheckService {

  private hubConnection!: signalR.HubConnection;
  private _result: Subject<Result> = new Subject<Result>();
  public result = this._result.asObservable();

  constructor(private http: HttpClient) {
  }
```

```typescript
  public startConnection() {
    this.hubConnection = new signalR.HubConnectionBuilder()
        .configureLogging(signalR.LogLevel.Information)
        .withUrl(environment.baseUrl + 'api/health-hub', { withCredentials:
false })
        .build();

    console.log("Starting connection...");
    this.hubConnection
      .start()
      .then(() => console.log("Connection started."))
      .catch((err : any) => console.log(err));

    this.updateData();
  }

  public addDataListeners() {
    this.hubConnection.on('Update', (msg) => {
      console.log("Update issued by server for the following reason: " + msg);
      this.updateData();
    });
  }

  public updateData() {
    console.log("Fetching data...");
    this.http.get<Result>(environment.baseUrl + 'api/health')
      .subscribe(result => {
        this._result.next(result);
        console.log(result);
      });
  }

export interface Result {
  checks: Check[];
  totalStatus: string;
  totalResponseTime: number;
}

interface Check {
  name: string;
  responseTime: number;
```

```
   status: string;
   description: string;
}
```

The above code might not be simple to understand at first glance, however, there are some useful console.log calls that can be used to understand what's going on.

As we can see, the important tasks are handled by three methods:

- **startConnection**. This method instantiates the hubConnection, a persistent connection to the SignalR endpoint that we've configured in our ASP.NET Core app, so that our client will be able to listen to the Hub events and act accordingly. It also executes the updateData method once to retrieve the initial data to display.

- **addDataListeners**. This method is meant to be executed right after the above one, since it requires an already-existing hubConnection, and registers a handler to the "Update" event: such a handler basically logs the received message and executes the updateData method to "refresh" the data shown by the UI.

- **updateData**. This method, as the name implies, performs a standard HTTP call to the HealthCheckMiddleware API endpoint to retrieve the health check data and emit a new value to the private _result *Subject*, thus notifying all the subscribers of the public result *observable* that encapsulates it.

As we can see, we're using the same *observable*-based logic that we adopted for the *WorldCities* app's AuthService in *Chapter 11*, *Authentication and Authorization*: the *result* observable will notify all the subscribed components about any updated *SignalR* result, so that they can act accordingly.

Moreover, since all the HTTP work is being performed here, we took the chance to move the Result and Check interfaces in this file (they are currently in the health-check.component.ts file): we've also added the export keyword to the Result interface, since we're going to use it in the HealthCheckComponent— as we'll see in a short while.

Refactoring the HealthCheckComponent

Now that we have the HealthCheckService performing the heavy lifting, we need to refactor the HealthCheckComponent, replacing the current HttpClient implementation with the service's methods.

Let's start with the TypeScript file.

health-check.component.ts

Open the /src/app/health-check/health-check.component.ts file and replace the existing content with the following code (relevant new lines are highlighted):

```typescript
import { Component, Inject, OnInit } from '@angular/core';
import { Observable } from 'rxjs';
import { HealthCheckService, Result } from './health-check.service';

@Component({
```

```
  selector: 'app-health-check',
  templateUrl: './health-check.component.html',
  styleUrls: ['./health-check.component.scss']
})
export class HealthCheckComponent implements OnInit {

  public result: Observable<Result | null>;

  constructor(
    public service: HealthCheckService) {
      this.result = this.service.result;
  }

  ngOnInit() {
    this.service.startConnection();
    this.service.addDataListeners();
  }
}
```

If we compare the new code with the old one, we can acknowledge how the new implementation is much swifter and easier to read, now that all the data-retrieval logic has been put away: that's what services are meant for.

 It's worth noting that the approach used to refactor the HealthCheckComponent is quite similar to what we did in the NavMenuComponent of our *WorldCities* app, since we need to fulfill the same task: updating the UI whenever new/fresh data is received from a dependency service. The only difference is that we've used an *async pipe* instead of a Subject, just like we did in *Chapter 9, Back-End and Front-End Debugging*.

Now we can move on to the template file.

health-check.component.html

The component's template file requires only minimal updates, mostly due to the fact that we're using HealthCheckService's result member instead of the previous local variable.

Open the /src/app/health-check/health-check.component.html file and perform the following changes (updated code is highlighted):

```
<h1>Health Check</h1>

<p>Here are the results of our health check:</p>

<p *ngIf="!(result | async)"><em>Loading...</em></p>
```

```
<table *ngIf="result | async as res">
  <thead>
    <tr>
      <th>Name</th>
      <th>Response Time</th>
      <th>Status</th>
      <th>Description</th>
    </tr>
  </thead>
  <tbody>
    <tr *ngFor="let check of res.checks">
      <td>{{ check.name }}</td>
      <td>{{ check.responseTime }}</td>
      <td class="status {{ check.status }}">{{ check.status }}</td>
      <td>{{ check.description }}</td>
    </tr>
  </tbody>
</table>
```

That's it: the style sheet file doesn't require changes, meaning that we're done.

Testing it all

It's finally time to test all we have done so far.

Launch the two projects in *Debug* mode and, from the Angular app, navigate to the HealthCheckComponent.

We should see no UI differences up to this point, since we're still performing the initial HTTP call to fetch the health checks data: however, if we take a look at the browser's console, we can already see the console.log entries showing that the connection with the Hub has been established successfully, as shown in the following screenshot:

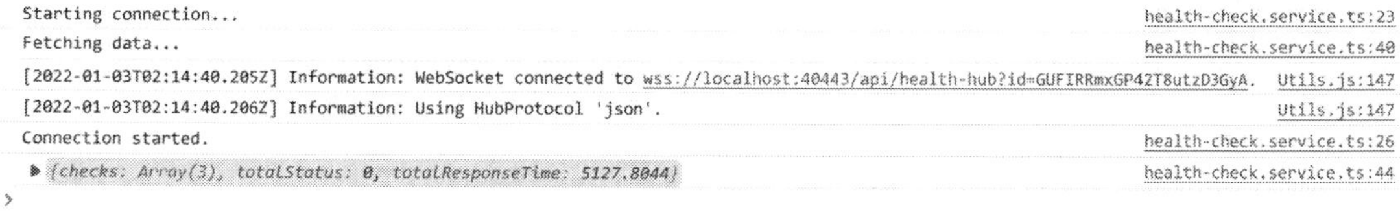

```
Starting connection...                                                                    health-check.service.ts:23
Fetching data...                                                                          health-check.service.ts:40
[2022-01-03T02:14:40.205Z] Information: WebSocket connected to wss://localhost:40443/api/health-hub?id=GUFIRRmxGP42T8utzD3GyA.   Utils.js:147
[2022-01-03T02:14:40.206Z] Information: Using HubProtocol 'json'.                                       Utils.js:147
Connection started.                                                                       health-check.service.ts:26
▶ {checks: Array(3), totalStatus: 0, totalResponseTime: 5127.8044}                        health-check.service.ts:44
>
```

Figure 14.1: SignalR connection started

Now we can test if the server-initiated update works as expected. To do that, open a different browser (or tab) and navigate to the following URLs:

```
https://localhost:40443/api/broadcast/update
```

```
https://localhost:40443/api/broadcast/update2
```

As we already know, the former endpoint is handled by the `BroadcastController` and the latter using the *Minimal API*. However, both of them should produce the same outcome: upon each request, the `HealthCheckComponent` should refresh the health checks data.

The refresh can be verified by looking at the **Response Time** values, in milliseconds, which will likely have a different value upon each update, and in the browser's console, where we should be able to see the server update request messages and the new data received by the subsequent HTTP call:

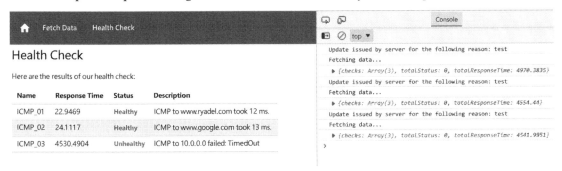

Figure 14.2: Console logs showing the server-initiated updates

Our basic implementation seems to be working.

Client-initiated Events

However, we've only worked on a server-to-client broadcast: what if we want to send something from our client to the server? It's true that we have a URL endpoint to test our update message, but could we send it from the `hubConnection` instead?

As a matter of fact, we can: and it's actually quite simple to implement, since we already did most of the required groundwork.

More precisely, here's what we need to do:

- **Update the HealthCheckHub** at the *server-side* level, to give clients the chance to invoke an *Update* method
- **Update the HealthCheckComponent** at the client-side level, to actually invoke the method
- **Test it** to see if everything works as expected

Let's do this.

Updating the HealthCheckHub

As we already know, the SignalR Hub allows a bi-directional data exchange, meaning that clients can send data through it: however, if we want to allow such behavior, we need to implement the necessary methods within the `Hub` itself.

To do that, open the `HealthCheckHub.cs` file and add the following `Update` method:

```
using Microsoft.AspNetCore.SignalR;

namespace HealthCheckAPI
{
    public class HealthCheckHub : Hub
    {
        public async Task ClientUpdate(string message) =>
            await Clients.All.SendAsync("ClientUpdate", message);
    }
}
```

The above code closely resembles what we've used in the BroadcastController and the *Minimal API*: however, this time we've used a different broadcast event, so that we'll be able to distinguish it from the server-initiated one. Furthermore, we took the chance to allow a custom message that clients might want to send, which will be transmitted together with the event.

Updating the HealthCheckService

Now that our Hub has an Update method, we just need to invoke it from our client.

Switch back to our Angular app, open the /src/app/health-check/health-check.service.ts file, and add the following method just below the existing updateData method, right before the end of the class:

```
// ...

  public sendClientUpdate() {
    this.hubConnection.invoke('ClientUpdate', 'client test')
    .catch(err => console.error(err));
  }

// ...
```

Since we're using a new event, we also need to add a new event handler for when we receive it. Scroll up on that same file and append the following code to the existing addDataListeners method:

```
this.hubConnection.on('ClientUpdate', (msg) => {
  console.log("Update issued by client for the following reason: " + msg);
  this.updateData();
  });
}
```

Now we just need to execute the sendClientUpdate method from the client. The best place to do that is the HealthCheckComponent.

Updating the HealthCheckComponent

Since we just need to execute a public method, a simple HTML button in the HealthCheckComponent's template file, like the following one, would be enough to do the trick:

```
<button (click)="service.sendClientUpdate()">
  Refresh
</button>
```

However, since we don't want to directly call that service's method through the component's HTML template, let's create a local method for that.

Open the /src/app/health-check/health-check.component.ts file and append the following method at the end of the file, right below the ngOnDestroy() existing method:

```
onRefresh() {
  this.service.sendClientUpdate();
}
```

Once done, open the /src/app/health-check/health-check.component.html file and append the following lines to the existing code to call the method we've just added:

```
<hr />

<button (click)="onRefresh()">
  Refresh
</button>
```

That's it: now we can test what we did.

Testing the new feature

To test the new feature, run the two projects in *Debug* mode, then use the Angular app to navigate to the HealthCheckComponent. Once there, click the refresh button and let the magic happen: if we did everything correctly, we'll be able to see the **Response Time** values, in milliseconds, vary upon each refresh, as well as seeing the client update messages in the browser's console, as shown in the following screenshot:

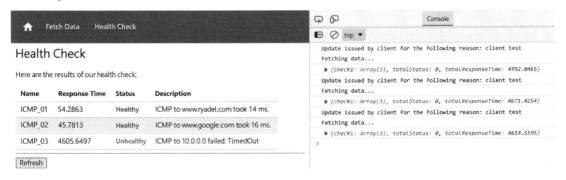

Figure 14.3: Client update test

With that, our ASP.NET Core SignalR overview is over.

Rest assured, we've only scratched the surface of the library's many built-in features and usage examples, but now that we've learned how to set up the Hub connection and send data from the server to clients and vice versa, we can definitely use it to bring real-time update capabilities to our projects.

Summary

This chapter was entirely dedicated to SignalR, an open-source library developed by Microsoft and shipped with ASP.NET Core that allows us to add real-time functionality to web applications.

We spent the first part of the chapter understanding the concepts of *Real-Time HTTP* and *Server-side Push*, reviewing the various techniques and workarounds used since the beginning of the Internet to achieve or emulate such capabilities; then we quickly reviewed the main features of SignalR, which leverages most of these techniques to provide an abstraction layer accessible through a proprietary API and built around concepts such as *hubs*, *protocols*, *connections*, *users*, and *groups*.

Right after that, we put our hand to code and implemented SignalR in ASP.NET Core and Angular, as well as setting up and configuring the required Microsoft NuGet and npm packages. More specifically, we started with implementing a server-initiated broadcast event that could be issued by executing a dedicated route: while we were there, we took the chance to implement such a route using either a dedicated *controller* or the *Minimal API* alternative approach introduced with .NET 6. Once done, we added a client-initiated event to see how the Hub connection that we implemented early on could be used the other way around.

Now we're ready to move on to the next—and final—topic of this book: app deployment.

Suggested topics

For further information, we recommend the following topics: SignalR, HTTP/1.0, HTTP/1.1, RFC 2616, Server Push, HTTP Long Polling, gRPC, WebRTC, WebSocket, WebSocketAPI, RFC 6455, Server-Sent Events (SSE), MessagePack, BlazorPack.

References

- *SignalR Hub Protocol:* `https://github.com/dotnet/aspnetcore/blob/068797e16a1bfe66461 e15c8a2ffa864369d384d/src/SignalR/docs/specs/HubProtocol.md`
- *ASP.NET SignalR GitHub repository:* `https://github.com/SignalR/SignalR`
- *@microsoft/signalr npm package:* `https://www.npmjs.com/package/@microsoft/signalr`

15

Windows, Linux, and Azure Deployment

Our valuable journey through ASP.NET Core and Angular development is coming to an end. The two projects we've been working on since *Chapter 1, Introducing ASP.NET and Angular*—HealthCheck and WorldCities—are now potentially shippable products and are mostly ready to be published in a suitable environment for evaluation purposes.

In this chapter, we'll deal with the following topics:

- **Preparing our app for production**, where we'll learn some useful optimization strategies to move our app into a production folder
- **Windows deployment**, where we'll see how we can deploy our HealthCheck web application to a Windows Server virtual machine and publish it over the web using **Internet Information Services (IIS)** with the new in-process hosting model
- **Linux deployment**, where we'll deploy our WorldCities web application to a Linux CentOS virtual machine and publish it over the web using the Kestrel web server over an Nginx-based proxy
- **Azure app service deployment**, where we'll deploy our HealthCheck web application to an MS Azure web app fully managed instance without the need to set up a VM-based infrastructure

The ultimate goal of this long and ambitious chapter is to learn the requisite tools and techniques to deploy an ASP.NET Core and Angular app on a production Windows and/or Linux hosting server, as well as within a cloud-based environment: let's embark upon this final effort!

Technical requirements

In this chapter, we're going to need all the previous technical requirements listed in *Chapters 1–14*, together with the following additional packages.

For Windows deployment:

- **IIS** (Windows Server)
- **ASP.NET Core 6.0 runtime (and the Windows Hosting Bundle installer for Win64** (Microsoft .NET official website))

For Linux deployment:

- **ASP.NET Core 6.0 runtime for Linux** (YUM package manager)
- **.NET 6 CLR for Linux** (YUM package manager)
- **Nginx HTTP server** (YUM package manager)

As always, it's advisable to avoid installing them straight away: we're going to bring them in over the course of the chapter to better contextualize their purpose within our project.

The code files for this chapter can be found here: `https://github.com/PacktPublishing/ASP.NET-Core-6-and-Angular/tree/main/Chapter_15`.

Getting ready for production

In this section, we'll see how we can further refine our apps' source code in order to get them ready for production usage. We'll mostly deal with server-side and client-side caching, environment configuration, and so on. While we're there, we'll take the chance to learn some useful production optimization tips offered by our *front-end* and *back-end* frameworks.

More specifically, we're going to cover the following:

- **Configuring the endpoints**, where we'll see how we will set up the production endpoints (hostnames, aliases, and IP addresses) and SSL certificates throughout the chapter
- **ASP.NET Core deployment tips**, where we'll learn how our *back-end* has been optimized for production usage
- **Angular deployment tips**, where we'll review some strategies used by the Visual Studio template to optimize the *front-end* production-building phase

Let's get to work!

Configuring the endpoints

When a web application is published in a *production* environment, it needs a public endpoint (URL) so that its users will be able to access it. Such an endpoint is typically a dedicated domain name (`www.myapp.com`), a third-level domain name (`myapp.someapps.com`), a path within a shared domain name (`www.someapps.com/myapp/`), or an IP address (`20.103.255.220`).

Sometimes these endpoints are also configured to use non-standard TCP ports (`www.myapp.com:8080`), just like the `40433` and `40080` ports we've used to locally host our projects during the development phase: however, this approach is rarely used in production, since it could easily cause compatibility issues, site reputation penalties, SEO drawbacks, and so on.

In our specific scenario, we're going to need several endpoints, since we're aiming to publish no less than four apps—HealthCheck, HealthCheckAPI, WorldCities, and WorldCitiesAPI—in multiple places. To address such a requirement without having to use non-standard TCP ports, rely upon subpaths, or purchase multiple domains, we suggest choosing between the following two routes:

- **Use third-level domain names** from a single domain under our possession, and map them to the production server's public IP address using the public DNS settings for that domain
- **Use "fake" domain names**, and map them to the production server's public IP address using the local machine's HOSTS file

Throughout this chapter we're going to take the first route, creating the following third-level domain names:

- healthcheck-2022.ryadel.com—for the HealthCheck Angular app
- healthcheck-api-2022.ryadel.com—for the HealthCheckAPI Web API
- worldcities-2022.ryadel.com—for the WorldCities Angular app
- worldcities-api-2022.ryadel.com—for the WorldCitiesAPI Web API

This convenient choice allows us to use a single domain and a single wildcard SSL certificate (*.ryadel.com) for all our needs, with considerable economic savings.

Those who don't have (or want to purchase) a domain and a wildcard SSL certificate can take the alternative route, creating some mappings between the public IP address assigned to the servers we're going to create and use and some "fake" hostnames, using the above names or even more elegant alternatives such as healthcheck.io, healthcheck-api.io, and the like: we're free to choose any name we like, since they will only exist in our local environment. In the next section we'll briefly explain how to create these mappings using the operating system's HOSTS file.

Tweaking the HOSTS file

The easiest and most effective way to map a hostname to a given IP address on any Windows, Linux, and macOS operating systems is by editing the HOSTS file, which is used by the OS to ultimately map hostnames to IP addresses before (and instead of) resolving them through the DNS lookup.

 For additional information about the Windows HOSTS file, check out the following URL: https://en.wikipedia.org/wiki/Hosts_(file).

In Windows systems, the HOSTS file is located at the following URL:

```
C:\Windows\System32\drivers\etc\hosts
```

In Linux and macOS systems, the HOSTS file is located at the following URL:

```
/etc/hosts
```

Such a file can be edited with a text editor in the following way:

```
<IP.ADDRESS.0.1> healthcheck.io
<IP.ADDRESS.0.2> healthcheck-api.io
<IP.ADDRESS.0.3> worldcities.io
<IP.ADDRESS.0.4> worldcities-api.io
```

We don't have to do this now, since we don't know those IP addresses yet: we're going to add the above entries throughout this chapter, replacing the various `<IP.ADDRESS.0.N>` entries with the public IP address of the virtual machine or app service we're going to use.

 In order to edit the Windows HOSTS file, we'll need administrative privileges for it; otherwise, we won't be able to permanently change it on disk.

As a matter of fact, creating these "overrides" within the local machine's HOSTS file is an easy and effective way to test our web apps in production using a "real" hostname (instead of a mere IP address) without having to actually purchase any domain or SSL certificate. However, such a choice comes with some obvious downsides, including:

- **Unreachability**. No one else will be able to reach these apps, unless they tweak the HOSTS file just like we do
- **TLS/SSL issues**. We likely won't have a valid TLS/SSL certificate for these "fake" domains, meaning that we'll have to live with browser warning pages, security exceptions, antivirus warnings, service worker registration failures, and so on—even if we use the MS Azure tenant certificate or a self-signed TLS/SSL certificate (more on that later on)

If you want to take the HOSTS file route, be sure to understand the full extent of these drawbacks.

Other viable alternatives

Those who don't want to follow our suggested routes are free to use any suitable alternative: owned domain names, additional IP addresses, DNS entries provided by third parties, and so on—as long as you know how to properly handle them.

The same goes for TLS/SSL certificates, which can be obtained free of charge using some dedicated services (such as *ZeroSSL*) or non-profit certificate authorities (such as *Let's Encrypt*) instead of having to purchase them.

To find out more about ZeroSSL, check out the following URL: `https://zerossl.com/`.

For additional info regarding Let's Encrypt, check out the following URL: `https://letsencrypt.org/`.

And here's a guide explaining how to use the above services to generate and configure a free TLS/SSL certificate for an MS Azure Windows virtual machine: `https://blog.kloud.com.au/2019/04/27/generating-and-configuring-free-ssl-certs-for-azure-windows-iaas-virtual-machines/`.

Furthermore, if we plan to host our app using Azure App Service (see the *Azure App Service deployment* section below), we can use the **App Service Managed Certificate** feature to create a free TLS/SSL certificate managed by Azure, which is actually very easy to pull off.

For further info about this technique, refer to the following guide from Microsoft Docs:

`https://docs.microsoft.com/en-us/azure/app-service/configure-ssl-certificate`

That said, for the sake of simplicity, in this chapter we're going to use (and take for granted) some third-level domains with a wildcard SSL certificate. Those who want to use one of the above alternatives can replace this technique with their preferred approach: just remember to change the ASP.NET Core projects' `appsettings.json` files and/or the Angular projects' `/environments/environment.prod.ts` files accordingly.

ASP.NET Core deployment tips

As you most likely already know, ASP.NET Core allows developers to adjust an application's behavior across many environments: the most common of these are development, staging, and production environments. The currently active environment is identified at runtime by checking an environment variable that can be configured and modified from the project's configuration files.

This variable is called `ASPNETCORE_ENVIRONMENT` and, while we're running our project on Visual Studio, it can be set by using the `/Properties/launchSettings.json` file, which controls various settings that will be applied to our local development machine upon our web application's launch.

The launchSettings.json file

If we take a look at the `launchSettings.json` file, we can see that it contains some specific settings for each execution profile of our project. To see a quick example of this, here are the contents of the `HealthCheckAPI` project's `/Properties/launchSettings.json` file:

```json
{
  "$schema": "https://json.schemastore.org/launchsettings.json",
  "iisSettings": {
    "windowsAuthentication": false,
    "anonymousAuthentication": true,
    "iisExpress": {
      "applicationUrl": "http://localhost:40080",
      "sslPort": 40443
    }
  },
  "profiles": {
    "HealthCheckAPI": {
      "commandName": "Project",
      "dotnetRunMessages": true,
      "launchBrowser": false,
      "launchUrl": "swagger",
      "applicationUrl": "https://localhost:40443;http://localhost:40080",
      "environmentVariables": {
        "ASPNETCORE_ENVIRONMENT": "Development"
      }
    },
    "IIS Express": {
      "commandName": "IISExpress",
      "launchBrowser": false,
      "launchUrl": "swagger",
      "environmentVariables": {
        "ASPNETCORE_ENVIRONMENT": "Development"
      }
    }
  }
}
```

As we can see, there are two execution profiles currently set:

- **The IIS Express profile**, which is related to the IIS Express HTTP server. This profile will be used whenever we launch our project in debug mode, which we can do by pressing *F5* (unless we changed the default debugging behavior).

- **The HealthCheckAPI profile**, which is related to the application itself. This profile will be used whenever we launch our project using the .NET Core CLI (in other words, the dotnet run console command).

For both of them, the ASPNETCORE_ENVIRONMENT variable is currently set to the Development value, meaning that we're always going to run our apps in *development* mode from Visual Studio, unless we change these values.

How do different environments affect our web application's behavior? In the next section we'll shed some light on that.

Runtime environments

Let's start by briefly explaining what happens at runtime.

Right after our web application starts, ASP.NET Core reads the ASPNETCORE_ENVIRONMENT environment variable and stores its value in the EnvironmentName property of our app's IWebHostEnvironment instance, which, as its name suggests, provides information about the web hosting environment our application is running in. Once set, this variable can be used programmatically—either directly or with some helper methods—to determine our app's behavior at any moment of our *back-end* life cycle.

We've already seen these methods in action in the Program class of our ASP.NET Core applications—for example, here's what we can find in HealthCheckAPI's Program.cs source code:

```
// ... existing code...

// Configure the HTTP request pipeline.
if (app.Environment.IsDevelopment())
{
    app.UseSwagger();
    app.UseSwaggerUI();
}

// ... existing code...
```

In the preceding lines, we're telling our app to register the Swagger and SwaggerUI middleware only if the app is running in a **development environment**. This condition, which is part of most Visual Studio web application templates, is there for a reason: it's a precautionary measure to prevent us from accidentally disclosing our OpenAPI documentation to the public—unless we explicitly choose to do that by rewriting that if block.

Given our current scenario, since our HealthCheckAPI project's sole purpose is to interact with our HealthCheck Angular project, there's no reason to release our Swagger JSON file or a UI that will make it more human-readable: for that very reason, we can just leave things like that. The same logic can be applied to the WorldCitiesAPI project as well.

The story would've been different if we were dealing with a Web API meant to be consumed from some third-party services or arbitrary clients: in those circumstances, providing detailed API documentation would have probably been a wise choice, provided that the necessary security measures were considered.

While we're here, we can take the chance to further improve the `Program.cs` file's configuration settings for the **staging** and **production environments** by using the `ExceptionHandler` middleware instead of the default `DeveloperExceptionPage`. However, before doing that, it could be wise to take a step back and briefly introduce the concept of error handling in ASP.NET Core to better understand the underlying context.

Error handling techniques

As per its default settings, all ASP.NET Core web applications show detailed stack traces for server errors using the `DeveloperExceptionPageMiddleware`. This middleware is inserted early in the middleware pipeline and can catch any unhandled exceptions thrown by any subsequent middleware, thus being very useful during the development phase; however, exception information and stack traces shouldn't be shown when the project is made available to the public.

For that very reason, a common security practice is to replace it with the `UseExceptionHandlerMiddleware` when the project runs in a **non-development environment**. Such middleware will still be able to catch (and potentially log) exceptions, but instead of printing all the relevant info within a dedicated error page it can be configured to redirect the request to a customizable "error" route, which can be handled using a controller's action method, a Minimal API method, or anything else.

Now that we know all that, we can set up the `UseExceptionHandlerMiddleware` by slightly updating that "conditional" part of the `Program.cs` file in the following way (new lines are highlighted):

```
// ... existing code...

// Configure the HTTP request pipeline.
if (app.Environment.IsDevelopment())
{
    app.UseSwagger();
    app.UseSwaggerUI();
}
else
{
    app.UseExceptionHandler("/Error");
    app.MapGet("/Error", () => Results.Problem());
}

// ... existing code...
```

As we can see by looking at the above code, we've configured the exception handler middleware to redirect errors to the /Error route, and we've also added a simple MinimalAPI method to handle it.

The Results.Problem() we're returning produces a ProblemDetails response, a JSON-formatted, machine-readable response message for specifying errors in HTTP APIs based on https://tools.ietf.org/html/rfc7807.

With such modifications applied, whenever our ASP.NET Core app crashes, its error page will conditionally show the following messages:

- **Development environment**: A low-level/detailed error message, such as the exception info and the stack trace (for developers only)
- **Staging or production environment**: A high-level/generic unavailability message (for all end-users)

The developer exception page includes a detailed series of useful information about the exception and the request, such as exceptions and inner exceptions, stack traces, query string parameters, cookies, and HTTP headers.

For additional information about this, and error handling in ASP.NET Core in general, visit the following URL: https://docs.microsoft.com/en-us/aspnet/core/fundamentals/error-handling.

While we're here, we can add another middleware to further increase the security posture of our non-*development* environments: the HSTSMiddleware, which adds the **HTTP Strict Transport Security** (**HSTS**) max age header value to all our responses.

Here's how we can do that (new code is highlighted):

```
// ... existing code...

// Configure the HTTP request pipeline.
if (app.Environment.IsDevelopment())
{
    app.UseSwagger();
    app.UseSwaggerUI();
}
else
{
    app.UseExceptionHandler("/Error");
    app.MapGet("/Error", () => Results.Problem());
    app.UseHsts();
```

```
    }

    // ... existing code...
```

The HSTS header complies with some good HTTP security practices and is therefore highly desirable for any app that is publicly facing the web; however, it is basically useless (and can be a hindrance) during debugging, which is the reason why we are only setting it for non-*development* environments, just like the custom error page.

Before moving on, let's copy all the updates we've made to the `HealthCheckAPI`'s `Program.cs` file to the `WorldCitiesAPI`'s `Program.cs` files, so that both our apps will benefit from these convenient settings.

Rule(s) of thumb

Now that we've seen how to programmatically determine our web app's execution environment and make our HTTP pipeline act accordingly, we should learn how to properly adopt, and adapt, these conditional practices to best suit those environments.

Since the development environment is only available to developers, it should always favor debugging capabilities over performance. Therefore, it should avoid caching, use in-memory loading strategies to quickly respond to changes, and emit as much diagnostic information as possible (logs, exceptions, and so on) to help developers promptly understand what's happening.

 If you remember what was said in *Chapter 10, ASP.NET Core and Angular Unit Testing,* regarding **Test-Driven Development (TDD)**, you should easily understand how the development environment is where the TDD practice shines the most.

Conversely, while addressing a production environment, a good way to make these decisions is by applying the following rules of thumb:

- **Turn on caching whenever possible** in order to save resources and increase performance
- **Ensure that all the client-side resources** (JavaScript, CSS files, and so on) are bundled, minified, and potentially served from a **Content Delivery Network (CDN)**
- **Turn off diagnostic error pages** and/or replace them with friendly, human-readable error pages instead
- **Enable production logging and monitoring** using application performance management tools or other real-time monitoring, auditing, and watchdog strategies
- **Implement the best security practices** made available by the frameworks
- **Implement Open Web Application Security Project (OWASP)** methodologies for software development, as well as network, firewall, and server configurations

These are the general guidelines (or good practices) that we should always take into serious consideration while refining the *back-end* part of our web applications for production usage.

What about the **staging environment**? It's mostly used as a preproduction environment where we can perform (or make some testers perform) our *front-end* testing before giving the OK for production deployment. Ideally, its physical characteristics should mirror that of production, so that any issues that may arise in production occur first in the staging environment, where they can be addressed without impacting users.

> Again, if we think back to our behavior-driven development analysis back in *Chapter 10, ASP.NET Core and Angular Unit Testing,* we can definitely acknowledge that the staging environment would be the perfect place to test for the expected behavior of any newly added features of our apps before releasing them into production.

Let's continue our learning path through the ASP.NET Core environments with another important question: how can we set the proper environment when we deploy our app(s)?

Setting the environment in production

What happens to the ASPNETCORE_ENVIRONMENT variable when we publish our web application for production deployment, just like we did during *Chapter 12, Progressive Web Apps,* when we configured a folder-based publish profile for our HealthCheckAPI and WorldCitiesAPI projects?

As we can see by looking inside those folders, the launchSettings.json file cannot be found there, since it is not being published. That is certainly to be expected, since it's only meant to be used by Visual Studio and other local development tools.

Whenever we host the app on a production server, we'll have to manually set that value using one of the following approaches:

* A dedicated **environment variable** with the same name
* Specific **platform settings**
* A **command-line** switch

These methods strongly depend on the server's operating system. In the upcoming sections, we'll see how we can perform them on Windows and Linux servers.

> It's important to remember that the environment, once set, can't be changed while the web app is running.

If no environment-related setting is found, the web app will always use the production value as the default, this being the most conservative choice for performance and security, since most debugging features and diagnostic messages will be disabled.

Conversely, if the environment is set multiple times (such as by the environment variable and then a command-line switch), the app will use the last environment setting read, thereby following a cascading rule.

Updating the appsettings.Production.json file(s)

We already know from *Chapter 3, Looking Around,* that the configuration settings contained in the appsettings.json file of our ASP.NET Core projects can be overridden for specific runtime environments using environment-specific files—such as appsettings.Development.json and appsettings.Production.json. Now that we're about to deploy our apps in production, we should take the chance to briefly review those file(s) and see if we need to change some of these settings.

HealthCheckAPI

Let's start with the HealthCheckAPI project. As a matter of fact, this project doesn't use connection strings, secret keys, or anything that could require an override for a production environment—except for the AllowedCORS key that we added in *Chapter 12, Progressive Web Apps.*

If we want to make our Web API only be accessible from the HealthCheck Angular app's host name, we'll need to create a new appsettings.Production.json file to override this key using the following command:

```
{
    "AllowedCORS": "https://healthcheck-2022.ryadel.com"
}
```

Needless to say, the above value would be OK only for our specific scenario, since we're using third-level domain names of the ryadel.com domain: those who are using different domains (or any alternative approach) should set that value according to their specific choice.

 The above appsettings.Production.json file has been added to the GitHub repository for this chapter for reference purposes only: however, putting that file under the same source control of the app is widely considered bad practice, even if it does not contain personal or sensitive info, since it could be inadvertently deployed in production and therefore override the file already present on the server, which could be subject to code-independent changes over time. To minimize this risk, it's better to have it stored in a separate location and manually copy it on the server whenever we need to.

If we don't want to restrict the CORS policy for our production app, we can avoid creating the appsettings.Production.json file for the HealthCheckAPI project.

Let's now move on to the WorldCitiesAPI project.

WorldCitiesAPI

The situation for our WorldCitiesAPI is slightly more complex, since we have several keys we might want to override in production: the connection string to access our SQL database and the whole JwtSetting block.

Here's what a suitable `appsettings.Production.json` file would look like (relevant settings are high-lighted):

```
{
    "ConnectionStrings": {
      "DefaultConnection": "PUT-YOUR-PRODUCTION-CONNECTION-STRING-HERE"
    },
    "JwtSettings": {
      "Audience": "https://worldcities-2022.ryadel.com"
    },
    "AllowedCORS": "https://worldcities-2022.ryadel.com"
}
```

Be sure to replace the `ConnectionStrings:DefaultConnection` value with your actual connection string; moreover, set the `JwtSettings:Audience` and `AllowedCORS` values to match the Angular app's production endpoint that you plan to use.

> Again, a sample `appsettings.Production.json` file for the `WorldCitiesAPI` project with the above values has been added to the GitHub repository for this chapter, for reference purposes only; what we should actually do is to create and/or update it on the production server (or service) after we've deployed our app.

We're now ready to proceed to the next steps: deploying our app in a *Production* environment on Windows, Linux, and Azure. However, before doing that, let's take a moment to discuss the deployment modes available to us.

.NET deployment modes

In *Chapter 12*, *Progressive Web Apps*, when we created our first publish profile to deploy our app to a local folder, we didn't change the **deployment mode** settings, leaving them as they were. Truth be told, we did that because it wouldn't have made any difference, since we used that build just to steal some **progressive web app** (PWA)-related generated files and use them to register our service worker from a standard Visual Studio debug run.

However, the .NET deployment mode is a very important configuration feature that we definitely need to understand in order to make the right choice whenever we have to deploy our application for production usage.

Let's now try to shed some light on the three different types of deployments available from Visual Studio for .NET applications:

- **Framework-dependent deployment (FDD):** As the name implies, such a deployment mode requires the presence of .NET Framework, which must be installed and available on the target system; in other words, we'll build a portable .NET application as long as the hosting server supports it.

- **Self-contained deployment (SCD):** This deployment mode doesn't rely on the presence of .NET components on the target system. All components, including the .NET libraries and runtime, will be included in the production build. If the hosting server supports .NET, the app will run in isolated mode, separating itself from other .NET applications. SCD builds will include an executable file (a `.exe` file on Windows platforms) as well as a `.dll` file containing the application's runtime.

- **Framework-dependent executable (FDE):** This deployment mode will produce an executable file that will run on the hosting server, which must have the .NET and ASP.NET Core runtimes installed. Therefore, such a mode is rather similar to FDD since both of them are framework-dependent.

Let's now try to understand the pros and cons of each deployment mode.

Framework-dependent deployment

Using the FDD mode grants the developer a number of advantages, including the following:

- **Platform independence:** There's no need to define the target operating system since the .NET runtime installed on the hosting server will seamlessly handle the app's execution, regardless of its platform.

- **Small package size:** The deployment bundle will be small since it will only contain the app's runtime and the third-party dependencies. .NET itself won't be there since we expect it to already be present on the target machine by design.

- **Latest version:** As per its default settings, FDD will always use the latest serviced runtime installed on the target system, with all the latest security patches.

- **Better performance in multihosting scenarios:** If the hosting server has multiple .NET apps installed, the shared resources will enable us to save some storage space and, most importantly, obtain reduced memory usage.

However, this deployment mode also has a number of weaknesses, including the following:

- **Reduced compatibility:** Our app will require a .NET runtime with a version compatible with the one used by our app (or later). If the hosting server is stuck to a previous version, our app won't be able to run.

- **Stability issues:** If the .NET runtime and/or libraries were to change their behavior (in other words, if they had breaking changes or reduced compatibility for security or licensing reasons), our app would potentially be impacted by these changes as well.

Self-contained deployment

Using the SCD mode has two big advantages that could easily outweigh the disadvantages regarding some specific scenarios:

- **Full control over the published .NET version,** regardless of what is installed on the hosting server (or what will happen to it in the future)

- **No compatibility issues,** since all the requisite libraries are provided within the bundle

Unfortunately, there are also some relevant disadvantages:

- **Platform dependency**: Providing the runtime with the production package requires the developer to select the target building platforms in advance.

- **Increased bundle size**: The additional presence of the runtime resources will definitely take its toll in terms of disk space requirements. This can be a heavy hit if we plan to deploy multiple SCD .NET Core apps to a single hosting server, as each of them will require a significant amount of disk space.

The self-contained deployment bundle size issue was addressed in .NET Core 3.0 with the introduction of the **app trimming** feature (also called **assembly linker**), which basically trims the unused assemblies. This approach has been further improved in the subsequent .NET versions, where assemblies get "cracked open" and purged of the types and members not used by the application, further reducing the size.

 For further info about the .NET **app trimming** feature, check out the following post by Sam Spencer (Program Manager, .NET Core team): https://devblogs.microsoft.com/dotnet/app-trimming-in-net-5/.

Framework-dependent executable

The FDE deployment mode was introduced in .NET Core 2.2 and, starting from version 3.0, is the default mode for the basic dotnet publish command (if no options are specified). This new approach has the following advantages:

- **Small package size, latest version**, and **better performance in multihosting scenarios**, just like FDD mode

- **Easy to run**: The deployed executable can be directly launched and executed, without having to invoke the dotnet CLI

This approach also has some disadvantages:

- **Reduced compatibility**: Just like FDD, the app requires an ASP.NET Core runtime with a version compatible with the one used by our app (or later)

- **Stability issues**: Again, if the ASP.NET Core runtime and/or libraries were to change their behavior, those changes could break the app or alter its behavior

- **Platform dependency**: As the app is an executable file, it must be published for each different target platform

As we can easily guess, all of these three deployment modes can either be good or bad, depending on a number of factors, such as how much control we have over the deployment server, how many ASP.NET Core apps we plan to publish, and the target system's hardware and software capabilities.

As a general rule, as long as we have the rights to install and update system packages on the deployment server, the FDD modes should work well; conversely, if we host our apps on a cloud-hosting provider that doesn't have our desired .NET runtime, SCD would arguably be the most logical choice.

The available disk space and memory size will also play a major role, especially if we plan to publish multiple apps.

 As a matter of fact, the requirement of being able to manually install and update the packages on the server should no longer be a hindrance since all .NET updates will now be released through the regular Microsoft Update channel, as explained in the following post by Jamshed Damkewala (Principal Engineering Manager, .NET): `https://devblogs.microsoft.com/dotnet/net-core-updates-coming-to-microsoft-update/`.

That said, we're going to use the FDD (default) deployment mode, since our current scenario requires the publication of two different apps that share the same ASP.NET Core runtime version on the same server.

Angular deployment tips

Let's now turn our gaze to the *front-end* to properly understand how the Visual Studio template that we've used to build our two apps handles Angular's production deployment tasks.

It goes without saying that the same good practices we've determined for the *back-end* retain their value at the *front-end* as well, as we'll see in a short while. In other words, performance and security will still be the principal goals in this regard.

Let's now try to understand how the Angular CLI handles our applications' publishing and deployment tasks.

ng serve, ng build, and the package.json file

As we should already know, whenever we run one of our Angular projects in Visual Studio, the actual app is served using an in-memory instance of the Angular CLI server: this server is launched by Visual Studio using the `ng serve` command, as we can see by looking at the console window that is automatically opened during the launch to host that process.

If we take a look at that window we can see this clearly, as shown in the following screenshot:

```
ng serve -ssl --ssl-cert C:\Users\DarkAngel\AppData\Roaming\ASP.NET\https\health-check.pem --ssl-key C:\User...    —    □    ×

> health-check@0.0.0 start C:\Projects\ASP.NET-Core-6-and-Angular\Chapter_15\HealthCheck\HealthCheck
> ng serve --ssl --ssl-cert %APPDATA%\ASP.NET\https\%npm_package_name%.pem --ssl-key %APPDATA%\ASP.NET
\https\%npm_package_name%.key

√ Browser application bundle generation complete.

Initial Chunk Files      | Names      |       Size
vendor.js                | vendor     |    3.80 MB
polyfills.js             | polyfills  |  339.61 kB
styles.css, styles.js    | styles     |  289.99 kB
main.js                  | main       |   41.59 kB
runtime.js               | runtime    |    6.86 kB

                         | Initial Total |  4.46 MB

Build at: 2022-03-15T19:05:21.390Z - Hash: f7795de558248515 - Time: 9341ms
```

Figure 15.1: Visual Studio output window during the initial debug phase

Conversely, whenever we want to compile our app for production, as we learned in *Chapter 12, Progressive Web Apps*, we need to use the `ng build` CLI command instead:

```
> ng build
```

The above command creates the Angular bundle with several optimization features meant for production deployment, including the following:

- **Ahead-of-time (AOT) compilation:** This converts the HTML and TypeScript code into efficient JavaScript code in order to provide faster rendering in the browser. The default mode (used for `ng serve`), called **just-in-time (JIT)** compilation, compiles the app in the browser at runtime and is, therefore, a much slower and less-optimized alternative.

- **Production mode:** This makes the app run faster by disabling some development-specific checks, such as the dual change detection cycles.

- **Bundling:** This concatenates the various app and third-party files (npm packages) into a few bundles.

- **Minification:** This removes whitespaces, comments, optional tokens, and any unnecessary characters and artifacts to HTML, JavaScript, and CSS files.

- **Uglification:** This internally rewrites the JavaScript code to shorten the variable and function names; this will also make our published code less readable, which is often a good thing since it will shield our app against malicious reverse-engineering attempts.

- **Dead code purging:** This removes any unreferenced modules and/or unused code files, snippets, or sections.

As we can see, all of the preceding features aim to increase the performance and security capabilities of our production build.

Differential loading

Another nice feature worth mentioning is differential loading, which was introduced in Angular 8 and enabled by default when using the `ng build` command.

Differential loading is Angular's way of overcoming the compatibility issues between various browsers, especially the older ones; in other words, those that are still based on older versions of JavaScript.

As we can see by looking at the `tsconfig.json` file placed at the root of our Angular projects, our TypeScript code will be transpiled and bundled into *ES2017*, also known as **ECMAScript** 2017, a JavaScript syntax that is compatible with the vast majority of modern browsers. However, there is still a number of users with older clients, such as old desktop, laptop, and/or mobile devices, that are bound to *ES5* and earlier versions.

To work around this, previous versions of Angular, as well as most other *front-end* frameworks, provided a number of support libraries (known as **polyfills**) that would have conditionally implemented the missing features for those browsers that didn't natively support them. Unfortunately, such a workaround massively increased the production bundle, thereby resulting in a performance hit for all users, including those using modern browsers that didn't need those polyfills to begin with.

Differential loading solves this issue by generating two separate bundle sets during the build phase:

- The first bundle contains the app's code, which has been transpiled, minified, and uglified using a modern ECMAScript syntax. This bundle ships fewer polyfills and therefore results in a much smaller size.

- The second bundle contains the same code transpiled in the old ES5 syntax, along with all the necessary polyfills. Needless to say, this bundle is much bigger than the first one in terms of file size, but properly supports older browsers.

The differential loading feature can be configured by altering two files:

- The `.browserlistrc` file, which lists the minimum browsers supported by our application
- The `tsconfig.json` file, which determines the ECMAScript target version that the code is compiled to

By taking both of these settings into consideration, the Angular CLI will automatically determine whether or not to enable the differential loading functionality.

This strategy is very effective since it will allow our Angular apps to support multiple browsers without forcing our *modern* users to retrieve all the unnecessary bundles.

The angular.json configuration file(s)

The most important difference between `ng serve` and `ng build` is that the latter is the only command that actually writes the build-generated artifacts to the output folder: those files are built using the webpack build tool, which can be configured using the `angular.json` configuration file.

The output folder is also set within that file, more precisely, in the **projects** | **[projectName]** | **architect** | **build** | **options** | **outputPath** section. In our sample apps, it's the `dist/[projectName]` folder, meaning that all the build-generated artifacts will be deployed in the `/dist/HealthCheck` and `/dist/WorldCities` folders.

Updating the environment.prod.ts file(s)

Another file we need to remember is the `/environments/environment.prod.ts` file of the `HealthCheck` and `WorldCities` Angular apps, where we must replace the `baseUrl` key value—currently set to `https://localhost:40443/`—with the actual endpoints that our `HealthCheckAPI` and `WorldCitiesAPI` apps will respond to.

In our specific scenario, since we're using third-level domain names of the `ryadel.com` domain, we need to change them in the following way:

- `https://healthcheck-api-2022.ryadel.com`
- `https://worldcities-api-2022.ryadel.com`

Those who used different domains (or any alternative approach) should update the above values according to their specific choice.

Automatic deployment

Angular 8.3.0 introduced the new `ng deploy` command, which can be used to deploy the Angular app to one of the available production platforms thanks to some third-party builders that can be installed using `ng add`.

Here's a list of the supported builders at the time of writing:

- `@angular/fire` (Firebase)
- `@azure/ng-deploy` (MS Azure)
- `@zeit/ng-deploy` (ZEIT Now)
- `@netlify-builder/deploy` (Netlify)
- `angular-cli-ghpages` (GitHub Pages)
- `ngx-deploy-npm` (NPM)

Although the `ng deploy` CLI option is not yet supported by Visual Studio, it can be very useful to instantly deploy our app using some presets that can be configured in the *deploy* section of the `angular.json` file. Such a section isn't available in the `angular.json` file of our projects, but it will be automatically added as soon as one of the preceding builders is installed using the `ng add` CLI command (with its corresponding default settings).

With this we are ready to begin the actual deployment phase.

Windows deployment

In this section, we'll learn how to deploy our `HealthCheck` web application on a Windows 2019 Datacenter edition server hosted on MS Azure.

Here's what we're going to do:

- **Create a new VM on MS Azure** using the Windows 2022 Datacenter Edition template and configure it to accept inbound calls to TCP ports 3389 (for Remote Desktop), 80 (for HTTP), 443 (for HTTPS), and 22 (for SSH)
- **Configure the VM** by downloading and/or installing all the necessary services and runtimes to host the `HealthCheck` app
- **Publish the HealthCheck app** to the web server we've just set up
- **Configure IIS to serve the app in the proper way**
- **Test the HealthCheck app** from a remote client

Let's get to work!

In this deployment example, we're going to set up a brand-new VM on the MS Azure platform, which requires some additional work; those users who already have a production-ready Windows server should skip the sections related to the VM setup and go directly to the publishing topics.

Creating a Windows Server VM on MS Azure

If we remember our journey through MS Azure in *Chapter 5*, *Data Model with Entity Framework Core*, when we deployed a SQL database there, we should already be prepared for what we're going to do:

- Access the MS Azure portal
- Add and configure a new VM
- Set the inbound security rules to access the VM from the internet

Let's do this.

Accessing the MS Azure portal

As usual, let's start by visiting the following URL, which will bring us to the MS Azure website: `https://azure.microsoft.com/`.

Again, we can either log in using an already-existing MS Azure account or create a new one (possibly taking the chance to use the free 30-day trial, if we haven't used it already).

Refer to *Chapter 5*, *Data Model with Entity Framework Core*, for additional information on creating a free MS Azure account.

As soon as we have created the account, we can go to `https://portal.azure.com/` to access the MS Azure administration portal, where we can create our new VM.

Adding a new Windows VM

Once logged in, click on the **Virtual machines** icon (refer to the following screenshot):

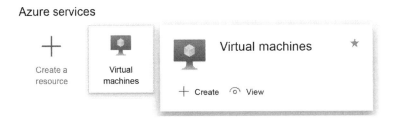

Figure 15.2: Clicking on the Virtual machines icon

From the next page, click **Add** (near the top-left corner of the page) to access the **Create a virtual machine** panel.

The **Create a virtual machine** panel is basically a detailed wizard that allows us to configure a new VM from scratch. The various configuration settings are split into a number of panels, each one dedicated to a specific set of capabilities, as shown in the following screenshot:

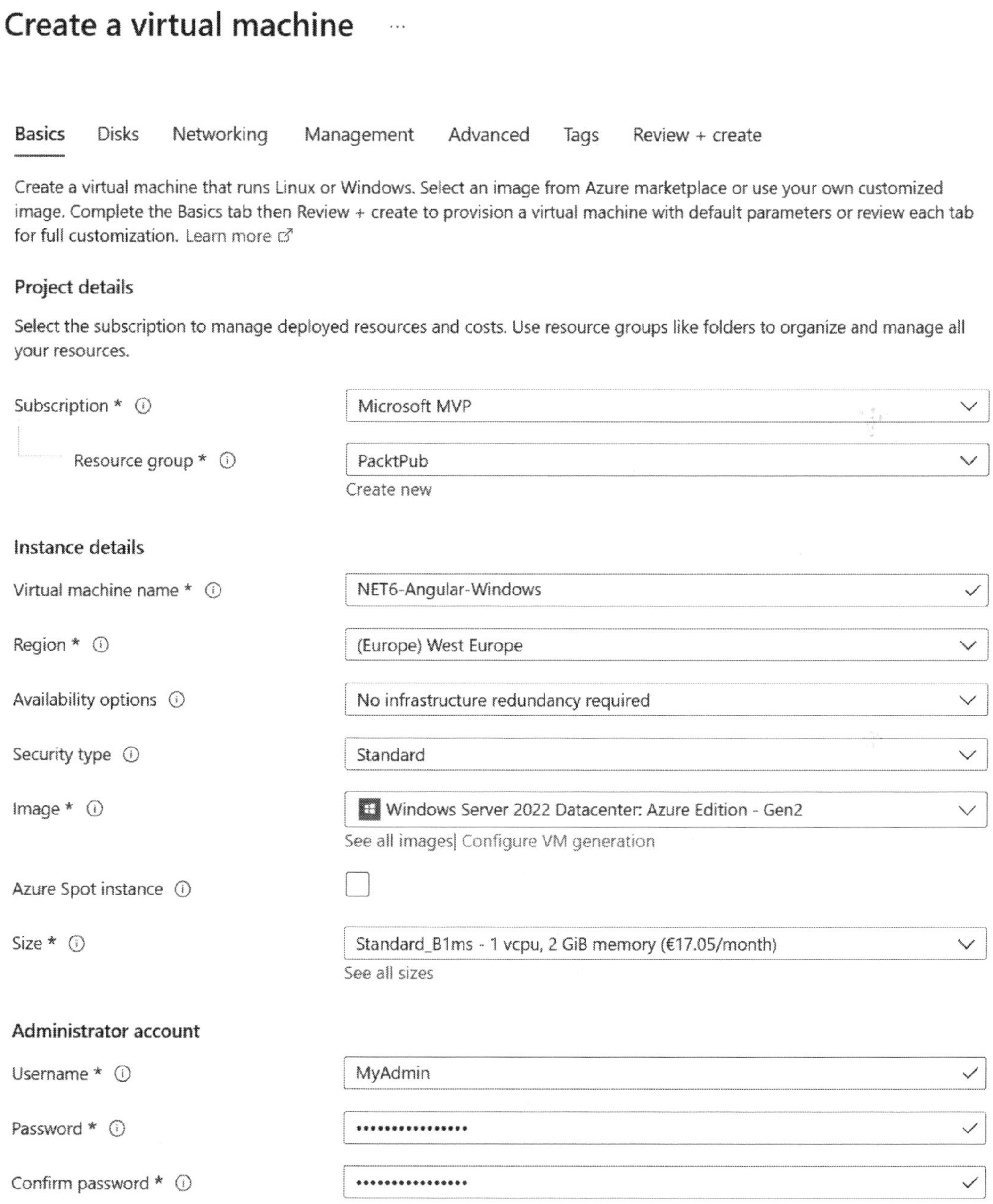

Create a virtual machine   ...

| **Basics** | Disks | Networking | Management | Advanced | Tags | Review + create |

Create a virtual machine that runs Linux or Windows. Select an image from Azure marketplace or use your own customized image. Complete the Basics tab then Review + create to provision a virtual machine with default parameters or review each tab for full customization. Learn more ☑

Project details

Select the subscription to manage deployed resources and costs. Use resource groups like folders to organize and manage all your resources.

Subscription * ⓘ	Microsoft MVP ⌄
Resource group * ⓘ	PacktPub ⌄
	Create new

Instance details

Virtual machine name * ⓘ	NET6-Angular-Windows ✓
Region * ⓘ	(Europe) West Europe ⌄
Availability options ⓘ	No infrastructure redundancy required ⌄
Security type ⓘ	Standard ⌄
Image * ⓘ	🔲 Windows Server 2022 Datacenter: Azure Edition - Gen2 ⌄
	See all images| Configure VM generation
Azure Spot instance ⓘ	☐
Size * ⓘ	Standard_B1ms - 1 vcpu, 2 GiB memory (€17.05/month) ⌄
	See all sizes

Administrator account

Username * ⓘ	MyAdmin ✓
Password * ⓘ	•••••••••••••••• ✓
Confirm password * ⓘ	•••••••••••••••• ✓

Figure 15.3: The Create a virtual machine panel

It's worth noting that the MS Azure settings we're going to review, as well as the look and feel of the various screenshots, might vary in the future, as Microsoft is continuously adding new features, control switches, and other UI/UX goodies to their wizards.

That said, here's a brief summary of the main settings panels:

- **Basics:** Subscription type, VM name, deployment region, image, login credentials, and so on
- **Disks:** The number and capacity of HDDs/SDDs to provide the VM with
- **Networking:** Network-related configuration settings
- **Management:** Monitoring features, auto-shutdown capabilities, backup, and more
- **Advanced:** Additional configuration, agents, scripts, extensions, and the like
- **Tags:** These allow some name-value pairs that can be useful in categorizing the various MS Azure resources to be set

In our current scenario, we just have to slightly modify the first four tabs, leaving the remaining ones as their default settings.

In the **Basics** tab:

- **Resource group:** Use the same resource group used for the SQL database (or create a new one).
- **Virtual machine name:** Use `NET6-Angular-Windows`, `HealthCheck`, or any other suitable name.
- **Region:** Choose the region closest to our geographical position.
- **Availability options:** No infrastructure redundancy required.
- **Image:** In our example, we're going to use the *Windows Server 2022 Datacenter* default image; feel free to use it as well or pick another one.
- **Azure Spot instance:** Select **Yes** if you want to create the VM using the Azure Spot feature, which allows us to take advantage of Azure unused capacity at a significant cost saving. However, since these VMs can be evicted at any point in time when Azure needs the capacity back, we should only use this feature for short-term testing purposes: if we want to create a permanent, production-like VM, we should definitely choose **No** and create a standard pay-as-you-go machine.
- **Size: Standard B1ms (1 vCPU, 2 GiB memory).** Feel free to choose a different size if you're willing to spend more: B1ms is an entry-level machine featuring a very limited set of resources that will suffice for this deployment sample, but won't perform well in production.
- **Administrator account:** Select the **Password authentication** type, and then create a suitable username and password set. Remember to write these down in a secure place, since we'll definitely need these credentials to access our machine in a while.

In the **Disk** tab:

- **OS disk type:** Select **Standard HDD**; this is the cheapest available choice
- **Data disks:** We do not need to create additional data disks for our current purposes

In the **Network** tab:

- **Virtual Network:** If you created a SQL database hosted on Azure in *Chapter 5, Data Model with Entity Framework Core*, select the same **VNet** used for it; otherwise, create a new one
- **Public inbound ports:** Choose **Allow selected ports**, then select the following ports from the list: **HTTP (80)**, **HTTPS (443)**, **SSH (22)**, and **RDP (3389)**

In the **Management** tab:

- **Monitoring | Boot diagnostics: Disable**

Leave all the other settings as their defaults.

 For further info regarding the Azure Spot feature, read the following article: `https://docs.microsoft.com/en-us/azure/virtual-machines/spot-vms`.

Once done, click the **Review + create** button to review our configuration settings and initiate the VM deployment process.

At the end of the process, we should see a screen like the following:

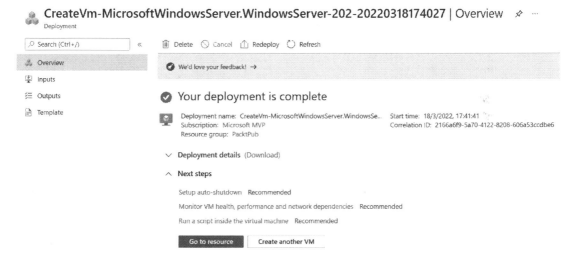

Figure 15.4: Deployment complete screen

From there, we can click the **Go to resource** button to access the VM's **Overview** panel.

Configuring a DNS name label

Now we have the chance to add a DNS name label to our VM, which will be used to generate a unique fifth-level domain name in addition to its unique numeric IP address.

To do this, locate the **DNS name** label in the virtual machine's **Overview** panel and click on the **Configure** link next to it, as shown in the following screenshot:

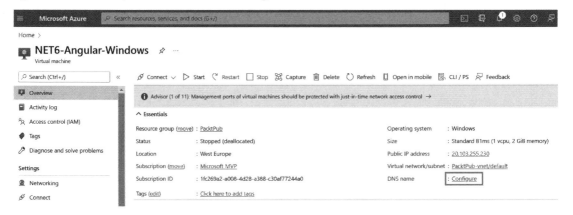

Figure 15.5: Configuring a DNS name label

Once generated, the DNS name will look like this: `your-chosen-name.westeurope.cloudapp.azure.com`.

> The DNS name label is basically an A record that will grant a "human-readable" public endpoint to your VM server. It goes without saying that the DNS name must be unique within the chosen Azure region.
>
> In our example, we're going to use the following DNS name:
>
> `healthcheck-2022.westeurope.cloudapp.azure.com`

Configuring the DNS name label and getting the DNS name can be useful if we want to access our web application from the web without having to configure anything on our end (such as a host mapping to the VM's IP address or something like that). We could even use it to replace one of the "fake" hostnames that we plan to put within our local machine's HOSTS file for our `HealthCheck` and `HealthCheckAPI` apps—`healthcheck.io` or `healthcheck-api.io`—if we want to.

Before leaving the **Overview** tab, be sure to take a note of the virtual machine's IP address and **DNS name**, since we're going to need them in a short while.

Setting the inbound security rules

Go to the **Settings | Networking** tab and ensure that the **Inbound port rules** tab contains the routes for the **public inbound ports** we specified when we created the VM: **HTTP (80)**, **HTTPS (443)**, **SSH (22)**, and **RDP (3389)**. In the unlikely case they are not here, we need to manually set them.

While we're here, we can also take the chance to restrict access to some of these rules instead of leaving them open to the public, depending on our specific needs; for example, it's strongly advisable to restrict access to the SSH and RDP inbound rules to a secure **source IP address** (or address range), which can be set to either our static IP address or our ISP's IP mask.

Such a setting will ensure that no third parties will be able to attempt Remote Desktop access or visit our web application.

> **IMPORTANT:** For reasons of space, we will not go into any more detail on the security aspects related to connections with MS Azure and the virtual machines hosted therein. Opening port 3389 and/or 22 to a single IP address is a simple solution that works well for our testing purposes, but for a production environment we should definitely switch to safer and stronger access protocols, such as *JIT access, Azure Bastion,* and/or secure SSH tunnels.
>
> For additional info on these security best practices, read the following guides:
>
> `https://docs.microsoft.com/en-us/azure/security-center/just-in-time-explained`
>
> `https://docs.microsoft.com/en-us/azure/bastion/`

Regardless of how we will eventually set these inbound rules, we take for granted that we leave the RDP port 3389 open for our local machine, so that we can connect to our VM using Remote Desktop.

Configuring the Windows VM

With TCP port 3389 open, we can launch the **Remote Desktop Connection** built-in tool from our local Windows-based development machine. Type in the public IP address of the Azure VM and click **Connect** to initiate an RDC session with our remote host:

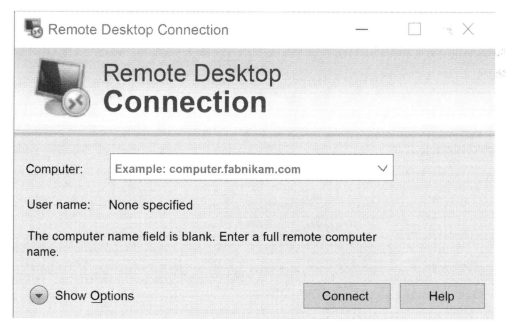

Figure 15.6: The Remote Desktop Connection tool

If the inbound security rule has been properly configured, we should be able to connect to our new VM's desktop and set up our VM for serving our ASP.NET Core and Angular HealthCheck web application. Doing this requires a series of configuration tasks that will be described in the next sections.

The first step, which we'll be dealing with in the following section, will be installing IIS, a flexible, secure, and manageable HTTP server that we'll use to host our ASP.NET Core and Angular application over the web.

For reasons of space, we're not going to talk about IIS or explore its functionalities: we'll just use the minimum amount of settings required to host our apps. For additional information regarding IIS, check out the following URL: https://www.iis.net/overview.

Adding the IIS web server

Once connected via Remote Desktop, we can access **Control Panel | Program and Features | Turn Windows features on and off** (or the **Add Roles and Features Wizard** from the **Server Manager** dashboard) to install IIS on the VM, as shown in the following screenshot:

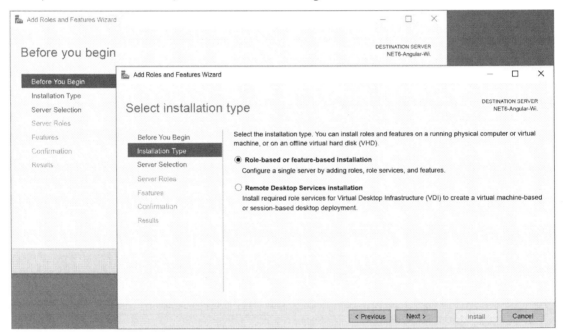

Figure 15.7: The Add Roles and Features Wizard

From the various roles available, select **Web Server (IIS)**, as shown in the following screenshot. Be sure that the **Include management tools** checkbox is checked, and then click **Add Features** to start installing it:

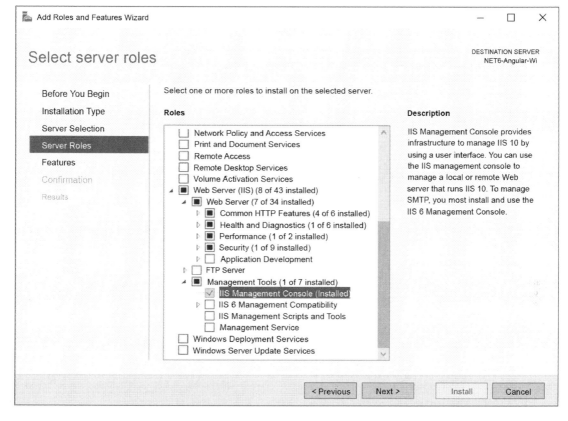

Figure 15.8: Selecting Web Server (IIS)

There's no need to change anything until the end of the installation phase; the default settings will work just fine for our deployment scenario.

Installing the ASP.NET Core Windows hosting bundle

Once IIS has been installed, we can proceed with downloading and installing the **ASP.NET Core runtime**.

It's strongly advisable to install the .NET runtime after installing IIS because the package bundle will perform some modifications to the IIS default configuration settings.

To download the .NET runtime, visit the following URL: `https://dotnet.microsoft.com/en-us/download/dotnet/6.0`.

Be sure to pick the **ASP.NET Core 6.0.1 Runtime – Windows Hosting Bundle installer** package for **Windows x64**, as shown in the following screenshot:

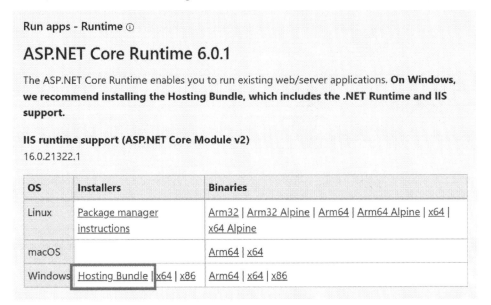

Figure 15.9: Picking the Windows Hosting Bundle installer package

The bundle includes the .NET runtime, the ASP.NET Core runtime, and the ASP.NET Core IIS module, everything we need to run our ASP.NET Core and Angular app from our VM.

Restarting IIS following ASP.NET Core runtime installation

Once the ASP.NET Core runtime installation process is complete, it's advisable to issue a stop/start command to restart the IIS service.

To do this, open a Command Prompt window with administrative rights and execute the following console commands:

```
> net stop w3svc /y
> net start w3svc
```

These commands will allow IIS to pick up a change to the system path made by the Windows Hosting Bundle installer.

Publishing HealthCheck and HealthCheckAPI

Now, we must find a way to publish the HealthCheck Angular app and HealthCheckAPI Web API and deploy them to our server.

As for the Angular app, we already know how to perform the first step from *Chapter 12, Progressive Web Apps*: we need to open a Command Prompt, navigate to the project's root path and run the ng build command; we just need a way to copy them to our new VM.

A simple way to do this is by using the Remote Desktop resource-sharing feature, which allows our local HDD to be accessed from a remote instance... or even a simple cut and paste. We can use one of these features to copy the whole content of our development machine's /build/HealthCheck/ folder into a new C:/inetpub/HealthCheck/ folder created to the remote VM.

As for the ASP.NET Core app, there are several alternative options to perform the publishing and deployment task, all accessible from the **publish profiles** feature.

Introducing Visual Studio publish profiles

Visual Studio's **publish profiles** feature allows us to build, publish, and sometimes even deploy a web application directly from the GUI, thus greatly simplifying the publishing process.

To create a publish profile, choose one of the following paths:

- Right-click the API project in **Solution Explorer** and select **Publish**
- Select **Publish {PROJECT NAME}** from the **Build** menu

Once we do that, we'll be asked to select one from several available publish targets, including:

- **Azure**
- **Docker Container Registry**
- **Folder**
- **FTP/FTPS Server**
- **Web Server (IIS)**
- **Import Profile**

Given our specific scenario, we should follow one of the following routes:

- Create a **Folder publish profile** to publish our app to a local folder of our development machine, and then copy the files to the web server somehow
- Install an FTP/FTPS server on our web server and then set up an **FTP publish profile**
- Use Visual Studio's **Azure Virtual Machine publish profile**
- Use Visual Studio's **Web Server (IIS) publish profile**

All the above options are viable. The last two require installing some additional components (*Web Deploy*) on the VM server: however, once we do that, they will work in an almost fully automated fashion (1-click deploy).

That said, in the following sections we'll briefly review all of them.

Folder publish profile

Here's what we need to do to create a new *Folder publish profile*:

1. Select the **Folder** option (or select the previous publishing profile).
2. Specify the path of the folder that will contain the published application.
3. Click the **Create Profile** button to create the profile.

4. Click the **Publish** button to deploy our `HealthCheckAPI` back-end to the chosen local folder. Visual Studio will suggest a path located within the application's `/bin/Release/` subfolder, such as `/bin/Release/net6.0/publish/`; we can either use this or choose another folder of our choice.

When the publishing task is complete, we can use the RDP resource-sharing feature to copy the whole content of our development machine's `/bin/Release/net6.0/publish/` folder into a new `C:/inetpub/HealthCheckAPI/` folder—just like we did with our Angular app.

FTP publish profile

If our web server can accept FTP (or FTPS) connections, then a suitable alternative way of publishing our project is to create an FTP-based *publish profile* that will automatically upload our web project to our web server using the FTP/FTPS protocol.

> If we don't want to use the built-in FTP server provided by Windows Server, we can install a third-party FTP server, such as FileZilla FTP Server, a great open-source alternative that comes with full FTPS support. You can find FileZilla FTP Server at the following URL: `https://filezilla-project.org/download.php?type=server`.

To make use of the FTP publish profile, we'll also need to open our VM's TCP port 21 (or another non-default port) by adding another inbound security rule, just like we did with ports 22, 80, 443, and 3389.

All we need to do is link the FTP destination folder to a new website project using IIS, and we'll be able to publish/update our website in a real-time fashion, as everything will be put online as soon as the publishing task is complete.

> As we said earlier, we're doing all this assuming that we have a web server accessible through FTP or that we're willing to install an FTP server. If that's not the case, you might as well skip this section and use a different publishing profile, such as Azure Virtual Machine or Folder.

To set up the FTP publishing profile, select IIS, FTP, and the other icons, wait for the wizard-like modal window to appear, and then select the following options:

- **Publish method**: Select **FTP**.
- **Server**: Specify the FTP server URL (IP address or domain name).
- **Site path**: Insert the target folder from the FTP server root, such as `/HealthCheckAPI/`.
- **Passive Mode, Username, Password**: Set these values according to our FTP server settings and given credentials. Activate **Save Password** if you want to let Visual Studio store it, so we won't have to write it with each publishing attempt.
- **Destination URL**: This URL will be automatically launched as soon as the publishing task successfully ends using the default browser. It's often wise to set it to our web application's base domain, such as `www.our-website-url.com`, or to leave it empty.

Once done, click on the **Validate Connection** button to check the preceding settings and ensure that you're able to reach the server through FTP. If you aren't, it might be wise to perform a full-scale network check, looking for firewalls, proxies, antivirus, or other software that could prevent the FTP connection from being established.

Azure Virtual Machine publish profile

The **Azure Virtual Machine** publish profile is a great way to enforce the **continuous integration** and **continuous delivery** (**CI/CD**) DevOps pattern because it will act as either a build system (for producing packages and other build artifacts) or a release management system to deploy our changes.

To use this, select the **Azure Virtual Machine** option, click **Browse**, and then select the VM that we created a moment ago (see the following screenshot):

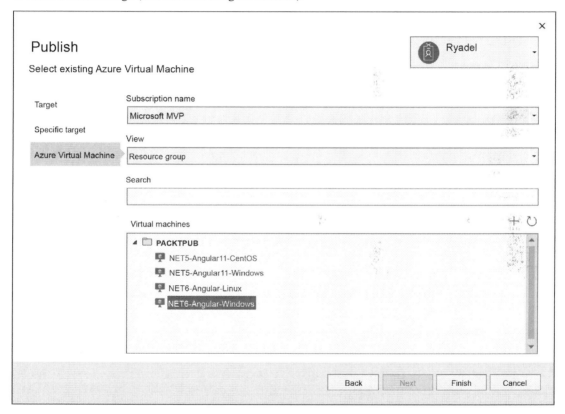

Figure 15.10: Selecting the newly created VM

However, in order to do this, we need to perform some additional configuration changes on our VM, including the following:

- Install the **Web Management Service** using the **Server Roles** interface, just like we did with IIS early on
- Start the **Web Management Service** and set its startup mode to *Automatic*

- Install the **Web Deploy** IIS extension package (available through the `https://www.iis.net/downloads/microsoft/web-deploy` website)
- Open the `8172` TCP port in the MS Azure Virtual Machine's **Networking** tab, just like we did with `22`, `80`, `443`, and `3389` a while ago
- Set up a globally unique DNS name for the VM (as explained in the *Configuring a DNS name label* section a while ago)

For reasons of space, we won't go through these settings. However, for additional information regarding the preceding tasks, check out the following guide: `https://github.com/aspnet/Tooling/blob/AspNetVMs/docs/create-asp-net-vm-with-webdeploy.md`.

Once we're done with these settings, we should be able to publish our web application to the VM in a seamless and transparent manner.

Configuring IIS

Regardless of the publishing technique we've used, by now our remote VM server should have the following folders:

- `C:/inetpub/HealthCheck/`—with our Angular app bundled files
- `C:/inetpub/HealthCheckAPI/`—with our ASP.NET Core Web API published files

Now is a good chance to create (or edit) our `HealthCheckAPI` app's `appsettings.Production.json` file, following the guidelines we explained early on.

As for the `appsettings.Development.json` file, we can just delete it, since we likely won't ever need to execute our app in a *development* environment on this VM server.

 If we want to never have to worry about deleting the development file, and minimize the risk of overwriting the production file, we can even configure our Visual Studio publish profile(s) to exclude them both using the following guide:

`https://weblog.west-wind.com/posts/2020/Jul/25/Excluding-Files-and-Folders-in-Visual-Studio-Web-Site-Project`

After doing that, we need to configure IIS to make these two apps available on the *World Wide Web*. To do that, we need to add two IIS website entries:

- `HealthCheck`, for the Angular app
- `HealthCheckAPI`, for the ASP.NET Core app

Let's start with the Angular app.

Adding the HealthCheck website entry

From the IIS Manager main page, expand the root node to show the **Sites** folder, then right-click it and select the **Add Website** option to create a new website.

Fill out the **Add Website** modal window, as shown in the following screenshot:

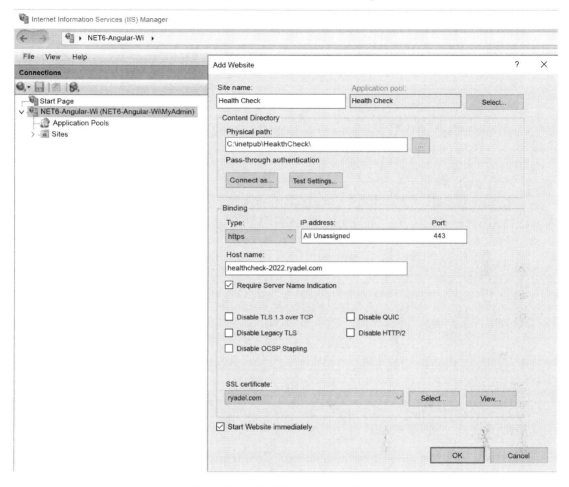

Figure 15.11: Add Website modal window

Here's a summary of the most relevant settings (and how we recommend they are set for our specific purpose):

- **Site name:** The name you want to give to your website; in our example we are using `HealthCheck`.
- **Physical path:** `C:\inetpub\HealthCheck` (the path where we've copied the Angular app's bundled files).
- **Binding Type:** `https`.
- **IP address:** `All Unassigned`.
- **Port:** 443.

- **Host name:** This is the endpoint the Angular app will respond to: in other words, the main entry point of our end-users. In the above screenshot we've used `healthcheck-2022.ryadel.com`, but you obviously need to use your actual hostname instead.
- **Require Server Name Indication:** Yes.
- **SSL certificate:** In our given scenario we're using our TLS/SSL wildcard certificate: if you don't have one, you can select the `TenantEncryptionCert` provided by Azure or use a self-signed TLS/SSL certificate (see below).
- **Start Website immediately:** Yes.

Once done, click **OK** to add the new website. A new entry will appear in the tree view on the right within the **Sites** folder.

Adding the HealthCheckAPI website entry

Right-click again on the **Sites** folder, then right-click it and select the **Add Website** option to create another website.

Repeat the same steps as before, with the following differences:

- **Site name:** In our example we're using `HealthCheckAPI`.
- **Physical path:** `C:\inetpub\HealthCheckAPI` (the path where we've copied the published files of our ASP.NET Core app).
- **Host name:** This is the endpoint the ASP.NET Core Web API will respond to: in other words, the endpoint we need to put in the Angular app's `environment.prod.ts` file. Put your chosen hostname there.

Once done, click **OK** to add the new website. Now we should have two website entries within the **Sites** folder, `HealthCities` and `HealthCitiesAPI`, each one configured to handle a different domain name.

Before going further, it might be wise to spend a couple of words on *SSL certificates*.

A note on TLS/SSL certificates

Since our apps are meant to be served using HTTPS, when we created the IIS website entries, we had to specify a TLS/SSL certificate for both of them. For the sake of simplicity, we assumed that we already have a valid TLS/SSL certificate compatible with the hostnames we've used. If we don't have them, we can either:

- **Purchase and install a TLS/SSL certificate** from a third-party reseller
- **Get a free TLS/SSL certificate** using a non-profit *certificate authority* such as *Let's Encrypt*
- **Use the MS Azure tenant certificate autogenerated by MS Azure when we created our VM**
- **Create a self-signed certificate** using the guide below

The first two routes will likely be the ways to go for any non-testing scenario. The other alternatives should be OK when performing the initial deployment tests, because they provide a faster (and cost-free) alternative to achieve our goal: that's why we're going to use them in our sample scenario.

However, an Azure-generated or self-signed certificate has the following downsides:

- All browsers (and antiviruses with web protection filters) will raise the typical SSL warnings and "unsecure website" messages, which we'll have to manually confirm/accept/skip
- We won't be able to properly test most of the PWA features of our app, because the service worker registration will fail

As we've seen in *Chapter 12*, *Progressive Web Apps*, a trusted HTTPS connection is one of the requirements for PWAs; unfortunately, a self-signed SSL certificate won't do the trick, unless we create a CA certificate, register it into our Chromium browser, and then use it to sign our own SSL certificate.

Those who want to try that route can follow the instructions explained in this Stack Overflow answer by *JellicleCat*: `https://stackoverflow.com/a/60516812/1233379`.

Or check other alternative methods discussed in that thread.

In the next section we'll briefly see how we can create a self-signed SSL certificate that can be used instead of the MS Azure ones.

Creating a Self-Signed SSL certificate

To create a self-signed SSL certificate, connect to the VM using Remote Desktop and perform the following steps:

1. Open the IIS Manager desktop app, select the root node from the tree view on the left, and then double-click the **Server Certificates** icon, as shown in the following screenshot:

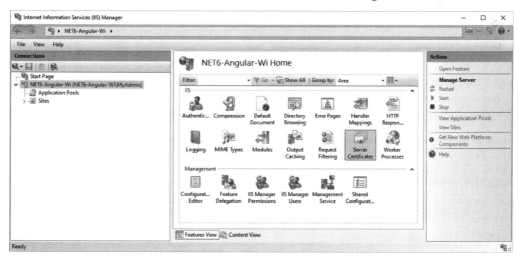

Figure 15.12: HealthCheck home view

2. Once in the **Server Certificates** panel, click the **Create Self-Signed Certificate** link in the **Actions** column on the right.

3. A modal window will appear (see the following screenshot), where we'll be asked to specify a friendly name for the certificate. Choose a friendly name for the certificate, select the **Personal** certificate store, and then click **OK** to create the self-signed certificate:

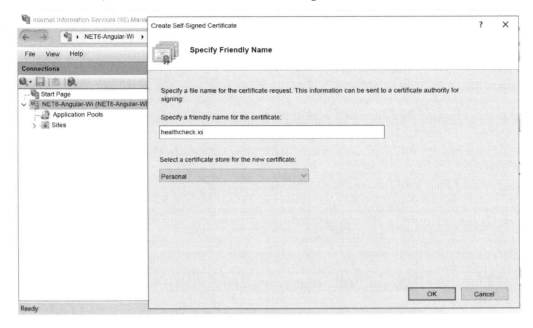

Figure 15.13: Create Self-Signed Certificate modal window

In the above example we're using the healthcheck.io friendly name for the certificate, but we're free to use any name we like: we're not using a specific domain name, since we're likely going to use that certificate for all the websites and services that can't rely upon a CA-signed certificate.

Once done, we'll be able to assign our new self-signed SSL certificate to all our website entries, replacing the MS Azure one.

Configuring the IIS application pool

As you may already know, the IIS service runs the various configured websites under one or more application pools. Each application pool configured will spawn a dedicated w3wp.exe Windows process that will be used to serve all the websites that have been configured to use it.

Depending on the publishing requirements of the various websites we need to host, we could run all websites in a few application pools (or even a single one) or each one with its own application pool. Needless to say, all the websites that share the same application pool will also share their various settings, such as memory usage, pipeline mode, identity, and idle timeout.

In our specific scenario, when we created our HealthCheck and HealthCheckAPI websites in the previous section, we chose to create a dedicated application pool with that same name—which is also the IIS default behavior. Therefore, in order to configure the website's application pool settings, we need to click on the Application Pools folder from the tree view on the left and then double-click each website entry from the Application Pools list panel, as shown in the following screenshot:

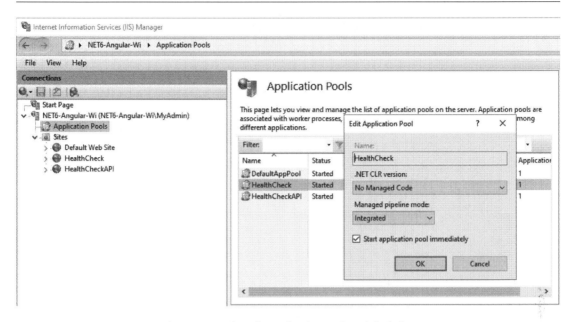

Figure 15.14: The Edit Application Pool modal window

In the **Edit Application Pool** modal window, choose the following settings, as shown in the preceding screenshot:

- **.NET CLR version: No Managed Code**
- **Managed pipeline mode: Integrated**

You might be wondering why we're also choosing **No Managed Code** for the API application pool, since we're clearly using the ASP.NET Core CLR. The answer is simple: since ASP.NET Core runs in a separate IIS process, there's no need to set any .NET CLR version on IIS.

> For additional information regarding the ASP.NET Core hosting model on IIS, including the various differences between the in-process and out-of-process hosting models, check out the following URL: `https://docs.microsoft.com/en-us/aspnet/core/host-and-deploy/iis/`.

The IIS configuration is almost done. However, before being able to test what we did, we need to perform a last task: add the .webmanifest file extension to the list of the IIS-supported *MIME types*.

Adding the .webmanifest MIME Type

As per its default settings, IIS does not serve any files with an extension that does not have a MIME map associated with it. Unfortunately, the .webmanifest extension—which we used in *Chapter 12, Progressive Web Apps*, for our PWA manifest file—is not associated with a MIME map, meaning that this file won't be sent to the browser.

To fix this issue, we need to perform the following tasks from the **IIS Manager** tool:

1. From the tree view on the left, select either the server's root node or the `HealthCheck` website, depending on if we want to add the new mapping to all the websites or to our Angular app's website only: in our scenario, both options will work, but we suggest adding the mapping to all the websites since it won't pose significant security issues.

2. Select **MIME Types** from the options listed in the right part of the window.

3. Once there, select **Add** from the menu to the right.

4. In the dialog box that opens, type `.webmanifest` in the file name extension box, and `application/manifest+json` in the **MIME type** box, as shown in the screenshot below:

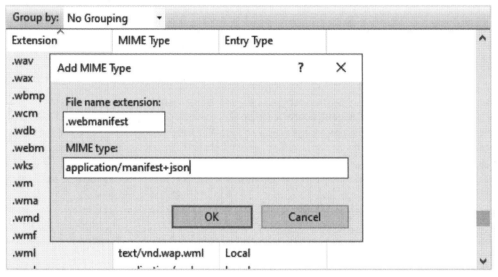

Figure 15.15: Mapping the .webmanifest file extension to the application/manifest+json MIME type

That's it: now we're ready to check our `HealthCheck` Angular app and `HealthCheckAPI` ASP.NET Core Web API and see if they are still able to work together like they did on our development machine.

Testing HealthCheck and HealthCheckAPI

Our web application should now be ready to receive HTTP requests; we only need to ensure that remote clients will be able to access it, including the machine we want to use to perform our first connection test.

More specifically, what we need to do depends on how we have configured the host name of our IIS websites:

- If we have used real domain names (or IP addresses, or DNS names), we just have to set the new DNS records and/or wait for them to propagate
- If we have used some "fake" hostnames, we need to map them to the remote VM server's IP address within the local machine's HOSTS file, as explained in the *Tweaking the HOSTS file* section above

Once both our websites' endpoints are reachable from our machine, we can proceed with the test.

Testing the app

Now, we can finally launch our favorite Chromium-based web browser and call the Angular app's endpoint that we configured early on.

 A Chromium-based browser, such as Google Chrome or Microsoft Edge, will make us able to immediately check out the Web App manifest file and the service worker, just like we did with the "local" publishing test that we performed in *Chapter 12*, *Progressive Web Apps*.

If we did everything correctly, we should be able to see our HealthCheck web application in all its glory:

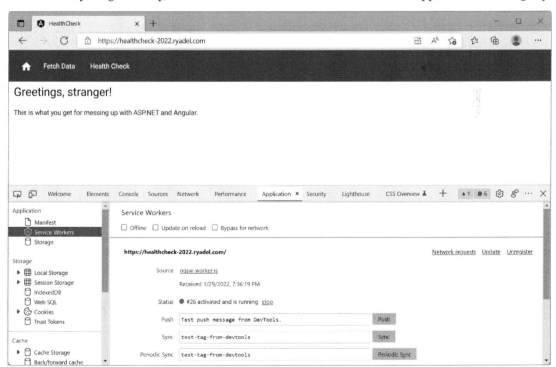

Figure 15.16: Launching our HealthCheck web application

Other than seeing the home view, we should also be able to see the following:

- The app manifest file (with all the *HC* icons) in the **Application | Manifest** panel of the browser's development console

- The service worker properly registered in the **Application | Service Workers** panel of the browser's development console

- The *send this page* and *install* icons in the rightmost part of the browser's address bar

In order to see those panels, remember to press *Shift + Ctrl + J* to bring the development console into view.

From there, we can now install the app and check/uncheck its offline status to test the service worker's behavior, just like we did in *Chapter 12, Progressive Web Apps*, when we tested our published app from a standard Visual Studio debug run; if we did everything properly, everything should work and behave in the same way.

With this, we've completed our Windows deployment journey; our HealthCheck and HealthCheckAPI web apps have achieved their ultimate goal.

In the next section, we'll see how we can deploy our WorldCities and WorldCitiesAPI web apps to a completely different machine.

Linux deployment

Throughout this section, we'll learn how to deploy our WorldCities web application on a Linux CentOS 8 server hosted on MS Azure.

More precisely, here's what we're going to do:

- **Create a new VM on MS Azure** using the CentOS-based 8.2 template
- **Configure the VM to accept inbound calls** to TCP ports 22 (for SSH), 80 (for HTTP), and 443 (for HTTPS), as well as setting up the Nginx + Kestrel edge-origin hosting model
- **Publish the WorldCities app** to the web server we've just set up
- **Test the WorldCities app** from a remote client

Let's get to work!

It's worth noting that the CentOS-based template that we're going to use in this deployment sample can be easily replaced—with minor variations—with any other Linux VM template available on MS Azure: as a matter of fact, the ASP.NET Core Linux runtime works well with most Debian-based and RPM-based Linux distributions, with a few minor differences mostly related to their package management systems.

Needless to say, those who already have a production-ready Linux server could probably skip the sections related to the VM setup and go directly to the subsequent publishing topics.

Creating a Linux CentOS VM on MS Azure

Once again, we need to perform the following steps:

- **Access the MS Azure portal**
- **Add and configure a new VM**
- **Set the inbound security rules** to access the VM from the internet

However, since we already explained the MS Azure VM creation process with Windows Server earlier on in this chapter, we're going to briefly summarize all the common tasks and avoid resubmitting the same screenshots.

 Those who require additional explanations regarding the various required steps can check out the *Creating a Windows Server VM on MS Azure* section.

Let's go back to MS Azure once more!

Adding a new Linux VM

Once again, we need to log in to MS Azure using our (existing or new) account and access the MS Azure portal administration dashboard.

Right after that, we can click on the **Virtual Machine** icon and click **Add** to access the **Create a virtual machine** panel and enter the following settings.

In the **Basics** tab:

- **Resource group:** Use the same resource group used for the SQL database (this is mandatory unless our database is not there).
- **Virtual machine name:** Use `NET6-Angular-Linux`, `WorldCities`, or any other suitable name.
- **Region:** Choose the region closest to our geographical position.
- **Availability options:** No infrastructure redundancy required.
- **Image:** In our example, we're going to use the *CentOS 8.3 Free* image by *Cognosys* (see below), which is provided free of cost; alternatively, you can choose any other Linux-based VM template as long as you're willing, and able, to adapt the following instructions according to the (arguably minor) differences between different Linux distributions.
- **Azure Spot instance:** Again, select **Yes** for an Azure Spot instance, or **No** for a standard pay-as-you-go instance.
- **Size: Standard B1ms (1 vcpu, 2 GiB memory):** Feel free to choose a different size if you're willing to spend more; *B1ms* is an entry-level machine featuring a very limited set of resources that will suffice for this deployment sample, but won't perform well in production.
- **Administrator account:** Select the **Password authentication** type, and then create a suitable username and password set. Remember to write these down in a secure place, since we'll definitely need these credentials to access our machine in a while.

For reference purposes, here's the link to the *CentOS 8.3 free* image we're going to use:

`https://azuremarketplace.microsoft.com/en-us/marketplace/apps/cognosys.`
`centos-8-3-free`

In the **Disk** tab:

- **OS disk type:** Select **Standard HDD**; this is the cheapest available choice. It goes without saying that those who want to instantiate a production environment (or are willing to pay some extra bucks) should choose a faster choice instead, such as **Standard** or **Premium SSD.**

- **Data disks:** Azure Linux VMs come with a temporary disk and an OS disk, which are good enough for our sample purposes; again, those who want to set up a production environment can (and should) add additional storage here.

In the **Network** tab:

- **Virtual Network:** Select the same VNet used for the SQL database (or create a new one)

- **Public inbound ports:** If the wizard allows this (depending on the chosen OS image), choose **Allow selected ports**, then select the following ports from the list: **HTTP (80)**, **HTTPS (443)**, **SSH (22)**

In the **Management** tab:

- **Monitoring | Boot diagnostics:** Off

Once done, click the **Review + create** button to review our configuration settings and initiate the VM deployment process.

Once deployment is complete, we can click the **Go to Resource** button to access the **Virtual Machine overview** panel.

Configuring a DNS name label

Again, we have the chance to add a DNS name label to our VM and generate a unique fifth-level domain name to conveniently access it. If we choose to do this we need to locate the **DNS Name** label in the virtual machine's **Overview** panel, click on the **Configure** link next to it, and perform the steps already explained for the Windows VM.

Before proceeding, take note of both the DNS name and the machine's IP address, as we'll likely need them later on.

Setting the inbound security rules

Go to the **Settings** | **Networking** tab and take note of the machine's public IP address. Then, check for the existence of the following inbound security rules, adding them if they're not already present:

- **TCP port 22**, so that we'll be able to access the machine using the Secure Shell protocol (also known as **SSH**)
- **TCP ports 80 and 443**, to access the HTTP server (and our WorldCities web app) from the internet using SSL

Again, if you want to increase the security posture of the VM, be sure to restrict access to these inbound rules to a secure **source IP address** (or address range), which can be set to either our static IP address or our ISP's IP mask.

Configuring the Linux VM

Now, we can use the SSH protocol to access our new Linux VM and perform two different (yet both required) sets of tasks:

- **Set up and configure the VM** by installing the various required packages (the ASP.NET Core runtime, the Nginx HTTP server, and the like)
- **Build, publish, and deploy the WorldCities and WorldCitiesAPI projects** using the Angular CLI and the Visual Studio publish profile, just like we did for the Windows VM

For the first set of tasks, we're going to use **PuTTy**, a free SSH client for Windows that can be used to remotely access a Linux machine's console. As for the deployment tasks, we'll handle them using **Secure Copy** (aka **SCP**), a Windows command-line tool that allows files to be copied from a (local) Windows system to a remote Linux machine.

PuTTy can be downloaded and installed from the following URL: https://www.putty.org/.

The **SCP** command-line tool is already shipped with most Windows versions, including Windows 10; for additional information on it, visit the following URL: https://docs.microsoft.com/en-us/azure/virtual-machines/linux/copy-files-to-linux-vm-using-scp.

Connecting to the VM

Once installed, launch **PuTTy** and insert the VM's public **IP address** (or DNS name), as shown in the following screenshot:

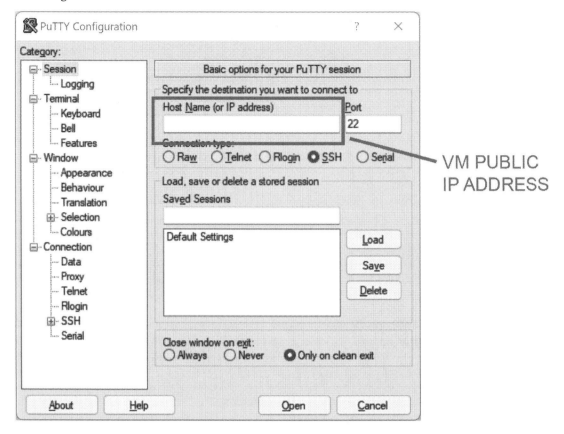

Figure 15.17: PuTTY Configuration window

Once done, click **Open** to launch the remote connection.

We'll be asked to accept the public SSH key. Once accepted, we'll be able to authenticate ourselves with the username and password specified a short time ago in the MS Azure portal's virtual machine setup wizard:

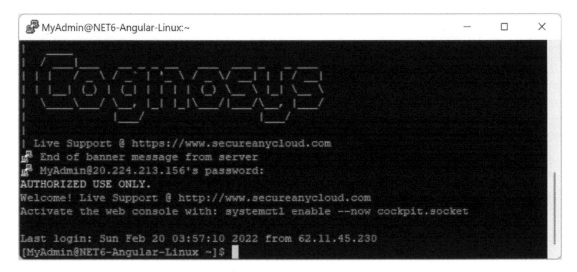

Figure 15.18: Command-line authentication

Once connected, we'll be able to issue terminal commands on the remote VM to set up and configure it according to our needs.

The configuration steps explained in the following sections are OK for the time being, but could change in the future following the release of new versions of .NET and/or CentOS. For up-to-date info, check out the following guide: https://docs.microsoft.com/en-us/dotnet/core/install/linux-centos.

Installing the ASP.NET Core runtime

Once we've successfully logged in to the Linux VM terminal, we can start to configure the remote system to enable it to run (and host) ASP.NET Core applications. To achieve this, the first thing to do is to download and install the ASP.NET Core runtime.

However, before we can do that, we need to execute the following required steps:

- Register the Microsoft key
- Register the product repository
- Install the required dependencies

These steps need to be done once per Linux machine. Luckily enough, all of them can be done with the following command:

```
$ sudo rpm -Uvh https://packages.microsoft.com/config/centos/8/packages-
microsoft-prod.rpm
```

Once this is done, we'll be able to install the ASP.NET Core 6.0 runtime in the following way:

```
$ sudo dnf install aspnetcore-runtime-6.0
```

The preceding command will ask us for confirmation a couple of times and will likely take a while to complete.

Alternatively, if we don't want to install the ASP.NET Core runtime on the Linux server, we could publish the app as an SCD, as explained in the first section of this chapter.

Once done, we can proceed to the next step: installing the web server.

Installing Nginx

The next thing we have to do involves installing the *Nginx* server package. For those that don't know it, Nginx is a free and open-source high-performance HTTP server, load balancer, and reverse proxy used by millions: this is the HTTP server we're going to use in Linux to serve our web application by reverse-proxying the Kestrel service.

In February 2020, Netcraft estimated that Nginx served 36.48 percent of all active websites ranked, ranking it first, above Apache, at 24.51 percent: however, according to W3Techs, Apache was ranked first at 40.1 percent and Nginx second at 31.8 percent around that same period. That said, we're going to use Nginx because it features a modular, event-driven, asynchronous, single-threaded architecture that scales well on generic server hardware and across multiprocessor systems, thus being an ideal partner for an ASP.NET Core web application hosted on Linux.

In previous versions of CentOS, before being able to do this, we had to add the EPEL repository, which was required for YUM to find the Nginx package to install:

```
$ sudo dnf install epel-release
```

However, starting with CentOS 8, Nginx can be installed without prerequisite steps in the following way:

```
$ sudo dnf install nginx
```

For additional information about installing an ASP.NET Core web application on Linux with Nginx, check out the following URL: https://docs.microsoft.com/en-us/aspnet/core/host-and-deploy/linux-nginx.

Now we need to configure Nginx to start automatically whenever the VM is started (or restarted).

Starting up Nginx

When we install IIS on Windows, the service will start automatically and will be configured with an automatic startup type by default. Conversely, Nginx does not start on its own and won't be executed automatically upon startup.

To start Nginx, execute the following command:

```
$ sudo systemctl start nginx
```

To set Nginx to run automatically on system startup, use the following command:

```
$ sudo systemctl enable nginx
```

After applying these settings, it would be wise to reboot the Linux machine to be sure that all the configured settings will be applied upon reboot. The reboot can be done with the following command:

```
$ sudo reboot
```

Now we can configure the machine's TCP and HTTP layers.

Checking the HTTP connection

The CentOS-based MS Azure VM template that we've used in this deployment scenario doesn't come with a local firewall rule blocking TCP ports 80 and/or 443. Therefore, as soon as Nginx is up and running, we should be able to connect to it properly by typing the VM's public IP address (or DNS name) in the browser's address bar from our development machine.

If we did everything correctly, we should see the Nginx welcome page, as shown in the following screenshot:

Welcome to nginx on Red Hat Enterprise Linux!

This page is used to test the proper operation of the **nginx** HTTP server after it has been installed. If you can read this page, it means that the web server installed at this site is working properly.

Website Administrator

This is the default `index.html` page that is distributed with **nginx** on Red Hat Enterprise Linux. It is located in `/usr/share/nginx/html`.

You should now put your content in a location of your choice and edit the `root` configuration directive in the **nginx** configuration file `/etc/nginx/nginx.conf`.

For information on Red Hat Enterprise Linux, please visit the Red Hat, Inc. website. The documentation for Red Hat Enterprise Linux is available on the Red Hat, Inc. website.

Figure 15.19: Connecting to the VM's Nginx HTTP server

If we can see the preceding response, it means that we likely have no firewall to worry about, therefore we can skip the following section and move on to the next. Conversely, if the connection cannot be established, we might have to perform some additional steps to open the VM's 80 and 443 TCP ports.

 Before altering the VM firewall rules, it might be wise to carefully check for the TCP **80** and **443** inbound security rules that we should have set on the MS Azure portal administration site, as explained in the *Setting the inbound security rules* section.

Opening the 80 and 443 TCP ports

Depending on the Linux template chosen, it could be necessary to change the local firewall settings to allow incoming traffic for the 80 and 443 TCP ports. The commands required to do this might vary, depending on the built-in firewall abstraction layer shipped with Linux distributions.

In Linux, the Kernel-based firewall is controlled by `iptables`; however, most modern distributions commonly use either the `firewalld` (CentOS, RHEL) or `ufw` (Ubuntu) abstraction layers to configure `iptables` settings.

 In a nutshell, both `firewalld` and `ufw` are firewall management tools that can be used by system administrators to configure the firewall features using a managed approach. We can think of them as front-ends for the Linux kernel's networking internals.

In VM Azure's CentOS-based Linux template, `firewalld` is present, but it's usually disabled (although it can be started and/or enabled to have it automatically run on each startup); however, if we're using a different template/VM/Linux distribution, it might be useful to spend a couple of minutes learning how we can properly configure these tools.

firewalld

Here's the command to check whether `firewalld` is installed:

```
$ sudo firewall-cmd --state
```

If the command returns something other than `not running` or `command not found`, this means that the tool is installed and active. Therefore, we need to execute the following `firewalld` commands to open TCP ports 80 and 443:

```
$ sudo firewall-cmd --permanent --add-port=80/tcp
$ sudo firewall-cmd --permanent --add-port=443/tcp
$ sudo firewall-cmd --reload
```

The `--reload` command is required to immediately apply the `firewalld` settings without having to issue a reboot.

ufw

Here's the command to check whether `ufw` is running:

```
$ sudo ufw status
```

If the preceding command returns something other than *command not found*, this means that the tool is installed and running.

Here's the `ufw` required terminal command to open TCP ports 80 and 443:

```
$ sudo ufw allow 80/tcp
$ sudo ufw allow 443/tcp
```

After executing these commands, we should be able to connect the Nginx HTTP server from our developer machine and receive the response page shown in the previous screenshot.

Publishing WorldCities and WorldCitiesAPI

Now we can publish the WorldCities and WorldCitiesAPI projects and deploy them to the Linux VM server.

Building the Angular app

As for the Angular app, we can generate the production bundle in the /dist/ folder using the ng build command of the Angular CLI, just like we did with the HealthCheck app early on.

Before doing that, be sure to check the /environments/environment.prod.ts file to ensure that the baseUrl key is set to the public endpoint that we plan to use for our WorldCitiesAPI ASP.NET Core WebAPI. In our current scenario, we're going to use the following URL:

```
export const environment = {
  production: true,
  baseUrl: "https://worldcities-api-2022.ryadel.com/"
};
```

Again, be sure to adapt the above value depending on the chosen approach to define the public endpoints.

That's it for the WorldCities Angular app; conversely, its WorldCitiesAPI counterpart needs some additional work.

Building the WorldCitiesAPI app

To publish the WorldCitiesAPI web app, we need to create another Visual Studio publish profile and then execute it to build the production files in the /bin/Release/net6.0/publish/ folder that we'll have to upload to the VM server, just like we did with the HealthCheckAPI early on.

However, before doing that, we need to ensure that our web application is properly configured to be served through a reverse proxy and will be able to access the production database.

In order to do the former, we need to use the **Forwarded Headers Middleware** from the Microsoft.AspNetCore.HttpOverrides package.

When HTTPS requests are proxied over HTTP using an edge-origin technique, such as the one we're pulling off with Kestrel and Nginx, the originating client IP address, as well as the original scheme (HTTPS), is lost between the two actors. Therefore, we must find a way to forward this information. If we don't do this, we could run into various issues while performing routing redirects, authentication, IP-based restrictions or grants, and so on.

The most convenient way to forward this data is to use the HTTP headers: more specifically, using the X-Forwarded-For (client IP), X-Forwarded-Proto (originating scheme), and X-Forwarded-Host (host header field value).

The built-in **Forwarded Headers Middleware** provided by ASP.NET Core performs this task by reading these headers and filling in the corresponding fields on the web application's HttpContext.

> For additional information regarding Forwarded Headers Middleware and its most common usage scenarios, check out the following URL: `https://docs.microsoft.com/en-us/aspnet/core/host-and-deploy/proxy-load-balancer`.

While we're there, we also need to properly check the connection string to the SQL database that we set up in *Chapter 5, Data Model with Entity Framework Core*, to ensure that it will still be reachable by the Linux VM (or change it accordingly). In the following two sections we will deal with both of these issues.

Adding the forwarded headers middleware

To add the Forwarded Headers Middleware, open the WorldCitiesAPI's Program.cs file and add the following highlighted lines to the existing code:

```
using Microsoft.AspNetCore.HttpOverrides;

// ...

app.UseHttpsRedirection();

// Invoke the UseForwardedHeaders middleware and configure it
// to forward the X-Forwarded-For and X-Forwarded-Proto headers.
// NOTE: This must be put BEFORE calling UseAuthentication
// and other authentication scheme middlewares.
app.UseForwardedHeaders(new ForwardedHeadersOptions
{
    ForwardedHeaders = ForwardedHeaders.XForwardedFor
    | ForwardedHeaders.XForwardedProto
});

app.UseAuthentication();
app.UseAuthorization();

// ...
```

As we can see, we're telling the middleware to forward the X-Forwarded-For and X-Forwarded-Proto headers, thereby ensuring that redirected URIs and other security policies will work properly.

> **IMPORTANT:** As written in the comments, this middleware must be put before calling UseAuthentication or other authentication scheme middlewares.

Now, we can move on to the following step: adding a connection string that lets us connect to the production database.

Checking the database connection string

From **Solution Explorer**, open the `secrets.json` file and check out the connection string that we set up in *Chapter 5, Data Model with Entity Framework Core*, which has worked flawlessly for our development machine since then. We need to be sure that such a connection string will work on our Linux VM as well.

If the SQL database is hosted on MS Azure or a publicly accessible server, we won't have to do anything; however, in the case where we've used a local SQL database instance installed on our development machine, we'll need to choose one of the following available options:

1. Move and/or copy the `WorldCities` SQL database to MS Azure
2. Install a local *SQL Server Express* (or *Development*) instance on the CentOS VM right after creating it
3. Configure an inbound rule to the custom local (or remote) SQL Server Express (or Development) instance that we set up in *Chapter 5, Data Model with Entity Framework Core*, possibly restricting external access to the new VM's public IP address only

For option #1, right-click the local SQL Database instance and select **Tasks | Deploy Database to MS Azure SQL Database**; check out *Chapter 5, Data Model with Entity Framework Core*, for additional details.

For option #2, take a look at the following SQL Server Linux installation guide: `https://docs.microsoft.com/en-us/sql/linux/sql-server-linux-setup`.

For option #3, check out the following URL: `https://docs.microsoft.com/en-us/sql/sql-server/install/configure-the-windows-firewall-to-allow-sql-server-access`.

Regardless of the option we choose to adopt, we'll eventually end up with a connection string that will allow us to connect to the production database. We can then create a new `appsettings.Production.json` file on the VM server and add the connection string there, together with the `JwtSettings` and the `AllowedCORS` keys, as explained earlier on in this chapter, in the *Updating the appsettings.Production.json file(s)* section.

 A sample `appsettings.Production.json` file for the `WorldCitiesAPI` has been added—for reference purposes only—in the GitHub repository for this chapter. Be sure not to do that in your non-sample projects and/or when dealing with actual database credentials, as doing that would negate the whole purpose of the *Visual Studio User Secrets* feature, which we introduced back in *Chapter 5, Data Model with Entity Framework Core*: keeping our credentials away from source control repositories.

It's worth noting that creating and setting up the `appsettings.Production.json` file is not a Linux-specific task; if we had published the `WorldCitiesAPI` app on a Windows server, we would have had to do the exact same thing.

As soon as we have built the production bundles for our WorldCities and WorldCitiesAPI apps, together with the required configuration files, we can finally deploy them to our VM server.

Deploying the files to the Linux VM

Copying the production bundles from our development machine to the Linux VM server is a task that can be fulfilled in many ways, including:

- Using our existing **Folder publish profile** and then copying the files to the web server using the SCP command-line tool
- Using our existing **Folder publish profile** and then copying the files to the web server using a GUI-based SFTP Windows client, such as:
  - **Using WinSCP:** A free SFTP, SCP, S3, and FTP client for Windows: https://winscp.net/
  - **Using FileZilla FTP Client:** Another free, open-source FTP client with FTP over TLS (FTPS) and SFTP support: https://filezilla-project.org/
  - Installing an FTP/FTPS server on our web server and then set up an **FTP publish profile**
  - Using Visual Studio's **Azure Virtual Machine publish profile**

In this deployment scenario, we'll go with the first option, which is arguably the easiest one to achieve; as for the other available alternatives, we've already talked about them in the previous section (*Windows Deployment*), so we won't repeat anything here.

Creating the /var/www folder

The first thing we need to do is create a suitable folder to store our application's published files on the Linux VM. For this deployment scenario, we're going to use the /var/www/<AppName> folder, thereby following a typical Linux convention; needless to say, since we're going to publish two apps, we're going to create two folders.

Since the Azure CentOS-based template doesn't come with an existing /var/www folder, we need to create that as well. To do this, execute the following command from the Linux VM console:

```
$ sudo mkdir /var/www
```

This /var/www/ folder will be our Linux equivalent of the Windows C:\inetpub\ folder, the directory that will contain our web applications' files.

Right after this, we can create two new subfolders there by means of the following command:

```
$ sudo mkdir /var/www/WorldCities
$ sudo mkdir /var/www/WorldCitiesAPI
```

These two folders will contain our application's published files.

Setting permissions

Now, we need to configure the access permissions to the /var/www/WorldCities folder of the Nginx default user.

In this deployment scenario, we're taking for granted the fact that the Nginx instance is running with its default nginx user and nginx group. In other Linux environments, the username and/or group might vary—for example, in some Linux distributions, the Nginx group is called www or www-data.

To determine which user Nginx is running in, use the following command:

```
$ ps -eo pid,comm,euser,supgrp | grep nginx
```

To list all available Linux users and/or groups, use the following commands:

```
$ getent passwd
$ getent group
```

Once we retrieve the user and group, we can use them to change the /var/www folder permissions. Assuming the default values (nginx user and nginx group), this can be done in the following way:

```
$ sudo chown -R nginx:nginx /var/www
$ sudo chmod -R 550 /var/www
```

This will make both the nginx user and its corresponding nginx group able to access the /var/www/WorldCities folder in read and execute mode, while blocking any access to every other user/group.

Before moving on, there's still one thing to do. If we aim to publish our app using FTP, FTPS, or SFTP, the above permissions won't be enough; we need to be sure to set them accordingly with our FTP server requirements and/or the account that we plan to use to perform the upload task.

Publishing permissions

The most common way to set up publishing permissions is to use the Linux setfacl command to grant read and write permissions to the /var/www folder for the publishing account.

If we plan to publish our app with the user account that we set up in MS Azure, we can do that in the following way:

```
$ sudo setfacl -R -m u:<USERNAME>:rwx /var/www
```

Be sure to replace the preceding <USERNAME> placeholder with the username that we previously set up on the Azure VM (the same one we used to log in to the VM terminal).

> Setting the permissions as explained previously should be enough for most scenarios; however, the server could require additional tweaking depending on the Linux distribution and version, system configuration, and other settings.

Now we can finally copy the files.

Copying the WorldCities publish folder

Once the /var/www/WorldCities and /var/www/WorldCitiesAPI folders have been properly set up on the Linux VM, we can open Command Prompt to our local development machine and initiate the copy.

Let's start with the WorldCities Angular app. Using Command Prompt, navigate to the app's root folder and issue the following SCP command to copy the production bundles built using the ng build command to the remote VM:

```
> scp -r dist/WorldCities/* <USERNAME>@<VM.IP.ADDRESS>:/var/www/WorldCities
```

> Remember to replace the <USERNAME> and <VM.IP.ADDRESS> placeholders with the actual values.

The SCP command will then ask us whether we want to connect to the remote folder, as shown in the following screenshot:

Figure 15.20: Authorizing the connection to the remote folder

Type yes to authorize the connection, and then repeat the command to copy the source folder to its destination. The SCP command will start to copy all the files from the local development machine to the VM folder, as shown in the following screenshot:

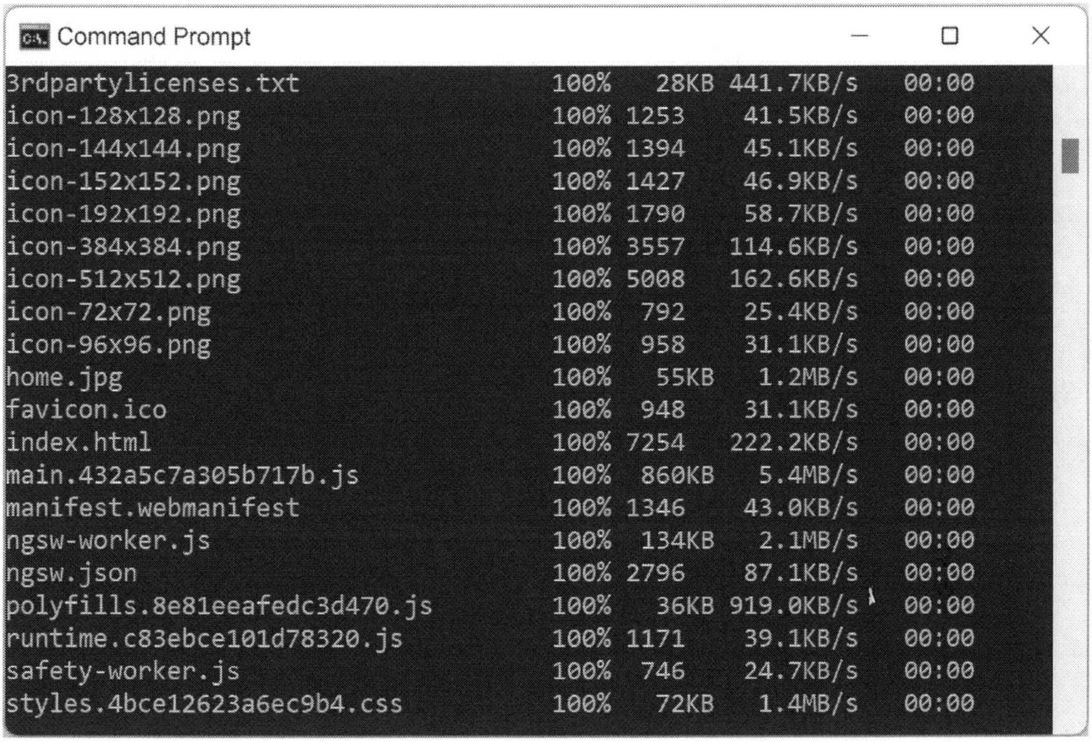

Figure 15.21: Copying all files from the local development machine to the VM folder

Right after that, we can do the same for the WorldCItiesAPI app—assuming we've already published it locally using a Folder publish profile.

To do that, navigate to the WorldCitiesAPI project's root folder and then launch the following SCM command:

```
> scp -r bin/Release/net6.0/publish/* <USERNAME>@<VM.IP.ADDRESS>:/var/www/
  WorldCitiesAPI
```

If we've created the appsettings.Production.json file within the project (bad practice) it will be deployed within the rest of the app, meaning that we'll need to manually edit it from the VM server; if we have created it separately (good practice), now we can take the chance to either create it locally and then upload it using the SCP tool, or directly create it in the VM server using a text editor such as *nano* or *vim*. Be sure to do that before proceeding.

Now that our WorldCities app files have been copied to the Linux VM, we just need to configure the Kestrel service and then the Nginx reverse proxy to serve it.

Configuring Kestrel and Nginx

Before starting, we will quickly explain how the Kestrel service and the Nginx HTTP server will interact with each other.

The high-level architecture is quite similar to the Windows out-of-process hosting model that has been used since ASP.NET Core 2.2:

- The Kestrel service will serve our web app on TCP port 5000 (or any other TCP port; 5000 is just the default one)
- The Nginx HTTP server will act as a reverse proxy, forwarding all the incoming requests to the Kestrel web server

This pattern is called the **edge-origin proxy**, and can briefly be summarized by the following diagram:

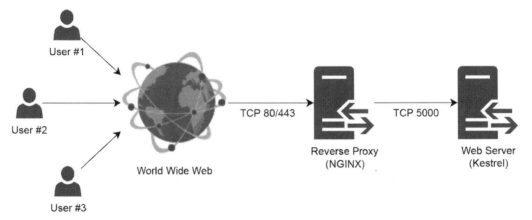

Figure 15.22: The edge-origin proxy

Now that we've understood the general picture, let's do our best to pull it off.

Since our app will be served using HTTPS, we need to either purchase and install a TLS/SSL certificate from a third-party reseller or create a self-signed one.

For this specific scenario, we'll take for granted that we have a valid certificate, just like we did with Windows: however, to benefit those who don't have one, we'll briefly explain how to create a self-signed certificate on Linux using the OpenSSL command-line tool.

Creating the self-signed SSL certificate

If you already have a valid TLS/SSL certificate you can skip the following guide and continue to the next section: we just need to copy the certificate files to the /var/www/ssl folder of the VM server machine, which can be done with SCP just like we did with the app's production files.

If you need to create a self-signed certificate, here's what you need to do:

1. Create the /var/www/ssl folder with sudo mkdir /var/www/ssl

2. Create the self-signed SSL certificate (worldcities.crt) and the private key file (worldcities. key) with the following command:

```
$ sudo openssl req -x509 -newkey rsa:4096 -sha256 -nodes -keyout /var/
www/ssl/worldcities.key -out /var/www/ssl/worldcities.crt -subj "/
CN=worldcities.io" -days 3650
```

3. Once done, merge the certificate and the private key into a single worldcities.pfx file:

```
$ sudo openssl pkcs12 -export -out /var/www/ssl/worldcities.pfx -inkey /
var/www/ssl/worldcities.key -in /var/www/ssl/worldcities.crt
```

When asked for the PFX file password, enter a random password and remember this as "the certificate password" for later use.

Setting the SSL folder permissions

Regardless of how we obtained it, now we should have a TLS/SSL certificate in the /var/www/ssl folder: this means that now we need to set the proper permissions to that folder to make it- accessible from both Nginx and the app, just like we did with the /var/www folder early on:

```
$ sudo chown -R nginx:nginx /var/www/ssl
$ sudo chmod -R 550 /var/www/ssl
```

In this specific case, we must perform an additional step: more precisely, we need to change the security context of the /var/www/ssl folder (and all its containing files) so that Nginx will be able to access it:

```
$ sudo chcon -R -v --type=httpd_sys_content_t /var/www/ssl
```

If we don't execute the preceding command, **Security-Enhanced Linux** (**SELinux**) will prevent httpd daemons from accessing the /var/www/ssl folder, causing unwanted "permission denied" errors during the Nginx startup phase. It goes without saying that if our Linux system is not running SELinux, or we have permanently disabled it, the preceding command can be skipped. However, since it's active in the MS Azure CentOS-based VM template, we might need to execute it.

SELinux is an access control (MAC) security mechanism implemented in the CentOS 4 kernel. It is quite similar to the Windows UAC mechanism and has strong default values that can be relaxed in case of specific requirements.

To temporarily disable it, run the `sudo setenforce 0` terminal command. Doing this can be useful when we run into permission issues to determine whether the problem is related to SELinux.

For additional information regarding SELinux and its default security settings, check out the following URLs:

`https://wiki.centos.org/HowTos/SELinux`

`https://wiki.centos.org/TipsAndTricks/SelinuxBooleans`

For additional information regarding the OpenSSL tool, check out the following URL:

`https://www.openssl.org/docs/manmaster/man1/openssl.html`

Now we have a valid self-signed TLS/SSL certificate that can be used by Nginx.

Configuring the systemd service

Now that we have a TLS/SSL certificate and we've set the proper permissions to its `/var/www/ssl` containing folder, we can create a `systemd` entry to register the `WorldCitiesAPI` as a service. The `WorldCities` Angular app doesn't need Kestrel and therefore will require much less work, since it's all about serving static files.

Let's start by creating the service definition file in the `/etc/systemd/system/` folder.

To do that, we'll use nano, an open-source text editor for Linux that can be used from a command-line interface (similar to `vim`, but much easier to use). Let's go through the following steps:

1. Execute the following command to create a new `/etc/systemd/system/kestrel-WorldCitiesAPI.service` file:

```
$ sudo nano /etc/systemd/system/kestrel-WorldCitiesAPI.service
```

2. Once done, fill the newly created file with the following content:

```
[Unit]
Description=WorldCitiesAPI

[Service]
WorkingDirectory=/var/www/WorldCitiesAPI
ExecStart=/usr/local/bin/dotnet /var/www/WorldCitiesAPI/WorldCitiesAPI.
dll
Restart=always
```

```
# Restart service after 10 seconds if the dotnet service crashes:
RestartSec=10

KillSignal=SIGINT
SyslogIdentifier=WorldCitiesAPI
User=nginx
Environment=ASPNETCORE_ENVIRONMENT=Production
Environment=DOTNET_PRINT_TELEMETRY_MESSAGE=false
Environment=ASPNETCORE_URLS=http://localhost:5000

# How many seconds to wait for the app to shut down after it receives the
initial interrupt signal.
# If the app doesn't shut down in this period, SIGKILL is issued to
terminate the app.
# The default timeout for most distributions is 90 seconds.
TimeoutStopSec=90

[Install]
WantedBy=multi-user.target
```

3. Once done, press *Ctrl + X* to exit and then *Y* to save the file on disk.

The `kestrel-WorldCitiesAPI.service` file is available in the `/_LinuxVM_ConfigFiles/` folder of this book's GitHub repository.

Depending on the Linux distribution, the `dotnet` executable might be located in different folders than `usr/bin`, such as `/usr/share/bin`, `/usr/local/bin`, or `/usr/share/dotnet`: be sure to check it out.

As we can see, this file's contents will be used by `systemd` to start the `WorldCitiesAPI` project with our app's production values, such as the `ASPNETCORE_ENVIRONMENT` variable, which we talked about earlier on, and the TCP port, which will be used to internally serve the app.

> The preceding settings are OK for our current deployment scenario; however, they should be changed to comply with different usernames, folder names, TCP ports used, the web app's main DLL name, and so on. When hosting a different web application, be sure to update them accordingly.

Now that we have configured the service, we just need to start it, which can be done using the following command:

```
$ sudo systemctl start kestrel-WorldCitiesAPI.service
```

If you also want to make the service automatically run on each VM reboot, add the following command:

```
$ sudo systemctl enable kestrel-WorldCitiesAPI.service
```

Immediately after this, it would be wise to run the following command to check whether the service is running without issues:

```
$ sudo systemctl status kestrel-WorldCitiesAPI.service
```

If we see a green `active (running)` message, such as the one in the following screenshot, this most likely means that our Kestrel web service is up and running:

```
MyAdmin@NET6-Angular-Linux:~                                                      —    □    ×
● kestrel-WorldCitiesAPI.service - WorldCitiesAPI
   Loaded: loaded (/etc/systemd/system/kestrel-WorldCitiesAPI.service; enabled; vendor preset: disabled)
   Active: active (running) since Fri 2022-03-18 22:30:27 UTC; 31min ago
 Main PID: 890 (dotnet)
    Tasks: 14 (limit: 12049)
   Memory: 117.3M
   CGroup: /system.slice/kestrel-WorldCitiesAPI.service
           └─890 /usr/local/bin/dotnet /var/www/WorldCitiesAPI/WorldCitiesAPI.dll
lines 1-8/15 39%
```

Figure 15.23: Seeing the green active (running) message

If the `status` command shows that something's off (red lines or advice), we can troubleshoot the issue by looking at the detailed ASP.NET Core application error log with the following command:

```
$ sudo journalctl -u kestrel.worldcities
```

The `-u` parameter will only return messages coming from the `kestrel-WorldCitiesAPI` service, filtering out everything else.

Since the `journalctl` log could easily become very long, even with the preceding filter, it could also be advisable to restrict its timeframe using the `--since` parameter in the following way:

```
$ sudo journalctl -u kestrel-worldcities --since "yyyy-MM-dd HH:mm:ss"
```

Be sure to replace the `yyyy-MM-dd HH:mm:ss` placeholders with a suitable date-time value.

Last but not least, we can just output the last-logged error with the `-xe` switch:

```
$ sudo journalctl -xe
```

These commands should be very useful in troubleshooting most error scenarios on Linux in an effective manner.

 For additional information regarding the `journalctl` tool, check out the following URL: https://www.freedesktop.org/software/systemd/man/journalctl.html.

If the `kestrel-worldcities.service` is up and running, our job here is done: we've successfully configured `systemd` to start the `WorldCitiesAPI` project as a service, which is hosted by ASP.NET Core using the Kestrel web server. Now we just need to set up Nginx to reverse proxy Kestrel and we're done.

However, before doing that, it might be wise to spend a minute understanding why we need to build such an *edge-origin* pattern in the first place.

Why are we not serving the web app with Kestrel directly?

We could be tempted to just configure the Kestrel web service on TCP port 443 (instead of TCP 5000) and get the job done now, without having to deal with Nginx, and skipping the whole reverse proxy part.

Despite being 100% possible, we strongly advise against doing this for the same reasons as stated by Microsoft here:

> *Kestrel is great for serving dynamic content from ASP.NET Core. However, the web serving capabilities aren't as feature-rich as servers such as IIS, Apache, or Nginx. A reverse proxy server can offload work such as serving static content, caching requests, compressing requests, and SSL termination from the HTTP server. A reverse proxy server may reside on a dedicated machine or may be deployed alongside an HTTP server.*
>
> *[Source:* https://docs.microsoft.com/en-us/aspnet/core/host-and-deploy/ linux-nginx*]*

In short, Kestrel is not intended to be used on the front line, at least for the time being; therefore, the correct thing to do is to definitely keep it far from the edge and leave such a task to Nginx.

Configuring Nginx for WorldCitiesAPI

The last thing we need to do is to configure the Nginx HTTP server to act as a reverse proxy for our Kestrel service. Take the following steps:

1. Type the following command to create a dedicated Nginx configuration file for this job:

```
$ sudo nano /etc/nginx/nginx-WorldCitiesAPI.conf
```

2. Then, fill the new file's content with the following configuration settings:

```
server {
    listen      80;
    listen      [::]:80;
    server_name worldcities-api-2022.ryadel.com;
    return      301 https://worldcities-api-2022.ryadel.com$request_uri;
}
server {
  listen 443 ssl http2;
  listen [::]:443 ssl http2;

  ssl_certificate /var/www/ssl/star_ryadel_com.crt;
```

```
    ssl_certificate_key /var/www/ssl/star_ryadel_com.key;

    server_name worldcities-api-2022.ryadel.com;

    root /var/www/WorldCitiesAPI/;
    index index.html;
    autoindex off;

    location / {
      proxy_pass http://localhost:5000;
      proxy_http_version 1.1;

      proxy_cache_bypass $http_upgrade;

      proxy_set_header Connection $http_connection;
      proxy_set_header Host $host;
      proxy_set_header Upgrade $http_upgrade;
      proxy_set_header X-Forwarded-For $proxy_add_x_forwarded_for;
      proxy_set_header X-Forwarded-Host $host:$server_port;
      proxy_set_header X-Forwarded-Proto $scheme;
      proxy_set_header X-Forwarded-Server $host;
    }
}
```

3. Once done, press *Ctrl* + *X* to exit and then *Y* to save the file.

4. Right after that, execute the following command to authorize the Nginx service to connect to the network:

```
$ sudo setsebool -P httpd_can_network_connect 1
```

The preceding command will probably take a while to complete; however, it is required to change the SELinux default settings, which prevents all `httpd` daemons (such as Nginx) from accessing the local network and, hence, the Kestrel service. If our Linux system is not running SELinux, or we have permanently disabled it, we don't need to execute the preceding command.

While we're here, we can take the chance to configure Nginx to serve the `WorldCities` Angular app as well.

Configuring Nginx for WorldCities

The Angular app is not served locally by Kestrel, hence there's no need to proxy it: Nginx just needs to serve its static files, thus acting like a standard web server.

To configure it to behave that way, create a new Nginx configuration file in the following way:

```
$ sudo nano /etc/nginx/nginx-WorldCitiesAPI.conf
```

And fill it with the following content:

```
server {
    listen          80;
    listen          [::]:80;
    server_name  worldcities-2022.ryadel.com;
    return          301 https://worldcities-2022.ryadel.com$request_uri;
}

server {
  listen 443 ssl http2;
  listen [::]:443 ssl http2;

  ssl_certificate /var/www/ssl/star_ryadel_com.crt;
  ssl_certificate_key /var/www/ssl/star_ryadel_com.key;

  server_name worldcities-2022.ryadel.com;

  root /var/www/WorldCities/;
  index index.html;
  autoindex off;
}
```

As we can see, this time we're dealing with a much simpler configuration file, since we don't have to proxy anything.

 The nginx-WorldCities.conf files are available in the /_LinuxVM_ConfigFiles/ folder of this book's GitHub repository.

Let's now see how we can instruct Nginx to read these new configuration files upon startup.

Updating the nginx.conf file

The two configuration files we've just added need to be referenced within the main Nginx configuration file; otherwise, they won't be read and applied.

To do this, edit the /etc/nginx/nginx.conf file with the following command:

```
$ sudo nano /etc/nginx/nginx.conf
```

Then, add the following highlighted lines near the end of the file, just before the final closing square bracket:

```
# ...existing code...

    location / {
    }

    error_page 404 /404.html;
        location = /40x.html {
    }

    error_page 500 502 503 504 /50x.html;
        location = /50x.html {
    }
}

server_names_hash_bucket_size 128;
include nginx-WorldCities.conf;
include nginx-WorldCitiesAPI.conf;

# ...existing code...

}
```

Those include lines will allow Nginx to read these configuration files and act accordingly: reverse-proxying the WorldCitiesAPI ASP.NET Core app, and directly serving the WorldCities Angular app. The new settings will be applied as soon as Nginx is restarted, which is something that we'll do in a short while.

 As we can see by looking at the above code, we also took the chance to increase the server_names_hash_bucket_size default value (64) to 128, which allows it to handle longer hostnames such as those used in our scenario.

All the required deployment tasks on Linux have been completed. Now, we just have to properly test the WorldCities and WorldCitiesAPI web applications to see whether it works.

Testing WorldCities and WorldCitiesAPI

The testing phase will be very similar to what we did at the end of the Windows deployment section. Observe the following steps:

1. Before leaving the Linux VM terminal, it would be wise to restart the Kestrel services and the Nginx service in the following way:

```
$ sudo systemctl restart kestrel-WorldCitiesAPI
$ sudo systemctl restart nginx
```

2. Immediately after this, check for their statuses with the following commands to ensure that they're up and running:

```
$ sudo systemctl status kestrel-WorldCitiesAPI
$ sudo systemctl status nginx
```

In production environments, it is advisable to test the updated Nginx configuration before restarting Nginx using the following command:

```
sudo nginx -t
```

That way the production site won't go down if Nginx fails to load due to a configuration error of any kind.

Now, we're ready to switch to our local development machine and start the test.

Testing the app

Again, we're going to perform these tests using a Chromium-based browser (Google Chrome or Microsoft Edge) because of their built-in development tools that conveniently allow us to check for Web App Manifest and service worker presence.

Launch Google Chrome and write the Angular app's public URL in the browser's address bar:

```
https://worldcities-2022.ryadel.com
```

If we have done everything correctly, we should be able to see the `WorldCities` Angular app's home view:

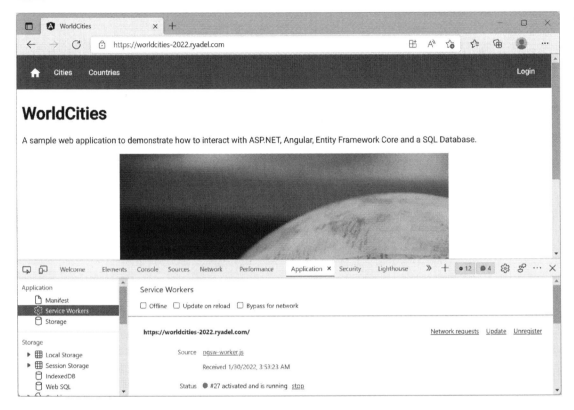

Figure 15.24: The WorldCities home view

From there, we should check for the presence/availability of the following goodies:

- The app manifest file (with all the *HC* icons) in the **Application | Manifest** panel of the browser's development console
- The service worker properly registered in the **Application | Service Workers** panel of the browser's development console
- The *send this page* and *install* icons in the rightmost part of the browser's address bar
- The service worker's behavior when checking and unchecking the offline status to test the service worker's behavior
- Access to the SQL database
- The **Edit City** and **Edit Country** reactive forms
- The login and registration workflows

If everything works as expected, we can say that our Linux deployment journey is over as well. In the next section we'll see how to deal with some typical ASP.NET Core error messages so we can understand potential issues that may arise during or after the deployment phase—and properly address them.

Troubleshooting

If the web application encounters a runtime error, the production environment won't show any detailed information about the exception to the end-user. For this reason, we won't be able to know anything useful about the issue unless we switch to **Development Mode** (refer to the following screenshot):

Figure 15.25: Error message in the production environment

This can be done in the following way:

1. Change the `ASPNETCORE_ENVIRONMENT` variable value to `Development` in the `WorldCitiesAPI` service settings file of the affecting app

2. Restart the service (and regenerate the dependency tree afterward) with the following commands:

```
$ sudo systemctl restart kestrel-WorldCitiesAPI
$ sudo systemctl daemon-reload
```

However, you are strongly advised to never do this in real production environments and inspect the `WorldCitiesAPI` service's journal logs with the following `journalctl` commands instead, as we suggested early on:

```
$ sudo journalctl -u kestrel-WorldCitiesAPI --since "yyyy-MM-dd HH:mm:ss"
$ sudo journalctl -xe
```

Such an approach will give us the same level of information without exposing our errors to the public.

Now that we're done with Linux, we're ready to explore our last—but not least—deployment alternative: *Azure App Service*.

Azure App Service deployment

Throughout this section, we'll learn how to deploy our `HealthCheck` and `HealthCheckAPI` web applications on **MS Azure App Service**, a fully managed platform for building, deploying, and scaling web apps.

As we'll be able to see, this deployment is considerably easier and faster than the previous ones, because we won't need to deploy a virtual machine; App Service's fully managed approach grants a deployment experience similar to the one we experienced back in *Chapter 5*, *Data Model with Entity Framework Core*, when we created an MS Azure database: we'll just get what we need to publish our app, without the need to perform any hardware and/or software setup.

This approach can be a tremendous advantage for most projects, as long as we don't need to perform complex low-level infrastructure configuration tasks.

Here's what we'll do in detail:

- **Create two Web App instances on MS Azure** for our `HealthCheck` and `HealthCheckAPI` apps, using the free-tier (F1) pricing plan
- **Adapt our apps** to make both of them work with the App Service public URLs
- **Publish our apps to Azure App Service** using FTPS (for the Angular app) and Visual Studio (for the ASP.NET Core app)
- **Test our new App Service instances** to ensure they work as expected

This is going to be our last set of tasks: let's get them done!

Creating the App Service instances

Go to `https://portal.azure.com/` and log in with your account. Once done, input `app service` in the search bar and select the **App Service** feature. From there, we need to create two new entries: let's start with the `HealthCheck` Angular app.

Adding the HealthCheck App Service

Once there, click on the **Add** button in the topmost menu to access the **Create Web App** form, shown in the following screenshot:

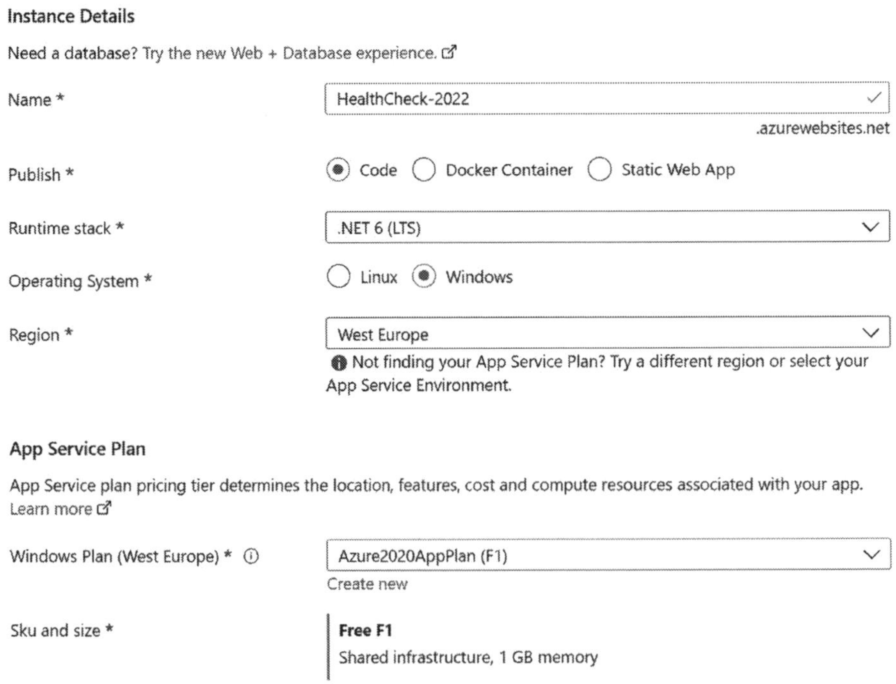

Instance Details

Need a database? Try the new Web + Database experience. ☐

Name *	HealthCheck-2022 ✓
	.azurewebsites.net
Publish *	⦿ Code ◯ Docker Container ◯ Static Web App
Runtime stack *	.NET 6 (LTS) ∨
Operating System *	◯ Linux ⦿ Windows
Region *	West Europe ∨
	ⓘ Not finding your App Service Plan? Try a different region or select your App Service Environment.

App Service Plan

App Service plan pricing tier determines the location, features, cost and compute resources associated with your app. Learn more ☐

Windows Plan (West Europe) * ⓘ	Azure2020AppPlan (F1) ∨
	Create new
Sku and size *	**Free F1**
	Shared infrastructure, 1 GB memory

Figure 15.26: The Create Web App form

Fill out the required fields in the following way:

- **Name:** This will be our web app instance's unique name, which will also be used as the public URL's subdomain. In the preceding screenshot we've used HealthCheck-2022, but any suitable name will do.

- **Publish:** Choose **Code**, unless you want to host the app within a managed Docker container.

- **Runtime stack:** Choose **.NET 6**. Truth be told, any stack would do, since we're going to use this App Service entry to publish the bundle of our Angular app, which is made of static HTML, JS, and CSS files only.

- **Operating System:** Choose **Windows**, since we've optimized our HealthCheck app for a Windows OS to deploy at the beginning of this chapter.

- **Region:** Choose the region closest to our geographical position.

- **App Service Plan:** Choose a suitable plan, or just pick the free plan (F1) if you only want to test the service—just like we did in the preceding screenshot.

- **Subscription:** Select your MS Azure subscription.

- **Resource group:** Use the same resource group used for the SQL database and/or the VMs (or create a new one).

Once done, click the **Review + Create** button at the bottom left of the page to access the review page. From there, click the **Create** button to start the deployment process. The whole operation will take a few seconds, after which we'll be able to go to our newly created resource:

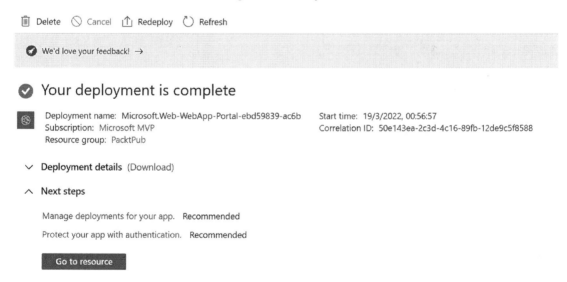

Figure 15.27: Deployment complete screen

If we click on the **Go to resource** button, we'll be taken to the Web App instance's configuration panel, which has a bunch of available options:

Figure 15.28: HealthCheck-2022 configuration panel

However, we don't need any of these settings for now; we just have to retrieve the public URL of our app, which will be in the `https://<appname>.azurewebsites.net/` format.

As we can see in the preceding screenshot, our sample web app instance's public URL is `https://healthcheck-2022.azurewebsites.net/`.

Take note of that URL, since we're going to need it in a short while. If we navigate to it, we'll see a welcome screen informing us that the managed instance is ready to host our web app and asking us to deploy our code, which is precisely what we're going to do in a short while—after creating another App Service instance for our `HealthCheckAPI` ASP.NET Core app.

Adding the HealthCheckAPI App Service

To add another App Service instance for our `HealthCheckAPI` ASP.NET Core app we have to repeat the same steps that we just did to create the previous one. The only setting we need to change is the instance **Name**, which we can set to **HealthCheck-API-2022**.

After the `HealthCheck-API-2022` instance has been created, we can take the chance to configure the *CORS* settings for this App Service instance, since these settings will override any CORS policies applied at the ASP.NET Core level.

Navigate to the **CORS** page using the left menu tree view and add the public URL of the `HealthCheck-2022` App Service instance that we created early on to the list of **Allowed Origins**, as shown in the following screenshot:

Figure 15.29: Azure App Service CORS setup

Once done, go back to the instance's **Overview** page and take note of the public URL, which should be something like the following: `https://healthcheck-api-2022.azurewebsites.net/`.

Now that we know the public URLs of our App Service instances, we can adapt our `HealthCheck` and `HealthCheckAPI` apps to work with them.

Adapting our apps for App Service

If we want our `HealthCheck` Angular app to properly work with the `HealthCheckAPI` Web API, we need to change the `baseUrl` value in the `/environments/environment.prod.ts` file, replacing the existing value.

Here's how we can do that (updated value is highlighted):

```
export const environment = {
    production: true,
    baseUrl: "https://healthcheck-api-2022.azurewebsites.net/"
};
```

In the GitHub repository for this chapter, instead of replacing the previous value, we've added a new `baseUrl_AppSettings` key and put the new value there, so that the reader will have both URLs available for review: needless to say, the `baseUrl_AppSettings` key won't have any effect—it's for reference purposes only.

As for the `HealthCheckAPI` app, there's nothing we need to do: we don't even have to change the `AllowedCORS` value in the `appsettings.Production.json` file, since the CORS headers are managed by Azure App Service.

That said, if we want to change them anyway to reflect the Angular app's location, here's how we can do that (updated value is highlighted):

```
{
    "AllowedCORS": "https://healthcheck-2022.azurewebsites.net/"
}
```

Again, in the GitHub repository for this chapter we've added a new `AllowedCORS_AppSettings` key instead of replacing the previous value to keep both URLs available for reference purposes.

Now we can move to the publishing tasks.

Publishing our apps to App Service

In this section we'll see how we can publish our `HealthCheck` and `HealthCheckAPI` apps to the App Service instance that we created a short while ago.

Publishing the Angular app

Let's start with our `HealthCheck` Angular app.

The first thing to do is to rebuild it using the `ng build` command, so that the Angular bundle will be updated with the latest changes that we made.

Right after that, go back to our new `HealthCheck-2022` App Service instance in the MS Azure management portal. Once there, navigate to the **Deployment** > **Deployment Center** menu item using the main tree view on the left, then select the **FTPS credentials** tab, as shown in the following screenshot:

Figure 15.30: HealthCheck-2022 Deployment Center

Take note of the **FTPS endpoint** URL, as well as the **Application Scope's Username** and **Password**. These are the settings that we need in order to upload the Angular bundle from our local development machine to the HealthCheck-2022 App Service instance using the FTP/FTPS protocol.

 For reasons of space, we will not explain how to establish an FTPS connection using the above info, due to it being a rather trivial task that can easily be managed through free software such as **FileZilla**, **FTP Voyager**, or **WinSCP**: instead, we'll trust that the reader is able to do that themselves.

While publishing our Angular app to the App Service instance, we can take the chance to delete the hostingstart.html file containing the HTML code for the App Service welcome screen that we saw early on, as we don't need it anymore.

Once the FTPS upload process is done, there's one last thing we need to do before publishing: add the .webmanifest file extension to the list of the MIME types supported by the App Service instance, otherwise it won't be served to the clients and the service worker won't work.

Configuring the webmanifest MIME type

Unfortunately, at the time of writing, App Service doesn't have a GUI section for configuring MIME types yet. The only way to do that is with a minimal web.config file with the following content:

```xml
<?xml version="1.0" encoding="utf-8"?>
<configuration>
  <system.webServer>
    <staticContent>
      <remove fileExtension=".webmanifest" />
      <mimeMap fileExtension=".webmanifest" mimeType="application/
manifest+json" />
    </staticContent>
  </system.webServer>
</configuration>
```

To quickly fulfill this task, we can create this web.config file on our development machine and then publish it on the production server using FTPS.

Alternatively, we can create that file using the MS Azure portal website GUI thanks to the **App Service Editor** feature, which is currently in preview but fully working for this specific purpose. To do that, perform the following tasks:

1. Go back to the MS Azure portal
2. Access the HealthCheck-2022 management page
3. Navigate to the **App Service Editor (preview)** tab

Once there, after skipping a couple of help/tutorial screens, we'll be able to access a neat web-based *File Manager* that allows us to browse and edit all the App Service instance files that we uploaded early on.

We can use that tool to create a new `web.config` file and fill it with the above content directly from the browser, as shown in the following screenshot:

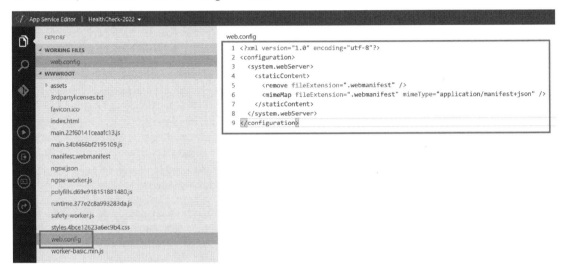

Figure 15.31: Using the App Service Editor feature to edit the web.config file

Right after that, we can move on to the `HealthCheckAPI` ASP.NET Core project.

Publishing the ASP.NET Core project

To publish our `HealthCheckAPI` ASP.NET Core project, we have two options:

- Create a Visual Studio *FTP publish profile* (or use an existing one) and then adopt the same FTPS-based upload method we've just used with our Angular project
- Create a Visual Studio Azure App Service publish profile and use it

As always, the choice is ours: since we've already seen how to handle this task with FTPS, let's briefly review the alternative route.

Switch back to Visual Studio. From **Solution Explorer**, right-click on the HealthCheckAPI project's root node and select **Publish** to access the publishing settings.

Once there, select **Azure** and then **Azure App Service (Windows)**, as shown in the following screenshot:

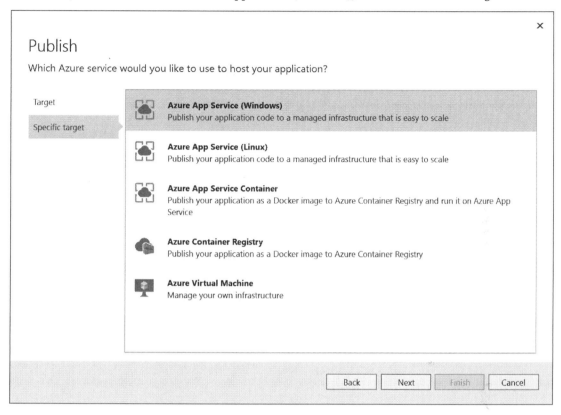

Figure 15.32: Selecting Azure App Service (Windows) in the Publish window

In the next section, we'll be asked to log in to our MS Azure account (unless we've already linked it to Visual Studio); once done, we'll be asked to select a **Resource group** and an App Service instance within it:

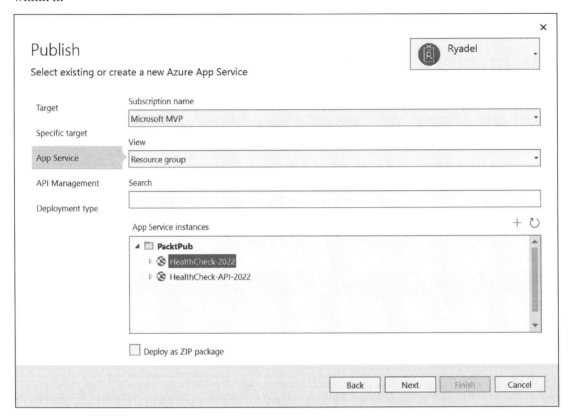

Figure 15.33: Selecting a Resource group and App Service instance

From here we can select the Web App instance we created a short while ago: once done, skip the **API Management** panel and click **Finish** to save the publish profile.

 HealthCheckAPI's App Service publish profile won't be available in the GitHub project for this chapter because it contains personal info regarding the Azure subscription: however, it shouldn't be a problem for the reader to create their own profile, it being a very simple and straightforward process.

Right after that, we can hit the **Publish** button and let Visual Studio work its magic on MS Azure: as soon as the publishing process completes, we'll finally be ready to perform our final test.

Testing HealthCheck and HealthCheckAPI

To test our new App Service instances, we just need to connect to the HealthCheck-2022 public URL: https://healthcheck-2022.azurewebsites.net/.

If we did everything correctly, we should be able to see our `HealthCheck` Angular app publicly available on the web and fully capable of connecting to the `HealthCheckAPI` ASP.NET Core app:

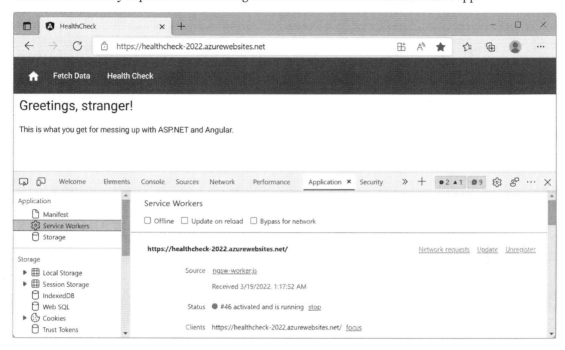

Figure 15.34: Our HealthCheck app on the web

As we can see in the preceding screenshot, the app is served in HTTPS thanks to the built-in wildcard certificate provided by MS Azure, meaning that we'll also be able to test our service worker without having to purchase an SSL certificate on our own.

That's it. Our ASP.NET Core and Angular deployment tasks have come to an end. We sincerely hope you've enjoyed reading the book as much as we've enjoyed writing it.

Summary

Finally, our journey through ASP.NET Core and Angular has come to an end. Our final task involved getting our SPAs—now empowered with the most relevant features of PWAs—ready to be published in a suitable production environment.

The first thing we did was explored some pivotal deployment tips for our *back-end* and *front-end* frameworks. Since the Visual Studio template already implements the most important optimization tweaks, we took some valuable time to properly learn and understand the various techniques that can be used to increase our web application's performance and security when we need to publish it over the web.

Right after that, we went through Windows deployment with a step-by-step approach. We created a Windows Server VM on the MS Azure portal, and then we installed the IIS service and properly configured it in order to publish our existing `HealthCheck` and `HealthCheckAPI` apps over the web.

Then, we switched to Linux, where we learned how to deploy our `WorldCities` and `WorldCitiesAPI` apps on a CentOS-based VM. After configuring it properly, we took the opportunity to implement the out-of-process hosting model using Kestrel and Nginx, which is the standard approach for serving ASP.NET Core web applications on Linux-based platforms. To achieve this, we had to change some of our `WorldCitiesAPI` app's *back-end* settings to ensure that they would be properly served behind a reverse proxy.

For both of the above scenarios we used real domain names and SSL certificates, which allowed us to properly test the *service workers*: however, we also learned how to create self-signed certificates and host-mapping techniques, which can be useful for handling testing or non-production deployment tasks in a cost-effective way.

We've also thoroughly tested the result of our deployment efforts with a web browser from our development machine.

The last thing we did was deployed our `HealthCheck` app to MS Azure App Service, a fully managed platform that can be a great fit for most projects that don't require complex low-level configuration settings.

Our adventure with ASP.NET Core and Angular has finally ended. This is such a rich topic that we could have spent even more time discussing the frameworks and perfecting our projects even more than what we did: that said, you should be satisfied with the results obtained and the lessons learned.

We hope you enjoyed this book. Many thanks for reading it!

Suggested topics

For further information, we recommend the following topics: HTTPS, Secure Socket Layer (SSL), ASP. NET Core deploy, HTTP Strict Transport Security (HSTS), General Data Protection Regulation (GDPR), Content Delivery Network (CDN) MS Azure, Open Web Application Security Project (OWASP), SQL Server, SQL Server Management Studio (SSMS), Windows Server, IIS, FTP server, publish profiles, ASP. NET Core In-process Hosting Model, ASP.NET Core Out-of-process Hosting Model, CentOS, Kestrel, Nginx, reverse proxy, Forwarded Headers Middleware, SCP, FileZilla FTP Client, WinSCP, journalctl, nano, HOST mapping, self-signed SSL certificate, openssl, Security-Enhanced Linux (SELinux).

References

- *ZeroSSL:* `https://zerossl.com/`
- *Let's Encrypt:* `https://letsencrypt.org/`
- *Generating and Configuring Free SSL Certs for Azure Windows VMs:* `https://blog.kloud.com.au/2019/04/27/generating-and-configuring-free-ssl-certs-for-azure-windows-iaas-virtual-machines/`
- *Host and deploy ASP.NET Core:* `https://docs.microsoft.com/en-us/aspnet/core/host-and-deploy/`
- *Host ASP.NET Core on Windows with IIS:* `https://docs.microsoft.com/en-us/aspnet/core/host-and-deploy/iis/`

- *ASP.NET Core Performance Best Practices*: `https://docs.microsoft.com/en-us/aspnet/core/performance/performance-best-practices`

- *Use multiple environments in ASP.NET Core*: `https://docs.microsoft.com/en-us/aspnet/core/fundamentals/environments`

- *Handle errors in ASP.NET Core*: `https://docs.microsoft.com/en-us/aspnet/core/fundamentals/error-handling`

- *Enforce HTTPS in ASP.NET Core*: `https://docs.microsoft.com/en-us/aspnet/core/security/enforcing-ssl`

- *.NET Core application deployment*: `https://docs.microsoft.com/en-us/dotnet/core/deploying/`

- *.NET Core 2.1, 3.1, and .NET 5.0 updates are coming to Microsoft Update*: `https://devblogs.microsoft.com/dotnet/net-core-updates-coming-to-microsoft-update/`

- *App Trimming in .NET 5*: `https://devblogs.microsoft.com/dotnet/app-trimming-in-net-5/`

- *Angular – Deployment Guide*: `https://angular.io/guide/deployment`

- *Enable cross-origin resource sharing*: `https://enable-cors.org/`

- *Angular: The Ahead-of-Time (AOT) compiler*: `https://angular.io/guide/aot-compiler`

- *Publish an ASP.NET Web App to an Azure VM from Visual Studio*: `https://github.com/MicrosoftDocs/azure-docs/blob/master/articles/virtual-machines/windows/publish-web-app-from-visual-studio.md`

- *Publish an application to IIS by importing publish settings in Visual Studio*: `https://docs.microsoft.com/en-us/visualstudio/deployment/tutorial-import-publish-settings-iis?view=vs-2019`

- *Use Spot VMs in Azure*: `https://docs.microsoft.com/en-us/azure/virtual-machines/spot-vms`

- *Quick reference: IIS Application Pool*: `https://blogs.msdn.microsoft.com/rohithrajan/2017/10/08/quick-reference-iis-application-pool/`

- *Configure the Windows Firewall to Allow SQL Server Access*: `https://docs.microsoft.com/en-us/sql/sql-server/install/configure-the-windows-firewall-to-allow-sql-server-access`

- *Configure ASP.NET Core to work with proxy servers and load balancers*: `https://docs.microsoft.com/en-us/aspnet/core/host-and-deploy/proxy-load-balancer`

- *Host ASP.NET Core on Linux with Nginx*: `https://docs.microsoft.com/en-us/aspnet/core/host-and-deploy/linux-nginx`

- *PuTTty: A free SSH and Telnet client for Windows*: `https://www.putty.org/`

- *Move files to and from a Linux VM using SCP*: `https://docs.microsoft.com/en-us/azure/virtual-machines/linux/copy-files-to-linux-vm-using-scp`

- *Install the .NET SDK or the .NET Runtime on CentOS*: `https://docs.microsoft.com/en-us/dotnet/core/install/linux-centos`

- *Installation guidance for SQL Server on Linux*: `https://docs.microsoft.com/en-us/sql/linux/sql-server-linux-setup`

- *Deploy an ASP.NET Core Web Application to Linux CentOS*: `https://www.ryadel.com/en/asp-net-core-2-publish-deploy-web-application-linux-centos-tutorial-guide-nginx/`
- *journalctl – Query the systemd journal*: `https://www.freedesktop.org/software/systemd/man/journalctl.html`
- *openssl – OpenSSL command-line tool*: `https://www.openssl.org/docs/manmaster/man1/openssl.html`

Packt>

packt.com

Subscribe to our online digital library for full access to over 7,000 books and videos, as well as industry leading tools to help you plan your personal development and advance your career. For more information, please visit our website.

Why subscribe?

- Spend less time learning and more time coding with practical eBooks and Videos from over 4,000 industry professionals
- Improve your learning with Skill Plans built especially for you
- Get a free eBook or video every month
- Fully searchable for easy access to vital information
- Copy and paste, print, and bookmark content

At www.packt.com, you can also read a collection of free technical articles, sign up for a range of free newsletters, and receive exclusive discounts and offers on Packt books and eBooks.

Other Books
You May Enjoy

If you enjoyed this book, you may be interested in these other books by Packt:

C# 10 and .NET 6 – Modern Cross-Platform Development, Sixth Edition

Mark Price

ISBN: 9781801077361

- Build rich web experiences using Blazor, Razor Pages, the Model-View-Controller (MVC) pattern, and other features of ASP.NET Core
- Build your own types with object-oriented programming
- Write, test, and debug functions
- Query and manipulate data using LINQ
- Integrate and update databases in your apps using Entity Framework Core, Microsoft SQL Server, and SQLite
- Build and consume powerful services using the latest technologies, including gRPC and GraphQL
- Build cross-platform apps using .NET MAUI and XAML

Software Architecture with C# 10 and .NET 6, Third Edition

Gabriel Baptista

Francesco Abbruzzese

ISBN: 9781803235257

- Use proven techniques to overcome real-world architectural challenges
- Apply architectural approaches such as layered architecture
- Leverage tools such as containers to manage microservices effectively
- Get up to speed with Azure features for delivering global solutions
- Program and maintain Azure Functions using C# 10
- Understand when it is best to use test-driven development (TDD)
- Implement microservices with ASP.NET Core in modern architectures
- Enrich your application with Artificial Intelligence
- Get the best of DevOps principles to enable CI/CD environments

An Atypical ASP.NET Core 6 Design Patterns Guide, Second Edition

Carl-Hugo Marcotte

ISBN: 9781803249841

- Apply the SOLID principles for building flexible and maintainable software
- Get to grasp .NET dependency Injection
- Work with GoF design patterns such as strategy, decorator, façade, and composite
- Explore the MVC patterns for designing web APIs and web applications using Razor
- Discover layering techniques and tenets of clean architecture
- Become familiar with CQRS and vertical slice architecture as an alternate to layering
- Understand microservices and when they can benefit your applications
- Build an ASP.NET user interfaces from server-side to client-side Blazor

Packt is searching for authors like you

If you're interested in becoming an author for Packt, please visit authors.packtpub.com and apply today. We have worked with thousands of developers and tech professionals, just like you, to help them share their insight with the global tech community. You can make a general application, apply for a specific hot topic that we are recruiting an author for, or submit your own idea.

Share your thoughts

Now you've finished *ASP.NET Core 6 and Angular, Fifth Edition*, we'd love to hear your thoughts! Scan the QR code below to go straight to the Amazon review page for this book and share your feedback or leave a review on the site that you purchased it from.

https://packt.link/r/1803239700

Your review is important to us and the tech community and will help us make sure we're delivering excellent quality content.

Index

63921974R00433